D0205700

American and Soviet Military Trends Since the Cuban Missile Crisis

AMERICAN AND SOVIET MILITARY TRENDS

Since the Cuban Missile Crisis

by

JOHN M. COLLINS

Douglas D. Mitchell
Research Assistant

With a Special Introduction
by
CONGRESSMAN JOHN B. BRECKINRIDGE

The Center for Strategic and International Studies
Georgetown University
Washington, D.C.

First Printing June 1978

Library of Congress Catalog Card Number: 78-58310
ISBN: 0-89206-002-6 paperbound
ISBN: 0-89206-003-4 hardbound

Author's Dedication

To
SWIFT,
the perfect partner.

Without her steadfast support,
this project would have been impossible.

Preface

The Center for Strategic and International Studies (CSIS), Georgetown University, takes pride in publishing a definitive study of the U.S.-Soviet military balance. It is the most comprehensive, authoritative assessment ever made available to the American public. The author, John M. Collins, one of the nation's leading defense experts, examines every main weapons system and all types of forces employed by the two superpowers. He demonstrates with massive detail that the United States is losing in the capability to deter Soviet aggression across the broad spectrum of possible conflicts.

For more than 15 years the Center's program for research and writing has focused on trouble spots, trying to anticipate crisis situations before they hit the policymaker. On every subject CSIS has provided the Administration, the Congress, businessmen, and the public alike with careful analyses, setting forth a wide range of pertinent facts. The Collins book fits squarely into this program. Congressman John B. Breckinridge has written a special introduction in which he indicates the critical importance of understanding the use of power in international affairs.

The book Congress did not print—*American and Soviet Military Trends Since the Cuban Missile Crisis* —is required reading for every concerned citizen.

Ray S. Cline
Executive Director of Strategic Studies
The Center for Strategic and
International Studies
Georgetown University

Special Introduction

Congressman John B. Breckinridge

The Communist Party leaders of the USSR since the time of Lenin have been great admirers of the German strategist Karl von Clausewitz, who reminded us nearly two centuries ago that power is more than the capacity to destroy. It is also the capacity to *influence*. His maxim that "war is the continuation of politics by other means" suggests that the exercise of political influence in "peacetime" is always one of the primary purposes governing force deployments.

In recent years the rulers of the USSR have announced that they believe what they term the world "correlation of forces" has shifted markedly, perhaps irreversibly, in the direction of the "socialist camp"—i.e., the cluster of Communist states dominated by Moscow. They point to the U.S. defeat in Vietnam, the lack of U.S. assistance to Angola, and U.S. acceptance of Soviet numerical superiority in the SALT I Treaty.

As the most obvious indicator of national strength, military power is taken by many international observers to be symbolic of a nation's destiny and purpose. The rapid and unprecedented decline of relative U.S. military power vis-a-vis Soviet strength outlined in the pages of this book by John M. Collins, therefore, is perceived by many to reflect a greater—and much more disturbing—national malaise: the decline of American political will and the growing ambiguity of American national purpose. While Americans may not acknowledge this publicly, or may not even be aware of it, others are. Europeans often say, some sorrowfully, others without regret, "the American era is past."

And yet the political and economic freedom embodied in U.S. society has within it a remarkable ability to rebound from self-defeating decisions of the past. It is my firm belief that the American people and their leaders stand at a critical and decisive juncture in history. On

August 4, 1914, just days after Germany had declared war on Russia and France, Edward, Viscount Grey of Fallodon, standing at the windows of his room in the Foreign Office watching the lamp-lighters extinguish the lights in St. James Park, solemnly declared: "The lamps are going out all over Europe; we shall not see them lit again in our lifetime." In this brief but poignant statement was expressed the destiny of Europe. No longer could it control the events that would determine its own fate.

In today's world there are only two global powers—the United States and the Soviet Union. These two nations do not share the same economic interests. They differ on most political issues and basic principles of society. And they both possess a military force structure designed to insure that their respective interests are protected. It is for these reasons that our military posture relative to the Soviet Union stands at the heart of our foreign policy, our collective security arrangements, and our force deployments in support of alliances around the world.

To permit the adverse trends of the past ten to fifteen years to continue would be tantamount to a conscious decision by the American people to allow their national independence and free institutions increasingly to become hostage to decisions made in Moscow by Soviet Communist Party leaders. This risk is unacceptable in a world more threatening than any we have known in our lifetime. It is an awesome fact that a misjudgment on our part about the nature and intentions of Soviet military power—and what is necessary to confront and neutralize that power—could well be fatal, not only for America but also for the fundamental values of 2,500 years of Western civilization.

Acknowledgments

A wide assortment of knowledgeable individuals contributed to this document, directly or indirectly. I owe a lasting debt to them all.

Senator John C. Culver (D-Iowa) started it all in November 1975, when he commissioned me to prepare "an in-depth conceptual analysis of the U.S./Soviet military balance, with special attention to: comparative strengths and weaknesses; significance; possible ways to redress the balance in U.S. favor wherever required, without increasing the defense budget." The Senate Armed Services Committee, at his request, published the resulting preliminary study in January 1976.

Cooperation by the U.S. Department of Defense throughout the subsequent gestation period of this book was superlative. Secretaries of Defense, the Chairman of the Joint Chiefs of Staff, and Chiefs of all four Military Services allowed me free access to their respective organizations and assigned subordinates as permanent points of contact.

As a result, I was able to draw on "research assistants" and reviewers throughout the entire defense establishment. Their input was indispensable. Special gratitude is due Andrew W. Marshall, DOD Director of Net Assessment, assisted by Majors Robert G. Gough and William Rennagel; Colonel Thomas W. Sherman, Executive Officer to the Director of the Joint Staff; Commander Roy N. Wallace, J-5 (Plans and Policy); Lieutenant Colonels Taylor N. Oncale and Edward V. Karl, Army; Edwin L. Woisard, Director of Navy Net Assessment and Captain William H. Cracknell, Naval Intelligence; Major General James R. Brickel, Air Force Director of Concepts, and Captain Frank G. Klotz; Lieutenant Colonel Norman H. Smith, Marine Corps; Joseph A. English, along with Robert O. Nevel, Military Sealift Command; and my next door neighbor, Colonel James N. Hockney, who furnished airlift materials.

No one, outside myself, made a greater contribution than members of DIA, at the behest of three successive Directors: Lieutenant Generals Daniel O. Graham, Samuel V. Wilson, and Eugene F. Tighe, Jr. Robert O. Duckworth, Deputy Chief, Soviet/East European Division was saddled with extra duty for the full period as my primary contact. John D. Donaldson and Bruce A. Hoffer handled Soviet manpower, working in close collaboration with David A. Smith from DOD Manpower and Reserve Affairs. Lieutenant Colonel Louis F. DeMouche was a key source of information on Soviet ground forces.

General Alexander M. Haig, Jr., Supreme Allied Commander Europe, was kind enough to set up conferences for me at SHAPE, then sent me to Headquarters, U.S. European Command, where General Robert E. Huyser acted as host.

Several "outsiders" assisted by supplying facts and critiquing in detail parts of successive drafts. Among them were William F. and Harriet Fast Scott, whose insights on Soviet defense organization were invaluable. William T. Lee helped balance my coverage of the Soviet budget.

Almost every defense analyst with the Library of Congress contributed in one way or another: Alva M. Bowen and Edmund Gannon, navy; Bert H. Cooper, Jr. and Anibal A. Tinajero, weapons systems; Richard P. Cronin, defense budgets; Robert L. Goldich, manpower; Mark M. Lowenthal, U.S. defense organization; Francis T. Miko, Soviet defense organization; Herbert Y. Schandler, NATO and military assistance. Robert G. Bell, Alva Bowen, John P. Hardt, Joseph Whelan, and William W. Whitson participated in the review process, along with James W. Robinson, who checked the draft for policy matters and provided substantive comments. Robert L. Bostick coordinated all graphics.

Douglas D. Mitchell, my Research Assistant, updated all statistical tables, and added a mountain of new information.

Finally, I salute Marjorie Cline and Sylvia Lowe, who put the finished product together, condoning last minute changes by me in galleys and page proofs, and shepherded it through the publishing process in record time.

In short, many other people did most of the work. I only wish I could share whatever recognition the study may attract. They, of course, are absolved of any blame.

John M. Collins
Alexandria, Virginia
May 14, 1978

TABLE OF CONTENTS

Table of Contents

Page

Page

Page

BOOK III. NATO AND THE WARSAW PACT

Page

BOOK IV. ISSUES AND OPTIONS

Figures

Graphs

Maps

American and Soviet Military Trends Since the Cuban Missile Crisis

Background, Purpose, and Scope

If we could first know *where* we are and *whither* we are tending, we could better judge *what* to do and *how* to do it.

Abraham Lincoln
Springfield, Illinois
June 16, 1858

America's armed services possessed unparalleled assets at the time of the Cuban missile crisis in 1962. We were the world's sole military superpower. Moscow's machine was still mainly second class.

Only the United States deployed diversified land, sea, and aerospace forces designed to function across the full conflict spectrum. Soviet nuclear capabilities at that stage featured a handful of heavy bombers and a few ballistic missiles. The Soviet Navy was suitable essentially for coastal defense. Tactical air arms were primitive by U.S. standards. A mammoth army, organized, trained, and equipped to protect Mother Russia comprised the principal sinew. Combined arms offensive strength was strictly circumscribed, even on the Eurasian land mass.

U.S. forces registered many improvements in the following 15 years, which brings us to the present, but their relative decline has been dramatic, when compared with Soviet counterparts. That trend continues.

The implications of that development are subject to interpretation. Some seers predict disaster, others disagree, but most parties seem to concur on one point: neither U.S. principles nor programs of any sort could prosper in peacetime or persist in war if the balance tipped too far in Soviet favor.

U.S. security architects, therefore, strive to maintain a military establishment that can deter and, if need be, defend successfully against Soviet aggression across the conflict spectrum, while retaining capabilities in reserve to safeguard U.S. regional interests against possible threats by lesser powers.

Presidential Review Memorandum (PRM)-10, the Carter Administration's first comprehensive survey of U.S. national security requirements, recognized five types of conflict that could involve U.S. armed forces in support of national interests: strategic nuclear war; combat in Central Europe between NATO and the Warsaw Pact; an "East-West" war elsewhere; altercations in East Asia, typfied by a showdown in Korea; and assorted contingencies, such as the conflict in Vietnam.[1] The Soviet Union would be our foremost foe in the first two cases, and a possible opponent in cases three and four.

What military balance would best satisfy associated U.S. requirements is a contentious matter.[2] To aid Congress in ascertaining "How much is enough?", the Congressional Research Service (CRS) compiled a frame of reference in 1976, with careful concern for force sufficiency criteria,[3] then used that treatise as a tool to trace the evolution of U.S. and Soviet military strength during this decade.[4]

This third-generation product, which supersedes its two predecessors, subsumes and supplements their contents, but serves the same four-fold purpose:

—Furnish facts.

—Outline opinions.

—Sharpen issues.

—Stimulate debate.

The scope not only includes force-shaping factors and a net assessment under the same cover, but isolates salient issues that could assist Congress in reviewing defense requirements, plus requests for funds.

—Book I sketches fundamental security interests, which form the foundation for force requirements.

—Book II assesses changes in separate U.S. and Soviet armed services since the late 1950s. Book III compares central alliances during that same period. Both amalgamate, augment, and amend contents from the previous studies. Four modifications merit special mention:

—Sections now open with a survey of security objectives, policies, and strategic concepts that condition the size, structure, and special characteristics of forces on each side.

—Geographic influences receive increased emphasis, along with several military subjects, such as comparative organization, doctrine, command/control and communications (C^3), tactical air defense, and readiness.

—NATO and Warsaw Pact statistics, formerly listed as lump sums, are broken out by country, with France included to show the strongest NATO case.

—Pertinent parts of the U.S. Coast Guard are compared with Soviet coastal combatants.

—Book IV, which addresses consequent issues, both present and projected, follows a format from the first report, with many refinements and a sharper focus.

Special attention is paid to trends that condition the size, composition, and capabilities of U.S. and Soviet armed services. Readers can readily see which currents are strong, which are weak, which are shifting, and which are steady. Even items as indelible as national interests indicate significant change during the past two decades.

The eight-year U.S. statistical spread is drawn directly in most cases from unclassified computer printouts produced by the Department of Defense (DOD) and the four military services. Defense Intelligence Agency (DIA) furnished most Soviet figures.[5] Some data differ in detail from those in classified documents, but the patterns portrayed are dependable.

Resultant summaries confirm which weapons are phasing in and out at what rates. Those indications, combined with organizational and hardware characteristics, spotlight qualitative, as well as quantitative, changes on both sides.

Data are displayed unconventionally whenever so doing clarifies comparison. U.S. strategic nuclear manpower figures, for example, normally are included in Army, Navy, and Air Force totals. This study shows them separately. Soviet Strategic Rocket Forces are subdivided, so that personnel for theater nuclear purposes are distinct from those that serve ICBMs. Division counts are somewhat different than Congress is used to seeing, even though totals tally the same. And so on.

This study, like its predecessors, is predicated on CRS guidelines, which insist on independent analyses that avoid advocacy. The author, therefore, considered constructive comments from a wide range of sources during the preparation and review process, but sought no official concurrence from any critic, and reserved all rights to accept or reject. Conflicting opinions were cast in relief by citing contrasting viewpoints.

The end product supports no special position. It simply depicts, as dispassionately as possible, the development of U.S. and Soviet armed services, describing where they have been, where they are now, and where they are going unless one or both sides change course. The resultant compendium thus lays part of the groundwork for congressional participation in a national decision-making process designed to ratify, reinforce, retard, or reverse present trends.[6]

Footnotes

1. Wilson, George C., "War Planners Note Soviet Grip on NATO's Oil," *Washington Post*, July 9, 1977, p. A3.

2. The U.S./Soviet *military* balance is just one component of the U.S./Soviet *strategic* balance, which is just one aspect of the U.S. *global* balance with other powers that

determines our total defense demands. Political, economic, geographic, social, psychological, scientific, and technological assets that are central to any strategic balance are considered here only as they directly affect relative strengths of U.S. and Soviet armed services, along with respective allies.

3. U.S. Congress. Senate. Committee on Armed Services. *United States/Soviet Military Balance: A Frame of Reference for Congress. A study by the Congressional Research Service.* 94th Congress, 2d Session. Washington: U.S. Govt. Print. Off., 1976. 86 pp.

4. Helms, Jesse A., "American and Soviet Armed Services, Strengths Compared, 1970–1976. Remarks in the Senate." *Congressional Record, Part 3, August 5, 1977, pp.* S14063–S14104.

5. All assessments of the U.S./Soviet military balance depend directly or indirectly on DOD and its affiliates for U.S. force levels. The intelligence community is the most important primary source of statistics concerning the Soviet side. Officials and observers both occasionally disagree with the basic data, but most disputes deal with differences in interpretation.

6. See Annex A for a glossary of selected terms. Annex B contains abbreviations used throughout this text. Annex C links nomenclatures with nicknames for major weapons systems.

I

SECURITY INTERESTS COMPARED

The Fundamental Focus

American and Soviet armed services exist essentially to satisfy security interests, which form the foundation for objectives, policies, commitments, and connected force requirements.[1] Some U.S. interests conflict with those of the Kremlin, others are compatible, but intensities seldom are the same, and opposing leaders tend to interpret them differently.

Selected Security Interests

A few fundamental interests have contributed significantly to asymmetries in the U.S./Soviet military balance since the Cuban missile crisis. Trends could change when successors replace the present Soviet hierarchy, but comparing perceptions and apparent priorities over the past 25 years provides important insights at this point.

Survival/Security

The only sacrosanct interests are survival and physical security, which must be satisfied if sovereign states hope to preserve their people and production base with territorial integrity, national institutions, and values acceptably intact.

Both interests were academic throughout most of America's history, partly because we were isolated by oceans and flanked by friendly countries. The Continental United States (CONUS) was immune to serious attacks by external powers from 1815, when British troops lost the Battle of New Orleans, until the mid-1950s, when the Soviets began to deploy long-range Bear and Bison bombers with nuclear delivery capabilities.

Thereafter, Moscow massed a missile strike force that could shatter the United States as a twentieth century society.[2] U.S. strategic nuclear forces consequently are crucial to interests in survival and homeland security. Our conventional components, however, are not directly connected, because no hostile country has amphibious assault, naval air, and transoceanic logistic capabilities needed to seize, secure, and sustain sizable lodgments on defended U.S. shores.

In sharp contrast, Czarist Russia and its successor the Soviet Union have been exposed to constant pressures from powerful foes along lengthy frontiers since times that predate Ivan the Terrible. Concerns for survival and security thus are immediate and immense. Influences on armed services are everywhere evident, especially in ground forces and air defense.

Peace

Peace, but not peace at any price, has been a high priority U.S. interest since the onset of the Nuclear Age.[3] Even limited strife involving superpowers or their proxies could suddenly escalate out of control, through intent or miscalculation.

U.S. leaders, however, traditionally tend to define "peace" as the absence of a shooting war.[4] They maintain military power in peacetime mainly to avert overt aggression by armed enemies.

The Soviet high command conversely is committed to an ideological premise that true peace theoretically can exist only when the socialist system prevails.[5] Peaceful coexistence, presently called detente, strives "to exclude war, and primarily world war, as a means of settling interstate disputes," but the Soviet Union, according to repeated pronouncements, competes "for keeps" with non-communist countries at every other level.[6] Military services play positive political and psychological roles in that continuous "peacetime" struggle, supplementing their utility as tools for deterrent purposes or for armed conflict.

Strategic Stability

The United States has a deep-seated desire for strategic stability, a state of equilibrium that, if attained, would eliminate U.S. and Soviet advantages which could cause either side to seek changes in the status quo through the use or threat of force. The search for stability colors the U.S. approach to Strategic Arms Limitation Talks (SALT), where our aim is essential equivalence.[7] It is equally apparent in official attitudes toward Mutual and Balanced Force Reductions (MBFR) for Europe.[8] U.S. attempts to avoid postures that might tempt the Soviets to preempt have been articulated many times by America's top decision-makers during this decade, despite the search for new nuclear options.[9]

Soviet leaders publicly proclaim identical interests in a stable balance. Brezhnev, as his country's senior spokesman, states categorically that the Soviet Union "will not seek military superiority" or in any way "upset the approximate equilibrium of military strength existing" in Central Europe or "between the U.S.S.R. and the U.S.A."[10]

In practice, however, the Soviets appear to lack our intense concern for strategic stability, probably because it would defer communist victory in the struggle with capitalism. U.S. arms controllers find their Soviet counterparts reluctant to settle for essentially equal aggregates whenever superior armed services truly seem to count.

Credibility

Credibility is an indispensable asset for any nation that aspires to international leadership or hopes to function effectively as a world power. Its ingredients must include clearly evident capabilities and intentions, coupled with strong national will, if they are to command the attention of adversaries, allies, and the uncommitted.

U.S. concern for credibility increased by orders of magnitude after World War II, when American military might became a Free World bulwark. The shift from Massive Retaliation to Flexible Response in 1961 and our current quest for alternatives to Assured Destruction reflect efforts to ensure continued credibility of U.S. deterrence across the conflict spectrum. NATO reluctantly switched its strategy in 1967 for similar reasons.[11]

Soviet leaders share our affinity for credibility as a crucial national interest, but record a far more consistent attitude toward affiliated requirements. Their military strength expands in most respects, even when ours contracts. Efforts to improve their relative posture are sometimes slow, but always steady.

Power

Force and power are frequently confused. Force is just one input to power which, when properly applied in its many modes, can culminate in influence or control over other countries.

The United States and the Soviet Union both express intense interests in power as a matter of principle. Both sometimes use force as a fulcrum to support specific objectives. The Kremlin, however, seems to apply power more consistently in pursuit of more power. Its requirements for armed services to underpin political and psychological purposes consequently appear greater than our own in most instances.[12]

Freedom of Action

Finally, freedom of action overlaps all other U.S. and Soviet interests. It is the key to strategic initiative, without which either country would be compelled to react, rather than act.

Mutual interests in freedom of action assumed special prominence when the United States and Soviet Union began to compete in the post-World War II period. Since then, some new Soviet options have opened. Some U.S. options have closed, as succeeding sections will show. Those developments relate directly to different deductions concerning demands for force flexibility.

Footnotes

1. For a concise review of interrelationships among national security interests, objectives, policies, and commitments, see Collins, John M., *Grand Strategy: Principles and Practices*. Annapolis, Maryland: Naval Institute Press, 1973, pp. 1–7.

2. Some authorities contend that effective steps following a full-scale nuclear exchange with the Soviet Union could restore the United States at an earlier stage than most skeptics suspect, but U.S. preparations are scarcely past the planning phase, and long-term consequences of intense radiation are largely incalculable. Civilization in its present form might not be cancelled permanently, but recovery would be prolonged even in optimum circumstances. Problems are described in *Long-Term Worldwide Effects of Multiple Nuclear Weapons Detonations*. Washington: National Academy of Sciences, 1975, 213 pp. See also Kahn, Herman, *On Thermonuclear War*, 2d Ed. New York: The Free Press, 1969, pp. 40–95.

3. General of the Army Omar N. Bradley, as Chairman of the Joint Chiefs of Staff, was one who saw peace as a salient U.S. interest shortly after the Soviets detonated their first nuclear device. U.S. Congress. House. Armed Services Committee, Doc. No. 600, *Unification and Strategy*. 81st Congress, 2d Session. Washington: U.S. Govt. Print. Off., 1950, p. 14.

4. One example of U.S. attitudes toward "peace" occurred late in the Vietnam War, when Kissinger, in his capacity as Special Assistant to the President for National Security Affairs, pronounced that "peace is at hand." A fragile cease-fire in fact commenced within 90 days, but final terms rid the region of U.S. power, leaving rival forces in place. There was no political settlement in that highly political contest. Accords were signed, but the conflict went on, with Saigon's survival at issue. Quote from White House Press Conference, Washington, News Release, Bureau of Public Affairs, Department of State, October 26, 1972, pp. 2–3. The cease-fire began on January 27, 1973.

5. Lenin, V. I., *Collected Works*. Vol I. Moscow: Progress Publishers, 1970, p. 771. U.S. Sovietologists are divided concerning the degree to which such scripture still governs Soviet policy.

6. Article by Observer, "For the Liquidation of Colonialism and the Triumph of Peace," *Pravda*, October 24, 1964. That position, stated during Brezhnev's early days, has stayed constant.

7. Essential equivalence as a U.S. SALT policy was emphasized in Section 3 of the Joint Resolution on Interim Agreement (Public Law 92–448, 86 Stat. 746, approved September 30, 1972), which stipulates that "the Congress recognizes the principle of United States-Soviet Union equality reflected in the anti-ballistic missile treaty, and urges and requests the President to seek a future treaty that, inter alia, would not limit the United States to levels of intercontinental strategic forces inferior to the limits provided for the Soviet Union. . . ."

8. The purpose of MBFR, according to the U.S. representative, is "to achieve a more stable balance at lower levels of forces with undiminished security" in Central Europe. Quoted in Hörhager, Axel, "The MBFR Talks—Problems and Prospects," *International Defense Review*, April 1976, p. 189.

9. President Nixon at an early date directed the Defense Department to limit the "numbers, characteristics, and deployments of our forces [to those] which the Soviet Union cannot reasonably interpret as being intended to threaten a disarming attack." DOD translated those instructions into planning criteria that prohibited "providing [any] incentive for the Soviet Union to strike the United States first in a crisis." That philosophy still prevails. Quotes are contained in Nixon, Richard M., *Foreign Policy for the 1970's: Building for Peace*, Washington: U.S. Govt. Print. Off., 1971, p. 131; and Laird, Melvin R., *Statement Before the House Armed Services Committee on the FY 1972–1976 Defense Program and the 1972 Defense Budget*, March 9, 1971, p. 62.

10. Brezhnev speech in "Kremlin Meeting Opens Revolution Anniversary Celebration," *FBIS, Daily Report, Soviet Union*, November 2, 1977, p. 15.

11. American interests in credibility were especially evident after U.S. combat forces were committed in Indochina. With the whole world watching and waiting the outcome, which would substantially influence future U.S. foreign policy and our alliance system, President Johnson concluded that "if we are driven from the field in Vietnam, then no nation can ever have the same confidence in American promises or American protection. We will stand in Vietnam." Quoted in Thompson, Robert, *No Exit From Vietnam*. New York: David McKay Co., Inc., 1969, p. 92.

12. For detailed discussion, see Luttwak, Edward N., "Perceptions of Military Force and US Defense Policy," *Survival*, January/February 1977, pp. 2–8.

II

SEPARATE STRENGTHS COMPARED

PART I

Analytical Problems

Good big armed services are almost always superior to good small ones, but "it is not true that more is always better than less, or that the nation could always use more. The United States could have 10 times as many . . . . forces as the Soviets and still not have enough, or one-tenth as many and have too much," if ends and means were mismatched.[1]

Comparing military debits and credits, however, is a complex process. Defects in the data base confront analysts with severe constraints at the onset. Simple alterations in assumptions can create radically different conclusions, even if the input is constant.[2]

Great size can impede rather than improve performance, unless needs and numbers mesh. Technology can not substitute completely for first-class strategy. Reserve components complement regular forces. Allies add to (and sometimes subtract from) regional strength. Present status may be less meaningful than projections. Finally, a good many non-military elements influence deterrent/defense equations. When political, economic, or psychological power can satisfy essential security interests, military requirements usually can be reduced. All such considerations must be called to account.

The following discourse identifies sample problems and pitfalls.

Quantitative Comparisons

Quantitative analyses illuminate important indicators for comparing competing forces, but difficulties in compiling compatible figures complicate the mere matching of raw statistics.

U.S. intelligence estimates of Soviet strengths, for example, are inexact, because of incomplete collection capabilities and uncertainties introduced by the Kremlin's cover and deception efforts.[3] Conclusions in some cases indicate nothing more than an order of magnitude.[4]

Just deciding how and what to count can be confusing.

Calculations may involve total inventories on both sides, or only those items in operational units. Stockpiles, particularly prepositioned equipment, can be included or ignored. Determining what fits in which category can be equally complicated. U.S. and Soviet definitions of "heavy" bombers and ICBMs differ drastically. Dual-purpose systems, such as air superiority aircraft that double as air defense interceptors, produce similar counting problems.

Large missiles, divisions, ships, and so on in any given class count the same as small ones. Old weapons count the same as new. Service troops count the same as combatants in basic manpower comparisons.

Deciding how to display statistics is also difficult. Schematics such as Graph 1, which condenses 17 subsequent summaries, are subject to all sorts of odd interpretations, unless tied tightly to analytical texts. "Side-by-side" comparisons of like systems, including tables contained in this study, are simple and convenient, but may also be misleading, because superior quantities and superior capabilities are not always synonymous. "Head-to-head" comparisons of competing systems (cruise missiles against air defense) are also suspect. In the absence of any accepted conversion formula, no one knows for sure what respective weights should be assigned. The full significance of numbers is revealed only in concert with other relevant factors, whatever the case.

Translating simple sums into comparative capabilities that connote *quantitative* "superiority," "inferiority," or "essential equivalance" (sometimes called "equal aggregates") thus is an imprecise art whose product portrays just one part of the U.S./Soviet military balance. Dogmatic conclusions postulated solely on comparative statistics occasionally are correct, but always bear close scrutiny.[5]

Qualitative Comparisons

Comparing qualitative characteristics of manpower, weapons, and equipment is an equally convoluted process, because key indicators are often concealed. Speeds, service ceilings, combat radii, and payload capacities of most Soviet aircraft, for example, are subjects of speculation in the United States.

Backfire bombers are a case in point. Several U.S. aircraft corporations in 1976 estimated effective ranges, using different sets of data from different sources that created different conclusions. Assessments at the lower end of the scale suggested a round trip limitation of

Graph 1
STATISTICAL BALANCE 1977

(Note Sliding Scale)

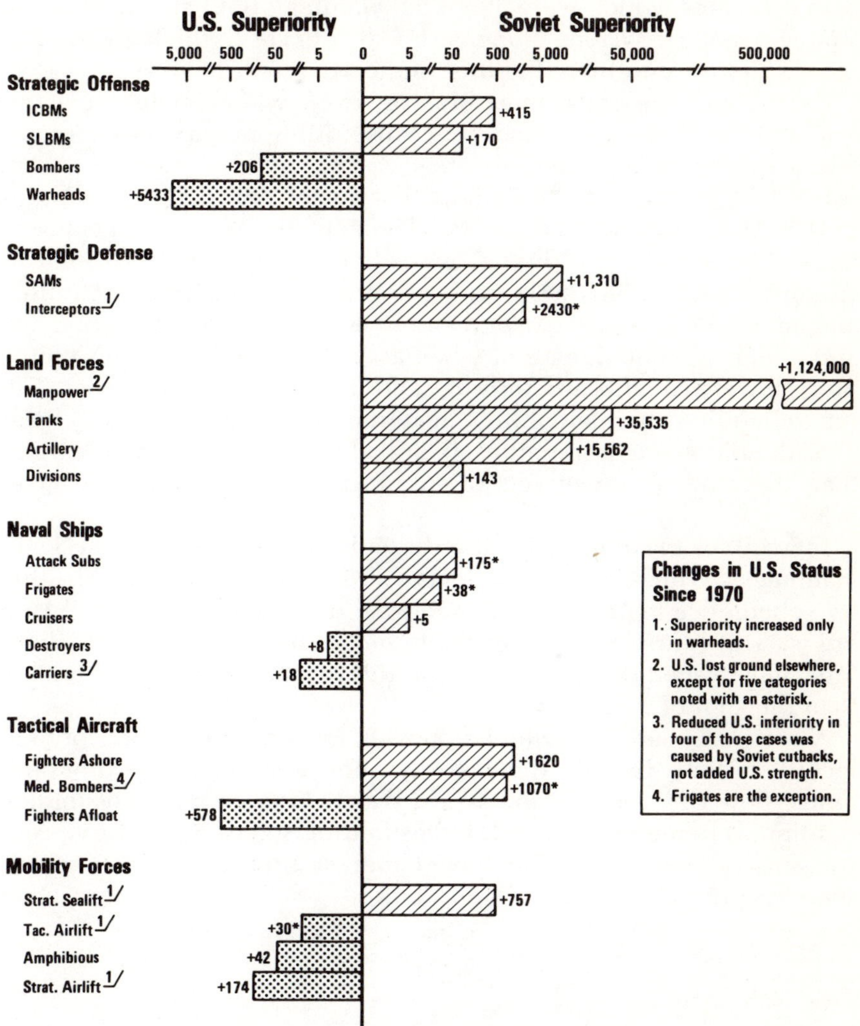

NOTES: 1/ Includes U.S. reserve components.
2/ Excludes high command and general support.
3/ Includes U.S. LHA & LPH helicopter carriers.
4/ Includes Navy.
5/ Some Soviet strength estimates are subject to substantial error.

roughly 3,500 nautical miles. If correct, that would classify Backfire as an intermediate-range aircraft in the same category as Soviet Badgers and Blinders. Other analyses, however, showed Backfire with nearly twice that reach, which clearly would give it intercontinental capabilities, like Bears, Bisons, and B-52s. This study sticks with median estimates, which were about 5,000 miles,[6] but lists Backfire as a strategic nuclear system, along with U.S. FB-111s, which are smaller, have a shorter unrefueled radius, and carry lesser loads.[7]

Evaluations are sometimes elusive, even when Soviet items are available for inspection, simply because different experts assign different weights to assorted aspects.

It is true, to cite just one sample, that Soviet T-62 tanks are superior to U.S. M-60s in several respects.[8] Their smaller size presents poorer targets. Less width and lighter weights make them better suited for crossing shaky bridges and slipping through crooked streets. Air filters and automatic aperture closings shield crews against radioactive dust and chemical contamination, whereas U.S. crews lack much protection. However, sights and turning spans are strictly second class. Taking reliability, maintainability, materials, craftsmanship, and other considerations into account, each tank obviously may be much better than the other in given sets of circumstances, depending on given tasks.

Intangibles make it even more difficult to compare U.S. and Soviet manpower. Which takes precedence: outstanding initiative or instinctive obedience to orders? Technological training or toughness? Modern wars, of course, are won by teams, not individuals. Analysts, therefore, must ascertain whether respective wholes equal more or less than the sum of their parts.

Assessing in advance which opposing attributes are most apt to affect the military balance in what ways, hence, poses perplexing problems.[9] Few U.S. seers before World War II foresaw Japanese soldiers fighting so fiercely, or French forces folding so fast. Qualitative comparisons between U.S. and Soviet men-at-arms might also contain some surprises.

Footnotes

1. Enthoven, Alain C. and Smith, K. Wayne, *How Much is Enough?*, New York: Harper and Row, 1971, p. 201.

2. Illustrations connected with a specific situation are contained in Chapter II, The Effect of Different Assumptions. *Assessing the NATO/Warsaw Pact Military Balance*, Washington, Congressional Budget Office, December 1977, pp. 9–25.

3. The dearth of reliable Soviet data puts U.S. negotiators at a disadvantage in attempts to conclude acceptable SALT, MBFR, and other arms control arrangements. American input provides hard facts to conferees. Statistics concerning Soviet and satellite forces consist exclusively of U.S. intelligence estimates, which are exceedingly imprecise in many instances. That situation only recently has started to change, according to U.S. officials. See, for example, Burt, Richard, "Soviets Begin Providing Missile Arsenal Data," *Washington Star*, March 14, 1978, p. A-5.

4. Soviet secrecy laws and procedures are outlined in U.S. Congress. Senate. *Soviet Space Programs, 1971–75*. Staff Report prepared for use of the Committee on Aeronautical and Space Sciences. Vol. 2. Washington: U.S. Govt. Print. Off., August 30, 1976, pp. 87–89.

5. Ambiguities involved in quantitative analysis led the Chief of Naval Operations to advise the author, "The greatest service you can provide is a concise and oft repeated caveat . . . . delineating just exactly what side-by-side comparisons are (a quantitative listing of forces in being) and are not (indicators of the military balance and relative effectiveness)." Attachment to a letter received from Admiral J. L. Holloway, III, dated September 23, 1977.

6. CIA provided accurate, but limited, information to McDonnell Douglas analysts in St. Louis, who concluded that Backfire has a range between 3,500 and 5,000 miles. Only the lower estimate was ever released. DIA provided detailed data to McDonnell Douglas analysts in California, and to other aircraft corporations, at about the same time in 1976. Ensuing studies contended that Backfire has a range of 4,500–6,000 miles, with 5,000+ being about average. Information provided telephonically by officials in McDonnell Douglas Corporation and DOD on February 22, 1977.

7. Congressional testimony in May 1976 concerning Backfire's role is still essentially correct. "The CIA is saying the aircraft is primarily built for a peripheral role, [although] it has a capability for an intercontinental mission . . . . Everybody agrees in the intelligence community on that." Disputes, however, arise over different opinions concerning intent, rather than capabilities. DIA and Air Force intelligence analysts, who are skeptical of U.S. abilities to assess Soviet plans accurately, would prefer to class Backfire as a strategic nuclear system. CIA considers it tactical. U.S. Congress. Subcommittee on Priorities and Economy in Government of the Joint Economics Committee. *Allocation of Resources in the Soviet Union and China–1976*. Part 2. Hearings. May 24, 1976. 94th Congress, 2d Session. Washington: U.S. Govt. Print. Off., 1976, pp. 71–72. Updated telephonically by DIA officials on November 3, 1977.

8. *Comparative Characteristics of Main Battle Tanks*. Fort Knox: Kentucky, U.S. Army Armor School, June 1973, pp. 11–1 through 11–4, 14–1 through 14–4.

9. One formula for comparing opposing armed forces is contained in Rosenberg, Ralph G., "Relative Combat Power," *Military Review*, March 1978, pp. 56–67.

PART II

Organization and Functions

Soviet armed services feature central control and long-term continuity for key leaders. Force structures, in the main, conform with functions. Politico-military integration is close to complete.

U.S. forces share few of those characteristics. Decentralization dominates. Executive and Legislative Branches share responsibilities. Civil and military roles, for the most part, are separate. So are command and support. Operating forces, as a general rule, are configured for regional, rather than functional, requirements. Tenure for top leaders is temporary.

Respective platforms for strategic planning and combat operations, thus, are clearly different.

U.S. Establishment

America's military high command reflects civilian control, in conformance with our Constitution. Subordinate echelons are shaped to shield this country's interests and strengthen its influence, at home and overseas.

Command Structure

The President formulates defense policy, assisted by advisors. As Commander-in-Chief, he also exerts active control over our armed forces.[1]

Principal deputies for plans and operations are his Special Assistant for National Security Affairs, installed solely by the President, and the Secretary of Defense, who is subject to Senate confirmation. Both are political appointees and civilians.[2] The Chairman of the Joint Chiefs of Staff, his closest military associate, is one layer removed. (Figure 1).

National Security Council (NSC)

The National Security Council advises "the President with respect to the integration of domestic, foreign, and military policies relating to national security so as to enable the military services and the other departments and agencies of the Government to cooperate more effectively." Part and parcel of that prescription is the duty "to assess and appraise the objectives, commitments, and risks of the United States in relation to our actual and potential military power."[3]

Those tasks have remained constant since 1947, but the NSC, which adapts to suit the personal style of each President, has experienced constant evolution and four sweeping revisions under the aegis of seven Administrations. Organizational and operational changes have been profound.

Statutory members include the President, Vice President, Secretary of State, and Secretary of Defense.[4] The Chairman of the Joint Chiefs of Staff, Director of Central Intelligence,[5] and Secretary of the Treasury have been regular attendees at meetings since Truman's time. The President's Special Assistant for National Security Affairs presently orchestrates NSC activities on a continuing basis. Most staff members are civilians.

The current NSC strives to stress long-range policy planning, instead of crisis management, which consumed extensive time in the recent past. CIA provides intelligence input. Other agencies, offices, and cabinet-level departments participate as required, to ensure comprehensive coverage. Products include the dissemination of Presidential decisions and assignment of connected tasks.

Office, Secretary of Defense (OSD)

The Secretary of Defense, who serves the President at Cabinet level, not only sets policy, but directs national defense plans, programs, and operations from his post in the Pentagon. Commissioned officers of armed services "may be detailed for duty as assistants," but "the Secretary may not establish a military staff."[6]

Fourteen incumbents have occupied the office since 1947, for an average tenure of two years.[7] Few had broad related experience, or previously studied the profession of arms seriously.[8]

Early Secretaries possessed little power, in contrast with successors since 1961 who, with one exception, have exerted close, continuous, central control within confines of their Department.[9] That trend seems stable.

Figure 1
U.S. HIGH COMMAND STRUCTURE

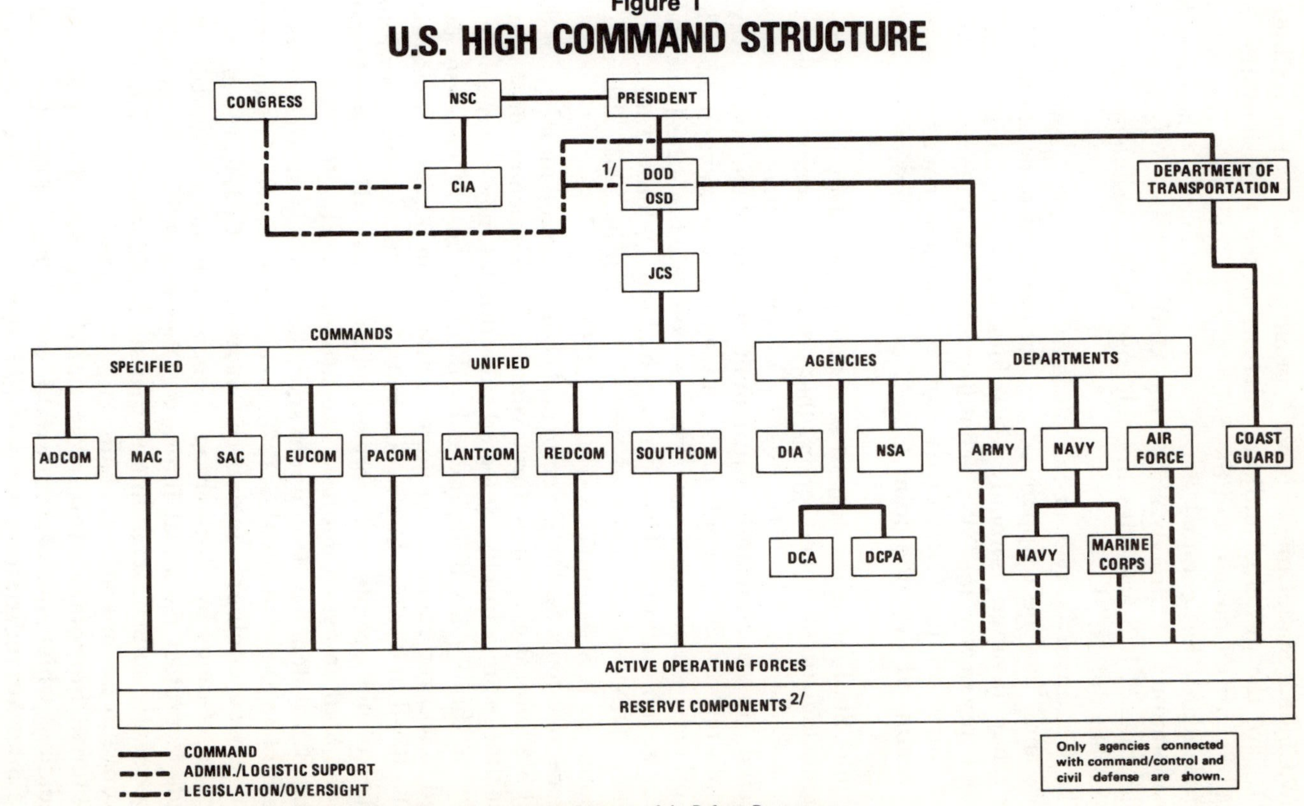
CONGRESS
NSC
PRESIDENT
CIA
1/
DOD
OSD
DEPARTMENT OF TRANSPORTATION
JCS
COMMANDS
SPECIFIED
UNIFIED
AGENCIES
DEPARTMENTS
ADCOM
MAC
SAC
EUCOM
PACOM
LANTCOM
REDCOM
SOUTHCOM
DIA
NSA
ARMY
NAVY
AIR FORCE
COAST GUARD
DCA
DCPA
NAVY
MARINE CORPS
ACTIVE OPERATING FORCES
RESERVE COMPONENTS 2/
COMMAND
ADMIN./LOGISTIC SUPPORT
LEGISLATION/OVERSIGHT
Only agencies connected with command/control and civil defense are shown.
1/ Congressional oversight extends throughout subordinate elements of the Defense Department.
2/ Come under unified/specified Commands only when called to active federal service.

Joint Chiefs of Staff (JCS)

The Joint Chiefs of Staff, whose members include a chairman, the Army Chief of Staff, Chief of Naval Operations, and Air Force Chief of Staff, "are the principal military advisors to the President, the National Security Council, and the Secretary of Defense." The Marine Commandant "has coequal status" when "any matter scheduled for consideration . . . . directly affects the Marine Corps," which is most of the time.[10] JCS activities in each case "take precedence over all their other duties."[11]

The Chairman "serves at the pleasure of the President" for two years, and "may be reappointed . . . . for one additional term." The four other members normally serve four years. Limitations can be waived only in wartime. "While holding office, the Chairman ranks all other officers of the armed forces. However, he may not exercise military command over the Joint Chiefs of Staff or any of the armed forces."[12]

A Joint Staff furnishes support as required, primarily in the form of strategic/logistic plans and reports that prepare JCS members to make recommendations.[13] Its core consists "of not more than 400 officers," selected "in approximately equal numbers" from the Army, Navy/Marines (an 80–20 percent mix[14]), and Air Force. Several agencies and officers, which strictly speaking are separate from the Joint Staff, act as augmentation.[15] They do *not* include Defense Intelligence Agency (DIA), which replaced the J-2 Section in 1961, although it responds to JCS requests, as well as DOD.

Peacetime tours for the Director and commissioned members of the Joint Staff are, at maximum, three years.[16] The Director cannot return thereafter in any capacity. Selected subordinates may resume duty in less than three years if approved by the Secretary of Defense, provided officer returnees never number more than 30. Such limitations can be lifted in wartime but, to ensure tight civilian control "the Joint Staff shall not operate or be organized as an overall Armed Forces General Staff and shall not have executive authority."[17]

The JCS system has been under sporadic attack for several years. A Blue Ribbon Defense Panel in 1970, for example, found it "a forum for inter-service conflict," in which overworked Chiefs reach compromise solutions by "log-rolling", when confronted with daily demands to protect parochial interests. Objective advice to superiors consequently suffers, according to that study, which also feared JCS influence in the operational chain.[18]

Defense Secretary Melvin R. Laird spurned Panel recommendations which, if accepted, would have redefined the JCS role.[19] The Carter Administration, less certain that the system is satisfactory, recently revived review.[20]

Unified/Specified Commands

Active operating forces of the U.S. armed services, other than those in overhead status, are assigned to seven commands with broad, continuing missions.[21] Commanders-in-Chief (CINCs) are four-star generals or flag officers, whose tenures average about three years.

Four unified commands, which amalgamate forces from two or more military services, have regional responsibilities (Map 1). Atlantic Command (LANTCOM) is mainly Navy and Marine, but has mixed staff representation. European Command (EUCOM), which contributes to NATO's forward defense, also covers Africa north of the Sahara and much of the Middle East. Pacific Command (PACOM) has purview for planning purposes from our own west coast through the Indian Ocean and most of Asia. Southern Command (SOUTHCOM) has responsibilities that reach across Latin America.

Three specified commands, manned mainly by the Air Force, are structured for functional purposes. Strategic Air Command (SAC), which contains all U.S. land-based ballistic missiles and long-range bombers, has a global mission. Aerospace Defense Command (ADCOM), an amalgam of active and reserve components, shields the United States.[22] Military Airlift Command (MAC) is single manager for all transport aviation serving U.S. armed services.

Readiness Command (REDCOM), a unified but nominally noncombatant command, controls Army and Air Force tactical units held in CONUS as central reserves.

The normal chain of command in all cases extends from the President, as Commander-in-Chief, to the Secretary of Defense. Their mandates are transmitted to unified and specified commanders through the Joint Chiefs of Staff, who maintain the World-Wide Military Command and Control System (WWMCCS).[23] Communications channels "for execution of the Single Integrated Operational Plan (SIOP)[24] and other time-sensitive operations" are directly to "executing commanders" at appropriate levels. In emergency, contact could be with Minuteman missile sites or Polaris/Poseidon submarines.

Military Departments/Services

Departments of the Army, Navy, and Air Force "at the seat of government" are separate DOD organizations. Civilian Service Secretaries operate "under the authority, direction and control of the Secretary of Defense."[25]

Active and reserve components of the Army, Navy, Air Force, and Marine Corps are subordinate elements within those Departments. Four-star Chiefs "rank above all other officers" on respective Service lists, less the Chairman of the Joint Chiefs of Staff.[26]

Map 1

U.S. UNIFIED AND SPECIFIED COMMANDS

NOTES: Whether or not there is a boundary between EUCOM and PACOM through the Soviet Union is classified information. Readers can presume that if such a line could be identified, it would in some way join the two water boundaries between those commands.

Canada and Mexico, being contiguous to the United States, enjoy special security relationships. No unified or specified command has responsibility for Africa South of the Sahara.

Still, their power in that capacity is limited. They organize, train, and equip forces for assignment to unified and specified commands, but exert no command authority after control passes, although administrative and logistic support continues. Other responsibilities, indirectly related, range from doctrine development to weapons research.[27]

Shared relationships of the sort just described produce inconsistent results. DOD holds each JCS member "responsible for keeping the secretary of his military department fully informed on matters considered or acted upon by the Joint Chiefs of Staff,"[28] but frictions arise when principles and practice fail to coincide.[29]

Force Functions

The Department of Defense deploys armed forces to support and defend the Constitution against all enemies, foreign and domestic; to insure, by timely and effective action, the security of the United States, its possessions, and areas vital to its interests; to uphold and advance national policies; and to safeguard internal security.[30]

Congress, in accord with Title 10, United States Code, confirms fundamental functions of the U.S. Army, Navy, Air Force, and Marines. DOD, with Presidential approval, spells out a series of Service duties in somewhat greater detail. (See Annex D for verbatim texts).[31]

The following sections summarize salient functions, Service-by-Service, stressing degrees of interdependence.

Army Roles and Missions

The U.S. Army prepares primarily to conduct prompt and sustained operations on land. It is suited specifically to close with and defeat large enemy ground forces and to secure, occupy, defend and, if necessary, govern strategic areas overseas. In some circumstances, it provides massive logistic and administrative support to sister services. The active Army and National Guard also assist in domestic security missions, when so ordered by competent higher authority.

The Army, however, depends on the Air Force and Navy for most of its aerial firepower, long-range reconnaissance, and aerospace defense,[32] plus all strategic mobility.

Navy Roles and Missions

General naval supremacy is the U.S. Navy's goal. It prepares to conduct prompt and sustained operations on, over, and under high seas; to destroy enemy naval forces; suppress the foe's ocean-going commerce at terminals and in between; control vital ocean areas; and protect U.S. maritime life lines. Only sealift can move mass tonnages transoceanically, given current states of technological art, or transport land forces for amphibious assaults.

There is no explicit statutory authorization for the Navy to conduct strategic nuclear operations. That function is implicitly included under "operations incident to war at sea," according to current interpretation.[33]

Navies, free afloat, depend on installations ashore, and lack abilities to project power far inland, except with aircraft and missiles.

Air Force Roles and Missions

The U.S. Air Force, our only Service with offensive strategic aerospace warfare as an official function, is also best adapted for some aspects of CONUS air defense. Its tactical air assets, unlike those of the Navy and Marine Corps, are tasked expressly to attain general air superiority and influence areas inland. They also conduct close combat, interdiction, and airlift operations for the Army.

Substantial assistance from other Services is essential for logistic support and local security overseas.

Marine Corps Roles and Missions

The U.S. Marine Corps, organized "to include not less than three [active] combat divisions and three air wings,"[34] is a combined arms force that specializes in amphibious operations. Marines are ideal for "showing the flag", seizing and/or defending advanced naval bases, and conducting land operations along a littoral that is essential to naval campaigns, under an organic air umbrella that assists in fleet defense and covers forces ashore.

Marine air/ground teams, however, are constrained by small size and lack staying power. When the Corps participates in protracted, large-scale campaigns, as it did during World War I, in Korea, and Vietnam, it needs substantial non-Navy assistance.

Congressional Influence

Congress, with legislative and oversight powers, brings great pressures to bear on the size, shape, characteristics, operational concepts, and consequent capabilities of U.S. armed services. Some controls are indirect, but still can be decisive.[35]

Budgetary Responsibilities

An annual confrontation occurs at budget time, when Congress and the Executive Branch strive to reconcile national security requirements with acceptable costs.[36]

The Armed Services committees, which establish pay scales for all U.S. armed forces, active and reserve, annually originate legislation that covers about one-third of all DOD expenditures, especially for research, development, and procurement. Appropriations committees may cut consequent authorizations approved by Congress and signed by the President, but cannot exceed such limits.

Two-thirds of the Pentagon's annual budget request are still handled exclusively by the Appropriations committees. Those expenditures involve semi-stable constants, rather than contentious variables like weapons procurement. Operations and maintenance funds, military pay and allowances, and retirement benefits are representative. Since the Armed Services and Appropriations committees often have differing views, the Executive Branch today must satisfy four reviewing authorities.

That fact of life is further complicated by a division of responsibility that places most foreign military aid under jurisdiction of the Senate and House Foreign Affairs/International Relations Committees.[37] Differences of opinion with the Executive Branch, and sometimes between themselves, can make it difficult to promulgate compromise policies.

Treaty Ratification

Article II of the U.S. Constitution permits the President to make treaties "by and with the advice and consent of the Senate, provided two thirds of the Senators present concur."

Eight mutual defense pacts, with more than 40 participants, all went through that process. (See subsequent section on U.S. commitments.) Panama Canal treaties were ratified in March and April 1978. SALT II negotiators have yet to present a pact.

Manpower Matters

Manpower procurement matters related to strength levels, the draft, and the All-Volunteer Force have been congressional concerns for many years. Congress also exercises increasing oversight responsibilities regarding personnel utilization.[38]

Investigations and subsequent actions address such diverse subjects as recruiting practices; a gamut of policies that affect the retention of career personnel (everything from housing to family separations); the problem of "grade creep," which many congressmen believe has produced too many "chiefs" in comparison with "Indians;" officer/enlisted ratios, which cause similar criticism; student loads for recruit and specialized training; flight schools; professional education in military and civilian institutions; ROTC and OCS; and the balance between combat and support personnel. Discipline, drug addiction, racial strife, and other morale indicators consume considerable time and energy.

War Powers

U.S. founding fathers intended that no one man should commit this country to war, but constitutional guarantees in that regard have been subject to elastic interpretation. The constitutional separation of powers on one hand reserves for Congress the right to declare wars. Custom recognizes that the Chief Executive must be able to respond rapidly in emergency.

The President traditionally played the dominant role. Congress has declared war only five times since 1789: the War of 1812; the Mexican War; the Spanish-American War; World War I; and World War II. Congress often assented to armed actions in ways that fell short of formal declarations, but many adventures occurred without congressional concurrence.

That situation has changed, at least in degree.

The War Powers Resolution of 1973 forbids the President to wage undeclared war for more than 60 days, unless Congress gives express consent by a majority vote in both chambers. That limitation would prevent minor incidents or emergency actions from developing into large-scale, prolonged hostilities without congressional concurrence. Nevertheless, the phraseology is loose enough to permit the President considerable leeway in situations that seem to call for force or the threat of force.[39]

Ambiguities will remain until applications and constitutionality are tested by the courts. Meanwhile, the War Powers Resolution puts on the books a law that sharply limits the President's authority to wage war solely on his initiative.[40]

Miscellaneous Oversight

Oversight and investigative powers of the House and Senate Armed Services Committees cover nearly every defense activity.[41] Other committee interests are important, but more intensive. Top leaders, military and civilian, can take office only if sanctioned by the Senate. The Secretary of Defense can neither transfer functions nor scrap weapons systems without concurrence by the full Congress.[42] The list of specifics is too lengthy to cite.

Legislation covers some situations. In others, congressional pressures cause Executive Branch officials to take corrective actions spontaneously.

Soviet Establishment

The Communist Party of the Soviet Union (CPSU), specifically the Political Bureau (Politburo) of its Central Committee, is at the pinnacle of Soviet power. It is "the leading and guiding force of Soviet society and the nucleus of its political system." The Presidium of a bicameral parliamentary body called the Supreme Soviet is the senior State authority on the governmental side.[43]

Interlocking, overlapping responsibilities for national security purposes permeate the system. Party leaders, who also hold key posts in government, are in total control at the top.[44]

Command Structure

Open source literature that specifically concerns Soviet high command of armed forces is strictly limited. Scraps available commonly do as much to cloud issues as to clarify.[45] The organizational chart at Figure 2 was pieced together from several sources. Components shown are reliable. Command relationships, camouflaged by "shell games" and clever charades, are considerably less certain, and would change conclusively if war should occur.

Council of Defense

Leonid Il'ich Brezhnev, current Secretary General of the CPSU, serves simultaneously as Chairman of the Presidium of the Supreme Soviet. He formed the Council of Defense in his latter capacity, and confirmed its composition, in accord with Article 121 of the Soviet Constitution. His promotion to Marshal of the Soviet Union on May 7, 1976 coincided with public disclosure that he personally chairs that conclave, which previously was secret.[46]

Council members apparently include several colleagues from the Politburo. Other Party dignitaries and military men doubtless attend some meetings, depending on the agenda. The powerful Minister of Internal Affairs (MVD) and Chairman of the Committee for State Security (KGB) may be among them.[47]

The Council of Defense in peacetime is slightly similar to the U.S. National Security Council, chaired by our President. Policies, plans, and preparations, for example, span political, economic, social, and psychological, as well as military, spectrums.[48] The Council reaches decisions and issues decrees but, unlike our NSC, can *direct* compliance by civilian sectors along with armed services.

Differences in wartime would be more dramatic if, as apparently advertised, the current Council of Defense converted to wield "the same powers as the State Committee of Defense [GKO] during the Great Patriotic War." Connections with the Central Committee CPSU definitely would be direct, in accord with contentions that concentrated control "of the country and its Armed Forces . . . . is a decisive condition" for victory.[49]

Figure 2.
SOVIET PEACETIME HIGH COMMAND STRUCTURE

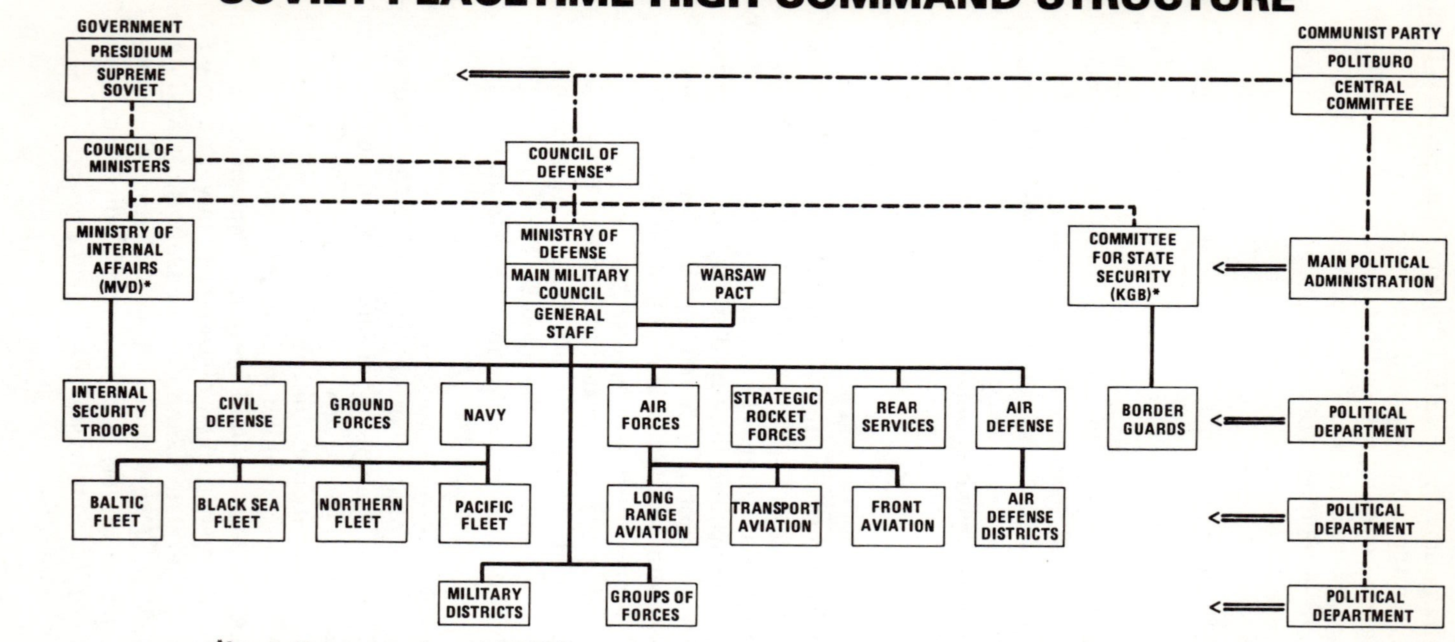

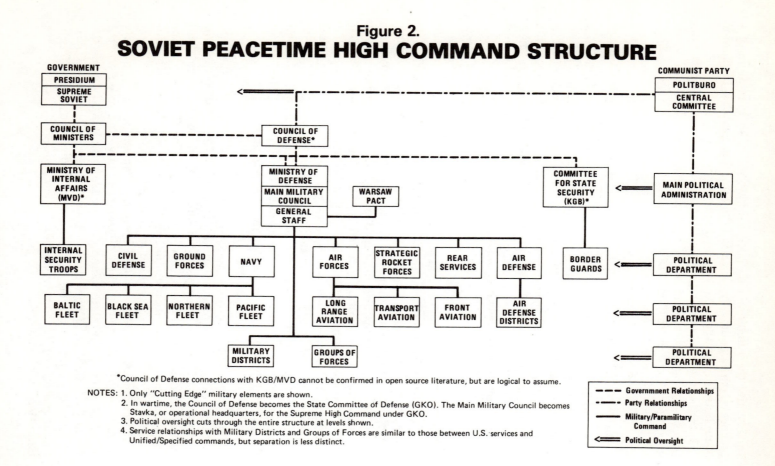

*Council of Defense connections with KGB/MVD cannot be confirmed in open source literature, but are logical to assume.

NOTES:
1. Only "Cutting Edge" military elements are shown.
2. In wartime, the Council of Defense becomes the State Committee of Defense (GKO). The Main Military Council becomes Stavka, or operational headquarters, for the Supreme High Command under GKO.
3. Political oversight cuts through the entire structure at levels shown.
4. Service relationships with Military Districts and Groups of Forces are similar to those between U.S. services and Unified/Specified commands, but separation is less distinct.

Ministry of Defense

The Soviet Ministry of Defense is mainly an administrative abstraction. Plans and actions are apportioned among components.

Main Military Council The Defense Ministry's Main Military Council, guided by the Council of Defense, generates policy for Soviet armed services.

Marshal D. E. Ustinov, the Minister of Defense, most likely is Chairman, in addition to his duties as Politburo member and on the Council of Defense.[50] Brezhnev probably participates, along with three First Deputy Ministers of Defense. Membership may also include the Chief of the Main Political Administration (a CPSU affiliate), all 10 Deputy Defense Ministers, Service commanders, and the Inspector General, plus Chiefs of Civil Defense and Rear Services.[51]

Should war occur, a transformed Main Military Council would take over immediately as operational headquarters, or Stavka, for a Supreme High Command under GKO. Some present members probably would become permanent advisors, vice participants, to concentrate central command and control even further.[52]

General Staff The Soviet General Staff, which has no equivalent in the United States, is executive agent for the Main Military Council in peacetime, and for Stavka in time of war.

Personnel policies strive to promote professional competence and stability. Senior officers often serve for more than a decade in key positions.[53] Graduation from a two-year course at the General Staff Academy is mandatory for many subordinate slots.[54] Tour lengths tend to suppress parochial Service ties.[55]

General Staff purview has expanded substantially since World War II, when "leadership of military actions" was confined mainly to Ground Forces.[56] It now coordinates "central administrations" of the Defense Ministry, together with staff activities of all armed services, civil defense, "military districts, groups abroad, air defense districts, and fleets," according to an official Soviet statement in December 1976. Tasks entail everything from trend analysis to certain aspects of training. The General Staff "researches actual problems of Soviet military science," then tests its theories in peacetime practice. Perhaps most important of all, it shapes a unified military strategy to support political doctrine promulgated by the Communist Party.[57]

In short, the Soviet General Staff cuts straight across a range of responsibilities shared by our National Security Council, DOD, JCS, and the U.S. armed services.

Military Services/Civil Defense Five military services, structured on functional lines, comprise the Soviet "cutting edge". All are subsidiary to the General Staff. Tenure for top leaders is about eight years.[58]

Strategic Rocket Forces (SRF) contain all land-based missiles with ranges that exceed 1,000 kilometers (600 miles). Unlike SAC, it lacks any aircraft.

Air Defense Forces (PVO Strany) control antiballistic missile (ABM), interceptor aircraft, and land-based surface-to-air missile (SAM) assets in the Soviet Union, along with ancillary installations. Air Defense Districts divide the active direction.

Headquarters, Soviet Ground Forces, which Khrushchev scuttled just before he himself stepped down,[59] was reinstated in 1968. Its subordinate arms and services are organized, trained, and equipped to wage land warfare with conventional or theater nuclear weapons. Control, however, passes to other parties for operational purposes, just as it does for U.S. counterparts.

Soviet Air Forces (VVS) include three main elements. Long-Range Aviation deploys two strategic nuclear air armies, the first in European Russia, a second in the Far East. Military Transport Aviation, the Soviet equivalent of MAC, retains a sizable pool of strategic and tactical aircraft in central reserve, but parcels out part of its holdings, including cargo helicopters, to joint combatant commands. Front Aviation, which furnishes its entire contingent of fighter/attack aircraft for joint use by Military Districts and Soviet Groups of Forces in Eastern Europe, focuses its energies on training and support.[60]

The Navy, with forces aloft, ashore, and afloat, subdivides into four fleets (Northern, Baltic, Black, and Pacific), plus a Caspian Sea flotilla. Strategic nuclear submarines, assigned mainly to the Northern and Pacific Fleets, concentrate on the east and west flanks, with access to open oceans. Naval air power is almost all land based.

Civil defense, in keeping with Soviet war survival strategy, is coequal in status with the five military services. Its chief, a four star general, is also a Deputy Minister of Defense. Each of the 15 Soviet Republics has a general officer in charge. Training programs are countrywide, comprehensive, and compulsory.[61] The small U.S. structure, which attracts little attention from superiors, stresses natural disasters, not national security.

Joint Combatant Commands Soviet Ground Forces and Front Aviation, along with combat and service support, are assigned to joint combatant commands that, in some respects, are similar to U.S. unified commands. Those self-contained entities, like the several Services and Civil Defense, come under direct supervision of the General Staff.

Sixteen Military Districts, which enjoy jurisdiction in the Soviet Union, differ in size and shape from the 15 Republics (Map 2). Concentrations generally are greatest in the smallest Districts that border Warsaw Pact states. They also show better readiness conditions, by and large, than those in Siberia or central reserve.[62]

Four Groups of Forces, or theater commands, hold sway outside Soviet frontiers: Group of Soviet Forces, Germany (GSFG), with headquarters at Wünsdorf, near Berlin; Northern Group (Poland), headquartered at Leignitz; Central Group (Czechoslovakia), at Milovce, near Prague; and Southern Group (Hungary), with its command post in Budapest.[63]

Static formations would convert to mobile "fronts" in wartime, somewhat like former U.S. army groups, but with strong tactical air components.

Internal Affairs/State Security

Finally, Soviet leaders are chronically concerned about domestic security, which creates requirements for two full-time force categories that are absent as such in the U.S. establishment: KGB Border Guards and internal security troops belonging to the MVD.[64] Both are heavily armed. Our National Guard, under State or Federal control, occasionally is called on to quell civil violence, if police or other authorities for any reason fail to preserve property or protect people, but it by no means is a close counterpart.[65]

Force Functions

Soviet force functions doubtless duplicate those described for U.S. counterparts in many respects, although few have ever been disclosed.[66] U.S. intelligence sources are classified.

Nevertheless, differences that contribute to asymmetries between the two sides can be deduced from Soviet force structure. Three disparities are dominant.

For openers, Title 10 obligates our Army, Navy, and Air Force to develop and deploy capabilities that could, if required, conduct "sustained" combat operations. Soviet services are improving their staying power, but still seem to be charged more with shock action. U.S. general purpose forces consequently are long on logistic support and sometimes short on combat power in comparison.

DOD Directive 5100.1 assigns primary amphibious assault responsibilities to the U.S. Marine Corps. It also instructs our Army to participate. The Soviet Union, which has amphibious ships for its naval infantry, marks no such mission for its Ground Forces, whose capabilities currently are confined to administrative landings from merchant ships.

Map 2

SOVIET MILITARY DISTRICTS

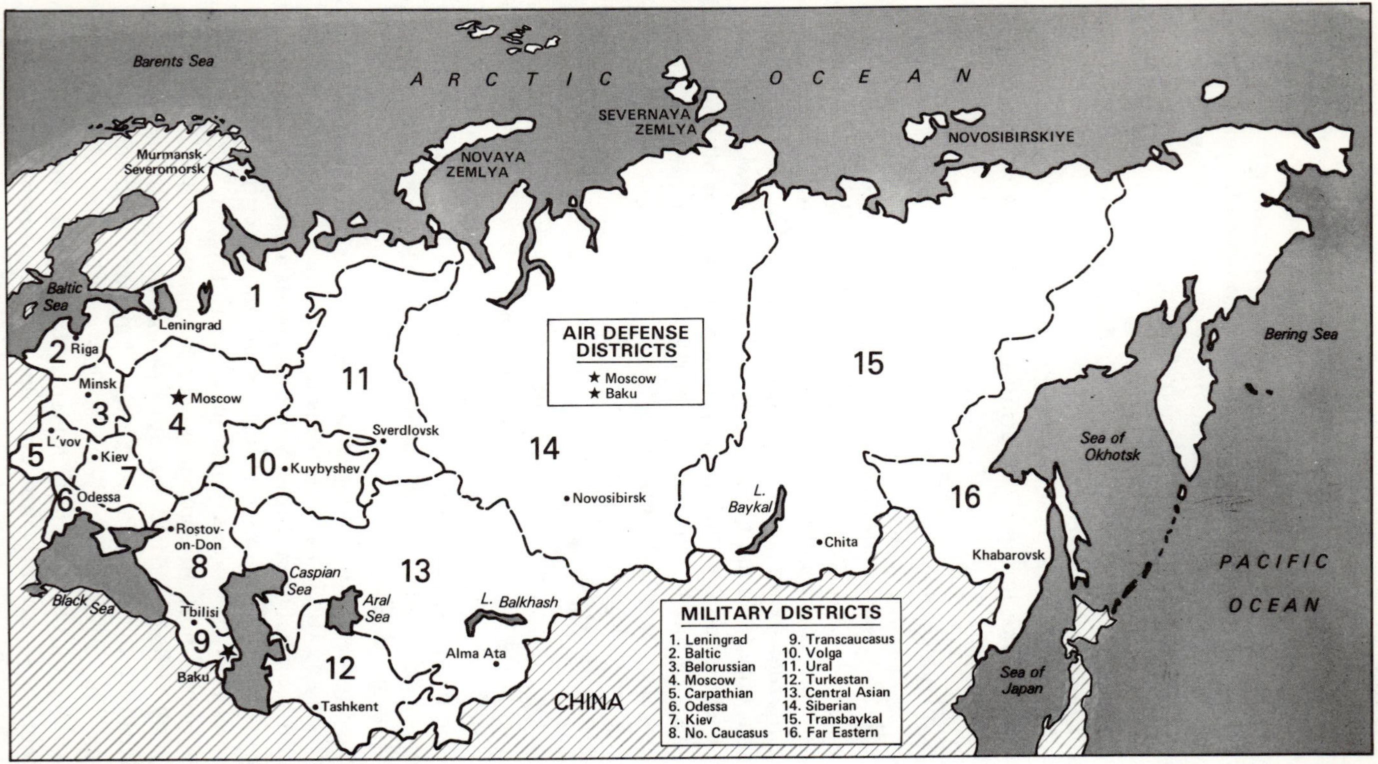

Source: Adapted from a map compiled by Harriet Fast Scott

U.S. Navy and Marine airmen are tasked to take care of aerial combat and ground attack missions. Soviet opposite numbers are not. Their naval infantry, which lacks organic air support and cannot count on carrier-based fighters for cover, is poorly suited for flexible options beyond reach of bombers ashore. Yak-36 fighters aboard the latest Soviet aircraft carriers afford the first indication that Soviet naval functions could change.

Overall Observations

U.S. and Soviet high commands and armed services are structured to serve essentially different political systems and security purposes. Neither has a corner on organizational assets or liabilities that materially affect the military balance.

The Soviet establishment accrues important advantages from secrecy, central control, and stable assignments for political leadership and military professionals in top echelons. Those strengths, however, contain the seeds of weakness. They inhibit the introduction of innovative ideas and reduce responsiveness among subordinates, whose tendencies to take initiative at critical times can best be described as "scant".[67]

The U.S. setup, subject to constant public scrutiny, is steered by civilians, who rarely have much military experience. It also is plagued by shared responsibilities and "revolving door" personnel policies in military ranks. Still, the ceaseless search for quality (sparked in part by critics in Congress) and abilities to accommodate quickly help compensate. So does displacing "dead wood". Those crucial credits counter debits so successfully that the system proves strong under pressure.

Footnotes

1. Article II, Section 2 of the U.S. Constitution designates the President as "Commander in Chief of the Army and Navy of the United States, and of the Militia of the several States, when called into the actual Service of the United States."

2. The Secretary of Defense, by law, "may not be appointed . . . . within 10 years after relief from active duty as a commissioned officer of a regular component of an armed force." Neither may his deputies. U.S. Congress. House. Committee on Armed Services. *National Security Act of 1947* (Public Law 253, 80th Congress, July 26, 1947. 61 Stat. 495), as amended. Washington: U.S. Govt. Print. Off., 1973, pp. 7, 13.

3. *Ibid.*, p. 2.

4. *Ibid.*

5. *Ibid.*, pp. 3–5. "At no time shall the two positions of the Director and Deputy Director [of CIA] be occupied simultaneously by commissioned officers of the armed services, whether on active or retired status."

6. *Ibid.*, p. 15. Four military men currently serve as Deputy Assistant Secretaries of Defense.

7. Elliot L. Richardson's term as Secretary of Defense, the shortest, totalled 114 days. Robert S. McNamara served seven years, from 1961 to 1968.

8. General of the Army George C. Marshall is the only military professional ever to hold the office of Secretary of Defense. His term during the Truman Administration was confined to parts of 1950–1951.

9. Defense Secretary Melvin R. Laird briefly recast DOD in a participative management mold (1969–1973) that contrasted with the so-called "McNamara Monarchy" (1961–1968). Laird's successors delegate less authority than he did.

10. *National Security Act of 1947*, as amended, p. 19.

11. Department of Defense Directive 5158.1, *Organization of the Joint Chiefs of Staff and Relationships With the Office of the Secretary of Defense,* December 31, 1958, as amended, p. 2.

12. Eight officers have served as Chairman of the Joint Chiefs of Staff since 1947. A ninth incumbent filled that slot in June 1978. Four were Army, three Navy, and two Air Force. General Maxwell D. Taylor served slightly less than one full term (October 1962–July 1964). Only one, General Earle G. Wheeler, was extended beyond four years, from July 1964 to July 1970, during the Vietnam War. Quotations are from *National Security Act of 1947,* as amended, pp. 19–20.

13. Full JCS responsibilities are contained in *Unified Action Armed Forces (UNAAF),* JCS Pub. 2, Washington: The Joint Chiefs of Staff, November, 1959, as amended, pp. 11–12.

14. The Joint Chiefs of Staff, *Commanders Digest,* January 6, 1977, p. 6.

15. The entire Organization of the Joint Chiefs of Staff (OJCS) approximates 1,285 military and civilian personnel. Total commissioned officer strength, including those on the Joint Staff, slightly exceeds 600.

16. Tour limitations do not apply to other elements of OJCS.

17. *National Security Act of 1947,* as amended, p. 20.

18. *Report to the President and the Secretary of Defense on the Department of Defense by the Blue Ribbon Defense Panel, July 1, 1970.* Washington: U.S. Govt. Print. Off., 1970, pp. 33–35.

19. Secretary Laird, speaking at a press conference, made his position clear concerning the Joint Chiefs: "I listen to their recommendations on a regular basis, and I don't believe that there has ever been a better working relationship." Deputy Secretary David Packard concurred with the comment, "The report greatly underrates the Joint Chiefs of Staff. DOD Adopts Contract Release Suggestion; Studies Conflicts of Interest," *Commanders Digest,* August 15, 1970, p. 8; Department of Defense News Release No. 681–70, p. 1.

20. Weinraub, Bernard, "Role of the Joint Chiefs Under Study; Overhaul of Command is Possible," *New York Times,* November 8, 1977, p. 1.

21. *National Security Act of 1947,* as amended, p. 12.

22. Continental Air Defense Command (CONAD), a unified command, included Army and Air Force components (ARADCOM and ADCOM). ADCOM, much reduced itself, replaced CONAD in 1975, recognizing the reduced role of CONUS aerospace defense in U.S. nuclear strategy. ARADCOM, whose responsibilities included antiballistic missile (ABM) and surface-to-air missile (SAM) defenses for the United States, disappeared in January that same year.

23. Department of Defense Directive 5100.30, *World-Wide Military Command and Control System (WWMCCS),* December 2, 1971, pp. 1–2.

24. The SIOP is America's strategic nuclear strike plan.

25. *National Security Act of 1947*, as amended, p. 10.

26. *Ibid.*, p. 18.

27. *Ibid.*, p. 12; JCS Pub. 2, p. 16.

28. Department of Defense Directive 5100.1, *Functions of the Department of Defense and its Major Components*, December 31, 1958, as amended, p. 2.

29. U.S. Congress. House. Committee on Government Operations. *Access of Service Secretaries to Military Information.* Hearings. 94th Congress, 1st Session. Washington: U.S. Govt. Print Off., 1975, 40 pp.; and 94th Congress, 2d Session. Washington: U.S. Govt. Print. Off., 1976, 22 pp.

30. JCS Pub. 2, p. 10.

31. Civil defense enjoys equal status with armed services in the Soviet establishment. Our Defense Civil Preparedness Agency (DCPA) does not. It is a small DOD subsidiary.

32. Army functions include aspects of strategic aerospace defense for the United States, a dormant demand at this time.

33. Strategic nuclear operations by the U.S. Navy have never been seriously challenged by other services, because so doing would open up the whole question of overlapping roles and missions.

34. *National Security Act of 1947*, amended, p. 16.

35. Article I, Section 1 of the U.S. Constitution grants Congress all legislative authority at the federal level. Section 8 prescribes powers to "provide for the common defense," by raising and supporting active armed forces and a militia. It also prescribes rules for their regulation.

36. For an extensive commentary on congressional budgetary processes, see Aspin, Les, "The Defense Budget and Foreign Policy: The Role of Congress," *Daedalus*, Summer 1975, pp. 155–174.

37. Rule XXV, 1j, 1, Committee on Foreign Relations. U.S. Congress. Senate. Committee on Rules and Administration, *Standing Rules of The United States Senate.* Washington: U.S. Govt. Print. Off., 1977; Rule XI, 7, Committee on Foreign Affairs (now the Committee on International Relations). U.S. Congress. House. *Rules of the House of Representatives* [by] Lewis Deschler, Parliamentarian. Washington: U.S. Govt. Print. Off., 1967.

38. Rule XXV, lb, 1, Committee on Armed Services, *Standing Rules of the United States Senate;* Rule XI, 3, Committee on Armed Services, *Rules of the House of Representatives.*

39. War Powers Resolution of 1973, PL 93-148, 87 Stat. 555.

40. The Senate approved the War Powers Resolution on October 10, 1973. The House followed suit two days later. President Nixon vetoed the bill on October 24, 1973, calling it "clearly unconstitutional," but was overriden by the Congress on November 7. "War Powers of Congress and the President—Veto." *Congressional Record*, November 7, 1973, pp. S20093–S20116; "War Powers Resolution—Veto Message From the President of the United States," *Congressional Record*, November 7, 1973, pp. H9641–H9661.

41. Rule XXV, ib, 1, Standing Rules of the United States Senate indicates that the Armed Services Committee shall "study and review, on a comprehensive basis, matters relating to the common defense policy of the United States, and report thereon from time to time." Oversight and legislative responsibilities are closely connected. The latter cover:

> "1) Aeronautical and space activities peculiar to or primarily associated with the development of weapons systems or military operations.
>
> 2) Common defense.
>
> 3) Department of Defense, the Department of the Army, the Department of the Navy, and the Department of the Air Force, generally.

4) Maintenance and operation of the Panama Canal, including administration, sanitation, and government of the Canal Zone.

5) Military research and development.

6) National security aspects of nuclear energy.

7) Naval petroleum reserves, except those in Alaska.

8) Pay, promotion, retirement, and other benefits and privileges of members of the Armed Forces, including overseas education of military and civilian dependents.

9) Selective Service system.

10) Strategic and critical materials necessary for the common defense."

The House Armed Services Committee has a similar charter.

42. *National Security Act of 1947,* as amended, pp. 7–9, 12–17, 19.

43. See Articles 6 and 108, *Constitution (Fundamental Law) of the Union of Soviet Socialist Republics,* Adopted at the Seventh (Special) Session of the Supreme Soviet of the USSR, Ninth Convocation on October 7, 1977, Moscow: Novosti Press Agency Publishing House, 1977, pp. 21, 81.

44. Keefe, Eugene K. et al., *Area Handbook for the Soviet Union,* DA Pam 550–95. Washington: U.S. Govt. Print. Off., 1971, p. 397 and pp. 419–424.

45. "Very few [U.S.] scholars or intelligence analysts," for example, "have specialized in the [Soviet] General Staff, and our data base in both the classified and unclassified worlds apparently is seriously deficient. References *to* the General Staff are fairly common, but hard information *about* it is rare. When limited information becomes available, it tends to raise more questions than are answered." JCS (J-5) written comments on a draft of this study, December 14, 1977.

46. Scott, Harriet Fast, "The Soviet High Command," Soviet Aerospace Almanac Issue, *Air Force Magazine,* March 1977, pp. 52–53.

47. *Ibid.* Membership in the State Committee for Defense (GKO) during World War II originally included Josef Stalin, as Chairman; V. M. Molotov, the Foreign Minister; Marshal K. E. Voroschilov, Commissar for Defense; G. M. Malenkov, who briefly succeeded Stalin as Premier in 1953; and L. P. Beria, Chief, Commissariat of Internal Affairs (NKVD). N. A. Bulganin, N. A. Vozhesenskiy, L. M. Kaganovich, and A. I. Mikoyen joined a bit later. *Soviet Military Encyclopedia,* Vol. 2, p. 622.

48. Scott, Harriet Fast, "The Soviet High Command," p. 53. "The preparation of a nation for war is accomplished along three main lines—the preparation of the armed forces, the preparation of the national economy, and the preparation of the population." Sokolovsky, V. D., *Military Strategy.* 3d Ed. Moscow: Military Publishing House, 1968. Translated and edited with an analysis and commentary by Harriet Fast Scott, New York: Crane, Russak & Co., Inc., 1975, pp. 306–333.

49. Sokolovsky, writing eight years before Soviet sources openly confirmed that a Council of Defense in fact exists, announced the "possible organization of a higher agency of leadership of the country," with GKO powers. *Military Strategy,* p. 361.

50. Marshal Georgi K. Zhukov, who served briefly as Minister of Defense in 1957, was the first active professional military officer to become a member of the Politburo. Since then, only Marshal A. A. Grechko (whose term was nine years) has been so honored. Ustinov, despite his marshal's baton, has no military background. *Understanding Soviet Military Developments.* Washington: Office of the Assistant Chief of Staff for Intelligence, Department of the Army, April 1977, p. 10.

51. Scott, Harriet Fast, comments on a draft of this study, February 22, 1978.

52. Scott, Harriet Fast, "The Soviet High Command," pp. 53–54; Sokolovsky, V. D., *Military Strategy,* p. 361.

53. Army General S. M. Shtemenko seems to hold the General Staff tenure record. He retained important posts from World War II until his death in 1976, a period of 30-plus years. JCS (J-5) comments on a draft of this study, December 14, 1977.

54. The U.S. Armed Forces Staff College is a JCS affiliate. Its courses run five months. The National War College and Industrial College of the Armed Forces are also

under JCS jurisdiction. Graduation from one of those courses, which cover 10 months, or from a Service war college with equivalent credit, is a prerequisite for many policy/plans posts in the Pentagon.

55. Scott, Harriet Fast, "The Soviet High Command," p. 55.

56. Sokolovsky, V. D., *Military Strategy*, p. 362.

57. Quoted in Scott, Harriet Fast, "The Soviet High Command," p. 55.

58. Current Air Defense, Ground Force, and Air Force commanders were installed in 1966, 1967, and 1969 respectively. Admiral of the Fleet S. G. Gorshkov has served as Navy Commander-in-Chief since 1956, 22 consecutive years.

59. Soviet Ground Force reductions during the late 1950s are discussed in Wolfe, Thomas W., *Soviet Power and Europe, 1945–1970*. Baltimore: The Johns Hopkins Press, 1970, pp. 160–166.

60. Erickson, John, *Soviet-Warsaw Pact Force Levels*, USSI Report 76-2. Washington: United States Strategic Institute, 1976, pp. 48–51.

61. Gouré, Leon, *Soviet Civil Defense in the Seventies*. Coral Gables, Fla.: Center for Advanced International Studies, University of Miami, September 1975, pp. 1, 37–47, 82–94; Scott, Harriet Fast, "Civil Defense in the USSR," *Air Force Magazine*, October 1975, pp. 29–33.

62. Central Asian and Far Eastern Military Districts also have large force concentrations. *Understanding Soviet Military Developments*, p. 11.

63. *Ibid.*, pp. 11–12; Erickson, John, *Soviet-Warsaw Pact Force Levels*, pp. 70–71.

64. KGB Border Guards are "entrusted" with "protection of the land and sea state border of the USSR." Many missions are assigned in Section III, Articles 29–30, 39, Statute on the Protection of the State Border of the Union of Soviet Socialist Republics, Vedmosti SSSR (1960), No. 34, Item 324, adopted August 5, 1960. English translation in *Soviet Statutes and Decisions*, Summer 1967, Vol. III, No. 4, pp. 18–23. MVD internal security functions are not available in unclassified English translations.

65. Army National Guard Regulation 350–1, October 31, 1975, enjoins each State "to provide units organized, equipped and trained to function effectively at existing strength in the protection of life and property and the preservation of peace, order and public safety under competent orders of Federal or State authorities." State authorization to use the National Guard for internal security purposes is contained in laws of the 50 States. Title 10, United States Code, Chapter 15, Section 333 permits the President to federalize the Guard "to suppress, in a State, any insurrection, domestic violence, unlawful combination, or conspiracy, if . . . . any part or class of [that State's] people is deprived of a right, privilege, immunity, or protection named in the Constitution and secured by law, and the constituted authorities of that State are unable, fail, or refuse" to provide proper protection.

66. Some insight into Soviet roles and missions is manifest in Kozlov, S. N., *USSR Officers' Handbook. Chapter 5. Moscow: USSR Ministry of Defense, 1971*, pp. 127–140. Contained in *Translations on USSR Military Affairs*, No. 742. Washington: Joint Publications Research Service, September 29, 1971 (JPRS 54154), pp. 52–64.

67. Interactions are addressed in Wolfe, Thomas W., *The Military Dimension in the Making of Soviet Foreign and Defense Policy*. Washington: The Rand Corporation, October 1977, 44 pp.

PART III

Building Blocks

Three basic building blocks contribute to military capabilities: money, manpower, and materiel. Those indices, however, are often misapplied in comparing competitors. This short section provides perspective.

Defense Budgets

Comparing defense budgets, an interesting intellectual pursuit, is among the most publicized, but least meaningful, means of measuring military power.

Purpose of Comparing Budgets

Budget studies concerning the U.S./Soviet military balance most often emphasize one of two issues, sometimes both:[1]

—Economic "burdens" that armed forces impose on respective societies, with special concern for national abilities to sustain particular pressures over specified periods at the expense of domestic priorities.
—The magnitude of respective military expenditures, with special attention to trends.

Methods of Calculating Soviet Budgets

The annual Soviet State Budget contains a solitary statistic in a single-line entry entitled "Defense". The figure fluctuates slightly to suit political purposes, but has stayed fairly constant at 17-some-odd billion rubles for several years.[2]

That scrap of unsubstantiated information reportedly reflects most Soviet outlays for personnel, operations, maintenance, and military construction. Additional costs may be concealed elsewhere, along with research, development, and procurement.[3] The Ministry of Education bears expenses for extensive basic training conducted in civilian schools. Most money for moving military units and materiel comes from the Ministry of Transportation. The Welfare Ministry administers military retired pay. And so on.[4]

U.S. calculations of Soviet defense budgets, therefore, must be devised, either in dollars or rubles. Both methods commonly begin with the same data base, which includes a detailed account of physical accoutrements and activities that constitute Soviet defense efforts for any given year.[5]

Dollar computations speculate how much it would cost to reproduce Moscow's military establishment in the United States, then contrast consequent estimates with confirmed U.S. expenditures. Such comparisons reveal rough budgetary relationships and trends, but no more.[6]

Ruble computations assist U.S. analysts in assessing actual Soviet expenditures and their impact on that country's economy. Appraisals rely on real Soviet prices to the extent possible, but straightforward statistics are scarce for about one-third of all military items. CIA in such cases first computes costs in dollars, then converts to rubles, using U.S. intelligence estimates of relative production and efficiency as indices. Determining ruble costs of U.S. forces is such a convoluted process, that no reputable comparisons of defense expenditures exist in that coin.[7]

Comparative Economic Burdens

Official U.S. estimates until 1975 suggested that Soviet outlays for defense equalled a steady 6–8 percent of that country's growing Gross National Product (GNP).[8] Recently revised evaluations by CIA, based on better measurement data, now indicate that the share is twice that amount, or 11–13 percent,[9] compared with a projected 5.2 percent for the United States in FY 1977.[10] Even the new assessment, however, has been seriously challenged.[11] Some authorities place the Soviet proportion as high as 20 percent.[12]

Increased U.S. estimates of the Soviet defense burden came as no surprise to experienced students of the subject. As the Congressional Budget Office put it, current conclusions "serve principally to resolve a paradox . . . .How could the Soviets squeeze such a large defense establishment out of such a small fraction [6–8 percent] of their GNP? It now appears they were not particularly efficient; rather, we simply underestimated how much of their budget went to defense."[13]

One conclusion, however, seems inescapable. Both sides could sustain current rates of expenditure indefinitely without serious strains. The United States devoted almost 40 percent of its GNP to national defense during World War II, but the civilian standard of living still was higher than in most countries today.[14] The annual growth in Soviet GNP seems sufficient to allow increased defense spending and slow improvements in living standards to proceed simultaneously.[15]

Comparative Defense Spending

Estimated total dollar costs of Soviet defense programs in 1976 exceeded U.S. budget authorizations by about one-third, according to CIA (40 percent, if pensions are excluded). Soviet expenditures have expanded about 3 percent per year since 1970, whereas U.S. outlays expressed in constant dollars have contracted steadily.[16]

Questionable Confidence in Estimates

Conclusions sketched above are subject to question, since dollar and ruble estimates of Soviet defense budgets both are subject to sizable error.

To begin with, compiling a sound data base is a treacherous task. Some counts of Soviet manpower and materiel are incomplete. Others admittedly are incorrect. The costs of Soviet weapons, equipment, and construction depend in large part on their physical and technological characteristics, which in many cases (such as ballistic missiles) are imprecisely known to U.S. analysts.[17]

Assuming U.S. estimates of Soviet force size and structure were entirely accurate, cost estimates would still be ambiguous "because there is no appropriate or universally agreed set of . . . . rules, and thus there is no objective standard by which to measure error." Assumptions and arbitrary judgments consequently abound.[18]

Two examples, one related to dollars, the other to rubles, serve as illustrations.

Determining dollar prices for Soviet items not in our possession is a very subjective process. Some weapons, when obtained, prove less sophisticated and cheaper by far than formerly presumed. Others, such as ZSU 23–4 anti-aircraft guns and BMP infantry combat vehicles, turn out to be much "more costly in dollars than their closest US counterparts."[19]

Manipulations by the Kremlin, which make it impossible for U.S. analysts to know what a ruble is worth, complicate computations.[20] Moreover, prices vary to fit the market. Trucks sold to collective farms may cost 40,000 rubles. The charge to some other State enterprise may be one-fourth that amount. Foreign sales customers may receive identical vehicles for fewer than 4,000 rubles. Our intelligence community is uncertain where Soviet armed forces fit on that sliding scale, but surmise that some parts of the Soviet civil economy subsidize defense spending.[21]

U.S. estimates of Soviet operations/maintenance expenditures are even less exact. Calculations concerning research, development, test, and evaluation (RDT&E)—which contributes to our opponent's future capabilities—are shakier still.[22] Some Soviet budget categories, such as military assistance and civil defense, escape assessment entirely, because evidence is inadequate.[23] Compound problems prevail when allies are considered (such as NATO and the Warsaw Pact).

In sum, the extent to which counting and costing errors overstate or understate Soviet defense budgets is an open debate.[24]

Practical Applications

It may indeed be true that "properly conceived and executed analyses of U.S. and Soviet defense expenditures can provide valuable insights into the status and trends of the two defense efforts."[25] Even rough estimates indicate relative willingness to commit sizable resources for politico-military purposes at the expense of domestic sectors. Statistics on investment versus consumption provide clues to long-range priorities. So do defense shares devoted to research and development, specific systems, and support.[26]

Nevertheless, costs do not measure effectiveness. "Budgets are, in an important sense, little more than a summary of other data. We could perceive changes in military capabilities *without* the aid of defense costing calculations" (emphasis added).[27]

The Manpower Cost Caveat

One caveat, however, is critical.

The cost of U.S. defense manpower has doubled during the past decade, owing to the initiation of annual comparability pay raises and a one-time increase to make an All-Volunteer Force feasible. Pay and allowances have absorbed more than half of our defense budget for several years. Associated outlays for troop housing, recruiting, human relations, and various other activities presently push the total close to 65 cents out of every dollar.[28] Relative shares for manpower have been stabilized, but absolute outlays will continue to climb as programmed cost-of-living increases periodically take effect.[29]

The impact on force modernization is immense. Manpower costs added to inescapable expenditures for operations and maintenance sharply reduce funds for research, development, and procurement programs in an inflationary environment that causes prices to escalate.[30] The Soviet Union, with lower pay scales, could afford a larger force and modernize at more rapid rates if its total defense budget were exactly the same as that of the United States, because a greater share of its money can be spent on machines.[31]

Defense Manpower

Manpower levies, like defense budgets, have some bearing on national economies, but are a marginal index for comparing rival military establishments in most respects, as this survey shows.

Opposing Manpower Policies

Three opposing policies bear directly on the U.S./Soviet quantitative and qualitative manpower balance.

All-Volunteer Force Versus Conscripts

Three decades of U.S. conscription ended in January 1973,[32] when draft calls registered zero, although the Selective Service System still survives on a "deep standby" basis.[33]

America's withdrawal from Indochina, implementation of the Nixon Doctrine (which demanded fewer general purpose forces than previous containment policies), budgetary difficulties, public opinion, and reevaluations of pressing threats led U.S. leaders to establish manpower requirements at 2.2 million in 1973.[34] That ceiling has remained almost constant.[35]

The United States probably could slightly exceed stated recruiting limits in these times of tight economy, but if society were more affluent, we would face serious problems filling quotas, given continued insistence on quality personnel. In either event, this country is *compelled* to stress reserve components, which constitute our only sustained combat capability, short of restoring the draft.

Influences on the balance between U.S. and Soviet forces thus are adverse, because the Kremlin imposes fewer constraints on the size and composition of its armed services, which still rely on conscripts.

Standing National Services Versus Total Force

The All-Volunteer Force, combined with retrenchment after the Vietnam War for political and economic reasons, has caused recent U.S. administrations to reinforce already strong emphasis on so-called Total Force Concepts, which count on allies and reserve components to offset reductions in our regular establishment.[36] Soviet leaders rely more on active national military forces and less on civilians, reserves, and allies to support national interests. The U.S./Soviet balance in NATO's center sector, where America's contribution is comparatively small, is especially sensitive to those conflicting policies. (Book III develops that theme.)

Firepower Versus Manpower

The United States places a high premium on human life. This country, therefore, replaces manpower with firepower wherever possible. High dollar costs for pay and allowances reinforce that policy, which keeps personnel strengths down and support requirements up in U.S. armed forces. Soviet concerns have always been less intense.

Quantitative Considerations

The present size of U.S. and Soviet armed services is important but, to be most meaningful, quantitative analyses must also relate respective populations to projected requirements. This section, therefore, addresses demographic trends before treating defense manpower directly.

Demographic Constraints

Both sides anticipate that smaller supplies of young people, especially men, will annually reach military age in the 1980s, but the implications are different (Figure 3).[37]

Czarist Russia and the Soviet Union suffered physical invasion during two great wars,[38] civil war, collectivization, famine, political purges, and pestilence for the first five decades of this century.[39] The people bounced back briefly in the 1950s with sharp population growth. That surge, however, has ceased. Soviet armed services, twice the size of U.S. counterparts, soon will find it difficult to fill conscription quotas. Needs will exceed the number of 18-year-old males beginning about 1983,[40] if current force strengths stay constant at plus or minus 4½ million.

Soviet leaders could alleviate serious shortfalls only by reducing quantitative and/or qualitative induction requirements; lengthening terms of military service and/or civilian workweeks; filling blank files from the manpower intensive economy; or otherwise altering allocations in some combination. Competition for scarce resources is bound to be acute.[41]

America's "baby boom" has also stopped. The slower rate of U.S. population increase parallels that of the Soviet Union but, as long as the U.S. active military establishment stays comparatively small, supply will substantially exceed demand. In fact, the pool of 18-year-old males will continually be sufficient to maintain a much larger force if mobilization should ever prove mandatory.[42]

The Statistical Base

U.S. armed services try to keep careful statistics concerning respective manpower levels. All sorts of activities and administrative actions depend on such lists: pay and allowances; rations; quarters and other

FIGURE 3 U.S. and Soviet Male Manpower Pools (In Millions)

	1975		*1980*		*1985*		*1990*	
	US	*USSR*	*US*	*USSR*	*US*	*USSR*	*US*	*USSR*
18-Year-Old Male Cohort	2.15	2.49	2.13	2.54	1.82	2.06	1.75	2.14
Disqualified, Deferred								
Medical,[1] Moral	.43	.25	.43	.25	.36	.21	.35	.22
Mental[2]	.28		.28		.24		.23	
School[3]	.02	.50	.02	.53	.02	.53	.02	.53
Total	.73	.75	.73	.78	.62	.74	.60	.75
Expired Exemptions		.21		.23		.22		.21
Net Males	1.42	1.95	1.40	2.01	1.20	1.54	1.15	1.60
Force Levels[4]	2.20	4.50	2.20	4.50	2.20	4.50	2.20	4.50
Annual Demand[5]	.38	1.69	.38	1.69	.38	1.69	.38	1.69
Over/Short	+ 1.04	+ .26	+ 1.02	+ .32	+ .82	− .15	+ .77	− .09

[1]The U.S. medical disqualification rate of about 16% and a moral rejection rate of about 4% were developed by DOD in 1963 for use by the President's Task Force on Manpower Conservation. Feshbach concludes that the corresponding Soviet rate for the two combined is about 10%.

[2]The U.S. mental disqualification rate of 13% is slightly less than current Army standards. An additional 5.8% of the 18-year-old cohort could be drafted if requirements were reduced to the minimum allowed by the Selective Service Act. The Soviets have no comparable criteria.

[3]U.S. educational deferments are confined to medical and dental schools. Soviet counts include special secondary schools, vocational/technical training, and college.

[4]Constant force levels shown correspond closely with current active military manpower strengths on both sides.

[5]Annual requirements, for males only, are calculated on about 2-year retention for Soviet conscripts and close to 5 years for U.S. volunteers.

Adapted from a table prepared by Frederick W. Suffa and Murray Feshbach. Contained in correspondence emanating from OASD (M&RA), subject: U.S./Soviet Manpower Pool Projections, February 10, 1977. 5 pp.

construction; clothing and personal equipment; medical support; training facilities; and miscellaneous services are representative. Reserve components and civilians, as well as uniformed regulars, are taken into account.

Conversely, the U.S. intelligence community accorded low priority to Soviet personnel statistics until the recent past, except for combat forces. Other problems were more pressing.[43]

Analysts traditionally scrutinized functional categories. Strategic attack forces, for example, included long-range aviation, plus all ballistic missiles ashore and afloat. Ground force, navy, and air force general purpose contingents were segregated into special groups. Command and general support (CGS) forces from all services coalesced into a separate class. Results, which related manpower statistics to *missions,* instead of *organizations,* contained significant oversights, double counting, and other inconsistencies.

A comprehensive reassessment, completed in 1975, reduced such shortcomings by combining functional and organizational approaches. For the first time, intelligence specialists from CIA and DIA addressed discrete, clearly defined entities: Strategic Rocket Forces (SRF); strategic defense forces (the PVO); and integrated ground, air, and naval services that included respective support. Navy statistics, for example, combined strategic nuclear submarines, general purpose forces, and naval infantry (herein called marines). The Ministry of Defense and Main Political Directorate were catalogued separately.[44] Sharp statistical revisions resulted.

The following review reflects current tabulations. Comparisons with U.S. forces are confined to 1976–1977, because our intelligence community has never published an agreed adjustment of estimated Soviet personnel strengths for the early part of this decade.[45] Trend tables and graphs in other documents, including those disseminated by DOD, should therefore be treated cautiously.

Active Armed Forces

Post-Vietnam cutbacks have *physically subtracted* over a million men from active U.S. roles since 1970 (from 3,088,000 to 2,073,000).[46] The U.S. *paper recomputation* added almost a million to previously estimated Soviet levels near the end of that period, largely in the command/support category.[47]

Official confidence in Soviet statistics is only about plus or minus 15 percent, but current consequences still show in stark relief on Graph 2 and Figure 4. Soviet ground forces exceed the aggregate of active U.S. forces by almost half a million. Total Soviet military manpower is more than twice ours (4,437,000 to 2,073,000). That circumstance reflects traditional stress on large standing armies since early Czarist times.

Nearly half a million paramilitary border guards and internal security troops supplement the regular establishment. Many are armed with automatic weapons, aircraft, and armored vehicles.[48] KGB divisions, like the Nazi SS, fought well during World War II, and could today if called on for homeland defense.

Perhaps 70,000 political officers, who parallel the military chain of command at almost every level, are soldiers in every sense.[49] Other forces are not. These include 400,000 support troops committed to construction projects, transportation, and part-time farm labor.[50] Their training is spotty and superficial, and units lack arms. Still, most of them contribute to military capabilities that bear on the balance of

Graph 2

COMPARATIVE MANPOWER
Statistical Summary - 1977

(In Thousands. Note Different Scales)

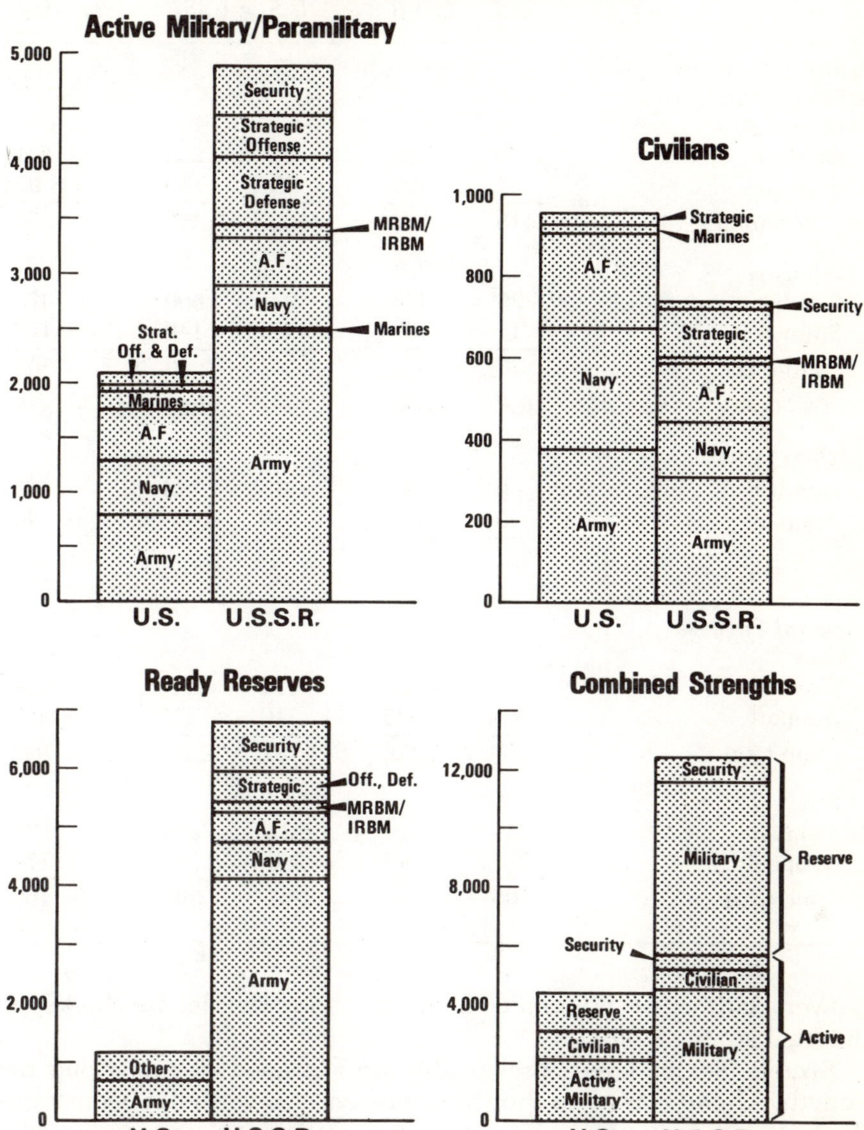

FIGURE 4 U.S. and Soviet Active Military/Paramilitary Manpower Strengths (Thousands)

	1976		1977		Current U.S. Standing
	U.S.	USSR	U.S.	USSR	
Military Services					
Strategic Nuclear[1]					
Offensive					
Combat	79	255	74	235	− 161
Support	44	135	35	130	− 95
Sub-total	118	390	109	365	− 256
Defensive					
Combat	26	475	24	500	− 476
Support	14	135	13	140	− 127
Sub-total	40	610	37	640	− 603
TOTAL	158	1000	146	1005	− 859
MRBM/IRBM					
Combat	0	85	0	85	− 85
Support	0	40	0	40	− 40
TOTAL	0	125	0	125	− 125
General Purpose					
Army					
Combat	462	1725	471	1710	−1239
Support	316	745	310	757	− 447
Sub-total	778	2470	781	2467	−1686
Navy					
Combat	234	310	238	308	− 70
Support	271	90	269	90	+ 179
Sub-total	505	400	507	398	+ 109

power. Railroads run by men in uniform, for example, are the key to internal strategic mobility.[51]

Sizable Soviet forces presumably are "pinned down" along the lengthy Chinese frontier, but their presence nevertheless constrains U.S. courses of action in East Asia. A Sino-Soviet thaw, a subject for speculation since Mao's death, could free some of those forces for duty elsewhere.[52]

As it stands, statistically superior active armed forces assist Moscow in at least two important ways:

FIGURE 4 (Con't)

	1976 U.S.	1976 USSR	1977 U.S.	1977 USSR	Current U.S. Standing
Air Force					
Combat	122	300	122	300	− 178
Support	331[2]	130	325[2]	130	+ 195
Sub-total	448	430	447	430	+ 17
Marines					
Combat	108	12	108	12	+ 96
Support	84	0	84	0	+ 84
Sub-total	192	12	192	12	+ 180
TOTAL	1923	3312	1927	3307	−1380
Military Services (Recap)					
Combat	1021	3162	1037	3150	−2113
Support	1060	1275	1036	1287	− 251
TOTAL	2081	4437	2073	4437	−2364
Paramilitary					
Frontier Security (MGB)	0	155	0	160	− 160
Internal Security (MVD)	0	300	0	300	− 300
TOTAL	0	455	0	460	− 460
GRAND TOTAL	2081	4892	2073	4897	−2824

[1]U.S. "combat" strengths equal undifferentiated DPPC totals. "Support" figures added are Air Force elements serving in strategic roles.

[2]Excludes support elements counted as strategic nuclear.

—They strengthen deterrent capabilities by influencing political and psychological impressions in this country and among our allies.

—They foster flexibility not available to U.S. forces.

Civilian Manpower

Civilians supplement active military manpower in both defense establishments to provide continuity and special skills.

Once again, U.S. statistics are solid.[53] Those for the Soviets are so spongy that confidence in present estimates approximates plus or minus 25 percent at best, a mighty high margin of error.[54]

Still, evidence seems to indicate that U.S. civilian strengths exceed the Soviets' somewhat in absolute terms, and are triple propor-

FIGURE 5 U.S. and Soviet Civilian Manpower Strength[1] (Thousands)

	1976		1977		Current U.S.
	U.S.	USSR	U.S.	USSR	Standing
Military Services					
Strategic Nuclear[2]					
Offensive					
Combat	2	30	5	30	− 25
Support	18	20	13	20	− 7
Sub-total	20	50	18	50	− 32
Defensive					
Combat	9	30	7	30	− 23
Support	5	35	4	35	− 31
Sub-total	14	65	11	65	− 54
TOTAL	34	115	29	115	− 86
MRBM/IRBM					
Combat	0	9	0	9	− 9
Support	0	6	0	6	− 6
TOTAL	0	15	0	15	− 15
General Purpose					
Army					
Combat	45	165	44	165	−121
Support	344	140	334	140	+194
Sub-total	389	305	378	305	+ 73
Navy					
Combat	5	110	5	110	−105
Support	295	25	293	25	+268
Sub-total	300	135	298	135	+163

tionately. We employ one civilian for every two military men. Their ratio is believed to be about one for six or seven (see Figure 5).

As a result, overall personnel comparisons that merge active military manpower with civilians reduce this country's quantitative deficit from 2:1 to 5:3 for forces in being. Narrowing the numerical gap, however, by no means indicates that civilian and military strengths are interchangeable. Civilians can substitute for uniformed specialists, but they are not combat forces in any sense of the word, nor are they readily redeployable in most instances.

Ready Reserves

U.S. Ready Reserve strengths[55] have dropped dramatically since 1970,

FIGURE 5 (Con't)

	1976 U.S.	*1976* USSR	*1977* U.S.	*1977* USSR	*Current U.S. Standing*
Air Force					
Combat	30	115	28	115	− 87
Support	208[3]	30	204[3]	30	+174
Sub-total	238	145	232	145	+ 87
Marines					
Combat	0	0	0	0	—
Support	19	0	20	0	+ 20
Sub-total	19	0	20	0	+ 20
TOTAL	946	585	928	585	+343
Military Services (Recap)					
Combat	91	459	89	459	−370
Support	889	256	868	256	+612
TOTAL	980	715	957	715	+242
Paramilitary					
Frontier Security (KGB)	0	8	0	8	− 8
Internal Security (MVD)	0	9	0	9	− 9
TOTAL	0	17	0	17	− 17
GRAND TOTAL	980	732	957	732	+225

[1]Soviet figures for 1977 are identical to those for 1976 because no revision has been conducted by U.S. intelligence community.

[2]U.S. "combat" strengths equal undifferentiated DPPC totals. "Support" figures added are Air Force elements serving in strategic support roles.

[3]Excludes support elements counted as strategic nuclear.

from 2,661,000 to 1,189,000.[56] Our Marine Corps, which lost 56 percent of assigned personnel, suffered worst, but the Army and Navy were also sliced in half. Decline will continue, because fewer forces annually enter reserve status at a slower rate from a smaller establishment than during days of the draft, when conscripts served two-year terms.

Soviet forces released from active service in the last five years are counterparts of the U.S. Ready Reserve for purposes of this study, although they are not precisely comparable and statistics shown in Figure 6 are questionable.[57] Their regular Air Force, for example, outnumbers the Soviet Navy and has a shorter term of service, yet accumulated 165,000 fewer reserves, according to official intelligence estimates.[58]

FIGURE 6 U.S. and Soviet Ready Reserve Strengths[1] (Thousands)

	1976		*1977*		*Current*
	U.S.	*USSR*	*U.S.*	*USSR*	*U.S. Standing*
Military Services					
Strategic Nuclear					
Offensive	4	520	10	520	− 510
Defensive	13	0[2]	10	0[2]	+ 10
Sub-total	17	520	20	520	− 500
MRBM/IRBM	0	170	0	170	− 170
General Purpose					
Army	798	4140	708	4140	−3432
Navy	203	625	199	625	− 426
Air Force	206	490	185	490	− 305
Marines	84	0	77	0	+ 77
Sub-total	1291	5255	1169	5255	−4086
TOTAL	1308	5945	1189	5945	−4756
Paramilitary[3]	0	855	0	855	− 855
GRAND TOTAL	1308	6800	1189	6800	−5611

[1]U.S. figures for Ready Reserve combine Individual Ready Reserve and Selected Reserve (including National Guard) strengths. Soviet figures for 1977 are identical to those for 1976 because no revision has been conducted by U.S. intelligence community.

[2]Soviet strategic defensive reserves appear as "0" because they are included in figures for Army Reserves, where defensive PVO forces are assigned on release from active duty.

[3]No breakout is available for frontier and internal components.

Nevertheless, it is certain that Soviet Army reserves alone would dwarf the combined size of all U.S. reserve components if their estimated numbers were reduced by half. That gap will grow, as U.S. reserves contract.

Aggregates Assessed

Soviet active military regulars, not counting security forces, exceed the entire U.S. establishment, including civilians and reserves (Figure 7). Soviet military/paramilitary regulars and reserves triple the U.S. total (4,219,000 to 12,429,000). Even if U.S. experts have overestimated Soviet active military strengths by 15 percent and all other personnel by 25 percent, the Kremlin still would have almost twice as many people in its military machine as we do (9,764,000 to 4,219,000).

Those statistics, however, can convey false impressions. Just as increased costs often fail to increase effectiveness, quantitatively superior personnel strengths frequently fail to create superior

FIGURE 7 U.S. and Soviet Combined Manpower Statistics Compared (Thousands)

	1976 U.S.	1976 USSR	1977 U.S.	1977 USSR	Current U.S. Standing
Military Services					
Strategic Nuclear					
Offensive	142	960	137	935	– 798
Defensive	67	675	58	705	– 647
Sub-total	209	1635	195	1640	–1445
MRBM/IRBM	0	310	0	310	– 310
General Purpose					
Army	1965	6915	1867	6912	–5045
Navy[1]	1008	1160	1004	1158	– 154
Air Force	892	1065	864	1065	– 201
Marines	295	12	289	12	+ 277
Sub-total	4160	9152	4024	9147	–5123
TOTAL	4369	11097	4219	11097	–6878
Paramilitary	0	1327	0	1332	–1332
GRAND TOTAL[2]	4369	12424	4219	12429	–8210

[1]The U.S. Coast Guard, with 37,450 military personnel and 6,250 civilians, is not shown, because only a small number represent combat capabilities in the context of this study.

[2]Figures include active military, reserves, and civilians.

capabilities. Threats posed by naval flotillas and fighter squadrons, for example, depend on material numbers, not human mass. Direct correlations between personnel statistics and power are confined not just to general purpose ground forces, both army and marines, but specifically to "cutting edge" elements that match man against man in mortal combat.

Qualitative Considerations

Whereas quantitative manpower comparisons are meaningful mainly in the ground combat context, qualitative characteristics affect the U.S./Soviet military balance in many important ways. This section is confined to a few general considerations. Comments keyed to specific armed services appear elsewhere, when appropriate.

Cultural Controls

The quality of U.S. and Soviet military manpower is conditioned from the crib by sharply different cultures. Our system, for example, puts a premium on individual competition. Soviet citizens are servants of the State, which stresses collective enterprise. Attitudes concerning military life are distinctly different. The American tradition of distrust toward standing armed services, for example, has no duplicate in the Soviet Union.[59]

The significance of cultural considerations, however, rarely is cleancut. "The Soviet soldier's greatest strength (obedience) is perhaps his greatest weakness (lack of initiative)."[60] Observers at one pole in fact opine that national character exerts "a permanent and often decisive influence upon the weight [any] nation is able to put into the scales of international politics."[61] Authorities at the antipode scoff at national stereotypes, which they contend are unsubstantiated.[62] Analysts consequently should apply prudence in sorting out vices and virtues associated with U.S. and Soviet society.[63]

Discipline

Disciplinary problems that plagued American communities late in the last decade devitalized U.S. troops during the early 1970s. Drug abuse, "underground" activities, crime, racial unrest, irresponsibility, and rebellion against authorities were rampant.[64] Those debilities, however, were only briefly dangerous to U.S. security, and now are better contained.[65]

Discipline in Soviet armed services has always been stringent by U.S. standards, but sometimes splits wide apart. Misdoings on U.S. ships in the recent past, for example, were minor compared with an attempted mass defection that mars the Soviet Navy's record.[66]

Despite such lapses, discipline normally is a poor criterion for assessing the U.S./Soviet military balance, because it affords neither side a consistently marked advantage.

Education and Training

Land, sea, and air forces on both sides all feature technical functions that demand high quality manpower.

U.S. Status The quality of nonprior service accessions, as measured by mental capacity, is higher today than in FY 1964, the last year in which we had a peacetime draft.[67] That bright trend, however, may be transitory, because national Scholastic Aptitude Tests (SATs) show a discouraging downward trend in reading and comprehension abilities of U.S. high school students. Beyond that, current employment rates create a "buyer's market" for our All-Volunteer Force. Resurgence could quickly reduce the roster of qualified recruits.[68]

Since 80 percent of all first-term U.S. enlisted men revert to reserve status after three or four active duty years,[69] retaining prime personnel is a pressing problem. Turnover causes instability within each Service, complicates training, and reduces readiness. The present pattern of careerists retiring after 20 years makes room at the top for younger men, but robs our armed forces of many mature and experienced members.

U.S. Ready Reserves are now better than ever in many respects,[70] but qualitative shortcomings of recent nonprior service recruits are more sharply pronounced than in the active services. Part-time leaders and part-time training impair proficiency least in Air Force airlift and air defense organizations. Most other elements suffer, despite strong command emphasis for the last several years.[71]

Soviet Status The 1967 Law of Universal Service theoretically obligates all 18-year-old Soviet males to serve the State in active armed forces. About 80 percent are conscripted annually, but those committed to "hot spots" constitute the cream of the crop. Culls go to construction gangs and general labor.[72]

Pre-induction preparation starts in grammar schools. Average results are approximately equal to a month of active basic training. About a third of all inductees take additional courses from DOSAAF.[73] City dwellers with mechanical skills are supplanting peasants as the primary source of manpower,[74] but specialists such as tank drivers still must spend six months in a "cram course" before being certified for duty with tactical units.[75]

Improved education, which makes it possible for present-day recruits to master military skills more quickly than their predecessors, probably prompted the Defense Ministry to cut draft age and conscript service a full year in 1967.[76] Still, the sacrifice in experience has been considerable. Turnover is terrific. Callups take place twice a year, spring and fall. A quarter of all draftees are discharged at the same time.[77]

Technical competence especially is afflicted by short tours. Civilians ashore, not seamen afloat, consequently service a high percentage of Soviet shipboard equipment. Aircraft maintenance is equally aggravating. Supervisory requirements in all skill areas are far greater than for U.S. forces.

Problems will compound by the end of this century, when provincial peoples with poor command of the Russian language will provide about one-third of each annual 18-year-old cohort. In 1970, for example, "slightly over 40 percent of the Kazakhs [spoke] Russian." Other minorities reported no more than 15–20 percent. Georgian recently replaced Russian as the official language in that Caucasian state after protests in Tbilisi, the capital. The situation may improve in coming generations, as a result of intensive study programs, but few will be truly fluent for a very long time.[78]

In sum, Soviet training and operational procedures are *effective,* but commonly *inefficient.* Efforts often are excessive in terms of ends achieved, partly because uncompromising dedication sets equal priorities for all objectives.

Soviet Political Indoctrination

Most Americans believe that political indoctrination is less important than "practical matters", but the Soviets consider it compulsory. Protracted and pervasive programs compete eternally with military training for time and attention, although there is no close linkage between professional competence and the Communist Party line. Conflicts of interest assume special significance in high technology units that can least afford the tradeoff.[79] Powerful political officers frequently second guess commanders, who must keep a tight rein on subordinates to minimize "mistakes".[80] As a result, innovation is a rare commodity.

Combat Experience

Soviet Ground Forces and Air Force since World War II have seen little combat. Organized units have been used mainly to suppress unrest in satellite states and skirmish on the Chinese border. The Soviet "blue water" Navy has never fired a shot in anger.

All four U.S. armed services, in contrast, were committed in the Korean War (1950–1953) and the Vietnam War (1965–1972), not to mention the Dominican Crisis (1965). Our Navy, however, was essentially unopposed at sea in every instance, and neither our Army nor Air Force encountered combat under conditions analogous to those that would pertain if war occurred in Central Europe between NATO and the Warsaw Pact. Whether U.S. experience constitutes pluses or minuses thus is contentious. Some lessons may indeed be sound in context with the U.S./Soviet military balance. Others might best be unlearned.

Concluding Comments

Soviet soldiers are not "10 feet tall" when compared with American counterparts, but neither are they 10 inches. Which opposing strengths outweigh which weaknesses may someday make a great difference, but judgments now are subjective.

Manpower qualities on both sides seem in the main sufficient to support most projected courses of action. Still, the will to endure unto death depends on more than physical training and technical excellence. The prime imponderable is performance under pressure, which turns on toughness of mind. Only the crucible of combat could confirm the presence or absence of that crucial characteristic.[81]

Defense Technology

Science and technology exert enormous influences on future U.S. and Soviet capabilities. Competition between the two countries is intense. Each side struggles ceaselessly to stock its arsenal with weapons and equipment that satisfy special needs under changing conditions.

Technological Warfare

Technological warfare, which connects science with strategy and tactics, is deliberately designed to outflank enemy forces by making them obsolete. Battles are won by budgeteers and men at drawing boards before any blood is shed.[82]

Technological surprise thus poses special perils in critical echelons of the conflict spectrum, where sudden, one-sided supremacy in aerospace defense, antisubmarine systems, super-smart weapons, chemical warfare, lasers, and the like could create spectacular shifts.[83] The Soviet penchant for secrecy prompts "worst case" U.S. estimates in such instances.

Classic dangers develop when new systems based on new technology burst on the scene (nuclear weapons, for example), but breakthroughs that combine new systems with old technology or vice versa can also create serious shocks. Still, creativity alone confers no advantage unless tied to procedures that translate inventive ideas into tangible instruments deployed in correct combinations and sufficient strength.[84] Tactical thought outweighs scientific theory as often as not.

"Victory" is achieved when one participant unveils technological superiority so pervasive and pronounced that opponents can neither cope nor catch up. Since indicators of rival success often surface slowly, losers sometimes cherish illusions of winning until too late. Conversely, they may long be aware that they have lost, but lack any way to rally.

Unfortunately, technological forecasting is at best imprecise.[85] Surprise can be intense when enemies are fully aware of their foe's R&D schemes, if they fail to sense the significance. Serendipitous offshoots of basic or applied research often alter perceived patterns in unexpected ways. Even so, estimating future states of the enemy's art may be the *easiest* prediction. Analysts must also account for educational, economic, institutional, bureaucratic, and doctrinal constraints.[86] The will to compete can be crucial.

Since surefire predictions perhaps are impossible, given the dearth of hard data, being "ahead" is important in technological areas that really count. Substantial leads lessen chances for surprise, by allowing friendly teams to explore frontiers before they are probed by enemies.[87]

Divergent R&D Guidelines

The United States and Soviet Union, in pursuit of separate goals, adhere to divergent R&D guidelines.

The traditional U.S. approach to research and development, trained on technological initiative, features "pioneering and aggressive innovation."[88] Quantum improvements are the aim. That policy stimulates creativity in one sense, but paradoxically cultivates conservatism. Many modest advancements are accused of approaching obsolescence before they can be deployed. Successors for aging systems thus are often delayed indefinitely while U.S. scientists strain for breakthroughs.

The Soviets for many years espoused incremental improvements, with few probes along scientific frontiers. Moderately modernized arms and equipment were procured as they became available. That procedure ensured continually improved capabilities which narrowed or closed qualitative gaps, while U.S. forces "made do" with products in hand.[89]

In present practice, neither the United States nor the Soviet Union promotes quantum jump or incremental improvement policies exclusively. U.S. tanks, guns, aircraft, and other items often undergo repeated modifications that add to or otherwise alter original capabilities without replacing basic systems. The Soviets began stressing *both* approaches early in the 1970s. Nevertheless, the differences described still strongly influence force postures on both sides.[90]

Soviet Challenges

The Soviet Union, as a closed society, enjoys a few advantages not duplicated in the United States.

Leadership, starting with Lenin, has stressed science and technology. Command emphasis and a cohesive strategy ensure an increasingly skilled cadre, sustained heavy investments in rubles and other resources, and solid continuity. Focus remains unflinchingly on military research and development, with scant fear of repercussions caused by domestic demands.[91]

Extreme secrecy shrouds Soviet efforts, often concealing courses of action and intent until field testing starts in full view. Shortcuts are possible, because published reports of U.S. plans and progress point them out. The Kremlin consequently can concentrate on carefully chosen goals that simplify the search for superiority in selected sectors.[92]

All, however, is not advantageous.

Surreptitious science carries severe penalties. It inhibits competition and free interchange of ideas (both essential stimulants) and protects poor programs from public opposition. The Socialist system excludes many incentives that generate growth. Civil and military R&D efforts are sometimes so segregated that neither sustains the other.[93] To compensate in part, the Soviets participate in exchange programs, purchase products and processes on the open market, perpetrate espionage, plagiarize ideas, and engage in technological piracy.[94]

In the past, Soviet scientists stuck closely to a policy of conservative incrementalism that featured slow but steady progress.[95] The R&D community designed around difficulties. Current indications, however, suggest a significant change, characterized by expansion in the scope of Soviet basic research, greater emphasis on innovation, and increasing inclination to take technological risks on speculative projects that promise big payoffs if successful.[96]

Soviet forces already feature a smorgasbord of brand-new systems based on technology well known in the West, but slightly exploited. Significant samples include intercontinental ballistic missiles (ICBMs) with "cold launch" capabilities;[97] mobile air defenses that can move with ground troops; satellite intercept and surveillance craft; armored vehicles and surface ships engineered expressly to operate in chemical/biological warfare environments; rapid-fire rocket launchers; anti-ship cruise missiles; and fire-control systems unmatched either in this country or among other NATO members.[98]

From the small fraction of Soviet exploratory efforts for which U.S. intelligence analysts have sound evidence, several now stressed could bear strongly on the future balance if breakthroughs occur.

Controlled thermonuclear fusion could pave the way for limitless power supplies. Wing-in-ground effect aircraft able to skim the sea's surface apparently offer great promise as part of an anti-submarine system. Techniques subjecting certain substances to pressures exceeding a million megabars could transform matter into new forms of unfathomed importance. Metallic ammonia, for example, could constitute the ideal propellant for space ships in its highly condensed stage, or furnish unstable materials for exotic munitions. High energy lasers have endless experimental applications, including space-borne satellite killers.[99]

Soviet progress in producing practical ABM weapons based on charged-particle beams (CPBs) is particularly controversial.[100] Major General George J. Keegan, former Air Force Assistant Chief of Staff for Intelligence, reportedly advised authorities about CPB programs in 1975. He sounded a public alarm two years later, after retiring from active service.[101] Detractors, however, doubt that any Soviet breakthrough will soon degrade U.S. deterrence. Technical difficulties are tremendous. Nuclear-tipped ABM interceptors, for example, have destructive radii measured in miles. CPBs must score direct hits on hostile warheads.[102] The Secretary of Defense and Director of Central Intelligence both express extreme skepticism.[103]

Other observers see a possibly ominous parallel between present debates and those about ICBMs 30-odd years ago. The U.S. chief of Scientific Research and Development, they recall, then told Congress that intercontinental missile attacks were technically "impossible". That prediction was patently false. We started funding full-scale efforts within a few years. Soviet testing flowered in the 1950s.[104]

U.S. Responses

The United States starts with the world's richest reservoir of scientific resources. Constant feedback between civil and military markets encourages entrepreneurism and technological chain reactions not remotely equalled by our Russian rival. As a result, options still closed to the Soviets are completely open to us.[105]

This country's predominance, however, shows signs of perishability that makes many intellectuals lament our lack of momentum.[106]

Causes include uncertain goals that make it troublesome to chart a sound course for defense technology. Insistence on practical products is becoming more pronounced. Fund requests for abstract research are frequently cut or cancelled. Sharp fiscal caution extends to other R&D sectors. Consequent tendencies to tolerate few failures sometimes impede rapid progress.[107]

Beyond that, technological transfers to Soviet competitors create sharp anxieties among some U.S. analysts, who see a "one-way street" that serves Soviet ends at U.S. expense.[108] The total impact on U.S. security is difficult to assess, because no focal center studies such trends. Still, a recent RAND report cautions that uncontrolled exports "of integrated circuit manufacturing plants, machinery, and know-how cannot but improve Soviet military computers."[109] Other items, such as those that contributed to Soviet wide-bodied aircraft technology, may also give inimical aid and comfort.

What to release and what to retain is contentious. U.S. companies, despite intense criticism, were permitted to provide precision grinders that polish miniature bearings for missile guidance systems, because "comparable machines were available from other supplying countries and quantities had been sold to the Soviet Union from Switzerland and Italy some years before."[110] The impending sale of sophisticated Cyber 76 computers[111] was reversed only after congressional petitions reached the President.[112]

Adverse publicity related to such issues points up increasing requirements to reconcile U.S. commerce with reasonable controls in ways that reduce risks to our security.[113] Since early resolution seems unlikely,[114] the Secretary of Defense has issued interim instructions on the subject. The primary objective is "to protect the United States' lead time relative to its principal adversaries in the application of technology to military capabilities .... In addition, it is in the national interest not to make it easy for any country to advance its technology in ways that could be detrimental" to our cause. Consequently, DOD seeks to regulate a range of exports that include technical data used to design, produce, test, employ, maintain, and recon-

FIGURE 8 The Technological Balance

General	*Specific*
United States Clearly Superior	
"Black box" electronics	Aircraft
Computers	Air-to-air missiles
Integrated circuits	Artillery ammunition
Microtechnology	ECM, ECCM
Night vision	Look-down shoot-down systems
Small turbofan engines	Precision-guided munitions
Space technology	Remotely piloted vehicles
Submarine noise suppressants	Strategic cruise missiles
Terrain-following radar	Survivable submarines
Soviets Closing Gap	
Aerodynamics	MIRVs
Composite materials	Missile accuracy
Inertial instrumentation	Satellite sensors
	Tactical nuclear systems
Soviet Union Clearly Superior	
Cast components	Air defense missiles
Commonality of components	Anti-ship missiles
Ease of maintenance	Armored fighting vehicles
High pressure physics	Artillery/rocket launchers
Magneto-hydrodynamic power	Chemical/biological warfare
Rockets and ramjets	Cold weather equipment
Simple systems for common use	Gas turbines for ships
Titanium fabrication	ICBM payloads, yields
Welding	Mobile ballistic missiles
	Ship size vs firepower
	Tactical bridging
Status Uncertain	
Acoustics	Antiballistic missiles
Adaptive optics	Antisubmarine warfare
High explosive chemistry	High energy lasers
Inductive storage and switching systems for pulsed power control	Satellite-borne radars
Reduced drag for submarines	

struct materials, as well as materials themselves, if they "embody extractable critical technology" and/or complete a process line.[115]

Comparative Competence

Relative standings of U.S. and Soviet defense technologies reflect a dynamic situation. Trends there, as elsewhere, are more revealing than static snapshots at any point in time. Figure 8 (see page 65) therefore should segregate sample comparisons into classes that show convergence, divergence, crossovers, static situations, and uncertainties,[116] but lack of information forces a simpler configuration. Confidence in categories shown is high where evidence is conclusive or Soviet leaders signal serious shortfalls by seeking U.S. assistance. It is low where clues are equivocal.

More importantly, some leads and lags on each side are deliberate, caused at least as much by different missions and developmental styles as by asymmetries in technological competence or failure to foresee demands. The United States, which still holds unsurpassed abilities to compete technologically, could quickly close any *current* gaps if our leaders chose to do so.

Consequently, technological comparisons can be quite confusing, unless linked with strategic concepts, significant threats, and associated force requirements.

Footnotes

1. Marshall, Andrew W., *Comparisons of US and SU Defense Expenditures.* A study prepared by Director of Net Assessment, Department of Defense, September 16, 1975. Contained in *Allocation of Resources in the Soviet Union and China—1975,* p. 155.

2. *Estimated Soviet Defense Spending in Rubles, 1970–1975,* Central Intelligence Agency, May 1976, p. 5; Graham, Daniel O., "The Soviet Military Budget Controversy," *Air Force Magazine,* May 1976, p. 34.

3. Lee, W. T., "Soviet Defense Expenditures," Chapter 7 in *Arms, Men, and Military Budgets: Issues for Fiscal Year 1977,* Ed. by William Schneider, Jr., and Francis P. Hoeber. New York: Crane, Russak & Co., 1976, p. 261.

4. Graham, Daniel O., "The Soviet Military Budget Controversy," p. 34.

5. *Estimated Soviet Defense Spending in Rubles,* CIA, p. 5.

6. *A Dollar Comparison of Soviet and US Defense Activities, 1967–1977,* Central Intelligence Agency, January 1978, 13 pp.

7. *Estimated Soviet Defense Spending in Rubles,* CIA, p. 5. W. T. Lee, for one, finds Soviet data reliable enough for sound computation purposes, and consequently arrives at different conclusions than CIA. See for example his critique entitled *Understanding the Soviet Military Threat: How CIA Estimates Went Astray.* New York: National Strategy Information Center, 1977, 73 pp.

8. Marshall, Andrew W., *Comparisons of US and SU Defense Expenditures*, p. 170; *Estimated Defense Spending in Rubles*, CIA, p. 16.

9. *Estimated Soviet Defense Spending in Rubles*, p. 16.

10. U.S. outlays for defense as a percent of GNP were calculated using statistics in U.S. Congress. Senate. *Second Concurrent Resolution on the Budget*, Fiscal Year 1978. Conference Report to accompany H. Con. Res. 341. 95th Congress, 1st Session. Washington: U.S. Govt. Print. Off., 1977, pp. 6, 7.

11. W. T. Lee, a specialist on Soviet economic and military affairs, shows a rising share of Soviet GNP for defense since 1958. He calculates it was 14–15 percent in 1975, and predicts as much as 23 percent in 1980. "Soviet Defense Expenditures," *Osteuropa Wirtschaft*, December 1977, pp. 273–292 (in English).

12. The Soviet defense budget equals 10–20 percent of GNP, according to Andrew Marshall in *Comparisons of US and SU Defense Expenditures*, p. 164. Daniel Graham cites 15–20 percent in "The Soviet Military Budget Controversy," pp. 36, 37.

13. Letter and accompanying staff paper submitted by the Congressional Budget Office to Brock Adams, Chairman of the House Budget Committee, subject: Replies to Chairman Adams' Questions in his letter of April 15, 1976. Dated July 21, 1976. Page 3 of cover letter.

14. Statistics from Braden, John B., *Comparison of U.S. Government Budget Data . . . . Related to Total Budget Outlays and to Gross National Product (GNP)*, Fiscal Years 1940–1976. Washington: Congressional Research Service, February 7, 1975, p. 7.

15. Future difficulties are discussed in U.S. Congress. Joint Committee Print. *Soviet Economic Problems and Prospects. A Study Prepared for the Subcommittee on Priorities and Economy in Government of the Joint Economic Committee.* 95th Congress, 1st Session. Washington: U.S. Govt. Print. Off., August 8, 1977. 30 pp.

16. *CIA Dollar Comparisons of Soviet and US Defense Activities*, 1967–1977, pp. 4, 13, plus DOD comments on a draft of this study. W. T. Lee shows a growth rate of 8–12 percent per annum for Soviet defense spending, according to a personal conversation with the author on February 22, 1978.

17. Congressional Budget Office Replies to Chairman Adams' Questions, pp. 1–2.

18. *Ibid.*, pp. 3–4.

19. Marshall, Andrew W., *Comparisons of US and SU Defense Expenditures*, p. 169.

20. The Soviet official rate of exchange for foreign trade purposes is $1.35 per ruble.

21. Graham, Daniel O., "The Soviet Military Budget Controversy," p. 34.

22. CIA acknowledges that its dollar estimates contain a "substantial" margin of error. Its analysts place "greatest confidence in the investment category—procurement of weapons and equipment and construction of facilities." Funds for manpower "are the largest and the most reliable component in the operating category." The estimated dollar costs for Soviet RDT&E "should be regarded as significantly less reliable than those for either investment or operating." *CIA Dollar Comparison of Soviet and U.S. Defense Activities*, 1967–1977, pp. 2–3.

Ruble estimates experience similar problems, with RDT&E once again being least reliable. "There is considerable uncertainty about the basic data, most of which comes from Soviet publications . . . . The division of expenditures between the military and civilian sectors is particularly uncertain." *Estimated Soviet Defense Spending in Rubles*, CIA, pp, 13, 15.

23. Marshall, Andrew W., *Comparisons of US and SU Defense Expenditures*, p. 167.

24. Congressional Budget Office Replies to Chairman Adams' Questions, pp. 1, 4, 6–8.

25. Marshall, Andrew W., *Comparisons of US and SU Defense Expenditures*, p. 153.

26. DIA comments on a draft of this study, September 9, 1977.

27. Cover letter, Congressional Budget Office Replies to Chairman Adams' Questions, p. 2.

28. Schlesinger, James R., *Annual Report to the Congress on the FY 1976 and Transition Budgets, FY 1977 Authorization Request, and FY 1976–1980 Defense Programs*, February 5, 1975, pp. 123–126. Relationships cited are still much the same.

29. Public Law 90–207, 90th Congress, (81 Stat. 649), Section 8, December 16, 1967.

30. Schlesinger, James R., *Annual Report to the Congress on the FY 1976 and Transition Budgets*, p. D–1.

31. Soviet pay and allowances were an estimated 18–25 percent of the total defense budget in 1969, the latest year for which unclassified data are available. Cohn, Stanley H., *Economic Burden of Defense Expenditures.* Contained in U.S. Congress. Soviet Economic Prospects for the Seventies, a Compendium of Papers Submitted to the Joint Economic Committee. 93d Congress, 1st Session. Washington: U.S. Govt. Print. Off., 1973, p. 150.

32. *Military Manpower Requirements Report for FY 1974.* Washington: Department of Defense, February 1973, pp. 1–2.

33. Young American males no longer need to register with Selective Service. In emergency, it would take "120 to 150 days to get 100,000 accessions," according to the Acting Director. DOD plans call for that many within 60 days after mobilization is ordered. Finegan, Jay, "Condition of Selective Service Shocks 'Hill' Personnel Panel," *Navy Times*, October 31, 1977, p. 3.

34. *Military Manpower Requirements Report for FY 1974*, p. 5.

35. The U.S. FY 1978 active military manpower authorization is 2,079,418. Public Law 95–111, September 22, 1977.

36. Laird, Melvin, *Statement on the FY 1972 Defense Budget*, p. 21. Specifically, Total Force Concepts emphasize "our need to plan for optimum use of all military and related resources available to meet the requirements of Free World security. [Those] include active and reserve components of the U.S., those of our allies, and the additional military capabilities of our allies and friends that will be made available through local efforts, or through provision of appropriate security assistance programs."

37. For U.S. statistics and summary discussion, see *Projections of the Population of the United States: 1977 to 2050.* Washington: U.S. Department of Commerce, Bureau of the Census, July 1977, pp. 4–9, 10–11. Soviet trends are described in Feshbach, Murray and Rapawy, Stephen, *Soviet Population and Manpower Trends and Policies.* Contained in U.S. Congress. Joint Committee Print, "Soviet Economy in a New Perspective, A Compendium of Papers Submitted to the Joint Economic Committee." Washington: U.S. Govt. Print. Off., October 14, 1976, pp. 113–114, 144–152.

38. The Second World War alone cost Soviet society something like 7.5 million military dead, along with 10–15 million civilians. Dupuy, R. E. and Dupuy, T. N., *The Encyclopedia of Military History.* New York: Harper and Row, 1970, p. 1198.

39. Collectivization and political purges, with fatal side effects, caused 20 million or more Soviet deaths, many of which were deliberate, between 1930 and 1950. U.S. Congress. Senate. *The Human Cost of Communism. A study prepared for a subcommittee of the Committee on the Judiciary.* Washington: U.S. Govt. Print. Off., 1970, pp. 1, 25.

Forty million *deaths* in 20 years, half of them self-inflicted, (20 percent of the population at that time) suggest that U.S. and Soviet views of Assured Destruction requirements may be somewhat different.

40. U.S. manpower experts are still uncertain what potential 18-year-old female cohorts have to replace male conscripts on either side at present or in the predictable future.

41. Feshbach, Murray and Rapawy, Stephen, *Soviet Population and Manpower Trends and Policies*, p. 114.

42. *Ibid.*, pp. 114–115. Additional details are contained in an inter-office memorandum, U.S./Soviet Manpower Pool Projections, OASD (M&RA), February 10, 1977. 5 pp.

43. This subsection originally was predicated on personal conversations between the author and DIA analysts in September and October 1976, together with written data

furnished by DIA in an informal fashion. Statistical updates draw on similar sources in November 1977.

44. Classified details are contained in *Reassessment, Soviet Armed Forces Personnel Strengths* (U). Washington: DIA, July 1975, 8 pp.; and Part II, November 1975, 61 pp.

45. The study of Soviet military manpower is starting to attract some attention. A major conference at the University of Edinburgh in April 1978 included participants from both sides of the Atlantic.

46. U.S. active military strengths were mainly derived from Manpower Statistics by Defense Planning and Programming Category for each military service and DOD agencies, a series of unpublished working papers prepared for OASD (M&RA), Program Division. Figures for 1970–74 were dated March 29, 1976. Figures for 1975, 1976, and 1977 were dated October 21, 1975, August 26, 1976, and August 31, 1977 respectively. OASD (M&RA) furnished supplemental statistics on U.S. strategic offensive and defensive forces to facilitate special displays.

47. Soviet active manpower strengths were derived from DIA.

48. Border Guards belong to the KGB, internal security troops to the MVD, according to John Erickson, who mentions accoutrements in *Soviet-Warsaw Pact Force Levels*, pp. 20–21.

49. DIA identifies about 12,000 personnel in the Main Political Directorate. The remaining 58,000 are diffused in military units.

50. Congressman Les Aspin, for example, calls 2,755,000 Soviet armed forces "non-threatening" to the United States. He credits each side with about 2,000,000 "comparable opposing forces." *Disarmament and International Views*, May 1976, pp. 5–7.

51. DIA comments on a draft of this study, March 2, 1977.

52. U.S. leaders are compelled to consider the eventual possibility of a new Sino-Soviet entente since, to paraphrase Lord Palmerston, there is no such thing as permanent friends or permanent enemies, only permanent interests.

53. U.S. civilian statistics include direct and indirect hire. The latter involves paying foreign governments, who in turn provide civilians to assist U.S. forces overseas. Contract services, which contribute a large but unknown number of man hours, supplement U.S. civilians shown on figures and graphs in this study. See Note 46 for sources of U.S. civilian statistics, which are the same as for active military.

54. Soviet civilian manpower strengths were derived from DIA.

55. U.S. Ready Reserves include personnel who enlist directly into Reserve and National Guard units of the top-priority Selected Reserve; prior service personnel who elect to join Selected Reserve units after stints with the active establishment; and prior service personnel released to Individual Ready Reserves, which are affiliated with no organization, but act as fillers.

56. U.S. Ready Reserve strengths were derived from *Selected Manpower Statistics, OASD (Compt), Directorate for Information, Operations, and Control*, April 15, 1971, p. 86; April 15, 1972, p. 89; April 15, 1973, p. 91; May 15, 1974, p. 91; May 15, 1975, p. 99; June 1976, p. 98. See also "Guard and Reserve Manpower: Strengths and Statistics, ODASD (RA)", flyleaf, June 1976 and July 1977.

57. Soviet forces released from active service during the period 1973–1977 total about 5,945,000. U.S. servicemen released during that same time frame total 2,843,000.

58. Soviet and NATO reserve systems are compared in Goldich, Robert L. *The Applicability of Selected Foreign Military Reserve Practices to the U.S. Reserves: Proposals Based on the Reserve Forces of the United Kingdom, Federal Republic of Germany, Israel, and the U.S.S.R.* Appendix D: Soviet Reserve Forces. Washington: Library of Congress, Congressional Research Service, processed, January 26, 1978. 23 pp.

59. "Soviet leadership has instituted for the young people essentially a military regime of indoctrination and training. . . ." Gist, David M., "The Militarization of Soviet Youth," *Naval War College Review*, Summer 1977, p. 14. Andrew W. Marshall, DOD Director of Net Assessment, stressed that point in comments on a draft of this study in September 1977.

60. FM 30–40, *Handbook on Soviet Ground Forces*. Washington: Headquarters, Department of the Army, June 30, 1975, pp. 3–30. For additional discussion, see pp. 3–7 through 3–30.

61. Morgenthau, Hans J., *Politics Among Nations*, 4th Ed. New York: Alfred A. Knopf, 1967, pp. 122, 127–128.

62. Organski, A. F. K., *World Politics*, 2d Ed. New York: Alfred A. Knopf, 1968, p. 87.

63. Soviet culture and society is discussed at length in Smith, Hedrick, *The Russians*. New York: Quadrangle/New York Times, 1976, 527 pp.

64. The Defense Manpower Commission (DMC) "found no evidence that any unit had been affected negatively by socioeconomic changes, either as to performance or mission capability. Generally, commanders [told DMC members] that these are the concerns of Washington, not of the field." Palmer, Bruce, Jr., and Tarr, Curtis W., "A Careful Look at Defense Manpower," *Military Review*, September 1976, p. 7.

65. Turner, Frederick C., "How Tall Are the Russians?," opening remarks in a panel discussion at the annual convention of the Association of the United States Army, Washington, October 12, 1976, p. 4.

66. "Russians Stung by Dissent in Armed Forces," *Baltimore News-American*, February 9, 1976, p. 4; "Soviet Mutiny Ended Swiftly," *Washington Post*, June 7, 1976, p. 18; "Mutinied Soviet Destroyer Dispatched on Long Voyage," *Christian Science Monitor*, June 29, 1976, p. 6.

67. Goldich, Robert L., *Military Manpower Policy and the All-Volunteer Force*, Issue Brief 77032. Washington: Congressional Research Service, April 6, 1977 (as updated). 22 pp.

68. Palmer, Bruce, Jr., and Tarr, Curtis W., "A Careful Look at Defense Manpower," p. 11.

69. Rumsfeld, Donald H., *Annual Defense Department Report, FY 1977*, p. 288.

70. *Ibid.*, p. 293.

71. *Defense Manpower: The Keystone of National Security, Report to the President and the Congress*. Washington: Defense Manpower Commission, April 1976, p. 2.

72. Goldhamer, Herbert, *The Soviet Soldier: Soviet Military Management at the Troop Level*. New York: Crane, Russak & Co., Inc., 1975, pp. 4, 36–37, 69; Turner, Frederick C., "How Tall Are the Russians?," p. 2; Lee, William T., "Military Economics in the USSR," *Air Force Magazine*, March 1976, p. 50; Feshbach, Murray and Rapawy, Stephen, *Soviet Economy in a New Perspective*, p. 148.

73. DOSAAF stands for the All-Union Voluntary Society for Assistance to the Army, Air Force, and Navy. Its clubs and schools play an important part in pre-induction training.

74. Turner, Frederick C., "How Tall Are the Russians?," p. 4.

75. Minckler, Rex; Ginsburgh, Robert N., and Rebh, Richard G., *Soviet Defense Manpower. A Summary Report on the Proceedings and Results of a Seminar for the DOD Director of Net Assessment and ASD (MRA&L)*. Washington: *Tempo*, General Electric Center for Advanced Studies, July 14, 1977, pp. 16, 23.

76. Turner, Frederick C., "How Tall Are the Russians?," p. 3. Callup age was cut from 19 to 18 years. Service with the Army, Air Force, naval air elements, and border/security troops was reduced from three to two years. Service on naval ships, with coast guard combat units, and with maritime units of border troops was cut from four years to three. For full details, see *Current Digest of the Soviet Press 19*, No. 45, November 29, 1967, pp. 4–10.

77. Goldhamer, Herbert, *The Soviet Soldier*, pp. 4–5, 39. Feshbach and Rapawy foresee an obligation to change the current system, perhaps by extending lengths of service once again. See *Soviet Population and Manpower Trends and Policies*, p. 149.

That trend may already be in motion (see Erickson, John, *Soviet-Warsaw Pact Force Levels*, pp. 17, 20). If so, and rates of induction were substantially reduced, no buildup would occur. Such action would simply confirm that shorter enlistments unduly degrade performance. Holding three age groups under arms at current conscription rates, however, would cause active duty strengths to shoot up by more than a third. A shift from selective extension of conscripts with critical skills to pervasive increases in length of service could be especially significant, according to Robert L. Goldich, a defense manpower analyst with the Congressional Research Service, who suggests that willingness to incur consequent economic liabilities for military purposes could signify major changes in Soviet intentions. Close scrutiny by U.S. intelligence analysts thus would be commendable.

78. Feshbach, Murray and Rapawy, Stephen, *Soviet Population and Manpower Trends and Policies,* pp. 113, 125–126; "Soviets Yield After Language Protest," *Washington Star,* April 18, 1978. p. A-2.

79. Goldhamer, Herbert, *The Soviet Soldier,* pp. 255–309, 324–327.

80. Present-day political officers lack the clout of World War II commissars. They neither countersign orders nor have an official say in operational command. All the same, their influence is still immense. DIA comments on the draft of this study, March 2, 1977.

81. Adapted from Hayward, T. E., "Mind Over Matter," *Marine Corps Gazette,* December 1976, p. 9. See also Azama, Rodney S., "The Psychology of the Soviet Army Commander," *Military Review,* September 1977, pp. 31–40.

82. For discussion, see Possony, Stefan T. and Pournelle, J. E., *The Strategy of Technology: Winning the Decisive War.* Cambridge, Mass.: Dunellen, 1970, pp. 1–20, 55.

83. Dr. George Heilmeier, Director of Defense Advanced Research Projects Agency (ARPA) outlines possibilities in "Guarding Against Technological Surprise," *Congressional Record,* June 22, 1976, p. S10139.

84. Research, development, test, and evaluation (RDT&E) precedes procurement. Abstract research improves prospects for a range of practical products by broadening the base of human knowledge. Applied technology supports specific goals. Stage I in the U.S. process identifies options, sets priorities, and defines projects. Stage II establishes program characteristics, including costs and schedules. Stage III produces prototypes. Civil contractors and military project managers complete technical tests during Stage IV, which culminates in operational assessments that are conducted by authorities who are independent of users as well as developers.

85. "In 1878, Frederick Engels stated the weapons used in the Franco-Prussian war had reached such a state of perfection that further progress which would have any revolutionary influence was no longer possible. Thirty years later, the following unforeseen systems were used in World War I: Aircraft, tanks, chemical warfare, trucks, submarines, and radio communications. A 1937 study entitled 'Technological Trends and National Policy' failed to foresee the following systems, all of which were operational by 1957: Helicopters, jet engines, radar, inertial navigators, nuclear weapons, nuclear submarines, rocket powered missiles, electronic computers and cruise missiles. The 1945 Von Karmann study entitled 'New Horizons' missed ICBMs, man in space [and so on], all operational within 15 years." Heilmeier, George, *Congressional Record,* June 22, 1976, p. S10139.

86. Knorr, Klaus and Morgenstern, Oskar, *Science and Defense: Some Critical Thoughts on Military Research and Development.* Princeton, N.J.: Princeton University Press, 1965, pp. 19–27.

87. George Heilmeier sketches a seven-step process that a free society can take to forestall technological surprise. Initiative is the most important. *Congressional Record,* June 22, 1976, p. S10139.

88. U.S. Congress. House. *Hearings on Department of Defense Appropriations for 1976 before a subcommittee of the Committee on Appropriations.* Part 4. Research, Development, Test, and Evaluation. 94th Congress, 1st Session. Washington: U.S. Govt. Print. Off., 1975, pp. 366–369, 531–532, 553–554.

89. *Ibid.*

90. *Ibid.,* pp. 553–554.

91. Background information is contained in *The Soviet Military Technological Challenge*, Washington: The Center for Strategic Studies, Georgetown University, September 1967, pp. 13–31; Harvey, Mose L. et al., *Science and Technology as An Instrument of Soviet Policy*. Coral Gables, Fla.: University of Miami, Center For Advanced International Studies, 1972, 219 pp.

92. Currie, Malcolm R., *Program of Research, Development, Test and Evaluation, FY 1977*. Washington: Department of Defense, February 3, 1976, pp. I–6, II–2.

93. Augenstein, Bruno, Military RDT&E, Chapter 6 in *Arms, Men, and Military Budgets, (FY 1977)* pp. 220–221; Currie, Malcolm R., *Program of Research, Development, Test and Evaluation, FY 1977*. pp. I–6, II–2.

94. Possony, Stefan T. and Pournelle, J. E., *The Strategy of Technology*, p. 22. None of the techniques noted is unique to the Soviet Union, but strong emphasis is evident.

95. Incremental improvements are important even when the main focus is on mighty leaps forward. Indeed, they serve a crucial purpose when opposing systems are essentially equal. "In an air battle conducted with air-to-air missiles . . . . a two mile difference in radar ranges can result in one side being destroyed even before it detects the other. Small improvements in missile accuracy can [immensely increase] kill probabilities." Possony, Stefan T. and Pournelle, J. E., *The Strategy of Technology*, pp. 30, 38–39.

96. Currie, Malcolm R., *Program of Research, Development, Test and Evaluation, FY 1977*, pp. I–5, II– 3–4.

97. A "pop-up" procedure that ejects ballistic missiles from silos or submarines using power plants that are separate from the missile body. Primary ignition is delayed until projectiles are safely clear of carriers/containers, preserving the launcher intact for reuse if required.

98. "The Russians are not coming, the Russians are there," in terms of RDTD&E, according to Anthony R. Battista, in the annual staff review for members of the R&D Subcommittee of the House Armed Services Committee. "Congress told Defense R&D does not keep pace with the Soviet threat," *Defense/Space Daily*, February 16, 1978, p. 17. See also Currie, Malcolm R., *Program of Research, Development, Test and Evaluation, FY 1977*, pp. I–7, 8, II–10, 17.

99. "Soviet R&D: No New Weapons Expected, But Surprises Still Possible," *Aerospace Daily*, August 13, 1976, p. 241. Supplemented telephonically by staff members of ARPA on December 3, 1976. See also Cooke, Robert, "The Lethal Laser is Here—Will it Be Added to US, Soviet Arsenals?" and "Lasers Turned to Spying on Spies," *Boston Globe*, May 23, 1976, p. 1 and May 24, 1976, p. 1.

100. Charged-particle beams, which focus and project atomic particles at the speed of light, require prodigious power approaching 10 joules per pulse. Each particle exerts anywhere from 1 to 100 giga electron volts. (One dyne is a basic unit of force that gives a free mass of one gram an acceleration of one centimeter per second per second. In the process, it produces one unit of work called an erg. One joule equals 10 million ergs. One giga volt is a billion volts). Potential power sources include fission or fusion energy; giant capacitors capable of storing great power for fractions of seconds; electron ejectors that produce high energy pulse streams at high velocities; collective accelerators for similar purposes; hot gas plasma to accelerate other subatomic particles; and flux compression to convert energy from explosive generators. Robinson, Clarence A., Jr., "Soviets Push for Beam Weapons," *Aviation Week and Space Technology*, May 2, 1977, pp. 16–23.

101. *Ibid.*

102. One skeptical account of CPBs is contained in Garwin, Richard L., "Charged-Particle Beam Weapons?" See *Congressional Record*, July 27, 1977, pp. S12931–S12933.

103. Defense Secretary Harold S. Brown has announced that "it is, in my view, and that of all the technically qualified people whom I know who've looked at this whole thing, without foundation. The evidence does not support the view that the Soviets

have made such a breakthrough or indeed that they are very far along in such a direction . . . . I think that not now nor in the foreseeable future would [a CPB] weapons system be a very useful one in terms of really changing the balance." "Brown Comments on Beam Weapons," *Aviation Week and Space Technology,* May 30, 1977, p. 12.

Stansfield Turner, Director of Central Intelligence, concurred when testifying before the Joint Economic Committee. "Most of the evidence adduced to the contrary is based on the assumption that a particular facility in the Soviet Union is dedicated to [CPB] purpose, and additional assumptions about their state of technology. We [the CIA] think all of these assumptions are questionable." In sum, he said, "we really do not know" the status of Soviet programs, and "cannot either confirm or deny" any progress. "CIA's Turner Says Soviets Not Near Particle Beam Weapon," *Defense/Space Daily,* August 18, 1977, p. 257.

104. Dr. Vannevar Bush was quoted in "Debate Seen on Charged-Particle Work," *Aviation Week and Space Technology,* May 2, 1977, p. 17.

105. Augenstein, Bruno, in *Arms, Men, and Military Budgets (FY 1977),* pp. 218, 220, 221, 244–247; Possony, Stefan T. and Pournelle, J. E., *The Strategy of Technology,* p. 51.

106. Senior members of the President's Committee on Science and Technology and the National Science Board, for example, recently expressed concern. Others share such sympathies. Participants at a symposium sponsored by Massachusetts Institute of Technology (M.I.T.) agreed that serious, speedy steps are needed to prevent further erosion of the U.S. position. Jerome B. Wiesner, M.I.T.'s President, predicted that "if we don't apply our enormous, unused capacity to technology, we face a problem of whether we shall survive 30 years from now." "R&D on the Skids," *Time,* May 3, 1976, p. 56; "Loss of Innovation in Technology is Debated," *New York Times,* November 25, 1976, p. 53.

107. Currie, Malcolm R., *Program of Research, Development, Test and Evaluation, FY 1977,* p. I–6; Possony, Stefan T. and Pournelle, J. E., *The Strategy of Technology,* pp. 23–25; "Weapons Research: Ivan's Edge is Our Bureaucracy," *Armed Forces Journal,* July 1976, pp. 16, 18.

108. "Since 1901 there have been 38 Americans among the 190 [Nobel physics prize] winners, and only 6 Russians. There have been 89 [chemistry] winners since the start, including 21 Americans. But only one Russian . . . . The Soviets put up the first Sputnik 20 years ago." Attempts "to mark the anniversary and to celebrate the 1917 October revolution with a new feat," however, "failed; they couldn't make the [publicized] linkup" in space. At this stage, we have more to offer than they do. TRB, "Russia Needs Our Technology—Badly," *Washington Star,* October 15, 1977, p. 11. Soyuz 26, a ferry craft, did dock with Salyut 6, a space station, on December 11, 1977 and set an endurance record. The United States has not yet duplicated those feats.

109. "Soviet Computer Technology: Catching Up," *Air Force Magazine,* November 1976, p. 67; Additional details are contained in *Long-Range U.S.-U.S.S.R. Competition: National Security Implications,* proceedings of a conference conducted by the National Defense University, July 12–14, 1976, pp. 208–246; and Augenstein, Bruno in *Arms, Men, and Military Budgets (FY 1977),* pp. 242–244.

110. Letter from Brent Scowcroft, Special Assistant to the President for National Security Affairs, to Congressman Jack F. Kemp, September 13, 1976. 2 pp.

111. Costick, Miles, "The Strategic Dimension of the U.S. Computer Exports to the U.S.S.R.," *Congressional Record,* May 19, 1977, pp. H4735–H4738.

112. "U.S., Citing Military Use, Bars Soviet Computer Deal," *Baltimore Sun,* June 24, 1977, p. 1.

113. Current controls include security classifications, applied primarily by the Department of Defense; The Arms Export Control Act, administered by the Department of State; the Export Administration Act affiliated with our Commerce Department; and informal regulatory agreements associated with the Consultative Group Coordinating Committee (CoCom), whose members include NATO countries (less Iceland) and Ja-

pan. Bucy, J. Fred, "On Strategic Technology Transfer to the Soviet Union," *International Security*, Spring 1977, pp. 34–36.

114. Bucy addresses a wide range of past, present, and projected problems concerning export controls. *Ibid.*, pp. 25–43.

115. Secretary of Defense Brown issues "Interim Policy on Export Control of United States Technology," *News Release*, Washington, OASD (Public Affairs), September 2, 1977, with inclosed memorandum. 5 pp.

116. Augenstein, Bruno, in *Arms, Men, and Military Budgets (FY 1977)*, pp. 216–217.

PART IV

Strategic Nuclear Trends

Strategic nuclear trends that shaped current capabilities on both sides started in the 1950s. This section connects force requirements with respective strategies, relating asymmetries in each case to divergent demands.[1]

Soviet Purpose

Soviet security objectives are subjects of speculation in the United States. Some specialists bank heavily on official publications as primary source materials. "If Western commentators are uncertain about [the Kremlin's] aims and aspirations," said one, "they have no one but themselves to blame. The record is clear."[2] Other analysts, however, contend that jargon-riddled and convoluted Soviet writings on national security rarely reveal real goals. As they see it, public pronouncements by top Soviet leaders may seem straightforward, but documentable facts are difficult to separate from dissemblance. A good deal must, therefore, be derived from deduction, which leaves the door wide open for different opinions.

One faction, for example, identifies world domination as a genuine Soviet goal.[3] Those who subscribe to that thesis say "compellence" overrides "deterrence" as the dominant aim, accompanied by quests for strategic supremacy.[4] A CIA estimate, presented to Congress in 1976, submitted that "the Soviets are committed to the acquisition of 'war-fighting capabilities', a decision which . . . . accords with a long-standing tenet of Soviet military doctrine that a nuclear war could be fought and won."[5]

Skeptics simply see an elemental Soviet drive for essential equality. Expansion that seems to exceed such limits is explained as Russian "over-reaction to past weakness." American innovations accelerate Soviet actions to catch up.[6] Responsibilities for a ceaseless arms spiral and chronic instability thus must be shared by both countries.[7]

Soviet Posture

Whatever purpose they serve, improvements in Soviet nuclear posture have created new problems for U.S. strategists since 1962.

The mythical "missile gap," which played a prominent part in our 1960 presidential campaign, proved to be in U.S., instead of Soviet, favor. This country's strategic nuclear superiority was still cleancut at the time of the Cuban crisis. Subsequent realignments, however, have had far-reaching ramifications.

For the first time since the American Revolution, a competitor has uncommitted capacities that could destroy the United States, if it cares to run reciprocal risks.[8] Calculated steps continue to strengthen Soviet nuclear strike forces and strategic defense as instruments of national policy. Efforts now under way emphasize counterforce capabilities against U.S. ICBMs, pre-launch protection for offensive assets, and survivable reserves. Active and passive shields increasingly cover command/control systems and critical civilian sectors.[9]

Some programs have proved more successful than others. Progress is incomplete. Proper equilibrium may still prevail, with forces, "at present, in rough equivalence," as highly-placed officials assert.[10] Nevertheless, the situation is significantly less salutary from our standpoint than it was in the early 1960s.

U.S. Response

Some shifts in the U.S./Soviet nuclear balance could have been short-stopped. Others were past control.[11] All, however, have compelled accommodations.

U.S. Strategic Nuclear Goals

Evolving Soviet nuclear capabilities have encouraged a series of U.S. Presidents to alter most objectives that underwrite our irreducible interest in survival (Graph 3).

Deterring atomic aggression against the United States dwarfs other American aims, as it has since the mid-1950s, when Soviet long-range aircraft first acquired abilities to engage targets in this country. If preventive measures had collapsed at that time, all efforts to the con-

Graph 3

U.S. Strategic Nuclear Objectives

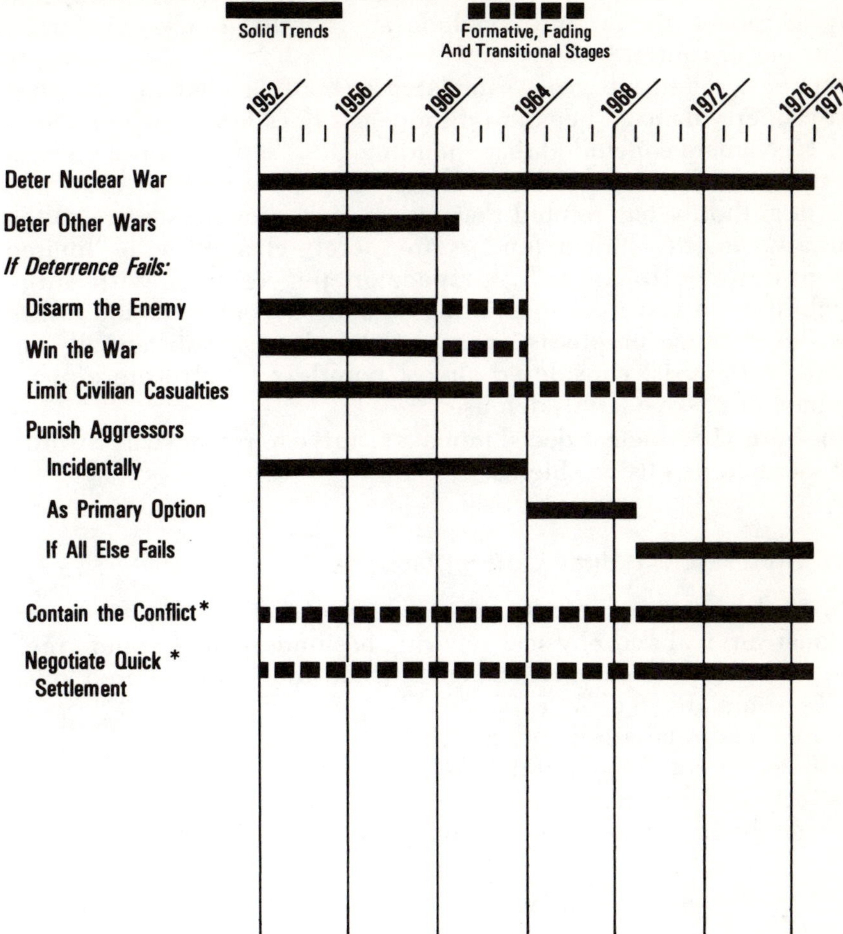

*Dotted line indicates period when objective may have been implicit, but was not articulated as an important goal.

trary, U.S. leaders planned on counterforce operations to disarm the opposition and "win" the ensuing conflict.[12]

Victory ceased to be America's consummate aim as soon as the Soviets deployed massive nuclear capabilities predicated on ballistic missiles instead of manned bombers. Successful counterforce operations were "simply unattainable" by 1964,[13] given our second-strike strategy.[14] Defense at that stage was impossible.

America's only objective if deterrence had failed in the next few years was "to destroy [any] aggressor as a viable society."[15] That vengeful purpose, however, by 1970 "appeared less and less credible" in response to "anything less than an all-out attack" on the United States and its cities.[16] Unrestrained reprisal thus remains as our last-ditch option, but U.S. Administrations now actively seek some way to cap escalation and conclude any conflict quickly, before it burns out of control.[17]

Strategic defensive goals calculated to confine civilian casualties and property damage began to disappear a decade ago, when Secretary McNamara concluded that shielding U.S. "cities against a Soviet [missile] attack . . . . would be a futile waste of our resources."[18] No one in authority has refuted that assertion, recent lip service to the contrary. America's air defenders are merely charged with "limited day-to-day control of U.S. airspace in peacetime," with surge capabilities to stave off small-scale assaults by bombers and cruise missiles.[19] Since emphasis on active defense is "substantially reduced, it [now is] considered almost pointless to advocate a major program of passive [civil] defense."[20]

In short, U.S. nuclear decision-makers strive to retain sharp swords, but sacrifice defensive shields.

U.S. Strategic Nuclear Concepts

U.S. nuclear strategy, contrived to satisfy objectives affiliated with national survival and physical security, has undergone frequent revision since 1962. Elemental changes, which reflect our altered aims, can be summarized as follows:

—Reduced retaliatory options
—Rejection of homeland defense
—Increased reliance on arms control

Three distinct stages of development stand out (Graph 4).[21]

The Age of Assured Ascendancy

America's deterrent strategy during the 1950s could have been defined as Assured Ascendancy. Our evident edge at that stage encouraged decisive concepts, despite second-strike constraints that precluded preemptive or preventive operations as policy options.

Counterforce operations of all kinds were conspicuous ingredients, designed to deliver crippling blows against attacking bombers, preserve U.S. cities, and pave the way for massive retaliation against Moscow's means of waging offensive war.[22]

Bald quantitative and qualitative superiority characterized U.S. force posture throughout the Age of Assured Ascendancy, which persisted into the early 1960s. At our zenith, diversified retaliatory arms in a high state of readiness were complemented by a multifaceted air defense system. The aggregate solidly enhanced this country's deter-

Graph 4

U.S. Nuclear Strategy

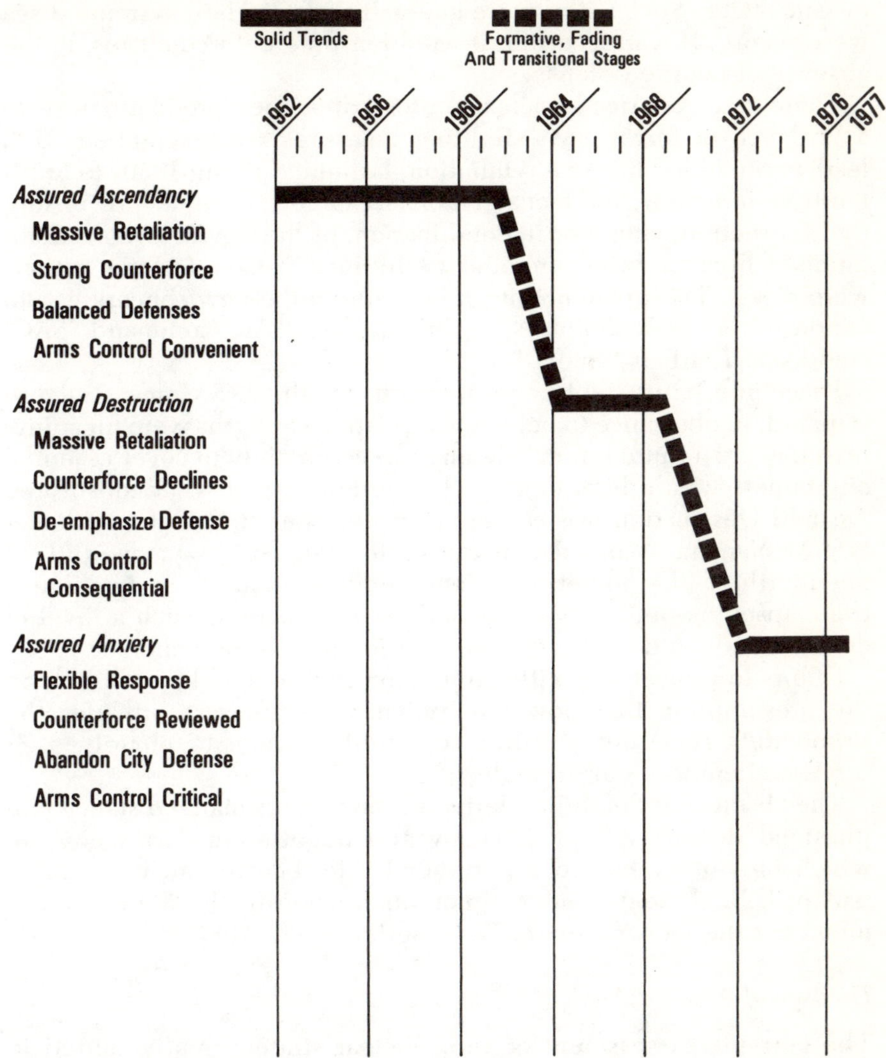

rent across the nuclear spectrum, by guaranteeing that we could conduct a general war victoriously, and handle atomic contingencies.

Arms control played an unprepossessing part in U.S. plans. It was simply a strategic adjunct.

The Age of Assured Destruction

The United States abandoned Assured Ascendancy concepts in 1963, and substituted Assured Destruction.[23]

The reason was elemental. Nothing we could do within the confines of second-strike concepts and existing states of technological art could protect the American people or production base against a full-scale missile attack. Soviet silos were generally safe.[24] Their systems at sea were secure. If war occurred, it would cripple both countries, in the absence of missile defense.

Thereafter, America's nuclear strategy depended predominantly on a "balance of terror". War-fighting measures were scrapped. U.S. leaders remolded massive retaliation, fashioned in the 1950s to fulfill multiple functions, and focused it on city targets, designed to "ensure the destruction, singly or in combination, of the Soviet Union, Communist China, and the communist satellites."[25] Counterforce actions were recast. Their paramount purpose under the new concept was to suppress the foe's defenses, so our Strategic Air Command (SAC) could smash urban centers.

Peacetime parity replaced superiority as the U.S. force structure standard, in obeisance to beliefs that relative strengths were meaningless, beyond a finite point. The mission was mainly to cover essential city targets with a high degree of confidence. Just what constituted Assured Destruction was contentious even then, but Defense Secretary McNamara assumed that means to eradicate "say, one-fifth to one-fourth of [the Soviet] population and one-half of [Soviet] industrial capacity would serve as an effective deterrent. Such a level of destruction would certainly represent intolerable punishment."[26]

Efforts to protect U.S. cities from atomization took low priority, on the presumption that power to pulverize aggressors provides the prime deterrent, not abilities to "limit damage to ourselves."[27] Strategic defenses started to decline.

The absence of flexibility derived from that specialized stance emphasized demands for diplomacy and negotiation. Arms control, which previously played a peripheral role, became an inseparable part of U.S. strategy, under direct supervision of the State Department, not the Department of Defense.[28]

The Age of Assured Anxiety

The current reassessment of U.S. nuclear strategy really started in 1969, when President Nixon asked an oft-quoted question: Should the President, in event of a nuclear attack, be left with the single option of slaughtering Soviet civilians, knowing that millions of Americans would be killed in return?[29]

Assured Destruction stood fast as the fundamental U.S. deterrent to general nuclear war, with one significant modification: targets were selected specifically to delay Soviet recovery indefinitely, instead of inflict intolerable punishment. Counterforce concepts came off the shelf to discourage and, if need be, deal with lesser challenges.[30]

The consequences, however, have been contestable.

Additional armaments of specialized character, some say, would allow the United States to meet measured aggression with increased confidence only if we could conduct a controlled counterforce war, which is no longer the case. The threat of massive retaliation was a credible constraint when SAC held all the "trump cards", but if executed today would stimulate escalation, instead of squelching nuclear sparring. With no clear way for this country to clamp on a lid, the scope and intensity of conflict could rocket out of control.[31]

Steps to shore up mutual vulnerability, America's deterrent mainstay, have met with mixed success.[32] On the positive side, the SALT I ABM Treaty, which deprived the United States and Soviet Union of missile defense,[33] may have strengthened deterrence temporarily, by ensuring the continued futility of a full-scale fusillade.[34] U.S. decision-makers, however, disregard air and civil defenses, while the Kremlin's stress in both sectors stays comparatively strong.[35] A Soviet ABM breakthrough, not soon expected but not impossible either, thus could shift the strategic nuclear balance suddenly in their favor.

Increased instability causes reciprocal arms control accords to assume a critical role. U.S. security now depends to unprecedented degrees on cooperation by Soviet competitors, whose incentives to compromise seem less intense than our own.

The SALT I interim agreement to limit selected delivery systems (see Annex E) may have slowed Moscow's momentum (a moot point), but it also contained inequities, which caused Congress to insist that SALT II not limit U.S. forces to levels lower than those allowed the Soviet Union.[36] The subsequent search for essential equivalence remains unsettled, despite repeated assurances from senior U.S. officials that a suitable SALT II treaty is close at hand.[37]

The cumulative course of events since 1962 consequently causes substantial uncertainties in the U.S. defense establishment and among many concerned citizens, who sense that America's nuclear deterrent powers, while still strong, could be slipping away. The Age of Assured Anxiety will thus be with us until U.S. strategists solve some critical problems.

Strategic Offensive Comparisons

Strategic nuclear forces are extremely specialized. Those fit for offensive purposes are poorly adapted for defense, and vice versa. This section, therefore, separates the two categories, while showing connections.[38]

Force Shaping Criteria

Several fundamental policy decisions and geographic circumstances, in addition to or elaboration of those already discussed, differentiate

U.S. nuclear strike forces from Soviet counterparts in size, structure, and technical characteristics.

Policy Decisions

Four deliberate U.S. policy decisions contribute to asymmetrical development and force deployments on opposing sides. Two have been constant for two or more decades. Two have been subject to change (Graph 5).

Mixed Force Concepts Flexibility is a time-tested Principle of War.[39] The experience of many millenia confirms that it rarely is wise to rely on a single weapons system, regardless of its attributes.

The mission in our case is to maintain diversified forces that can support deterrent concepts under worst-case circumstances. As a minimum, they must be able to survive a savage first strike by any enemy and still retain infallible Assured Destruction abilities. The mix must also afford a range of flexible responses within the framework of our second-strike strategy, minimize probabilities that all U.S. systems could be compromised concurrently by technological surprise, and contribute to stability.

Congress in the 1950s put its seal of approval on a triad of manned penetrating bombers, fixed-site ICBMs, and submarine-launched ballistic missiles (SLBMs). Designated tactical aircraft reinforce as required. Each component is significantly different in terms of pre- and post-launch survivability, range, reliability, responsiveness, accuracy, adaptability, and cost. Each has shortcomings, but components complement each other nicely.

That combination sufficed until the 1970s, when system costs and Soviet capabilities began to cast doubts on its continued suitability. The required mix and degree of redundancy currently are under official review, with four systems in various R&D stages as potential supplements or replacements: air- and sea-launched cruise missiles (ALCMs, SLCMs); air-launched ballistic missiles (ALBMs); and land-mobile ICBMs.[40]

The Soviets, for all practical purposes, rely on a dyad of massive, land-based ballistic missiles coupled with SLBMs. They still downplay aircraft, which would add flexibility, although Backfire bombers now augmenting their arsenal could be assigned significant roles. The two sides thus are quite dissimilar.

Force-Sizing Standards U.S. force-sizing standards have shifted four times since the early 1960s.

Clearcut quantitative and qualitative superiority supported U.S. deterrent strategy at the onset of the Atomic Age. Until 1956, the United States enjoyed a monopoly of nuclear weapons that could be delivered

Graph 5

U.S. Nuclear Retaliatory Force Posture Policies

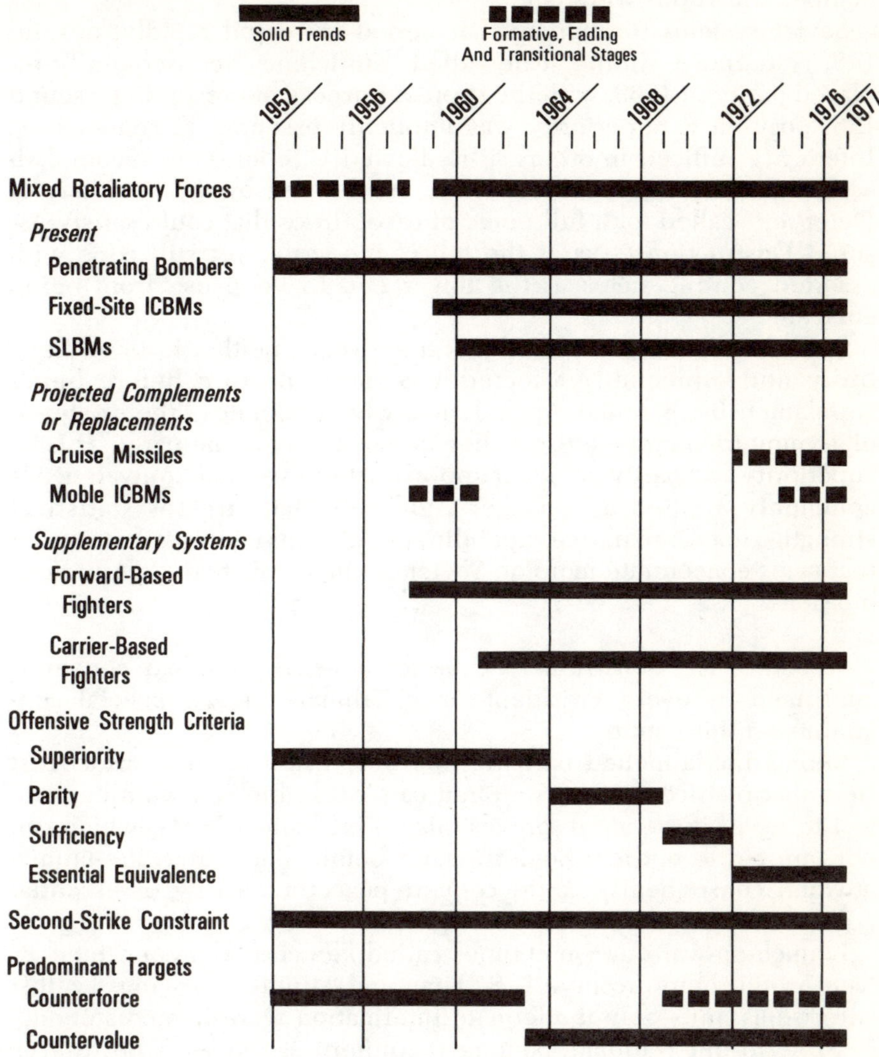

intercontinentally. We retained unquestioned supremacy well into the succeeding decade. Assured Ascendancy depended on that solid advantage.

Parity replaced superiority in 1964, when America's mixed matrix was focused on city targeting. To attain desired ends, DOD stressed numbers of nuclear bombs and warheads, not delivery vehicles.[41] That tack strongly influenced decisions to install multiple independently-targetable reentry vehicles (MIRVs), instead of adding launchers. We stopped adding missile systems in 1967, when the total reached 1,000 Minutemen and 656 Polaris/Poseidon SLBMs. SAC's bomber squadrons were cut.

Soviet systems throughout that period increased rapidly, despite U.S. restraint. A sliding scale called "sufficiency" consequently replaced parity in 1969, with the express purpose of preserving a sound U.S. position.[42] Superiority was implicitly essential in some cases. Inferiority sufficed in others, if it allowed U.S. forces to accomplish assigned missions. Specific criteria, spelled out by the Secretary of Defense,[43] called for a full range of capabilities that could satisfy Assured Destruction tasks at the top of the scale, yet still cope with assorted contingencies at the lower end to keep us "from being coerced."[44]

Sufficiency, which survived just three years, neither fostered flexibility nor appreciably affected U.S. force posture before being supplanted by essential equivalence, which tolerates "the existence of asymmetries provided . . . . they do not all favor one party."[45] Like superiority and parity, which it approximates, essential equivalence is commonly applied as a rather rigid rule that stresses statistical strengths, not comparative capabilities. U.S. arms control efforts under that aegis concentrate more on Soviet deployments than on American missions.

Second-Strike Constraints U.S. second-strike nuclear concepts, confirmed by every President since Truman, impose special constraints on this country.

Submarine-launched ballistic missiles, when at sea, suffer least from that restriction. SAC's aircraft can "scramble" on warning, subject to recall if the alarm proves false. Fixed-site ICBMs, which can not, must ride out any Soviet assault before retaliating. Pre-launch attrition consequently could convert peacetime parity or essential equivalence into inferiority very quickly.

Launch-on-warning (sometimes called launch under confirmed attack) would help preserve U.S. Titan and Minuteman wings against surprise assaults only if adequate information were immediately accessible to our National Command Authorities (NCA), who reserve exclusive rights to sanction retaliatory strikes.[46] As a minimum, rational response would depend on sufficient data to determine the magnitude and impact areas (cities or silos) of a Soviet missile attack. Should the U.S. alert apparatus fail to function for any reason, including early enemy action, chances are slim that *any* decision to launch could be made, much less implemented, in the few minutes available.[47]

Soviet leaders seem less preoccupied with such problems. Readiness conditions indicate a relaxed attitude. Only a small fraction of their ICBMs, for example, are considered to be on peak alert, compared with close to 100 percent on our side.[48] Slightly more than a tenth of their SLBMs usually are at sea. We keep half of ours on open water.[49] Technical problems contribute to their poor preparedness, but that posture also suggests that Soviet fears of a U.S. first strike are subdued. Should preemptive or preventive war ever appear attractive, they would have plenty of time to improve their position.

Types of Targets Concentration on countervalue targeting during the days of Assured Destruction shaped a specialized force for the United States.

By coincidence, rather than design, U.S. decision-makers deployed sufficient counterforce capabilities with which to engage in constrained nuclear conflict of a considerable order. Contrary to popular misconception, U.S. strategic retaliatory forces always retained respectable powers to destroy most Soviet military targets, including bombers and their bases, ballistic missile submarines in and near ports, ABM and air defense installations, certain command/control facilities, and nuclear stockpiles.

U.S. weapons, however, were never expressly engineered with requisite combinations of accuracy, payload, yield, and responsiveness needed to neutralize time-sensitive, hardened point targets (such as missiles in silos), because cities as a general rule are soft, static, sprawling areas.[50] Congress routinely rebuffed fund requests to create single-shot hard target kill capabilities for Minuteman and Poseidon, which Administration spokesmen sought in the early 1970s to support controlled counterforce concepts.[51] Mark 12A MIRV warheads for Minuteman III, with impressive yield/accuracy improvements, have since been developed, but deployment will not be complete before the end of this decade, even if present plans bear fruit.[52]

The Soviets, in contrast, have been amassing big boosters for land-based ballistic missiles. Consequent payload capacities, combined with better accuracy, create increasingly ominous counterforce capabilities against U.S. second-strike ICBMs, which are "sitting ducks" in their silos. Instability in that leg of our triad thus is acute.[53]

Target Dispersion

The United States and U.S.S.R. both encompass immense expanses,[54] but Soviet targets dispersed deep in that country are somewhat less accessible than U.S. assets, which are confined to fewer contiguous sites close to our east and west coasts.

Core Areas Core areas are geographically distinct aggregations that contain countervalue targets of great political, economic, and/or cultural significance, the seizure, retention, destruction, or control of which would afford marked advantage to any opponent.[55]

Only two out of nine Soviet nodes, at Leningrad and Vladivostok, touch the sea (Map 3). Neither is truly vital.[56] Four of the five crucial centers in European Russia lie several hundred miles or more behind air defense shields, and make U.S. SLBMs stretch from most launch

Map 3
SOVIET CORE AREAS

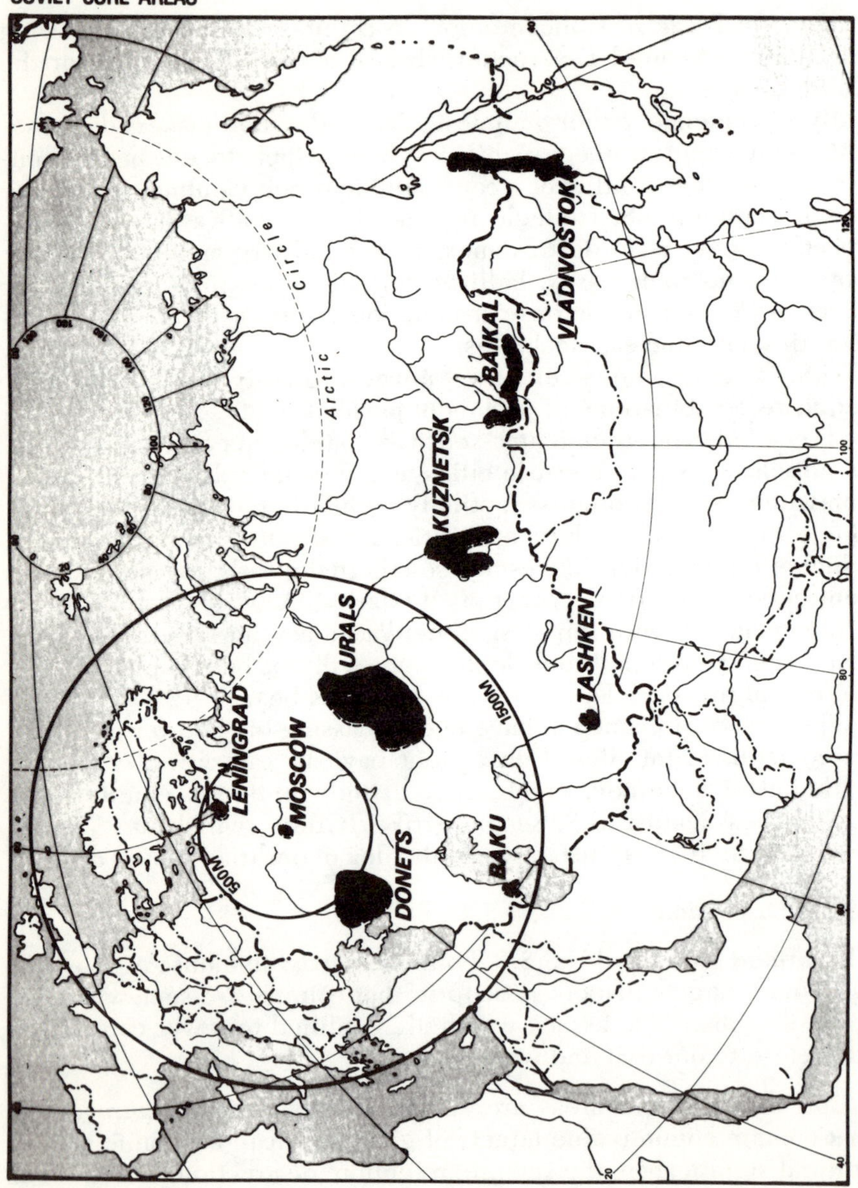

points. All five are essential to, or emotionally allied with, Soviet interests in national survival and security.

Moscow, the capital city and nerve center, has a population exceeding 7,000,000, plus focal points for politico-military control, transportation, communications, commerce, finance, diversified industry, research, and education.

Leningrad, the second city, is celebrated for culture, science, and technology. It produces precision instruments; optics; plastics and pharmaceuticals; ships, including submarines. The port is important. So are Kronstadt Naval Base and several airfields.

The Donets Basin boasts Kharkov, Donetsk, Lugansk, Nikopol, Krivoy Rog, Dnepropetrovsk, and Zaporozh'ye. It is famed for iron, coal, steel, industrial machinery, thermal and hydroelectric power, fertilizer plants, explosives manufacture, locomotive production, ball bearings, and factories for guided missiles.

The Urals are noted for iron ore at Magnitogorsk, along with the largest steel mill in the Soviet Union. Perm produces arms, ammunition, aircraft engines, and chemicals. It also features oil fields and a refinery. Sverdlovsk is the natural gateway through those mountains. Chelyabinsk contains a cluster of heavy industry, and so on.

Baku is renowned for petroleum and its products.

Four subsidiary core areas are regionally vital, but the Soviet Union could survive as a strong state without them.

Tashkent is noted, among other things, for nuclear research. The Kuznetsk complex, which covers Barnaul, Novosibirsk, Novokuznetsk, and Kemerovo, is the foremost mining and manufacturing region in Siberia. Baikal, embracing Bratsk, Irkutsk, and Ulan-Ude, is a bottleneck on the ribbon-like Trans-Siberian Railway, an important source of raw materials, local industries, and a huge hydroelectric power plant. Vladivostok and vicinity, as far north as Nikolaevsk, contains major manufacturing centers that serve the Soviet Far East, and affords commercial access to the open ocean.

Core areas in CONUS, by way of contrast, are accessible. The Atlantic seaboard, 150 miles wide at best, comprises a single string of strategic targets. That narrow strip, including our national nerve center, is essential to security. Similar concentrations are spaced along the Pacific coast from Seattle to San Diego. Both flanks thus already lie within easy reach of Soviet submarines armed with short-range SLCMs. Those boats could, if considered expendable, launch surprise attacks from positions astride our continental shelf. A third U.S. core abuts the Canadian border along the line of Great Lakes. It is more remote, but still affords the easiest possible access from Russian bomber bases. U.S. defense demands consequently could soar if the Soviets deployed medium-range cruise missiles in strength, or substantially augmented their Long Range Aviation.[57]

Population Centers Urban patterns are particularly important, because deterrent powers predicated on Assured Destruction depend on abilities to destroy cities.[58]

Half the American people live in 140 poorly-protected cities, according to census surveys. Millions are massed in 35 metropolitan areas.[59] Most skilled labor, the lion's share of corporate management, and many indispensable defense industries are found in those same centers, which mainly crown five strategic cores in our north-central Atlantic states, the Great Lakes region, Texas, California, and the Pacific Northwest.

The Soviet population, although concentrated in the Leningrad-Odessa-Kusnetsk triangle, still is considerably less compressed.[60] The 1,000 largest cities contain fewer than 50 percent of the people.[61]

That fact of life, coupled with U.S. second-strike concepts, calls for more American nuclear weapons to hold Soviet citizens "hostage" than the Kremlin would need to cripple this country if its forces struck first.

Counterforce Targets U.S. strategic nuclear submarine support bases[62] and the Soviet counterpart on Kamchatka are equally exposed to aircraft and cruise missile assaults launched from positions offshore. Pens on the Barents Sea, behind Norway's northernmost nob, are better protected.

Every SAC bomber squadron in the United States (Map 4) is fair game for Soviet second-generation SLBMs, not to mention their modern successors. Prelaunch survival prospects are somewhat more sanguine for Soviet aircraft dispersed deep in that country's centrum.

Distance, however, is no defense against ICBMs. U.S. land-based missile wings are concentrated in nine compact clusters, all west of the Mississippi. Soviet silos are scattered along a single swath that cuts east-west across the continent (Map 5). Geographic distribution affords no distinct advantage in either case, since the two forces can easily target each other.

Contemporary Force Trends

Force deployments give shape and substance to U.S. and Soviet strategies already described. Some changes in U.S. retaliatory posture correlate closely with essential security interests and stated concepts. Others seem out of kilter.[63]

Intercontinental Ballistic Missiles

All U.S. and Soviet ICBMs still seem to be cased in subterranean concrete silos, although our rival reportedly has produced and stored at least 100 SS-16 land-mobile models since testing was terminated in 1975.[64] (See Figure 9.)

Map 4

MISSILE/BOMBER BASES IN THE UNITED STATES

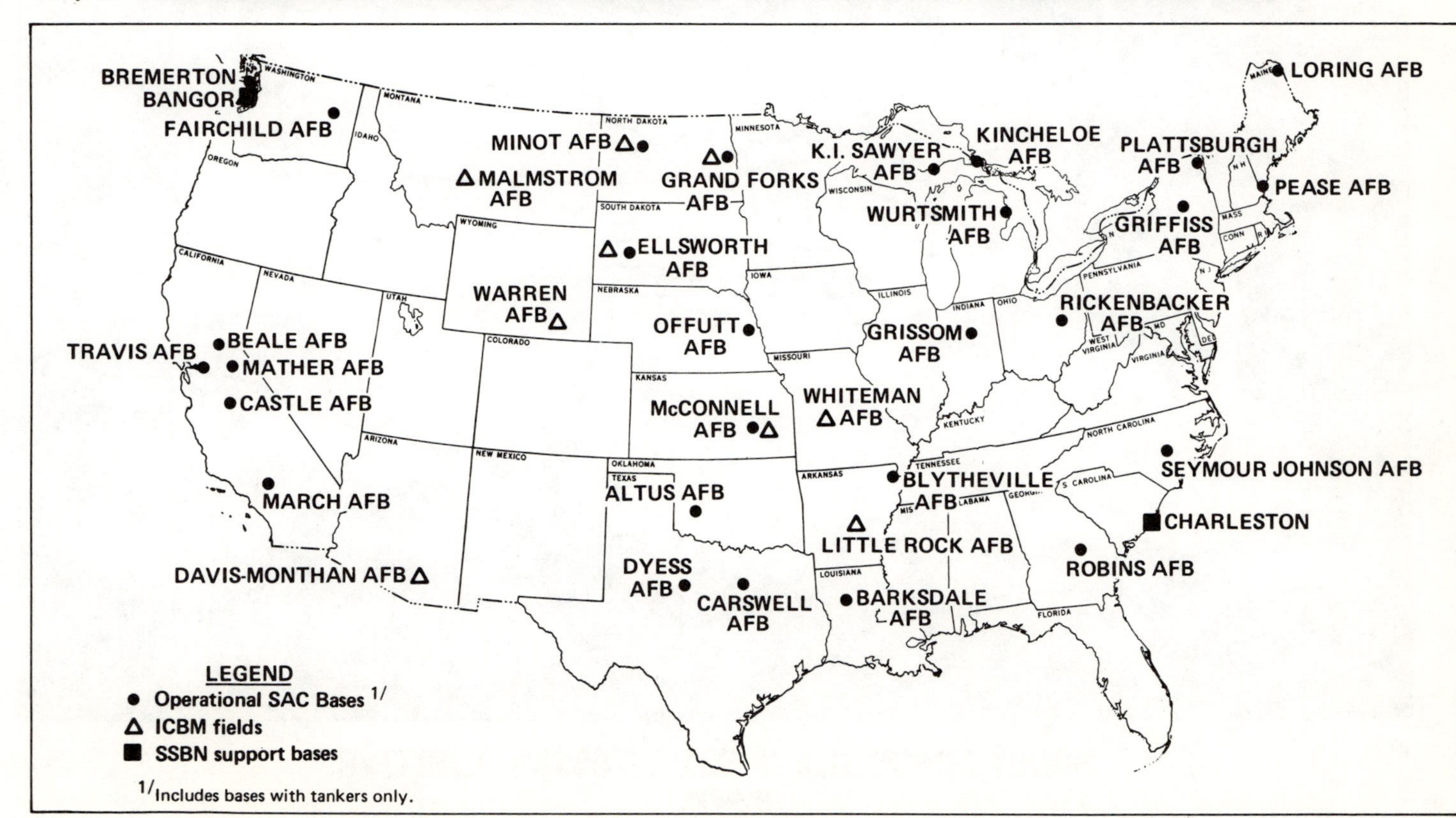

Map 5
BALLISTIC MISSILE SITES IN THE SOVIET UNION

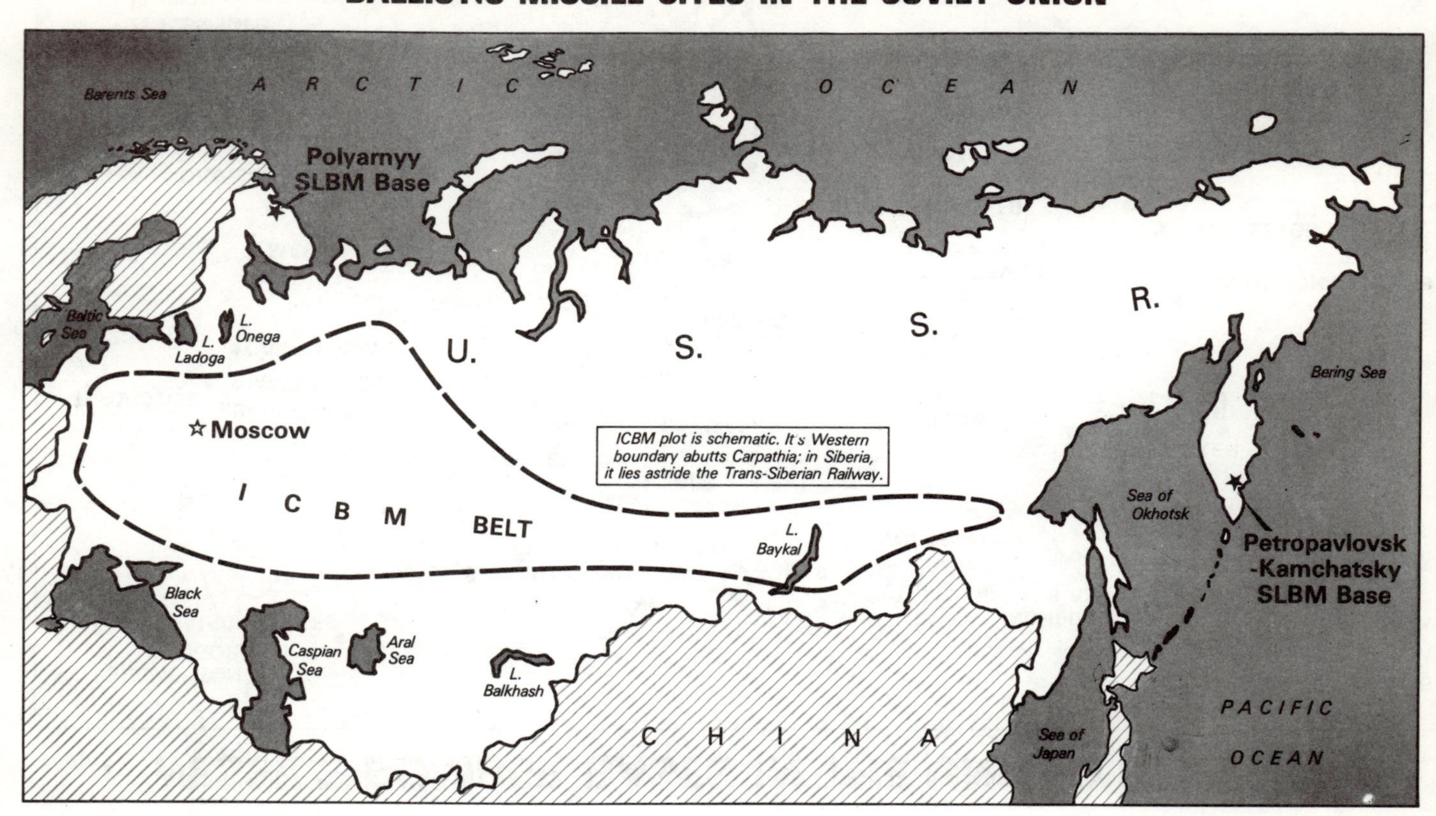

FIGURE 9 INTERCONTINENTAL BALLISTIC MISSILES, Statistical Trends and System Characteristics

Launchers	*1970*	*1971*	*1972*	*1973*	*1974*	*1975*	*1976*	*1977*	*Net Change 1970–77*
HEAVY ICBMs									
United States									
Titan II	54	54	54	54	54	54	54	54	0
Soviet Union									
SS-7	190	190	190	190	190	190	140	80	−110
SS-8	19	19	19	19	19	19	19	9	− 10
SS-9	228	270	288	288	288	288	264	200	− 28
SS-18[1]	0	0	0	0	0	10	36	100	+100
SS-19[2]	0	0	0	0	0	60	100	120	+120
Total	437	479	497	497	497	567	559	509	+ 72
U.S. Standing	− 383	− 425	− 443	− 443	− 443	− 513	− 505	− 455	− 72
LIGHT ICBMs									
United States									
Minuteman I	490	390	290	140	21	0	0	0	−490
Minuteman II	500	500	500	510	450	450	450	450	− 50
Minuteman III	10	110	210	350	529	550	550	550	+540
Total	1000	1000	1000	1000	1000	1000	1000	1000	0

[1]This summary considers 48 out of 100 Soviet SS-18s are Mod 2s. Warhead totals count eight (rather than 10) MIRVs for each of those missiles in 1977.

[2]Although SS-19 ICBMs are not classified as "heavy" for purposes of Strategic Arms Limitation Talks (SALT), they are included in that category here for most accurate comparability of strategic forces.

FIGURE 9 (Con't)

Launchers	*1970*	*1971*	*1972*	*1973*	*1974*	*1975*	*1976*	*1977*	*Net Change 1970–77*
Soviet Union									
SS-11	970	970	970	970	1030	960	910	850	−120
SS-13/16[3]	20	40	60	60	60	60	60	60	+ 40
SS-17	0	0	0	0	0	10	20	50	+ 50
Total	990	1010	1030	1030	1090	1030	990	960	−30
U.S. Standing	+10	−10	−30	−30	−90	−30	+10	+40	+ 30
TOTAL ICBMs									
United States	1054	1054	1054	1054	1054	1054	1054	1054	0
Soviet Union	1427	1489	1527	1527	1587	1597	1549	1469	+ 42
U.S. Standing	− 373	− 435	− 473	− 473	− 533	− 543	− 495	− 415	− 42
Warheads									
United States									
MIRV	30	330	630	1050	1587	1650	1650	1650	+1620
Other	1044	944	844	704	525	504	504	504	− 540
Total	1074	1274	1474	1754	2112	2154	2154	2154	+1080
Soviet Union									
MIRV	0	0	0	0	0	400	680	1304	+1304
Other	1427	1489	1527	1527	1587	1528	1429	1251	176
Total	1427	1489	1527	1527	1587	1928	2109	2555	+1128
U.S. Standing	− 353	− 215	− 53	+ 227	+ 525	+ 226	+ 45	− 401	− 48

System Characteristics

	First Deployed	*Number RVs* Single	MRV[4]	MIRV	Warhead Yield	CEP (Nautical) Miles)	Range (Miles)	Cold Launch	Propellant
United States									
Titan II	1963	1			9 MT	0.8	7250	No	Liquid
MM I	1962	1			1 MT	0.5	7500	No	Solid
MM II	1965	1			1 MT	0.3	8000	No	Solid
MM III	1970			3	170 KT ea	0.2	8000	No	Solid
Soviet Union									
SS-7	1962	1			3–5 MT	1.0	6500	No	Liquid
SS-8	1963	1			2–4 MT	1.0	6900	No	Liquid
SS-9	1967	1			18–25 MT	0.4	7000	No	Liquid
Mod 4	1971		3		2–5 MT ea	1.0	5500	No	Liquid
SS-11	1966	1			1–2 MT	0.7	6000	No	Liquid
Mod 3	1973		3		500 KT–1 MT ea	0.6	5500	No	Liquid
SS-13	1969	1			500 KT–1 MT	1.0	5000	No	Solid
SS-16[3]	1978?	1			1 MT	0.3	5000	No	Solid
SS-17	1975			4	500 KT–1 MT ea	0.3	5500	Yes	Liquid
SS-18	1974	1			18–25 MT	0.3	6000	Yes	Liquid
Mod 2	1976			8–10	1–2 MT ea	0.3	5500	Yes	Liquid
SS-19	1974			6	500 KT–1 MT ea	0.25	5000	No	Liquid

[3]The deployment status of SS-16s is uncertain.

[4]The three MRVs on each SS-9 Mod 4 and SS-11 Mod 3 count as single warheads in this summary.

U.S. Trends The total number of U.S. ICBMs and the "heavy-light" mix of 54 Titan IIs and 1,000 Minutemen has stayed static since 1967. Converting half the force to MIRVed Minuteman IIIs[65] drastically reduced weapons in the megaton range (only 504 remain), but concurrently doubled our warheads from 1,054 to 2,154.

Titans have ample explosive power to crack hard structures, such as Soviet silos, but lack the accuracy to "kill" point targets consistently. Minuteman missiles, which mount smaller warheads, still lack sufficient yield (although Mark 12As, soon to be deployed, will correct that condition).[66] Consequently, U.S. ICBMs at this stage are essentially designed to fulfill Assured Destruction functions against Soviet population/production centers and other soft targets.[67]

Soviet Trends Moscow has stressed land-based ballistic missiles since the early 1960s. Deployments soared during that decade, then slowed when the tally outstripped our own by almost a third. U.S. intelligence confirms just 122 new Soviet silos since 1970, but all are in the "heavy" category, which includes five systems (SS-7, SS-8, SS-9, SS-18, and SS-19).[68]

Fifteen percent of all Soviet warheads are in the 5–25 megaton range, versus fewer than five percent for our ICBM force (380 to 54). The least lethal tips have three times the yield of those on Minuteman III. That disparity derived from a conscious U.S. decision to emphasize precision, when the Soviets stressed raw power. The Kremlin now strives for both. If, as reported, post-boost control will soon allow SS-18 and SS-19 ICBMs to approach a CEP of 0.1 nautical miles (a 50–50 chance of hitting within 600 feet of any aiming point), their capabilities against the hardest U.S. silos would be credible.[69]

Systems with MIRV capabilities are now supplanting those with single weapons. If, indeed, all SS-17s and SS-19s are MIRVed (which intelligence can not deny or confirm), the Soviets already have twice as many ICBM *warheads* as we have missile *silos*. Their count now outnumbers ours slightly (2,555 to 2,154), but larger Soviet missiles with greater MIRV capacities put Moscow in position to pass us quickly, and Soviet craftsmen have the competence to develop deadly accuracies if ruling councils so choose.

The complete package is imposing. Soviet Strategic Rocket Forces are receiving "uniformly first class" ICBMs at a rate of 100–150 a year (not counting SS-16s, whose status is uncertain), have a fifth-generation family of four new models in different R&D stages, and are modifying four more.[70]

Consequences The present and projected balance between U.S. and Soviet ICBMs creates two central consequences. One concerns the prelaunch survival of undefended American missiles, whose power to perform Assured Destruction tasks is by no means permanent. The other concerns comparative counterforce capabilities.[71]

Survival Prospects for U.S. ICBMs Defense Secretary Brown predicts that Soviet SS-17s, SS-18s, and SS-19s could "pose a substantial threat [to our ICBMs] in the 1980s." The Federation of American Scientists has concurred, with the comment that "our fixed land-based missiles in silos will look more and more vulnerable to attack if MIRV and increases in accuracy cannot be prevented."[72]

Corrective courses of action are subject to question.

Installing more U.S. ICBMs would prove impractical, because the Soviets could add hard target warheads much faster than we could build silos and fill them with missiles, at a fraction of the cost.

Prospects for reinforcing U.S. silos face finite limitations (the ultimate compressive strength of cement approximates 3,000 psi, to cite just one criterion). After maximum practical hardness has been achieved, an advanced generation of Soviet warheads with appropriate yields and pinpoint precision could strike each silo in a closely spaced ICBM field with far less fear of "fratricide" than saturation attacks would currently cause.[73]

Launch-on-warning policies might help preserve U.S. ICBMs in specialized circumstances, but limitations are severe. (See section on second-strike constraints).

Even so, undefended U.S. ICBMs in concrete silos could serve deterrent purposes for an extended period, according to some authorities.[74] All, however, seem to agree that the key question is not *whether* the Soviets could eventually crush them with a first strike, only *when* they could achieve that capability.

Substituting some sort of mobile system for all or part of our stationary ICBMs therefore might make military sense. Costs would be considerable but, because mobile missiles are more survivable than those in silos, there would be no need to replace Minutemen on a one-for-one basis.[75]

Freely-mobile models, whether launched from land or air, would present fewer promising counterforce targets. Moscow's immense missiles and high-yield MIRVs would lose much of their practical meaning. Relative combat power *really would* be less relevant if U.S. ICBMs, as well as SLBMs, were generally safe before launch. U.S. force requirements would be less related to Soviet order of battle. The need to verify numbers on each side would be less pressing. Temptations to engage in an endless offensive arms race should be reduced.

Fiscal constraints and critics, however, caused DOD to terminate air-mobile programs at least temporarily after the Air Force successfully test-launched an ALBM from a C-5A aircraft in October 1974.[76] Freely-mobile missiles on land mounts fell prey to environmental and other considerations somewhat earlier.

Two concepts for land-mobile MX missiles remain under serious consideration.[77] One involves a "shell game", in which several shelters would serve each ICBM. Aggressors would have to ascertain which were empty and which concealed lucrative targets. An alternative configuration would move missiles at random within a covered trench, perhaps 12 miles long.[78]

Deterrent properties in each case depend on proliferating, rather than removing, aim points. Rivals, faced with prospects of expending huge numbers of nuclear weapons without assurance of preventing U.S. response, reputedly would find risk-versus-gain ratios poor.

That conclusion, however, is by no means foregone.[79] Should it prove false, the side effects of saturation attacks, especially fallout, could create more U.S. problems than they solve.[80] A fresh look at free-mobility concepts might find a more favorable option.

Comparative Counterforce Capabilities America's second-strike ICBMs are unlikely to match Moscow's counterforce capabilities, whether or not we "go mobile".

SAC, if provided with bigger missiles, more MIRVs, and better accuracy, could conduct surgically-precise operations with tight control over collateral casualties and damage. U.S. hard target kill capabilities would also reduce Soviet incentives to conduct a surprise first strike on Minutemen with part of their ICBMs, since reserves would be less survivable.[81]

Should the Kremlin choose to launch reserves on warning, however, U.S. advantages would be much reduced.[82] SAC could finish rival silos, but not before the missiles in them took flight. Such action actually could invite additional devastation in the United States. Catching a few Soviet reserves in their silos and preventing refirings from cold launch facilities would afford cold comfort in such circumstances.

Ballistic Missile Submarine Systems

All U.S. and Soviet sea-launched ballistic missiles (SLBMs) are carried by submarines, which are the most survivable of all strategic nuclear systems, when on station at sea. "Hair-trigger" action would not be needed to avoid heavy losses from surprise attacks. Decisions to fire against Assured Destruction type targets could be delayed indefinitely without degrading deterrence or countervalue capabilities. (See Figure 10.)

U.S. Trends The total number of U.S. nuclear-powered ballistic missile submarines has stayed constant at 41 since 1967. Each, regardless of class, still carries 16 SLBMs. Missile counts remain at 656, but the mix is decidedly different than it was early in this decade.

All single-warhead Polaris A-2s have phased out. MRVs on the 10 remaining A-3s have larger yields than most U.S. ICBMs, but poorer CEPs. Preponderant power now lies with MIRVed Poseidon missiles,

FIGURE 10 BALLISTIC MISSILE SUBMARINE SYSTEMS, Statistical Trends and System Characteristics

Submarines	*1970*	*1971*	*1972*	*1973*	*1974*	*1975*	*1976*	*1977*	*Net Change 1970–77*
Nuclear Power									
United States									
Poseidon	1	7	12	22	24	28	28	31	+30
Polaris A2	13	10	8	0	0	0	0	0	−13
Polaris A3	27	24	21	19	17	13	13	10	−17
Total	41	41	41	41	41	41	41	41	0
Soviet Union									
D-class	0	0	0	1	5	11	17	26	+26
Y-class	13	20	26	31	33	34	34	34	+21
H-class	7	7	7	7	7	7	7	7	0
Total	20	27	33	39	45	52	58	67	+47
U.S. Standing	+21	+14	+ 8	+ 2	− 4	−11	−17	−26	+47
Diesel power									
United States	0	0	0	0	0	0	0	0	0
Soviet Union									
G-class	20	20	20	20	20	20	19	19	− 1
U.S. Standing	−20	−20	−20	−20	−20	−20	−19	−19	+ 1

FIGURE 10 (Con't)

Submarines	*1970*	*1971*	*1972*	*1973*	*1974*	*1975*	*1976*	*1977*	*Net Change 1970–77*
Total									
United States	41	41	41	41	41	41	41	41	0
Soviet Union	40	47	53	59	65	72	77	86	+46
U.S. Standing	+ 1	− 6	−12	−18	−24	−31	−36	−45	−46

SLBMs	*1970*	*1971*	*1972*	*1973*	*1974*	*1975*	*1976*	*1977*	*Net Change 1970–77*
United States									
Polaris A-2	128	128	128	128	64	32	0	0	−128
Polaris A-3	512	416	336	176	208	176	208	160	−352
Poseidon	16	112	192	352	384	448	448	496	+480
Total	656	656	656	656	656	656	656	656	0
Soviet Union									
SS-N-4	27	27	27	21	21	21	18	12	− 15
SS-N-5	54	54	54	60	60	60	60	60	+ 6
SS-N-6	208	320	416	496	528	528	528	532	+324
SS-N-8	0	0	0	12	60	132	220	274	+274
Total	289	401	497	589	669	741	826	878	+589
U.S. Standing	+367	+255	+159	+ 67	− 13	− 85	−170	−222	−589

Warheads	*1970*	*1971*	*1972*	*1973*	*1974*	*1975*	*1976*	*1977*	*Net Change 1970–77*
United States									
MIRV	160	1120	1920	3520	3840	4480	4480	4960	+4800
Other	640	544	464	304	272	208	208	160	– 480
Total	800	1664	2384	3824	4112	4688	4688	5120	+4320
Soviet Union									
MIRV	0	0	0	0	0	0	0	0	0
Other	289	401	497	589	669	741	826	878	+ 589
Total	289	401	497	589	669	741	826	878	+ 589
U.S. Standing	+511	+1263	+1887	+3235	+3443	+3947	+3862	+4242	+3731

FIGURE 10 (Con't)

Submarine characteristics

Class	*No. March 1978*	*First Deployed*	*Power Plant*	*SLBMS Type*	*No.*	*Torpedo Tubes*	*Speed in Knots (submerged)*
United States							
Benjamin Franklin	12	1965	Nuclear	Poseidon C-3	16	4	30
Lafayette	19	1963	Nuclear	Poseidon C-3	16	4	30
Ethan Allen	5	1961	Nuclear	Polaris A-3	16	4	30
George Washington	5	1959	Nuclear	Polaris A-3	16	4	30
Soviet Union							
Delta-I	17	1972	Nuclear	SS-N-8	12	6	20-30
Delta-II	4	1973	Nuclear	SS-N-8	16	6	25
Delta-III	5	1977	Nuclear	SS-NX-18	16	6	?
Golf-I	4	1961	Diesel	SS-N-4	3	10	17
Golf-II	13	1967	Diesel	SS-N-5	3	10	17
Golf-III[1]	1	1977	Diesel	SS-N-8	6	10	17
Golf-IV[1]	1	1976	Diesel	SS-N-6	4	10	17
Hotel	7	1958	Nuclear	SS-N-5	3	10	22
Yankee-I	33	1967	Nuclear	SS-N-6	16	8	30
Yankee-II[2]	1	1977	Nuclear	SS-NX-17	12	8	30

Missile Characteristics

		Number RVs						
	First Deployed	Single	MRV[5]	MIRV	Warhead Yield	CEP (Nautical) Miles	Range (Miles)	Propellant
United States								
Polaris A-2	1962	1			800 KT	0.5	1750	Solid
Polaris A-3[3]	1964		3		200 KT ea	0.5	2880	Solid
Poseidon	1971			10	40 KT ea	0.3	2880	Solid
Soviet Union[4]								
SS-N-4	1961	1			1 MT	1.5	300	Solid
SS-N-5	1963	1			1–2 MT	1.5	900	Solid
SS-N-6	1968	1			500 KT–1 MT	.7	1500	Liquid
Mod 3	1974		3		500 KT–1 MT ea	.7	1600	Liquid
SS-N-8	1973	1			500 KT–1 MT	0.8	4800	Liquid

[1]Golf-III and IV submarines are essentially Golf-II with new missiles.
[2]Yankee II is essentially Yankee I with a new missile. Delta III is a new submarine.
[3]The last Polaris A-3 submarine being converted to Poseidon left the shipyard on February 22, 1978.
[4]SS-NX-17 and SS-NX-18 SLBMS are deployed aboard submarines but are not yet operational, and do not count against totals in this summary.
[5]The three MRVs on Polaris A-3 and SS-N-6 Mod 3 count as single warheads in this summary.

which may carry as few as 6 or as many as 14 warheads. Most are tipped with 10, for an average of 160 per boat. Accuracy, however, at a third of a mile, is still less than the best ICBMs, and 40 KT yields are only one-fourth as much as Minuteman's MIRVs. Their lethality against hard targets is commensurately less.

U.S. submarine missile systems, therefore, afford an effective Assured Destruction force for use against most surface structures in Soviet cities, but several warheads would be needed to crumple a single silo. Flight times to bomber bases deep in Soviet territory allow enemy aircraft on alert ample opportunity to "scramble".

Switching to many small MIRVs had other side effects. The current Poseidon complement concentrates 4,960 weapons on 31 boats, of which about a third are tempting targets immobilized in port for maintenance at any given time.[83] Each submarine at sea, however, poses deterrent threats of immensely greater magnitude than its 1970 predecessors.

Trident submarines, each carrying 24 long-range missiles with 10 much larger, more accurate warheads,[84] are designed to ensure a strong U.S. sea-based deterrent in the mid-1980s. The number of U.S. SLBMs will nevertheless decline, because Polaris/Poseidon submarines must retire at more rapid rates than Trident can replace them. A low-water mark of 312 tubes (less than half the current complement) will occur in 1986, if phaseouts take place when each boat reaches the end of its normal 20-year service life. Reductions will stop at 512 in 1992 if Poseidon boats can be retained for 25 years.[85] Improved readiness can compensate only partly.

Covert operations on station would be enhanced considerably if the Trident systems were coupled with secure, continuous communications from National Command Authorities to submarines submerged at safe depths. Current Very Low Frequency (VLF) links "are not effective beyond antenna depths of 25 to 30 feet below the ocean surface." Risks of detection and destruction increase when captains receive instructions under those circumstances.[86] Response times could be considerable, because radio contacts, which cannot be constant, are separated by several hours.

Seafarer, the Navy's star-crossed replacement, has collided head-on with influential critics, who score it unacceptable on several counts.[87] Whether that solution or some other would be most satisfactory is yet to be resolved, but requirements remain.

Soviet Trends Antiquated submarines armed with three short-range SLBMs each accounted for much of Moscow's sea-launched missile strength as late as 1970. Half were diesel powered.

Since then, 47 new nuclear subs have hoisted the total to over twice our own. The number of tubes has more than tripled (from 289 to 878).

Only 72 short-range missiles remain. Other types could obliterate U.S. bomber bases (but not alert aircraft) from firing positions on our continental shelf and in the Caribbean, using yields measured in megatons. Short flight times would allow fewer than 10 minutes warning. SS-N-8s, currently deployed, have a 4,800-mile range that American SLBMs will not match until Trident I missiles load aboard Poseidon submarines, beginning in 1979. Immense launch areas, which complicate U.S. search procedures, enhance survivability.[88] A new submarine, the first of a class called Typhoon, is under construction, according to intelligence sources. Few details have been released, but reports compare its size to Trident.[89]

Even so, Soviet submarine systems are inferior to U.S. counterparts in most crucial respects. Diesel-powered types still comprise a substantial share. Late-model nuclear boats, being noisier than Polaris and Poseidon, are more susceptible to compromise. On-station time is only about 10 percent, as opposed to 50 percent for our force[90] (although Soviet surge capabilities are considerable).

Total target coverage currently is a fifth that afforded by our SLBMs (878 to 5,120), since none of their missiles as yet are MIRVed.[91] Long-range SS-N-8s must sacrifice security for counterforce capabilities. Even at best, technical limitations on trajectories prevent sneak attacks from point-blank range.[92] Should they launch from points in the Barents Sea, where most are stationed, flight times to the closest U.S. bomber bases would triple, and threats would be much reduced.

ASW Problems Eternal invulnerability for U.S. ballistic missile submarines is by no means certain, despite some authorities who seek to convey that impression.

Traditional detection methods count on acoustical apparatus that identify distinctive submarine sounds. Alternatively, they try to find anomalies that submerged submarines make in the earth's magnetic field. No major breakthrough based on such conventional technologies will soon "paint the ocean transparent," according to Old Salts, but Soviet scientists and seamen seem to be studying other prospects. Moving submarines, for example, cause thermal disruptions. They also leave biological tracks of dying micro-organisms in their wake, and disturb ultraviolet radiations in sea water. The larger the submarine, the more likely hydrodynamic disturbances can be detected. Radar at "exceptionally high frequencies" can recognize submarine signatures in atmosphere *above* the ocean. Collating and coordinating data via satellite communications could help.[93]

"Even when they go to sea, the Russians still think like artillerymen." Some U.S. analysts consequently accord considerable credibility to Soviet press reports that ballistic missiles ashore and afloat could serve as ASW weapons. Thirty-four Yankee class submarines with short-range SLBMs, for example, may be devoted partly to antisubmarine purposes. SS-18 ICBMs, which have more range than they need to strike targets in the United States, could saturate likely U.S. SLBM launch sites, if detection systems located our submarines within small enough grid squares. Other possibilities, perhaps unforeseen by our side, might fit Soviet plans.[94]

How soon the Soviets can put proper combinations together is uncertain. No evidence at this stage suggests that workable ASW solutions are close, but indications are strong that Soviet efforts are intensive and intense.

Consequences The expanding strength of Soviet submarine-launched missile systems in no way endangers U.S. counterparts, except for those in port, nor does it degrade their deterrent capacities. Matching Moscow's buildup with more submarines, SLBMs, and MIRVs would, therefore, serve little purpose in terms of essential missions.

Reinforcing SLBMs with bigger warheads and better accuracy would improve U.S. hard target kill capabilities from firing positions close to Soviet shores, since flight times would be shorter than those for ICBMs. Each submarine, however, would run serious risks in enemy coastal waters, and chances of catching Soviet missiles in silos would be slight, given our second-strike strategy.

Qualitative changes centered on continued pre-launch survivability, therefore, seem to proffer the best prospects for preserving the deterrent powers of American SLBMs, despite Soviet ASW efforts.

Strategic Bombers

The United States and Soviet Union both based strategic nuclear strength on manned bombers until ballistic missiles were deployed en masse, beginning early in the 1960s. Thereafter, the U.S. accent on air power stayed comparatively strong, while Soviet stress has been slight. (See Figure 11.)[95]

Assured Destruction is the principal capability in each case, because opposing alert forces (aircraft and ICBMs) have adequate time to launch before bombers could arrive. That characteristic, which makes aircraft a poor first-strike system, enhances strategic stability.

U.S. Trends B-52s assigned to Strategic Air Command (SAC) as unit equipment have decreased 30 percent since the start of this decade, from 465 to 316. The oldest airframes have been flying for 20 full years, the newest for 15.[96] They still pack a powerful wallop, but impressive improvements in Soviet air defense cause hot debates over penetration prospects in the 1980s.

Figure 11 STRATEGIC NUCLEAR BOMBERS, Statistical Trends and System Characteristics

Aircraft	*1970*	*1971*	*1972*	*1973*	*1974*	*1975*	*1976*	*1977*	*Net Change 1970–77*
Heavy Bombers									
United States									
B-52	465	435	397	397	372	330	330	316	−149
Soviet Union									
TU-95 Bear	100	100	100	100	100	100	100	100	0
MYA-4 Bison	40	40	40	40	40	40	40	40	0
Total	140	140	140	140	140	140	140	140	0
U.S. Standing	+ 325	+ 295	+ 257	+ 257	+ 232	+ 190	+ 190	+ 176	−149
Modern Medium Bombers									
United States									
FB-111	4	66	66	66	66	66	66	60[1]	+ 56
Soviet Union									
TU-26 Backfire-B	0	0	0	0	0	10	20	30	+ 30
U.S. Standing	+4	+66	+66	+66	+66	+56	+46	+30	+ 26

[1]Six overstrength FB-111s were dropped from SAC units in 1977 to reduce manpower and maintenance overhead to a level matching actual operational capability.

FIGURE 11 (Con't)

Aircraft	*1970*	*1971*	*1972*	*1973*	*1974*	*1975*	*1976*	*1977*	*Net Change 1970–77*
Grand Total									
United States	469	501	463	463	438	396	396	376	– 93
Soviet Union	140	140	140	140	140	150	160	170	+ 30
U.S. Standing	+ 329	+ 361	+ 323	+ 323	+ 298	+ 246	+ 236	+ 206	–123
Nuclear Weapons[2]									
United States	2226	1762	1842	1206	1426	1658	2058	2034	–192
Soviet Union	140	140	140	140	140	160	180	200	+ 60
U.S. Standing	+2086	+1622	+1702	+1066	+1286	+1498	+1878	+1834	–252

[2]Nuclear Weapons include only deliverable bombs and ASMs; reserve weapons are not counted.

Since actual bomber force loads vary according to assigned missions, weapons figures above are best estimates. U.S. values for FY 1970–75 were derived by subtracting ICBM/SLBM warheads from total loads published in Annual DOD Reports; those for FY 1977 use average loadings of 2 bombs and 2 SRAMs per FB-111, and 1.6 bombs and 3.84 SRAMs per B-52, as calculated in A.A. Tinajero, *Projected Strategic Offensive Weapons Inventories (1977)*, pp. 36–38. For FY 1976, both methods were used to yield identical results.

Soviet figures reflect one large bomb or ASM per Bear/Bison, and two ASMs per Backfire. Backfire bombers shown as land-based tactical air systems in Figure 28 are the same as those shown on this table.

Bomber Characteristics

	First Deployed	*Unrefueled Combat Radius (Miles)*	*Bomb Load (Lbs)*	*ASM*	*Max Speed (Mach)*	*Engines Nr*	*Engines Type*
United States							
B-52 G	1959	3,385[1]	60–70,000	SRAM	0.95	8	Jet
FB-111	1969	1,550	13,500	SRAM	2.5	2	Jet
Soviet Union							
TU-95 Bear	1955	3,900	35,000	AS-3	0.78	4	Turbo-prop
MYA-4 Bison	1956	3,000	20,000		0.87	4	Jet
TU-26 Backfire-B[2]	1974	2,500	10,000	AS-4	2.5	2	Jet

Air-To-Surface Missile Characteristics

	First Deployed	*Warhead Yield*	*Range (Miles)*
United States			
SRAM	1972	200 KT	100
Soviet Union[2]			
AS-3 Kangeroo	1961	1 MT	400
AS-4 Kitchen	1967	? KT	300
AS-6 Kingfish	1970	1 MT	200

[1]B-52G combat radius reflects maximum high altitude mission armed with average load of bombs and SRAMs. B-52H radius under those conditions is 4060 nautical miles. FB-111 radius is with SRAMs only. The 1550-mile combat radius would be reduced if the load were 13,500 lbs of nuclear bombs.
[2]Backfire characteristics are based on a hi-lo-hi mission profile, without external weapons.

Multimegaton gravity bombs come in various sizes, one of which offers assorted yields. B-52s carry up to four as their basic load.[97] They could also be fitted for up to 20 nuclear-tipped Short-Range Attack Missiles (SRAMs), although only 1,500 were produced, an average of four per plane. Those weapons are designed primarily to destroy terminally-defended targets, but can also assist aircraft penetration by suppressing enemy SAMs and radar sites.[98]

Sixty smaller, less capable FB-111s supplement U.S. "heavy" bombers. Payloads are roughly half that of B-52s, and ranges are less than one-third, but each can carry six slim bombs, six SRAMS, or some combination (an average of two SRAMs per aircraft is in stock).[99]

SAC tanker squadrons furnish aerial refueling support that assures intercontinental range for B-52s and FB-111s under combat conditions.

Flexible force loadings for U.S. bombers are adjusted to suit changing missions and target assignments, as Figure 11 shows. As currently armed, SAC's air wings account for 20-plus percent of all allocated U.S. weapons and about half of all megatonnage.[100] Fewer aircraft lift larger loads than in the recent past.

Soviet Trends Soviet heavy bomber strength peaked at about 210 turboprop Bears and jet-powered Bisons in 1966, then steadily dropped to 140, the current tally. Something like 80 tankers serve those aircraft, whose penetration prospects would be poor if we possessed sound defenses. Both types probably average just one large gravity bomb as the basic load, although B-Model Bears may carry a single AS-3 Kangaroo missile, which could be released 400 miles from its target.[101]

Supersonic Backfire, the first new Soviet bomber deployed in the past 15 years, is smaller but much more sophisticated. That modern aircraft probably threatens sea lanes and NATO more than North America, but could strike U.S. cities without resorting to tanker support, then recover in Cuba or another "neutral" country. In-flight refueling is technically possible, because all Backfires are fitted with probes. Standoff missiles extend their range by as much as 500 miles.[102]

Medium-range Badgers could attack undefended targets in CONUS on one-way missions or strike Alaska and return. They are considered "tactical" aircraft in this study, however, and are covered as such in sections concerning theater nuclear and land-based naval systems.

Consequences The U.S./Soviet bomber balance affects SAC's force requirements in two significant ways. One, connected with "mirror image" problems, concerns perceptions, and the other concerns our security.

U.S. Requirements Related to Backfire Soviet Backfire bombers may have some bearing on U.S. needs for improved air defense, but are completely unrelated to offensive force requirements.

Backfire squadrons, which currently contribute less to Soviet strategic nuclear capabilities than forward-based fighters add to ours, could double in number or disappear without diluting any advantages that accrue from SAC's aircraft. Manned bombers may indeed be a legitimate leg of the U.S. triad, but maintaining superiority, essential equivalence, or any other military balance with Backfire would serve some cosmetic or symbolic purpose, nothing more.

Bombers Replaced by Cruise Missiles President Carter on June 30, 1977 disclosed his decision to cancel prospective production of B-1 bombers, which were scheduled to strengthen our triad in the 1980s. Simultaneously, he announced plans to substitute air-launched cruise missiles (ALCMs), which could be cut loose from B-52s before they entered Soviet air space.[103] Only a handful of bombers will be modernized to improve penetration probabilities for manned aircraft.[104]

Complete implications of that determination are inconclusive. SALT II issues are still intense.[105] Cruise missile tactics are uncertain. Nevertheless, several conclusions concerning system characteristics are conspicuous.[106] Some suggest strength. Others show weakness.

Pre-launch survival prospects would be best if all ALCMs were mounted on B-52s, which could carry up to eight in the bomb bay, with six more under each wing. Widebodied transports, such as C-5s and converted commercial aircraft, would take longer to taxi and take off (if finally allowed by SALT).

Once aloft, security would improve temporarily, but interceptor aircraft almost certainly would try to destroy U.S. carriers before they launched their missiles. Otherwise, Soviet air defenders would face a spate of separate projectiles, instead of one compact target. Barrage attacks against flight corridors over U.S. soil thus might be conducted, if any breakdown in deterrence led to large-scale nuclear war.

Cruise missiles proceeding under their own power depend on compact radar cross-sections, indistinct infrared "signatures", and terrain-hugging capabilities to assist in breaching defenses. They currently lack active penetration aids and elaborate electronic countermeasures (ECM) packets, are unable to take evasive action, and can not cope with contingencies.

Supersonic speeds would help, but U.S. systems now in development are subsonic. Low, slow approaches, however, encourage accuracies that as yet are unattainable by ballistic missiles. An inertial guidance system, periodically updated enroute, can reduce errors to a few feet. Missiles fitted with warheads of sufficient yield could crush very hard structures, but most time-sensitive and mobile targets would remain immune.

How well cruise missiles could pierce Soviet defenses-in-depth consequently is the main matter in dispute, considering test performance[107] (see Map 1 for selected target locations). The swarms once contemplated could have saturated Soviet systems, but they are no longer planned, and SALT II approval of such strength is problematic.

In the final analysis, therefore, U.S. security will be well served only if satisfactory capabilities can be deployed at acceptable costs in time to support stated strategy. If not, our deterrent could suffer.

Triads Assessed in Tandem

Separate assessments of triad components supply incisive insights, but only a survey of interactions on competing sides can measure complete effectiveness.

Comparative Patterns The basic composition of both triads has stayed constant during this decade. Only sizes and shapes have changed. (See Graphs 6 and 7, together with Figure 12.)[108]

America maintains a balanced structure of ballistic missiles and bombers. The Soviet Union does not. Most of its might will remain with large, land-based missiles, even if Moscow MIRVs SLBMs, because bigger, more numerous ICBMs can carry many more warheads.[109] The importance of manned bombers is minuscule in comparison.

Soviet delivery systems are somewhat more numerous than in 1970, while our count is slightly smaller, but MIRV programs caused U.S. weapon holdings to rise at a rapid rate until they reached a plateau not yet approached by our rival. America's transcendence, however, may be transitory. The Soviets have established a solid expansion base, and growth could be just beginning.

Cogent Implications U.S. bombers and ICBMs are more vulnerable than ever before. That condition erodes stability, even though no current combination of assaults could smother the two systems simultaneously.[110] Soviet counterparts are comparatively secure, because of our second-strike strategy. SLBMs are still safe at sea.

Both sides consequently display awesome Assured Destruction abilities, but neither could neutralize the other by adding offensive power under current conditions. Defensive measures, discussed in the following section, may endanger U.S. survival to a greater degree.

Graph 6

STRATEGIC OFFENSIVE FORCES
Statistical Summary

(Note Different Scales)

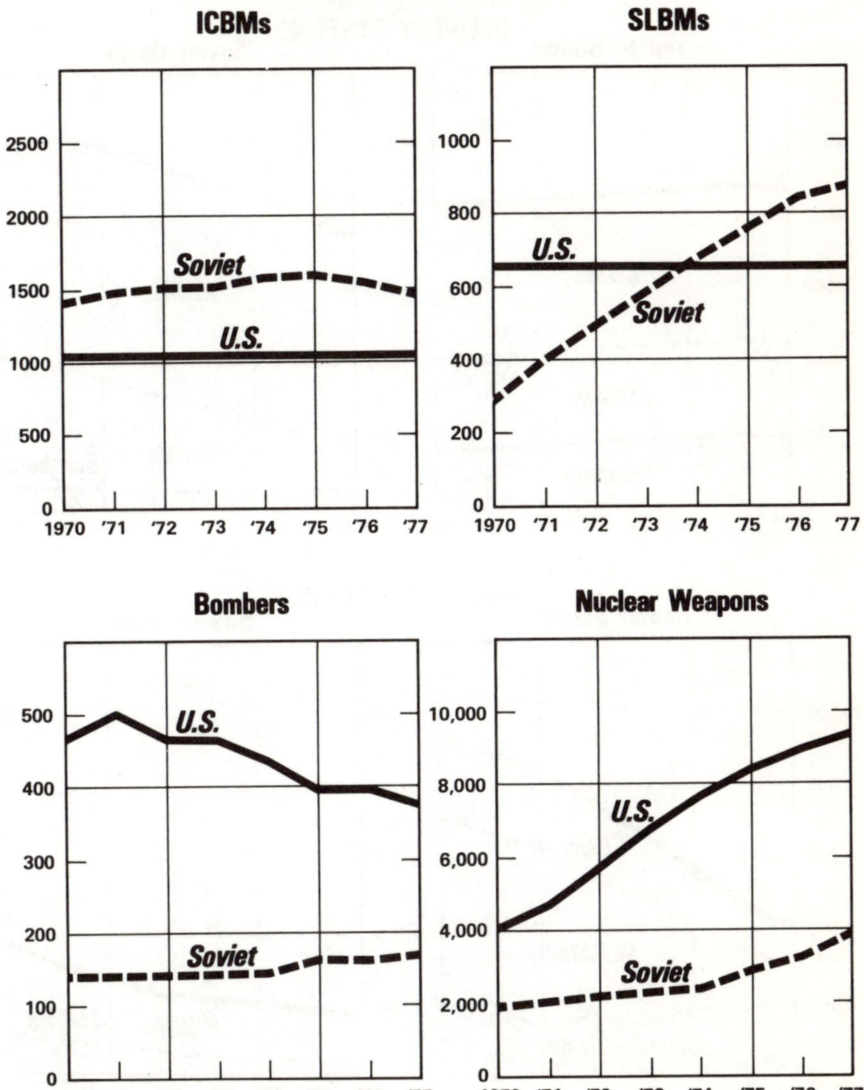

Graph 7

TRIADS COMPARED STATISTICALLY

(Note Different Scales)

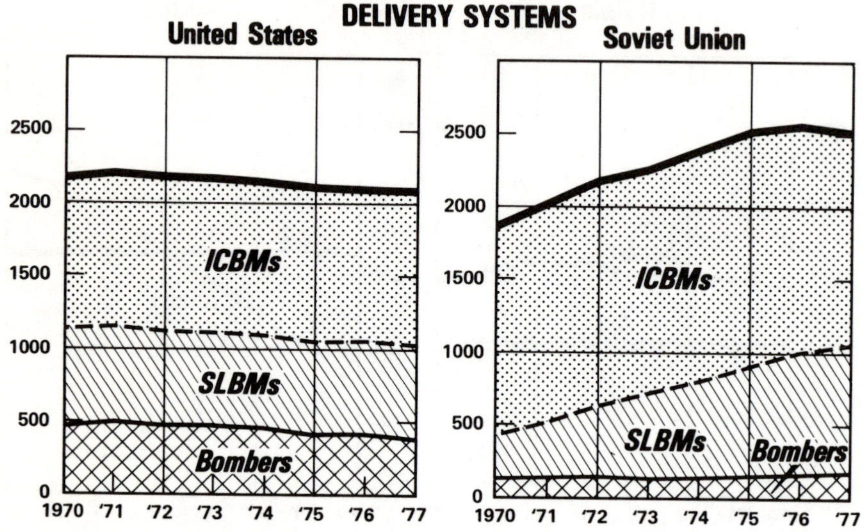

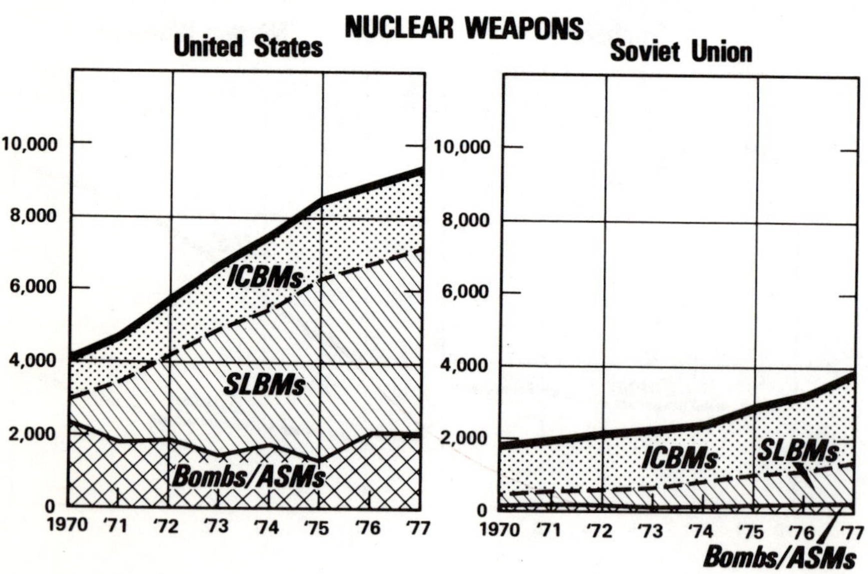

FIGURE 12 STRATEGIC OFFENSIVE FORCES, Statistical Recapitulation

Systems	*1970*	*1971*	*1972*	*1973*	*1974*	*1975*	*1976*	*1977*	*Net Change 1970–77*
United States									
ICBM	1054	1054	1054	1054	1054	1054	1054	1054	0
SLBM	656	656	656	656	656	656	656	656	0
B-52	465	435	397	397	372	330	330	316	−149
FB-111	4	66	66	66	66	66	66	60	+ 56
Total	2179	2211	2173	2173	2148	2106	2106	2086	− 93
Soviet Union									
ICBM	1427	1489	1527	1527	1587	1597	1549	1469	+ 42
SLBM	289	401	497	589	669	741	826	878	+589
Bear/Bison	140	140	140	140	140	140	140	140	0
Backfire-B	0	0	0	0	0	10	20	30	+ 30
Total	1856	2030	2164	2256	2396	2488	2535	2517	+661
U.S. Standing	+ 323	+ 181	+ 9	− 83	− 248	− 382	− 429	− 431	−754

FIGURE 12 (Con't)

Weapons	*1970*	*1971*	*1972*	*1973*	*1974*	*1975*	*1976*	*1977*	*Net Change 1970–77*
United States									
ICBM	1074	1274	1474	1754	2112	2154	2154	2154	+1080
SLBM	700	1664	2384	3824	4112	4688	4688	5120	+4420
Total	1774	2938	3858	5578	6224	6842	6842	7274	+5500
Soviet Union									
ICBM	1427	1489	1527	1527	1587	1928	2109	2555	+1128
SLBM	289	401	497	589	669	741	826	878	+ 589
Total	1716	1890	2024	2116	2256	2669	2935	3433	+1717
U.S. Standing	+ 58	+1036	+1834	+3462	+3968	+4173	+3907	+3841	+3783
Bombs/ASMs									
U.S.	2226	1762	1842	1206	1426	1658	2058	2034	− 192
Soviet	140	140	140	140	140	160	180	200	+ 60
U.S. Standing	+2086	+1622	+1702	+1066	+1286	+1498	+1878	+1834	− 252
Grand Total									
United States	4000	4700	5700	6784	7650	8500	8900	9308	+5308
Soviet Union	1856	2030	2164	2256	2396	2829	3115	3633	+1777
U.S. Standing	+2144	+2670	+3536	+4528	+5254	+5671	+5785	+5675	+3531

Footnotes

1. A compendium of recent official documents, policy statements, and analyses related to nuclear strategy and force posture is available in *Nuclear Strategy and National Security Points of View,* Ed. by Robert J. Pranger and Roger P. Labrie. Washington: American Enterprise Institute for Public Policy Research, 1977. 515 pp.

2. Gray, Colin, "War and Peace—The Soviet View," *Air Force Magazine,* October 1976, p. 28.

3. See, for example, Kohler, Foy D., "The Communist Objective: Domination of the Entire World Society is the Ultimate Goal," *Congressional Record,* November 8, 1971, pp. S17753–S17755.

4. Pipes, Richard, "Why the Soviet Union Thinks It Could Fight and Win a Nuclear War," *Commentary,* July 1977, p. 34. For a rebuttal, see Rosenfeld, Stephen S., "A Hawkish Argument With Holes," *Washington Post,* July 8, 1977, p. A25.

5. U.S. Congress. Subcommittee on Priorities and Economy in Government of the Joint Economics Committee. *Allocation of Resources in the Soviet Union and China–1976.* Hearings Part II, May 24, June 15, 1976. Washington: U.S. Govt. Print. Off., 1976, p. 68.

6. Johnson, David T., "Soviet Fears and Objectives: The Need for Clarification," *Defense Monitor.* Washington: Center for Defense Information, May 1977, pp. 1, 2–3; and "U.S. Strategic Momentum," *Defense Monitor,* May 1974. 8 pp.

7. Some cause/effect relationships connected with U.S. and Soviet strategic nuclear deployment programs since 1962 were discussed by Albert Wohlstetter in *Foreign Policy:* "Is there a Strategic Arms Race?," Summer 1974, pp. 3–20; "Rivals, But No 'Race'," Fall 1974, with comments by Paul H. Nitze, Joseph Alsop, Morton H. Halpern, and Jeremy J. Stone, pp. 48–92. Rebuttals in *Foreign Policy* were published by Johan Jorgen Holst, "What is Really Going On?," Summer 1975, pp. 155–163 and Michael Nacht, "The Delicate Balance of Error," Summer 1975, pp. 163–177. Wohlstetter replied in "Optimal Ways to Confuse Ourselves," Fall 1975, pp. 170–198.

8. A truncated United States would have survived, if the Union had lost the Civil War. Hitler lacked amphibious assault and logistic capabilities to bridge the English Channel, much less the broad Atlantic.

9. Strategic nuclear forces must satisfy five prerequisites before they can become rational instruments of national policy in active rather than passive roles, according to Paul H. Nitze. Four are cited in the text above. The fifth involves the means and mind to insure initiative and preserve predominant power, by preemption if necessary. "Deterring Our Deterrent," *Foreign Policy,* Winter 1976–77, pp. 197–198.

10. "The strategic balance is maintained," according to Paul C. Warnke, Director of the U.S. Arms Control and Disarmament Agency. "This view is, of course, shared by the Secretary of Defense and the other senior government officials with responsibility for national security policy." Statement in response to a request by Congressman David F. Emery, October 19, 1977.

11. Secretary of Defense Robert S. McNamara, speaking in the late 1960s, announced that the U.S.S.R. had "achieved, and most likely will maintain over the foreseeable future, an actual and credible second strike capability . . . ." Certainly, he continued, "nothing short of a massive pre-emptive first strike on the Soviet Union in the 1950s" could have precluded that development. *Statement Before the Senate Armed Services Committee on the FY 1969–73 Defense Program and the 1969 Defense Budget,* January 22, 1968, pp. 46, 47.

12. President Truman in the 1950s elected "to build up U.S. strategic nuclear forces—both as a deterrent to Communist aggression and as a war-winning capability." The succeeding Eisenhower Administration "never wavered" in its intent to win "if

general war were thrust upon us." Twining, Nathan B., *Neither Liberty nor Safety*. New York: Holt, Rinehart, and Winston, 1966, pp. 146–147.

13. McNamara, Robert S., *Statement Before the Senate Armed Services Committee and the Subcommittee on DOD Appropriations on the FY 1965–1969 Defense Program and the 1965 Defense Budget*, January 27, 1964, p. 31.

14. The United States has never subscribed to a nuclear first strike as the opening move of any war, but has always reserved rights to use nuclear weapons first in response to aggression. For background discussion and citations, see U.S. Congress. House. *Hearings Before the Subcommittee on International Security and Scientific Affairs of the Committee on International Relations concerning First Use of Nuclear Weapons: Preserving Responsibile Control.* Washington: U.S. Govt. Print. Off., 1976, 246 pp.

15. McNamara, Robert S., *Statement Before the House Armed Services Committee on the FY 1966–1970 Defense Program and 1966 Defense Budget*, February 18, 1965, p. 38.

16. Schlesinger, James R., *Annual Defense Department Report on the FY 1975 Defense Budget and FY 1975–1979 Defense Program*, March 4, 1974, p. 38.

17. Strategic nuclear objectives to afford added flexibility date from early days of the Nixon Administration. As the President put it, "If war occurs—and there is no way we can absolutely guarantee that it will not—we should have means of preventing escalation while convincing an opponent of the futility of continued aggression." Nixon, Richard M., *Foreign Policy for the 1970's: Shaping a Durable Peace*. Washington: U.S. Govt. Print. Off., 1973, p. 184.

18. McNamara, Robert S., *The Essence of Security*. New York: Harper and Row, 1968, p. 63; and McNamara, Robert S., *Statement on the FY 1969 Defense Budget*, p. 63.

19. Rumsfeld, Donald H., *Annual Defense Department Report on the FY 1977 Budget and its Implications for the FY 1978 Authorization Request and the FY 1977–1981 Defense Programs*, January 27, 1976, p. 88; Weinraub, Bernard, "[Defense Secretary] Brown Says Stronger Air Defense is Needed to Face Soviet Bomber," *New York Times*, April 7, 1978, p. 3.

20. Rumsfeld, Donald H., *Annual Defense Department Report on the FY 1978 Budget, FY 1979 Authorization Request, and FY 1978–1982 Defense Programs*, January 17, 1977, p. 77. Additional details on current U.S. objectives are contained in Brown, Harold, *Department of Defense Annual Report, Fiscal Year 1979*, February 2, 1978, p. 45.

21. Sections on U.S. nuclear strategy were first published in similar form as Collins, John M., *Defense Trends in the United States, 1952–1973*. Washington: Congressional Research Service, May 14, 1974, pp. 27–34. That material also appeared, slightly modified, in *Orbis*, Fall 1974, pp. 750–753.

22. Counterforce characteristics are summarized in Collins, John M., *Counterforce and Countervalue Options Compared.* Washington: Congressional Research Service, December 7, 1972, 45 pp.

23. Defense Secretary McNamara reviewed strategic nuclear decisions that accompanied the switch to Assured Destruction in his *Statement on the FY 1969 Defense Budget*, pp. 41–76. His discourse covers calendar years 1961–1968.

24. The U.S. R&D community long ago had the technical competence to create missile warheads with accuracy/yield combinations that could crush Soviet ICBMs encased in concrete silos. Their practical value, however, is still strictly limited in context with our second-strike strategy.

25. McNamara, Robert S., *Statement on the FY 1965 Defense Budget*, pp. 31–32.

26. McNamara, Robert S., *Statement on the FY 1969 Defense Budget*, p. 50.

27. McNamara, Robert S., *Statement Before the House Armed Services Committee on the FY 1968–1972 Defense Program and 1968 Defense Budget*, January 23, 1967, pp. 38–39.

28. The U.S. Arms Control and Disarmament Agency (ACDA) was established in 1961. Five U.S. arms control initiatives were concluded during the Age of Assured

Destruction, in attempts to strengthen stability: the Washington-to-Moscow "Hot Line" (1963); the Limited Test Ban Treaty (1963); a treaty excluding mass destruction weapons from outer space (1967); a treaty prohibiting nuclear weapons in Latin America (1967); and a non-proliferation treaty (1968). *Arms Control and Disarmament Agreements, 1959–1972.* Washington: ACDA, 1972, pp. 10–76.

29. Nixon, Richard M., *U.S. Foreign Policy for the 1970's: A New Strategy for Peace.* Washington: U.S. Govt. Print. Off., 1970, p. 122.

30. Details are described in Schlesinger, James R., *Annual Defense Department Report on the FY 1975 Defense Budget,* pp. 3–6, 25–80. See also Davis, Lynn Etheridge, *Limited Nuclear Options: Deterrence and the New American Doctrine,* Adelphi Papers No. 121. London: International Institute for Strategic Studies, 1976, 22 pp.

31. Defense Secretary Brown, for one, believes that "any use of nuclear weapons would run the risk of rapid escalation." Consequently, he is luke warm toward limited nuclear options. *Statement to the Congress on the Amendments to the FY 1978 Budget and FY 1979 Authorization Request,* February 22, 1977, p. 6.

32. One U.S. school of thought believes that a "balance of terror" based on mutual vulnerability best preserves deterrence by making victory impossible. Populations are perpetual hostages, according to their strategy. Prospects of prodigious casualties if war should occur are an imperative part of the concept. Any move to mitigate the threat of mutual suicide by shielding population and production base thus would dilute deterrence by making war seem acceptable. U.S. Congress. Senate. *United States and Soviet City Defense: Considerations for Congress.* Prepared by the Congressional Research Service. 94th Congress, 2d Session. Washington: U.S. Govt. Print. Off., 1976, pp. 5–8.

33. Article III of that treaty limits each side to two sites with "no more than one hundred ABM launchers and no more than one hundred ABM interceptor missiles" apiece. A Protocol in 1974 reduced the authorization to a single such site in each country. U.S. decision-makers dispensed with that prerogative, but the two sides are still essentially equivalent. The Soviets have deployed only 64 missiles that could be smothered by a U.S. attack. We have none.

34. Some proponents of strategic defense concede that *mutual* vulnerability might assist in strengthening deterrence. *Unilateral* vulnerability most surely would not. They believe that sound protective measures would best preserve peace over the long term, because no strategic deadlock in history has endured. For details, see section on Strategic Defensive Comparisons, Connections Between Deterrence and Defense.

35. U.S. Congress. *United States and Soviet City Defense,* pp. 13–17.

36. Section 3 of the Joint Resolution on Interim Agreement "recognizes the principle of United States-Soviet Union equality reflected in the antiballistic missile treaty . . . ." *Ibid.,* pp. 858–859.

37. The proper relation of SALT to U.S. nuclear strategy is increasingly in question. See for example Burt, Richard, "Arms Control and Soviet Strategic Forces: The Risks of Asking SALT to Do Too Much," *The Washington Review of Strategic and International Studies,* January 1978, pp. 19–33.

38. Current U.S. philosophy is found in Brown, Harold, *Department of Defense Annual Report, FY 1979,* pp. 42–66.

39. The Principles of War comprise many lists. The British subscribe to 10; Moscow to half that many. Flexibility is missing from American versions. For general background discussion, see Willoughby, Charles A., *Maneuver in War,* Harrisburg, Pa.: Military Services Publishing Co., 1939, pp. 25–44.

40. For associated issues, see Collins, John M. and Mitchell, Douglas D., *Strategic Force Options Related to SALT II.* Issue Brief 77046. Washington: Congressional Research Service, May 1, 1977, 23 pp. Updated periodically.

41. Atlas ICBMs retired in 1964. The Minuteman program was compressed from 1,200 to 1,000 that same year. Plans for 45 Polaris submarines with 720 missiles were cut to 41 boats with a total of 656. B-52 strengths today are half what they were 10 years ago.

42. "There is an absolute point below which our security forces must never be allowed to go. That is the level of sufficiency. Above or at that level, our defense forces protect national security adequately. Below that level is one vast undifferentiated area of no security at all. For it serves no purpose in conflicts between nations to have been almost strong enough." Nixon, Richard M., *U.S. Foreign Policy for the 1970s: Building for Peace,* p. 167.

43. Defense Secretary Melvin R. Laird identified four criteria for strategic nuclear sufficiency:

—Maintaining an adequate second-strike capability to deter an all-out surprise attack on U.S. forces.

—Providing no incentive for the Soviet Union to strike the United States first in a crisis.

—Preventing the Soviet Union from gaining abilities to cause considerably greater urban/industrial destruction than we could inflict on the Soviets in a nuclear war.

—Defending against damage from small attacks or accidental launches.

—Statement Before the House Armed Services Committee on the FY 1972–1976 Defense Program and the 1972 Defense Budget, March 7, 1971, p. 62.

44. Nixon, Richard M., U.S. *Foreign Policy for the 1970s: Building for Peace,* p. 70.

45. Schlesinger, James R., *Annual Defense Department Report on the FY 1975 Defense Budget,* p. 43.

46. U.S. National Command Authorities are limited to the President, the Secretary of Defense, and their duly deputized alternates or successors.

47. U.S. launch under attack policies appear to be under advisement. As Defense Secretary Brown puts it, "the question is, would you launch land-based missiles before explosion of nuclear weapons on the United States?" He indicates "that it is not our doctrine to do so—neither is it our doctrine that under no circumstances would we ever do so." "Sec. Brown: 'Launch on Warning or Launch Under Attack'?", *Defense/Space Daily,* November 11, 1977, p. 68. For connected issues, see Bell, Robert G., *Launch on Warning: Pros and Cons.* Washington: Congressional Research Service, July 7, 1976, 9 pp.

48. U.S. Congress. Subcommittee on Priorities and Economy in Government of the Joint Economics Committee. *Allocation of Resources in the Soviet Union and China–1977.* Hearings. Part 2, June 30, 1977. Washington: U.S. Govt. Print. Off., 1977, p. 77.

49. Brown, George S., *United States Military Posture for FY 1978.* Washington: The Joint Chiefs of Staff, January 20, 1977, p. 14.

50. Civil defense measures that put critical installations underground or otherwise provide blast protection for population and/or production base can "harden" selected sections of cities. Few facilities, however, are likely to become as resistant to nuclear assault as missile silos.

51. A 1969 DOD proposal to improve Poseidon's guidance system was withdrawn spontaneously "in view of the serious fiscal situation." The 1970 request for Advanced Ballistic Reentry System (ABRES) was cut to forestall efforts "in support of any future hard-target kill capability." Three amendments to the military procurement authorization bill, all counterforce connected, were defeated in 1971. DOD asked for a $20 million add-on in 1972 to improve missile accuracy, but lost out in conference. Discussion and citations are contained in Appendix 2 to Collins, John M., *Counterforce and Countervalue Options Compared,* pp. 32–45.

52. Mark 12A deployment reportedly will occur in two stages. Modifications to Minuteman III's guidance system started in October 1977. New warheads are scheduled to be installed in 1979. Leubsdorf, Carl P., "Carter Approves More Accurate Missile," *Baltimore Sun,* June 2, 1977, p. 4.

53. Defense Secretary Brown, speaking on American Broadcasting Company's Issues and Answers TV interview program, November 6, 1977, disclosed that Soviet ICBMs will threaten Minuteman's survival in the early 1980s, whether or not current SALT II negotiations are concluded successfully.

54. The Soviet Union, a continental colossus that sprawls over half of Europe and 40 percent of Asia, spans 7,000 miles from the Baltic Sea to Bering Strait, a distance comparable to the straight-line course between Baltimore and Rangoon, Burma. The Soviet's southern border with Afghanistan and bleak Taymyr Peninsula, on the frozen arctic shore, are separated by the same longitudinal spread as Chattanooga, Tennessee and Thule, Greenland (about 3,000 miles).

55. Core areas, sometimes called strategic areas, commonly include military, as well as civilian, components. This study, however, segregates counterforce targets in a separate section.

56. The term "vital", by definition, deals with the difference between life and death. Neither Leningrad nor Vladivostok is necessary for continued survival of the Soviet state.

57. The Soviet SALT II team originally insisted that air- and sea-launched cruise missiles (ALCMs, SLCMs) with ranges in excess of 600 km (320 nm) should count against the ceiling on systems allowed each side. Weapons of that sort would be worthless against targets in most Soviet strategic areas, unless mounted on manned bombers with credible penetration capabilities. Missiles with a 1,500 nm range now are being bandied about, but even if allowed would barely be able to reach Moscow from practical launch points, much less breach defenses in depth over that distance (Map 1). As a result, cruise missiles might afford America short-term tactical advantages, because we are ahead technologically, but geographic circumstances could cause them to become strategic liabilities over the long run, if Soviet leaders start to deploy modern models. A total ban might work better for the United States, provided proscriptions could be policed. As it stands, two types of Soviet SLCMs (SS-N-3s and SS-N-12s), whose estimated effective ranges are 150–250 nm, could hit half the U.S. population, plus many industrial and military targets, if used for preemptive purposes from positions outside the 100-fathom curve.

58. Assured Destruction prospects depend on highly reliable abilities to inflict unacceptable damage on any aggressor or combination of aggressors during the course of a nuclear exchange, even after absorbing a surprise first strike. Cities contain essential targets, including people and production facilities.

59. Official summaries showed 162 U.S. cities with populations of at least 100,000 in 1975. Clusters of a million or more (many more, in some cases) included:

Anaheim-Santa Ana
Atlanta
Baltimore
Boston
Buffalo
Chicago
Cincinnati
Cleveland
Columbus
Dallas-Fort Worth
Des Moines
Detroit
Houston
Indianapolis
Kansas City
Los Angeles area
Miami
Milwaukee
Minneapolis-St. Paul
Nassau-Suffolk
New Orleans
New York area
Newark
Philadelphia
Phoenix
Pittsburgh
Portland
Riverside/San Bernardino
St. Louis
San Diego
San Francisco area
San Jose
Seattle area
Tampa-St. Petersburg
Washington area

60. Open sources showed 254 Soviet cities with populations of at least 100,000 in 1975, about a third more than the United States. Just 13 of those exceeded a million:

Baku
Gorki
Kharkov
Kiev
Kuibyshev
Leningrad
Minsk
Moscow
Novosibirsk
Odessa
Sverdlovsk
Tashkent
Tbilisi

61. Post Nuclear Attack Study (PONAST) II briefing prepared by the Studies Analysis and Gaming Agency, Joint Chiefs of Staff, May 23, 1973. No census has been taken since.

62. U.S. Polaris/Poseidon submarine bases currently are located at Charleston, South Carolina; Holy Loch, Scotland; Rota, Spain; and Guam. A fifth installation, to serve Trident, is under construction at Bangor, Washington. Kings Bay, Georgia is scheduled to replace Rota in the early 1980s.

63. Statistics in this section cover the period 1970–1977. Future trends are addressed in Tinajero, A. A., *Projected Strategic Offensive Weapons Inventories of the U.S. and U.S.S.R.: An Unclassified Estimate.* Washington: Congressional Research Service, March 24, 1977, 180 pp. See also U.S. Congress. House. *Hearings on H.R. 8390 Supplemental Authorization for Appropriations for FY 1978 and Review of the State of U.S. Strategic Forces.* Committee on Armed Services. 95th Congress, 1st Session. Washington: U.S. Govt. Print. Off., 1977, 471 pp.

64. The Soviets are introducing two-stage SS-20 mobile MRBMs into their active inventory. That system, which could strike targets in China and NATO Europe, converts to SS-16s with intercontinental range by adding a third stage. A few SS-16s have been encased in silos. Whether all mobile versions have gone into storage is debatable, since detection is difficult. "Soviets deploy SS-16 ICBM," *Aviation Week and Space Technology,* February 27, 1978, p. 15; Weinraub, Bernard, "Pentagon Aides Say Moscow Has Mobile Missiles Able to Reach U.S.," *New York Times,* November 3, 1977, p. 3.

65. Multiple reentry vehicles (MRVs) on any ballistic missile are similar to the pellets in a shotgun shell. They saturate a single target. Multiple independently targetable reentry vehicles (MIRVs) also are carried by a single missile, but engage several separate targets.

66. Yields expressed in kilotons or megatons and accuracies expressed in circular errors probable (CEPs) are subject to considerable speculation. Unclassified documents universally agree on estimates for some U.S. and Soviet systems, but disagree on others. Those used in this study have been carefully checked by officials in U.S. military services and DIA.

67. Warhead lethality, derived from accuracy and yield, is expressed as K. More than 30 K reputedly is required to destroy a silo hardened to resist overpressures of 330 pounds per square inch (psi). About 50 K could crack one hardened to 500 psi. A 1,000 psi silo could survive a shock of almost 80 K. Titan II's largest warhead is rated at less than 20 K. Each MIRV on Minuteman III exerts about 8 K. Several such weapons would be needed to neutralize the weakest Soviet silo.

68. A unilateral U.S. statement associated with the 1972 SALT I interim agreement on the limitation of selected strategic offensive systems identified "heavy" ICBMs as those having "a volume significantly greater than that of the largest light ICBM", which then was the SS-11. Since no different definition has been formally adopted, this study considers SS-19s to be "heavies". They exceed SS-11s by about 60 percent in volume and 350 percent in payload capacity, which enables them to handle half a dozen MIRVs rated at roughly 500 KT to 1 MT each.

69. Lethality (K) is directly proportional to yield 2/3 and inversely proportional to CEP^2. Thus, increasing any weapon yield by a factor of eight produces just four times more lethal power. Reducing the same weapon's CEP by a factor of eight multiplies K 64 times. Improving accuracy *and* yield by factors of eight increases K 256 times.

Six recent tests from Tyuratom on the Aral Sea to Kamchatka consistently scored CEPs of 0.1 nm or better for SS-18s and SS-19s, according to Robinson, Clarence, "Soviets Boost ICBM Accuracy," *Aviation Week and Space Technology,* April 3, 1978, pp. 14–16.

70. Wilson, George C., "Brown Cites Discovery of New Soviet ICBMs," *Washington Post,* September 16, 1977, p. A–12.

71. A survey of the situation is contained in Gray, Colin, *The Future of Land-Based Missile Forces,* Adelphi Papers No. 140. London: International Institute for Strategic Studies, 1978, 36 pp.

72. Brown, Harold, News Conference, The Pentagon, October 4, 1977. Cited in *Selected Statements.* Washington: Department of the Air Force, November 1, 1977, p. 40; *Solution to Counterforce: Land-Based Missile Disarmament,* Public Interest Report, Federation of American Scientists, February 1974, p. 1.

73. The simultaneous explosion of two or more nuclear weapons over any target is almost impossible to plan. "Fratricide" occurs when blast, heat, or radiation from the first detonation destroys or deflects other warheads in the salvo. If successive shots delay until adverse conditions dissipate, slightly damaged silos can launch missiles through the resultant "window." McGinchley, Joseph J. and Seelig, Jakob W., "Why ICBMs Can Survive a Nuclear Attack," *Air Force Magazine,* September 1974, pp. 82–85.

74. Uncertainties surely assist this country's deterrent. "Any reasonably cautious Soviet planner or policy-maker contemplating a nuclear strike on the Minuteman force (which—if it failed—could result in the destruction of the power base of the Communist Party of the Soviet Union) would entertain the following sorts of doubts . . . . Would the Soviet missiles work with the reliability estimated from limited peacetime tests? Would there be previously undetected bias errors which degrade accuracy? Would the U.S. silos be 'harder' than anticipated? Would the surviving U.S. ICBMs in silos still possess sufficient destructive power to pose a significant threat to the Soviets because of their multiple warheads?" From letters to the author written by Major General Richard L. Lawson on August 17 and 21, 1976, when he was Air Force Chief of Plans.

75. The Air Force has reviewed many basing modes for mobile ICBMs, which could be mounted on railway flat cars, trucks, tracked vehicles, river barges, ground effects machines, and aircraft. Each is more survivable than fixed-site systems, despite distinctive shortcomings, but all lost out to silos in the early 1960s, essentially because of costs. As Secretary McNamara put it, "a mobile squadron of 30 missiles" on rails would have had the same price tag "as a fixed-base squadron of 50 missiles." U.S. Congress. House. *Defense Appropriations for 1962,* Part 3. Secretary of Defense, Joint Chiefs of Staff, Service Secretaries, and Chiefs of Staff. 87th Congress, 2d Session. Washington: U.S. Govt. Print. Off., 1961, p. 9.

76. "Drop of Minuteman By C-5A Tests Air-Mobile Concept," *Aviation Week and Space Technology,* November 11, 1974, pp. 20–21.

77. Pro/con arguments, with special concern for cost, are contained in Tinajero, A. A., *M-X Intercontinental Ballistic Missile Program.* Issue Brief 77080. Washington: Congressional Research Service, June 29, 1977 (periodically updated). 20 pp.; See also Ball, Desmond J. and Coleman, Edwin, "The Land-Mobile ICBM System: A Proposal," *Survival,* July/August 1977, pp. 155–163.

78. *MX Vehicles Design and Critical Tests, Phase I Summary Report, D295-10009-6.* Seattle: Boeing Aerospace Company, June 1977. 68 pp. Covers shelter-based and buried trench concepts, equipment, estimated costs, and associated subjects. See also *Status of the Air Force's Missile X Program.* Washington: General Accounting Office, March 31, 1978, 14 pp.

79. A special scientific task force, for example, reportedly recommends that the President delay full-scale deployment of MX on grounds that such a decision would be premature, despite Minuteman's decreasing survival prospects. Evans, Rowland and Novak, Robert, "The 'Fixed Theology' of Carter's Arms Advisors," *Washington Post,* December 9, 1977, p. A–19. See also Burt, Richard, "M.I.T. Team is Critical of Proposal to Base Mobile Missiles in Tunnels," *New York Times,* March 25, 1978, p. 8.

80. Selected arms control implications of MX are contained in U.S. Congress. Senate Committee on Foreign Relations and House Committee on International Relations.

Analysis of Arms Control Impact Statements Submitted in Connection With the FY 1978 Budget Request. Joint Committee Print. 95th Congress, 1st Session. Washington: U.S. Govt. Print. Off., 1977, pp. 40–45.

81. One prevalent scenario postulates a surprise first strike, in which part of the Soviet ICBMs cripple ours completely during an intense crisis that threatens Soviet crucial interests. Such a ploy would pay off hugely in terms of political and psychological power, if U.S. leaders accepted the loss without "appropriate" response. The Kremlin could dictate terms concluding that particular showdown, and might be tempted to precipitate others. Few "appropriate" U.S. responses would be available. Soviet counterforce capabilities in reserve would greatly exceed those carried by U.S. bombers and SLBMs. If we chose to strike their cities, they could strike ours in return. Still, that scenario has serious shortcomings, since it would work well only if the Soviets were sure our President would capitulate, which could never be confirmed. A first strike on American ICBMs consequently would incur enormous known risks in return for uncertain gains, unless (as some claim) the Soviets could absorb a U.S. second strike successfully.

82. A Soviet decision to launch reserve ICBMs on warning during a full-scale exchange would depend to a large extent on what type targets remained undamaged in the United States. Russian cities could be ruined in return if the Kremlin struck U.S. centers indiscriminately. Allowing reserve missiles to be destroyed by our second strike might, therefore, be the best option in some cases.

83. In the past, U.S. ballistic missile submarines averaged 60 days on patrol and 30 days in port. Transit times to launch stations and return still take 2–10 days, depending on base locations. Improved boats, better maintenance procedures, and longer range missiles will enable each Polaris/Poseidon boat to stay on station for longer periods, but a sizable percentage must always be in port for repair and crew rest. The same will be true for Trident.

84. Trident I missiles, like Poseidon, can carry 6 to 14 warheads. The average will be about 10. The reported range is 4,000 miles. Trident II missiles, with much greater payload capacity, will be able to deliver more and/or larger MIRVs (average 17) with improved precision on targets 6,000 miles distant. For technical characteristics of Trident submarines and missiles, together with a summary discussion of development difficulties, basing, and costs, see Tinajero, A. A., *Trident Program.* Issue Brief 73001. Washington: Congressional Research Service, 1977 (periodically updated), 13 pp.

85. Vice Admiral C. H. Griffith, Deputy Chief of Naval Operations (Submarine Warfare), quoted by George C. Wilson, "The Coming Sub Missile Gap," *Washington Post,* March 19, 1978, p. C–1.

86. *Seafarer ELF Communications Systems Final Environmental Impact Statement for Site Selection and Test Operation.* Washington: Department of the Navy, December 1977, (6 Vol.). See Summary Statement, p. 1.

87. Critics of Seafarer, which exploits extremely low frequencies, levy at least four charges, all of which are contentious: it is ineffective; it is environmentally inexcusable; it is extravagantly expensive; it is not the best elective. Issues and alternatives are addressed in Gannon, Edmund, *Seafarer,* Issue Brief 78015. Washington: Congressional Research Service, March 2, 1978 (updated periodically). 17 pp.

88. DIA declares that 80 SS-NX-18 and 12 SS-NX-17 SLBMs have been deployed with Soviet fleets. When officially designated operational systems, they will raise total Soviet SLBM holdings to 970. Telephonic conversations in February 1978.

89. Burt, Richard, "Soviet is Reported Building a New Missile Submarine," *New York Times,* October 29, 1977, p. 3.

90. *Ibid.,* p. 14.

91. Eighty SS-NX-18 SLBMs carry three MIRVs each for a total of 240 warheads. Twelve SS-NX-17s carry single warheads. When those systems are officially designated operational, Soviet SLBM warheads will jump from 878 to 1130.

92. The minimum range of ballistic missiles, with either minimum energy or depressed trajectory, is about one-third the maximum range. DIA comments on a draft of this study, September 9, 1977.

93. Bradsher, Henry S., "Vulnerability Growing for U.S. Sub-Based Missiles?," *Washington Star,* December 12, 1977, p. 1.

94. *Ibid.*

95. Statistics in this section refer only to unit equipment (UE) aircraft. Those in storage, being cannibalized, or used for training purposes do not count. Significant numbers of U.S. land- and carrier-based tactical aircraft, for which the Soviets have no counterparts, are excluded, although they act as strategic nuclear auxilliaries.

96. About 75 B-52Ds, delivered to SAC in 1957, still were assigned in March 1978, according to Air Force staff officers. The last B-52H models entered service in 1962.

97. Covault, Craig, "B-52 Training Stresses Timing, Realism," *Aviation Week and Space Technology,* May 10, 1976, p. 127.

98. *Annual Air Force Almanac Issue, Air Force Magazine,* May 1976, p. 123.

99. *Ibid.,* p. 112.

100. Air Force comments on a draft of this study, September 10, 1977.

101. "Second Annual Soviet Aerospace Almanac," *Air Force Magazine,* March 1976, pp. 94–95, 105.

102. *Ibid.,* pp. 95–96, 105. Backfire's capabilities and limitations still cause controversies that will not likely be soon resolved. See Book II, Part I (Qualitative Problems) for a sample. There are indications that tanker support may be forthcoming. Cordray, Charles W., "Soviet Believed to be Developing Tanker To Refuel Backfire," *Baltimore Sun,* February 7, 1978, p. 1.

103. Defense Secretary Brown reviews rationale in "The B-1 Cruise Missile Decision," *Commanders Digest,* September 15, 1977, 12 pp.

104. Some combination of SAC's B-52G and H models reportedly will carry cruise missiles. The Air Force plans to modify the 75 B-52Ds for penetration purposes, an expensive proposition. (One wag says, "the required upgrade is roughly equivalent to jacking up the tail number and putting a new airplane under the number.") "Perry Gives Cruise Missiles Edge Over B-1 in Penetration," *Aerospace Daily,* July 28, 1977, p. 144; "Air Force Officer Disagrees With Perry's B-1/Cruise Missile Views," *Aerospace Daily,* August 10, 1977, p. 222.

105. Collins, John M. and Mitchell, Douglas D., *SALT II Problems and Prospects.* Issue Brief 77030. Washington: Congressional Research Service, 1977 (periodically updated), p. 6. Other arms control implications are contained in U.S. Congress. *Analysis of Arms Control Impact Statements Submitted in Connection With the FY 1978 Budget Request,* pp. 80–89.

106. For technical characteristics of air-, sea-, and land-launched cruise missiles, see Tinajero, A. A., *Cruise Missiles (Subsonic): U.S. Programs.* Issue Brief 76018. Washington: Congressional Research Service, 1977 (updated periodically), 23 pp.

107. Some critics cite computer studies that conclude U.S. Hawk air defense missiles would defeat ALCMs under development. DOD officials contend that simultations and live tests are successful if they assist corrective actions. Evans, Rowland, and Novak, Robert, "The Vulnerability of the Cruise Missile," *Washington Post,* October 29, 1977, p. A-15; Weinraub, Bernard, "Pentagon Aides Call Cruise Missile Able to Penetrate Soviet," *New York Times,* November 2, 1977, p. 6; "Cruise Missile to be Tested Against F-14, Hawk," *Aerospace Daily,* November 4, 1977, p. 28.

108. The U.S. triad is under serious study. Weinraub, Bernard, "Pentagon Reviewing Strategic Posture," *New York Times,* December 1, 1977, p. 21.

109. ICBMs presently carry 70 percent of all Soviet warheads. That share could increase to 90 percent or more if SS-19 deployments are large and SS-18s mount maximum MIRVs. By way of contrast, U.S. ICBMs carry fewer than a fourth of our strategic nuclear weapons.

110. Soviet SLBMs, with flight times of 6 to 10 minutes if fired close to U.S. coasts, might catch some of SAC's aircraft on strip alert, but still lack sufficient accuracy/yield combinations to crush concrete silos. Soviet ICBMs, which take about 30 minutes to reach targets, pose greater threats to American land-based missiles, but would allow authorities ample time to launch bombers. Scheduling problems of that sort are close to insoluble.

Strategic Defensive Comparisons

CONUS defense plays almost no part in U.S. nuclear strategy.[1] Deterrence depends almost entirely on powers to survive preemptive strikes, then savage the aggressor.[2]

Soviet policy is of a different persuasion. Consistent efforts to develop credible safeguards for Mother Russia are everywhere evident.

Components of Strategic Defense

Homeland defense depends on specialized tools that suit active and passive defense purposes. (See Figure 13.)

Early Warning

The first prerequisite for successful defense is a reliable early warning apparatus that can identify attacks, impending or in progress, and alert authorities rapidly. Surveillance and tracking capabilities must cope with the full range of threats from aircraft and missiles, some of which can approach targets from any point on the compass or from platforms suspended in space.

Strategic Warning Strategic warning, which indicates that enemy offensive operations may be imminent, could alert authorities days (perhaps weeks) before aggression commenced. Clues derive from disparate sources, such as political analysts, photographs, sensors, and secret agents.

Limitations, however, are sweeping and severe. Most strategic nuclear preparations, which take place in subterranean silos and submarines at sea, are well concealed. Uncertainties call for caution, be-

FIGURE 13 ACTIVE AND PASSIVE DEFENSES,
Types and Characteristics

	Timing		*Type defense*		*Type protection*	
	Before enemy launch	*After enemy launch*	*Terminal*	*Distant*	*People*	*Property*
Early warning:						
Strategic	X				X	X
Tactical		X			X	X
Active defense:						
Strike forces:						
Bombers[1]	X			X	X	X
ICBMs	X			X	X	X
SLBMs[2]	X			X	X	X
Submarines	X			X	X	X
ABM		X	X	X	X	X
Air Defenses:						
Interceptors[3]		X		X	X	X
SAMs		X	X		X	X
Passive defense:						
Blast shelters[4]		X	X		X	
Fallout shelters[5]		X	X		X	
City evacuation	X			X	X	
Industrial:						
Dispersal	X		X			X
Hardening[6]	X		X			X

[1]The slow flight time of bombers affords them little ability to destroy time-sensitive targets, such as missiles in silos.
[2]Small warheads and short flight times make SLBMs best suited to strike bombers and their bases.
[3]Interceptor aircraft conduct terminal defense as a secondary mission.
[4]Expedient blast shelters provide some protection to industry.
[5]Fallout shelters protect perishables, such as food supplies, as well as people.
[6]Includes earth or sandbag covering for machinery and components essential to economic recovery.

cause premature counteractions (other than preemption, which U.S. policy presently precludes) could catalyze instead of circumvent nuclear conflict.

Tactical Warning Tactical warning addresses attacks already in progress. Advance notice could amount to several hours for bombers speeding over polar flight paths, but only a few minutes for missiles fired at seaboard cities by submarines close to coasts.

Positive warnings for battle management purposes include numbers of hostile aircraft and missiles, axes of attack, altitudes or trajectories, and known penetration aids.

Negative warnings, such as enemy jamming efforts and assaults on opposing sensors, would alert defenders just as definitely as news from a notification network, but decision-makers would lack data needed to assess threats accurately and react most ably.

Defensive Actions

Comprehensive defenses orchestrate complementary efforts of active and passive elements, which protect points and/or areas, depending on their characteristics. Defenses-in-depth that capitalize on systems with dissimilar capabilities are least subject to compromise.

Active Defense A good offense reduces the need for defense, if enemy weapons can be destroyed *before* they swing into action. The side that strikes first thus has a theoretical advantage.

Defensive actions *after* hostile aircraft and missiles are airborne can occur any place along flight paths, from enemy airspace to impact zones. Active ABM and air defenses attempt to defeat attackers en route before they hit cities or counterforce targets.

Passive Defense Civil defense, which is entirely passive, supplements active measures. Lifesaving efforts and damage limitation both are essential elements. Fallout shelters can greatly moderate mass fatalities caused by surface bursts upwind from cities. Expedient blast shelters promise poor protection for property exposed to direct hits or near misses by megaton weapons, but even simple sandbags would provide impressive shields against less severe shocks.[3]

Connections Between Deterrence and Defense

Responsible champions and critics of defense both believe that nuclear deterrence is the basic U.S. security goal, but concepts for achieving credibility create serious schisms. One school declares that defense strengthens deterrence. Another school demurs. There are compromise convictions.

Opponents of Defense

Three negative views are worth note.

Position "A" Patrons of Position "A" believe that a "balance of terror" based on mutual vulnerability would best preserve deterrence, by making victory impossible. Populations are perpetual hostages, according to their strategy. Prospects of prodigious casualties if war should occur are an imperative part of the concept. Any move to mitigate the threat of mutual suicide thus would dilute deterrence by making war seem acceptable. Paradoxically, there is nothing callous about that philosophy, which is calculated to *conserve* human life, not *squander* it.

Position "B" A second group, less certain that defense is intrinsically undesirable, downgrades connected programs on technological grounds. They opine that impervious protection is a practical impossibility, since saturation assaults could overload any system. A porous screen actually would *invite* casualties, rather than *inhibit* them, by ensuring intemperate attacks. For those who escaped incineration, life in the post-war world would be "poor, nasty, brutish, and short," as Hobbes once put it. Survivors would envy the dead.

Position "C" A third faction concludes that city defense would compel opponents to produce new and exotic weapons with sure-fire penetration prospects. Stability, if restored at all, would be at some stratospheric level. The price paid for dubious improvements in deterrent powers thus would prove improvident.

Proponents of Defense

Some proponents of defense concede that *mutual* vulnerability might ensure deterrence. *Unilateral* vulnerability most certainly would not. Since no strategic deadlock in history has endured, they therefore prefer preparedness across the nuclear spectrum to preserve continuous peace. Even an offensive arms race in response to sound U.S. defenses could hold positive promise. U.S. and Soviet weaponry today, for example, is far superior quantitatively and qualitatively to that deployed 15 years ago, but the nuclear standoff seemed much more stable until the Kremlin unilaterally began to buttress city defense.

Leaving American people and our production base exposed is morally impermissible, according to this view. Leakproof defenses may indeed be impossible,[4] but a pervious shield would be better than none. Inability to protect everyone and everything does not mean that no one and nothing should be safe. At the very least, fears of small-scale, accidental, unauthorized, exemplary, or nuisance attacks would substantially diminish.

Partial defense would complicate Soviet tactics in event of a nuclear war. Aircraft and missiles both would face more difficult missions. Days of the "free ride" would be over. Some assets would be lost to saturation attacks, but others would last, because no foe has unlimited weapons to expend.[5] End results might well make the difference between restoring the pre-war way of life and remaining a pitiful remnant of modern America.

Changing U.S. Concepts

Official U.S. policies pertaining to CONUS defense shifted from one pole very nearly to the other as America's decision-makers sought the key to credible deterrence during the past two decades.

Defense Emphasized, 1955–1962

Defense was a solid U.S. goal in the 1950s, when manned bombers constituted the only intercontinental threat. The United States met Soviet challenges head-on with conventional, time-tested methods.

Working hand-in-glove with Canadian neighbors, we installed multifaceted point and area defenses-in-depth, calculated to preserve American people and our production base by downing aggressor aircraft. At its peak, the aggregate was penetrable, but provided great protection.[6]

When ballistic missiles began to complicate matters, U.S. leaders shifted emphasis, but sound defenses were still a salient objective. An active ABM R&D program was in being by the mid-1950s, well before Sputnik demonstrated Soviet abilities to deploy ICBMs.[7] The first site in our Ballistic Missile Early Warning System (BMEWS) became operational at Thule, Greenland, in 1961. Technological problems delayed decisions to deploy antimissile missiles, but the intent was incessant. Civil defense reached its apogee shortly after the Cuban missile crisis. Public interest and perceived needs were both intense.

Defense Deemphasized, 1963-Present

The architects of U.S. deterrent strategy charted a different course in the early 1960s, when Moscow's missiles emerged. As Defense Secretary Robert S. McNamara saw it, a "nuclear-armed offensive weapon which has a 50/50 chance of destroying its target would be highly effective, but a defensive weapon with the same probability of destroying incoming nuclear warheads would be of little value."[8] Improved offensive capabilities ostensibly could cancel out any defense at a fraction of the cost. Damage limitation consequently became an unstressed secondary mission.

Anti-ballistic missile options almost disappeared on May 26, 1972, when the SALT I ABM Treaty was signed. The United States and Soviet Union, according to those accords, renounced the right to erect area defenses of respective homelands and agreed that point defenses should comprise no more than two sites each.[9] A subsequent Protocol cut the allocation to one, but U.S. decision-makers dispensed with that prerogative.[10]

America's air defenders have since received drastically reduced missions. The aim now is merely early warning, surveillance, token control of U.S. peacetime airspace, and sufficient strength in reserve to stave off small-scale assaults by bombers and cruise missiles.[11]

Civil defense measures lost momentum rapidly after the Cuban missile crisis. Interest evaporated in most official circles. Public apathy is still evident.

Constant Soviet Concepts

Soviet leadership subscribes to Lenin's sanctified saying that "the primary producer of all mankind is the laboring man, the worker. If he survives, we save everything . . . . but if he dies, so does the State."

Soviet strategic defense certainly exhibits continuity that contrasts sharply with U.S. inconsistency. Protecting the population enjoys high priority. *Abilities* to attain that end are incomplete, but the *aim* appears unswerving. There is no conviction that deterrence and defense are incompatible.[12] On the contrary, Soviet spokesmen assert that homeland defense "strengthens international security as a whole."[13]

Contemporary Force Trends

U.S. and Soviet strategic defensive force trends reflect the concepts just described.

Ballistic Missile Defense

America's ballistic missile defenses once seemed expansive on paper, but little more than early warning sites ever materialized.

U.S. Warning Systems The U.S./Canadian North American Air Defense Command (NORAD) presently relies on several complementary warning systems whose dissimilar characteristics lessen the likelihood of surprise attacks and false alarms. At least two different devices that sense different phenomena survey each relevant launch site.[14] (See map 6.)

ICBM Warning An early warning satellite in synchronous orbit over the Indian Ocean uses infrared sensors to sight rocket plumes of Soviet ICBMs within 90 seconds after blastoff.[15] The system could handle many contacts simultaneously before becoming saturated. Signals from the satellite to control stations on Guam and near Alice Springs, Australia, are relayed to NORAD almost instantaneously.[16]

Still, U.S. satellites may not be survivable.[17] In any case, they are poorly equipped to predict probable impact areas and, being dependent on infrared emissions, lose track of enemy missiles in midcourse, *after* boosters burn out, but *before* payloads and penetration aids (penaids) separate.[18]

Consequently, BMEWS takes up tracking and target identification tasks where the satellite stops. Three huge overlapping fans extend northward for 3,000 miles from radar sites in Clear, Alaska; Thule, Greenland, and Fylingdales Moor, England. Missiles launched north from the Eurasian land mass must pass through those detection arcs.

Map 6

BALLISTIC MISSILE WARNING SITES

(Except Satellites)

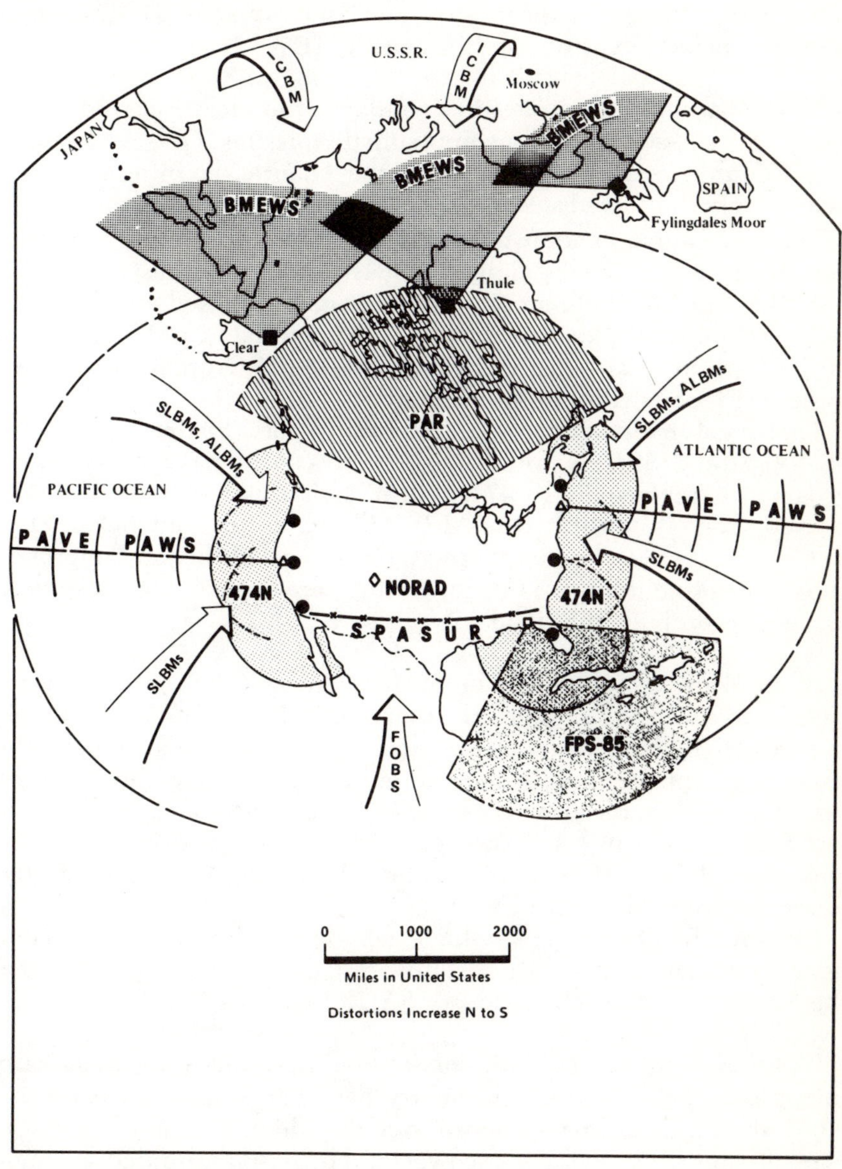

Tracking radars then compute trajectories and general impact areas for missile bodies, but not MIRVs.[19]

One Perimeter Acquisition Radar (PAR), the sole active survivor of our ABM complex at Grand Forks, North Dakota, refines warning data within its 1,800 mile radius, which spans a 120-degree arc.[20] It can provide accurate RV counts and predict impact points for large-scale raids.[21]

No basic changes in procedure are contemplated. DOD simply plans to upgrade existing satellites and BMEWS.[22]

SLBM Warning Two satellites similar to the one discussed above scan U.S. flanks for sea-launched ballistic missiles. One is stationed over Central America, another above the Atlantic. Warning times are exceedingly short for close-in shots, but better for firings farther out.[23]

The mid-course handoff for tracking purposes presently passes to one of six 474N radars along our east and west coasts, because BMEWS and PAR both are out of position.[24] A phased-array radar at Eglin AFB, Florida, keeps a sharp eye on potential SLBM launch sites in the Caribbean and guards against Fractional Orbit Bombardment System (FOBS) strikes from the south.[25]

That combination, however, has blind spots. Soviet SS-N-8 and SS-N-6 Mod 2 SLBMs, for example, both can by-pass the system.[26] Programs to replace the six 474N "dish" radars with two PAVE PAWS phased array systems at Otis AFB, Massachusetts, and Beale AFB, California, are therefore in progress. Greater reliability and improved capabilities (including a 3,000-mile range) are expected to fill surveillance gaps on both U.S. flanks.[27]

Soviet Warning Systems The Soviet Galosh system lacks forward-based early warning stations like the U.S. BMEWS, but compensates in part with high-powered phased array Hen House radars around the nation's periphery. Target acquisition and initial tracking tasks are assigned to two large phased array Dog House radars (counterparts of our PAR), which in turn pass control to one of four Try Add sites (analogous to our Missile Site Radars (MSR)) near the capital city. Space satellites play a part.[28]

Rigorous R&D programs, which include rapidly deployable components, remain in progress,[29] stimulating claims by some critics that the Soviet Union is "cheating" on SALT I accords.[30]

Weapons Systems Ballistic missiles on both sides are essentially unopposed, because neither country has ever erected an extensive ABM shield. The Soviet Galosh system, which comprises 64 launchers in four sites around Moscow, could be easily saturated. A single U.S. Safeguard installation opened operations with 100 Sprint missiles in an ICBM field near Grand Forks, North Dakota, in October 1975, but shut down one month later.[31] (Figure 12).

Scientists on both sides still pursue credible ABM capabilities within confines imposed by the SALT I Treaty and subsequent Protocol. Those documents restrict development and deployments, but not basic research. The stakes are high, because a breakthrough by either side could suddenly shift the strategic balance. There is no consensus in the U.S. intelligence community concerning Soviet progress in that regard.[32]

Air Defense

Air defense systems must be able to cope with land- and carrier-based aircraft, plus cruise missiles of all kinds, which can challenge from ground level to 100,000 feet or more in darkness and dismal weather.

America's air defenses, unlike ABM, once encompassed full-scale deployment programs for weapons systems as well as early warning. Threat perceptions and budgetary priorities, not technical problems, played predominant roles in decisions to reduce our efforts. Soviet defenses, in contrast, are the world's strongest and most sophisticated.

U.S. Warning and Control NORAD's early warning apparatus was considerable in the early 1960s, when surveillance capabilities reached their peak.

The most direct avenue of approach, then as now, was from the north. Eighty-one Distant Early Warning (DEW) stations were draped across arctic wastes from the Aleutians to the Atlantic as an outer alert perimeter (Map 7). The Mid-Canada and Pine Tree Lines were positioned closer in, augmented by a generous group of gap-filler radars. Navy picket ships, Texas Towers, and Air Force early warning aircraft covered both flanks.

That complex has since been cut drastically. Picket ships, Texas Towers, gap-filler radars, and the Mid-Canada line have completely disappeared. Surveillance still in existence displays technology that, in the main, dates back two decades or more.

Remaining ground-based radars can detect high-flying (40,000 feet) aircraft and cruise missiles at a distance of about 200 nautical miles, but would be essentially useless against small cross-section targets (such as cruise missiles) skimming the surface.[33] DEW stations and their Greenland-Iceland-U.K. extension could be easily bypassed unless assisted by offshore airborne patrols, which now operate only on call. Long-range radar coverage in the Pine Tree Line exhibits significant gaps, especially at low altitudes.[34]

As a hedge against Soviet bomber threats in the 1980s, DOD presently is experimenting with Over-the-Horizon Backscatter (OTH-B) radars, whose fans would extend more than 1,800 nautical miles from

Map 7
U.S. AIR WARNING SITES

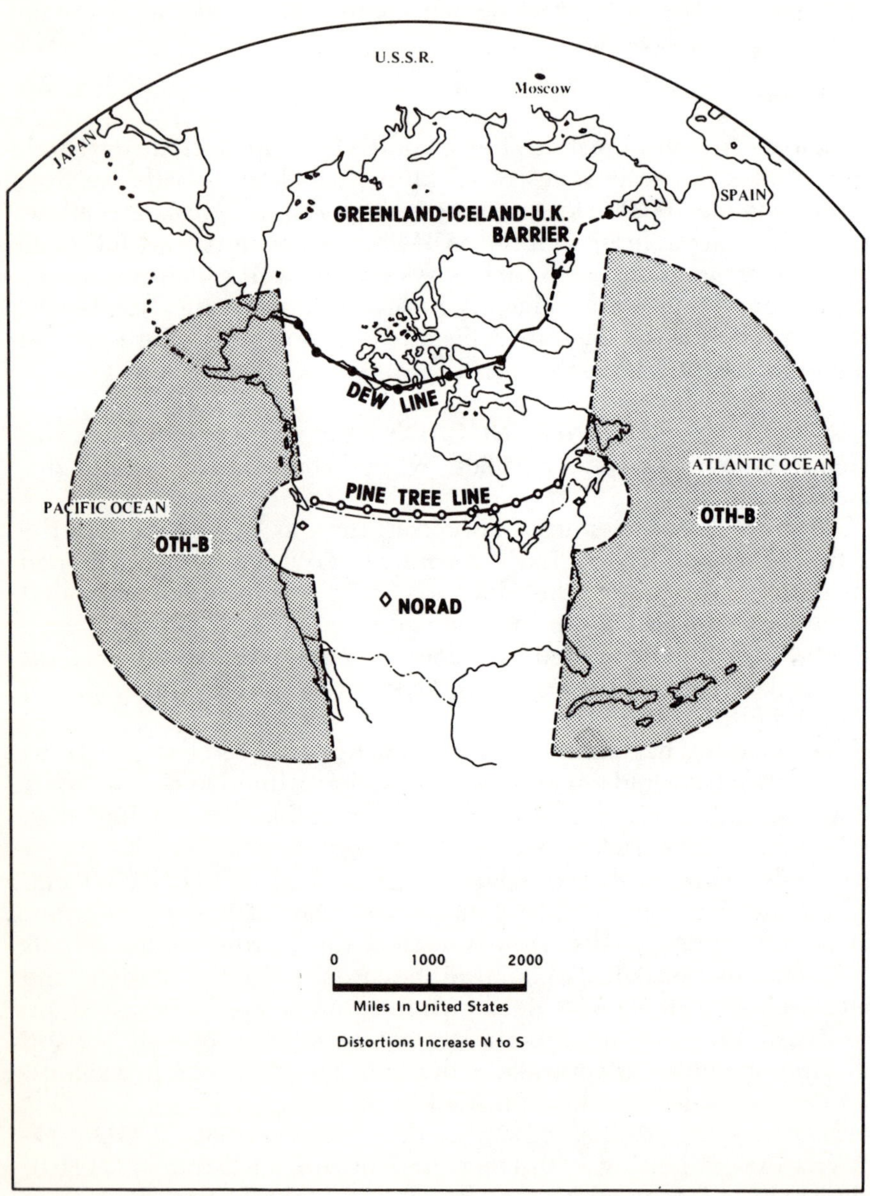

sea level to the ionosphere (with a nominal dead zone that circles the site for 500 miles in all directions.)[35] However, several technical problems remain. Auroral disturbances, for example, preclude surveillance of polar approaches.[36]

Provided most wrinkles can be ironed out, DOD plans to deploy two sites only if Soviet bomber threats warrant: one near Cutler, Maine, the other somewhere in the Pacific Northwest. Two additional installations, one looking north, the other south, would assure complete coverage, but neither is now programmed. The remnants of our DEW Line (perhaps enhanced) and a reduced number of long-range radars will remain in operation to compensate.[37] Six Airborne Warning and Control System (AWACS) aircraft, scheduled to complete the U.S. screen by about 1980, will add new capabilities for detecting aircraft flying at low levels over land. In times of crisis, they could be "augmented with additional aircraft from the general purpose AWACS force."[38] Map 8 shows the surveillance spread of a single set.

Map 8

AWACS SURVEILLANCE COVERAGE

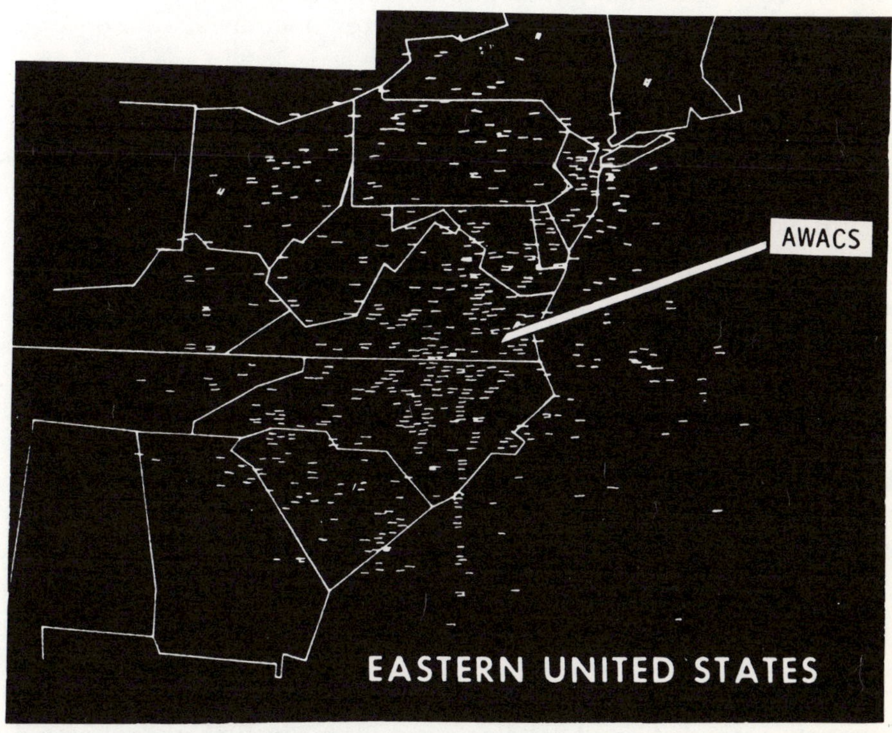

NOTE: One dash indicates one aircraft on the AWACS radar screen.

Six Semi-Automatic Ground Environment (SAGE) sites, the residue of more than 20 installed in the early 1960s, will disappear by 1981. So will our single Manual Control Center (MCC). Five Regional Operations Control Centers (ROCCs)—four in CONUS, one in Alaska—will accomplish peacetime airspace sovereignty missions in their stead. Each ROCC reportedly could handle data from 15 surveillance radars, most of which jointly serve the U.S. Armed Forces and Federal Aviation Administration, then control all intercepts in its sector.[39]

ROCCs, however, could no more survive a missile attack than SAGE,[40] since both are housed in buildings open to bombardment. U.S. concepts therefore call for one AWACS aircraft to be based at each ROCC. If an attack seems imminent, each AWACS will update its computer base and embark a battle management staff. Once aloft, its ability to direct defensive efforts would be much enhanced.[41]

Soviet Warning Systems More than 6,000 ground radars support the Soviet air defense structure. Quality ranges from impressive to poor, because the expanding base includes many old models. Capabilities against low-flying aircraft, for example, are still far from complete. Moss aircraft, comparable to U.S. EC-121s (ancestors of AWACS) work well over water, but not over land, which creates radar "clutter". Corrective efforts are in progress, but the network even now is effective enough to cause concern among SAC crew members who, on call, would have to take the trip.[42]

Weapons Systems

U.S. and Soviet air defense weapons reflect diametric differences in perceived threats and policy. (See Graph 8 and Figures 14–15 for statistical summaries at the end of this section.)

U.S. Interceptors and SAMs The world's best interceptor aircraft, including F-101Bs, F-102As, and F-106As, furnished air defenses for CONUS in the early 1960s (the last F-106A was accepted in July 1961). At that time, 67 active and 55 Air National Guard (ANG) squadrons, broadcast on 42 bases across the United States, were backed up by seven Bomarc anti-aircraft missile squadrons.[43] Nike-Ajax, first deployed in 1954, provided point defenses for something like 30 key cities before the end of that decade.[44] Those early SAMs, with conventional warheads, were replaced by nuclear-capable Nike-Hercules, which had a slant range of about 100 miles and could engage attacking enemy aircraft from medium altitudes to 100,000 feet. Hawk missiles were set to shoot down low-flying bombers by 1960.[45] Canadian forces added depth.

Projected threats, however, never developed. Soviet heavy bomber strength peaked at about 210 Bears and Bisons in 1966, then dropped to 140, the current tally. That fact, combined with Assured Destruction policies, caused U.S. air defense activities to decline before deployment plans were complete.[46] Cutbacks accelerated sharply after 1970. Active interceptor squadrons have lost two-thirds of their aircraft. Nike-Hercules batteries, which once defended CONUS cities, disappeared in FY 1974, except for three batteries located in Alaska. All other SAMs are in Florida[47], in position to protect that state against surprise attacks from Cuba, but unable to cope elsewhere without prior alert and redeployment. Point defense, for all practical purposes, thus is no longer possible.[48]

To compensate, our Aerospace Defense Command (ADCOM) now is compelled to supplement dedicated interceptors with F-4 fighters from the general purpose pool. F-15 allocations for that purpose are planned, although the force will not be trained specifically for CONUS air defense. Its primary mission in emergency is to reinforce NATO in an air superiority role. Conflicting priorities are readily apparent.[49]

As it stands, the attrition of aging interceptors will make it impossible for our Air National Guard to maintain even the present minimum number of alert sites in the late 1970s without replacements. In recognition, F-4s recently relieved a squadron of F-101s. A second squadron of F-4s is scheduled to replace an F-106 outfit in FY 1979, freeing aircraft for use as fillers in other organizations. There are no plans to replace any SAMs.[50]

Soviet Air Defense Weapons The Soviet Union, in stark contrast, has amassed the world's most impressive array of air defenses, which currently includes 2,700 interceptor aircraft and 12,000 SAMs.[51] Numerical strengths are slightly larger than they were in 1970. Sheer mass serves a useful purpose, even though half the inventory consists of items outmoded according to U.S. standards.

Overall effectiveness against U.S. low-level tactics and standoff missiles, such as SRAM, would be less than statistics suggest. DOD, for example, still cannot identify a "look-down shoot-down" system for the MIG-25 Foxbat or any other interceptor. Radar coverage constrains SAMs.[52] Still, SAC bombers fighting their way through Soviet defenses-in-depth face increasing competition that reduces penetration probabilities considerably. So will ALCMs.

Passive Defense Programs

Active defenses employ arms and equipment to deter, deflect, or otherwise defeat enemy offensive forces. Passive defenses apply cover, concealment, dispersion, protective construction, maneuver, and deception to minimize damage and casualties. The two types can be used separately or in tandem.

Defense for Delivery Systems

Pre-launch survival of U.S. nuclear delivery systems is predicated completely on passive defense. Fixed-site ICBMs, required to ride out any enemy first strike before retaliating, rely on hard silos to reduce initial attrition. Our bombers and SLBMs depend on mobility and dispersion.

Soviet passive protective measures are comparable, but security for land-based components in that country is enhanced considerably, because active defenses assist and U.S. second-strike concepts reduce potential threats.

Civil Defense

Civil defense (CD) in the United States is designed in the main to mitigate natural disasters, such as cyclones and floods. The Kremlin connects it with national security.

U.S. Avoidance Fifteen years ago the civil defense dole bought "an organization, but [did] not buy a program."[53] Nothing essential has changed.

Shelter Programs The Berlin crisis of 1961 precipitated our first shelter program. A crash survey then identified sites in existing structures. Only half the spaces were ever marked or stocked with the simplest survival kits. Half, being remote from residential areas, are accessible to most citizens only during normal working hours.[54]

Proposed plans to include fallout shelters in new construction were scrapped after the Senate rejected requests for authorizing legislation in 1963. Single-purpose public shelters were never seriously considered for similar reasons.[55] "Do-it-yourself" family shelter programs, which died in the early 1960s, were unsuccessful.[56]

Reduced funds currently cause sad side effects. The Defense Civil Preparedness Agency (DCPA) suffers from ever-greater shortages of engineers with CD experience, shelter managers, public information specialists, and trained radiological monitors. If "the chips were down," U.S. communities in the main would be poorly prepared to implement plans, even where shelters are marked and stocks are in place.[57]

City Evacuation The best defense against nuclear weapons is to be somewhere else when they detonate. City evacuation, a cheap substitute for costly shelters, therefore comprised the core of U.S. CD planning in the late 1950s, when subsonic bombers posed the sole threat and *tactical warning* times promised to be several hours long.[58]

Tactical evacuation plans were shelved in the early 1960s, when ballistic missiles first burgeoned. Times between detection and detonation would be so short that populations caught departing would incur more casualties than if they stayed in place.

No more was heard of crisis relocation for a full decade, until 1972, when DOD, spurred by Soviet initiatives, started to develop contingency evacuation plans for "high risk" areas. Some 250 urban centers whose 1970 census count exceeded 50,000 currently qualify.[59]

The new concept, unlike its ancestor, assumes a prolonged period of *strategic warning,* which would afford ample opportunity to evacuate cities if a nuclear conflict seemed imminent. Pilot projects are in progress at eight potential target sites, each close to military installations.

The practical problems of implementing crisis relocation plans in emergency, however, would be immense, even if we had strategic initiative, which is unlikely in light of second-strike concepts. At this point, the program is marked by public indifference and widespread opposition in the U.S. official community.

Soviet Accent Soviet stress on civil defense is very strong.[60] Efforts and investment increased substantially after Brezhnev expressed personal interest at the 23d Party Congress in 1966, and intensified six years later, after the SALT I Treaty put brakes on active defense.

Primary emphasis reportedly entails clearing cities in times of intense crisis. That decision coincides with the decline of ABM deployments. Protecting the population in place apparently seemed an impossible aim in the absence of any ability to intercept ballistic missiles. Elaborate displacement plans emphasize that essential enterprises continue to function until tension ends or nuclear conflict erupts. Fallout shelters, an associated element, would combine existing structures with expedients prepared in emergency.[61]

Long-range survival prospects are further improved by urban planning, which restricts population density, develops satellite towns around large cities, and creates firebreaks. New production plants are dispersed and "hardened" to extents possible, along with industries already in place. Prescriptions include replacing glass with solids and constructing fireproof roofs; reinforcing weak structures; burying utility stations, plus conduits for power and water; and improvising shields for installations on the surface. Redundant facilities, stockpiles, and war reserves all are standard procedure.[62]

Such *plans* are impressive on paper. How practical they would be in *practice* is problematical.

Simultaneous mass movements in the Soviet Union would create staggering economic and social problems attendant to feeding, housing, and ministering to millions of displaced persons during periods that could be prolonged. If evacuation were ordered in winter, severe cold would complicate matters immensely.

No one as yet has satisfactorily answered hard questions, such as:

—How would evacuating people from cities ensure Soviet survival, if the production base that sustains them were smashed?

—How would permanently displaced people survive if many cities of residence were destroyed?

—How could evacuees escape heavy cumulative casualties if U.S. saturation attacks used MIRVs en masse against many reception sites at an early stage?

—How could anything less than full-scale evacuation cut casualties during a limited nuclear war, unless the Soviets knew in advance which cities/areas we would strike?

Plausible explanations are essential. In their absence, U.S. leaders risk crediting the Soviet Union with CD capabilities that result in considerable part from rhetoric.

The Upshot American forces, people, and production base are naked to nuclear attack. A "vulnerability gap" of disputed proportions grows, because Soviet leaders stress defense, while U.S. leaders do not.

Cassandras at one end of the spectrum contend that emerging Soviet abilities, abetted by detailed plans, psychological conditioning, and physical preparations, already degrade U.S. deterrence and place this country in peril.[63]

Some noted U.S. specialists speculate that crisis relocation procedures would limit Soviet fatalities to four or five percent during a general war, under worst-case conditions.[64] Official estimates indicate that almost half the American people would die under similar circumstances. Another 35 million would demand medical attention.[65] If those casualty ratios were even close to correct, U.S. Assured Destruction capabilities would indeed be "a myth", as some claim.[66]

Skeptics, whose ranks include the present Secretary of Defense,[67] draw less drastic conclusions.

Most concede that the Kremlin stresses city defense, but doubt that U.S. deterrence is in danger. Followers of one faction, for example, see the so-called civil defense gap as a spurious issue, because they believe that nuclear blasts can break through the best protection.[68] Others, whose opinions are widely shared, suspect that Soviet CD capabilities, while significant, are overstated.[69] U.S. over-reaction, they contend, could be just as ruinous as complacency.

Which claims are correct is still not clear.

The U.S. intelligence community accorded such a low priority to Soviet civil defense for so many years that crash efforts to estimate current effectiveness are inconclusive.[70] Classified studies, as well as open assessments, thus lack sufficient hard data and depth to support solid conclusions concerning Soviet strengths and weaknesses.

All the same, Cassandras and skeptics seem to agree that Soviet CD capabilities would considerably exceed our own if the security they promise were overstated by several hundred percent and U.S. casualty statistics were high by, say, half.

Active and passive defenses in combination *are* beginning to create a survivability imbalance that favors the Soviets. Assertions that they soon could survive a general war appear premature, but long-term consequences could be severe if the trend proceeds too far. Civil defense in fact would assume a completely different connotation, if accompanied by Soviet breakthroughs in ASW[71] or ABM.[72] Active defense in that case would provide the primary shield. Civil defense, as part of a strategic defensive triad, would simply take care of the "slop over."

Any amalgam that allowed the Soviets to evade Assured Destruction, while America still could not, would dilute our bargaining powers and discredit this country's deterrent concept based on *mutual* dangers. Our only serious opponent would in fact have satisfied the true aim of strategy, spelled out first by Sun Tzu[73] and later by Liddell Hart, which is "not so much to seek battle as to seek a . . . . situation so advantageous that if it does not of itself produce the [desired] decision, its continuation by a battle is sure to achieve this."[74]

Graph 8

AIR DEFENSE FORCES
Statistical Summary - 1977

(Note Different Scales)

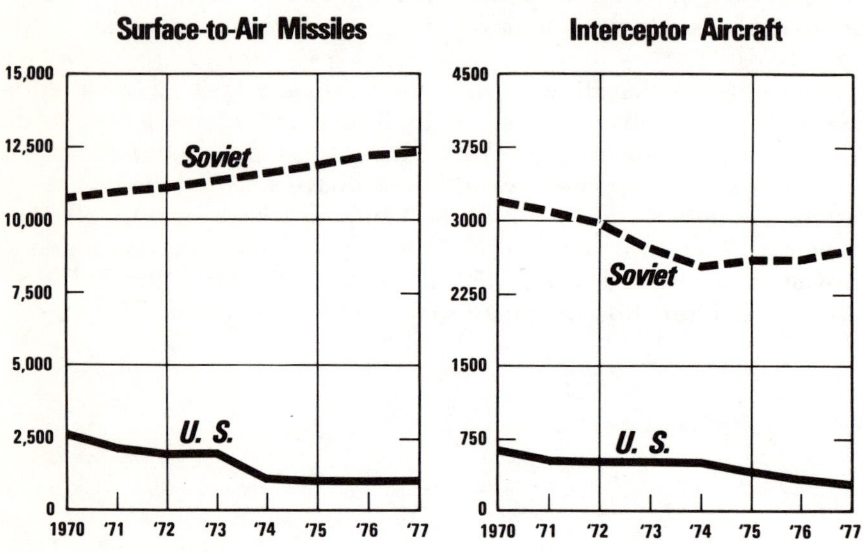

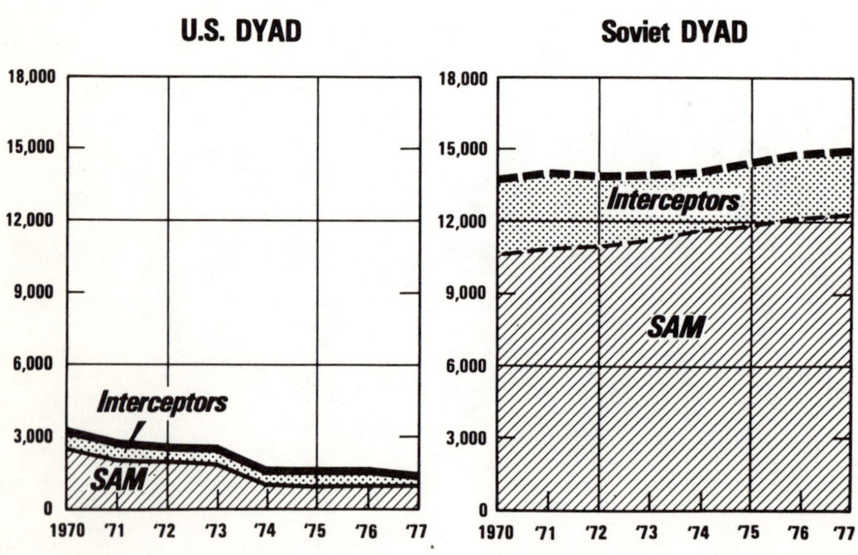

FIGURE 14 STRATEGIC DEFENSIVE MISSILE SYSTEMS, Statistical Trends and System Characteristics

	1970	*1971*	*1972*	*1973*	*1974*	*1975*	*1976*	*1977*	*Net Change 1970–77*
ABM LAUNCHERS									
United States	0	0	0	0	0	100	0	0	0
Soviet Union	64	64	64	64	64	64	64	64	0
U.S. Standing	−64	−64	−64	−64	−64	+ 36	− 64	− 64	0
SAM LAUNCHERS									
United States									
Active									
Hawk[1]									
Launchers	(288)	(288)	(288)	(288)	(288)	(288)	(288)	(288)	0
3 Arms Each	864	864	864	864	864	864	864	864	0
Nike Hercules[2]	792	504	504	504	126	126	126	126	− 666
Bomarc	196	196	84	0	0	0	0	0	− 196
Total	1852	1564	1452	1368	990	990	990	990	− 862
National Guard									
Nike Hercules[2]	684	486	486	486	0	0	0	0	− 684
Grand Total	2536	2050	1938	1854	990	990	990	990	−1546

FIGURE 14 (Con't)

	1970	1971	1972	1973	1974	1975	1976	1977	Net Change 1970–77
Soviet Union									
SA-1 Guild	3200	3200	3200	3200	3200	3200	3200	3200	0
SA-2 Guideline	4600	4500	4300	4100	3700	3500	3400	3300	−1300
SA-3 Goa[1]									
Launchers	(900)	(1000)	(1100)	(1100)	(1150)	(1200)	(1300)	(1300)	(+400)
Rails	1800	2000	2200	2600	3100	3500	3700)	4000	+2200
SA-5 Gammon	1100	1200	1300	1400	1500	1600	1800	1800	+ 700
Total	10,700	10,900	11,000	11,300	11,500	11,800	12,100	12,300	+1600
U.S. Standing[3]	−8164	−8850	−9062	−9446	−10,510	−10,810	−11,110	−11,310	−3146

[1]All Hawk launchers have three arms. SA-3s originally had 2 rails, but some were deployed with 4 rails, beginning in 1973. Each arm/rail holds one missile.
[2]Three Nike-Hercules batteries now are in Alaska. All other U.S. SAMs are in Florida, on call, but out of position to deal with surprise attacks.
[3]SA-4 and SA-6 through SA-9 all are tactical missiles associated with battlefield air defense. So are many Hawk and Nike Hercules. Those weapons are excluded from this summary, although some Soviet launchers could contribute to strategic defense if properly positioned at appropriate times. So could air defense artillery.

MISSILE SYSTEM CHARACTERISTICS

	First Deployed	*Nr Rails, Arms*	*Type Warhead*	*Slant Range (miles)*	*Combat Ceiling (Feet)*	*Launch Site*
United States						
Hawk	1960	3	HE	25	Lo-Med	Mobile
Nike Hercules	1958	1	HE, Nuke	100	100,000	Fixed
Bomarc	1958	1	HE, Nuke	200–400	70,000	Fixed
Soviet Union						
ABM						
ABM-1 Galosh	1964	1	Nuke	200		Fixed
SAM						
SA-1 Guild	1956	1	HE/Nuke			Fixed
SA-2 Guideline	1958	1	HE/Nuke	25	Med-80,000	Fixed
SA-3 Goa[1]	1961	2,4	HE/Nuke	18	Lo-40,000	Mobile
SA-5 Gammon	1963	1	HE/Nuke	50–150	95,000	Fixed

[1]An improved version of SA-3, first displayed in 1967, may have a nuclear warhead. A 4-rail version began replacing the standard 2-rail system beginning in 1973.

FIGURE 15 STRATEGIC DEFENSIVE INTERCEPTORS
Statistical Trends and System Characteristics

	1970	*1971*	*1972*	*1973*	*1974*	*1975*	*1976*	*1977*	*Net Change 1970–77*
United States[1]									
Active									
F-106 Delta Dart	207	199	162	126	120	115	114	108	− 99
F-102 Delta Dagger	58	14	16	5	0	0	0	0	− 58
F-101 Voodoo	56	1	4	3	0	0	0	0	− 56
Total[2]	321	214	182	134	120	115	114	108	−213
National Guard									
F-4 Phantom	0	0	0	0	0	0	0	18	+ 18
F-106 Delta Dart	0	0	33	67	68	90	90	90	+ 90
F-102 Delta Dagger	255	192	157	172	167	44	19	0	−255
F-101[3] Voodoo	45	110	102	107	117	122	87	54	+ 9
Total	300	302	292	346	352	256	196	162	−138
Grand Total	621	516	474	480	472	371	310	270	−351

[1]Figures above reflect Unit Equipment (UE) aircraft only.
[2]Thirty-six U.S. F-4s are dedicated to strategic air defense. None are in CONUS; 24 are in Alaska, 12 in Iceland.
[3]Three squadrons of Canadian F-101s, which total about 44 aircraft, are assigned to North American Air Defense Command (NORAD). They complement U.S. capabilities by covering northern approaches to the United States, which strengthens defense-in-depth.

Soviet Union									
MIG-17 Fresco	1000	800	650	400	200	150	100	100	−900
MIG-19 Farmer	350	350	350	300	200	200	150	100	−250
MIG-23 Flogger[1]	0	0	0	0	0	0	100	250	+250
MIG-25 Foxbat[1]	0	50	100	150	200	200	300	300	+300
SU-9 Fishpot	750	750	750	750	750	700	650	650	−100
SU-15 Flagon	400	550	550	600	650	850	850	850	+450
TU-28 Fiddler	150	150	150	150	150	150	150	150	0
YAK-25 Flashlight	200	100	50	0	0	0	0	0	−200
YAK-28 Firebar	350	350	350	350	350	350	300	300	− 50
Total	3200	3100	2950	2700	2500	2600	2600	2700	−500
U.S. Standing	−2579	−2584	−2476	−2220	−2028	−2229	−2240	−2430	+149

[1]MIG-23 and MIG-25 are the only interceptor aircraft presently being produced for Soviet air defense squadrons.

FIGURE 15 (Con't)

AIRCRAFT CHARACTERISTICS

	First Deployed	*Nr Jet Engines*	*Combat[1] Radius (Miles)*	*Max Speed (Mach)*	*Typical Armament*	
					Guns	*Missiles*
United States						
F-106 Delta Dart	1959	1	600	2.0	0	4 AIM-4F/G, 1 AIR-2
F-102 Delta Dagger	1959	1	450	1.5	0	3 AIM-4C/D, 1 AIM-26
F-101 Voodoo	1958	2	400	1.8	0	2 AIM-4D, 2 AIR-2
Soviet Union						
MIG-17 Fresco	1953	1	300	Subsonic	3X23 mm	
MIG-19 Farmer	1955	2	300	1.0	3X30mm	2 Atoll
MIG-23 Flogger	1972	1	700	2.5	Gatling	2 Apex, 2 Aphid
MIG-25 Foxbat	1970	2	500	3.2	0	4 Acrid
SU-9 Fishpot	1959	1	685	2.2	0	4 Alkali
SU-15 Flagon	1967	2	800	2.5	0	2 Anab
TU-28 Fiddler	1966	2		1.7	0	4 Ash
YAK-25 Flashlight	1953	1		Subsonic	2X37 mm	2 (Mixed)
YAK-28 Firebar	1961	2	575	1.1	0	2 Anab, 2 Atoll

[1]Combat radius is with external fuel tanks.

AIR-TO-AIR MISSILE/ROCKET CHARACTERISTICS

	First Deployed	*Guidance*	*Range (Miles)*	*Speed (Mach)*	*Warhead*	
					Type	*Yield*
United States						
Rockets						
AIR-2 Genie	1957	None	6	3.0	Nuclear	1.5 KT
Missiles						
AIM-4C,D Falcon	1956	Infrared	6	2.0	HE	
AIM-4F,G Falcon	1960	Radar	7	2.5	HE	40 lbs
AIM-26A Superfalcon	1960	Radar	5	2.0	Nuclear	
AIM-26B Superfalcon	1963	Radar	5	2.0	HE	
Soviet Union						
AA-1 Alkali	1960	Radar, IR	5	1–2	HE	
AA-3 Anab	1961	Radar, IR	15	2.5	HE	
AA-5 Ash	1965	Radar, IR	15	2.5	HE	
AA-6 Acrid	1970	Radar, IR	15	2.2	HE	
AA-7 Apex	1974	Radar, IR	15		HE	
AA-8 Aphid	1975	Radar, IR	3–4		HE	

Footnotes

1. This section extracts extensively from U.S. Congress. Senate. *United States and Soviet City Defense,* pp. 3–17.

2. A huge body of literature illuminates fundamentals of nuclear deterrence. See for example, Kahn, Herman, *Thinking About the Unthinkable.* New York: Horizon Press, 1962, pp. 101–126 and Harkabi, Yehoshafat, *Nuclear War and Nuclear Peace.* Tel Aviv: Israel Defense Forces, 1964, pp. 9–40.

3. For a concise discussion of civil defense measures to protect the production base, see Jones, T. K., testimony before the Civil Defense Panel of the Investigations Subcommittee of the House Committee on Armed Services. *Hearings. Civil Defense Review.* 94th Congress, 2d Session. U.S. Govt. Print. Off., 1976, pp. 206–267.

4. City defense specialists assigned to the Director of Defense Research and Engineering (DDR&E) indicate that they are unable to identify leakproof air or ABM defenses at any cost, even in the long-term future. Enemies with adequate assets could always concentrate great power on a few targets of greatest concern to them, but by doing so would dilute their abilities elsewhere.

5. Soviet counts of strategic nuclear warheads could exceed 10,000 in the foreseeable future if MIRV deployments proceed as U.S. intelligence presently predicts. Given estimated yields and accuracies, a high proportion would be required to produce high confidence "kill" probabilities under general war conditions. Targets would include 1,054 U.S. ICBM silos. Pattern coverage of air corridors emanating from 27 SAC bomber bases would be required. Defended cities would deplete the residue much more rapidly than if they remained exposed.

6. Murphy, Charles H., *The Decision to Curtail Strategic Air Defense Programs in FY 1975: Rationale and Implications.* Washington: Congressional Research Service, April 5, 1974, p. 6.

7. U.S. Congress. Senate. *Hearings on Study of Airpower before the Subcommittee on the Air Force, Armed Services Committee.* 84th Congress, 2d Session. Washington: U.S. Govt. Print. Off., 1956, p. 726.

8. McNamara, Robert S., *Statement on the FY 1969 Defense Budget,* p. 42.

9. Just why Brezhnev bargained away Soviet ABM defense by signing the SALT I Treaty is still unclear, since no spokesman on either side has shed official light. Speculators suggest that the apparatus, being neither extensive nor very effective, was expendable in the give and take.

10. See Annex E for full text of the SALT I ABM Treaty and associated statements.

11. Brown, Harold, *Department of Defense Annual Report, FY 1979,* p. 120. Backfire may yet reverse that trend, which has created a U.S. "Coast Guard of the Air." Weinraub, Bernard, "[Defense Secretary] Brown Says Stronger Air Defense Needed to Face Soviet Bomber," *New York Times,* April 7, 1978, p. 3.

12. Erickson, John, *Soviet Military Power, Report No. 73–1.* Washington: United States Strategic Institute, 1973, pp. 42, 45, 47, 49; Wolfe, Thomas W., *Soviet Power and Europe, 1945–1970.* Baltimore: The Johns Hopkins Press, 1970, pp. 186, 439–440.

13. Quotation from *The Political Heritage of V. I. Lenin and Problems of Contemporary War.* Ed. by Maj. Gen. A. S. Milovidov. Moscow: Voenizdad, 1972, p. 351.

14. Rumsfeld, Donald H., *Annual Defense Department Report, FY 1977,* pp. 92–93; Ulsamer, Edgar, *Strategic Warning: Cornerstone of Deterrence,* p. 41.

15. Miller, Barry, "U.S. Moves to Upgrade Missile Warning," *Aviation Week and Space Technology,* December 2, 1974, p. 18.

16. Ulsamer, Edgar, *Strategic Warning: Cornerstone of Deterrence,* pp. 41–42; Miller, Barry, "U.S. Moves to Upgrade Missile Warning," pp. 16–17; Klass, Philip J., "Early Warning Satellites Seen Operational," *Aviation Week and Space Technology,* September 20, 1971, pp. 18–19.

17. Bradsher, Henry, "Soviets Ahead in Satellite Killers," *Washington Star,* October 5, 1977, p. 3; "Defense Secretary Says Soviets Have Operational Anti-Satellite," *Defense/Space Daily,* October 5, 1977, p. 162; Fuller, Jack, "Turner Confirms Russ Killer Satellites," *Chicago Tribune,* February 2, 1978, p. 2.

18. Miller, Barry, "U.S. Moves to Upgrade Missile Warning," p. 17.

19. *Ibid.;* Ulsamer, Edgar, *Strategic Warning: Cornerstone of Deterrence,* p. 43; written comments on this study by Army Ballistic Missile Defense Program Office (BMDPO), June 15, 1976.

20. Written comments on this study by BMDPO, June 15, 1976.

21. Point Paper, "PAR Attack Characteristics," BMDPO, May 24, 1976.

22. Rumsfeld, Donald H., *Annual Defense Department Report, FY 1977,* p. 93.

23. Klass, Philip J., "Early Warning Satellites Seen Operational," p. 18.

24. The six 474N radars are located at Mount Laguna, near San Diego; Mill Valley, near San Francisco; Mount Hebo, Oregon; Charleston, Maine; Fort Fisher, North Carolina; and McDill AFB, Florida. For details, see Miles, Marvin, "Radar System Guards Against Attack by Subs," *Los Angles Times,* December 23, 1972, pp. 1, 5.

25. FOBS launches ballistic missiles into low orbit (about 100 miles). Retrorockets fired after less than one revolution permit rapid descent to targets, reducing defensive radar reaction times. Klass, Philip J., "FPS-85 Radar Expands to Cover SLBMs," *Aviation Week and Space Technology,* February 19, 1973, pp. 61–66.

26. Schlesinger, James R., *Annual Defense Department Report, FY 1976,* p. II–48; "DOD Heats Up Debate on Phased Array Radars for SLBM Detection," *Aerospace Daily,* December 5, 1973, p. 188.

27. *Ibid.*, pp. II–48, 49; "Radar Sites Picked," *Aviation Week and Space Technology,* April 12, 1976, p. 13; Brown, Harold, *Department of Defense Annual Report for FY 1979,* p. 123.

28. Ulsamer, Edgar, "The USSR's Military Shadow is Lengthening," *Sov-Aerospace Almanac 1977, Air Force Magazine,* March 1977, p. 42; Perry, G. E., "Russian Geostationary and Early-Warning Satellites," *Royal Air Force Quarterly,* Autumn 1977, pp. 272–279.

29. Fact Sheet, "Why BMD R&D on Limited Defense," Army Ballistic Missile Defense Program Office, undated (1976).

30. Laird, Melvin R., "Arms Control: The Russians Are Cheating!," *Reader's Digest,* December 1977, pp. 97–101; Robinson, Clarence A., Jr., "DOD Presses for ABM Fund Restoration," *Aviation Week and Space Technology,* June 7, 1976, pp. 16–17; Robinson, Clarence A., Jr., "Soviets Push ABM Development," *Aviation Week and Space Technology,* April 7, 1975, pp. 12–14; Laird, Melvin R., "Is This Detente?" *Reader's Digest,* July 1975, pp. 54–55; Hussein, Farooq, "Is Soviet Technology Side-Stepping SALT?," *New Scientist,* August 21, 1975, p. 432; and Gray, Colin S., "SALT I Aftermath: Have the Soviets Been Cheating?," *Air Force Magazine,* November 1975, pp. 28–33.

31. Rumsfeld, Donald H., *Annual Defense Department Report, FY 1977,* pp. 70, 91.

32. Personal conversations between the author and Air Force analysts in December 1977. Also "Soviets Said to Double U.S. BMD Effort," *Defense/Space Daily,* July 28, 1977, p. 138; Bradsher, Henry, "Soviet ABM Efforts Have Pentagon Worried," *Washington Star,* February 16, 1978, p. 11.

33. Written comments submitted by DDR&E on June 15, 1976.

34. U.S. Congress. House. Committee on Armed Services. *Cuban Plane Incident at New Orleans.* Hearings Before a Subcommittee . . . 92nd Congress, 1st Session. Washington: U.S. Govt. Print. Off., 1972, p. 77.

35. NORAD working papers, undated. Furnished on May 26, 1976.

36. Currie, Malcom R., *The Department of Defense Program of Research, Development, Test and Evaluation, FY 1977,* Statement to the 94th Congress, 2d Session, February 3, 1976, p. III–38; Rumsfeld, Donald H., *Annual Defense Department Report, FY 1977,* pp. 89–90; Ulsamer, Edgar, "Strategic Warning, Cornerstone of Deterrence," p.

47; DMS Market Intelligence Report, Electronic Systems Volume, OTHR, December 1975, p. 2.

37. *Ibid.;* Moorer, Thomas H., testimony before the Senate Armed Services Committee, February 5, 1974, p. 9 of the prepared statement; Brown, Harold, *Department of Defense Annual Report for FY 1979,* p. 123.

38. EC-121s now in operation are effective in detecting low-flying aircraft only over open water. Brown, Harold, *Department of Defense Annual Report for FY 1979,* p. 122. Supplemented by JCS (J-5) on April 20, 1978.

39. Brown, Harold, *Department of Defense Annual Report, FY 1979,* pp. 121–122.

40. The NORAD command center, buried deep in Cheyenne Mountain outside Colorado Springs, is less secure since Soviet SS-18s were first deployed in 1975. If it were lost early in a nuclear war, the U.S. early warning net would be less flexible. Freed, David, "NORAD Complex Now 'Vulnerable'," *Colorado Springs Sun,* July 28, 1977, p. 1.

41. Written comments by Air Force Assistant Chief of Staff for Studies and Analysis, June 18, 1976.

42. Brown, George S., *United States Military Posture for FY 1978,* pp. 24–25.

43. *Air Force and Space Digest, Almanac Issue,* September 1961, pp. 118–122.

44. Quester, George H., "Population Defenses: Have We Been Through It All Before?" *Public Policy,* Fall 1970, p. 723; and *Army Blue Book,* Vol. I, 1961, p. 289.

45. For characteristics of Hawk and Hercules missiles, see *The World's Missile Systems,* 2d Ed. Washington: General Dynamics, October, 1975, pp. 176–182.

46. U.S. Congress. House Document No. 432. *United States Defense Policies in 1959.* 86th Congress, 2d Session. Washington: U.S. Govt. Print. Off., 1960, pp. 38–39.

47. Brown, Harold, *Department of Defense Annual Report for FY 1979,* p. 121.

48. Brown, George S., *United States Military Posture for FY 1978,* pp. 28–29.

49. Conversations between the author and air defense specialists with NORAD and JCS (J-5) on December 14, 16, 1977. Brown, Harold, *Department of Defense Annual Report, FY 1979,* pp. 120–121.

50. *Ibid.*

51. The SA-10, with a speed approximating Mach 5 and acceleration up to 100 times the force of gravity, has recently been deployed, according to Rowland Evans and Robert Novak, "Does Russia's SA-10 Eclipse the Cruise Missile?," *Washington Post,* February 17, 1978, p. A–17. DIA analysts that date, in telephonic conversation, said acceleration claims in that article "overstated capabilities by a magnitude of five." They predict deployment in "two or three years."

52. Brown, George S., *United States Military Posture for FY 1978,* pp. 25, 27.

53. "Civil Defense in the Mid-1970s and Beyond" (in-house draft), Defense Civil Preparedness Agency, February 14, 1975, p. 18. Quotes Defense Secretary McNamara.

54. *Ibid.*, pp. 17–18, 33, 42–44.

55. *Ibid.*

56. See, for example, Schlesinger, Arthur M., Jr., *A Thousand Days.* Boston: Houghton Mifflin Co., 1965, p. 748.

57. "Civil Defense in the Mid-1970s and Beyond," pp. 43–46.

58. A key study group stated, "The Federal, State, County, and municipal governments should begin immediately to develop coordinated evacuation plans which could be put into effect without delay in the event of an emergency." *Report of Project East River, Part I, "General Report,"* Associated Universities, Inc., New York, July 15, 1952, p. 80.

59. Laird, Melvin R., *Annual Defense Department Report for FY 1973,* pp. 78–79. Some of the 250 urban centers actually are fourth priority high-risk areas. They are preceded by about 150 military installations; industrial, transportation, and logistics facilities that support military activities, including Washington, D.C.; and other basic

industries/facilities that "contribute significantly to the maintenance of the U.S. economy." *High Risk Areas*. Washington: Defense Civil Preparedness Agency, April 1975. 107 pp.

60. Representative Soviet writings on the subject include Yegorov, P. T., Shlyakhov, I. A., and Albin, N. I., *Civil Defense: A Soviet View*. Translated and ed. by Oak Ridge National Laboratory. Published under auspices of the U.S. Air Force. Washington: U.S. Govt. Print. Off., no date. 374 pp.; and Titov, N. M., Yegorov, P. T., Gayko, B. A., and others, *Civil Defense*. Translated and ed. by G. A. Cristy, Oak Ridge National Laboratory, (Document ORNL-TR-2845), July 1975. 118 pp.

Unclassified U.S. studies include Gouré, Leon, *War Survival in Soviet Strategy*. Center for Advanced International Studies, University of Miami, 1976, 218 pp.; *Industrial Survival and Recovery After Nuclear Attack: A Report to the Joint Committee on Defense Production, U.S. Congress*. Seattle: The Boeing Aerospace Company, November 18, 1976, 81 pp.; and U.S. Congress. House. *Civil Defense Review*. Hearings by the Civil Defense Panel of the Subcommittee on Investigations of the Committee on Armed Services. 94th Congress, 2d Session. Washington: U.S. Govt. Print. Off., 1976, 428 pp.

61. Titov, M. N. et al., *Civil Defense*, pp. v, vii, 23–25; Gouré, Leon, *Soviet Civil Defense in the 1970s*. Center for Advanced International Studies, University of Miami, September 1975, pp. 50–56.

62. Gouré, Leon, *War Survival in Soviet Strategy*, pp. 131–160.

63. Leon Gouré, T. K. Jones, George J. Keegan, and Harriet Fast Scott are among authoritative students of Soviet civil defense. All generally concur (as Jones put it before the Joint Committee on Defense Production in November 1976) that "Soviet preparations substantially undermine the concept of deterrence that forms the cornerstone of U.S. security."

64. Gailar, Joanne S. and Wigner, Eugene P., "Civil Defense in the Soviet Union," *Foresight*, May-June 1974, p. 10; and "Will Soviet Civil Defense Undermine SALT?," *Human Events*, July 8, 1972, pp. 497–498. The latter article refers to Wigner's original estimate in "The Myth of Assured Destruction," *Survive: An American Journal of Civil Defense*, July-August 1970, pp. 2–4.

65. U.S. Congress. Senate. *Analyses of Effects of Limited Nuclear Warfare*. Committee Print. Prepared for the Subcommittee on Arms Control of the Committee on Foreign Relations. Washington: U.S. Govt. Print. Off., 1975, pp. 112, 119; *Post Nuclear Attack Study (PONAST) II* briefing prepared by Studies Analysis and Gaming Agency, Joint Chiefs of Staff, May 23, 1973. See also, Kozicharow, Eugene, "Nuclear Attack Survival Aspects Studied," *Aviation Week and Space Technology*, November 14, 1977, pp. 52–54.

66. Wigner, Eugene P., *The Myth of Assured Destruction*, p. 4.

67. Brown, Harold, *Department of Defense Annual Report, FY 1979*, p. 64.

68. La Rocque, Gene R., "Danse Macabre in a Divided Ballroom," *New York Times*, October 14, 1976, p. 37; see also "The New Nuclear Strategy: Battle of the Dead?," *Defense Monitor*. Washington: Center for Defense Information, July 1976, 8 pp.

69. Aspin, Les, "Soviet Civil Defense: Myth and Reality," *Arms Control Today*, September 1976, p. 1–4.

70. Bradsher, Henry S., "Civil Defense Plans Compared," *Washington Star*, November 9, 1976, p. 2.

71. Imaginative Soviet approaches to ASW problems are outlined in Bradsher, Henry, "Vulnerability Growing for U.S. Sub-Based Missiles?," *Washington Star*, December 12, 1977, p. 1.

72. A case could be built for more and bigger U.S. ballistic missiles, more MIRVs, and MARV if the Soviets deployed a credible ABM system and/or secured major elements of the population and production base in hard shelters. Deterrence would be

well served, because U.S. weapons that survived a first strike would be numerous enough and possess sufficient lethal power to saturate defenses and ensure Assured Destruction.

73. Sun Tzu, circa 500 B. C. or thereabouts, was the first towering strategic theoretician to put his thoughts on paper. No one in the twentieth century has a better feel for concepts and constraints. Most of his ideas make just as much sense in the Nuclear Age as they did in the Classical Era. Two of his premises are particularly applicable to this text. "To subdue the enemy without fighting," he said, "is the acme of skill." Soviet leaders seem to understand that "what is of supreme importance in war is to attack the enemy's strategy," if they intend to attain that aim. "The worst policy," in his opinion, "is to attack cities," since the cornered foe will likely fight to the death. Assured Destruction policies would not have pleased him. Sun Tzu, *The Art of War*. Translated and introduced by Samuel B. Griffith. New York: Oxford University Press, 1963, pp. 77–79.

74. Liddell Hart, B. H., *Strategy*, 2d Rev. Ed. New York: Praeger, 1967, p. 339.

PART V

General Purpose Force Trends

America's army and tactical air power are designed primarily to help NATO allies deter, and if need be defeat, Soviet armed aggression in Europe. Navy and Marine needs are more global in nature, but preserving sea lanes for NATO takes a high priority.

Simultaneously, without undercutting those essentials, U.S. general purpose forces should be sufficient to discourage Soviet aggression elsewhere, if it endangers U.S. security; deal with such ventures if they do develop; and cope with selected contingencies caused by other countries, when U.S. decision-makers deem armed force advisable. Robbing Peter to pay Paul, as we did during the Vietnam and Yom Kippur Wars, intensifies risks in Western Europe, where we can ill afford it.

Coverage herein consequently compares total U.S. and Soviet general purpose forces, service by service, with the focus on flexibility. Regional interactions are reviewed in Book III, which assesses NATO and Warsaw Pact partners.

Soviet Strength in Context

Soviet aims that conceivably could conflict with U.S. regional interests are increasingly ambiguous.

Fifteen years ago, there was little question in the minds of U.S. leaders or among the American people that international communism, controlled by Moscow, was an immediate military threat to Free World survival and security.

Potential perils to the United States currently are less explicit. A subtle blend of political, military, economic, and psychological powers, applied indirectly, has been the preferred Soviet instrument since the Cuban missile crisis, our last armed confrontation. Even Brezhnev's attempt at brinkmanship during the Arab-Israeli showdown in 1973 was low key in comparison with probes that directly endangered U.S. security in the post-World War II period.[1] Proxies now substitute for Soviet troops in the Middle East, Africa, and South Asia.

The steady buildup of Soviet general purpose force strength, however, is creating a new strategic environment. Their posture is increasingly characterized by offensive capabilities not present in the past. Future risk-versus-gain ratios consequently could slant in Soviet favor if progress is one-sided.

Changing American Strategy

U.S. general purpose force goals and policies are shaped by many considerations. Those discussed below directly affect the U.S./Soviet military balance.

Shifts in U.S. Purpose

U.S. regional security aims stem from interests identified in Book I. A few are fairly constant. Most, however, have changed since the 1950s. Nearly all have scaled back, although the challenge increased. Only one, deterrence, has strengthened. (See Graph 9.)

A key U.S. goal, subscribed to by four Presidents (Truman, Eisenhower, Kennedy, and Johnson), was "containment", despite the demands of conservative critics, who called for "rollback". The original intent was to stop "Communist expansion . . . . without resorting to total war, if that be possible to avoid."[2] We meant to deter and, if required, defeat that foe everywhere in whatever disguise.[3]

"Winning" conventional conflicts, however, ceased to be a solid aim in the traditional sense when U.S. limited war concepts started to surface in Korea, although men like General Douglas MacArthur saw no suitable substitute.[4] Limited strife between the United States and Soviet clients could cause costs to escalate unacceptably even then, five years before the Kremlin deployed intercontinental delivery systems.[5] Once Moscow amassed its missile strike force, regional combat in context with U.S./Soviet competition could quickly become "irreversibly irremediable", as one expert put it.[6]

Defeating subversive insurgencies first surfaced as an American aim in Greece, China, and the Philippines well before 1961, when Nikita Khrushchev proclaimed communism's "sacred duty" to sponsor and/or support "just wars of national liberation" around the world.[7] Presidents Johnson and Kennedy both accepted that position as "a

Graph 9

U.S. General Purpose Force Goals

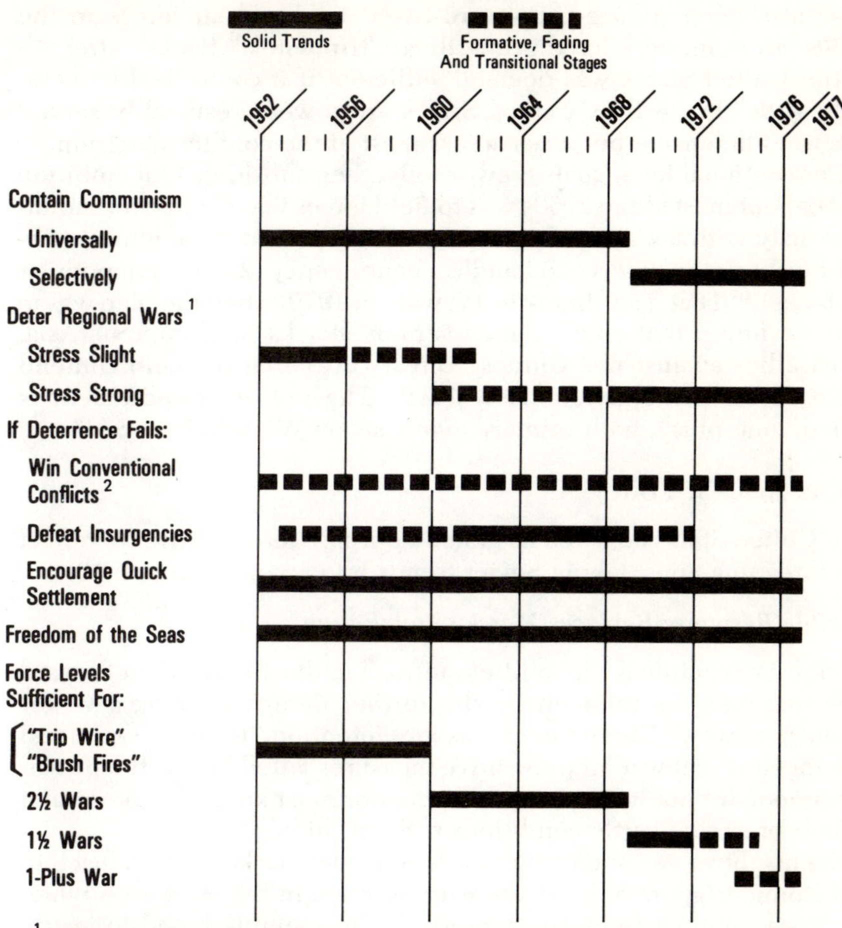

[1] Conventional conflicts and insurgencies.

[2] "Winning" never explicitly excluded as a U.S. goal. No test case involving Soviet allies since Korea. Last clear indication of resolve to "win" by military means came during the Cuban missile crisis, when U.S. invasion forces actually assembled.

challenge we must meet if we are to defeat the Communists,"[8] but sad experience in Vietnam cut that objective short.

The goal of curbing Soviet influence by military means under all conditions therefore gave way gradually to selective containment, which is closely linked with our search for a stable world balance. Deterring local, as well as global, wars has become the basic U.S. aim.[9] If deterrence should fail for any reason, attempts to stabilize the situation swiftly and conclude any conflict on favorable terms now would take top priority in most instances.

Freedom of the seas, as a U.S. objective, dates to the eighteenth century. (See naval section for discussion.)

America's general purpose force goals, which long were unrealistic, have also been reduced. Forward-based land and air forces in the 1950s, for example, served primarily as "trip wires." Backup strength in the United States was deemed sufficient if it could deal successfully with "brush fires", since SAC's air power presumably served deterrent/defensive purposes across most of the conflict spectrum.

Conventional force goals grew briefly, then subsided. Our ambition throughout most of the 1960s was to field forces that could cope simultaneously with major conflagrations in Europe *and* Asia, while withholding assets in reserve to handle a contingency (2½ wars in popular parlance).[10] That goal shrank to 1½ wars in 1970, when the plan was to provide forces that could stanch serious attacks in Europe *or* Asia, assist allies against non-Chinese threats in the Orient, and contend with a lesser emergency elsewhere.[11] The present requirement is called "one plus", with primary emphasis on Western Europe.[12]

Shifts in U.S. Policy

The United States adjusted its general purpose force policies to reflect the foregoing aims, taking Soviet trends into account. (Graph 10).

Flexible Response Replaces Massive Retaliation

Modest conventional capabilities sufficed in the 1950s, when forward defenses were "reinforced by the further deterrent of massive retaliatory power." There never was any intention "to turn every local war into a global war" if preventive measures failed but, as the principal proponent put it, "a potential aggressor must know that he cannot always prescribe battle conditions that suit him."[13]

Events, however, indicated that U.S. leaders lacked the stomach to trip atomic triggers in local altercations, even in the early days when we were immune from direct reprisal. Ends simply failed to justify such means. President Truman, in fact, refrained from using nuclear weapons in Korea on *any* scale, although many detractors disagreed with that decision.[14]

The search for more versatile policies centered on perceived needs "to react across the entire spectrum of possible challenge . . . . It is just as necessary to deter or win quickly a limited war as to deter general war. Otherwise, the limited war which we cannot win quickly may result in our piecemeal attrition or involvement in an expanding conflict. . . . "[15]

That thesis was repudiated when it came to a vote by the Joint Chiefs of Staff in March 1956, but was resurrected by President Kennedy five years later. It has been in effect ever since. The term "Flexible Response" is no longer fashionable, but the policy still is to maintain a full range of options.

Graph 10

U.S. General Purpose Force Policies

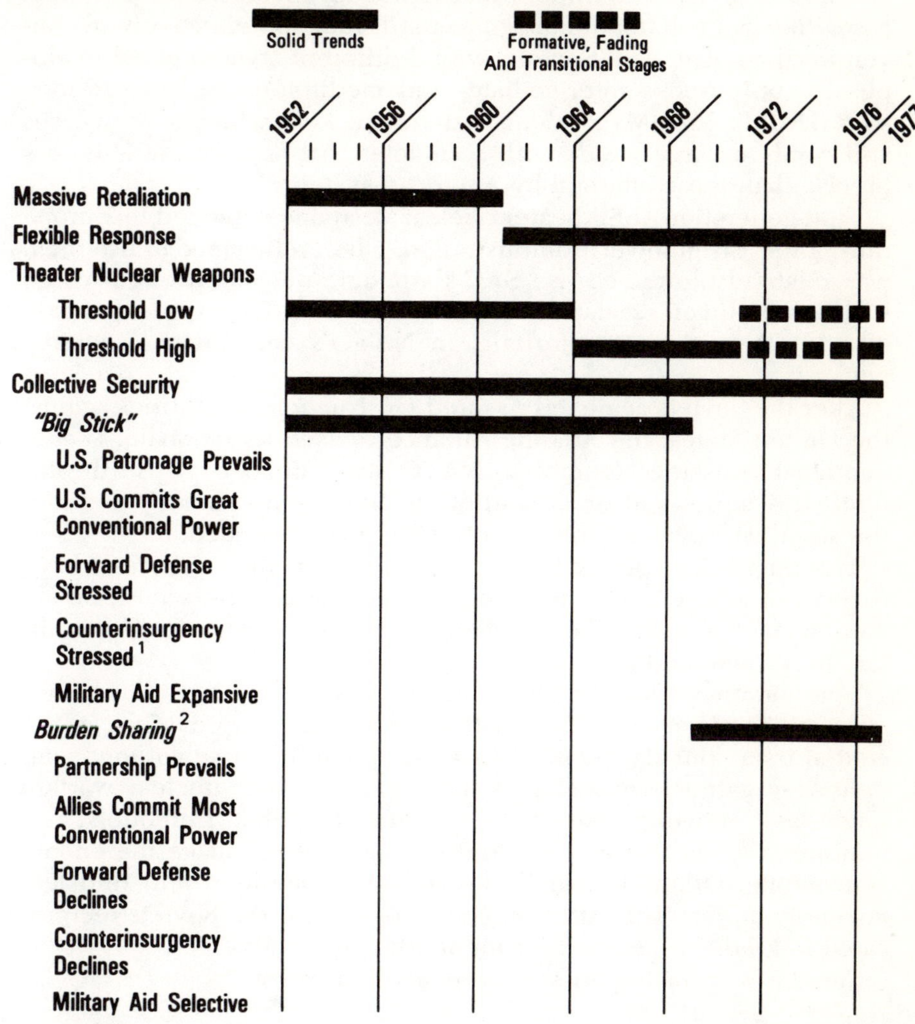

[1] Beginning in 1961.

[2] Originally called the Nixon Doctrine. The name has been dropped, but the concept stays constant.

The Role of Theater Nuclear Weapons

Nuclear weapons, originally suitable only for strategic bombardment purposes, were adapted for battlefield use in the 1950s. Land- and carrier-based tactical aircraft, tube artillery, free rockets, a variety of guided missiles, and atomic demolitions all put in an early appearance as delivery systems.

America's defense decision-makers experimented with all or most before deciding to stress adaptable aircraft and artillery. Our systems are designed to deliver small, accurate nuclear weapons in crowded spots, such as NATO Europe, without causing unconscionable civilian casualties and collateral damage, yet still function effectively in conventional combat. The Soviets, with a different style, elected to emphasize unipurpose intermediate- and medium-range ballistic missiles (IRBMs, MRBMs),[16] along with free rockets, which in most cases still combine large yields with accuracies that are considerably less precise than those attained by American systems.[17]

First-generation U.S. theater nuclear weapons deployed to Europe during the Eisenhower Administration, when reluctance to use them was relatively low, because SAC's strategic nuclear strength could still clamp a lid on escalation if conflict occurred. The express purpose was to offset obvious shortfalls in NATO's conventional combat power.[18]

After the Soviets achieved Assured Destruction capabilities against the United States, the Atlantic Alliance revised its rationale. If conventional resistance crumbled, NATO still intended to use theater nuclear weapons after consultation among members,[19] but the threshold was raised[20] and "hair-trigger" plans receded.

Theater nuclear policy today is again in transition. Interests have revived in smaller, "cleaner", more discrete weapons, whose timely employment in emergency might reduce requirements for U.S. military manpower and materiel.[21]

The tendency toward a lower nuclear threshold, however, encourages critics. They cite U.S. inability to control any conflict as the central issue, but also contend that risks could increase without compensatory gain, because forces needed for theater nuclear warfare might well outweigh those for conventional combat. Defenders, as a minimum, would depend on sufficient strength to make the enemy concentrate. Otherwise, mass destruction weapons would find few favorable targets. U.S. attrition could be rapid if the Soviets reciprocated in kind.[22] (See Book III for additional details.)

Some compromise policy thus seems imperative.

Collective Security

Collective security has been a pillar of U.S. defense policy since World War II, although interpretations have undergone a marked metamorphosis in recent years. The concept is increasingly restrictive.

Characteristics Through 1968 When America's aim was to contain communism universally and deal successfully with all manner of regional wars, U.S. collective security policy was calculated to underwrite world order. The pattern established by President Truman was perpetuated by Eisenhower, Kennedy, and Johnson.

Security Commitments Successive Administrations, with congressional concurrence, created a global alliance system between 1947 and the mid-1960s, during Cold War confrontations that preceded the present period called "detente". The current list (Figure 16) includes eight mutual defense pacts, whose membership totals 40 countries. Executive agreements and other formal pledges tie us to something like 30 more, not counting emotional and moral commitments not confirmed in writing.[23] U.S. support for Israel lies in the latter category.[24] As President Carter indicated on May 12, 1977, "We have a special relationship with Israel. It's absolutely crucial that no one in our country or around the world ever doubt that our number one commitment in the Middle East is to protect the right of Israel to exist, to exist permanently, and to exist in peace. It's a special relationship."

The United States, in accord with such agreements, is theoretically duty bound to help defend Latin America, most of Western Europe, and several countries (such as Japan, Taiwan, and the Philippines) along the Sino-Soviet rim. (See Map 9.) Responsibilities, however, are ranked in order of priority. None, for example, are nearly as compelling as those connected with NATO, and none are so specific. Automatic response is not a requirement even there, but cumulative assurances nevertheless are considerable (Annex F).

The Soviet Union, in contrast, has concluded alliances with many countries that speckle Asia, Africa, and the Middle East, not to mention Cuba (Figure 17),[25] but solid defense commitments still seem to be slanted toward satellite states, notably the Warsaw Pact (Annex G) and North Korea.[26]

Except for Canada and Mexico, U.S. lines of communication to allies have always crossed high seas.[27] Soviet commitments until recent times were reserved essentially for countries reached by rail and road.

Asymmetries between American and Soviet force structures accommodate those conditions. The U.S. Navy, for example, accents carrier-based fighter, attack, and reconnaissance aircraft that can conduct campaigns where support from shore-based counterparts could prove impractical or impossible.[28] The Soviet Navy, which had no need in the past, is just starting to deploy high performance carrier air power. U.S. strategic airlift capabilities also surpass the Soviets'. They accurately reflect requirements to move men and materials rapidly to far distant points. Longstanding Soviet superiority in conventional sealift has been an anomaly in this context.

FIGURE 16 U.S. Collective Security System

MULTILATERAL TREATIES

Inter-American Treaty of Reciprocal Assistance (Rio Pact) 1947[1]

United States	Dominican Republic	Nicaragua
Argentina	Ecuador	Panama
Bolivia	El Salvador	Paraguay
Brazil	Guatemala	Peru
Chile	Haiti	Trinidad and Tobago
Colombia	Honduras	Uruguay
Costa Rica	Mexico	Venezuela

North Atlantic Treaty (NATO) 1949

United States	Iceland	Portugal
Belgium	Italy	United Kingdom
Canada	Luxembourg	Greece (1952)
Denmark	Netherlands	Turkey (1952)
France	Norway	Federal Republic of Germany (1955)

Security Treaty between the United States and Australia and New Zealand (ANZUS) 1951

United States	New Zealand
Australia	

Southeast Asia Collective Defense Treaty (SEATO) 1954[2]

United States	Philippines
Australia	Thailand
France	United Kingdom
New Zealand	

BILATERAL TREATIES

U.S.-Canada Permanent Joint Board on Defense Declaration (1940)
Mutual Defense Treaty with the Philippines (1951)
Mutual Defense Treaty with South Korea (1953)
Mutual Defense Treaty with Republic of China (Taiwan) (1954)
Treaty of Mutual Security and Cooperation with Japan (1960)
Treaty of Friendship and Cooperation with Spain (1976)

[1]Cuba was excluded from the Rio Pact in 1962.

[2]The Southeast Asia Treaty Organization held its last meeting on June 30, 1975, but the Treaty remains in effect for those countries shown. The security of Thailand remains a U.S. commitment as expressed in the Treaty and in the 1962 Rusk-Thanat communique, although the force of each is subject to debate. All other SEATO countries remain linked to the United States through additional multilateral or bilateral treaties, as shown. The Republic of Vietnam, Laos, and Cambodia were not SEATO signatories, but were covered by a protocol.

CONGRESSIONAL RESOLUTIONS

There have been five Congressional resolutions since 1945. Each of these has been requested by the President to mobilize Congressional support at times of foreign policy crisis. Dates of the joint resolutions refer to the day they were signed into law. The date for H. Con. Res. 570 is the day the resolution was cleared by Congress. It did not require the President's signature and does not carry the force of law.

Formosa resolution, H.J. Res. 159, Jan. 29, 1955, covering Formosa (Nationalist China) and the Pescadores Islands against "armed attack" from Communist China.

Middle East resolution, H.J. Res. 117, March 9, 1957, proclaiming U.S. policy to defend Middle East countries "against aggression from any country controlled by international communism."

Cuban resolution, S.J. Res. 230, Oct. 3, 1962, to defend Latin America against Cuban aggression or subversion and to oppose the deployment of Soviet weapons in Cuba capable of endangering U.S. security.

Berlin resolution H. Con. Res. 570, Oct. 10, 1962, reaffirming the U.S. determination to use armed force, if necessary, to defend West Berlin and the access rights of Western powers to West Berlin.

Vietnam resolution, H.J. Res. 1145, Aug. 10, 1964, known as the Tonkin Gulf resolution, authorizing the President to use armed forces to repel attacks against U.S. forces and affirming U.S. determination to defend any SEATO treaty member or protocol state requesting assistance.

EXECUTIVE AGREEMENTS

The United States has entered defense arrangements by executive agreement with the following countries:

Denmark 1951
Iceland 1951
Spain 1953
Canada 1958
Liberia 1959
Iran 1959
Turkey 1959
Pakistan 1959
Philippines 1959, 1965

POLICY DECLARATIONS, COMMUNIQUES

The State Department's 1967 compilation of U.S. commitments includes 34 Executive Branch policy declarations and communiques issued jointly with foreign governments. The following areas and nations are covered by these pledges: Latin America (Monroe Doctrine), Berlin, Iran, India, Jordan, Israel, Thailand, South Vietnam, the Republic of China, and the Philippines.

With the exception of India and Israel, these policy declarations and communiques cover nations which also have received U.S. pledges under treaties, executive agreements or Congressional resolutions.

Map 9

U.S. AND SOVIET SECURITY TREATIES

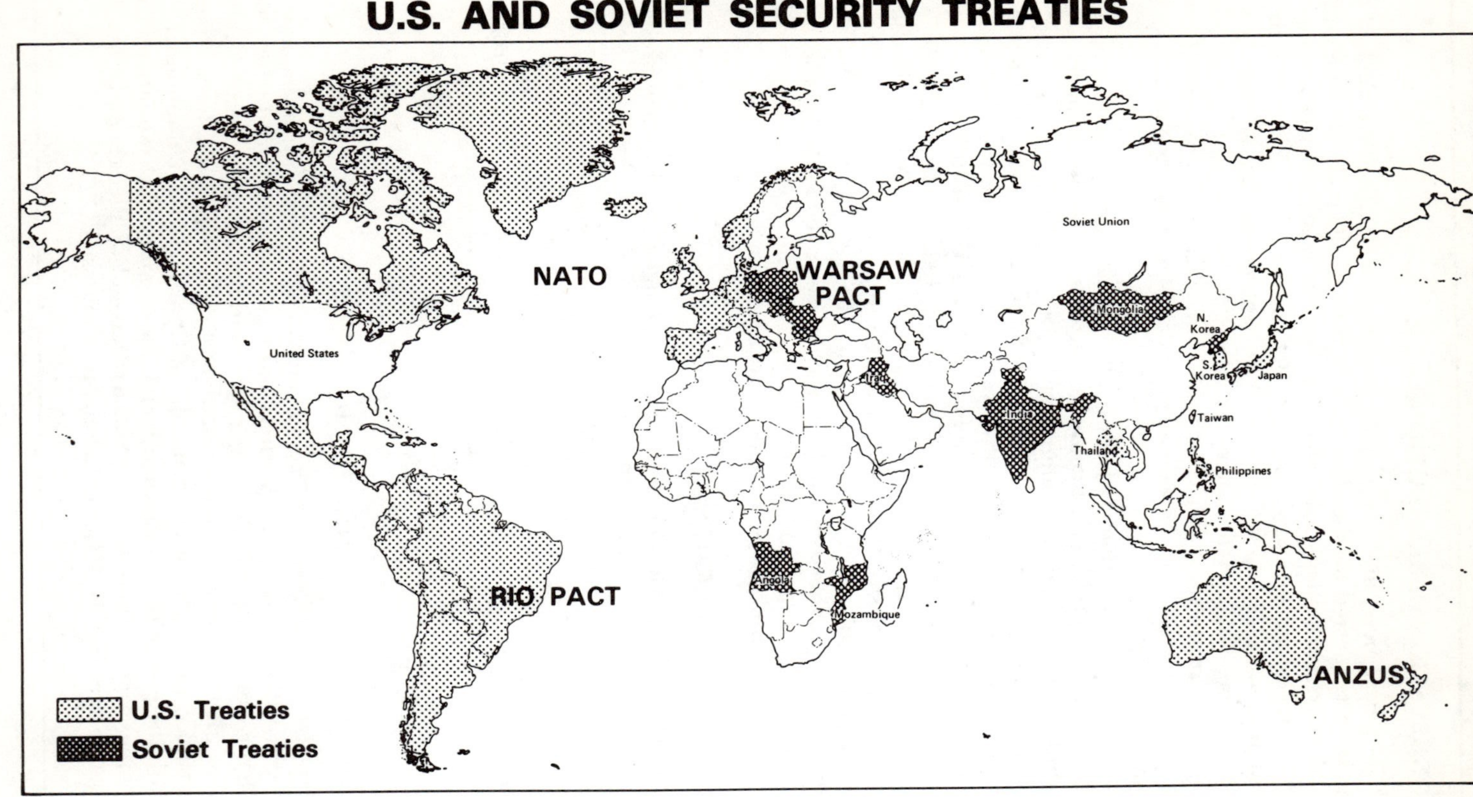

FIGURE 17 Soviet Collective Security System

MULTILATERAL TREATY

The Warsaw Treaty of Friendship, Cooperation, and Mutual Assistance 1955

Union of Soviet Socialist Republics	Hungary
Bulgaria	Poland
Czechoslovakia	Romania
German Democratic Republic	

BILATERAL TREATIES[1]

Treaties of Friendship, Cooperation, and Mutual Assistance

Angola (1976)	Iraq (1972; 1976)
Bulgaria (1967)	DPR Korea (1961)
Czechoslovakia (1970)	DPR Mongolia (1966)
German Dem. Rep. (1964; 1975)	Mozambique (1977)
Hungary (1967)	Poland (1965)
India (1971)	Romania (1970)

[1]The Treaty of Friendship, Cooperation, and Mutual Assistance between the USSR and Somalia, concluded in November 1974, was abrogated by Somalia on November 14, 1977. Diplomatic relations with Cuba were also severed by Somalia.

U.S. Contributions When U.S. patronage prevailed, we provided a strategic nuclear shield for the entire Free World, plus the lion's share of materiel support, funds, and (in many cases) conventional forces as well. That trend, established when our most effective allies were still recovering from the ravages of World War II, was little altered after they regained full strength.

In consonance with the policy of forward defense, American bases proliferated along the Sino-Soviet periphery. Discounting peaks during the Korean and Vietnam Wars, we habitually positioned approximately a quarter of our armed forces outside the Continental United States through 1968, afloat and in 30 some foreign countries. More than half were dedicated to or associated with NATO. Most of the remainder were in the Pacific and around the rim of Asia.[29]

To buttress the military capabilities of our allies, we sponsored expansive military assistance programs (MAP), beginning in 1947. Grant aid in the form of free arms, equipment, training, and services was originally bestowed on "forward defense countries", but 78 states eventually were recipients, despite charges that many of them were only remotely associated with U.S. national security needs.[30]

Current Characteristics About the time that unequivocal containment of communism expired as an American security objective, a collection of other compelling pressures, mainly the Vietnam War and economic problems, prompted new policies aimed at better burden sharing.

Partnership In place of patronage, we now strive to institute genuine partnerships. America will no longer conceive *all* the plans, design *all* the programs, and execute *all* the defense under any conditions. U.S. leaders promise to "provide a shield if a nuclear power threatens the freedom of a nation allied with us or of a nation whose survival we consider vital to our security", but "in cases involving other types of aggression . . . we shall look to the nation directly threatened to assume the primary responsibility of providing the manpower for its defense." That is not to say that the United States will arbitrarily abstain from committing armed forces in such conflicts. The policy still provides for U.S. military participation whenever "our interests dictate, but as *a* weight—not *the* weight—in the scale."[31]

Adjustable forward defense policies have derived from those guidelines. The Administration proposes to continue a strong U.S. presence in Europe until mutual force reductions can be negotiated with the Soviet Union.[32] In contrast, our military silhouette in Southeast Asia and the Western Pacific shrank in the early 1970s[33]; then stabilized, except for Korea.[34]

Military Aid Whereas U.S. bounties once were broadcast with abandon, security assistance has become circumspect. Even so, military aid in the Nixon and Ford Administrations retained an authoritative role, to sustain allied support of American interests, despite our reduced presence.[35]

That concept, however, is now in decline. Grant aid, which totalled $5.7 billion in FY 1952, was reduced to $250 million in FY 1978. Distribution currently is confined to eight countries. Credit and cash sales soon will replace all "giveaway" programs.[36] The consequences, which are still unclear, cause continuing concern in Congress.

Counterinsurgency Concepts U.S. counterinsurgency concepts, which had been evolving since the early 1960s, took an entirely different tack.

The failure of American arms to attain victory in Vietnam at any acceptable cost caused U.S. leaders to redefine relationships between "helpers and the helped". Present policy stresses preventive measures, rather than military action, with the local populace, not U.S. forces, as prime participants.[37]

Force Comparisons

U.S. general purpose forces, within the framework just described, have developed quite differently than Soviet counterparts.

Soviet leaders, who implicitly prefer a Principle of War called Mass, rarely reduce force levels, and winnow out stocks only when they cease to serve useful purposes.[38] U.S. defense decision-makers are partial to Economy of Force.[39] Quality, not quantity, is considered essential. America's armed services consequently are cut severely after every war. Outmoded weapons customarily retire when new ones enter the inventory.[40]

Soviet strength thus most often dilates, even when ours declines.[41] U.S. quality at this stage can no longer compensate completely for the lack of flexibility caused by quantitative inferiority.

Armies

A mammoth conscript army is the traditional source of Soviet general purpose force strength.[42] Other services are subsidiary, despite the emergence of a modern air force and navy. The much smaller U.S. Army currently consists of volunteers. Quantitative gaps that favor the Soviet Union are great in nearly every category.

Components

U.S. and Soviet land power is predicated on assorted branches of service that, when combined, can conduct conventional and nuclear operations in accord with assigned roles and missions. (See Part II and Figure 18.)

Combat Arms

Both sides are built around combat arms that superficially seem similar, but there are basic differences in structure and balance.

The U.S. Army, never intrinsically intended for combat in the United States, is tasked to fight wherever American interests are put in possible peril. That involves lands where mountains, jungles, swamps, and/or cities are the foremost features. Consequently, traditional infantry, free to move when other forces are mired, takes up to a third of our active maneuver strength, 45 percent including airborne and airmobile elements, more than half if reserve components count.[43]

Not so in the Soviet Union, which possesses unsurpassed maneuver room. There are no "foot soldiers" in Soviet Ground Forces. All infantry, from rifle squad to regiment, rides to keep up with tank troops, whose ratio compared with other combat arms is much higher than that of any prospective opponent. Neither the United States nor NATO has any such strength.[44]

Soviet forces allocated to battlefield air defense (which are different than and separate from the PVO) are present in proportions that U.S.

FIGURE 18 U.S. AND SOVIET GROUND ARMS AND SERVICES

United States	Soviet Union
Combat Arms	
Armor	Artillery
Air Defense Artillery	Air Defense
Engineers[1]	Airborne Troops
Field Artillery	Motorized Rifle
Infantry[2]	Tank Troops
Combat and Service Support	
Adjutant General	Administrative
Chaplains	Chemical
Chemical	Engineers
Judge Advocate	Highway Commandant
Medical	Intendance[3]
Military Intelligence	Justice
Military Police	Medical
Ordnance	Motor Transport
Quartermaster	Radio Technical[4]
Signal	Railway Troops
Transportation	Road (Building) Troops
	Signal
	Topopgraphic
	Transportation
	Veterinary

[1]U.S. engineers perform many support missions, but the branch as a whole is considered a combat arm.
[2]U.S. infantry includes mechanized, airborne, airmobile, and foot soldiers.
[3]Intendance is similar to U.S. quartermaster.
[4]Includes radar and electronic warfare.

units do not duplicate. So is field artillery,[45] in conformance with concepts that call for mass. Airborne troops, in contrast with U.S. counterparts, comprise a separate branch.[46]

Support Forces

Combat arms cannot exist without support forces to feed, clothe, shelter, arm, equip, maintain, administer, discipline, transport, and control the establishment. Both sides consequently maintain a sizable complement of service troops.

Some asymmetries shown on Figure 18 are mainly semantic. U.S. and Soviet designations differ, but the duties are identical. Several, however, are substantive. The Communist Party, for example, permits no equivalent of our chaplains. Internal security troops of the MVD, supplemented by militia and traffic control detachments from motor transport, take the place of U.S. military police. Chemical corps show in both columns, but ours is insignificant, while Soviets in that field are strong.[47]

The U.S. Army consolidates more support functions in fewer services than are found in Soviet Ground Forces. Scales that balance our combat forces with backup, however, sag under the weight of support elements, reflecting a persistent trend that dates from the Civil War.

The proportion of Army combat troops to organic and direct mission support, which excludes central supply, maintenance, training facilities, and administrative overhead, is of greatest concern to Congress. Still, using the Army's *total* strength as the criterion, support personnel outnumbered combat personnel at their peak in Vietnam by more than 3-to-1 (77.8 to 22.2 percent), versus 2-to-1 during the Korean conflict.[48]

That increase can be traced to technological advances and tactical refinements. Progress improved combat effectiveness, thereby reducing requirements for front-line soldiers. Battle casualty rates were cut in half, from 6.4 to 3.6 per 1,000, because fewer men were exposed to hostile fire and medical coverage was better. Modern weapons, however, demand more attention. Support costs climbed simultaneously, until they consumed anywhere from a quarter to half the defense budget in the early 1970s, depending on who did the counting.[49]

The U.S. Army has redressed "tooth-to-tail" ratios in recent years, by adding active combatants while slicing service support. Current reliance on reserve components for support courts calculated risks that some officials accept and others would like to skirt.[50]

Soviet Ground Forces, in search of extra staying power, expanded supporting services during that same period, but their proportion of "teeth-to-tail", while closer to ours than in the past, no doubt will never coincide. Force configurations and doctrines are too different.[51]

Military Doctrines

U.S. and Soviet doctrines for land combat share few similarities. Theirs is predicated on offensive operations, from a strategic standpoint. Ours, in essence, stresses defense.

U.S. Concepts

"We cannot know when or where the US Army will again be ordered into battle," but it "must, above all else, *prepare to win the first battle of the next war,*" because the first could well be the last, if we lose it. Once that end has been achieved, our Army aims at "emerging triumphant from the second, third, and final battles," if a series is essential.[52]

U.S. ground combat forces, if committed against Soviet counterparts, would (in some crucial cases) face a foe that could initiate conflict at his convenience, with sophisticated weapons, quantitative superiority, and short supply lines. Our side, as Army strategists see it, must be sufficiently strong *"to fight outnumbered and win."*[53]

Compulsory emphasis on economy of force, coupled with second-strike, selective containment policies, dictates a defensive posture for our Army at the onset of any conflict against powerful opponents, such as major Soviet forces or the Warsaw Pact.

That demand denies us initial initiative, but defense dispenses advantages that can be decisive: intimate knowledge of terrain, including avenues available to aggressors; cover and concealment; obstacles; and mutually supporting positions, with the best possible observation and fields of fire for flat trajectory weapons, such as small arms, machine guns, and wire-guided missiles. Defenders consequently should be able to defeat attackers, as long as "they are never outnumbered or outgunned more than 3:1 at the point and time of decision."[54]

Soviet armored spearheads could quickly penetrate traditional U.S. defenses, which deployed most strength along a single thin line, backed by modest reserves.[55] U.S. commanders instead are advised to concentrate winning combinations at proper times and places, "using reserves from the rear" and forces "from less threatened flanks," which remain lightly covered. Should concentration occur at the wrong spot, the mission is to countermarch mobile elements immediately. Success is contingent in any case on sound intelligence and "continuous, reliable, secure communications," because "outnumbered forces cannot afford mistakes."[56]

"The farther forward the battle can be fought, the better," but "defense must be elastic—not brittle." Successive positions in depth are preferable to strong points, where U.S. forces could be bypassed or fixed impotently by the foe's pressure.[57]

Offensive action *"is a vital part of all [U.S. Army] defensive operations."* Sallies against "weakened enemy elements" take precedence over "sweeping counterattacks which expose our forces to heavy losses." Such steps should be condoned "only when the gains to be achieved are worth the risks" involved in surrendering crucial advantages available to defenders.[58]

Should concentrated forces fail to achieve requisite "combat power ratios, then . . . . commanders must trade space for time," compelling aggressors to assault successive positions at great expense, while friendly forces drop back until reinforcements arrive, or they are overrun.[59]

Army doctrine recognizes that *"delay is the most demanding of all ground combat operations.* It requires highly competent, well-trained small units, and skillful small unit leaders."[60] It is also contingent on defensible terrain (delay on a tabletop would be tantamount to defeat); uncommitted troops to take up the slack; and sufficient space to trade along with front-line forces before time runs out, and retrograde actions turn into rout.

Finally, "firepower saves manpower and thus saves lives." Whether on offense or defense, the U.S. Army looks to the "new lethality" of modern weapons linked with modern mobility as a substitute for shortages. "Swiftly massed field artillery, totally mobile tank and mechanized infantry battalions, airmobile antiarmor weapons, attack helicopters, close air support aircraft and, in some circumstances, tactical employment of nuclear weapons offer us the means to concentrate overwhelming combat power and to decisively alter force ratios when and where we choose."[61]

Soviet Concepts

Soviet Ground Forces, much larger than U.S. counterparts, have developed a piledriver doctrine that relies somewhat less on finesse. Five proven Principles of War predominate: Objective; Offensive; Surprise; Maneuver; and Mass.[62]

Doctrine from Stalin's time until the late 1960s put a premium on defense, designed to protect Mother Russia by repelling invaders.[63] Offensive concepts have since replaced that passive scheme. The absolute aim is victory, complete and unequivocal, regardless of how the conflict starts or which side is responsible.[64] Limited war strategies, which settle for less, are conspicuous by their absence.

Soviet Ground Forces since the 1950s have been developing dual capabilities to conduct conventional and theater nuclear operations separately or in combination. The latter take top priority. Key leaders concede that combat conceivably could include a sustained conventional stage at the onset, but see no cleancut "firebreak".[65] On the contrary, all systems, counting chemical, are considered part of a package.[66]

Staging for assaults takes place in short periods to ensure surprise. Dispersed forces take full advantage of darkness and foul weather to avoid detection. Deception plans assist.[67]

Prodigious firepower preparations, calculated to create shock effects, most often precede attempts to penetrate. Divisions then attack on narrow fronts, massing combat power that sometimes outstrips defense at points of decision by several orders of magnitude. Regiments and larger elements commonly deploy in two echelons. Armies and fronts may form three waves to overwhelm the enemy.[68]

When the crust cracks, Soviet armored formations on multiple axes seek to fan out fast, driving for deep objectives.[69] The main mission is to maintain momentum. Heliborne forces seize river crossings; parachute troops drop farther out. Follow-on forces take over whenever spearheads slow. They bypass bottlenecks where necessary, but otherwise "pass through". Depleted divisions are replaced. Sustained rates of advance under conventional conditions should average 30 km (18 mi) per day against determined defense, according to Soviet doctrine. Nuclear weapons would double that prospect. Quick success compensates for heavy casualties, which commanders anticipate and accept.[70]

The whole concept bears some semblance to fluid Nazi-style Blitzkrieg operations, but supplements high-speed maneuver with massed firepower to a much greater extent.[71] Mobile artillery, including air defense guns and missiles, moves with every element down to regimental level. Hand-held Grails (like our Redeyes) are found in rifle companies. Breakthrough forces consequently feature lethal power along with psychological leverage.[72]

Soviet doctrine deems defense a temporary expedient (as U.S. doctrine once did), adopted only when circumstances compel, for the shortest possible periods.[73] It combines offensive and defensive characteristics, with massed fires and maneuver supporting positions in depth. Strong counterattacks by tanks receive special stress. No other army has practiced chemical, biological, and radiological (CBR) defense as religiously in peacetime.[74]

Interactions

Both sides confront doctrinal dilemmas, when faced with the other's stance.

U.S. Doctrinal Difficulties Critics take U.S. doctrine to task on several counts concerning objectives and tactics. Basic disagreements and point-by-point rebuttals have appeared in the press.[75]

Defensive U.S. postures, for example, are political facts of life at present. Soviet Ground Forces currently can mass superior military power. America's Army leaders contend that those conditions *compel* them to adopt an aim called "fight outnumbered and win".[76] Detractors, who deplore doctrinal accommodations of that sort, suggest that U.S. decision-makers would do well to "redesign . . . . our military force posture and possibly our diplomatic commitments," rather than encourage a "can-do" attitude in the Army that risks almost certain defeat.[77]

The Army's aim of winning the first battle "is not a short war concept." Rather, it attempts to offset "assumptions which have governed US military policy in the past: that time and material will eventually rectify an initial disadvantage," after American reserves from CONUS reach the scene of combat.[78] Critics, however, ask an annoying question. If there is a *second* battle, will winning the first help or hinder? Soviet doctrine, after all, allows for winning with follow-on waves, and accepts the loss of the first. "In some circumstances," therefore, concentrating "all efforts on winning the first battle" could "leave [U.S.] forces deployed in the wrong places for meeting a second [and decisive] thrust."[79]

Firepower doctrines embrace maneuver, and vice versa, but in different proportions and for different purposes. Forces devoted to the former seek to close with and destroy the enemy. Mobility merely puts firepower in place. Maneuver doctrines, by way of contrast, substitute balance for brute force to break the opponent's will. Firepower facilitates, but killing hostile troops is incidental. Maneuver advocates argue that our Army would do well to consider "ju jitsu", instead of a slam-bang defense that pits U.S. forces against numerically superior Soviets. Skeptics say the Army has no choice, since most opportunities to maneuver over large areas are open to the *offensive* side, which strives to seize, rather than safeguard, objectives.[80]

Finally, critics score any "precisely choreographed" U.S. "rolling defense" that depends on "reinforcing laterally with on-line battalions from the flanks," followed by "a series of well-timed withdrawals to prepared secondary . . . . positions." Such a procedure, they say, is sufficiently complicated in peacetime, when unopposed.[81] Under pressure, it could prove impossible. U.S. success, for example, relies extensively on electronic intelligence, but the Soviets assemble and attack in radio silence. They are also expert at disrupting communications. That capability has great significance, since our side needs tight command/control to concentrate power properly, then redeploy in response to changing conditions.[82]

Soviet Doctrinal Difficulties Soviet doctrine considers shock action[83] as a *strategic* tool to influence conflict at theater level.[84] Among land forces, tanks en masse, accompanied by mechanized firepower and mobile infantry, perform that mission best. As the opening move of any major war, Soviet concepts therefore call for armor to exploit penetrations made by other means,[85] perhaps including tactical nuclear weapons. The task is to envelop enemy defenses at an early stage.[86]

Armor, however, currently is confronted by precision-guided munitions and swarms of antitank (AT) missiles. Its future has been less secure since Israel suffered staggering losses during the 1973 Yom Kippur conflict.[87] Heliborne hunter-killers, with special capabilities and limitations, cause particular problems,[88] when mixed with man-packed systems and weapons mounted on trucks.

"Using *Soviet* figures," for example, a motorized rifle division "committed to high-intensity operations would be completely expended after *five days*." Total loss rates of "30 percent over some seven days as an average," including those in armored divisions, are indicated.[89]

Soviet decision-makers now debate the subject. The susceptibility of highly-touted BMP personnel carriers to AT weapons "starts a chain reaction which seems to threaten the entire structure of Soviet offensive doctrine. If BMPs are significantly more vulnerable than tanks they are accompanying, they may be destroyed at a much faster rate; the infantry may then have to dismount in order to carry out the attack on foot . . . ." Tanks in such case must proceed unescorted, at increased risk, or reduce the speed of attack. Either event would adversely affect offensive plans predicated on speed to enhance shock.[90]

Three possible cures appear to be considered.

Armored vehicles would be less vulnerable in nuclear environments. Enemy defenders would have to disperse to survive, and riflemen could ride rapidly through wrecked positions. Massive suppressive fires from conventional artillery might accomplish the same task, if weapons were well-protected and self-propelled. The third choice would capitalize on surprise, speed, and offensive flexibility—mainly maneuver, instead of fire. Whether one course or some combination will carry still is not clear.[91]

How well service support could keep pace stirs contention in any case. Soviet combat-to-support ratios currently are such that "not much more can be squeezed from the lemon." Changes now in progress stress improved staying power "right across the board."[92] Until programs pay off, however, logistic shortcomings could cut combat capabilities sharply after the first few days.

Tools of the Trade

Tools of the trade that give substance to U.S. and Soviet ground force doctrines for land combat include manpower, firepower, and mobility components. Comparative summaries follow. (See Graph 11 and Figures 21–22 at the end of this section.)

Comparative Manpower

Armies everywhere are still manpower intensive, even in this mechanized age. Active deployable personnel strengths displayed in Figure 21 thus are significant.[93]

U.S. Army rolls, drastically reduced by retrenchment after the Vietnam War, bottomed out at 420,000 in 1972, then began to recover by swapping overhead for sinew within a constant ceiling.[94] Still, Soviet increases during this decade cause the net U.S. loss to total almost half a million men. Soviet personnel, less command/support, now outnumber our own by almost three-to-one (1,722,000 to 598,000).[95]

Comparative Firepower

Firepower statistics in Figure 22 speak for themselves. Soviet quantitative superiority stands in stark relief. Qualities are competitive with (sometimes superior to) U.S. counterparts. A new main battle tank, a fine armored fighting vehicle (the BMP), a family of battlefield air defense weapons, and several artillery pieces, two self-propelled, are being deployed at rather rapid rates. Our Army's much-discussed main battle tank, infantry/cavalry fighting vehicle (IFV/CFV), and Patriot air defense system are still in gestation.

All the same, the U.S. Army has access to firepower unprecedented in its past. The "new lethality" is not just a slogan.

American tank gunners in World War II, for example, could puncture fewer than five inches of frontal armor plate on a German Panther at 500 meters. Sharpshooters in our current M-60s can score through nearly twice that thickness at four times the range. Armed with TOW AT weapons,[96] they expect first-round hits 9 out of 10 times at 3,000 meters. Stabilized turrets and night sights enable tanks to acquire and attack targets on the move, in daylight or darkness. What they see, they can stop.[97]

U.S. AT systems not only exceed the range of Soviet tank cannons, but possess penetration powers that outpaced armor protection anywhere in the Warsaw Pact by the mid-1970s.[98]

Improved artillery ammunition can cause up to four times as many personnel casualties per round as conventional high explosives could in past conflicts. Projectiles with time-delay submunitions extend suppression capabilities for protracted periods after impact. Laser range finders for forward observers reduce target estimation errors from 400 meters to about 10, hugely increasing probabilities of first-round hits. Response times have been cut from minutes to seconds. Precision-guided artillery projectiles, when perfected, should cause a quantum jump in destructive power.[99]

The U.S. Army R&D community increased land mine lethality dramatically during this decade, while decreasing size. Tactical commanders now can sow large fields in front of or atop advancing enemy troops in a matter of minutes, using an interim system scattered by helicopters.[100] Artillery-delivered mines are scheduled to follow. That tack immensely improves American AT capabilities, by channeling enemy approaches and slowing rates of advance.[101]

Comparative Mobility

Both sides are highly mobile. The Soviets specialize in armored personnel carriers and assorted fighting vehicles, some on wheels, others on tracks. The latest versions are amphibious. All are easily air transportable. Every front-line soldier reportedly rides. The U.S. Army lags.[102]

Heliborne forces, however, can move about the battlefield eight times faster than mechanized infantry and 20 times as fast as "foot sloggers".[103] U.S. Army utility helicopters still hold a strong edge, but Soviet forces are closing fast in numbers and know-how. (See Part VI for added discussion.)

Major Maneuver Units

Any army's cutting edge comprises maneuver and fire support components, of which divisions most affect the U.S./Soviet military balance. The following discourse compares overall structures, before assessing debits and credits on both sides.

Comparative Organization

U.S. and Soviet ground forces feature similar building blocks that fit many combinations:

United States	*Soviet Union*
	Front
Corps	Army
Division	Division
Brigade/Regiment	Regiment
Battalion/Squadron	Battalion
Company/Battery/Troop	Company/Battery
Platoon	Platoon

Each Soviet front typically contains three or four combined arms armies (15–20 divisions), one tank army (4–5 divisions), a tactical air army, and appropriate support.[104] This country has no counterpart. U.S. army groups, along with field armies, disappeared in the early 1970s.[105]

The largest U.S. maneuver units are corps, which equate most closely with Soviet armies. Both control two or more divisions, commonly four or five. Both have combat and support functions. Forces Command at Fort McPherson, Georgia, controls our two CONUS-based corps in peacetime. Theater headquarters take charge overseas. If conflict occurred, operational responsibility for committed U.S. corps would pass from those static centers to a combined command (such as NATO's Central Army Group), a joint U.S. task force (JTF) of two or more Services, or to a reconstituted field army. In special cases, corps carry out missions independently.[106]

Primary maneuver power on both sides is vested in divisions. The U.S. Army concentrates on three types: armored, mechanized, and infantry. Two divisions, one airborne, one air assault, add special capabilities. Motorized rifle and tank divisions contain most Soviet strength. Seven airborne divisions add flexibility. (See Figures 19–20 for comparative structures.)

Figure 19.
SOVIET DIVISION ORGANIZATION

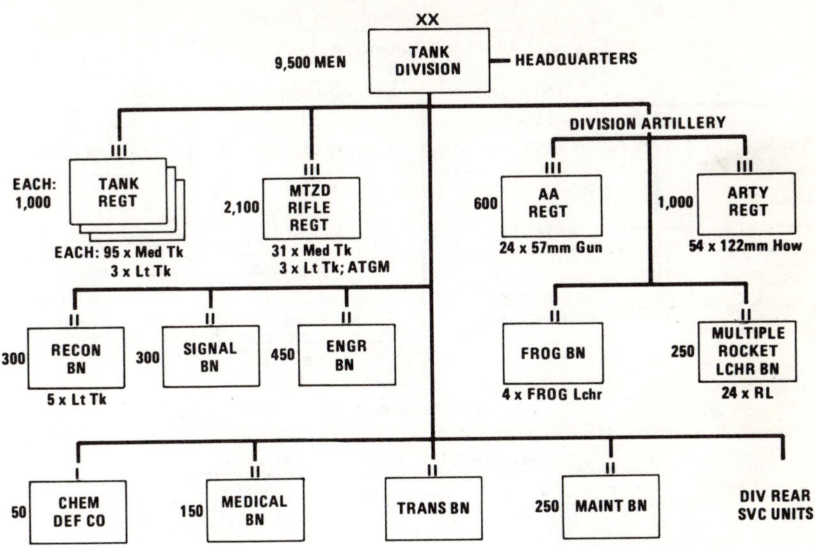

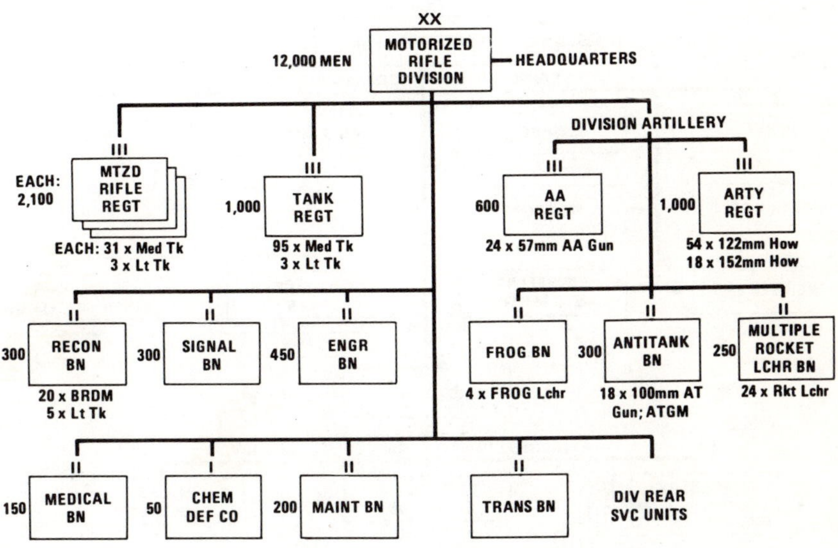

NOTES: 1. Motorized Rifle Battalions may have more than 31 tanks.
2. Tank Divisions have about 150 aromored carriers; Motor Rifle Divisions have about 375.
3. Light AA and AT weapons are omitted.

Figure 20.
U.S. DIVISION ORGANIZATION

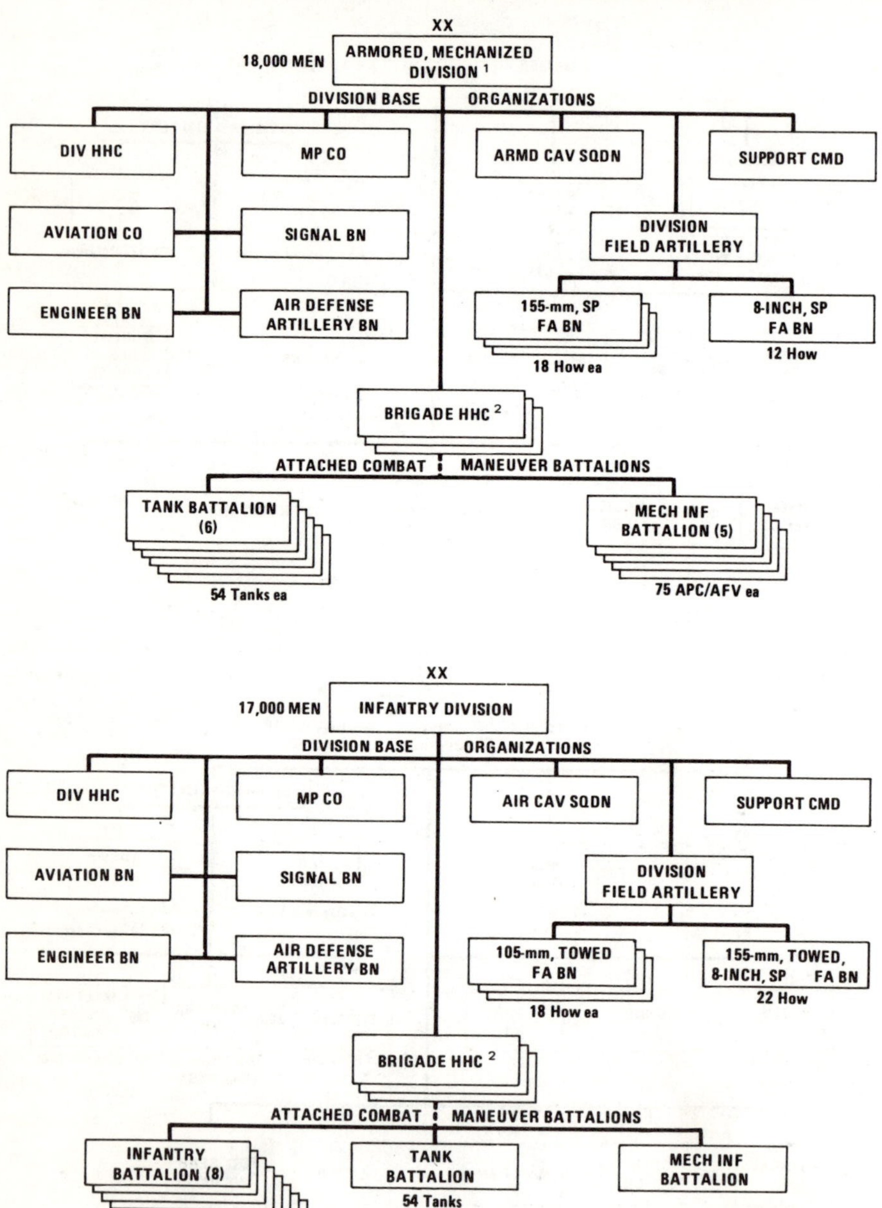

[1] Armored Division has 6 Tank, 5 Mech Battalions. Mechanized Division has 6 Mech and 4 Tank Battalions. Otherwise, organization is similar.

[2] Battalions are attached to brigades in the mix and for times desired.

Soviet divisions contain fewer troops than U.S. counterparts. Firepower is comparable or superior in most respects, but staying power is less commendable.

Ready Divisions

The U.S. Army has never exceeded 16 active divisions since 1970. A maximum of about 19 might be attained if All-Volunteer Force recruiting standards were relaxed or incentives raised.[107] (Figure 23).

Four Army divisions lack one regular brigade. Others lack one or more active maneuver battalions. Division readiness is unavoidably reduced, even though reserve component "roundouts" receive priority treatment and train part time with parent units.[108]

A fourth of our active divisions are stationed in Western Europe as part of NATO's on-site deterrent. Three in CONUS are earmarked to reinforce that force in emergency.[109] One is in Korea. Perhaps six in the United States should serve as a rotation base for troops returning from overseas.[110] Thus, only two divisions (one in CONUS, one in Hawaii) are free for contingency purposes without spreading the force very thin or federalizing parts of the National Guard.

Five separate brigades and three armored cavalry regiments (ACRs) afford extra U.S. strength, but are not the equivalent of two or three divisions, because they lack staying power and the capacity for large-scale combined arms action. Three brigades serve special purposes in Alaska, Berlin, and Panama. Two ACRs and equipment for the third (now in CONUS) are positioned in Germany. Only two brigades remain in general reserve.

In contrast, 55 Soviet Category I divisions are kept at 75–100 percent of top personnel strength, with complete equipment. Another 32 in Category II maintain average manning levels of about 60 percent. All officers, non-commissioned officers (NCOs), and key specialists are on tap to train as teams. Materiel shortages are minor. Experienced fillers thus can bring 87 divisions close to full strength in a few days.[111]

Capabilities in the recent past have been buttressed considerably by beefing up manpower and firepower. Each tank division has 1,000 more men than in 1970, mainly mechanized infantry. Motor rifle divisions each have been bolstered by 2,000 troops and 67 tanks. Both types are buttressed with additional artillery, some of it self-propelled. Personnel strengths stay small compared with U.S. counterparts, but striking power is potent.[112]

Nevertheless, the reservoir of Soviet ready divisions is reduced by restrictions much like our own.

Thirty-one of those ready divisions form the core for four Groups of Forces stationed in European satellites. Twenty-one that act as Warsaw Pact reinforcements are conveniently located in Military Districts abutting Russia's western border. Twenty-four more man the Chinese frontier. Ten are held in strategic reserve, including seven airborne divisions. Guards divisions around major cities, like Moscow and Leningrad, never move far from home stations. Perceived requirements, of course, could change, but few of the 87 ready divisions currently are uncommitted.[113]

First-Line Reserves Since most U.S. and Soviet ready divisions are tied to continuing tasks, first-line reserves fulfill a crucial function.[114]

Eight Army National Guard (ARNG) divisions comprise the U.S. complement.[115] That number has stayed constant since 1968. Fifteen separate brigades and three armored cavalry regiments not affiliated with active division roundout or augmentation programs complete the list of major maneuver units in the U.S. reserve.

ARNG infantry divisions, as a general rule, would require 10 weeks of intensive preparation before being fully ready to fight, although deployment might take place a month earlier in emergency. Post-mobilization training for armored and mechanized divisions would take almost four months, if tank gunners and signal troops in particular were allowed time to attain proficiency. Minimum combat standards could be achieved in nine or ten weeks.[116] Any National Guard division, however, could replace Regular Army forces in CONUS soon after entering federal service.

Nothing in the Soviet inventory is really comparable to our National Guard.

Twenty-some-odd so-called "mobilization divisions", not carried on active order of battle lists, could fill in 30 days, but manning levels now are minimal (200–300 men), stocks are in dead storage, and training would take several months.[117]

Eighty-four Category III divisions come closer to corresponding with U.S. reserve components, although all have substantial active elements. The best are at about one-third strength. The poorest are simply cadres, that total 10 percent. Combat equipment is almost complete, if elderly items count. Severe transport shortages would be solved in crises by taking trucks from the civil economy.[118]

Most such divisions, being stationed in densely populated regions with many reservists, could fill in about three days. Delays would be longer for those that rely on distant replacements. Redeployment to relieve Category I and II divisions in static sectors could commence as soon as units were up to strength, but considerable cramming would be required to create cohesive divisions.[119] Total elapsed times would be directly proportionate to training standards and percentages on active duty.

The Soviet aggregate, 11 times larger than our National Guard, allows the Kremlin latitude not available to U.S. leaders. Twenty-five Category III divisions stand guard along the Sino-Soviet frontier.[120]

Forty along western borders back up the Warsaw Pact. About twenty remain as first-line strategic reserves.

Marines and Naval Infantry

The main mission of U.S. Marines is to seize and secure hostile coasts by amphibious assault,[121] but the Corps is capable of sustained operations ashore, independently or in concert with our Army, if assisted logistically.

Active ground force components comprise 70,000 men in three divisions that are backed by extensive combined arms combat and service support.[122] (See Figures 21–23.)

Three divisions are positioned to cope promptly with assorted global contingencies and, after assembly, could contribute significantly to U.S. deterrent/defense capabilities vis-a-vis the Soviet Union. If those forces were committed, the Marines' reserve division/wing team would provide the sustaining base.[123]

Soviet naval infantry, with a total strength of 12,000, compose six regiments of fewer than 2,000 men each. As currently constituted, with minimum fire support and not much staying power, they are suitable mainly for commando-style raids and amphibious operations close to Soviet flanks.[124]

Combined Land Force Flexibility

U.S. active ground combat power, pooled with that of allies, presently serves deterrent purposes in Northeast Asia and NATO Europe. Five divisions (two Army, three Marine) are free to contend concurrently with contingencies elsewhere, if the situation stays stable in those theaters. Additional "brush fires" adverse to American interests would burn beyond our control, unless we called up reserves. Such action, however, could dilute essential U.S. deterrent powers by reducing abilities to reinforce rapidly at either point of primary decision.

Soviet flexibility seems more favorable. As matters now stand, Moscow has 30 divisions in strategic reserve, including 10 that are combat ready.

None, however, have recently been deployed beyond Soviet borders, except in satellite states, and abilities to sustain large-scale forces on far foreign shores are subject to serious question.[125] Proxies, largely Cubans, take their place.

The likelihood thus seems low that Soviet divisions will be used for distant initiatives in the short-range future. Immense geographic impediments and mobility problems inhibit employment in hot spots, such as the Middle East.[126] Huge Soviet reserves consequently bolster Warsaw Pact capabilities, as assessed in Book III, but bear less on the global balance.

Graph 11

SELECTED GROUND FORCE STRENGTHS COMPARED
Statistical Summary
(Note Different Scales)

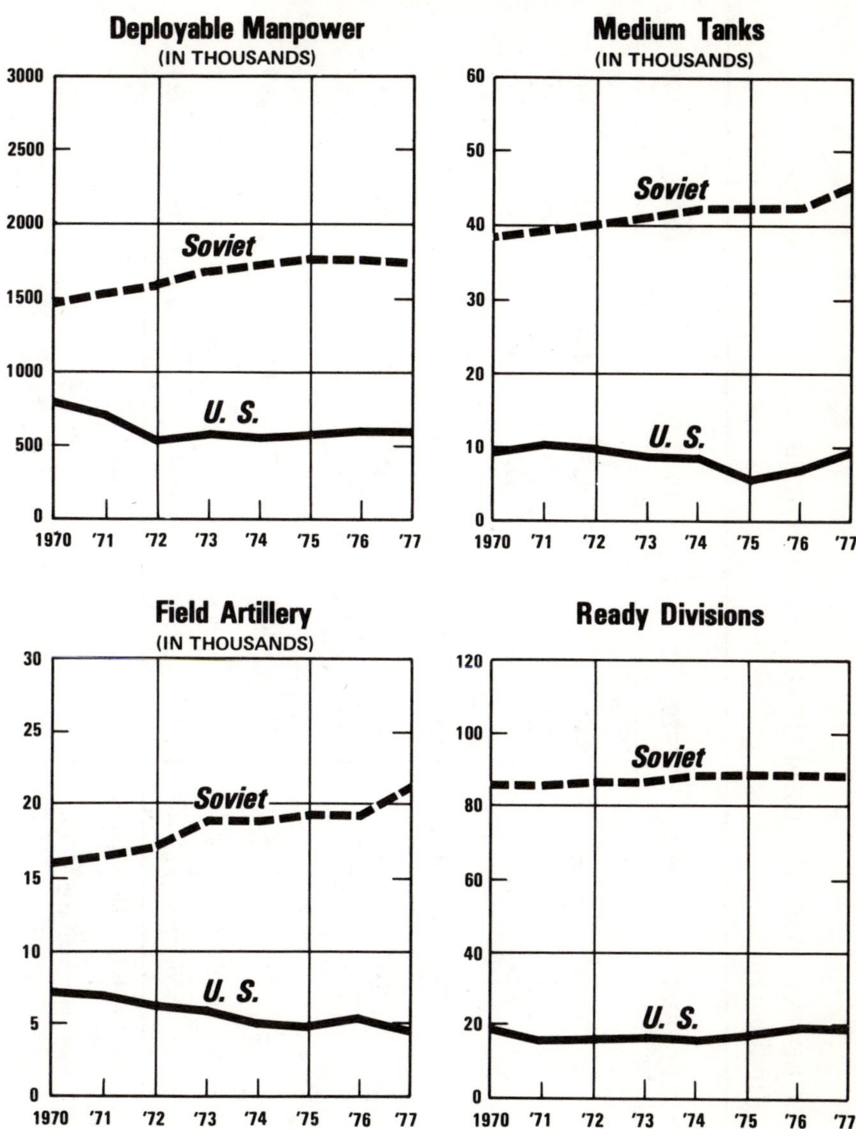

NOTE: U.S. includes Army and Marines.

FIGURE 21. GROUND FORCES, DEPLOYABLE MANPOWER
(in thousands)

	1970	*1971*	*1972*	*1973*	*1974*	*1975*	*1976*	*1977*	*Net Change 1970–77*
United States									
Army[1]	684	594	420	477	463	485	502	501	−183
Marines[2]	121	99	93	98	94	101	99	97	− 24
Total	805	693	513	575	557	586	601	598	−207
Soviet Union[3]									
Army	1,450	1,510	1,570	1,650	1,700	1,720	1,725	1,710	+260
Naval Infantry	10	10	10	11	11	12	12	12	+ 2
Total	1,460	1,520	1,580	1,661	1,711	1,732	1,737	1,722	+262
U.S. Standing									
Army	− 766	− 916	−1,150	−1,173	−1,237	−1,235	−1,223	−1,209	−443
Marines/Naval Infantry	+ 111	+ 89	+ 83	+ 87	+ 83	+ 89	+ 87	+ 85	− 26
Total	− 655	− 827	−1,067	−1,086	−1,154	−1,146	−1,136	−1,124	−469

[1]U.S. Army strengths include field commands and mission-oriented base operating support.
[2]Marine air wings are excluded.
[3]Soviet forces exclude command and general support forces.

FIGURE 22 SELECTED GROUND FORCE WEAPONS
Statistical Trends and System Characteristics

Ground Combat Weapons	*1970*	*1971*	*1972*	*1973*	*1974*	*1975*	*1976*	*1977*	*Net Change 1970–77*
ARMY									
HEAVY AND MEDIUM TANKS									
United States	9.520	10,180	9,435	8,430	8,400	5,195	6,265	9,465	−55
Soviet Union	38,000	39,000	39,500	40,500	42,000	42,000	42,000	45,000	+7,000
U.S. Standing	−28,480	−28,820	−30,065	−32,070	−33,600	−36,805	−35,735	−35,535	−7,055
LIGHT TANKS[1]									
United States	1,660	1,600	1,600	1,575	1,575	1,570	1,570	2,065	+405
Soviet Union	3,000	3,000	3,000	3,000	3,000	3,000	3,000	3,000	0
U.S. Standing	− 1,340	− 1,400	− 1,400	− 1,425	− 1,425	− 1,430	− 1,430	− 935	+405

[1]U.S. light tanks indicate Sheridan armored assault vehicles.

FIGURE 22 (Con't)

Ground Combat Weapons	*1970*	*1971*	*1972*	*1973*	*1974*	*1975*	*1976*	*1977*	*Net Change 1970–77*
ARMY									
APC/AFV[1]									
United States	11,875	13,000	11,860	11,775	10,510	10,480	11,245	11,370	–505
Soviet Union	30,000	30,000	30,000	35,000	35,000	38,000	38,000	44,000	+14,000
U.S. Standing	–18,125	–17,000	–18,140	–23,225	–24,490	–27,520	–26,755	–32,630	–14,505
ARTILLERY									
United States	6,885	6,635	5,840	5,540	4,710	4,625	4,885	4,440	– 2,445
Soviet Union	16,000	16,500	17,000	18,500	18,500	19,000	19,000	21,000	+ 5,000
U.S. Standing	– 9,115	– 9,365	–11,160	–12,960	–13,790	–14,375	–14,115	–15,562	– 7,445
ANTI-TANK GUIDED MISSILES									
United States	2,710	11,770	21,415	32,695	44,690	64,690	77,105	123,100	+120,390
Soviet Union	4,500	4,700	4,800	5,000	5,500	6,000	6,000	7,000	+ 2,500
U.S. Standing	– 1,790	+ 7,010	+16,540	+27,620	+39,115	+58,600	+71,105	+116,100	+117,890

[1]Armored personnel carriers (APC) and armored fighting vehicles (AFV) include wheeled and tracked vehicles.

Ground Combat Weapons	*1970*	*1971*	*1972*	*1973*	*1974*	*1975*	*1976*	*1977*	*Net Change 1970–77*
ARMY									
HEAVY MORTARS[1]									
United States	*	*	1,530	1,603	1,597	1,574	1,687	1,685	+ 155
Soviet Union	5,000	6,000	7,000	7,000	7,000	7,100	7,200	7,200	+2,200
U.S. Standing	*	*	−5,470	−5,397	−5,403	−5,526	−5,513	−5,515	− 45[2]
TACTICAL MISSILES[3]									
United States									
Pershing	108	108	108	108	108	108	108	108	0
Lance	0	0	6	24	36	42	48	48	+ 48
Total	108	108	114	132	144	150	156	156	+ 48
Soviet Union									
SCUD	300	300	300	350	400	400	450	500	+ 200
FROG	500	550	600	650	650	650	650	650	+ 150
Total	800	850	900	1,000	1,050	1,050	1,100	1,150	+ 350
U.S. Standing	− 692	− 742	− 786	− 868	− 906	− 900	− 944	− 994	− 302

[1]Heavy Mortars are U.S. 4.2-inch and Soviet 120mm and 240mm mortars.
[2]U.S. net change since 1972.
[3]Numbers indicate launchers, not missiles.
*Data not available.

FIGURE 22 (Con't)

Ground Combat Weapons	*1970*	*1971*	*1972*	*1973*	*1974*	*1975*	*1976*	*1977*	*Net change* 1970–77
U.S. MARINES									
Medium Tanks	175	175	175	175	175	175	175	176	+1
LVTPs	330	330	525	525	525	525	525	470	+140
Artillery	250	250	250	250	270	270	270	276	+ 26
Antitank Missiles	0	0	0	0	0	0	70	144	+144
Heavy Mortars	0	0	18	18	18	18	18	18	+18
SOVIET NAVAL INFANTRY									
Light Tanks	140	140	175	175	175	200	200	200	+ 60
APC/AFV	500	500	600	600	600	750	750	750	+250
Heavy Mortars	120	120	150	150	150	180	180	180	+ 60
Antitank Missiles	60	60	75	75	75	90	90	90	+ 30
GRAND TOTALS, ARMY/MARINES									
Medium Tanks									
U.S.	9,695	10,355	9,610	8,605	8,575	5,370	6,440	9,641	–54
U.S.S.R.	38,000	39,000	39,500	40,500	42,000	42,000	42,000	45,000	+7,000
U.S. Status	–28,305	–28,645	–29,890	–31,895	–33,425	–36,630	–35,560	–35,359	–7,054
APC/AFV/LVTPs									
U.S.	12,205	13,330	12,330	12,245	10,980	10,950	11,715	11,841	–364
U.S.S.R.	30,500	30,500	30,600	35,600	35,600	38,750	38,750	44,750	+14,250
U.S. Status	–18,295	–17,170	–18,270	–23,355	–24,620	–27,800	–27,035	– 32,909	–14,614

ARTILLERY									
U.S.	7,135	6,885	6,090	5,790	4,980	4,895	5,155	4,714	−2,421
U.S.S.R.	16,000	16,500	17,000	18,500	18,500	19,000	19,000	21,000	+5,000
U.S. Status	− 8,865	− 9,615	−10,910	−12,710	−13,520	−14,105	−13,845	− 16,286	−7,421
ANTITANK MISSILES									
U.S.	2,710	11,770	21,415	32,695	44,690	64,690	77,175	123,244	+120,534
U.S.S.R.	4,560	4,760	4,875	5,075	5,575	6,090	6,090	7,090	+2,530
U.S. Status	− 1,850	+ 7,010	+16,540	+27,620	+39,115	+58,600	+71,085	+116,154	+118,004
HEAVY MORTARS									
U.S.	*	*	1,548	1,621	1,615	1,592	1,705	1,703	+155
U.S.S.R.	5,120	6,120	7,150	7,150	7,150	7,280	7,380	7,380	+2,260
U.S. Status	*	*	− 5,602	− 5,529	− 5,535	− 5,688	− 5,675	− 5,677	−75

*Not available

FIGURE 22 (Con't)

U.S. GROUND COMBAT
SYSTEM CHARACTERISTICS

	First Deployed	Combat Weight (Tons)	Road Speed (mph)	Range (Miles)	Primary Arm Type	Primary Arm Range (Meters)	Crew/ Passengers	CBR Protection
ARMOR								
TANKS								
M-48A3	1963	52	30	310	90mm	900	4	No
M-60A2	1971	57	30	280	152mm	Classified	4	No
M-60A1, A3	1961/1976	53	30	310	105mm	4,400	4	No
Sheridan	1966	17	43	375	152mm	Classified	4	No
					Shillelagh	Classified		
APC/LVTP[1]								
M-113	1962	12	40	300	50 cal mg	1,000	1/8	No
LVTP-7	1972	25	40	300	50 cal mg	1,000	3/25	No

[1]LVTP speed in water is 7.5 knots; endurance at sea 15 hours.

	Type	*Transport*	*Effective Range (Meters)*	*Nuclear Capable*
ARTILLERY				
175mm	Gun	SP	32,800	No
8-in M-110	How	SP	16,800	Yes
155mm M-109A1	How	SP	18,000	Yes
155mm M-114	How	Towed	14,600	Yes
105mm M-101	How	SP	11,500	No
105mm M-102	How	Towed	11,000	No

ANTITANK GUIDED MISSILES	*Type*	*Caliber*	*Effective Range (Meters)*	*Guidance*	*Weight (lbs)*	*Crew*
Dragon	Medium	5-in	1,500m	Wire	30.5	1
TOW	Heavy	5.8-in	3,000m	Wire	228	4

FIGURE 22 (Con't)

SOVIET GROUND COMBAT
SYSTEM CHARACTERISTICS

	First Deployed	Combat Weight (Tons)	Road Speed (mph)	Aux Tanks (Miles)	Primary Arm Type	Primary Arm Range (Meters)	Crew/ Passengers	CBR Protection
ARMOR								
TANKS								
T-72	1975	40	30	[1]	115mm[1]	1,500	3	Yes
T-62	1962	40	30	310	115mm	1,500	4	Yes
T-55	1961	40	30	375	100mm	1,000	4	Yes
PT-76	1952	14	28	260	76mm	1,000	3	No
APC/AFV								
BTR-152	1959	9	45	390	None		19	No
BTR-50P	1957	15	25	170	None		22	Yes
BTR-60P	1961	10	48	300	None		16	Yes
BMP	1967	14	40	240	73mm	1,000	11	Yes
					Sagger AT	3,000		

[1]T-72 range not available. Gun may be 122mm, which has 2000+ meter range.

	Type	*Transport*	*Effective Range (Meters)*	*Nuclear Capable*
ARTILLERY				
203mm	Gun/How	Towed	27,000	Yes
180mm	Gun	Towed	30,000	?
152mm	Gun/How	Towed	17,000	?
152mm	Gun/How	SP	16,500	?
152mm	How	Towed	12,000	No
130mm	Gun	Towed	27,000	No
122mm	How	SP	15,300	No
122mm	How	Towed	16,000	No
100mm	Gun/AT	Towed	8,500	No

ANTITANK GUIDED MISSILES	*Type*	*Caliber*	*Effective Range (Meters)*	*Guidance*	*Weight (lbs)*	*Number Rails*
Sagger	Medium	5.5-in	3,000	Wire	25	1 on BMP, 6 on BRDM
Swatter	Heavy		2,500	Radio	45	4 on BRDM
"1977 Moscow Parade Missile"	Medium	*	*	*	*	5 on BRDM

*Not available.

FIGURE 22 (Con't)

TACTICAL AIR DEFENSE WEAPONS

	1970	1971	1972	1973	1974	1975	1976	1977	Net Change 1970–77
SAM LAUNCHERS									
United States									
Chapparral	290	435	450	450	435	435	435	435	+ 145
Soviet Union									
SA-4	200	300	400	500	600	700	800	1,000	+ 800
SA-6	30	100	200	300	400	400	500	600	+ 570
SA-8					20	50	100	200	+ 200
SA-9	200	400	700	1,000	1,400	1,700	2,100	2,400	+2,200
Total	430	800	1,300	1,800	2,420	2,850	3,500	4,200	+3,770
U.S. Standing	−140	−365	− 850	−1350	−1985	−2415	−3,065	−3,765	−3,625
A A GUNS									
United States									
Vulcan-SP	259	309	337	332	336	343	328	332	+ 73
Vulcan-Towed	70	165	212	210	186	188	198	211	+ 141
Total	329	474	549	542	522	531	531	543	+ 214
Soviet Union[1]									
ZSU 57/2							400	300	− 100
ZSU 23/4							1,800	2,300	+ 500
ZU 23/2							3,000	2,000	−1,000
57mm 5-60							3,500	3,000	− 500
Total							8,700	7,600	−1,100
U.S. Standing							−8,169	−7,057	+1,112

[1]Soviet statistics for years 1970–1975 are not available. Net change is from 1976 to 1977.

TACTICAL AIR DEFENSE: SYSTEMS CHARACTERISTICS

SAMS	*First Deploy*	*Range (Miles)*	*Target Acquisition*	*Tracking/ Guidance*	*Ceiling (Feet)*	*Speed (Mach)*	*Warhead/ Yield*	*Missiles*
UNITED STATES								
Chapparral M-48	1966	2	Optical	Optical/ IR homing	3,000	Super-sonic	HE	4 rails 1 missile ea
SOVIET UNION								
SA-4 (Ganef)	1967	50	Surveillance and acqui-sition radar	Command guidance	80,000	4	HE 300 lbs	1 launcher 2 missiles
SA-6 (Gainful)	1970	15	Search and acquisition radar	Radar/Comd, semi-active radar homing	40,000	3	HE 100 lbs	1 launcher 3 missiles
SA-8 (Gecko)	1975	7.5	Search and tracking radar	Command guidance	40,000	2	HE 50 lbs	2 launchers 2 missiles ea
SA-9 (Gaskin)	1968	5	Optical	Optical/ IR homing	15,000	2	HE 15 lbs	4 launcher containers

FIGURE 22 (Con't)

TACTICAL AIR DEFENSE: SYSTEMS CHARACTERISTICS

A A GUNS	*First Deploy*	*Range (Meters)*	*Target Acquisition*	*Fire Control*	*Barrels*	*Transport*	*Basic load (Rounds)*
UNITED STATES							
Vulcan XM-167	1966	1500	Visual, w/lead-computing gunsight	Manual/ radar	6 20mm	Towed	2000
Vulcan M-163	1966	1500	& range-only radar	Manual/ radar	6 20mm	SP	2000
SOVIET UNION							
ZSU 23/4	1965	2500	Radar or visual (Visual=2000m range)	Radar or Optical	4 23mm	SP	2000
ZU 23/2	1961	2500	Visual	Optical	2 23mm	Towed	2400 rounds
ZSU 57/2	1957	4000	Visual	Optical	2 57mm	SP	300 rounds
57mm S-60	1950	6000	Radar or visual (Visual =4000m range)	Radar or Optical	1 57mm	Towed	200

FIGURE 23 GROUND FORCE MANEUVER UNITS
Statistical Trends and Division Characteristics

Divisions	*1970*		*1971*		*1972*		*1973*		*1974*		*1975*		*1976*		*1977*	
UNITED STATES[1]																
Army																
Armor	4	2	3	2	3	2	3	2	3	2	4	2	4	2	4	2
Mechanized	4	1	4	1	4	1	4	1	4	1	4	1	5	1	5	1
Infantry	5	5	3	5	3	5	3	5	3	5	4	5	5	5	5	5
Airmobile	2	0	1	0	1	0	1	0	1	0	1	0	1	0	1	0
Airborne	1	0	1	0	1	0	1	0	1	0	1	0	1	0	1	0
Tricap	0	0	1	0	1	0	1	0	1	0	0	0	0	0	0	0
Sub-Total	16	8	13	8	13	8	13	8	13	8	14	8	16	8	16	8
Marine	3	1	3	1	3	1	3	1	3	1	3	1	3	1	3	1
Grand Total	19	9	16	9	16	9	16	8	16	9	17	9	19	9	19	9
SOVIET UNION[2]																
Tank	32	13	32	13	32	14	32	14	32	14	32	14	32	15	32	15
Motor Rifle	46	60	46	63	47	65	47	69	48	68	48	68	48	68	48	68
Airborne	7	1	7	1	7	1	7	1	7	1	7	1	7	1	7	1
Total	85	74	85	77	86	80	86	84	87	83	87	83	87	84	87	84
U.S. STANDING	−66	−65	−69	−68	−70	−71	−70	−76	−71	−74	−70	−74	−68	−75	−68	−75
GRAND TOTAL																
U.S.	28		25		25		25		25		26		28		28	
U.S.S.R.	159		162		166		170		170		170		171		171	
U.S. Standing	−131		−137		−141		−145		−145		−144		−143		−143	

See page 199 for footnotes.

FIGURE 23 (Con't)

Separate Brigades	*1970*		*1971*		*1972*		*1973*		*1974*		*1975*		*1976*		*1977*	
UNITED STATES[3]																
Roundout	0	0	0	0	0	1	0	2	0	1	0	3	0	4	0	4
Augment	0	0	0	0	0	0	0	0	0	4	0	4	0	4	0	4
Separate	7	21	7	21	5	20	4	19	3	17	4	15	5	15	5	15
Total	7	21	7	21	5	21	4	21	3	22	4	22	5	23	5	23
GRAND TOTAL	28		28		26		25		25		26		28		28	
SOVIET UNION[4]	0		0		0		0		0		0		0		0	
U.S. Standing	+ 28		+ 28		+ 26		+ 25		+ 25		+ 26		+ 28		+ 28	

Separate Regiments	*1970*		*1971*		*1972*		*1973*		*1974*		*1975*		*1976*		*1977*	
UNITED STATES[3]																
Armored Cav	5	4	4	4	3	4	3	4	3	4	3	3	3	3	3	3
SOVIET UNION[4]																
Naval Inf	5		5		5		5		5		6		6		6	

See page 199 for footnotes.

DIVISION CHARACTERISTICS

	Personnel Strength	*Medium Tanks*	*Armored Carriers LVTPs*	*Artillery Pieces*	*Anti-tank Missiles*[5]	*Maneuver Battalions* *I*	*T*	*M*	*Total*[6]
UNITED STATES									
Army									
Armor	18,000	324	450	66	376	0	6	5	11
Mechanized	18,000	270	490	66	422	0	4	6	10
Infantry	17,000	54	120	76	366	8	1	1	10
Airborne	16,000	0	0	54	417	9	1	0	10
Air Assault	18,000	0	0	54	372	9	0	0	9
Marine[7]	19,830	70	187	102	288	9	1	0	10
SOVIET UNION									
Tank	9,500	325	150	80	105	0	10	3	13
Motor Rifle	12,000	255	375	110	135	0	6	9	15
Airborne	8,000	0	100	54	145	9	0	0	9

[1]Column one for each year indicates active forces. Column two indicates Army National Guard and Marine Corps Reserve.
[2]Column one for each year indicates categories I and II. Column two indicates category III.
[3]Column one for each year indicates active forces. Column two indicates reserve components.
[4]All Soviet forces are active.
[5]U.S. Light Anti-tank Weapons (LAWs) and Soviet rocket-propelled grenades (RPG-7s) are excluded. Soviet anti-tank missiles include about 100 on BMP armored carriers in each type division.
[6]For maneuver battalions, I = infantry; T = tank; M = mechanized.
[7]U.S. Marine division depicted includes personnel and weapons attached from Force Troops.

Footnotes

1. With their "Arab client about to suffer a major defeat [in October 1973] . . . . Soviet leaders decided to pressure Israel and the United States by alerting Soviet airborne divisions . . . . The United States quickly reacted to the Soviet threat as Nixon called a nuclear alert." The crisis thereafter was quickly defused. U.S. Congress. House. *The Middle East, 1974: New Hopes, New Challenges.* Hearings Before a Subcommittee on the Near East and South Asia of the Committee on Foreign Affairs. 93d Congress, 2d Session. Washington: U.S. Govt. Print. Off., 1974, pp. 190–191.

2. Marshall, George C., *Statement Before the Senate Committees On Armed Services and Foreign Relations on the Military Situation in the Far East.* (Known as the MacArthur Hearings). 1951. pp. 365–366.

3. Containment principles have not always coincided with practice. Lebanon in the 1950s was conveniently situated for the execution of connected policies, as was Taiwan, where the U.S. Seventh Fleet then, as now, stood guard, but there was no practical way for the United States to apply military power effectively in Tibet, where Mao suppressed a popular uprising in 1959. Rebellions against Soviet control in East Germany, Poland, and Hungary in the 1950s elicited no military retort from the United States, partly because distance and lack of direct contact prevented U.S. forces from concentrating quickly at points of decision in Soviet-held territory. Communist influence in Indonesia, which peaked in 1965, provoked no response by this country for several reasons: the threat was indistinct; neither the U.S.S.R. nor China was directly involved; and U.S. leaders already were preoccupied with problems in Vietnam. Such exceptions, however, did not eliminate universal containment as an American goal.

4. Military victory is a traditional U.S. aim. Inconclusive Korea left a sour taste. General MacArthur, in his farewell address to Congress in 1951, featured the theme "there is no substitute for victory." He echoed that conviction at West Point 12 years later. "Your mission," he told the cadets, "is to win our wars." MacArthur, Douglas, *Duty, Honor, Country: A Pictorial Autobiography.* New York: McGraw-Hill Book Co., 1965, pp. 198, 218.

5. General Omar N. Bradley, speaking as Chairman of the Joint Chiefs of Staff on May 15, 1951, concluded that "enlargement of the war in Korea . . . . would involve us in the wrong war, at the wrong place, at the wrong time, and with the wrong enemy." Quoted in Collins, J. Lawton, *War in Peacetime.* Boston: Houghton Mifflin Co., 1969, p. 290.

6. McClintock, Robert, *The Meaning of Limited War.* Boston: Houghton Mifflin Co., 1967, p. 205.

7. Strausz-Hupe et al., *Protracted Conflict: A Challenging Study of Communist Strategy.* New York: Harper and Row, 1963, p. 158. Khrushchev's speech was made on January 6, 1961.

8. McNamara, Robert S., *Statement on the FY 1963 Defense Budget,* p. 20.

9. U.S. leaders since the early 1970s have sought "to further the [interest] of peace by deterrence of armed conflict at all levels." Laird, Melvin R., *Statement on the FY 1972 Defense Budget,* p. 1.

10. McNamara, Robert S., *The Essence of Security,* pp. 79–80.

11. Nixon, Richard M., *U.S. Foreign Policy for the 1970's: A New Strategy for Peace.* Washington: U.S. Govt. Print. Off., 1970, p. 129.

12. Information received telephonically from J-5 (Plans and Policy), Office of the Joint Chiefs of Staff, September 19, 1977.

13. Dulles, John Foster. *Address to Council on Foreign Relations, January 12, 1954.* Department of State Bulletin. Washington: U.S. Govt. Print. Off., p. 108; and *Statement Before the Senate Foreign Relations Committee,* March 19, 1954, pp. 4, 5.

14. General Nathan B. Twining, Chairman of the Joint Chiefs of Staff from 1957 to 1960, later suggested that "had we dropped one A-bomb on a tactical target during the Korean War . . . . there might have been no Chinese invasion . . . . Furthermore, Dien Bien Phu might not have happened, nor would Vietnam have been partitioned." *Neither Liberty Nor Safety*, p. 117.

15. Taylor, Maxwell D., *The Uncertain Trumpet*. New York: Harper and Brothers, 1959, pp. 5–7.

16. There is no U.S. consensus concerning Soviet theater nuclear capabilities. Some students of the subject contend that their MRBMs/IRBMs are better adapted than official studies now conclude. See for example, Douglass, Joseph D., Jr., "Soviet Military Doctrine and Strategy as Related to Nuclear War in Europe," a seminar paper prepared on February 11, 1978, 25 pp.

For general background, see Schlesinger, James R., *The Theater Nuclear Posture in Europe: A Report to the United States Congress in Compliance With Public Law 93-365*. Washington: Department of Defense, 1975. 30 pp.

17. U.S. R&D programs for mobile MRBMs were cancelled in 1964, the same year we removed Thor and Jupiter IRBMs from Turkey and Western Europe. That decision may soon be reversed. See Andrews, Walter, "Defense Chief Said to Plan '80 Development of Medium-Range Missile for Use in Europe," *Washington Post*, February 27, 1978, p. 7.

18. Proxmire, William, "Excellent Report on Tactical Nuclear Weapons by Senator Nelson." Remarks in the Senate. *Congressional Record*, July 20, 1971, p. S11626.

19. *Ibid*., pp. S11626–S11627; and *NATO Facts and Figures*. Brussels: NATO Information Service, January 1976, p. 108.

20. Policy predicated on a low threshold proposes to cross the line from conventional to nuclear combat with scant regret. A high threshold is crossed only with reluctance, after other responses fail.

21. Honest John rockets, the least accurate U.S. theater nuclear weapons, have been replaced by Lance missiles, which present proposals would fit with neutron warheads that have a comparatively small blast killing radius.

22. Enthoven, Alain C. and Smith, K. Wayne, *How Much is Enough?*, p. 125.

23. Collective security *policy* simply sets forth a philosophy that links a country loosely with a community of other nations that have common wants and needs. *Commitments*, in contrast, pledge the parties concerned to take promised steps under prescribed conditions.

24. The State Department in 1967 assured members of the Senate Foreign Relations Committee that the United States has no national obligation to shore up Israel or any Arab state in military emergency. We support "the political independence and territorial integrity of the countries of the Near East," the communication said, but that was "a statement of policy, not a commitment to take particular actions in particular circumstances." Those relationships remain. *Global Defense: U.S. Military Commitments Abroad*. Washington: Congressional Quarterly Service, 1969, pp. 24–25.

25. Haselkorn, Avigdor, *The Evolution of Soviet Security Strategy, 1965–1975*. New York: Crane, Russak & Co., 1978, 139 pp.

26. Bilateral pacts that supplement the Warsaw Treaty of Friendship, Cooperation, and Mutual Aid are published verbatim in Remington, Robin A., *The Warsaw Pact*. Cambridge, Mass.: The M.I.T. Press, 1971, 268 pp. Summary discussion is contained in Mackintosh, Malcolm, *Evolution of the Warsaw Pact*, Adelphi Papers No. 58. London: Institute for Strategic Studies, June 1969, 25 pp.

Soviet mutual defense arrangements with North Korea provide that "should either of the contracting parties suffer armed attack by any state or coalition of states . . . . the other contracting party shall immediately extend military and other assistance with all the means at its disposal." Testimony of Hon. William J. Porter, Ambassador, in U.S. Congress. Senate. Committee on Foreign Relations. *United States Security Agreements and Commitments Abroad: Republic of Korea*. Hearings. 91st Congress, 2d Session. Washington: U.S. Govt. Print. Off., 1970, p. 1577.

27. U.S. allies in Central America are accessible by road, but overland routes would not sustain heavy military traffic without upgrading at great cost in time, money, and effort.

28. Carrier-based aircraft were in the U.S. inventory long before our alliance system was installed, but power projection has always been one of their salient functions. Other important tasks include fleet air defense and antisubmarine warfare.

29. Murphy, Charles H. and Evans, Gary Lee, *U.S. Military Personnel Strengths by Country of Location Since World War II, 1948–73.* Washington: Congressional Research Service, November 13, 1973, pp. 1–10.

30. *Global Defense; U.S. Military Commitments Abroad.* Washington: Congressional Quarterly Service, September 1969, pp. 37–44.

31. Quotations were taken from the now-defunct Nixon Doctrine, but the policies expressed are essentially unchanged. Nixon, Richard M., *U.S. Foreign Policy in the 1970's: Building for Peace,* pp. 13–14.

32. President Carter, at a meeting of NATO foreign ministers on May 10, 1977, promised to "continue to provide our share of the powerful forces adequate to fulfill (a defense) strategy," in consonance with assurances that NATO continues to be "the heart of our foreign policy." Wilkie, Curtis, "Allies Welcome Pledge to Strengthen NATO," *Boston Globe,* May 11, 1977, p. 1.

33. Murphy, Charles H. and Evans, Gary Lee. *U.S. Military Personnel Strengths by Country of Location,* pp. 4–8; and *U.S. Military Strengths Outside the United States, as of March 31, 1973.* Washington: Office of Assistant Secretary of Defense (Comptroller), Directorate of Information Operations, undated.

34. "U.S. Troops Abroad: New Beef-up Begins." *U.S. News and World Report,* December 26, 1977/January 2, 1978, pp. 48–49.

35. U.S. military assistance programs in the past have been sponsored for several reasons, especially to: insure the survival and security of U.S. allies and associates; strengthen regional stability and/or stability within the states concerned; attain or retain military base rights; encourage self-reliance by recipients; promote bilateral relations; provide public evidence of U.S. interest and support; preclude influence by unfriendly powers in the affairs of U.S. allies or uncommitted countries whose future is linked with our own. Schandler, Herbert Y., *Summary of U.S. Arms Transfer and Security Assistance Programs,* draft report. Washington: Congressional Research Service, December 5, 1977, p. 29.

36. Schandler, Herbert Y., *U.S. Arms Sale: Debate.* Issue Brief 77097. Washington: Congressional Research Service, 1977 (updated periodically), p. 1.

37. "The best means of dealing with insurgencies is to preempt them through economic development and social reform and to control them with police, paramilitary and military action by the threatened government.

"We may be able to supplement local efforts with economic and military assistance. However, a direct combat role for U.S. general purpose forces arises primarily when insurgency has shaded into external aggression or when there is an overt conventional attack. In such cases, we shall weigh our interests and commitments, and we shall consider the efforts of our allies, in determining our response." Nixon, Richard M., *U.S. Foreign Policy for the 1970's: A New Strategy for Peace,* p. 127.

38. Lieutenant General Samuel V. Wilson, when Director of Defense Intelligence Agency, assessed Soviet preference for Mass as follows: "when we approach a position of parity . . . . we are comfortable with that kind of arrangement because we have confidence in ourselves and our materiel. . . . " The Soviets, however, have "often been defeated by numerically inferior but higher quality forces. Thus, their concept of what constitutes the necessary numerical superiority is totally different from our own." U.S. Congress. Subcommittee on Priorities and Economy in Government of the Joint Economics Committee. *Allocation of Resources in the Soviet Union and China—1977. Part II.* Hearings. 95th Congress, 1st Session. Washington: U.S. Govt. Print. Off., 1977, p. 80.

39. For a concise discussion of Principles of War, see Collins, John M., *Grand Strategy*, pp. 22–28.

40. The United States retains some major materiel items on active service when new ones enter the inventory (F-4 aircraft, for example, will phase out slowly in favor of F-14s and F-15s), but they are exceptions rather than rules, and numbers normally are reduced. U.S. reserve components and allies routinely continue to use selected systems after they retire from the regular establishment.

41. The evolution of Soviet general purpose forces is addressed, for example, in *The Russian War Machine, 1917–1945*. Ed. by S. L. Mayer. Secaucus, N. J.: Chartwell Books, Inc., 1977, 257 pp.; *The Soviet War Machine: An Encyclopedia of Russian Military Equipment and Strategy*. Ed. by Ray Bonds. Secaucus, N. J., 1976, 247 pp.; and Wolfe, Thomas W., *Soviet Power and Europe, 1945–1970*, 534 pp.

42. The Czars stressed mass in medieval times. "For centuries," in fact, "it has been the custom of Russian rulers to maintain in being, even in time of peace, ground forces larger than anyone else could see the necessity for." Kennan, George F., "The United States and the Soviet Union, 1917–1976," *Foreign Affairs*, July 1976, p. 680.

43. "The infantryman of airmobile, airborne, or infantry type divisions fights afoot, but, in some cases, *his mobility can be greater than that of his mechanized counterpart*. Strategically, he is easier to deploy. . . . On the battlefield, he and his weapons can be moved about by helicopter . . . . Dug in, he is difficult to dislodge." *FM 100–5, Operations*. Washington: Department of Army, July 1, 1976, pp. 2–11.

44. *FM 30–40, Handbook on Soviet Ground Forces*. Washington: Department of the Army, June 30, 1975, pp. 6–1, 6–17, 6–21.

45. U.S. field artillery and Soviet artillery serve the same purpose: indirect and direct fire support for ground force maneuver units, using mortars, cannons (guns and howitzers), free rockets, and short-range ballistic or cruise missiles.

46. *FM 30–40, Handbook on Soviet Ground Forces*, pp. 4–6. Forces from every branch of service fill U.S. airborne units. Positions are so scarce that only a few soldiers have stable career patterns as paratroops.

47. The Soviets subdivide ground support forces into Special Troops which, in the main, are assigned to combat formations (such as divisions, armies, and fronts) and Rear Services. That pattern, however, is not constant. Medical Troops, for example, are officially assigned to Rear Services, but in fact combat medics are also organic at levels as low as motor rifle and tank battalions. Similar inconsistencies exist on the U.S. side, which includes Combat Support and Combat Service Support categories. Engineers, medics, and military police fit in both. Figure 18 therefore dispenses with any such differentiation.

48. U.S. Congress. Senate. *Hearings Before a House Subcommittee of the Appropriations Committee on Department of Defense Appropriations for FY 1973. Part 5*. Washington: U.S. Govt. Print. Off., 1972, pp. 162–164.

49. *Military Manpower Requirements Report for FY 1973*. Washington: Department of Defense, February 1972, pp. 69–75. See also Binkin, Martin, *Support Costs in the Defense Budget: The Submerged One-third*. Washington: The Brookings Institution, 1972. 49 pp.

50. Paul Phillips, Acting Assistant Secretary of the Army for Manpower and Reserve Affairs, expressed the following opinion on February 9, 1977. "We are taking measures to improve the readiness and overall capability of the Reserve Components to accomplish this [essential support] mission; however, it is now clear that we should not proceed further in converting active Army support units to combat units. . . . The balance is a delicate one. . . . Indeed, by adding combat units at the expense of support units we may actually decrease early useable combat power." U.S. Congress. House. *Hearings on Military Posture and H.R. 5068, Department of Defense Authorizations for Appropriations for Fiscal Year 1978*. Before the Committee on Armed Services. 95th Congress, 1st Session. Part 5 of 6 Parts, Military Personnel etc. Washington: U.S.

Govt. Print. Off., 1977, pp. 347–348.

See also Stillman, Jack, "Singlaub Says Reserves Top Problem," *Atlanta Constitution*, March 13, 1978, p. 3c.

51. Soviet concepts, for example, envision "the rapid overwhelming of an enemy through high-speed attack, which obviously reduces the long-term logistic requirement—with a penetration achieved, then little fire and logistic support is needed. In sum, the logistics imbalance is a calculated but rational risk in Soviet operational thinking. . . . " Erickson, John, *Soviet-Warsaw Pact Force Levels*, p. 33.

52. *FM 100–5, Operations*, p. 1–1. The term "battle" in the cited text is used generically to include related engagements in a specific campaign, rather than a single spasm.

53. *Ibid.*, p. 1–2.

54. *Ibid.*, p. 3–4. Army doctrine contends that "weapons of the attacker are not as effective as the weapons of the defender, and his forces are more vulnerable." Attackers therefore "should seek a combat power ratio of at least 6:1," in accord with the adage that great captains never send a boy to do a man's job. "Obviously, these ratios [3:1, 6:1] are not fixed, but they convey a realistic approximation of the requirement."

55. *Ibid.*, p. 5–3. "A defense which spreads two brigades thinly across a wide area and holds one brigade in reserve for counterattack will be defeated by a breakthrough attack. It will in effect be defeated piecemeal because everywhere it will be too weak and thus overwhelmed." The same is true for corps and armies.

56. *Ibid.*, pp. 3–5/3–6, 3–15, 5–3, 7–1.

57. *Ibid.*, pp. 5–3, 5–13/5–14.

58. *Ibid.*, pp. 5–2, 5–7, 5–14.

59. *Ibid.*, pp. 5–3, 6–2/6–3.

60. *Ibid.*, pp. 6–2/6–4.

61. *Ibid.*, pp. 2–1, 3–4/3–5. A concise survey of the "new lethality" is contained in Chapter 2, "Modern Weapons on the Modern Battlefield," pp. 2–1/2–32.

62. Soviet Principles of War are Quantity and Quality of Divisions, Armament, Ability of Commanders, Morale, and Stability of the Rear. Principles cited in the text were lifted from the U.S. Army's list. Karl von Clausewitz first formally identified all five in his treatise *On War*. Ed. and translated by Michael Howard and Peter Paret. New Jersey: Princeton University Press, 1976, 717 pp. Soviet doctrine draws heavily on that document.

63. *FM 30–40, Handbook on Soviet Ground Forces*, pp. 5–7; "Understanding Soviet Military Developments," p. 24.

64. Donnelly, Christopher, "The Soviet Ground Forces." Chapter 10 in *The Soviet War Machine*, p. 163.

65. "Capabilities . . . . cannot be taken as a clear indication of intended action. Soviet leaders realize that armed conflict has never before been surrounded by such uncertainty. While the destructiveness of a single nuclear weapon can be precisely calculated, the cumulative effect of many . . . . on morale and discipline of the armed forces, on logistics, on the civilian population, and on the whole fabric of society can neither be calculated nor predicted." "Understanding Soviet Military Developments," p. 23.

66. *Ibid.*, p. 24; Erickson, John, "Soviet Ground Forces and the Conventional Mode of Operations," *Military Review*, January 1977, p. 50.

67. *FM 30–40, Handbook on Soviet Ground Forces*, p. 5–1.

68. "About two-thirds of the total strength is assigned to the first echelon . . . . There is no US Army equivalent to the second [or third] echelon." *Ibid.*, p. 5–7; *FM 100–5, Operations*, pp. 3–6, 5–2; Erickson, John, "Soviet Ground Forces and the Conventional Mode of Operations," p. 54.

69. Soviet division objectives currently are 10 times deeper than during early days of World War II. *FM 100–5, Operations*, pp. 2–32.

70. *Ibid.; FM 30–40, Handbook on Soviet Ground Forces*, pp. 5–11, 5–13; Erickson, John, "Soviet Ground Forces in the Conventional Mode of Operations," p. 54.

71. German generals during World War II developed dive bombers as a substitute for towed artillery, which could not keep up with tanks in Blitzkrieg (lightning war) operations. When the Luftwaffe lost air superiority to Allied fighters, Panzer columns deep in hostile territory lacked fire support, and failed. Soviet leaders seem to have learned that lesson. Owens, M. J., "Artillery is the Real Threat in the Soviet Weapons Arsenal," *Marine Corps Gazette,* July 1977, p. 37.

72. *Ibid.*, pp. 35–42; Erickson, John, "Soviet Ground Forces and the Conventional Mode of Operations," p. 50–51; *FM 100–5, Operations,* pp. 2–13; *FM 30–40, Handbook on Soviet Ground Forces,* pp. 5–3, 5–5.

73. Soviet "defense is employed locally while on the offensive in other sectors, or during consolidation after taking an important objective, to gain time, cover a withdrawal, or repel an attack by a superior enemy force." *FM 30–40, Handbook on Soviet Ground Forces,* pp. 5–15.

74. *Ibid.*, pp. 5–15/5–19.

75. *Field Manual 100–5, Operations;* "Banned at Fort Monroe, or the Article the Army Doesn't Want You to Read;" "TRADOC's Reply;" "Dynamic Doctrine for Dynamic Defense." All in *Armed Forces Journal,* October 1976, pp. 23–29.

76. "TRADOC's Reply," p. 27.

77. Lind, William S., "Some Doctrinal Questions for the United States Army," *Military Review,* March 1977, pp. 55–57.

78. "TRADOC's Reply," p. 27.

79. Lind, William S., "Some Doctrinal Questions for The United States Army," p. 57.

80. Maneuver has enabled numerically inferior forces to prevail many times in the past. Historical examples cited by Lind to make his case all concerned offensive operations. *Ibid.*, pp. 55, 57–61; "TRADOC's Reply," p. 27; "Dynamic Doctrine for Dynamic Defense," pp. 28–29.

81. Simplicity is a Principle of War. U.S. Army schools and colleges all stress the acronym "KISS", which stands for "keep it simple, stupid!" German Field Marshal Paul von Hindenburg summarized requirements nicely with his comment, "In war, only the simple succeeds."

82. Lind, William S., "Some Doctrinal Questions for the United States Army," pp. 55, 61–65.

83. Shock action depends on violent impact to disrupt and demoralize opponents in combat. Surprise and speed assist. Success is in direct proportion to power employed sharply at points of decision.

84. Armor was the decisive U.S. ground-gaining arm in Western Europe during World War II, but the situation has changed. The mission then was offensive. Now it is mainly defense. Allied armored divisions outnumbered the Nazis by about 4:1 in autumn 1944. The present NATO/Warsaw Pact ratio is nearly reversed. Today, the U.S. Army would have to content itself with shock action as a *tactical* instrument, designed to dominate local contests, rather than large-scale campaigns in contest with the Soviet Union.

85. Marshal of Tank Troops A. Babadzhanyan confirms that "Soviet military art assigns to tank troops the role of the main strike and maneuver force . . . ." In his opinion, tanks "are the least 'susceptible' of all to [neutralization by] new means of armed struggle . . . ." "Soviet Defends Tank Role," *Defense/Space Daily,* October 5, 1976, p. 189.

86. For discussion of Soviet nuclear doctrine connected with tanks as a shock force, see for example Douglass, Joseph D., Jr., "The Soviet Theater Nuclear Offensive," *Studies in Communist Affairs, Vol. 1,* published under auspices of the U.S. Air Force. Washington: U.S. Govt. Print. Off., 1976, 127 pp. Tanks as shock troops in conventional combat are covered in Erickson, John, "Trends in the Soviet Combined Arms Concept," *Strategic Review,* Winter 1977, pp. 38–53, together with his "Soviet Ground Forces and the Conventional Mode of Operations," pp. 49–56.

87. Skeptics, such as Marine Lieutenant General Robert H. Barrow, Deputy Commandant of the U.S. Marine Corps, believe that "we have at least reached the threshold, and maybe crossed it, in making the tank obsolete, or near obsolete . . . . Ten years from now the guy who brings a lot of tanks to the battlefield may be bringing liabilities rather than assets." Quoted in Crown, John, "Tanks on Way Out," *Atlanta Journal*, August 15, 1977, p. A–14.

Not everyone agrees. See for example Hatcher, Michael J., "The Tank is Alive and Well," *Military Review*, February 1978, pp. 75–87; McMaster, A. W., III, "Soviet Armor: A Study in Efficiency," *Armor*, January-February 1978, pp. 30–33.

88. Chuyko, L., "Tanks in the Sights." *Red Star*. Contained in *Soviet Press, Selected Translations*. Armed Forces Information Center, September 1977, pp. 242–244; Coniglio, Sergio, "Dragonflies Against Tanks," *Aviation and Marine International*, December 1976, p. 47.

89. Erickson, John, "The Ground Forces in Soviet Military Policy," lecture text, delivered at a symposium of the American Association for the Advancement of Slavic Studies, October 1977, p. 21.

90. Karber, Philip A., "Anti-Tank Weapons and the Future of Armor: Soviet Thought and NATO's Procrastination," *Armed Forces Journal*, November 1976, p. 20.

91. *Understanding Soviet Military Developments*, pp. 27–28.

92. Erickson, John, "The Ground Forces in Soviet Military Policy," pp. 29–30, and "Trends in the Soviet Combined Arms Concept," pp. 44, 46.

93. Total army strengths are compared in Part II. This section subtracts high command and general support forces, which amount to approximately a third of a million men in the U.S. Army, and nearly three-quarters of a million in the Soviet Union.

94. Brown, George S., *United States Military Posture for FY 1976*, p. 68.

95. The 3:1 ratio counts 97,000 U.S. Marines in the combat category.

96. TOW AT stands for tube-launched, optically-tracked, wire-guided antitank missile.

97. *FM 100-5 Operations*, pp. 2–2/2–6.

98. *Ibid.*, pp. 2–7/2–9.

99. Soviet artillery has a longer reach than our own (up to 40 km with rocket assist for some models), which complicates U.S. counterbattery fires. Fire direction on the Soviet side is centralized "at very high levels, reducing responsiveness to the maneuver units," but provides "effective massed firepower in support of breakthrough operations." *FM 100-5, Operations*, pp. 2–13/2–15.

100. Average U.S. infantry companies take about eight hours to hand lay a 250×350 meter minefield, carefully marked so someone later can safely pick them up. Scatter-type mines, which self-destruct after a predetermined period, thus are much more convenient.

101. *FM 100-5, Operations*, pp. 2–25.

102. Brown, George S., *United States Military Posture for FY 1978*, p. 65.

103. *FM 100-5, Operations*, pp. 2–11.

104. *FM 30-40, Handbook on Soviet Ground Forces*, p. 47.

105. Seventh U.S. Army in Europe and Eighth U.S. Army in Korea are remnants of formerly full-fledged field armies. They currently are headquarters that control no troops.

106. U.S. data derived from telephone conversations with officers at the Army Command and General Staff College and on the Army Staff (DCSOPS), January 10, 1978.

107. *U.S. Army Force Design: Alternatives for Fiscal Years 1977–1981*. Washington: Congressional Budget Office, July 16, 1976, pp. 45–49.

108. The U.S. Army began its "roundout" program in 1972, when one reserve brigade and four separate battalions were designated to replace components missing from *under-strength* active divisions. Four brigades and 11 separate battalions (6 tank, 4 mechanized, and 1 infantry) now serve that purpose. All such elements must be ready to deploy with parent divisions on demand. Four other independent reserve brigades

participate in an "augmentation" program intended to increase the combat power of designated *full-strength* divisions. These forces must also be ready to deploy with associated divisions on short notice, but requirements to do so depend on contingency plans. Data derived from Army staff officres in January 1977.

109. Four U.S. divisions are currently stationed in Germany. All others likely would be required as reinforcements if a major war occurred, but only three in CONUS (minus one brigade each already in Europe) are earmarked for early deployment. Heavy equipment for two of them is prepositioned. Facts corroborated by Army staff officers (DCSOPS), February 1978.

110. No rotation base would be needed if a general war erupted in Europe. *All* U.S. divisions were committed overseas during World War II. Most men returning to CONUS were separated from the Service, attended schools, or were assigned to staffs.

In peacetime, and during limited conflicts like those in Korea and Vietnam, U.S. divisions stay overseas, while personnel serve specified tours and then return to CONUS. Most men must receive assignments related to their skills, or readiness levels lapse. A satisfactory balance can be maintained if about 60 percent of the force stays in the United States, according to Army staff officers. When fewer than 40 percent serve as a rotation base, combat effectiveness suffers seriously.

Four U.S. divisions, for example, served as a rotation base for 15 others overseas in the late 1960s. Insufficient slots existed, especially for specialists. Training everywhere suffered. The four divisions, which played parts in NATO plans, were combat ineffective for a protracted period, because equipment was stripped and personnel passed through too rapidly.

111. Data derived from personal conversations with DIA analysts in January 1977.

112. *Ibid.* See also Erickson, John, *Soviet-Warsaw Pact Force Levels,* pp. 31–39.

113. DIA comments on a draft of this study, September 9, 1977.

114. The generic term "reserves", as used in this study, refers to all reserve components, including the National Guard.

115. Twelve divisions in the U.S. Army Reserve are regional replacement training centers, rather than maneuver units. The Executive Director of the National Guard questions whether *any* organized reserves could contribute effectively to our Total Force Concepts. "The Individual Ready Reserve has been destroyed," he said. "The Selective Service System has been destroyed. The [Army] guard and reserve would have to fill individual slots as replacements in an emergency, which would destroy their unit roles." Hearing before the House Armed Services Committee, reported in *Army Times,* February 27, 1978, p. 4.

116. Readiness Condition 1 (REDCON-1 or C-1) requires U.S. units to be "fully capable of performing missions for which organized or designed." Such units, with 95 percent of authorized manpower and 90 percent of material, "may be deployed to a combat theater immediately" after mobilization. C-3 units, which are marginally ready, have deficiencies that severely constrain capabilities, but could be committed in combat "under conditions of grave emergency." *Army Regulation 220-1, Unit Readiness Reporting,* March 17, 1975, pp. A–1, 2.

Times it would take for ARNG divisions to reach C-1 or C-3 status were furnished by Army staff officers in January 1977.

117. Data derived from personal conversations with DIA analysts in January 1977.

118. *Ibid.* The U.S. intelligence community counted 65 Category III divisions in 1976. That total increased in 1977, after analysts reevaluated readiness conditions, and reclassified several divisions formerly carried as Category II.

119. *Ibid.* Some sources contend that Cat III divisions can fill in 24 hours.

120. About half of all Soviet divisions on the Chinese border are Category III. The Kremlin apparently anticipates no early aggression by either side in that area.

121. Marine missions are much in dispute. See for example West, Francis J., "Marines for the Future," *U.S. Naval Institute Proceedings,* February 1978, pp. 34–42 and Salzer, Robert S., "The Navy's Clouded Amphibious Mission," *U.S. Naval Institute*

Proceedings, February 1978, pp. 24–33.

122. U.S. Marines are organized, trained, and equipped as an air-ground team whose divisions are never committed to combat without associated tactical air wings. This section arbitrarily separates the two components to facilitate U.S./Soviet comparisons.

123. The 4th Marine Division, manned by 19,000 reservists in paid drill status, has the goal of reaching full readiness 60 days after recall. Its units maintain only about 50 percent of their equipment allowance at home armories. Shortages must be made up in emergency from Prepositioned War Reserves at the same time active divisions are expected to tax the supply system. Individual Ready Reserves normally receive at least 30 days notice before call-up. If that requirement were waived, combat proficiency could be achieved more rapidly. U.S. Congress. Senate. *Hearings before the Armed Services Committee on FY 1977 Authorization. Part 3. Manpower.* 94th Congress, 2d Session. Washington: U.S. Govt. Print. Off., 1976, pp. 1846–1850.

124. DIA analysts identify a naval infantry division structure in the Soviet Far East, but its elements still exercise separately.

125. Several Soviet divisions were stationed in northern Iran during World War II. They stayed from August 25, 1941 until May 9, 1946, when U.S. and U.N. pressures prompted withdrawal.

126. Difficulties are described in U.S. Congress. House. *Oil Fields as Military Objectives: A Feasibility Study*, prepared for the Special Subcommittee on Investigations of the Committee on International Relations by the Congressional Research Service. 94th Congress. 1st Session. Washington: U.S. Govt. Print. Off., 1975, pp. 18–21.

Land-Oriented Tactical Air Power

Dissimilar doctrines, geographic circumstances, and technologic competence caused U.S. and Soviet tactical air combat power to develop along different lines that left our rival disadvantaged until recently.[1]

Assorted U.S. assets, positioned in allied countries and on aircraft carriers, possess global capabilities that can be supplemented swiftly with responsive reserves. Assigned missions span a wide spectrum. Soviet Front Aviation, dedicated to battlefield air defense in decades past, first began to deploy diversified aircraft and adjust its doctrine in the early 1970s. Transition continues.[2]

Air Combat Missions

The degree to which tactical air forces help deter or defeat opponents depends on abilities to attain air superiority over key contested areas, cut off enemy supplies/reinforcements, and furnish close support for ground forces. Few aircraft serve more than one mission equally well.[3] (See Figure 24.)

"Counter air operations are conducted to gain and maintain air superiority by destroying or neutralizing an enemy's . . . . air capability." Offensive sweeps against hostile airfields, command/control installations, and associated targets in hostile territory "are the most effective means," since they cripple assets "that constitute or support the enemy air order of battle." Defensive counter air campaigns, which are fought over friendly terrain in the form of air-to-air combat, seek to intercept and shoot down intruders.[4]

Air interdiction strives to destroy, deflect, or delay enemy naval and ground force formations "before they can be brought to bear." It also

FIGURE 24 TACTICAL AIRCRAFT PERFORMANCE CRITERIA CONNECTED WITH COMBAT MISSIONS

	Counter Air		*Interdiction*	*Close*
	Offensive	*Defensive*		*Support*
Speed	X	X		
Maneuverability	X	X		
Fast Climb		X		
High Ceiling		X		
Long Radius	X		X	
Loiter Ability			X	X
Payload				
Diversified	X		X	X
Heavy	X		X	X
Protection Against Ground Fire	X		X	X

NOTES:

[1]Characteristics shown are essential for missions cited. Nothing "nice to have" is noted.

[2]Offensive counter air strikes against aircraft and installations on the ground are identical with interdiction, but targets of opportunity are exceptions, rather than rules. Most strikes are preplanned.

[3]Aircraft designed solely for interdiction or close support require air cover when opponents have strong counter air capabilities.

[4]A fourth tactical air mission, not shown, is reconnaissance.

constrains antagonists by reducing supplies and disrupting lines of communication. Participating forces range over wide areas to attack preplanned objectives and time-sensitive targets of opportunity, such as truck columns and ship convoys.[5]

Close air support activities "provide responsive, sustained and concentrated firepower" that is carefully integrated "with the fire and maneuver of surface forces."[6] Munitions are delivered directly against enemy troops in contact with, or contiguous to, friendly contingents. Controllers on the ground identify targets and transmit requests. They also assess damage, "so decisions can be made to re-strike or divert sorties" elsewhere.[7]

Opposing Priorities

U.S. resources are structured to accomplish those tasks under a range of conditions. The Soviets are still somewhat confined, for good reasons.

America has enjoyed total air supremacy, not just local air superiority, in every land combat area since Axis air power was suppressed in the early 1940s.[8] Just two Luftwaffe fighters tried to strafe Allied troops when they stormed Norman shores on D-Day, 1944.[9] Communist air forces in Korea and Vietnam never posed serious problems.

Policy over the past 30 years consequently promoted the full-time application of U.S. multipurpose fighter-attack aircraft to deep interdiction missions and close support for ground combat formations.[10]

Soviet lessons learned in World War II were quite different. Operation Barbarossa, Hitler's invasion of Russia, "kicked off" before dawn on June 22, 1941. Roughly 1,800 Red Air Force aircraft were ruined by dusk. (America was "shocked" when U.S. Eighth Air Force lost 60 bombers in the Schweinfurt raid of October 14, 1943.)[11] The first week's tally was close to 4,000.[12] Whether those figures are inflated is irrelevant. The havoc still was horrible.

As a direct result, battlefield air defense took top priority for Soviet post-war tactical fighters, which lacked range and payload combinations needed to perform interdiction or close air support roles very well in the 1950s and 1960s. Policy decisions developed and deployed MRBMs and IRBMs to take care of the former task in a nuclear war. Massed artillery, mortars, and multitube rocket launchers reduced requirements for tactical air power along lines of contact in conventional conflicts. Most Soviet aircraft of course have always had some ground attack capabilities, but modern types procured especially for that purpose began to appear only in recent years.[13]

Organization

The United States Air Force (USAF) is tasked to gain and maintain general air supremacy, defeat enemy air forces, and control vital areas.[14] Army, Navy, and Marine Corps air arms assist.[15] (Annex D). All four Services are configured to cope with contingencies on a global scale. Soviet structure reflects responsibilities that are still largely regional.

This section on organization addresses tactical air combat components of our Air Force and Soviet Front Aviation, the two principal opponents. Some characteristics are shared, but differences are greater than similarities:

United States	*Soviet Union*
Tactical Air Command	Military District
Unified Command	Group of Forces
Air Force	Air Army
Division	Division
Wing	Regiment
Squadron	Squadron

U.S. Structure

Numbered U.S. air forces normally supervise two or more tactical fighter wings, whose subordinate squadrons, which average 24 aircraft each, comprise the "cutting edge". Divisions coordinate two or more wings only if circumstances, such as great distance, complicate direct air force control.

Slightly more than half of USAF's fighter/attack strength is assigned to Tactical Air Command (TAC), with headquarters at Langley AFB, Virginia. TAC organizes, trains, and equips rapid-reaction CONUS reserves for use by all five U.S. unified commands. It also acts as the air component for Atlantic Command (as AFLANT), Readiness Command (as AFRED), and Southern Command (as AFSO). Combat power reposes in the Ninth and Twelfth Air Forces, which total 15 fighter wings.[16] (Figure 25).

Another 30-plus percent of USAF's tactical combat aircraft are allocated to U.S. Air Forces Europe (USAFE). Third Air Force in England, Sixteenth in Spain, and Seventeenth in West Germany account for eight wings that would come under Allied Air Forces Central Europe (AAFCE) in event of conflict between NATO and the Warsaw Pact.[17]

Pacific Air Forces (PACAF), headquartered at Hickam AFB near Honolulu, cover a huge area with strict economy. Fifth Air Force, which deploys two divisions and two separate wings, scatters fighter squadrons from Okinawa to Korea and Japan. Thirteenth Air Force has just one wing, at Clark AB in the Philippines. An independent division based in Hawaii is backed by a group from the Air National Guard (ANG).[18]

Soviet Structure

Each of the 16 Soviet Military Districts contains a tactical air army. (See Figure 26 and Map 2.) Four more are assigned to Groups of Forces outside Soviet frontiers in East Germany, Poland, Czechoslovakia, and Hungary.[19] Should war occur, all 20 would come under control of ground commanders as integral elements of active "fronts".[20]

The 16th Air Army in East Germany includes two corps headquarters. Each superintends two or three air divisions. In every other instance, divisions are directly subordinate to armies. No air army has more than three divisions. Some have less. Divisions contain fighter or ground attack regiments, but not both. Three regiments of three squadrons each (half the size of U.S. counterparts) are standard.[21]

Soviet Badger, Blinder, and non-naval Backfire bombers remain under central control. All belong to Long-Range Aviation, but contribute to Soviet tactical air capabilities. Basic organization is similar to that just discussed, except that corps replace air armies as the senior elements. Each comprises three divisions of two or three regiments each.

Figure 25.

USAF TACTICAL AIR ORGANIZATION

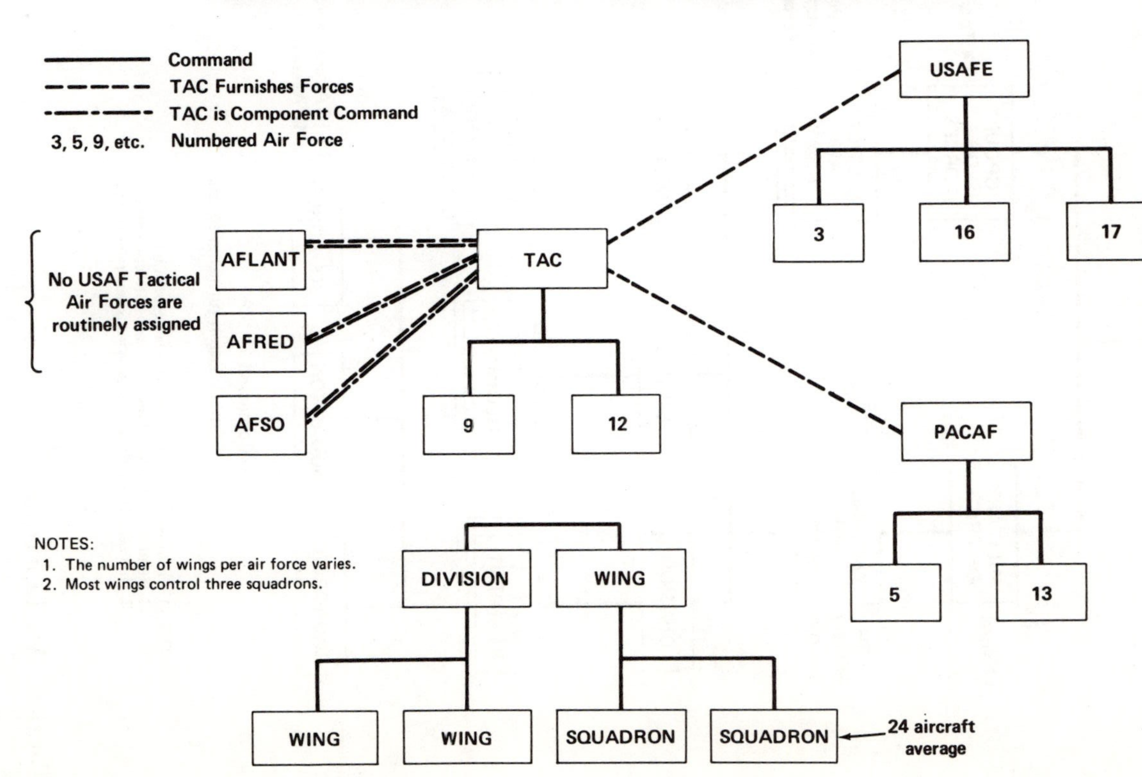

NOTES:
1. The number of wings per air force varies.
2. Most wings control three squadrons.

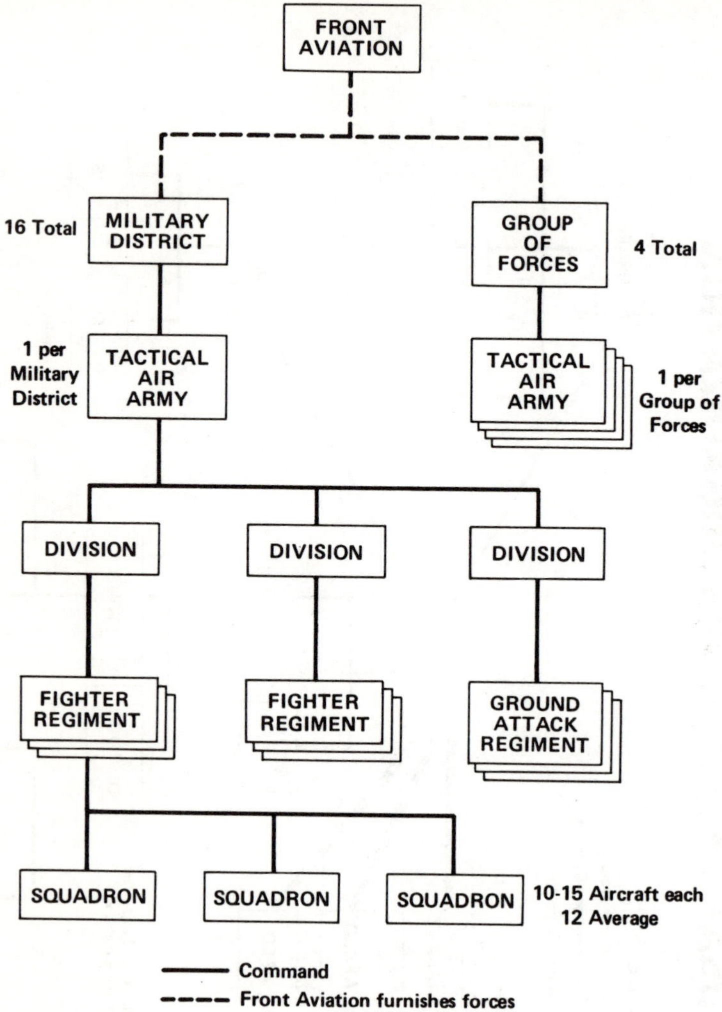

Tactical Air Doctrine

USAF tactical air doctrine has always stressed offensive action. Soviet concepts, inseparable from those of controlling Ground Forces, put most stock in defense during past decades. The shift now in progress is shaped by new needs to facilitate fast-moving breakthrough operations and maintain momentum.

Tactical air combat power can "respond to crises and armed conflicts more rapidly, with a wider range of options, than [most] other military forces . . . . Centralized control, decentralized execution and coordinated effort are fundamental." Power can best be applied by a single commander who possesses overall responsibility and commensurate authority to allocate air assets throughout the theater concerned.[22]

CONUS reserves stand ready to reinforce forces routinely stationed in forward areas. F-111s from Mountain Home AFB, Idaho, assisted by in-flight refueling, reportedly took just 19 hours to arrive in Korea during the 1976 DMZ incident in which two Americans were killed.[23] Air Force Reserve and National Guard squadrons can move out smartly soon after receiving orders. "Virtually all . . . . can reach Europe within a month or less."[24]

TAC also serves U.S. interests as required in remote regions. Self-sustaining squadrons equipped with "bare base" kits that contain portable shelters, power generators, field kitchens, fuel storage containers, and a few other essentials can function almost anywhere, provided a suitable runway, aircraft parking areas, and potable water supplies are present. War reserve materials (WRM) are stocked at squadron level as stopgaps to ensure uninterrupted emergency or wartime operations until standard logistic support can be instated.[25]

Response times can be much reduced if preparations take place before overseas crises occur. Tactical air reconnaissance units therefore are tasked to keep tab on the disposition, composition, and movement of enemy forces in selected trouble spots, along with activities at associated installations and along lines of communication. Near real time target coverage, combined with post-strike damage assessments, make it possible for U.S. tactical air forces to cope with fluid situations once armed conflict starts.[26]

Contingencies include incipient insurgency at one end of the scale and nuclear combat at the other. U.S. tactical air doctrine consequently demands flexible capacities to apply appropriate power against decisive objectives from widely dispersed locations under assorted circumstances. Employment principles call for offensive action, especially "at the very onset of hostilities," to seize initiative, preserve freedom of action, and impose U.S. will on opposing forces in "a minimum amount of time." Military and psychological advantages accruing from surprise can overcome superior forces, if massed firepower strikes swiftly where and when the enemy least expects.[27]

Theater nuclear concepts seek first and foremost to deter armed conflict, by convincing foes that "ultimate potential losses would not be worth the potential gains." If war should erupt, all efforts to the contrary, fear of lethal power loaded aboard U.S. tactical aircraft might still prevent opponents from crossing the "firebreak" between conventional and nuclear operations. Failing that, uncommitted U.S. nuclear strength conceivably could inhibit any enemy penchant for uncontrolled escallation, and perhaps encourage early termination. Weapons systems that diminish collateral damage and casualties presumably contribute to credible deterrence by making nuclear combat possible in circumstances that would otherwise prove impractical.[28]

Soviet Concepts

Reams have been written about Soviet tactical aircraft, but very little hard information concerning current concepts has appeared in public print. Since the subject is open to speculation, this précis quickly proceeds from the few known facts to unconfirmed opinion.

Soviet Front Aviation, bolstered by medium bombers, exists essentially as part of a combined-arms air-ground strike force configured for offensive shock action on a grand scale. Like the ground components they support, dual-capable tactical air forces are suitable for nuclear and conventional combat.

Doctrine still seems to dedicate substantial strength to battlefield air defense, but most new aircraft now in production are designed for offensive counter air or ground attack missions. Many older models have been modified for the latter purpose. Greater payload and range capabilities improve prospects for surprise, because squadrons far from present or prospective fronts could strike deep without refueling at forward bases, a requirement that afforded clear tipoffs to opposing intelligence in the recent past.[29]

Planned employment, however, is secret. Soviet tube artillery, for example, provides massive firepower that reduces requirements for close air support. Land-mobile air defense systems release fighter interceptor resources for different duties. Short-, medium-, and intermediate-range ballistic missiles are better than bombers for many interdiction missions. Tasks for tactical aircraft thus would likely be contingent on the intensity of conflict and its character, whether nuclear or conventional.

Short-range SCUD B and Scaleboard missiles, MRBMs, and IRBMs most likely would atomize high-value installations, including enemy air bases, early in any nuclear war, no matter who started it. If so, Soviet tactical aircraft might best be used to attack mobile targets (especially nuclear weapons systems) and sweep air space clean over essential areas of operation.[30] Close support for Soviet ground columns could take third priority.

Doctrine doubtless would be different if Soviet leaders elected or allowed a conventional opening phase. Deep interdiction and offensive counter air campaigns against command/control centers, theater nuclear delivery systems, air bases, and nodes along crucial lines of communication could contribute to quick air superiority, destroy or deflect rival reserves, create chaos in the enemy camp "and, perhaps above all, help deny [opposing ground divisions] an orderly fighting withdrawal."[31]

Alternatively, "it could well be sufficient for [Front Aviation] to be active in the counterair role early in the war, in order to reduce the [foe's] sortie rate" and the effectiveness of his strikes.[32] Close air support could wait until Soviet SAMs and interceptors sapped opposing strength. One student of the subject in fact suggests that "the conspicuous absence of Soviet-trained Egyptian fighter forces during the early battles of the 1973 Yom Kippur War may be an indication of Soviet employment concepts . . . . We may well have witnessed a conscious effort by the Egyptians to withhold fighters from the battle area until duels between the [Israeli Air Force and Arab] surface-to-air weapons had run their course."[33]

Only one thing seems certain at this stage: U.S. officials are uncertain which courses constitute Soviet doctrine.

Comparative Aircraft Inventories

Most U.S. and Soviet fighter/attack aircraft incorporate engine and air frame technology developed in the 1950s and early 1960s. Computer-assisted fire-control systems and other refinements came later. Improvement programs presently are in progress on both sides. The Soviets are refurbishing at a faster rate, but also have farther to go.

Fighter/Attack Aircraft

High performance aircraft from three U.S. services, the Air Force, Navy, and Marine Corps, contribute to America's land-oriented tactical air capabilities. Soviet competition constitutes a much different mix.

U.S. Status

USAF Trends Nuclear deterrent and defense requirements dominated U.S. tactical air research and development in the late 1950s and early 1960s.

"Dogfighting" was a dead issue. Cannons were excluded, because tactics called for theater interceptors to engage enemy bombers with conventional or atomic-tipped missiles long before visual contact occurred. A new family of attack aircraft, such as F-105s and F-111s, took over deep interdiction tasks, but close air support became a step-child. Vulnerability to ground fire caused little concern in any case, since aerial combat and weapon release would take place at lofty altitudes. There was no need for high sortie rates or sustained capabilities. Nuclear combat, as then conceived, would be bloody but brief.[34]

The strategic switch from Massive Retaliation to Flexible Response in 1961 demanded different tactical aircraft characteristics, but USAF bogged down in Vietnam before the transformation took place. Problems were soon apparent.

Rules of engagement that demanded visual identification were revived at an early date to avoid self-inflicted losses over the Red River Delta.[35] Scrapping with Soviet-made MIGs, however, was hazardous to the health of U.S. fighter pilots, whose air combat training had downplayed dogfighting since the Korean war.[36] Air-to-air missiles, designed to destroy bombers with straight and level shots, could not be launched on tight turns. Lightly-gunned American aircraft still managed impressive "won-lost" ratios,[37] but the outcome might have been different against massive Soviet opposition.

Target acquisition plagued pilots of high-performance jets, who were hard pressed to pinpoint and hit elusive troops and transport on the Ho Chi Minh Trail. "Soft-skinned" aircraft and occupants suffered such attrition from ground fire that defense suppression became a separate (although still unofficial) mission.[38] "Standoff" capabilities became almost essential. The entire experience had a pervasive influence on mission planning, tactics, and flight techniques.

Cost-effectiveness, combined with limitations on force size in the 1960s, led defense decision-makers to "insist that each airplane be fully capable of performing more than one mission[39] and, hopefully, for more than one [military] service."[40] A few exceptions have since emerged—the F-15, for example, is tailored for tactical air combat, the A-10 to attack tanks—but the all-purpose syndrome still shapes most systems. The so-called "hi-lo" concept, which mixes costly, sophisticated aircraft with simpler, cheaper counterparts, encourages competition and thereby tries to shave expenses.[41]

The current U.S. land-oriented tactical air inventory (Graph 12 and Figure 28), conditioned by compromise and cost constraints, is still the world's best. New aircraft now entering active service are superior to, or competitive with, the best Soviet products, regardless of mission. Our ground attack arsenal is undergoing a real revolution in technological terms.[42] Precision-guided munitions (PGMs) in particular promise to improve U.S. capabilities many-fold.[43] The imaging infrared (IIR) Maverick, an air-to-ground missile, can already kill tanks in daylight or dark. Close air support at night is still difficult, but USAF nevertheless can deliver ordnance "with a fairly high degree of confidence using long range navigation (LORAN), ground mapping radar, beacon bombing techniques . . . . [and] ground-based radar control systems."[44]

Marine Air Wings The Soviets have no air power comparable to U.S. Marine air wings, which include more than 300 fighter/attack aircraft in active squadrons (Figure 28).[45] Crews specialize in air cover and close support for Marine divisions during amphibious assaults and sustained operations, but are prepared to participate in overall air efforts as directed.[46]

Marine forces exhibit adaptability unequalled by sister Services, being able to function effectively either ashore or afloat.[47] Optical landing aids, arresting gear, lights, and other accoutrements associated with expeditionary airfields reduce requirements to seize or construct strips for high performance fighters at an early stage. Marine VSTOL aircraft transferred ashore on amphibious ships can commence operations even before installation is complete.[48]

U.S. Navy Contributions The U.S. Navy, with more than 600 carrier-based fighter/attack aircraft and collateral functions connected with land combat,[49] can supplement or supplant Air Force and Marine squadrons in many circumstances that call for air power. (See Figure 30 at the end of the next section for statistics.)

The Soviet Navy cannot yet compete. A few YAK-36 Vertical Takeoff and Landing (VTOL) aircraft aboard the carriers Minsk and Kiev constitute its sole fighter/attack capability. They reputedly are better than British-built AV-8 Harriers flown by U.S. Marines, but are too few to tip the U.S./Soviet military balance.[50]

Soviet Status Soviet statistical strengths have stabilized at a level twice our own, counting U.S. Marine Corps aircraft (Graph 12 and Figure 28).[51] The changing complexion, however, is more significant than mere numbers.

The lightly-armed, short-range, fair-weather MIG-17, 19, 21 air superiority series, supplemented by SU-7s, a rather shoddy ground attack product, afforded Front Aviation few advantages in 1970. Badger and Blinder bombers added deep interdiction potential of a sort, but penetration prospects were becoming dim by that date. Nothing was well-suited for close air support. The shortage of electronic countermeasures (ECM) was severe.[52]

Multimission fighters with advanced armaments, first-class avionics, and impressive penetration aids now augment Moscows's tactical air arsenal. All systems entering the inventory can deliver nuclear weapons as well as conventional ordnance, with much improved accuracy under adverse weather conditions. Older mainstays, mainly MIG-21s, undertake new tasks after modernization.[53] The combat radius and destructive power of some ground attack regiments consequently have quadrupled in recent years.[54]

SU-19 Fencer-A, commonly considered the first Soviet airframe created specifically for ground attack, comes complete with swing-wings, terrain-avoidance radar, and laser range finder, like a scaled-down F-111.[55] Its much-publicized low-level penetration profile at close to supersonic speeds may some day fill a long-standing gap for Front Aviation. In fact, however, acquisition thus far has been slow.

Meanwhile, interdiction duties seem to devolve mainly on MIG-23s (Flogger-D) and SU-17s (Fitter-C/D), buttressed perhaps by Backfire bombers.[56]

The MIG-23 air superiority model, Flogger-B, is clearly Front Aviation's first-line fighter. A 23mm twin-barrel gun and air-to-air missiles make it a worthy rival for the best U.S. aircraft, if the 1977 Air Intercept Missile Evaluation (AIMVAL) exercise at Nellis AFB was a competent test. F-14 and F-15 fighters both suffered heavy attrition under the stated rules.[57]

Conversion, however, is still incomplete. The newest Fitters and Fencers are not nearly as numerous as the fast-growing force of MIG-23s. Air intercept training retains its traditional emphasis on strict ground control, which has strong points, but allows little latitude for free air combat purposes. Soviet fighters, which cannot refuel in flight, are difficult to redeploy long distances over land without "stepping stones", and depend on ships for movement over open seas.[58]

Fire Support Helicopters

U.S. Army helicopter gunships, many armed with TOW antitank missiles, afford significant close air support that is immediately responsive to ground force commanders, regardless of mission priorities assigned to high-performance assets in other Services. Tactics, which were combat-tested in Vietnam, have been refined in the course of continual training.[59]

Soviet counterparts, controlled by front commanders, are closing fast from a standing start in 1973. Accelerated accession rates are erasing "the last area in tactical weaponry where the [United States] has held any production lead over the Soviet Union."[60] Deployments thus far have more than doubled every two years.

MI-24 (Hind) helicopters include four or five configurations. D-models, which mount Sagger AT missiles, 57mm rockets, and guns,[61] are formidable fire support systems. All versions serve several purposes simultaneously. Each, for example, can carry considerable cargo and 14 fully-armed troops.[62]

Air Defense Implications

Tactical air combat forces, to be effective in most respects, must successfully penetrate high-density ground gunfire and SAM defenses that cover key targets in forward as well as rear areas. Otherwise, they perish or fail to accomplish assigned purposes, even if favored with air superiority.

Difficulties today are dramatically different than during World War II, when each U.S. division had just 64 air defense weapons. Some anti-aircraft artillery tubes were aimed by radar, but none were very accurate, and ranges at best were restricted. The current divisional complex, including guns and missiles, can reach four times as far and control 36 times as much air space volume.[63]

American capabilities, however, have by no means kept pace with Soviet progress. (See Figure 22, at end of section on Armies.) The opposition actually practices what U.S. strategists preach when they say no army "can expect to win in battle unless its maneuver forces operate under a cohesive, extensive, and mobile umbrella of modern air defense."[64] Their all-altitude array, deployed in depth throughout each army area, furnishes Soviet Ground Forces a pervious, but still unparalleled shield for fixed and fast-moving targets, such as armored columns on the march.

The average aggregation with armies in East Germany features five kinds of crew-served mobile missiles (which excludes manpacked SA-7 Grails), plus four types of anti-aircraft artillery (Figure 27). The compilation confronts U.S. defense suppression forces with 750 firing points. Except for SA-2s, every SAM carrier mounts two or more missile launchers. Most guns also come in clusters. Vehicles in the main are tracked to accompany tanks. Every system has substantial shortcomings, but synergistic capabilities are considerable when they interlock.[65]

A complex of that sort need not be airtight to function efficiently. Defense suppression demands could divert many U.S. tactical air sorties from armor to SAMs during crucial early days of any conflict, when Soviet forward momentum would be most dangerous. Front Aviation, freed in part from air defense duties, could release some squadrons for more positive purposes. A sizable number of Soviet aircraft doubtless would be downed by their own defenses, since coordination would be exceedingly complex, but pluses apparently outweigh minuses from a practical standpoint.[66]

DOD spokesmen concede that "classic close air support (CAS) as practiced in World War II, Korea, and Vietnam may be an outmoded concept, except under benign conditions. . . ." Even so, "when enemy armor is moving rapidly, the associated defenses are much reduced in effectiveness. This fact coupled with new [U.S.] tactics, area munitions, the GAU-8 gun and a tough aircraft like the A-10 in conjunction with Army attack helicopters, should afford our air forces an opportunity" to score.[67]

Soviet Front Aviation and medium bombers at this stage face fewer constraints from skimpy U.S. systems.

Combined Flexibility

America's tactical air combat assets furnish flexibility not available to the Soviet Union, whose Front Aviation is largely confined to the

Figure 27

AIR DEFENSE FOR ONE SOVIET ARMY

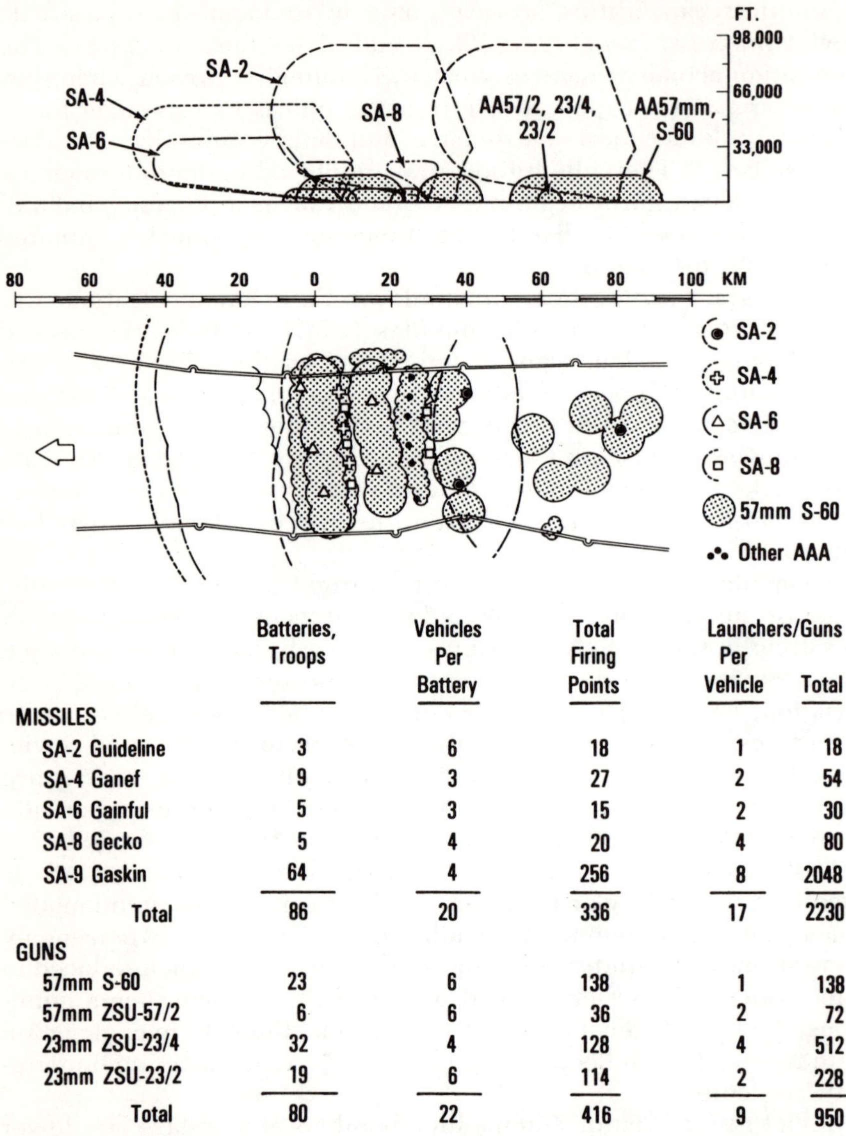

	Batteries, Troops	Vehicles Per Battery	Total Firing Points	Launchers/Guns Per Vehicle	Total
MISSILES					
SA-2 Guideline	3	6	18	1	18
SA-4 Ganef	9	3	27	2	54
SA-6 Gainful	5	3	15	2	30
SA-8 Gecko	5	4	20	4	80
SA-9 Gaskin	64	4	256	8	2048
Total	86	20	336	17	2230
GUNS					
57mm S-60	23	6	138	1	138
57mm ZSU-57/2	6	6	36	2	72
23mm ZSU-23/4	32	4	128	4	512
23mm ZSU-23/2	19	6	114	2	228
Total	80	22	416	9	950

NOTE: SA-9s do not show on diagram.

Eurasian land mass. Our clear qualitative edge is still evident in most respects, although the gap is closing.

Small size, however, creates an Achilles' heel. The several U.S. Services are insufficient to cope with large-scale contingencies, unless they assist each other. Even then, difficulties develop. Air Force-Navy-Marine collaboration, for example, was compulsory in Korea and Vietnam, to such a degree that deterrent/defense capabilities suffered in Central Europe.

Quantitative shortages could prove critical in a showdown with the Soviet Union, since "many-on-one" seems to be Moscow's rule. The few U.S. aircraft, compared with Front Aviation, will find it increasingly perilous to compete if current trends (including those connected with air defense) continue.

Projected U.S. procurement programs do little to brighten the picture.

Graph 12

TACTICAL AIR COMBAT FORCES
Statistical Summary - 1977

(Note Different Scales)

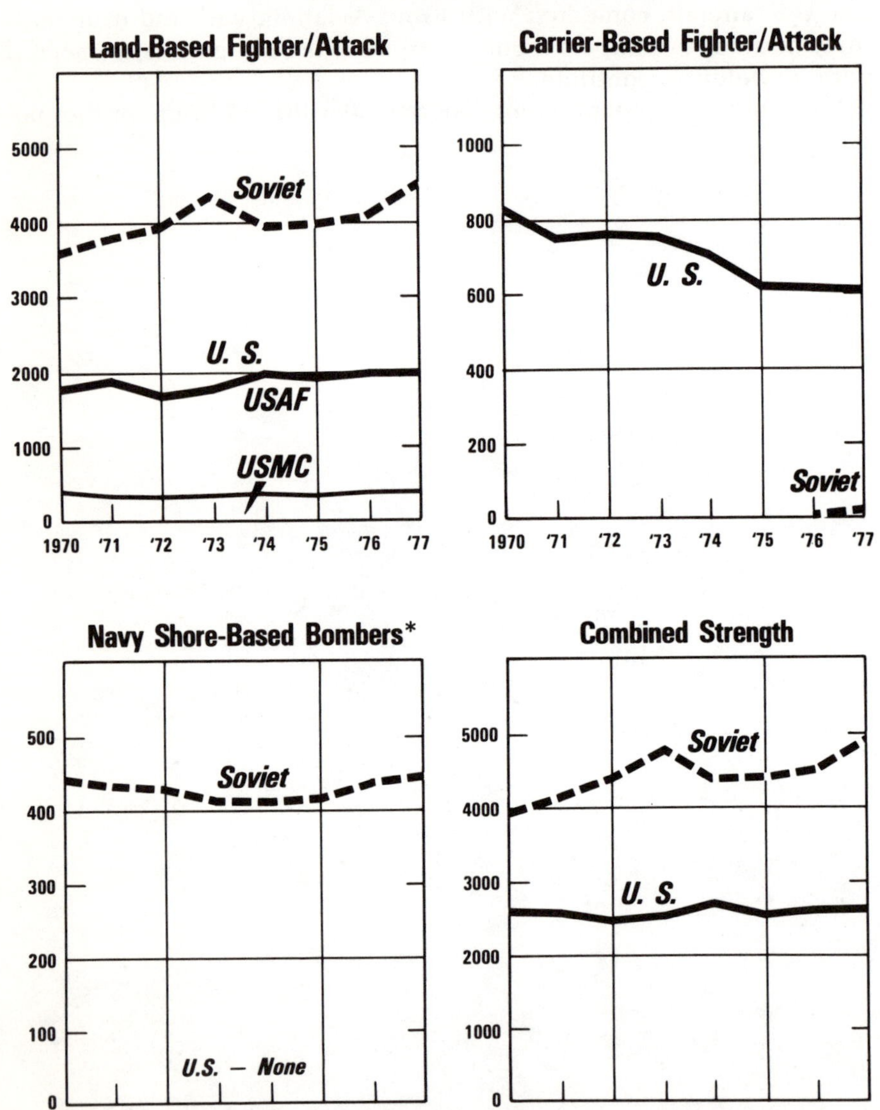

* Not normally directed against targets ashore, but possess such capability.

FIGURE 28 LAND-ORIENTED TACTICAL AIR FORCES
Statistical Trends and System Characteristics

FIGHTERS/BOMBERS[1]	*1970*	*1971*	*1972*	*1973*	*1974*	*1975*	*1976*	*1977*	*Net Change 1970–77*
UNITED STATES[2]									
Air Force									
A-7 Corsair	4	80	144	144	253	224	210	144	+140
A-10 Thunderbolt II	0	0	0	0	0	0	0	24	+ 24
F-4 Phantom	968	971	933	965	1056	1055	1091	1026	+ 58
F-15 Eagle	0	0	0	0	0	0	0	144	+144
F-100 Super Sabre	282	209	9	0	0	0	0	0	−282
F-105 Thunderchief	145	104	66	31	55	38	37	36	−109
F-111	26	158	211	283	311	333	312	282	+256
Total	1425	1522	1363	1423	1675	1650	1650	1656	+231
Marine									
A-4 Skyhawk	94	101	67	89	85	65	76	81	− 13
A-6 Intruder	76	47	45	49	49	56	57	57	− 19
AV-8 Harrier	0	6	13	32	59	53	53	51	+ 51
F-4 Phantom	184	154	144	130	128	130	132	135	− 49
Total	354	308	269	300	321	304	318	324	− 30
Grand Total	1779	1830	1632	1723	1996	1899	1968	1980	+201

[1]All aircraft are unit equipment (UE).
[2]For carrier-based tactical aircraft, see Figure 30.

FIGURE 28 (Con't)

FIGHTERS/BOMBERS	*1970*	*1971*	*1972*	*1973*	*1974*	*1975*	*1976*	*1977*	*Net Change 1970–77*
SOVIET UNION									
Bombers									
TU-16 Badger	500	500	500	500	500	475	475	475	− 25
TU-22 Blinder	175	200	200	200	200	170	170	150	− 25
TU-26 Backfire[3]	0	0	0	0	0	10	20	30	+ 30
IL-28 Beagle	220	180	180	180	180	170	70	0	−220
Total	895	880	880	880	880	825	735	655	−240
Fighter/Attack									
MIG-17 Fresco	800	800	800	900	900	900	600	200	−600
MIG-19 Farmer	100	200	100	50	0	0	0	0	−100
MIG-21 Fishbed	1400	1500	1600	1700	1500	1600	1700	1500	+100
MIG-23 Flogger	0	0	100	200	350	450	900	1100	+1100
SU-7 Fitter	500	500	500	500	400	400	400	300	−200
SU-17 Fitter-C	0	0	50	100	200	200	200	350	+350
SU-19 Fencer	0	0	0	0	0	0	50	150	+150
YAK-28 Firebar	50	50	100	200	50	0	0	0	− 50
Total	2850	3050	3250	3650	3400	3550	3850	3600	+750
Grand Total	3745	3930	4130	4530	4280	4375	4585	4255	+510
U.S. STANDING	−1966	−2100	−2498	−2807	−2284	−2476	−2617	−2275	−309

[3]Backfire bombers are the same aircraft shown on Figure 11.

RECONNAISSANCE[1]	*1970*	*1971*	*1972*	*1973*	*1974*	*1975*	*1976*	*1977*	*Net Change 1970–77*
United States									
RF-101 Voodoo	54	0	0	0	0	0	0	0	− 54
RF-4 Phantom	288	252	234	234	234	216	162	162	−126
Total	342	252	234	234	234	216	162	162	−180
Soviet Union									
MIG-17 Fresco	20	0	0	0	0	0	0	0	− 20
MIG-21 Fishbed	200	320	370	350	330	310	310	310	+110
MIG-25 Foxbat	0	0	10	20	40	70	100	130	+130
YAK-25 Flashlight	120	100	100	100	80	20	0	0	−120
YAK-28 Brewer	120	170	220	220	170	200	190	190	+ 70
IL-28 Beagle	190	220	220	190	130	120	80	40	−150
Total	650	810	920	880	750	720	680	670	+ 20
U.S. Standing	− 308	− 558	− 686	− 646	− 516	− 504	− 518	− 508	−200
HELICOPTER GUNSHIPS[4]									
United States	635	520	535	730	715	685	690	647	+ 12
Soviet Union	0	0	0	100	125	200	300	450	+450
U.S. Standing	+ 635	+ 520	+ 535	+ 630	+ 590	+ 485	+ 390	+ 197	−438

[1]All aircraft are unit equipment (UE).

[4]U.S. armed helicopters are AH-1s. Soviet counterparts are MI-24s and some MI-8 versions.

FIGURE 28 (Con't)

AIRCRAFT CHARACTERISTICS

	First Deployed	Combat[1] Radius (Miles)	Max Speed (Mach)	Payload[2] (lbs)	Typical Weapons		Nuclear Capable	All Weather
					Guns	Missiles/Bombs		
United States								
A-6 Intruder	1963	750	0.9	10,000	None	18 Mk-82	Yes	Yes
A-7D Corsair	1966	550	0.9	7,200	1 20mm	12 Mk-82	Yes	Yes
A-10 Thunderbolt II	1977	300	400 kt	16,000	1 30mm	6 AGM-65	No	Yes
AV-8 Harrier	1969	200	0.9	2,500	2 30mm	AIM-9	No	Yes
F-4 Phantom	1963	550	2.2	16,000	1 20mm	4 AIM-7E 11 Mk-117	Yes	Yes
F-15 Eagle	1977	990	2.5	14,000	1 20mm	4 AIM-9 4 AIM-7E	Yes	Yes
F-100 Super Sabre	1954	450	1.3	9,000	4 20mm	2 AIM-9 or 2 AGM-12	Yes	No
F-105 Thunderchief	1959	625	2.1	10,200	1 20mm	4 AGM-45 or 2 AGM-78	Yes	Yes
F-111	1967	745	2.2	14,500	1 20mm	24 Mk-82	Yes	Yes
Soviet Union								
MIG-17 Fresco	1953	300	0.9	1,100	3 23mm	4 Alkali	No	No
MIG-19 Farmer	1955	425	1.0	1,100	3 30mm	4 Alkali	No	No
MIG-21 Fishbed	1956	400	2.1	2,000	1 23mm	4 Atoll	Yes	No
MIG-23 Flogger	1971	700	2.5	2,800	1 23mm	4 AS-7	Yes	Yes
MIG 25 Foxbat	1970	500	3.2	NA	None	4 Acrid	No	Yes
SU-7 Fitter	1960	300	1.6	5,500	2 30mm	2 Atoll	No	No
SU-17 Fitter-C	1972	600	1.7	5,500	2 30mm	2 Atoll	Yes	Yes

SU-19 Fencer	1974	525	2.0	3,000	1 23mm	4 ?	Yes	Yes
TU-16 Badger	1955	1500	0.8	20,000	7 23mm	2 AS-5, AS-6	Yes	No
TU-22 Blinder	1962	1500	1.4	12,000	1 23mm	1 AS-4	Yes	No
TU-26 Backfire	1974	2500	2.5	10,000	None	2 AS-4	Yes	Yes
YAK-28 Firebar	1961	600	1.1	4,400	None	2 Anab	No	Yes

MISSILE CHARACTERISTICS

					Warhead	
	First Deployed	*Guidance*[3]	*Range (Miles)*	*Speed (Mach)*	*Type*	*Weight, Yield (lbs)*
UNITED STATES						
Air-to-Air						
AIM-7E Sparrow	1963	Radar	14	3.5+	HE	65
AIM-7F Sparrow	1976	Radar	28	3.5+	HE	86
AIM-9 Sidewinder	1958	Infrared	2	2.5	HE	22.5
Air-to-Ground						
AGM-12B Bullpup	1959	Radio	7	1.2	HE	250
AGM-12C Bullpup	1959	Radio	10	1.5	HE	1000
AGM-45 Shrike	1964	PH	10	2.0	HE	145
AGM-65 Maverick	1969	TV	8	*	HE	27
AGM-78 Standard Arm	1968	PH	15.5	2.0	HE	*

[1]Combat radii correspond with payloads shown under average conditions, except Backfire, which is hi-lo-hi, without external weapons.
[2]Payloads are merely representative. External fuel tanks are included where applicable.
[3]IR missile guidance is infrared. PH is passive homing.
*Unclassified data not available.

FIGURE 28 (Con't)

MISSILE CHARACTERISTICS

	First Deployed	Guidance	Range (Miles)	Speed (Mach)	Warhead Type	Warhead Weight, Yield (lbs)
SOVIET UNION						
Air-to-Air						
AA-1 Alkali	1959	Radar, IR	3	*	HE	*
AA-2 Atoll	1960	Radar, IR	3	*	HE	*
Advanced Atoll	1973	IR	5	*	HE	*
AA-3 Anab	1961	Radar, IR	15	*	HE	*
Air-to-Ground						
AS-3 Kangeroo	1960	Preprogrammed Autopilot	350	2.0	Nuke	5000
AS-4 Kitchen	1967	Preprogrammed Auto & Radar	250	4.0	HE/Nuke	2200
AS-5 Kelt	1965	Preprogrammed Autopilot	150	1.0	HE/Nuke	2200
AS-6 Kingfish	1970	Preprogrammed Autopilot	200	3.0	HE/Nuke	1100
AS-7 Kerry	1971	Command	6	1.0	HE	200
AS-9	1975	?	50	subsonic	HE	330

Footnotes

1. For general discussions of U.S. tactical air power see White, William D., *U.S. Tactical Air Power: Missions, Forces, and Costs.* Washington: The Brookings Institution, 1974, 121 pp.; and *Planning U.S. General Purpose Forces: The Tactical Air Forces.* Washington: Congressional Budget Office, January 1977, 51 pp.

2. The evolution of Soviet air power is elaborated in Boyd, Alexander, *The Soviet Air Force Since 1918.* New York: Stein and Day, 1977. 260 pp.; also Menaul, S.W.B., "The Soviet Air Forces." Chapter 6 in *The Soviet War Machine,* pp. 64–112; Berman, Robert P., *Soviet Air Power in Transition,* Washington: The Brookings Institution, 1978, 82 pp.

3. Whether multipurpose aircraft can serve as well as those designed for specific missions is a central issue under consideration by Congress.

4. Air Force Manual (AFM) 1-1, *United States Air Force Basic Doctrine.* Washington: Department of the Air Force, January 15, 1975, p. 3–2. Now under revision.

5. *Ibid.* Political constraints in Korea and Vietnam created "privileged sanctuaries" that contained crucial supply points. American campaigns against moving targets north of the 38th Parallel and along the Ho Chi Minh Trail consequently compelled U.S. air power to "swat flies in the kitchen, instead of spraying the compost." High costs compared with gains under those conditions still make interdiction the most controversial of all U.S. tactical air combat missions.

6. *Ibid.,* p. 3–2/3–3. Among U.S. Services, only the Marine Corps, with its close-knit division-wing teams, permanently rates close air support as the primary mission as a matter of policy. Fleet air defense is the first concern of Navy fliers. Air superiority is always atop the Air Force list, in accord with the axiom that secondary missions cannot otherwise be accomplished. U.S. Congress. Senate. *Close Air Support.* Report of the Special Subcommittee on Close Air Support of the Preparedness Investigating Subcommittee of the Committee on Armed Services. 92d Congress, 1st Session. Washington: U.S. Govt. Print. Off., 1972, pp. 7–9.

7. Close air support is mainly a uniservice matter in the U.S. Marine Corps. "Because the Army and Air Force are separate services . . . . the requirement for [a joint] air-ground communications system and an agreed employment concept (followed by joint training in operational procedures and frequent exercises) is essential." *FM 100-5, Operations,* p. 8–5.

8. Air superiority requires a degree of dominance that permits friendly land, sea, and air forces to operate at specific times and places without prohibitive interference by enemy air activity. Air supremacy allows one side complete freedom of action without effective opposition anywhere in the theater.

9. Ryan, Cornelius, *The Longest Day.* New York: Simon and Schuster, 1959, pp. 270–272.

10. "About one-third of the aircraft in the U.S. combat inventory were designed primarily for attacking surface targets. In the Air Force the duties of these more specialized types (all are subsonic and considered to be limited in air combat capability) were assimilated following World War II by long-range fighters, and the attack designation was discontinued." Until the Air Force adopted A-10s, "all the new designs of this kind [were] developed by the Navy, although the Air Force has adopted some for its use." White, William D., *U.S. Tactical Air Power,* p. 55. Further discussion of missions and airplanes is found on pp. 61–79.

11. *The War Reports of General George C. Marshall, General H. H. Arnold, Admiral Ernest J. King.* New York: J. B. Lippincott, Co., 1947, p. 435.

12. Boyd, Alexander, *The Soviet Air Force Since 1918,* pp. 110–111.

13. Some of the controversy concerning ground attack versus air superiority roles for U.S. and Soviet tactical aircraft is summarized in *Planning U.S. General Purpose Forces: The Tactical Air Forces.* Washington: Congressional Budget Office, January 1977, pp. 12–15.

14. Aerospace Defense Command, a NORAD component, is responsible for counter-air missions in CONUS. See Part IV for discussion.

15. "Under existing law and DOD/JCS directives, the Army has no [close air support] mission," but its attack helicopters assist. U.S. Congress. House. *Tactical Air Warfare.* Hearings Before the Task Force on National Security and International Affairs of the Committee on the Budget. 95th Congress, 1st Session. Washington: U.S. Govt. Print. Off., 1977, p. 154.

16. "Tactical Air Command: Modernization and Management." Special Report. *Aviation Week and Space Technology,* February 6, 1978, 250 pp. See also *Tactical Air Command, Air Force Fact Sheet 77-6.* Washington: Office, Secretary of the Air Force, February 1977, p. 2. Strength figure was drawn from U.S. Congress. Senate. *Seminars: Service Chiefs on Defense Missions and Priorities.* Hearings Before the Task Force on Defense of the Committee on the Budget. Part III. Air Force. Washington: U.S. Govt. Print. Off., 1976, pp. 70–72.

17. "United States Air Forces In Europe," *Air Force Magazine,* May 1977, pp. 84–85; U.S. Congress. Senate. *Seminars: Service Chiefs on Defense Missions and Priorities,* pp. 70–72. USAFE's Commander-in-Chief also commands AAFCE, which includes British, Belgian, Canadian, Dutch, and German squadrons.

18. "Pacific Air Forces," *Air Force Magazine,* May 1977, pp. 73–74. Tactical fighter groups in the ANG control squadrons that are widely separated from parent wings.

19. Ten Soviet squadrons, totalling 150 MIG 21J interceptors, helped defend the Suez Canal before Sadat expelled them in 1972, along with two reconnaissance squadrons. No Soviet Front Aviation is now stationed on foreign soil, except in satellite states. Erickson, John, *Soviet Military Power,* USSI Report 73-1. Washington: United States Strategic Institute, 1973, pp. 62, 64.

20. Erickson, John, *Soviet-Warsaw Pact Force Levels,* p. 48; Gray, Colin, "Soviet Tactical Air Power," Soviet Aerospace Almanac, *Air Force Magazine,* March 1977, pp. 62–63.

21. Open source surveys concerning the structure of Soviet tactical air power conflict in several respects. Data above were derived from written comments by DIA on a draft of this study, February 1978.

22. AFM 1-1, *United States Air Force Basic Doctrine,* pp. 2–2, 3–1.

23. "Tactical Air Command," *Air Force Magazine,* May 1977, p. 80.

24. *Planning U.S. General Purpose Forces: The Tactical Air Forces.* Washington: Congressional Budget Office, January 1977, pp. ix, 27.

25. AFM 1-1, *United States Air Force Basic Doctrine,* p. 2–3; Air Force Fact Sheet 77-6, Tactical Air Command, p. 2.

26. AFM 1-1, *United States Air Force Basic Doctrine,* pp. 2–1, 3–3.

27. *Ibid.,* pp. 2–1, 2–2.

28. *Ibid.,* pp. 1–1, 3–5.

29. Gray, Colin, "Soviet Tactical Air Power," pp. 63–64, 71; Erickson, John, *Soviet-Warsaw Pact Force Levels,* p. 49.

30. Gray, Colin, "Soviet Tactical Air Power," p. 71.

31. *Ibid.*

32. *Ibid.*

33. Dotson, Robert S., "Tactical Air Power and Environmental Imperatives," *Air University Review,* July-August 1977, p. 35.

34. Statement of Charles E. Myers, Jr., Assistant Director of Defense Research and Engineering. Contained in U.S. Congress. House. *Tactical Air Warfare.* Hearings Before the Task Force on National Security and International Affairs of the Committee on the Budget. 95th Congress, 1st Session. Washington: U.S. Govt. Print. Off., 1977, p. 3.

35. *Ibid.*, p. 4. When defending against high-performance aircraft armed with nuclear weapons, consequences of failure are so severe that it often is acceptable to destroy unidentified intruders. The slogan, not much overstated, is "shoot 'em all down, and sort out friend from foe on the ground!"

36. Nothing in the 1950s or 1960s, for example, compared with TAC's realistic "Red Flag" training program, which presently pits U.S. fighter pilots against Soviet tactics in simulated air-to-air combat with a special "aggressor" squadron. Both active and reserve components participate. TAC's "Red Flag" "Getting Ready for the Fatal Test," and TAC's "Red Flag" "Better Training Than Combat." Both by Benjamin F. Schemmer, *Armed Forces Journal*, April 1977, pp. 6, 29 and May 1977, pp. 15, 26–27.

37. Guns are more reliable than most missiles. They can be fired repeatedly at short range during drastic air combat maneuvers. Moreover, aircraft armed with two, or even four, missiles can quickly exhaust supplies, a possibly fatal flaw when opponents are many. Finally, guns and ammunition are cheap compared with missiles. One Sidewinder costs close to $50,000; each Sparrow twice that amount. Telephone conversation with senior U.S. Air Force officers who have extensive practical experience, January 19, 1978.

38. Myers, Charles E., Jr., in *Tactical Air Warfare*, p. 4. "It was common," for example, "to run both sets of [hydraulic] lines right down the strong back of the airplane." If that area was struck, "both the primary and secondary . . . . systems were damaged and control was lost. Fuel cells did not have to be lined to prevent leakage, and so on. The lack of resilience contributed to the high losses from simple enemy [anti-aircraft artillery] AAA defenses."

39. *Ibid.*, pp. 4–5. Recall that the TFX (now known as the F-111A) was expected to "combine deep all-weather nuclear and conventional strike, all-weather intercept, close air support, reconnaissance and air fighting both from land or aircraft carrier. And, it was to be more [cost-effective] at this combination than any existing aircraft."

40. The search for "common" Air Force and Navy tactical aircraft, such as the F-4, causes both Services to compromise on requirements and sometimes increases, rather than reduces, costs. Satisfactory products, as one cynic put it, are "as difficult to create as breeding a desert lizard with a salamander: the offspring will either drown or dry out." Stevenson, James P., "F-14 Versus F-15 Flyoffs: Who Would the Real Winner Be?," *Armed Forces Journal*, June 1975, pp. 40–43.

41. "Hi-lo" is no longer a popular term, but the concept persists. USAF's F-15/F-16 mix is matched by F-14/F-18 in the Navy. Foster, John S., Jr., *The Department of Defense Program of Research, Development, Test and Evaluation, FY 1974.* Statement Before the Defense Subcommittee of the Senate Appropriations Committee, March 28, 1973, pp. 3–1 to 3–8; Schlesinger, James R., *Annual Defense Department Report on the FY 1975 Defense Budget*, p. 223.

42. P-47 fighter bombers in World War II "could fly 100 miles to a target, stay for less than half an hour, deliver .50 cal. machine gun fire and two 250 pound bombs," then return to base. The A-10 carries 16,000 pounds (cannon ammunition, missiles, and bombs in some combination), can cover a combat radius of 250 miles with that cargo, yet still loiter around target areas for two hours before heading for home. Its 30mm GAU-8 gatling gun is seven times more lethal than the standard 20mm cannon. *FM 100-5, Operations*, pp. 2–20.

43. Air-delivered PGMs got their baptism of fire in May, 1972, when a few F-4s destroyed Paul Doumer bridge in the heart of Hanoi and another in Than Hoi, a town farther south. Both bridges had withstood six years of conventional assaults by several hundred sorties at the expense of 18 aircraft.

44. Currie, James B., USAF Director of Programs, in *Tactical Air Warfare*, pp. 155–156. For present limitations of most PGMs, see *Planning U.S. General Purpose Forces: The Tactical Air Forces*, p. 23.

45. Marine aircraft are an integral part of Navy tactical air power, procured with Navy dollars, supplied and serviced by a Navy system. Pilots in large part use Navy training

facilities. This section, however, considers the special contribution of Marine air wings to land-oriented air power.

46. Title 10, United States Code, Chapter 503, Section 5013 and Department of Defense Directive 5100.1, Collateral Functions.

47. "Bare base" kits would allow Navy fighter/attack aircraft to operate off primitive strips ashore, but supply, maintenance, and other support facilities now aboard carriers would be costly to duplicate. Carrier aircraft could, however, share established installations with other services.

48. Marine Corps comments on a draft of this study, September 1977. VSTOL stands for Vertical and/or Short Takeoff and Landing.

49. Title 10, United States Code, Chapter 503, Section 5012 and Department of Defense Directive 5100.1, Collateral Functions.

50. Prina, Edgar L., "Soviet Jet Called Superior to U.S. Version," *San Diego Union*, August 20, 1976, p. 21. Quotes Navy Secretary J. William Middendorf, II. For U.S. details, see Cooper, Bert, *V/STOL Developments: Background and Status of Navy/Marine Corps Vertical and Short Take-off and Landing Aircraft Programs*. Washington: Congressional Research Service, March 1, 1978. 157 pp.

51. Soviet strategic air defense forces could supplement Front Aviation for air superiority purposes, if threats to the homeland did not seem pressing. Squadrons now stationed near national frontiers could be committed quickly.

52. The evolution of aircraft types is described in Erickson, John, *Soviet Military Power*, pp. 62–66.

53. Deployment of new types along with the latest MIG-21 variants, has completely recast Soviet Front Aviation. "Approximately 70% of the fighter and fighter-bomber force comprises modern aircraft introduced since 1970." DIA comments on a draft of this study, September 9, 1977.

54. JCS (J-5) comments on a draft of the study, March 4, 1977.

55. DIA analysts indicate that SU-19 may be a medium-range bomber, rather than a close support aircraft. "If so, this would invalidate the above statement." Comments on a draft of this study, February 1978.

56. SU-17, successor to the aging SU-7, is a more versatile model that can operate efficiently from short, improvised strips, such as country roads, which endows it with admirable dispersal abilities. Its payload is about double that of the MIG-23B, but neither can compare with the highly touted SU-19 as a deep interdiction tool.

57. AIMVAL tests at Nellis AFB, Nevada, terminated in June 1977. F-14 and F-15 fighters armed with Sparrow missiles faced Sidewinders mounted on F-5s, which simulated MIG tactics and flight techniques. Sparrows have about 10 times the Sidewinder's range, but that advantage is dubious if rules of engagement or missile guidance requirements make close contact with enemy aircraft mandatory. Visual identification was essential in this case, which posed no problem for F-14s with TV sighting units aboard. They got clear pictures of "bogey" F-5s at 10–12 miles, safely outside the Sidewinder's range, but crews could not fire and forget their Sparrows, which must be guided to impact by the aircraft's radar. By the time they broke off, F-5 pilots had them in view, and shot a short-range Sidewinder back. Since neither side could evade, not many winners emerged. F-15s, with no long-range identification system, suffered similar fates. Blesse, Frederick C., "The Changing World of Air Combat," *Air Force Magazine*, October 1977, pp. 34–37.

58. JCS (J-5) comments on a draft of this study, March 4, 1977.

59. Helicopter gunships and fixed-wing attack aircraft are complementary, rather than competitive, weapons systems. Helicopters are slower, carry less payload, and have a shorter combat radius. They require more maintenance, as a general rule, and lack comparable passive protection, such as ECM and armor plate. Helicopters, however, can approach target areas at "nap-of-the-earth" altitudes, taking full advantage of terrain features to ward off enemy weapons. They can launch and recover without any

need for large, sophisticated operating bases, loiter at length, and strike with precision under circumstances that sometimes prove impossible for fast-flying fixed-wing aircraft.

60. "Congress Concerned Over Soviet Helos," *Armed Forces Journal,* January 1978, p. 8. Quotes Anthony R. Battista, a staff member of the House Armed Services Committee Research and Development Subcommittee.

61. Turbiville, Graham H., "The Attack Helicopter's Growing Role in Russian Combat Doctrine," *Army,* December 1977, pp. 28–33.

62. Tradeoffs, of course, are required, as with all other multipurpose platforms. Schemmer, Benjamin F., "Soviet Armed Helicopter Force Said to Double By Middle of 1977," *Armed Forces Journal,* December 1976, pp. 28–29.

63. *FM 100–5, Operations,* pp. 2–18/2–19.

64. *Ibid.,* p. 2–19.

65. Menaul, S. W. B., Chapter 6 and Gatland, Kenneth W., Chapter 13 in "The Soviet War Machine," pp. 55–58, 214–215, 225–229; *International Defense Review,* April 1975, p. 183; and "Modernization Marks Soviet Missiles," *Aviation Week and Space Technology,* December 21, 1977, pp. 82–83. Supplemented by telephone conversations with DIA analysts on January 23, 1978.

66. Gray, Colin, *Soviet Tactical Airpower,* pp. 63, 64–65, 69.

67. Myers, Charles E., *Tactical Air Power,* p. 44. Specific countermeasures are summarized on pp. 44–45, 154.

General Purpose Navies

Sea power is a necessity for the United States. Soviet naval needs, by and large, are less compelling.[1]

Commerce, always a U.S. tradition, assumes a salient role as dwindling natural resources increase our dependence on other countries for critical supplies. Petroleum products are most publicized,[2] but mineral shortages are also important.[3] Routes must therefore be secured for friendly merchant ships under adverse conditions.[4] Essential sea lines of communication must also be kept open in wartime to ensure the free flow of military forces and logistic support between America, its allies, and/or contested areas.[5]

The Soviet Union, with far fewer requirements for foreign raw materials and intrinsic interests that center on the Eurasian land mass, has only recently begun to break out of its continental cocoon. Its Navy is still cast as a spoiler that emphasizes negative sea denial, rather than positive sea assertion, capabilities.[6]

This section shows how differences in geographic advantage, size, composition, concepts, and accoutrements influence abilities of U.S. and Soviet general purpose navies to accomplish assigned tasks.[7] Naval forces for strategic nuclear purposes were surveyed in Part IV, specifically the section on ballistic missile submarines. For sealift, including amphibious assault, see Part VI, which concerns mobility.

Geographic Circumstance

Alfred Thayer Mahan, America's great naval strategist at the turn of this century, contended that States which control the Seven Seas can dictate decisions ashore. That contention may have been overstated, but geographic circumstance shapes U.S. and Soviet sea power potential more than any other factor.[8]

U.S. Strengths

The United States is twice blessed with sheltered ports on ice-free coasts that open on the world's largest oceans and, in turn, on every continent. Power can shift easily in response to requirements. Forces from European waters, for example, could reinforce the Far East with relative rapidity, passing through the Panama Canal (as long as it is secure) to weight whatever effort takes priority.[9] No other nation enjoys such freedom and flexibility.

Access to oceans, of course, also exposes this country's flanks to assault from the sea. Multiple entry points are available along our Atlantic seaboard, which comprises a single strategic area from Boston to Norfolk Naval Base. Once ashore, enemy forces could fan out fast on the world's finest roads. Similar concentrations are spaced along the Pacific coast from Seattle to San Diego.[10] No prospective opponent, however, is yet able to take advantage, except with sea-launched missiles. U.S. defense demands would soar only if the Soviet Navy combined extensive amphibious capabilities with command of the seas, an unlikely prospect at present.

Soviet Constraints

The U.S.S.R., with the world's longest coastline, is actually all but landlocked, being bottled up in poorly-placed ports that lack convenient outlets.

Ice impedes most Soviet ports every winter, except for bases in the Black Sea and along the Kola coast just east of Norway, where the Gulf Stream warms arctic waters (Map 10). The White Sea, including Arkhangel'sk, is closed six months each year, on the average, although icebreakers can occasionally open interior channels. The entrance, however, is hard to unblock. The Baltic is better, but the Gulf of Finland often freezes solid (three feet thick at Leningrad). Fast ice fills bays and inlets for three months or so as far south as Riga. Icebreakers keep bases clear in those areas only with great difficulty. Kaliningrad and Baltiysk are best sited, because of strong cross currents close to shore. Pacific ports stay in operation with the aid of icebreakers, which are busy from November through March as a minimum, even at Vladivostok.

When weather is favorable, Soviet naval forces in the main must funnel through natural choke points that pose no crucial problems in peacetime, but would seriously inhibit abilities to use home bases once a war started, if opponents employed blockades to bar passage. Only Petropavlovsk-Kamchatskiy on the Pacific, completely cut off

Map 10
SELECTED SOVIET NAVAL BASES

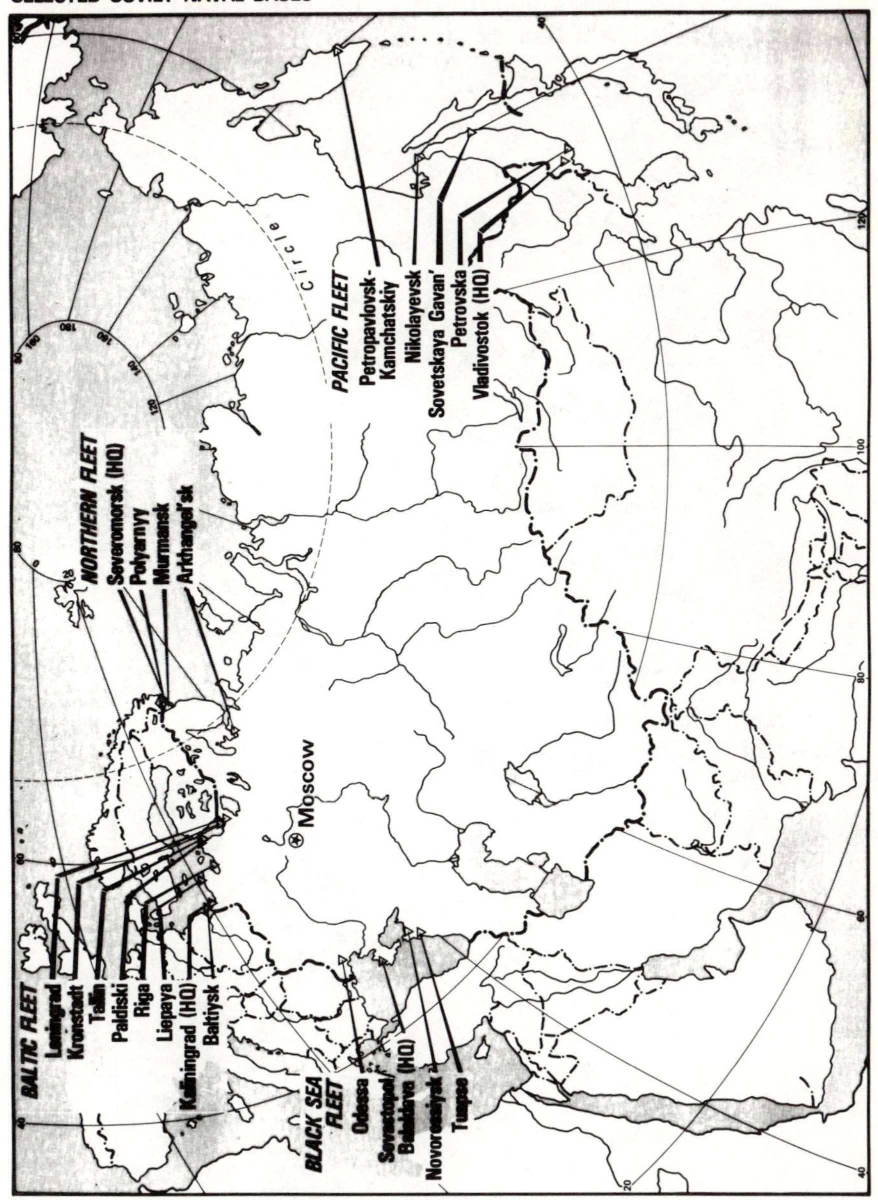

from land routes to civilization, enjoys easy entrance to and egress from open oceans (Map11).

The Greenland-Iceland-Faeroes-U.K. Gap seems porous on the map, but restricted passage reduces search areas for NATO's ASW

Map 11

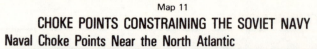

CHOKE POINTS CONSTRAINING THE SOVIET NAVY

Naval Choke Points Near the North Atlantic

Naval Choke Points Near the North Pacific

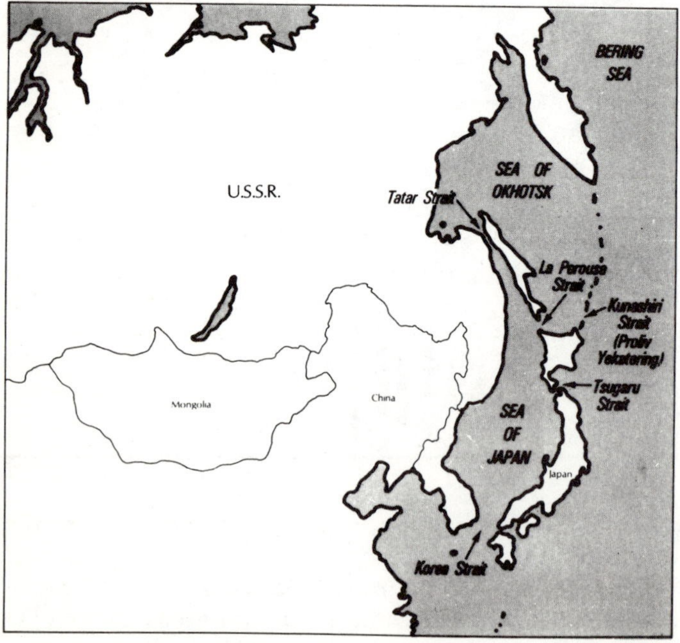

forces, which in wartime would oppose Soviet submarines passing in either direction between the Arctic Ocean and North Atlantic. The seabed there is also suitable for Captor mines, great numbers of which could lie passively on the bottom until activated by passing Soviet submarines.[11]

Other bottlenecks are much more confined. The Baltic's mouth, called the Skagerrak, is only 80–90 miles wide. The Turkish Straits are somewhat tighter. The Bosporus, for example, is bridged at Istanbul and the Dardanelles are nearly as narrow (¾ mile minimum). Shore-based guns guard Gibraltar. Hand grenades could hit ships in the Suez Canal, which is just 179 feet from shore to shore. That sluice likely would be closed in wartime, separating Soviet flotillas in the Indian Ocean from the Black Sea Fleet and its components in the Mediterranean. Korea Strait, at 110 miles, is the widest of five passages that connect the Sea of Japan with the North Pacific. Tsushima Island in its center sharply reduces usable channel space. Tatar Strait is especially slim.[12]

Comparative Structures

Geographic circumstance to a decisive degree dictates the organizational structure of U.S. and Soviet navies.

U.S. Commands

Two unified commands, one for the Atlantic (LANTCOM), a second for the Pacific (PACOM), serve America's needs. (See Figure 1 for interrelationships.)

LANTCOM's naval component is the Atlantic Fleet, whose operational element is Second Fleet. Norfolk is home port for both. Ships and crews therefrom regularly rotate into and out of Sixth Fleet in the Mediterranean, where they come under operational control of U.S. Navy Europe (USNAVEUR), the Navy component of European Command (EUCOM).

Relationships are less complex in PACOM, whose regional responsibilities reach from our own west coast through most of the Indian Ocean (Map 1). PACOM's naval component, the Pacific Fleet, is headquartered at Pearl Harbor, along with Third Fleet, one of its operational elements (although most of Third Fleet is stationed in San Diego). Seventh Fleet, whose Flagship works out of Yokosuka, Japan, patrols the Western Pacific, with Subic Bay as its center of gravity.[13]

Soviet Fleets

The Soviet Navy must maintain three separate fleets in the Baltic, Black, and Barents Seas, plus a fourth in the Northwest Pacific (Map 10). Those splintered elements operate in perpetual isolation from each other. Northern and Black Sea Fleets both furnish forces for the Mediterranean, but mutual support in the main is severely limited.

The Northern Fleet is stationed mainly in a sheltered inlet on the Kola coast, where three important bases string out north to south: Fleet Headquarters at Severomorsk; the ballistic missile and attack submarine complex at Polyarny; and Murmansk, a major logistic center. An affiliate at Arkhangel'sk, on the White Sea, is of secondary significance. The Northern Fleet furnishes submarines for Soviet forces in the Mediterranean, among other things. It also is home for the carrier Kiev.

Soviet naval strength in the Baltic began to branch out about 1940, after absorbing assets that belonged to other states. Kaliningrad, which houses Fleet Headquarters, is collocated with Baltiysk, its biggest operating base, near the present Polish border. Other ports are spotted along the East Baltic coast from Liepaya to Kronstadt and Leningrad. Surface ships and support for Atlantic excursions, including those to Angola and Cuba, come from this source.

The Black Sea Fleet, with Headquarters at Sevastopol/Balaklava, feeds all Soviet naval forces into the Mediterranean, less submarines, whose passage through the Turkish Straits is severely constrained in peacetime by Article 12, Section II of the Montreux Convention. Three of four Soviet aircraft carriers (Leningrad, Moskva, and Minsk) operate from Black Sea bases.

Submarines can navigate inland waterways that connect the Black and Baltic Seas. Warm weather passage from the Baltic to Barents Sea is possible for destroyers and smaller ships. Nuclear submarines built at Gorky, east of Moscow, follow a similar system to Leningrad, where they are fitted out, before joining the Northern Fleet.

The Soviet Pacific Fleet has its headquarters and principal support facilities at Vladivostok. Subsidiary installations hug the shore of Maritime Province as far north as Nikolayevsk, at the mouth of the Amur River. Others, like Magadan on the Sea of Okhotsk, are minor, with one exception: Petropavlovsk-Kamchatskiy, at the southern tip of a huge peninsula, is on truly open water. It provides the primary operating base for Soviet strategic nuclear and attack submarines in the Pacific.

Comparative Missions

U.S. deterrent/defense capabilities must be sufficient to satisfy several interlocking, overlapping naval missions in peacetime and in war.[14] Some Soviet aims are the same. Others are quite different.[15]

Peacetime Naval Presence

Peacetime presence to influence perceptions serves political and military purposes. This country consistently stresses one purpose. The Soviets strongly stress both.[16]

Men who fashion America's foreign policy perceive the U.S. Navy mainly as a military tool for deterrent and defense purposes. It is a peripheral and part-time instrument to exploit political, economic, and social opportunities. The Soviet Navy, in contrast, is routinely used to reap or retain an international reservoir of good will, which Soviet leaders (despite setbacks) try to translate into political persuasion, basing privileges, and other practical products that can have a significant bearing on the U.S./Soviet balance.[17] Their outposts along the African littoral, for example, overlook U.S. and NATO oil LOCs to ports in the Persian Gulf.[18]

Both sides periodically parade flotillas or fleets as deterrent threats in times of tension or crisis to impress each other with intent or resolve. Four such confrontations have taken place in this decade, twice in the Mediterranean during Arab-Israeli disputes, twice in the Indian Ocean.[19]

Sea Control

Freedom of the seas was a self-satisfying U.S. interest from late 1944, after the battle for Leyte, until increased Soviet capabilities started causing serious concerns in the mid-1960s. Since then, sea control, the prime prerequisite for all positive naval operations, has been a U.S. imperative.[20]

Positive U.S. aims demand abilities to deter or defeat enemy aircraft, submarines (including those bearing ballistic missiles), and surface combatants that try to interfere with friendly activities along selected ocean avenues or in associated areas. Local superiority (not necessarily numerical) is essential at specified times and places.[21]

Sea denial, the Soviet specialty, is simpler to satisfy, since the Kremlin can apply power at times, places, and under circumstances of its choosing to prevent the accomplishment of U.S. tasks.

Power Projection

Naval air and/or amphibious forces can assist in controlling seas by projecting power ashore to seize and secure, damage, destroy, or otherwise exert control over critical terrain features (such as Norway's North Cape or the Dardanelles), enemy installations, and ships in port. Power projection capabilities can also support national purposes not associated with sea control, as occurred during U.S. campaigns in Korea and Vietnam.[22]

American stress on such missions has been evident for many years. Soviet interest cropped up in a rather small way only recently.[23]

Comparative Naval Doctrines

U.S. naval doctrine has been in development since the days of John Paul Jones. Soviet doctrine dates back less than three decades. U.S.

concepts, which stress sea control, demand deployments and a general purpose force structure quite different than that needed by the Soviet Navy for sea denial.

U.S. Concepts

Contemporary U.S. strategy dictates that oceans act as "barriers for defense of the Continental United States, as avenues for extension of military and political influence abroad, and for international commerce which is essential to the sustained industrial output of the United States and its allies."[24]

The U.S. Navy, in consonance with resultant requirements, currently assigns about a third of its active operating forces to fleets in the Mediterranean, Western Pacific, and Indian Ocean (Map 12). Another third, located in Hawaii and along CONUS coasts, is ready to reinforce as required, or contend with contingencies in respective areas of responsibility. The remaining third usually is "in depot maintenance or undergoing basic training." Perhaps half of that relaxed reserve could contribute "on short notice to . . . . combat operations at sea." The consequent posture puts U.S. fleets in position to "attack the most probable adversaries, reinforce rapidly and protect [essential] sea lines of communication [SLOC]."[25]

"Sea control is the fundamental function of the U.S. Navy," but admirals and captains make no attempt to attain simultaneous ascendancy over all open seas, or even a single ocean. Fleets simply seek to deter or destroy enemy air, surface, and/or subsurface forces that impinge on U.S. interests in specific areas of competition. "Destruction is preferable," because deterrence permits the foe to fight another day under conditions we might find less favorable.[26]

U.S. *strategic* sea control forces engage "enemy threats at or near their source," bombarding bases, installing barriers, and instigating blockades to prevent opposing ships and aircraft from participating in offensive operations against the United States or its associates. Failing that, contingents seek and "destroy hostile naval combat units on the high seas." *Tactical* sea control connotes "perimeter defense" of designated sites, such as amphibious assembly and assault areas, security for convoys, and mine countermeasures to clear harbors, choke points, and other selected sectors.[27]

"Experience has shown that . . . . integrated operations are the most effective way to fight wars." U.S. Navy doctrine therefore depends on task forces tailored to accomplish particular assignments at particular times and places. Components include aircraft carriers, surface combatants (cruisers, destroyers, frigates, and mine warfare vessels), attack submarines, amphibious forces (both Navy and Marine), patrol craft (aloft and afloat), and support ships. Proper combinations create capacities greater than the strongest ships could ever command in isolation, regardless of quantities or characteristics.[28]

Map 12
U.S. Naval Deployment

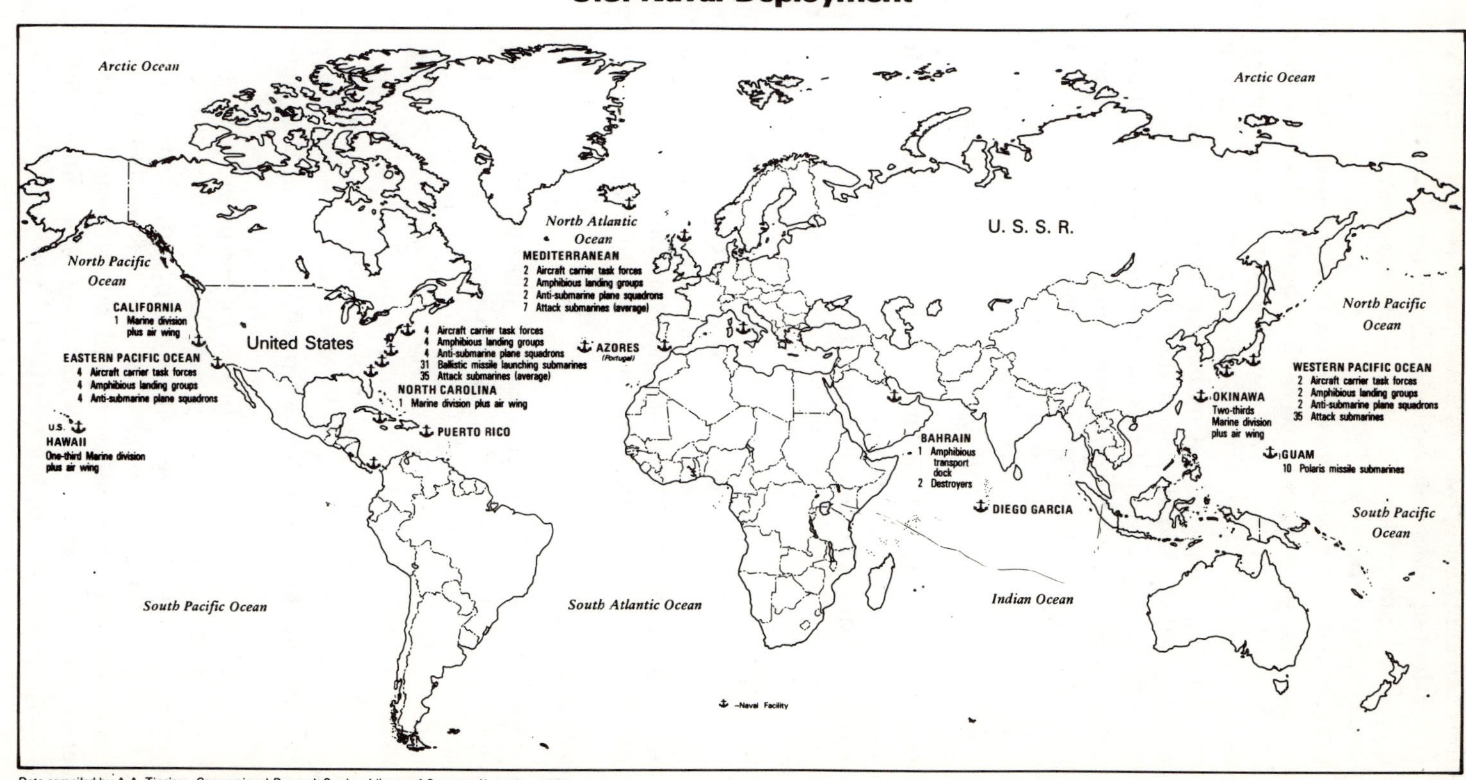

Data compiled by A.A. Tinajero, Congressional Research Service, Library of Congress, November, 1977.
SOURCE: U.S. Navy.

Allies can contribute, but "on a comparative unit for unit basis they are generally not as capable as their U.S. counterparts. In a worldwide conflict allied participation is most likely; in lesser contingencies it is highly scenario dependent."[29]

Overseas bases simplify operation in forward areas. However, they "are becoming more expensive both economically and politically," and their availability when the crunch comes cannot be assured. In direct consequence, U.S. Navy doctrine advises "a high degree of logistical independence. . . . Combatant ships must be able to carry large quantities of combat consumables such as fuel and ammunition; have good sea keeping qualities to ride out heavy weather for long periods . . . . ; and be able to steam long distances without the requirement for refueling stops." Underway replenishment and other special-purpose ships assist. So do Naval Construction Battalions (Seabees), which build and maintain base facilities overseas where suitable structures either do not exist or are not available for U.S. use.[30]

Finally, our Navy, like the Air Force, needs a worldwide command/control and communications (C^3) network to coordinate physically separate but strategically connected activities. The Navy Command and Control System (NCCS) performs that function from fixed and mobile stations. It seeks "to ensure that the National Command Authorities, unified commanders, naval component commanders, and subordinate naval commanders are able to discharge their individual responsibilities by receiving sufficient, accurate and timely information on which to base their decisions and by having available the means to communicate those decisions to the forces involved."[31]

Soviet Concepts

The Soviet Navy had no "blue water" strategy in the 1950s. Desire was present, but no doctrine.[32] That developed under the guiding hand of Fleet Admiral Sergei G. Gorshkov, who spells out his concepts for naval superiority in *Sea Power of the State.*[33] As a Deputy Minister of Defense and Commander-in-Chief of the Soviet Navy since 1956, he has converted principle to practice with unprecedented continuity of purpose.[34] The U.S. Navy has seen nine Service Secretaries and eight Chiefs of Naval Operations during that same 22-year period.

To begin with, Gorshkov believes in sea power as a geopolitical package, in which a strong navy, merchant marine, and sea research activities all play important, mutually-supporting parts, in peacetime and in war. Soviet commercial ships regularly replenish combatants. Fishing fleets collect intelligence and, on call, could quickly convert to active security tasks. Political and economic competition, particularly in the Third World, serves strategic purposes.[35]

Gorshkov's modern Navy started to emerge in the mid-1950s, reputedly in response to perceived threats by Western powers, whose island strongholds surrounded the Soviet Union and its "Socialist Commonwealth." Since navies, as he sees it, must fight future wars with forces on hand and on station at the start, his concept stresses plentiful weapons on the cheapest practical platforms to produce quantities that, combined with quality, could prevail in armed combat. The result is an innovative Service that consciously avoids copying its U.S. counterpart for the sake of essential equivalence.[36]

The focus shifted from coastal defense to sea-based deterrence in peacetime and power projection in event of nuclear war. Submarines armed with ballistic missiles comprise the primary instruments. Most other forces contribute to their security and seek out U.S. SSBNs. Fleet-against-fleet confrontations are strictly secondary in any other context. So are excursions against extended enemy SLOCs, which could be cut quickly and effectively by attacking terminals.[37] Deployment patterns, he implies, are "selected by the Soviet command . . . . not imposed by the enemy."[38] (See Map 13 for typical peacetime dispositions.)

The principal purpose of Soviet sea control is to safeguard ballistic missile submarines from home ports to patrol stations, including passage through choke points held by hostiles, if necessary.[39] Soviet surface ships and aircraft consequently are configured essentially for ASW,[40] but cruise missiles afford them tactical strike capabilities that Gorshkov feels are "practically unstoppable" against floating targets.[41]

Stress on conventional power projection and sea control seems to be increasing, but current capacities are most suitable for small-scale activities in lightly-contested areas. The Soviet Navy has not yet produced credible wartime capabilities to protect its own sea lines of communication against attack by a first-class power. (Larger Soviet aircraft carriers in greater numbers could signal significant change.) Underway replenishment capabilities to offset the shortage of secure overseas bases are still insufficient to support sustained combat operations in remote regions.[42]

Consequently, Gorshkov's doctrine indirectly identifies peacetime presence, including gunboat diplomacy short of shooting wars, as the most realistic role for the Soviet Navy wherever U.S. regional interests outweigh those of the Kremlin.[43]

Comparative Force Structures

U.S. and Soviet naval strategists recognize that specialized forces are required to satisfy respective doctrines, as shown on Figures 29–30. The two sides are structured asymmetrically as a direct result. (See Graph 13 and Figures 31–34 at the end of this section.)

Map 13
Soviet Naval Deployment

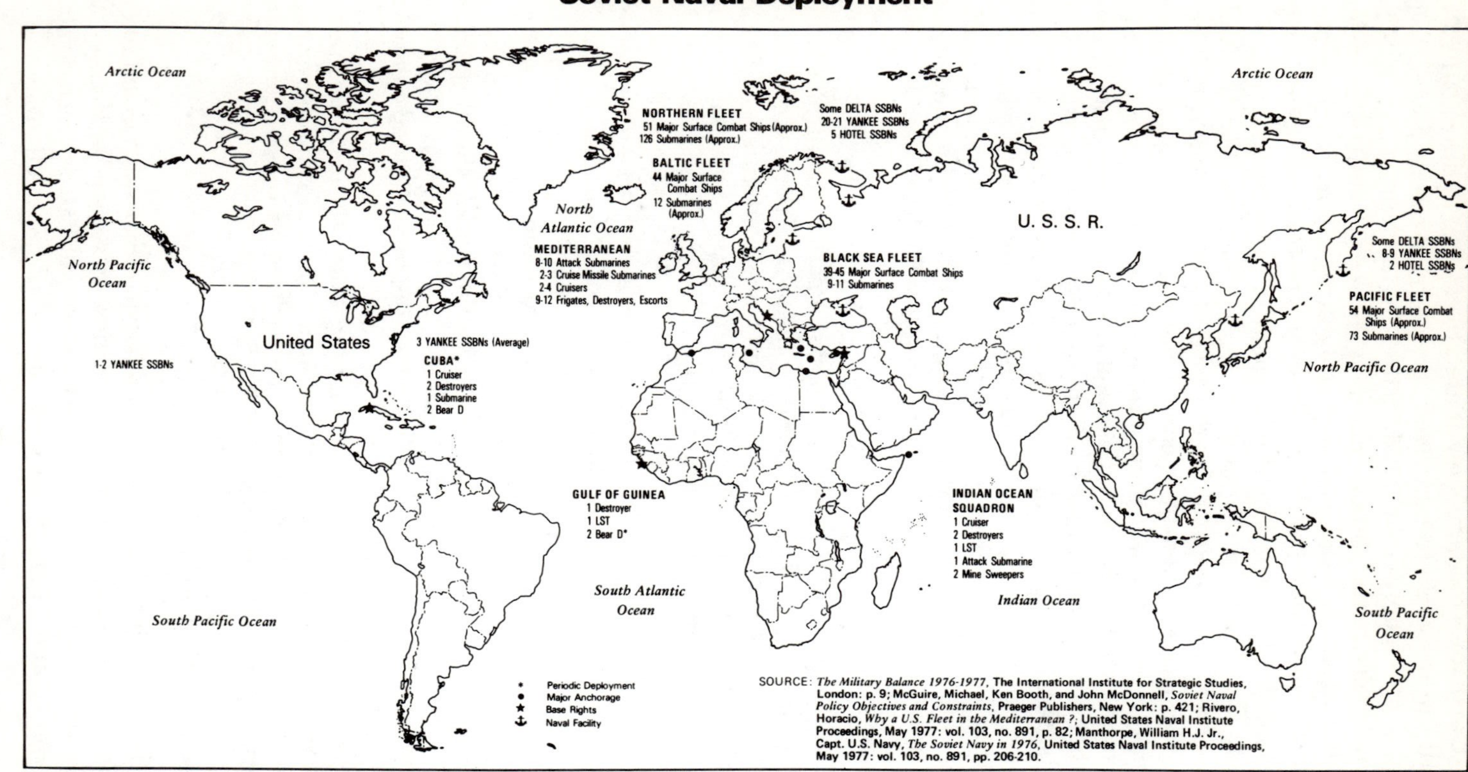

SOURCE: *The Military Balance 1976-1977*, The International Institute for Strategic Studies, London: p. 9; McGuire, Michael, Ken Booth, and John McDonnell, *Soviet Naval Policy Objectives and Constraints*, Praeger Publishers, New York: p. 421; Rivero, Horacio, *Why a U.S. Fleet in the Mediterranean ?*; United States Naval Institute Proceedings, May 1977: vol. 103, no. 891, p. 82; Manthorpe, William H.J. Jr., Capt. U.S. Navy, *The Soviet Navy in 1976*, United States Naval Institute Proceedings, May 1977: vol. 103, no. 891, pp. 206-210.

Data compiled by A.A. Tinajero, Congressional Research Service, Library of Congress, November, 1977.

Figure 29.

TASKS RELATED TO U.S. NAVAL CAPABILITIES

TYPE	CARRIERS	SURFACE COMBATANTS					SUB-MARINES		AMPHIB-IOUS		SUPPORT SHIPS	PATROL AIRCRAFT
	CV CVN	CG CGN	DD	DDG	FF FFG	MSF	SSBN	SS SSN	LHA LPH	LCC LKA LPD LSD LST	AO AE AOR AFS AK AOE AD AS	P-3
SEA CONTROL TASKS												
Anti-Air Warfare:												
Air Superiority	☆								•			
Air Defense	☆	□	•	□	•				•	•		
Anti-Submarine Warfare:												
Long-Range Operations	□							☆				□
Short-Range Operations	□	□	□	□	□			☆				□
Anti-Surface-Ship Warfare:												
Long-Range Operations	☆	(A)	(A)	(A)	(A)		•	□				•
Short-Range Operations	☆	□	□	□	□		•	□	•	•		•
Mine Warfare:												
Offensive	☆							□				□
Countermeasures						☆			□	•		
PROJECTION TASKS												
Strike Warfare:												
Nuclear	□	(B)	(B)	(B)	(B)		☆	(B)				
Conventional	☆	(C)	(C)	(C)	(C)			(C)				
Amphibious Warfare:												
Vertical Assault	•								☆	•		
Over the Beach									•	☆		
Close Air Support	☆								•			
Shore Bombardment		•	☆	☆	•				•			
Special Warfare:								☆	☆	☆		
SUPPORT TASKS												
Intelligence:												
Imagery	☆											
Reconnaissance	☆	•	•		•	•	•	□	•	•		□
Surveillance	☆	•	•	•	•	•		□	•	•		□
Command, Control, and Communications	☆	□	•	•	•		□	□	•	•		□
Electronic Warfare:	☆	□	□	□	□		•	•	•	•		□
Logistics:												
Long-Haul Resupply	□								•	•	☆	
Local Resupply	☆								•	•	☆	
Maintenance and Repair	☆	•	•	•					•	•	☆	

☆ High capability compared to other platforms.
□ Different method of achieving capability compared to ☆
• No extensive capability compared to ☆

(A) Sea-launched cruise missile (SLCM) with extended range, over-the-horizon targeting.
(B) SLCM with terrain contour matching (TERCOM) will provide nuclear strike capability.
(C) SLCM (2nd generation) with guidance accuracies to permit use of conventional warheads.

Data compiled by A.A. Tinajero and Ray F. Bessette, Congressional Research Service, Library of Congress.

Figure 30.

TASKS RELATED TO SOVIET NAVAL CAPABILITIES

	CARRIERS	SURFACE COMBATANTS					SUB-MARINES		AMPHIB-IOUS	SUPPORT SHIPS	PATROL AIRCRAFT
TYPE	CVSG CHG	CG CL	DD	DDG	FF FFL	MSF	SSBN SSB	SS SSN SSG SSGN	LST LSM	AOR AS AG AGI AK AR	TU-95 IL-38
SEA CONTROL TASKS											
Anti-Air Warfare:											
Air Superiority											
Air Defense	☆	□	•	□	•				•		
Anti-Submarine Warfare:											
Long-Range Operations	□							☆			□
Short-Range Operations	□	□	•	•	•			☆			□
Anti-Surface-Ship Warfare:											
Long-Range Operations	☆ (A)	☆ (B)					•	☆ (C)			
Short-Range Operations	□	□	•	•	•		•	☆			
Mine Warfare:											
Offensive	•	□	□	□	•			☆			□
Countermeasures						☆					
PROJECTION TASKS											
Strike Warfare:											
Nuclear	□ (A)	□ (B)					☆	□ (C)			
Conventional	☆ (A)	□ (B)									
Amphibious Warfare:											
Vertical Assault	☆										
Over the Beach									☆		
Close Air Support	☆ (A)										
Shore Bombardment		☆ (D)	☆	☆	•						
Special Warfare:								☆	□		
SUPPORT TASKS											
Intelligence:											
Imagery	☆										□
Reconnaissance	☆	•						□	•	□	□
Surveillance	☆	□	•	•	•	•		□	•	□	□
Command, Control, and Communications:	☆	☆	•	•	•	•	□	□	•		□
Electronic Warfare:	☆	☆	•	•	•	•		•	•		□
Logistics:											
Long-Haul Resupply	□									☆	
Local Resupply	□									☆	
Maintenance and Repair	•	•	•	•					•	☆	

☆ High capability compared to other platforms.
□ Different method of achieving capability compared to ☆
• No extensive capability compared to ☆

(A) Kiev CVSG only.
(B) Kynda, Kresta I CG's only.
(C) Echo II SSGN, Juliet SSG only.
(D) Sverdlov CL only.

Data compiled by Ray F. Bessette, on contract to Congressional Research Service, Library of Congress.

Aircraft Carriers

America's air power afloat has been quantitatively cut in half since 1965, when 25 carriers (not counting helicopter platforms for amphibious assault) were still in active service. Flexibility was first-rate. This country truly had two-ocean offensive capabilities at that time.[44]

Reductions to the current complement of 13 carriers (Figure 31) have caused drastic revisions in forward deployment patterns since the start of this decade. Just four are positioned permanently overseas—two in the Western Pacific, two in the Mediterranean. Those in the Pacific take care of the Indian Ocean. One in the Mediterranean is on call for excursions into the North Atlantic. Surge capabilities are slight.[45] Still, 200 U.S. fighter/attack aircraft are available in key areas at all times.[46]

The Soviet Navy, in contrast, has no attack carriers (CVA) comparable to our Midway class (in service since 1945), much less the nuclear-powered Enterprise, Nimitz, or Eisenhower (CVAN).[47] The Kiev (CVS-G), with its few high performance aircraft, is essentially an ASW platform, despite formidable missile armament. Its sister ship, the Minsk, is nearing operational status, but has not yet joined any fleet.[48] Moskva and Leningrad (CHG), which come equipped with ASW helicopters, apparently are the first and last in their class, which was designed to destroy ballistic missile submarines when short-range U.S. SLBMs required launch positions near European coasts. Land-based aircraft could cover the Soviet search. That situation changed when Polaris A-3 and Poseidon missiles replaced Polaris A-2s. Their range, 1,100 miles longer, allowed them to launch from stations beyond the effective reach and search capabilities of most reconnaissance craft tied to distant shores. The Soviet Navy has no counterparts for eight U.S. helicopter carriers (LPH, LHA), which support amphibious assault forces and perform other useful functions.

Other Major Surface Combatants

Numbers of U.S. major surface combatants assigned to the Regular Navy have declined dramatically during this decade, while Soviet strength stayed steady (Figure 32). America's cruiser (CG, CGN) quantities are still roughly the same, but 94 destroyers (DD, DDG) were decommissioned, while only four were delivered.[49]

Quality tells an even more telling tale.

Ships on the Soviet side are somewhat smaller than those in the U.S. Navy. Kresta cruisers, for example, displace 7,500 tons, slightly less than a U.S. Spruance class destroyer. Krivak DDs, at 4,000 tons, are a little larger than our latest frigates (FF, FFG). One new cruiser may be nuclear-powered. The United States has eight nuclear surface ships, including three aircraft carriers.

Soviet ships, however, are generally faster and, as every captain knows, an edge of one or two knots can be crucial in evading, engaging, or simply keeping station with the enemy. Major combatants mount a total of 72 cruise missiles created expressly to kill surface ships. Something like 175 SS-N-14 ASW missiles may also have anti-surface ship capabilities.[50] Endurance and seaworthiness have increased, along with offensive combat power. Krivak DDs, for example, are "ton-for-ton the heaviest armed and most effective [destroyers] afloat."[51] Several classes, such as Sverdlov, Kilden, and Kotlin, are reaching the theoretical end of their hull life (25–30 years, depending on ship type and circumstance), but many have been remodelled or reconstructed.

Coastal Combatants

The Soviet Union has more coastal combat craft, including minesweepers, than the rest of the world combined.[52] Neither the U.S. Navy nor Coast Guard has anything to equal 15 Nanuchka class coastal combatants or 120 Osa patrol boats with cruise missiles for shore-line defense (Figure 32).

Attack Submarines

The excellence of U.S. nuclear-powered attack submarines (SSNs) is widely acknowledged. They are not as fast as some Soviet boats (their Victors are the world's speediest), but are quieter and better equipped. The new Los Angeles class (SSN-688), now entering our inventory with wire-guided acoustic homing torpedoes and improved sonar systems, should strengthen the U.S. position.[53] So should Harpoon missiles, which presently are deployed on just one U.S. submarine.

Qualitative superiority, however, is insufficient when quantity is also essential.

U.S. attack submarines share ASW missions with several other fixed and mobile systems, but they play the paramount role. The 74 that remain after recent reductions therefore face distinct disadvantages trying to check three times their number in open oceans, even though most of their prey are diesel-powered and many are well past their prime (Figure 33). The balance would be better with the order of battle reversed.

Sixty-seven Soviet submarines, which account for more than a fourth of the force, are fitted to fire anti-ship cruise missiles. Total tubes exceed 400. Papa and Charlie classes can shoot from submerged positions. All classes carry torpedoes for close combat.

U.S. naval air power is mainly afloat. Soviet strength is almost all ashore (Figure 34).[54]

Land-based aircraft on both sides engage in ASW activities, active as well as passive, but only the Soviet Navy specializes in anti-surface ship strike forces. More than 300 aging Badger bombers, the basic component, can reach about 1,600 miles from home stations without refueling.[55] Their ability to pierce U.S. protective fighter shields would be poor if they carried gravity bombs, but cruise missiles can be launched at least 100 nautical miles from targets. Supersonic Backfires, whose naval numbers are increasing, open up new options. Others in Long-Range Aviation could act as backup.

B-52s armed with precision-guided munitions recently joined the competition, in accord with collateral functions of long standing,[56] which heretofore were finessed. Air Force tactical aircraft could augment SAC's shore-based strike capabilities, especially if forces receive Harpoon.[57]

Soviet Shortcomings

The "new" Soviet Navy suffers from several chronic shortcomings that it shares with the "old", not counting geographic constraints.

All Soviet surface ships would contend with lack of air cover if they swept far from friendly shores. Land-based bombers for area defense and on-board SAM clusters for short-range and point defense are poor substitutes for defenses-in-depth that feature carrier-based fighters.

Soviet naval forces are also short on stamina, except for late-model ships, such as Kiev, Kara, and Krivak. Small surface combatants, lacking large fuel capacities or nuclear power, have limited ranges. Restricted space for rations, ammunition, and other stores prohibit prolonged operations without resupply. Merchant tankers routinely refuel Soviet ships at sea, and trawlers serve some logistic purposes, but underway replenishment procedures are substandard compared with U.S. skills. Lengthy, large-scale operations would be next to impossible in sea areas remote from friendly port facilities.[58]

Finally, most conscripts quit after three years' service. Problems attendant to training 100,000 recruits every year (a fifth of the total force) almost beggar imagination in this specialized age, even though commissioned officers act as technicians in many cases.[59]

Soviet Strengths

Abilities of the Soviet Union to satisfy positive sea control and conventional power projection missions against U.S. opposition will generally be restricted to regions along its periphery until limitations just outlined are alleviated. The capacity for coordinated attacks on U.S. men-of-war and merchant shipping, however, could menace American missions. Eight task forces, totalling more than 200 surface ships and submarines, plus land-based naval aviation, deployed in diverse ocean areas during "Okean-75". Satellite surveillance, computerized data flow, and almost simultaneous communications reportedly coordinated functions that included convoy tracking and simultaneous cruise missile launches from widely-separated sites.[60]

Threats to the U.S. Surface Navy

A recent National Security Council study of U.S. strategy and naval missions reportedly revealed three major Soviet threats to the U.S. surface navy. All three concern anti-ship missiles.[61]

Anti-Ship Missiles and Strategy America's general purpose Navy depends on carrier aircraft for offensive sea power. The Soviet Navy specializes in ship-killing cruise missiles.

That imbalance began about two decades ago, when U.S. policy decisions scrapped our pioneer cruise missile programs and shifted funds to other systems that took priority.[62] Admiral of the Fleet S. G. Gorshkov, who took the opposite tack, watched Egypt test his theories in 1967 by sinking the Israeli destroyer Eilath with Soviet-supplied SS-N-2A Styx. He is now convinced that not even well-screened, nuclear-powered aircraft carriers could withstand assaults "delivered by a group of ships armed with cruise missiles." His conviction "pertains in equal measure to independent naval air operations" by shore-based bombers. "A single submarine is capable of destroying a major surface ship with a salvo of cruise missiles."[63]

Fifteen sorts of Soviet surface warships, submarines, and aircraft consequently carry at least one kind of cruise missile.[64]

Most Soviet long-range missiles (more than 100 miles) are jet propelled. Many short-range models are solid-fuel rocket powered. Speeds vary from 600 knots to several times faster than sound. Some, with small visual and radar cross-sections, confound anti-aircraft gun crews by skimming across the sea's surface. Others, with steep terminal trajectories, dive straight onto targets. In-flight corrections and terminal homing are the rule. The weight of some warheads exceeds a ton.[65]

Soviet strategy seems designed to seize and secure initiative with a single killing salvo. Missile-carrying surface ships, submarines, and aircraft, moving without any semblance of tactical formation, could trigger surprise preemptive strikes on signal, converging on targets from many directions, and perhaps from point-blank range.[66] U.S. aircraft carriers, cruisers, and support ships comprise high-contrast concentrations for Soviet missile seekers. To infrared scanners, they seem hot against cool sea backgrounds; to radars, they are large corner reflectors; to radiometric sensors, such as magnetic anomaly detectors, they are massive metal structures.[67]

Tactics close to shore tend to be somewhat different. Small, missile-bearing boats (nicknamed Wasp, Gnat, and Mosquito[68]) are difficult to distinguish in the coastal clutter of shallow-draft civilian craft and other reflectors. Short ranges and awesome weapons power could overwhelm warships caught unaware. Low-flying Soviet aircraft with cruise missiles complicate U.S. defensive problems. The impact on American power projection missions, particularly amphibious assaults, could be profound.[69]

U.S. Countermeasures U.S. sea control tactics traditionally try to destroy enemy weapons before they endanger our ships. Surprise first strikes by Soviet cruise missiles, launched at close range, could make that approach obsolete.

Active defenses alone appear inadequate. America's current ship-launched SAMs would be essentially ineffective against concerted attacks. "The time from detection to target engagement is [still] excessive and coordination among missile batteries on different ships . . . is poor. These difficulties are compounded by [SAM] system vulnerability to electronic counter-measures."[70] Even Phoenix-armed F-14s, which can engage six targets simultaneously, are subject to easy saturation if large-scale attacks box the compass.[71]

Diverting, rather than destroying, enemy missiles in flight therefore assumes increased importance. Authorities, however, generally agree that any navy which relies solely on decoys, jammers, chaff, and other electronic countermeasures for defense is doomed to take heavy losses when counter-countermeasures come into play.[72]

Successful defense likely will depend on SAMs and interceptor aircraft systems in combination with ECM, strategy, tactics, and doctrine. An appropriate package is not yet available.

Threats to Merchant Shipping

Soviet submarine threats to friendly merchant shipping are potent and potentially pervasive.

The Soviet Submarine Challenge Cruise missiles, with ranges from 25 to 250 miles, supplement new Soviet families of homing, acoustic, and wire-guided torpedoes. Submarines that serve as launch platforms can swim farther, faster, and deeper than predecessors, while suppressing sound more effectively. Special features include inertial navigation, highly-directional passive sonar, and receivers to warn of airborne and seaborne radar.[73]

Recent deployments have been unprecedented.[74] Submarines from the Northern Fleet, for example, surged between Norway and North America in April 1977, severely straining NATO's surveillance apparatus. Most intruders were attack types. At least 40 cruised across crucial shipping lanes south of Iceland. Soviet surface flotillas and missile-bearing aircraft acted as ASW "shotguns."[75]

America's ASW Response Successful ASW operations depend on abilities to find, fix, and finish enemy undersea raiders before they can wreak heavy damage.

Sensitive sensors on, over, and under the sea assist skilled crews in the U.S. search. Systems are active and passive, point and area, fixed and mobile. Some record radiations. Others register sound. Each is coupled with sophisticated torpedoes, depth charges, "smart" mines, and missiles mounted on improved platforms.[76] The aggregate, which causes cautious optimism among responsible U.S. officials,[77] is highly automated. "Sensors, navigation instruments, flight controls and weapons delivery systems are digitally interconnected. Computers can . . . . detect and identify a hostile submarine, select the appropriate weapon, and then photograph the results after that weapon is fired."[78]

Prospects for U.S. success thus are more favorable than they were a few years ago. Even so, breakthroughs in detection are still in the blueprint stage. Beyond that, the size of America's specialized force seems insufficient. ASW is mainly a time-consuming matter of attrition, in which numbers count more and more as friendly losses mount. Some authorities conclude that America at most might sink 20 percent of all Soviet submarines before they took serious toll among merchantmen.[79] Consequently, Soviet capacities to interfere with U.S. lifelines at sea could prove to be low-cost, low-risk operations under certain circumstances, at least as long as a "Mexican standoff" persists at strategic nuclear levels.

Protection for petroleum tankers plying routes from the Persian Gulf to U.S. and European ports is a case in point.

Convoys would reduce attrition, but U.S. escorts currently are inadequate even to shepherd ships along the 5,000-mile course to Capetown, if the Suez Canal were closed. Combat losses would cut effectiveness further. Land-based aircraft could provide part-time cover for unarmed, unaccompanied tankers following random tracks across the Atlantic, provided appropriate base rights could be obtained in neutral or allied countries, but would be a poor substitute for on-the-scene ASW support.[80]

Similar problems are apparent in the Pacific, where our Navy reputedly could keep sea lanes open to Alaska and Hawaii. It would, however, be hard pressed to control seas farther west against Soviet attack.[81]

Mine Warfare

The U.S. Navy has long been skilled at mine warfare, which helped strangle Japanese shipping in World War II and sealed off Haiphong harbor 30 years later. Still, Soviet mine*laying* capabilities are much more extensive (most ships have significant capacity) and generally superior, although tactics are somewhat different.[82]

The Soviet edge in mine*sweeping*, where we have better techniques but no numbers, is even more evident.[83]

America's active minesweeping ships (as opposed to aerial platforms) have all but disappeared. Sixty have been decommissioned since 1970, leaving only three. Twenty-two in the Naval Reserve would be hard pressed to clear important CONUS harbors expeditiously if extensive mine warfare occurred. U.S. mine clearance capabilities in support of amphibious assault operations are also strained. Rotary-wing aircraft supposedly supplant our former surface force for that purpose, but many Soviet mines are laid at depths beyond their reach. Moreover, Marines and minesweeping helicopters would compete for space on aircraft carriers at times when that could affect operations adversely. NATO navies could not take up the total slack if war occurred in Europe.

The Soviets, in contrast, maintain more than 360 ocean-going and coastal craft for minesweeping purposes. Their efforts might be easier than we would like if they were called on to break up U.S. barriers, because our clearance of Haiphong harbor and the Suez Canal were conducted in full view of Gorshkov's intelligence agents, who could copy techniques.

The U.S. Coast Guard

The U.S. Coast Guard, in accord with Title 14, Section 2 of the United States Code, is directed to "develop, establish, maintain and operate, with due regard to the requirements of national defense," facilities for specialized "service in the Navy in times of war."[84]

Consequently, the Coast Guard owns assorted airplanes and 2,000-odd surface craft. Not many more than 100, however, are armed. Thirty some cutters carry artillery. Twelve come equipped with torpedoes. Eighty patrol boats boast nothing bigger than mortars and machine guns. (See Figure 35.) Wartime utility of that small complement is conditioned by peacetime tasks. Rescue operations, for example, require shallow-draft hulls that are incompatible with ASW sonars. Search radars in most cases displace deck guns.

Correlation between U.S. Coast Guard and Soviet coastal combatant capabilities is accordingly low.

Current U.S. Flexibility

The current status of U.S. sea power is contentious.[85] Prophets at opposite poles probably will prove false, but present trends, even so, provide poor support for complacency. Serious students of naval strategy sum up the situation with one succinct statement: the U.S. Navy now enters an era of reduced options and reinforced risk.[86]

Graph 13

NAVAL COMBATANTS
Statistical Summary

(Note Different Scales)

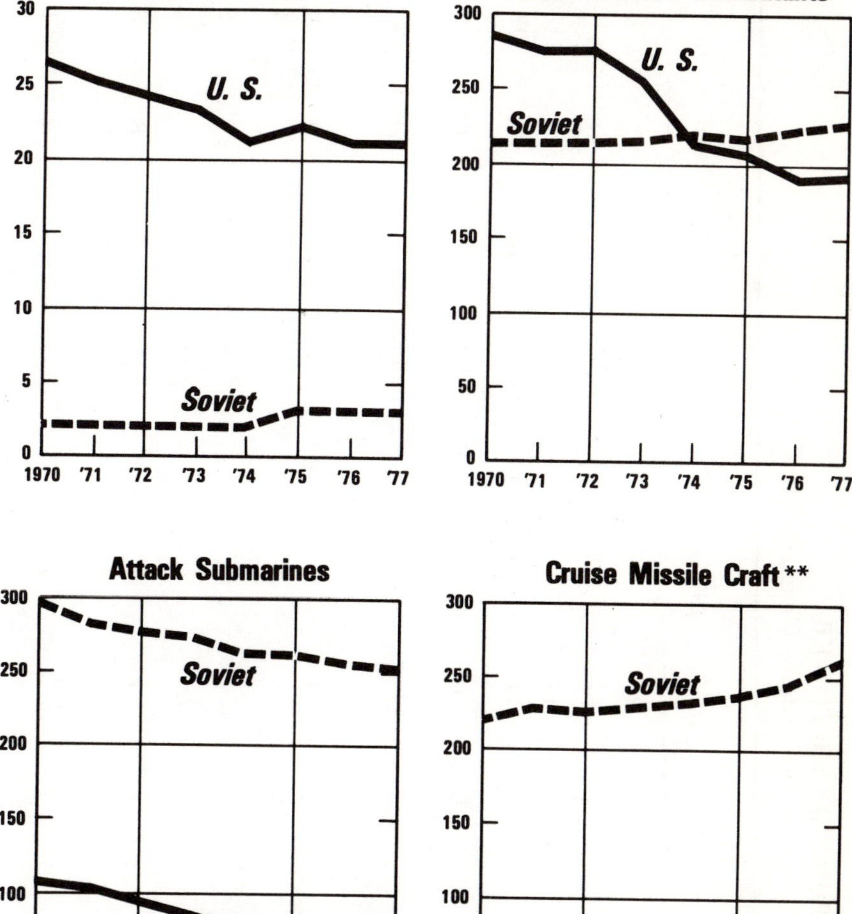

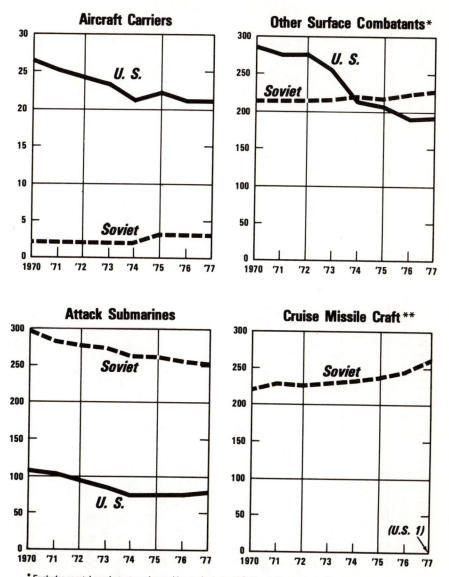

* Excludes coastal combatants and patrol boats; includes U.S. Naval Reserve ocean-going escorts.
** Includes cruise missile patrol boats.

FIGURE 31 CARRIER-BASED AIR POWER
Statistical Trends and Systems Characteristics

	1970	*1971*	*1972*	*1973*	*1974*	*1975*	*1976*	*1977*	*Net Change 1970–77*
ATTACK CARRIERS									
United States									
Nuclear	1	1	1	1	1	2	2	2	+1
Oil	14	13	13	13	13	13	11	11	−3
Total	15	14	14	14	14	15	13	13	−2
Soviet Union	0	0	0	0	0	0	0	0	0
U.S. Standing	+15	+14	+14	+14	+14	+15	+13	+13	−2
ASW CARRIERS									
United States	4	4	3	2	0	0	0	0	−4
Soviet Union[1]	2	2	2	2	2	3	3	3	+1
U.S. Standing	+ 2	+ 2	+ 1	Par	− 2	− 3	− 3	− 3	−5
HELO CARRIERS									
United States[2]	7	7	7	7	7	7	8	8	+1
Soviet Union	0	0	0	0	0	0	0	0	0
U.S. Standing	+ 7	+ 7	+ 7	+ 7	+ 7	+ 7	+ 8	+ 8	+1

GRAND TOTAL									
United States	26	25	24	23	21	22	21	21	−5
Soviet Union	2	2	2	2	2	3	3	3	+1
U.S. Standing	+24	+23	+22	+21	+19	+19	+18	+18	−6
FIGHTER/ATTACK AIRCRAFT[3]									
United States									
A-4 Skyhawk	147	38	41	42	30	40	0	0	−147
A-6 Intruder	119	118	105	113	115	97	104	107	− 12
A-7 Corsair	254	308	312	312	283	300	274	255	+ 1
F-4 Phantom	229	246	253	238	209	95	139	125	−104
F-8 Crusader	78	41	45	45	43	38	0	0	− 78
F-14 Tomcat	0	0	0	0	23	50	93	121	+121
Total	827	751	756	750	703	620	610	608	−219
Soviet Union									
Yak-36 Forger	0	0	0	0	0	0	15	30	+ 30
U.S. Standing	+827	+751	+756	+750	+703	+620	+595	+578	−249

[1]Soviet ASW Carriers include the Moskva, Leningrad, and the Kiev.
[2]"Helo Carriers" are U.S. Marine amphibious assault carriers, LPH and LHA. These carriers are the same ships shown in Figure 38, Amphibious Sealift.
[3]UE aircraft only, excluding reconnaissance, training, and special-purpose versions.

FIGURE 31 (Con't)

	1970	1971	1972	1973	1974	1975	1976	1977	Net Change 1970–77
ASW AIRCRAFT									
United States									
S-2 Tracker	91	83	73	68	52	31	5	0	−91
S-3 Viking	0	0	0	0	0	28	73	118	+118
SH-3 (Helo)	54	62	60	56	56	56	56	80	+ 26
LAMPS (Helo)	0	0	11	17	37	43	56	57	+ 57
Total	145	145	144	141	145	158	190	255	+110
Soviet Union									
KA-25 Harp (Helo)	80	95	95	145	160	170	180	190	+110
U.S. Standing	+ 65	+ 50	+ 49	− 4	− 15	− 12	+ 10	+ 65	par

AIRCRAFT CARRIER CHARACTERISTICS

	Fighter Aircraft	*Attack Aircraft*	*Recon Aircraft*	*ASW Aircraft*	*Average Age (Years)*	*Cruise Missiles*	*Other Weapons*	*Speed (Knots)*
United States								
Attack (CVA)	24 F-4/F-14	24–36 A-7, A-6	10 RA-SC	10 S-2/S-3	23	None	Sea Sparrow/ Terrier	35
Helicopter (LPH)	Carries a mix of about 20 CH-46, Ch-53, UH-1, AH-1 HELOS				12	None	Sea Sparrow/ 4 3in .50 cal	20

Helicopter (LHA)	Carries a mix of about 16 CH-46, 6 CH-53, 4 UH-1E helicopters AV-8s may replace some helos.				1	None	Sea Sparrow 3 5-in .54 cal	22
Soviet Union								
ASW (CVS-G)[1]	Carries up to 30 YAK-36 and/or ASW Helicopters				2	8 SS-N-3/12	Torpedoes, ASW Rockets, SUW-N-1	30+
Helicopter (CHG)	0	0	0	20 Helo	10	None	Torpedoes, ASW Rockets	30

AIRCRAFT CHARACTERISTICS

	First Deployed	*Combat Radius (Miles)*[2]	*Max Speed (Mach)*	*Payload (lbs)*[3]	*Typical Weapons*		*Nuclear Capable*	*All Weather*
					Guns	*Missiles/bombs*		
FIGHTER/ATTACK								
United States								
A-6 Intruder	1963	750	0.9	10,000	None	18 Mk-82	Yes	Yes
A-7D Corsair	1966	550	0.9	7,200	1 20mm	12 Mk-82	Yes	Yes

[1]Kiev class carriers can carry a mix of up to 30 fixed- and rotary-wing aircraft. All 30 could be Yak-36, but 10–15 seems standard.
[2]Combat radii correspond with payloads shown under average conditions.
[3]Payloads are merely representative. External fuel tank are included wherever applicable.

FIGURE 31 (Con't)

AIRCRAFT CHARACTERISTICS

	First Deployed	*Combat Radius (Miles)*[1]	*Max Speed (Mach)*	*Payload (lbs)*[2]	*Typical Weapons*		*Nuclear Capable*	*All Weather*
					Guns	*Missiles/bombs*[3]		
United States								
F-4J Phantom	1961	475	2.2	15,500	None	8 AIM-7/9	Yes	Yes
F-14 Tomcat	1973	580	2.3	17,600	1 20mm	8 AIM-7/9 6 AIM-54	No	Yes
Soviet Union								
YAK-36 Forger	1976	300	Subsonic	*	*	*	No	Yes
ASW AIRCRAFT			*Patrol Speed (mph)*	*ASW Weapons*			*Detection Devices*	
United States								
S-2 Tracker	1954	675	150	2 torpedoes or depth charges			MAD, radar, sonobuoys	
S-3 Viking	1974	1,200+	200	4 torpedoes or other mix			MAD, radar, sonobuoys	
SH-3 (Helo)	1961	100	135	2 torpedoes or other mix			MAD, radar, dipping sonar	
LAMPS (Helo)	1973	60	150	1 torpedo			MAD, radar, sonobuoys	
Soviet Union								
KA-25 Harp (Helo)	1967	200	120	2 torpedoes or depth charges				

[1]Combat radii correspond with payloads shown under average conditions.

[2]Payloads are merely representative. External fuel tanks are included wherever applicable.

[3]AIM-54 Phoenix, first deployed 1973; max speed Mach 5; guidance semi-active radar; detection range 120 nm; missile range 100+ nm; warhead HE. For other missile characteristics, see Figure 28, page 229.

*No unclassified data.

FIGURE 32 NAVAL SURFACE COMBATANTS (LESS AIRCRAFT CARRIERS)
Statistical Trends and System Characteristics

	1970	*1971*	*1972*	*1973*	*1974*	*1975*	*1976*	*1977*	*Net Change 1970–77*
CRUISERS									
United States									
SSM	0	0	0	0	0	0	0	0	0
Other									
Nuclear	3	3	3	3	4	5	5	8	+ 5
Oil	24	24	25	26	24	22	21	20	– 4
Total	27	27	28	29	28	27	26	28	+ 1
Soviet Union									
SSM[1]	9	10	12	15	17	19	21	23	+14
Other	15	15	15	13	12	11	10	10	– 5
Total	24	25	27	28	29	30	31	33	+ 9
U.S. Standing	+ 3	+ 2	+ 1	+ 1	– 1	– 3	– 5	– 5	– 8
DESTROYERS									
United States									
Active									
SSM[1]	0	0	0	0	0	0	0	0	0
Other	159	141	131	108	69	70	69	69	–90
Total	159	141	131	108	69	70	69	69	–90

[1]Soviet SSM figures include surface-to-underwater missiles that probably have SSM capabilities.

FIGURE 32 (Con't)

	1970	1971	1972	1973	1974	1975	1976	1977	Net Change 1970–77
DESTROYERS									
Reserve[2]	28	28	31	31	37	32	30	28	0
Grand Total	187	169	162	139	106	102	99	97	−90
Soviet Union									
SSM	6	7	7	10	13	16	20	35	+29
Other	71	70	70	67	67	65	64	54	−17
Total	77	77	77	77	80	81	84	89	+12
U.S. Standing	+110	+ 92	+ 85	+ 62	+ 26	+ 21	+ 15	+ 8	−102
FRIGATES[3]									
United States									
Active									
SSM	0	0	0	0	0	0	0	7	+ 7
Other	47	57	66	67	64	64	64	58	+ 11
Total	47	57	66	67	64	64	64	65	+ 18
Reserve[2]	6	4	4	4	0	0	0	0	− 6
Grand Total	53	61	70	71	64	64	64	65	+ 12
Soviet Union									
SSM	0	0	0	0	0	0	0	0	0
Other	111	111	110	109	108	105	106	103	− 8
Total	111	111	110	109	108	105	106	103	− 8

U.S. Standing	– 58	– 50	– 40	– 38	– 44	– 41	– 42	– 38	+ 20
SMALL COMBATANTS									
United States	0	0	0	0	0	0	0	0	0
Soviet Union									
SSM[4]	0	0	6	6	8	10	14	15	+ 15
Other[5]	70	75	77	80	85	88	88	90	+ 20
Total	70	75	83	86	93	98	102	105	+ 35
U.S. Standing	– 70	– 75	– 83	– 86	– 93	– 98	–102	–105	– 35
SHORE PATROL									
United States									
SSM	0	0	0	0	0	0	0	0	0
Other	16	17	16	14	14	14	8	3	– 13
Total	16	17	16	14	14	14	8	3	– 13
Soviet Union									
SSM[6]	140	145	136	129	127	123	121	120	– 20
Other[7]	665	555	480	460	430	394	391	380	–285
Total	805	700	616	589	557	517	512	500	–305
U.S. Standing	–789	–683	–600	–575	–543	–503	–504	–497	+292

[2]U.S. Naval Reserve ships shown are immediately available to augment active forces in emergency.
[3]Includes ships formerly called destroyer escorts and comparable craft over 1,200 tons. Seven U.S. frigates were armed with Harpoon in 1977.
[4]Soviet small combatants with SSM are Nanuchka.
[5]Soviet small combatants without SSM are Grisha and Poti.
[6]Soviet shore patrol craft with SSM are Osa and the few remaining Komar.
[7]Soviet shore patrol craft without SSM include fast torpedo boats, submarine-chasers, hydrofoils, and the like.

FIGURE 32 (Con't)

SHIP CHARACTERISTICS

	NR[1]	*First Deployed*	*Average Displace (Tons)*	*AAA SAM*	*ASW Weapons*[2]	*Major Guns*	*Power Plant*[3]
UNITED STATES CRUISERS							
Bainbridge (CGN)	1	1962	8,580	2 Terrier (Twin) 4 3-in	ASROC 2 Torpedo (Triplet)	None	Nuclear
Belknap (CG)	9	1964	7,930	1 Terrier (Twin) 2 3-in	ASROC (Twin) 2 Torpedo (Triplet)	1 5-in	Steam
California (CGN)	2	1974	10,150	2 Tartar	ASROC (Twin) 4 Torpedo	2 5-in	Nuclear
Leahy (CG)	9	1962	7,800	2 Terrier (Twin) 4 3-in	ASROC 2 Torpedo (Triplet)	None	Steam
Truxton (CGN)	1	1967	9,200	1 Terrier (Twin) 2 3-in	ASROC (Twin) 4 Torpedo	1 5-in	Nuclear

Virginia (CGN)	3	1976	11,000	2 Tartar(Twin)	ASROC (Twin) 2 Torpedo (Triplet)	2 5-in	Nuclear
DESTROYERS							
Charles F. Adams (DDG)	23	1960	4,500	1 Tartar (Single or Twin)	ASROC 2 Torpedo (Triplet)	2 5-in	Steam
Coontz (DDG)	10	1960	5,800	1 Terrier (Twin)	ASROC 2 Torpedo (Triplet)	1 5-in	Steam
Forest Sherman (DDG) (DDG)	14 4	1955 1967	4,050 4,150	None 1 Tartar	ASROC on 8 2 Torpedo (Triplet)	2/3 5-in 1 5-in	Steam Steam
Gearing (DD)	42	1945	3,500	None	ASROC 2 Torpedo (Triplet)	4 5-in	Steam
Spruance (DD)	8	1975	7,800	None	ASROC 2 Torpedo (Triplet) 1 ASW Helo	2 5-in	Gas Turbine

[1]Column 1 totals do not equal entire inventory, because several classes are not shown.
[2]Torpedoes are launch tubes only, not numbers of weapons.
[3]Speeds average slightly over 30 knots.

FIGURE 32 (Con't)

SHIP CHARACTERISTICS

	NR[1]	*First Deployed*	*Average Displace (Tons)*	*AAA SAM*[2]	*ASW Weapons*[3]	*Anti-Surface Ship Weapons*[4]	*Power Plant*[5]
SOVIET UNION CRUISERS							
Kara (CLGM)	5	1973	10,000	2 SA-N-3 2 SA-N-4 2-76 mm (Twin) 4 Gatling	8 SS-N-14 ASW rockets	10 Torpedo	Gas Turbine
Kresta I (CG)	4	1967	7,500	2 SA-N-1 2 57 mm (Twin)	ASW Rockets	4 SS-N-3 10 Torpedo	Steam
Kresta II (CG)	9	1970	7,500	2 SA-N-3 2 57 mm (Twin)	8 SS-N-14 ASW Rockets	10 Torpedo	Steam
Kynda (CG)	4	1962	5,500	1 SA-N-1 2 76 mm (Twin)	ASW Rockets	8 SS-N-3 6 Torpedo	Steam
Sverdlov (CL)	10	1952	17,500	32 37mm Some SA-N-4 Some Gatling		12 6-in Guns 12 3.9-in Guns	Steam

DESTROYERS							
Kanin (DDG)	7	1968	4,500	1 SA-N-1 2 57 mm (Quad)	ASW Rockets	10 Torpedo	Steam
Kashin (DDG)[6] (Converted)	6	1963	4,500	2 SA-N-1	ASW Rockets	4 SS-N-2 5 Torpedo Mines	Gas Turbine
Kotlin (DD)	15	1954	3,500	4 45mm (Quad)		4 5.1 in Guns 10 Torpedo Mines	Steam
Kotlin (DDG)	8	1962	3,500	1 SA-N-1 2 57 mm (Twin) 2 30 mm (Quad)		2 5.1 in Guns 5 Torpedo	Steam
Krivak (DD)	16	1971	4,000	2 SA-N-4 2 76 mm (Twin)	4 SS-N-14	8 Torpedo	Gas Turbine

[1]Column 1 totals do not equal entire inventory, because several classes are not shown.
[2]SA-N-3 probably has anti-surface ship as well as antiaircraft capabilities. All SAM launchers are twin-armed.
[3]SS-N-14 aerial torpedoes probably have anti-surface ship as well as ASW capabilities.
[4]Conventional torpedoes may have ASW as well as anti-surface ship capabilities. Numbers shown are launch tubes, not weapons.
[5]Kara, Kresta, Krivak, and Sverdlov ships have a top speed of about 32 knots; Kynda 34 knots; Kanin, Kashin, and Kotlin 35 knots.
[6]Fourteen Kashin destroyers lack anti-surface ship missiles.

CG is guided missile cruiser; CL is light cruiser; CLGM is light guided missile cruiser; DD is destroyer; DDG is guided missile destroyer.

FIGURE 32 (Con't)

PARTOL CRAFT CHARACTERISTICS

	NR	*First Deployed*	*Speed*	*Average Displace (Tons)*	*SAM AAA*	*Cruise Missiles*	*Other Arms*	*Power Plant*
SOVIET UNION								
Komar (PTG)[1]	Few	1960	40	80	2 25mm	2 SS-N-2	None	Diesel
Osa (PTG)[1]	120	1960	35	220	4 30mm	4 SS-N-2	None	Diesel
Nanuchka (PGG)[2]	15	1969	30	1000	1 SA-N-4 2 57mm	6 SA-N-9	None	Diesel

[1]PTG is guided missile patrol boat.
[2]PGG is patrol combatant.

ANTI-SHIP MISSILE/ROCKET CHARACTERISTICS

	First Deployed	*Range (Miles)*	*Warhead*	*Payload or Yield*
UNITED STATES				
ASROC	1961	6	HE, Nuke	[1]
Harpoon	1977	100	HE	500 lbs
SOVIET UNION				
SS-N-14	1974	30	HE, Nuke	KT?
SS-N-12	*	345	*	*
SS-N-9	*	150	HE, Nuke	*
SS-N-3[2]	1960	150–250	HE, Nuke	*
SS-N-2	1960	30	HE	*
SS-N-1	1958	130	HE, Nuke	*

[1]ASROC launch weight is 960 lbs. Payload is classified.
[2]Deployment date for SS-N-3 mounted on submarines is 1962.
*Unclassified data not available.

FIGURE 33 ATTACK SUBMARINES
Statistical Trends and Systems Characteristics

	1970	*1971*	*1972*	*1973*	*1974*	*1975*	*1976*	*1977*	*Net Change 1970–77*
UNITED STATES									
SSM	0	0	0	0	0	0	0	1[1]	+ 1
Other									
Nuclear	46	51	56	60	61	64	64	66	+20
Diesel	59	50	38	24	12	11	10	10	−49
Total	105	101	94	84	73	75	74	76	−29
Grand Total	105	101	94	84	73	75	74	77	−28
SOVIET UNION									
SSM									
Nuclear	35	38	40	41	42	42	43	44	+ 9
Diesel	28	27	26	25	24	24	23	23	− 5
Total	63	65	66	66	66	66	66	67	+ 4
Other									
Nuclear	24	26	28	31	34	37	38	37	+13
Diesel	210	190	180	175	160	156	150	148	−62
Total	234	216	208	206	194	193	188	185	−49
Grand Total	297	281	274	272	260	259	254	252	−45
U.S. Standing	−192	−180	−180	−188	−187	−184	−180	−175	−17

[1]The first U.S. attack submarine was armed with Harpoon in 1977.

FIGURE 33 (Con't)

ATTACK SUBMARINE CHARACTERISTICS

	Current Number[1]	*First Deployed*	*SUBROC, Cruise Missiles*	*Sub-Surface Launch*	*Torpedo Tubes*	*Power Plant*
UNITED STATES[2]						
688 Class (SSN)	6	1975	SUBROC	Yes	4	Nuclear
637 Class (SSN)	37	1966	SUBROC	Yes	4	Nuclear
594 Class (SSN)	13	1962	SUBROC	Yes	4	Nuclear
Skate Class (SSN)	4	1957	None		8	Nuclear
Skipjack Class (SSN)	5	1959	None		6	Nuclear
SOVIET UNION						
Cruise Missile						
Charlie (SSGN)	14	1968	8 SS-N-7	Yes	8	Nuclear
Echo II (SSGN)	29	1963	8 SS-N-3/12	No	10	Nuclear
Juliett (SSG)	16	1962	4 SS-N-3/12	No	6	Diesel
Papa (SSGN)	1	1973	8 SS-N-7	Yes	8	Nuclear
Attack						
Echo I (SSN)	5	1960	None		10	Nuclear
Foxtrot (SS)	60	1958	None		10	Diesel
November (SSN)	12	1958	None		8	Nuclear
Romeo (SS)	10	1961	None		8	Diesel
Tango (SS)	6	1973	None		6	Diesel
Victor (SSN)	20	1968	None		8	Nuclear
Whiskey (SS)	40	1951	None		6	Diesel
Zulu (SS)	10	1952	None		10	Diesel

[1]Column 1 numbers do not equal entire inventory, because some classes are not shown. A few U.S. diesel-powered submarines, all commissioned in the 1940s and 1950s, are omitted. So are "one-of-a-kind" classes, like nuclear Lipscomb and Narwhal.

[2]SS = Diesel Submarine; SSN = Nuclear Submarine; SSG = Diesel Cruise Missile Submarine; SSGN = Nuclear Cruise Missile Submarine.

FIGURE 33 (Con't)

ANTI-SHIP MISSILE/ROCKET CHARACTERISTICS

	First Deployed	*Range (Miles)*	*Warhead*	*Payload or Yield*
UNITED STATES				
Subroc	1966	30–35	Nuke	[1]
Harpoon	1977	100	HE	500 lbs
SOVIET UNION				
SS-N-12[2]	*	345	*	*
SS-N-7	1968	30	HE, Nuke	Kiloton
SS-N-3[3]	1962	150–250	HE, Nuke	Range

[1]Subroc launch weight is 4,075 lbs. Payload is classified.
[2]SS-N-12 is replacing SS-N-3. No data are available for items marked with an asterisk.
[3]Deployment date for SS-N-3 mounted on surface ships is 1960.

FIGURE 34 SHORE-BASED NAVAL AIRCRAFT
Statistical Trends and System Characteristics

	1970	*1971*	*1972*	*1973*	*1974*	*1975*	*1976*	*1977*	*Net Change 1970–77*
ANTI-SURFACE SHIP BOMBERS[1]									
United States	0	0	0	0	0	0	0	0	0
Soviet Union									
IL-28 Beagle	60	50	50	30	30	30	20	10	−50
SU-17 Fitter-C	0	0	0	0	0	0	Few	30	+30
TU-16 Badger	320	320	320	320	320	320	320	320	0
TU-22 Blinder	60	60	60	60	60	60	60	50	−10
TU-26 Backfire	0	0	0	0	0	0	30	35	+35
Total	440	430	430	410	410	410	430	445	+ 5
U.S. Standing	−440	−430	−430	−410	−410	−410	−430	−445	− 5
ASW AIRCRAFT[1]									
United States									
P-3 Orion	210	210	213	214	202	199	203	203	− 7

[1]UE aircraft only, excluding training and special-purpose versions.

FIGURE 34 (Con't)

	1970	*1971*	*1972*	*1973*	*1974*	*1975*	*1976*	*1977*	*Net Change 1970–77*
Soviet Union									
BE-6 Madge	30	10	0	0	0	0	0	0	−30
BE-12 Mail	60	75	75	100	100	100	100	100	+40
IL-38 May	20	20	40	40	55	55	55	55	+35
MI-4 Hound (Helo)	130	130	130	130	115	105	70	60	−70
TU-95 Bear-F	0	0	0	0	0	15	20	20	+20
Total	240	235	245	270	270	275	245	235	− 5
U.S. Standing	− 30	− 25	− 32	− 56	− 68	− 76	− 42	− 32	− 2
Grand Total									
United States	210	210	213	214	202	199	203	203	− 7
Soviet Union	680	665	675	680	680	685	675	680	0
U.S. Standing	−470	−455	−462	−466	−478	−486	−472	−477	− 7

AIRCRAFT CHARACTERISTICS

	First Deployed	Crew	Nr Engines	Patrol Radius (Miles)	Detection Devices[1]	Anti-Ship Weapons
ANTI-SURFACE SHIP BOMBERS						
Soviet Union						
IL-28 Beagle	1950	3	2	600		Bombs or torpedoes
SU-17 Fitter-C	1972	1	1	500		Rockets
TU-16 Badger	1955	7	2	1600		Bombs or ASM
TU-22 Blinder	1962	3–4	2	1700		Bombs
TU-26 Backfire	1975	2–4	2	2500		ASMs
TU-95 Bear-F	1971	5	4	3900		
ASW AIRCRAFT						
United States						
P-3 Orion	1962	10–12	4	1200	MAD, radar, sonobuoy	Torpedoes or mines
Soviet Union						
BE-12 Mail[2]	1965	4	2	1000	MAD, radar, sonobuoy	Bombs, mines, depth charges, torpedoes (various mixes)
IL-38 May	1968	12	4	2000	MAD, radar, sonobuoy	Bombs, mines, depth charges, torpedoes (various mixes)
MI-4 Hound (Helo)	1958		1	100	MAD, radar, sonar	None

[1]MAD stands for Magnetic Anomaly Detector.
[2]BE-12 (and its predecessor BE-6) is a flying boat.

FIGURE 35 COAST GUARD COMBATANTS
Statistical Trends and System Characteristics

	1970	1971	1972	1973	1974	1975	1976	1977	Net Change 1970–77
HIGH ENDURANCE CUTTERS									
Hamilton (378)	12	12	12	12	12	12	12	12	0
Campbell (327)	6	6	6	6	6	6	6	6	0
Owasco (255)[1]	12	12	9	11	5	5	0	0	−12
Casco (311)	11	7	0	0	0	0	0	1	−10
Total	41	37	27	29	23	23	18	19	−22
MEDIUM ENDURANCE CUTTER									
Reliance (210)[2]	16	16	16	16	16	15	15	15	− 1
PATROL BOATS									
Cape[3]	26	26	26	26	22	23	26	22	− 4
Point	53	54	53	53	53	53	53	53	0
Total	79	80	79	79	75	76	79	75	− 4

[1]Originally designated as gunboats.
[2]Reliance class cutters, originally designated as patrol craft, serve in a search and rescue role and would continue to do so in time of war. So would Cape and Point Class Patrol Boats.
[3]Entire class undergoing modernization, beginning with one ship in 1977.

COAST GUARD COMBATANTS

	First Deployed	*Speed (Knots)*	*Displace (Tons)*	*Guns*	*ASW Weapons*	*Power Plant*
HIGH ENDURANCE CUTTERS						
Hamilton (378)[1]	1967	29	2716	1 5in .38 DP 2 .50 MG	2 Triple Torpedo Tubes	2 Gas turbines & 2 Diesels
Campbell (327)	1936	19.8	2216	1 5 in .38 DP	None	Geared Turbine
Casco (311)[2]	1943	18.2	2800	1 5 in .38 DP	None	Diesel
MEDIUM ENDURANCE CUTTER						
Reliance (210)	1964	18	950	1 3in .50 Antiaircraft 2 .50 MG	None	2 Turbo-Charged Diesels
PATROL BOATS						
Cape	1953	20	98–106	1 81mm Mortar 2 .50 MG	None	4 Diesels
Point[3]	1960	22.6	67–69	1 81mm Mortar 2 .50 MG	None	2 Diesels

[1]Three Hamilton cutters commissioned after 1969 are also called Hero.
[2]One Casco refurbished for South Vietnam has been retained in active U.S. service.
[3]Some boats are unarmed.

Footnotes

1. "Fundamental asymmetries between the United States and the Soviet Union cannot be overstressed. The United States is a maritime nation. . . . [Its] international relations, be they economic, political, or military, are influenced by this heavy dependence on free and unimpeded passage on the oceans of the world." The Soviet State, by way of contrast, "has evolved through history as a continental power . . . . largely independent of sea lines of communication." Admiral J. L. Holloway, III, Chief of Naval Operations, in comments on a draft of this study, September 23, 1977, p. 2.

2. Imports currently account for about 45 percent of all petroleum consumed in the United States. *International Energy Bi-weekly Statistical Review*. Washington: Central Intelligence Agency, Office of Economic Research, February 8, 1978, pp. 10, 16.

3. Rumsfeld, Donald H., *Annual Defense Department Report for FY 1978*, p. 17.

4. For a summary of commodities imported and exported by the United States over 31 sea routes to foreign countries, see *Essential United States Foreign Trade Routes*. Washington: U.S. Government Printing Office, June 1975, 79 pp.

5. For general coverage of the U.S. Navy in concert with allies, see Crowe, William, "Western Strategy and Naval Missions Approaching the 21st Century," paper presented at an American Enterprise Institute Symposium in Washington, D.C., October 6, 1977, 54 pp.

6. For general coverage of the Soviet Navy, see Breyer, Siegfried and Polmar, Norman, *Guide to the Soviet Navy*, 2d Ed., Annapolis: U.S. Naval Institute Press, 1977, 610 pp.; Manthorpe, William, H. J., Jr., "The Soviet Navy in 1976," *U.S. Naval Institute Proceedings*, May 1977, pp. 202–214; McConnell, James M., "The Russian Navy in the Year 2000," paper presented at an American Enterprise Institute Symposium in Washington, D.C., October 6, 1977, 48 pp.; LeBourgeois, Julian, "What is the Soviet Navy Up To?," The Atlantic Council of the United States, Policy Paper, Washington, 1976, 15 pp.; Polmar, Norman, *Soviet Naval Power: Challenge for the 1970's*, Rev. Ed., New York: Crane, Russak & Co., Inc., 1974, 129 pp., and *Understanding Soviet Naval Developments*. Washington: Office of the Chief of Naval Operations, January 1978, 106 pp.

7. Alva M. Bowen, Jr., specialist in naval affairs for the Congressional Research Service, acted as technical advisor and data source during the preparation of this section.

8. A centrally situated strategic position, which combines secure land boundaries with access to one or more bodies of open water, took top place on Mahan's list. Those basic geographic conditions must be coupled with a coastline that features deep-draft harbors and defensible shores. Mahan, Alfred Thayer, *The Influence of Sea Power Upon History*. New York: Hill and Wang, 1957, pp. 25–39. First published in 1890.

9. Two examples illustrate the practical utility of the Panama Canal for naval purposes, if ships (excluding large aircraft carriers and supertankers) maintain a steady 20 knots:

San Diego to Eastern Mediterranean		
Via Panama Canal	8,875 nm	21 Days
Around Cape Horn	13,850 nm	30 Days
Difference	4,975 nm	9 Days
Norfolk to Pusan, South Korea		
Via Panama Canal	9,900 nm	22 Days
Around Good Hope	14,825 nm	31 Days
Difference	4,925 nm	9 Days

10. Few strategic areas in any major country are as geographically susceptible to assault from the sea as those in the United States. Entry points along our Atlantic coast include Boston Harbor and nearby strands on Cape Cod; New Bedford; Narragansett Bay; Jones Beach, Coney Island, and the Port of New York; Asbury Park and Atlantic City; Baltimore; Virginia beaches; Newport News and Norfolk. Favorable ports and landing sites farther south lead to locally significant strategic areas, but are physically separate from the primary core.

Splendid ports and beaches serve each U.S. Pacific core area: Seattle and Tacoma team up with Puget Sound; San Francisco is on one of the globe's finest bays; Santa Monica and Long Beaches bracket Los Angeles; San Diego has a companion called Coronado. Obstacles, such as Oregon's rocky coast and California's Big Sur, are lonely stretches far removed from any strategic area.

11. Some details are contained in "A New First Line of Defense Against Subs," *Business Week,* March 15, 1976, pp. 60J, 60L.

12. For elaboration, see Griswold, Lawrence, "The Chokepoint War," *Sea Power,* July 1973, pp. 11–18.

13. Additional details are contained in "Command Organization and Staff Structure for the Operating Forces of the U.S. Navy," *All Hands,* October 1977, pp. 12–13.

14. Naval missions are addressed by Admiral J. L. Holloway, III, Chief of Naval Operations, in U.S. Congress. House. U.S. Navy Analysis of Congressional Budget Office Budget Issue Paper *General Purpose Forces: Navy.* Prepared for the Committee on Armed Services. 95th Congress, 1st Session. Washington: U.S. Govt. Print. Off., January 12, 1977, 23 pp. See also Turner, Stansfield, "Designing a Modern Navy: A Workshop Discussion," contained in *Power at Sea, II. Super-powers and Navies,* Adelphi Papers 123. London: International Institute for Strategic Studies, 1976, pp. 25–27; and "The Naval Balance: Not Just a Numbers Game," *Foreign Affairs,* January 1977, pp. 342–347.

15. To answer the question, Why does any country need a navy?, see Booth, Ken, "Roles, Objectives and Tasks: An Inventory of the Functions of Navies," *Naval War College Review,"* Summer 1977. pp. 83–97.

16. U.S. Naval doctrine considers peacetime presence, "visible or invisible, large or small, provocative or peaceful," mainly in context with "international crisis short of conflict." Naval warships, in conjunction with marines, provide latent power for deterrent and/or compellent purposes. Political connotations are not covered in *NWP-1, Strategic Concepts of the U.S. Navy,* January 1977, p. 5–5.

17. MccGwire, Michael, "The Overseas Role of a 'Soviet Military Presence'." Chapter 2 in *Soviet Naval Influence.* Ed. by Michael MccGwire and John McDonald. New York: Praeger, 1977, pp. 31–57.

18. Every pro-Soviet country in Africa is a coastal state. Guinea-Bissau, Benin, People's Republic of the Congo, Angola, and Mozambique currently are in the Soviet camp, although Marxist Mozambique shows signs of cooling. The Soviet Navy lost important base rights in Somalia on November 14, 1977, but influence in Ethiopia increased simultaneously.

19. *Understanding Soviet Naval Developments,* pp. 5–6; 13; U.S. Congress. House. *Means of Measuring Naval Power: With Special Reference to U.S. and Soviet Activities in the Indian Ocean.* Prepared for the Sub-committee on the Near East and South Asia of the Committee on Foreign Affairs by the Congressional Research Service. Washington: U.S. Govt. Print. Off., 1974, pp. 1–5.

20. Title 10, United States Code, Chapter 503, Section 5012 and Department of Defense Directive 5100.1.

21. Admiral J. L. Holloway, III, Chief of Naval Operations, expressed related ideas in a letter to the author in September 1977:

"While it may often be necessary to distinguish between sea control and power projection, I would like to stress the close interrelationship of these two functions. Sea control is the fundamental function of the U.S. Navy and is a prerequisite for all other naval operations. The capability to project power was developed in naval forces largely as an adjunct to strategic sea control. It can be used for such operations as striking enemy bases to destroy ships and aircraft before they can take part in offensive operations against U.S. naval forces or for seizing limited strategic land areas such as narrow straits or an enemy forward base. Conversely, depending on the type of force employed, some degree of sea control is necessary in the sea area from which power is to be projected. Thus, it is necessary to look at and think of naval forces as a multipurpose entity rather than individual units designed for specific functions."

22. Title 10, United States Code, Chapter 503, Section 5012 and Department of Defense Directive 5100.1.

23. Turner, Stansfield, "The Naval Balance: Not Just a Numbers Game," pp. 342, 343.

24. *NWP 1, Strategic Concepts of the U.S. Navy,* p. 2–3.

25. *Ibid.*

26. *Ibid.*, p. 5–1.

27. *Ibid.*, p. 5–2.

28. *Ibid.*, pp. 5–4, 6–2, 6–3.

29. *Ibid.*, p. 5–4.

30. *Ibid.*, pp. 5–4, 6–1, 6–2, 6–3.

31. *Ibid.*, p. 5–3.

32. For formative years, when the Soviet Navy was not much more than a coastal defense force, and times of transition in the 1960s, see Herrick, Robert W., *Soviet Naval Strategy: Fifty Years of Theory and Practice.* Annapolis: United States Naval Institute, 1968, 197 pp.

33. Gorshkov, Sergei G., *Sea Power of the State.* Moscow: Military Publishing House, 1976. Translated by U.S. Naval Intelligence Support Center, July 27, 1976, 363 pp.; translated and excerpted by Reuben Ainsztein of the Sunday Times (London) in *Survival,* January-February 1977, pp. 24–29. See also Watson, Bruce W., "Comments on Gorshkov's 'Sea Power of the State'," *Naval Institute Proceedings,* April 1977, pp. 42–47, and Kenney, David Joseph, "Review Article: A Primer on S. G. Gorshkov's *Sea Power of the State," Naval War College Review,* Spring 1977, pp. 94–104.

34. Mahan, in the *Introductory to The Influence of Sea Power Upon History,* noted that "an improvement of weapons is due to the energy of one or two men, while changes in tactics have to overcome the inertia of a conservative class." That case is not precisely correct, but Gorshkov could move surely, because he was never "burdened by the baggage of victory." Purges in the 1930s and disasters during the Great Patriotic War left "no hoary wardroom traditions" to frustrate fresh concepts for a new Soviet Navy. Consequently, Gorshkov has written freely on a blank slate. Kenney, David Joseph, "Review Article," pp. 101–102.

35. Gorshkov, Sergei G., *Sea Power of the State,* pp. 1, 24, 26–27, 32, 34, 42–48, 53.

36. *Ibid.*, pp. 207, 218, 221–223, 285, 297, 324, 345, 359.

37. The Soviet Navy, if so desired, could mount a massive campaign against U.S. and NATO SLOCs, using attack submarines, aircraft, and (to a lesser extent) surface ships, many armed with cruise missiles. Our Navy is very vulnerable. A sizable part of their forces, however, seem committed to security for Soviet SLBMs, with attempts to sink U.S. counterparts as a secondary task. The timing and intensity of Soviet anti-SLOC attacks thus is subject to considerable speculation and controversy in the U.S. intelligence community and among other Western analysts, although there is consensus on one point: strong early assaults on SLOCs would weaken Soviet strategic defense of the homeland to some uncertain degree under general war conditions.

38. Gorshkov, Sergei G., *Sea Power of the State,* pp. 187, 277, 282–283, 286, 288. See also Rees, David, "The Gorshkov Strategy in The Far East," *Pacific Community,* January 1978, pp. 143–155.

39. Some U.S. analysts suggest that Soviet SLBMs would remain in strategic reserve during early stages of a general nuclear war for use as a political or military lever later.

Prelaunch security problems associated with such a withholding strategy would help explain reports that torpedo-attack and ballistic missile submarines patrol together in the Atlantic. McConnell, James M., *The Russian Navy in the Year 2000,* pp. 7, 9, 11–12.

40. Soviet cruisers and destroyers in the 1950s stressed anti-carrier capabilities, not ASW. Those ships, now nearing the end of active service, "show the flag" and confront U.S. naval contingents during mini-crises much more often than newer models, which are reserved for less mundane tasks.

41. Gorshkov, Sergei G., *Sea Power of the State,* pp. 248, 253, 255.

42. LeBourgeois, Julian, "What is the Soviet Navy Up To?," pp. 9–10, 14.

43. Gorshkov, Sergei G., *Sea Power of the State,* pp. 298–312.

44. The complement in 1965 included 16 attack carriers and 9 ASW carriers. Roughly a third were commonly forward- deployed, three with Sixth Fleet in the Mediterranean and five with Seventh Fleet in the Western Pacific.

45. Rumsfeld, Donald H., *Annual Defense Department Report for FY 1977,* p. 160.

46. For general background, see Bowen, Alva, *Roles and Missions of Aircraft Carriers in the U.S. Navy: Budgetary and Force Structure Implications.* Prepared for Senator Wendell Anderson. Washington: Congressional Research Service, March 17, 1978, 32 pp.; see also Polmar, Norman, "The Future of Sea-Based Air," paper presented at an American Enterprise Institute Symposium in Washington, D.C., October 6, 1977. 24 pp.

47. The Eisenhower, our newest nuclear-power aircraft carrier, was commissioned on October 18, 1977.

48. The Kiev seems less seaworthy than U.S. intelligence specialists first surmised. Open ocean cruises reportedly totalled just two weeks during its maiden year with the Northern Fleet. YAK-36 VTOL fighters hover so long they are burning flight deck plates, which may need to be replaced. Foley, James, "Soviet Aircraft Carrier Gets Little Ocean Duty," *Washington Post,* November 25, 1977, p. A32. Nevertheless, something like 10 carriers of this class eventually will join Soviet fleets, according to an Associated Press report. "[British Prime Minister James] Callaghan: Soviet Union Plans 10 Aircraft Carriers," *Washington Star,* April 22, 1978, p. A-2.

49. U.S. and Soviet ship deliveries from 1965 through 1976 are contained in MccGwire, Michael, "Western and Soviet Naval Building Programmes 1965–1976," *Survival,* September/October 1976, pp. 204–209. U.S. Navy and DIA sources provided 1977 updates.

50. Seven U.S. frigates were armed with Harpoon late in 1977. The number of missiles is classified.

51. Quote by the Chief of Naval Operations is contained in *Understanding Soviet Naval Developments,* p. 31. For comparisons between Krivak and U.S. Perry class frigates, which began deploying in 1977, see Heinl, Robert D., Jr., "Navy Lagging in Surface Sea Power," *Detroit News,* August 22, 1976, p. 1 and a rebuttal by John B. Shewmaker, "U.S. Destroyer Seen Superior: Col. Heinl Overrated Soviet Warship?," *Detroit News,* September 18, 1976, Letter to the Editor.

52. *Understanding Soviet Naval Developments,* p. 32.

53. Brown, Harold, *Department of Defense Annual Report, FY 1979,* pp. 173–175.

54. For general background concerning the use of land-based naval aircraft, see Zakheim, Dov S., "The U.S. Sea Control Mission: Forces, Capabilities, and Requirements." Washington: Congressional Budget Office, June 1977. 86 pp.

55. About 100 TU-16s are configured as tankers for aerial refueling. Soviet Long-Range Aviation units could augment them under some circumstances. In-flight refueling for aircraft committed to surprise first strikes could take place with impunity, but slow-flying Badgers would be tempting targets during that process thereafter.

56. Department of Defense Directive 5100.1 assigns the Air Force collateral functions in the field of sea interdiction, ASW, and aerial mine-laying.

57. Ginsburgh, Robert N., "A New Look at Control of the Seas," *Strategic Review,* Winter 1976, pp. 86–89. See also Silber, Howard, "B-52 Testing Its Ship-Sinking Abil-

ity," *Omaha World-Herald*. December 26, 1976, p. 1; Silber, Howard, "B-52s Track Soviet Carrier: Fleet Maneuvers Watched," *Omaha World Herald*, April 14, 1978, p. 1.

58. U.S. Congress. House. *Means of Measuring Naval Power*, pp. 9–13; *Understanding Soviet Naval Developments*, p. 17.

59. Merry, Robert, "Janes' Editor Sings Russ Navy Blues," *Chicago Tribune*, March 8, 1976, p. 1.

60. The Soviet Navy has conducted two world-wide exercises, one in 1970, the other in 1975. The most recent, code named "Okean-75", demonstrated dramatic progress during the intervening five years. For unclassified details, see Watson, Bruce W. and Walton, Margurite A., "Okean-75," *Naval Institute Proceedings*, July 1976, reprinted in *Congressional Record*, August 24, 1976, pp. 524339–41; and "Soviets Seen Operating Two Types of Ocean Surveillance Satellite," *Aerospace Daily*, June 2, 1976, p. 169.

61. "The Three Major Threats to U.S. Fleet," *Defense/Space Daily*, October 15, 1976, p. 246. Problems and prospects are further addressed in "Special Issue: Surface Warfare," *United States Naval Institute Proceedings*, March 1978. 176 pp.

62. Regulus I, first procured in 1951, was the first anti-ship missile to arm U.S. fleets. SS-N-1 Scrubbers, the earliest Soviet competitor, did not enter the inventory for seven years. The Regulus I turbo-jet power plant with solid propellant booster projected conventional or nuclear warheads for about 500 miles. Coastal cities as well as ships were potentially typical targets. Plans at one time called for 10 U.S. carriers, four cruisers, and two submarines to mount Regulus I. More than 500 were purchased, but only a few deployed over a 15-year period that fizzled out in 1966. Regulus II, rated at Mach 2 with a thousand-mile range, was the scheduled replacement, but funds were diverted in 1958 before development was complete. U.S. Congress. Senate. "The United States Guided Missile Program." Prepared for the Preparedness Investigating Subcommittee of the Committee on Armed Services by Charles H. Donnelly, Legislative Reference Service, Library of Congress. 86th Congress, 1st Session. Washington: U.S. Govt. Print. Off., 1959, pp. 61 facing, 71–72.

63. Gorshkov, Sergei G., "The Development of the Art of Naval Warfare," *U.S. Naval Institute Proceedings*, June 1975, p. 56.

64. U.S. naval intelligence specialists during the past year or more have begun to credit many Soviet ships with cruise missile capabilities in the ASW category, rather than against surface ships. SS-N-10s, once considered a surface-to-surface missile, have been dropped entirely from U.S. lists in favor of SS-N-14s, an aerial torpedo that probably poses some threat to surface ships, but is designed primarily for ASW purposes. For some detail, see Polmar, Norman, "Comment and Discussion," *U.S. Naval Institute Proceedings*, July 1977, p. 91.

65. Ruhe, William J., "Cruise Missile: The Ship Killer," *U.S. Naval Institute Proceedings*, June 1976, pp. 46, 47–48; and "Navy Faces Grave Cruise Missile Threat," *Aviation Week and Space Technology*, January 17, 1975, p. 101.

66. Ruhe, William J., "Cruise Missile: The Ship Killer," p. 47.

67. "Navy Faces Grave Missile Threat," p. 101.

68. Osa stands for Wasp; Nanuchka for Gnat; Komar for Mosquito.

69. Ruhe, William J., "Cruise Missile: The Ship Killer," pp. 48, 49, 52.

70. *Ibid.*, quoting the NSC study cited in Note 61. "There is indeed some doubt as to whether the Terrier system could effectively defend against cruise missiles fired from a single 'Charlie' -class submarine," according to a Congressional Budget Office study entitled *Planning U.S. General Purpose Forces: The Navy*. Washington: U.S. Govt. Print. Off., December 1976, p. 41. See also Rumsfeld, Donald H., *Annual Defense Department Report for FY 1978*, pp. 111, 112.

71. Turner, Stansfield, "The Naval Balance: Not Just a Numbers Game," p. 350.

72. Israeli patrol boats stymied Arabs armed with Styx missiles (SS-N-2s) during the Yom Kippur conflict in 1973, assisted by chaff umbrellas and clever tactics. Roughly 50

missiles were fired without one hit, because the Arabs were still unequipped to wage electronic warfare. Surprises could be expected from sophisticated Soviets. *Aviation Week and Space Technology,* January 27, 1975, p. 121. See also Eustace, Harry F., "A U.S. View of Naval EW" and Sunderam, G. S., "Electronic Warfare at Sea," both in *International Defense Review,* April 1976, pp. 4, 217.

73. Lindsay, George R., "Tactical Anti-Submarine Warfare: The Past and the Future," contained in *Powers at Sea, I. The New Environment,* Adelphi Papers 122. London: International Institute for Strategic Studies, 1976, p. 33; Merry, Robert, "Jane's Editor Sings Russ Navy Blues," p. 1.

74. General George S. Brown, Chairman of the Joint Chiefs of Staff, recently estimated that only 11 percent of the total Soviet submarine force is at sea during normal peacetime periods. Aldridge, Robert C., "The Pentagon is Working on It," *The Nation,* June 11, 1977, p. 711.

75. Foley, James, "Soviet Subs Swamp Spotters," *Philadelphia Inquirer,* July 29, 1977, p. 1. Intelligence analysts indicate that Soviet strength was less than press reports claimed, but confirm that no such surge had occurred before.

76. Lucas, Hugh, "ASW: Threat and Counterthreat," *Sea Power,* May 1977, pp. 9–15; "Detection and Destruction," *Maritime Defense,* July 1977, pp. 214–215; "Anti-Submarine Warfare," *Maritime Defense,* August 1977, pp. 246–250; Stevenson, John, "Antisubmarine Warfare Crucial, Complex, and Costly," *Norfolk Virginian-Pilot,* March 27, 1977, p. B1.

77. Admiral Thomas B. Hayward, who assumed command as Chief of Naval Operations in June 1978, admits that "we've got some distance to go before we can say we have the problem in hand," but emphasizes that, "I'm as optimistic as I have ever been in my naval career that the Soviet submarine is in for trouble." Corddry, Charles W., "Navy Gains Confidence in Facing Soviet Subs," *Baltimore Sun,* September 6, 1977, p. 1.

78. Aldridge, Robert C., "The Pentagon is Working on It," pp. 711–714.

79. Polmar, Norman, "Thinking About Soviet ASW," *U.S. Naval Institute Proceedings,* May 1976, p. 110.

80. U.S. Congress. House. "Oil Fields as Military Objectives," pp. 19–20, 66–67.

81. Admiral J. L. Holloway, III, Chief of Naval Operations, quoted in "The Naval Balance: Not Just a Numbers Game," p. 351.

82. Taylor, Jeremy D., "Mining: A Well Reasoned and Circumspect Defense," *U.S. Naval Institute Proceedings,* November 1977, pp. 40–45; Hoffmann, Roy F., "Offensive Mine Warfare: A Forgotten Strategy," *U.S. Naval Institute Proceedings,* May 1977, pp. 142–155.

83. Alva M. Bowen, Jr., specialist in naval affairs for the Congressional Research Service, Library of Congress, was the principal source for coverage concerning defensive mine warfare.

For written remarks, see Brown, Harold, *Department of Defense Annual Report, FY 1979,* pp. 177–178.

84. Title 14, Section 2 of the United States Code prescribes Coast Guard "aids to maintain navigation, icebreaking facilities, and rescue facilities for the promotion of safety on, under and over the high seas and waters subject to the jurisdiction of the United States. . . . " Section 3 elaborates: "Upon the declaration of war or when the President directs, the Coast Guard shall operate as a service in the Navy, and shall continue until the President, by executive order, transfers the Coast Guard back to the [Transportation] Department." Chapter 5 delineates four discrete functions, namely law enforcement, aids to navigation, saving life and property, and providing for the safety of naval vessels.

85. Two examples, neither extreme, suffice. Bagley, Worth H., "The Decline of U.S. Sea Power," *Orbis,* Summer 1977, pp. 211–226. Navy Secretary R. James Woolsey

conversely contends that "The U.S. Navy is in better shape, although lower in numbers, than it was six years ago. . . . " Quoted in "Is the U.S. Navy sinking?," *Armed Forces Journal*, November 1977, p. 35.

86. Stansfield Turner, Director of Central Intelligence, substantiates that view. "The Naval Balance: Not Just a Numbers Game," p. 339. See also Kelly, Orr, "U.S. Navy in Distress," *U.S. News and World Report*, March 6, 1978, pp. 24–28.

PART VI

Strategic and Tactical Mobility Trends

The proper mix and amount of land, sea, and air transportation needed to shift general purpose forces, supplies, and equipment depends on how much must be moved how far how fast under specific conditions to serve particular purposes. Prepositioning selected stocks (such as armor, artillery, and ammunition) in or near prospective employment areas can reduce demands, but only up to some changeable point, beyond which such steps can be counterproductive.[1]

Intercontinental lift over open oceans is a U.S. essential. Russian requirements thus far have been more regional. Dissimilar demands, coupled with policy peculiarities and geographic circumstance, consequently foster mobility force structures that are quite different in size as well as composition.[2] (See Graph 14 and Figures 36–38 at the end of this section.)

Military Airlift

There is no clean dividing line between strategic and tactical airlift, both of which specialize in rapid redeployment to serve deterrent and other purposes. The former, however, stresses long, secure hauls, while the latter takes care of shorter hops, including combat operations.[3]

Strategic Airlift

America's strategic airlifters are still peerless. Soviet counterparts are just starting to compete. (Figure 36).

Transoceanic airlift came into its own in the early 1950s, when USAF's newly-activated Military Air Transport Service (MATS), supplemented by commercial airlines, shuttled troops and cargo from our west coast to Korea.

An expanding alliance system and increased emphasis on general purpose forces reinforced U.S. requirements for rapid response capabilities, beginning about 1960. A succession of subsequent crises, first in Berlin, then in Cuba, and finally in Vietnam, underscored "the importance of adequate airlift."[4]

The Defense Department has accentuated "airlift enhancement" ever since. An all-jet force, comprising active military and civilian components, long since replaced propeller-powered predecessors.[5] In-flight refueling, facilitated in the future by advanced tankers, is the announced aim for all transport aircraft in Military Airlift Command (MAC).[6] Present generation cargo craft can operate off strips that their forebears found impossible. Wide-bodied and stretch versions are becoming available, including commercial aircraft in the Civil Reserve Air Fleet (CRAF). Tactical airlift, integrated into MAC in March 1975,[7] are more readily available to augment strategic squadrons than they were in the recent past.[8]

Current Capabilities Major emphasis on modernization has paid off. Our present all-jet force, less than half the size of its propeller-powered predecessor in the late 1960s, can lift loads more than three times larger.[9] Seventy C-5s can accommodate outsize, oddly-shaped cargo, such as heavy helicopters, tanks, and 20-ton cranes.[10] Aircraft and crews are qualified for in-flight refueling, which makes non-stop performance possible at unrestricted range.[11] C-141s, proved over a seven-year period on the trans-Pacific "pipeline" to Southeast Asia, are still reliable mainstays that make up 75 percent of our strategic airlift stable. Utilization rates could be increased in emergency by mobilizing associate reserves that lost their last aircraft in 1975, but are collocated with active squadrons, and participate in operations.[12] C-130 E/H models, available for augmentation under certain circumstances, could increase strategic capabilities by about 8,500 tons in fifteen days.[13]

The U.S. Civil Reserve Air Fleet, with roughly 135 long-range cargo and 94 passenger aircraft,[14] all modern jets, can be committed during crises in accord with contracts that connect commercial carriers with Military Airlift Command.[15]

Combined military/CRAF 30-day lift capabilities reportedly total 180,000 tons, 50,000 of which (28 percent) comprise C-5 sorties with outsize equipment.[16]

Continuing Constraints Absolute airlift abilities, however impressive in abstract terms, must be related to the real world and real requirements if they are to be meaningful.

The time required to deploy Army divisions with unit integrity intact depends entirely on C-5s, the only aircraft (including those in CRAF) that can carry outsize cargo.[17] The current complement of 70 clearly is too few to implement NATO plans in prescribed time frames.

Nearly five trips, for example, would be needed to move the medium tanks of one armored division, at the rate of two per load. One official study concludes that eight days would elapse before all outsize equipment could reach NATO airports after C-141s and CRAF delivered an inter-service package composed of 300,000 troops and 169,000 tons of cargo.[18]

C-141s, which "cube out" quickly,[19] fly many sorties with substantial lift capacity unused. Their inability to refuel in flight causes operational costs to soar and constrains mobility options.[20] Huge numbers are needed even to lift the combat elements of a light airborne division over long distances with a basic load of ammunition and five-day suppies of rations and fuel. A move from Fort Bragg, North Carolina, to the Middle East would consume more than 700 sorties,[21] not counting airlift required for associated Army support and forces from other services.[22]

CRAF equipment compensates less effectively than first glance suggests. Only 12 are wide-bodied freighters. Another 13 could be converted from passenger to cargo configuration.[23] None of those are (or could be) configured to carry outsize cargo.[24]

Finally, SAC's fleet of 615 KC-135 tankers[25] is sufficient to serve concurrently the peacetime U.S. B-52 alert force, transoceanic fighter redeployments, and strategic airlift operations only during small-scale, medium-range contingencies. Competition could delay supplies and reinforcements under more stringent circumstances.[26]

Soviet Posture

AN-22 Cocks, with a cargo capacity second only to U.S. C-5s, can lift outsize items like T-62 tanks, Frog-3 rockets, and SA-4 SAMs on tracked launchers. Flashy turbofan Candids (IL-76), which are just starting to see service, have some features similar to C-141s. Taken together, however, they total just 130 aircraft, a small fleet compared with the titanic armed force they are tasked to support. Neither is fitted for in-flight refueling.[27]

Both types, however, have engaged in successful supply operations to Ethiopia, overflying foreign countries without official clearance from departure bases in the Caucasus and near Tashkent. Some cargo reportedly offloads at Aden for transshipment, but most arrives in

Addis Ababa nonstop.[28] Large-scale airlift of that sort to southern Africa, Latin America, or other spots far from the Soviet Union would require "stepping stones" in neutral or friendly states.

Aeroflot, the Soviet state-controlled counterpart of U.S. civil airlines, could increase military cargo capacities about 35 percent, and triple spaces for passengers.[29] Its aircraft and crews may not yet match, say, Pan American, but its crews are gaining experience in long-range operations over strange territory. They serve 72 countries on every continent except Australia and Antarctica, as it currently stands.[30]

Tactical Airlift

Tactical transports suitable for airlandings and/or aerial delivery constitute the lion's share of all airlift aircraft on both sides. (Figure 36).

U.S. Posture

America's tactical airlift, long the world's best, is still unexcelled. Tried, true, and time-tested C-130s, which make up most of the force, are ideally suited for medium-range missions. They adapt equally well for logistic support and parachute assaults.

MAC's active force, however, is much smaller than in 1970. Reserve components, equipped mainly with older model C-130s, are much larger. Composite strengths have therefore stayed constant statistically, but combined capabilities have decreased. Reliance on reserve components, once modest, is now marked.

Beyond that, C-130 cargo compartments are too tight for loads like self-propelled artillery,[31] which C-141s can lift only by slighting strategic airlift missions. We also are losing any capacity to conduct operations off crude strips less than 2,000 feet long. A few C-7 and C-123 aircraft, approaching the end of their service life, are still assigned to squadrons in reserve, but capabilities are absent in the active inventory.

Soviet Posture

AN-12 Cubs, which account for almost 85 percent of Soviet tactical airlift, are inferior to U.S. C-130s in every respect. Still, they find space for all equipment assigned to airborne divisions.[32]

Cubs, assisted by Candids, are adequate to airlift one airborne division about 1,000 miles with all combat equipment and three days[1] worth of accompanying supplies. They could move assault elements of two divisions the same distance, provided heavy items were prepositioned. Augmentation from Aeroflot could triple the number of personnel.[33] Shorter hops increase capabilities, because turnaround times are reduced. Major elements thus could move rapidly to, say, the Middle East from departure airfields in the Caucasus, especially if committed in waves over several days.[34]

Reliable fighter support, however, could be a critical limiting factor in any objective area far from Soviet frontiers or satellite states. Forward basing conceivably could be found in friendly countries, such as Syria, but complexities would increase. The likelihood that large-scale Soviet airborne operations would occur under any conditions that exclude local air superiority seems slight.[35]

Battlefield Mobility

Dual-purpose Soviet MI-24 Hind helicopters, which serve as weapons platforms as well as cargo/troop carriers, possess great possibilities.[36] Their growth rate is very rapid. Training is "highly professional." Hook helicopters provide heavy lift. Hip and Hare/Hoplite models, both available in large numbers, can accomplish a wide range of mobility missions (Figure 36).

The combined U.S. Army and Marine Corps fleets of cargo/utility helicopters, cut by almost 60 percent since 1970, still possess battlefield mobility that the Soviets cannot yet match. That advantage, however, could disappear, if present stocks are not replaced with more capable models.

Military Sealift

Military sealift essentially serves two purposes: administrative movements and amphibious assaults. Once again, asymmetries between U.S. and Soviet structures are clearly apparent (Figure 37).

Administrative Sealift

Only sealift can carry mass tonnages over transoceanic distances to sustain forward deployed forces or move strategic materials in amounts essential for national security. The United States, as a maritime power, possessed capabilities that envious Soviets could only emulate in the not-so-distant past. Roles in recent years have reversed.

Comparative Priorities

America's airlifters enjoy consistent attention at budget time. Sealift gets short shrift. Interest in the 1960s centered on quick reaction instead of sustained support,[37] but few funds were forthcoming for forces afloat, even for that purpose. Consequently, U.S. assets, which reached their apogee during World War II, have been on a down-hill slide for three decades.[38]

The conversion has been from many ships to few; from military ships to civilian carriers; from U.S. ships to foreign flags; from general cargo to container ships; from small, adaptable ships to large ones whose applications are limited. Our "mothball" fleet, which once served well, is suitable mainly for scrap.[39] Those trends in combination make it infeasible for Military Sealift Command (MSC) and the U.S. Merchant Marine to satisfy large-scale contingency requirements without massive aid from allies.[40] Policy, in short, consistently causes sealift "dehancement".[41]

The balance between Soviet strategic airlift and sealift is precisely opposite. Moscow's merchant fleet, already much larger than our own, is growing at a more rapid rate. Ship characteristics are chosen carefully to serve politico-military as well as economic purposes, especially in areas where large, specialized vessels can not conveniently venture.[42] The impact of such policies on comparative mobility postures is profound.

Comparative Control

State-controlled Soviet maritime resources, military and "civilian", are all part of a carefully coordinated sea power package.[43] Strategic sealift is no exception. Centralized control of its assets and activities in conjunction with those of the Navy is constant and close to complete. Satellite states are included.[44] The contribution of merchant shipping to large-scale exercises, such as Okean-75,[45] gives clear evidence that cohesive plans and programs, first conceived by Khrushchev in the late 1950s, are impressively productive.[46]

The U.S. Merchant Marine, unlike its Soviet counterpart, is privately owned. Dovetailing with the Defense Department is spotty and sporadic. Steamship directing boards, which strive to show profits, are slow to finance ships or stress defense features that fail to pay off for stockholders.

A few organized attempts are being made to connect American merchantmen with strategic mobility,[47] but consultations on long-term needs are nearly nonexistent. The presidents of seven cargo-carrying lines, when recently canvassed on this subject, knew of no "plans to utilize the strategic capability of their fleets beyond the routine control measures in place for the past 25 years."[48] That deficiency is doubly important, because meaningful team efforts amount to more than managing ships. Mobilization must also include an intricate infrastructure of seamen, specialized support craft, and port facilities.[49]

Consequently, the U.S. Merchant Marine may remain marginally suitable for economic purposes, but will be poorly prepared to support security plans until decision-makers take positive action to correct deficiencies.

Present U.S. Merchant Fleet Posture

Military Sealift Command (MSC), the active U.S. Merchant Marine, National Defense Reserve Fleet (NDRF), and Effective U.S. Controlled Fleet (EUSC) serve this country's security purposes in different degrees and in different ways. Other flags under foreign control could contribute if conditions favored.

Military Sealift Command Military Sealift Command is the operating agency through which the Secretary of the Navy exercises single manager responsibilities for all U.S. strategic sealift. Six government-owned and 21 chartered dry cargo ships currently constitute its core—166 less than those assigned at the start of this decade. Thirty-three tankers make up the remainder. (Figure 37).

Active Merchant Marine Capabilities so slight would be quickly exhausted in wartime. Consequently, MSC leans ever more heavily on our active Merchant Marine, which is also shrinking.

Ships now in the inventory are tailored expressly for foreign trade, not military emergencies. The U.S. break-bulk tramp fleet has broken up.[50] Specialized container ships, which now predominate, capitalize on speed at sea and at pierside.[51] Loading and offloading can take less than 24 hours, versus several days for conventional freighters.

Unfortunately such vessels are ill-configured to carry vehicles. They lack onboard gantry cranes, which increases container capacities and decreases cost/maintenance problems, but makes discharge difficult in undeveloped ports. Heavy-lift helicopters, balloon-supported aerial tramways (like those used by lumber companies), and equipment on self-sustaining ships currently serve as expedients to unload container ships in such circumstances. Efforts of that sort, however, are expensive and inefficient.[52]

Even if the U.S. Merchant Marine were structured perfectly, potential problems would still exist, given existing legal limitations. Emergency callups are politically sensitive matters, and, in prolonged conflict, could weaken this country's already poor competitive commercial position by diverting ships for defense.[53]

Sharp distinctions consequently are made between major wars and minor contingencies. No emergency requisitioning, for example, ever occurred in the Vietnam War, although the President had such powers. As a direct result, civilian ships offered for charter were often second class in terms of requirements.[54]

National Defense Reserve Fleet Marginal abilities of the active Merchant Marine to satisfy national needs (with or without compulsory callups) reinforce reliance on the National Defense Reserve Fleet (NDRF), which is maintained by the Maritime Administration (MARAD), an arm of the Commerce Department.

NDRF proved reliable in the past. Most recently, 172 recalled ships moved 40 percent of all military cargo to Vietnam during peak periods.[55] Current capabilities, however, are miniscule. The "mothballed" fleet of World War II transports, which once numbered thousands, is now reduced to 146 that are worth reactivating. Law once allowed owners to trade in aging but effective Mariner class ships for clunkers they could sell for scrap, but no one stepped forward, so the NDRF rusts and rots.[56]

Those still seaworthy are small and slow,[57] but their self-sustaining characteristics and ability to accept outsize items like tanks, trucks, locomotives, rolling stock, and harbor craft makes them easily adaptable for military missions. Perhaps even more importantly, requirements for break-bulk ships will remain critical until commercial containers are approved for ammunition carriage sometime in the early 1980s.[58]

Current DOD plans call for supplementary sealift from NDRF storage sites to report ready for duty within 10–15 days after American servicemen and/or materiel are committed to contingency operations, but refurbishment in fact would take 30 days or more in many instances. Drydock schedules are cramped. Labor skills are short in some shipyards. The passage of time will only aggravate the availability of repair parts, which already are scarce. Union assurances that sufficient qualified crews could assemble in short order may prove optimistic. About eight months reputedly would transpire before all NDRF Victory ships could pass muster, if reactivation took place on a "business as usual" basis. Time could be cut to something like three months if crash programs were implemented.[59]

A program now is afoot to refit 20–30 NDRF ships fast enough to satisfy 5-to-10-day force generation requirements by 1982, if plans proceed on schedule.[60] Rapid reinforcement, however, using that Ready Reserve Force (RRF), will soon be overtaken by events, unless the President extends the National Emergencies Act (Public Law 94–412), which expires on September 14, 1978. Authority to activate *any* ships in the NDRF, including the RRF, or to requisition *any* commercial vessels for contingency purposes, will terminate on that date. Attempts to reach some other solution agreeable to all beneficiaries have thus far been fruitless. Funds to form a Ready Reserve Force would thus be wasted, if that impasse remains unresolved.[61]

Effective U.S. Controlled Fleet The Effective U.S. Controlled Fleet (EUSC) of 321 ships, owned by Americans but flying flags from Liberia, Panama, and Honduras, offers a fallback position of sorts. Written agreements list which ships might reasonably be available in emergency. How reponsive they would actually be is arguable. Their military value is minimal in any case, since all but 11 are tankers or bulk cargo carriers best suited for hauling petroleum products and natural resources.[62]

Other Foreign Flags Other foreign-flag ships completely beyond U.S. control are more than ample to meet America's major contingency requirements. Dependability, however, could be poor if perceived interests of the countries concerned (including NATO allies) fail to coincide with those of the United States during crises. Even if *owners* show good will, there is no certainty that alien *crews* will agree to traffic in war zones, with or without a big bonus.[63]

Salient U.S. Shortcomings U.S. strategic sealift suffers from insufficient ships that can assemble in acceptable times and carry military type cargo to points where facilities are undeveloped or destroyed.

Army armored and mechanized divisions, with many more vehicles than predecessors, would strain merchant shipping, not just during initial deployment, but on a continuing basis, if ground combat losses were large. The trend toward fewer ships, constructed essentially to carry containers, thus is inversely proportionate to military demand. Even modest attrition from Soviet attacks could cripple our abilities to accomplish essential missions.

Soviet Strategic Sealift

The Soviet merchant marine, controlled by the Navy, currently includes 1,750 modern, highly-automated ships whose characteristics have been shaped more by sea power concepts than purely commercial considerations.[64] Most, being self-sustaining[65] and smaller than U.S. counterparts, are better able to operate in ports plagued by shallow harbors and skimpy facilities. Abilities were displayed to advantage during the Vietnam War, when Soviet merchantmen moved millions of tons 14,000 nautical miles around the Cape of Good Hope to Haiphong.[66]

Present trends tend toward Roll-on Roll-off (Ro/Ro) vessels, with ramps that allow wheeled and tracked vehicles to board and debark at will from open piers, with or without containers. Something like 20 now are in service. Finland is building two "Seabee" ships, based on U.S. technology. Barges, stowed topside and between decks, can be loaded and unloaded easily, and integrate nicely with feeder systems that navigate inland waterways. The applicability to operations in out-of-the-way areas is apparent.[67]

Amphibious Sealift

Soviet amphibious sealift is still limited (Figure 38). Active U.S. assets are comparatively strong, although they dropped from 162 ships to 62, after reaching their apogee in 1967.

The residue is satisfactory for battalion- and regimental-size landings, but lift requirements for a single Marine division/wing team would absorb all but four operational ships scattered from Manila to the Mediterranean:

Command/control ship (LCC)	1
Amphibious assault ship (LPH)	6
Amphibious transport (LPA)	2
Amphibious transport dock (LPD)	12
Landing ship dock (LSD)	9
Amphibious cargo ship (LKA)	5
Landing ship tank (LST)	14–16
Total	49–51

Current assets are limited to 62 ships, of which 15 percent are normally in overhaul. Lead times for assembly would be long, and combat losses irreplaceable.[68]

Road and Rail

Except for one gravel road that links CONUS with Alaska, the United States has no overland routes to any prospective areas of possible confrontation with the Soviet Union, which relies heavily on road and rail links that lead to NATO territory, the Indian subcontinent, China, and the Middle East.

Soviet networks generally compare poorly with those in this country. Not many highways are paved. Trucks are plentiful, but maintenance is poor. Railways are still restricted, although traffic has doubled in the last decade. Trains enroute to and from central Europe (or China, for that matter) must change wheels at the border, because Russian broad gauge tracks are incompatible with those of satellite states.[69] The process takes about two hours for a 20-car train.

Nevertheless, Soviet land lines of communication constitute impressive mobility means that are more important than airlift and sealift for many missions.

Combined Flexibility

Composite Soviet mobility forces are sufficient to influence a range of low-key contingencies in widely-separated areas, such as Angola and the Arab States, but airlift/sealift shortages are still strong limiting factors for major military operations almost anywhere outside the home country or contiguous satellites.

Quick and efficient logistic support for allies is a U.S. airlift specialty. MAC's squadrons also afford means of reinforcing forward deployed forces rapidly or shifting sizable combat power anywhere in the world. Apparent flexibility, however, is conditioned by the dearth of sealift, which makes it almost impossible to sustain major efforts without allied assistance. That dangerous combination calls for caution under most conceivable circumstances, since aid is by no means assured.

Graph 14

AIRLIFT AND SEALIFT
Statistical Summary - 1977

(Note Different Scales)

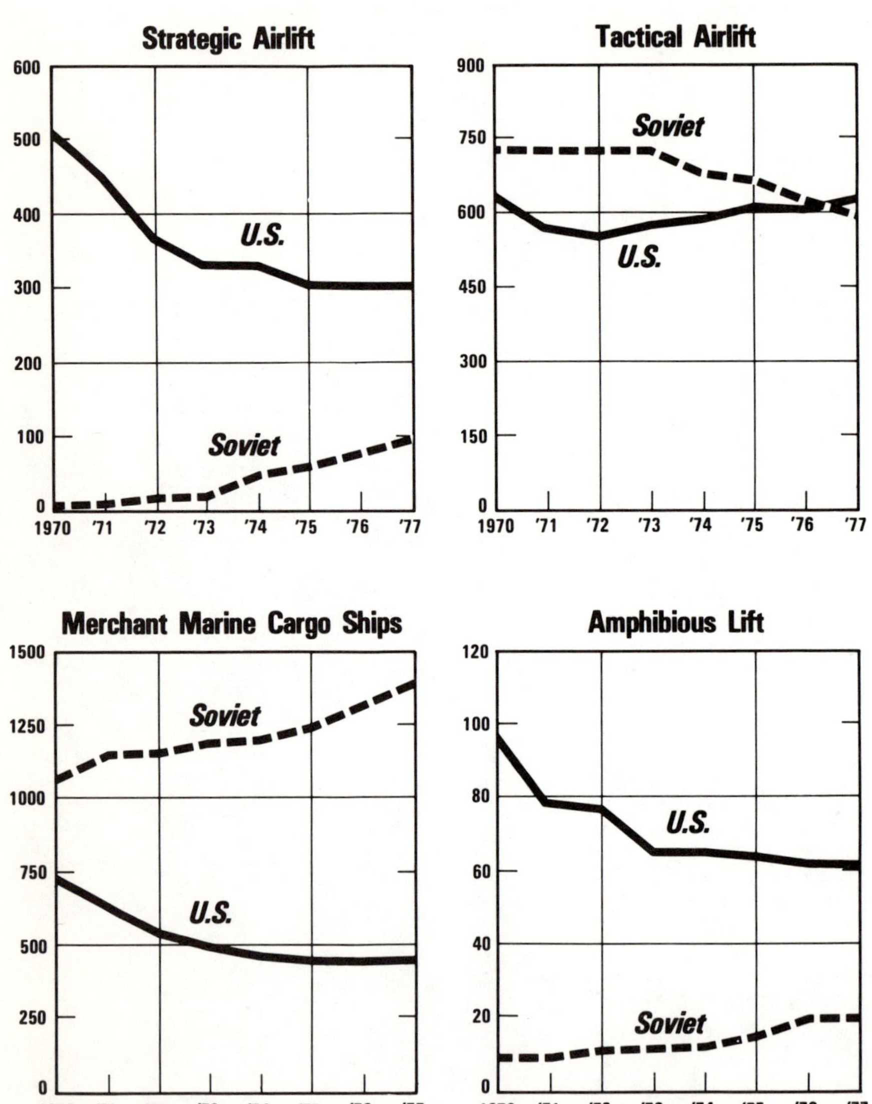

Note: U.S. airlift and merchant ships include reserve components.

Figure 36 MILITARY AIRLIFT
Statistical Trends and System Characteristics

	1970	1971	1972	1973	1974	1975	1976	1977	Net Change 1970–77
STRATEGIC AIRLIFT									
United States[1]									
Active									
C-5 Galaxy	2	28	49	70	70	70	70	70	+ 68
C-133 Cargomaster	38	14	0	0	0	0	0	0	– 38
C-141 Starlifter	234	234	234	234	234	234	234	234	0
Total	274	276	283	304	304	304	304	304	+ 30
Reserve									
C-97 Stratofreighter	32	8	8	0	0	0	0	0	– 32
C-124 Globemaster	208	168	72	24	24	0	0	0	–208
Total	240	176	80	24	24	0	0	0	–240
Grand Total	514	452	363	328	328	304	304	304	–210
Soviet Union									
AN-22 Cock	10	10	20	20	50	50	50	50	+ 40
IL-76 Candid	0	0	0	0	0	10	40	80	+ 80
Total	10	10	20	20	50	60	90	130	+120
U.S. Standing	+504	+442	+343	+308	+278	+244	+214	+174	–330

[1]U.S. aircraft are unit equipment (UE) only.

FIGURE 36 (Con't)

	1970	1971	1972	1973	1974	1975	1976	1977	Net Change 1970–77
TACTICAL AIRLIFT									
United States[1]									
Active									
C-7 Caribou	80	80	4	0	0	0	0	0	− 80
C-123 Provider	60	38	0	0	0	0	0	0	− 60
C-130 Hercules	394	332	288	272	272	272	234	234	−160
Total	534	450	292	272	272	272	234	234	−300
Reserve									
C-7 Caribou	0	0	32	48	48	48	48	48	+ 48
C-119 Flying Boxcar	48	0	0	0	0	0	0	0	− 48
C-123 Provider	8	8	40	72	72	72	64	64	+ 56
C-130 Hercules	44	114	188	188	198	222	262	284	+240
Total	100	122	260	308	318	342	374	396	+296
Grand Total	634	572	552	580	590	614	608	630	− 4
Soviet Union									
AN-12 Cub	730	730	730	730	680	670	630	600	−130
U.S. Standing	− 96	−158	−178	−150	− 90	− 56	− 22	+ 30	+126

[1] U.S. aircraft are unit equipment (UE) only.

Grand Total									
United States	1148	1024	915	908	918	918	912	934	−214
Soviet Union	740	740	750	750	730	730	710	700	− 40
U.S. Standing	+408	+284	+165	+158	+188	+188	+202	+234	−174
UTILITY/CARGO HELICOPTERS									
United States[1]									
Army									
CH-34 Choctaw	185	40	0	0	0	0	0	0	−185
CH-37 Mojave	25	0	0	0	0	0	0	0	− 25
CH-47 Chinook	480	460	345	380	365	330	325	306	−174
CH-54 Flying Crane	70	55	50	50	50	50	50	32	− 38
UH-1 Iroquois	4030	3750	2810	2680	2945	2440	2358	2303	−1727
Total	4790	4305	3205	3110	3360	2820	2733	2641	−2149
Marine									
CH-46 Sea Knight	224	164	133	140	91	118	141	146	− 78
CH-53 Sea Stallion	113	95	101	107	101	97	101	99	− 14
Total	337	259	234	247	192	215	242	245	− 92
Grand Total	5127	4564	3439	3357	3552	3035	2975	2886	−2241
Soviet Union	800	900	950	1100	−1325	1350	1475	1600	+800
U.S. Standing	+4327	+3664	+2489	+2257	+2227	+1685	+1500	+1286	−3041

[1]Strengths for U.S. Army helicopters reflect active inventory aircraft only.

FIGURE 36 (Con't)

TRANSPORT AIRCRAFT CHARACTERISTICS

	NR	Power Plant Type	Cruising Speed (Knots)	Maximum Cargo Load (lbs)	Range with Max Load Nautical (miles)[1]	Minimum Runway Length (Feet)[2]		Troops[3]	
						T/0	Land	Pax	Para
United States									
Active									
C-5	4	Jet	450	209,000	2,565[4]	7700	4610	343	0
C-130E	4	Turbo prop	280	42,000	2,000	2600	2700	91	64
C-141	4	Jet	425	63,600	2,835	6300	3840	131	123
Reserve									
C-7	2	Prop	140	6,000	100	1000	1000	31	25
C-123K	4	2 Jet 2 Prop	145	17,600	100	1325	1150	58	58
C-130A	4	Turbo prop	290	25,000	1,075	1850	1850	89	64
C-130B	4	Turbo prop	290	35,000	1,575	2400	2400	91	64
Soviet Union[5]									
AN-12 Cub	4	Turbo prop	320	44,000	400	2300	1640	90	60
AN-22 Cock	4	Turbo prop	350	176,200	2,200	4260	2620	175	0
IL-76 Candid	4	Jet	430	88,000	2,700	3300	1600	140	140

[1]Ranges correspond with loads shown. Performance data predicated on wartime maximum gross takeoff weights, no wind, and maximum fuel reserves. Lighter loads allow longer ranges.

[2]Minimum runway lengths shown above apply to *average*, not *maximum*, gross takeoff weights.

[3]Pax stands for passengers; para for paratroops.

[4]C-5 range is unrefueled.

[5]Coke (AN-24) and Curl (AN-26), both similar to Fokker F-27s, are scarcely suitable for most airlift purposes. Coot (IL-28), a medium transport, is assigned almost exclusively to Aeroflot, rather than Soviet Air Force units. All three are therefore excluded.

FIGURE 37 MERCHANT MARINE
Statistical Trends and System Characteristics

	1970	*1971*	*1972*	*1973*	*1974*	*1975*	*1976*	*1977*	*Net Change 1970–77*
UNITED STATES									
MILITARY SEALIFT COMMAND									
Nucleus									
Cargo	69	66	63	30	12	9	6	6	– 63
Tanker	25	24	17	16	20	19	21	21	– 4
Total	94	90	80	46	32	28	27	27	– 67
Charter									
Cargo	123	76	91	43	34	22	21	21	–102
Tanker	36	31	34	23	22	13	9	12	– 24
Total	159	107	125	66	56	35	30	33	–126
Grand Total	253	197	205	112	88	63	57	60	–193
REMAINDER ACTIVE MERCHANT MARINE									
Cargo	351	300	205	249	257	272	268	267	– 84
Tanker	187	183	176	176	169	181	180	182	– 5
Total	538	483	381	425	426	453	448	449	– 89

FIGURE 37 (Con't)

	1970	1971	1972	1973	1974	1975	1976	1977	*Net Change 1970–77*
EFFECTIVE U.S. CONTROLLED FLEET									
Cargo	34	22	20	18	14	11	10	11	– 23
Tanker	265	269	276	301	319	299	304	310	+ 45
Total	299	291	296	319	333	310	314	321	+ 22
TOTAL ACTIVE									
Cargo	577	464	379	340	317	314	305	305	–272
Tanker	513	507	503	516	530	512	514	525	+ 12
Total	1090	971	882	856	847	826	819	830	–260
NATIONAL DEFENSE RESERVE FLEET									
Cargo	170	175	168	149	138	139	139	146	– 24
Tanker	20	27	28	26	24	28	19	18	– 2
Total	190	202	196	175	162	167	158	164	– 26
U.S. RECAP									
UNITED STATES									
Cargo									
Active	577	464	379	340	317	314	305	305	–272
NDRF	170	175	168	149	138	139	139	146	– 24
Total	747	639	547	489	455	453	444	451	–296

Tanker									
Active	513	507	503	516	530	512	514	525	+ 12
NDRF	20	27	28	26	24	28	19	18	− 2
Total	533	534	531	542	554	540	533	543	+ 10
All Active	1090	971	882	856	847	826	819	830	−260
All NDRF	190	202	196	175	162	167	158	164	− 26
Total	1280	1173	1078	1031	1009	993	977	994	−286
SOVIET UNION									
Cargo	1075	1150	1150	1200	1200	1250	1325	1400	+325
Tanker	325	300	300	300	300	300	325	350	+ 25
Total	1400	1450	1450	1500	1500	1550	1650	1750	+350
U.S. Standing									
Cargo	−328	−511	−603	−711	−745	−797	−881	−949	−621
Tanker	+208	+234	+231	+242	+254	+240	+208	+193	− 15
Total	−120	−277	−372	−469	−491	−557	−673	−756	−636

FIGURE 37 (Con't)

CARGO SHIP CHARACTERISTICS

UNITED STATES	*Marad Design*	*Ship Class*	*Capacity (M/T)*[1]	*DWT*[2]	*Speed (Knots)*	*Boom/ Capacity (Tons)*	*Container Capacity*[3]	*Lighters/ Barges*
Break Bulk	VC2-S-AP2	Adelphi Victory	11325	7400	15	1 50	None	None
	C3-S-37c	Sheldon Lykes	14300	9610	18	1 60	None	None
	C4-S-57A	Challenger	16072	10290	20	4 10 2 15 1 70	None	None
Partial Containership	C4-S-64A	Austral Pilot	17176	9800	20	4 15 2 10	203–20	None
Self-Sustaining Containership	C6-S-1Qc	President Polk	26700	17300	20	2 10 4 22 1 60	380–20 198–40	None
Containership Non Self-sustaining	C5-S-73b	C. V. Lightning	23800	11700	20	None	928–20	None
	C6-S-IN	American Ace	26100	17100	22	None	463-20 234–40	None

		Sea-Land Galloway (SL-7)	59300	20060	30	None	896–35 200–40	None
Lash[4]	C8-S-81b	Lash Italia	32655	17990	21	1 30 1 500 (Crane)	248–20	49 with containers, 62 without
Sea Bee[5]	C8-S-82A	Doctor Lykes	37187	25550	20	2000 (Elevator)	None	38 Barges
RO/RO		Ponce	49200	11192	25	None	None	None
	C7-S-95	Maine	43390	11980	23	2 15	None	None

[1]Measurement ton (M/T) equal to 40 cubic feet
[2]DWT stands for deadweight tons
[3]203–20 indicates 203 20-foot containers, and so on.
[4]Lash Lighter Capacity 475 M/T
[5]SeaBee Barge Capacity 1000 M/T

FIGURE 38 AMPHIBIOUS SEALIFT
Statistical Trends and System Characteristics

	1970	*1971*	*1972*	*1973*	*1974*	*1975*	*1976*	*1977*	*Net Change 1970–77*
UNITED STATES									
LCC	2	4	3	2	2	2	2	2	0
LKA	12	7	6	6	6	6	5	5	– 7
LPA	4	3	3	2	2	2	0	0	– 4
LPD	12	14	15	14	14	14	14	14	+ 2
LPSS	1	1	1	1	1	0	0	0	– 1
LSD	13	12	12	13	13	13	13	13	0
LST	46	30	30	21	20	20	20	20	–26
Total	90	71	70	59	58	57	54	54	–36
LPH/LHA	7	7	7	7	7	7	8	8	+ 1
Grand Total	97	78	77	66	65	64	62	62	–35
SOVIET UNION									
LST	10	10	12	12	12	15	20	20	+10
U.S. STANDING	+87	+68	+65	+54	+53	+49	+42	+42	–45

LCC = Amphibious Command Ship
LKA = Amphibious Cargo Ship
LPA = Amphibious Transport
LPD = Amphibious Transport Dock
LPSS = Amphibious Transport Submarine
LSD = Landing Ship Dock
LST = Landing Ship Tank
LCM = Landing Craft, Merchanized
LCPL = Landing Craft, Personnel
LCU = Landing Craft, Utility
LCVP = Landing Craft, Vehicle, Personnel
LVTP = Landing Vehicle, Tracked, Personnel

Soviet LSMs (Landing Ships, Mechanized) correspond more closely with U.S. landing craft than with amphibious ships, and are so listed. They currently have 65.

AMPHIBIOUS SHIP CHARACTERISTICS[1]

	Speed (Knots)	Troops	General Cargo (Cu ft)	Vehicles (Sq ft)	Ammo (Cu ft)	Fuel Drums	Fuel Bulk (Gal)	Booms, Cranes, (Tons)	Boats	Helos
UNITED STATES										
LKA Rankin Class	16	138	42,518	21,798	39,988	600	None	4 35T 2 10T 6 5T	6 LCM-6 6 LCVP 2 LCPL 1 LCM-8	None
LPA Paul Revere CL	20+	1657	135,457	10,132	11,471	905	AVGAS: 5900	2 60T 1 30T 3 10T 2 8T 2 5T	7 LCM-6 10 LCVP 5 LCPL	1 CH-53
LPD[2] Austin Class	20+	925	2,176	11,127	16,660	MOGAS: 22,335 AVGAS: 97,328 AV-LUB: 4,500 JP-5: 224,572		1 30T 6 4T 2 1.5T	2 LCPL 2 LCVP	2 CH-53
LSD Thomaston Class	20+	341	N/A	8,754	3,000	AVGAS: 1200 or MOGAS: 1200 Diesel: 39,000		2 50T	Ship's Boats 2 LCVP 2 LCPL [3]	1 CH-53

[1]Each class is different. Ships above are currently in widest use.
[2]LPD can carry ammunition or general cargo, but not both.
[3]Sample loads: 3 LCU; or 19 LCM-6; or 9 LCM-8; or 48 LVTP.

FIGURE 38 (Con't)

LST CHARACTERISTICS								
	Speed (knots)	*Troops*	*General Cargo (Tons)*	*Vehicles (Sample loads)*	*Ammo (Cu ft)*	*Bulk Fuel (Gal)*	*Boats*	*Helos*
UNITED STATES								
LST 1179 Class	20+	431	500 (beach) 2000 over LST-installed causeway	25 LVT, 17 2½ T Trucks or 21 M-60 Tanks 17 2½T Trucks	2,552	254,000 Diesel; 7197 MOGAS; 134,438 AVGAS	3 LCVP 1 LCPL	1 CH-53
SOVIET UNION								
LST Alligator	15	375		26 Tanks				

LANDING CRAFT CHARACTERISTICS

UNITED STATES				
LCM-6	9	80	34	3 ¼-T Trucks or 1 2½-T Truck/Trailer
LCM-8	12	150	60	1 M-60 Tank
LCU[1]	8	400	180	3 M-60 Tanks
LCVP	8	36	8100	1 ¼-T Truck/Trailer
LVTP	7	28	None	None
SOVIET UNION				
LSM				
Polnocny A	18	200		6 Tanks
Polnocny C	18	30		5 Tanks

[1]LCU is 1610 series

Footnotes

1. Prepositioned stocks require protected facilities. Duplicate sets of equipment (one in use, one in storage) not only double costs, but some items are difficult to maintain, much less modernize, at rates equal to those of items in active units. Land-based depots in particular are susceptible to preemptive destruction in some deployment areas. Relocating caches in emergency can *add* to, rather than *reduce*, demands on airlift and sealift. Rainville, R. C., *Strategic Mobility and the Nixon Doctrine.* Washington: The National War College, 1971, pp. 60–61.

2. U.S. plans, programs, and alternatives are addressed in Rumsfeld, Donald H., *Defense Department Report for FY 1978,* pp. 228–237; Brown, George S., *United States Military Posture for FY 1978,* pp. 93–98; and "Mobility Forces: An Interim Report," prepared by the Congressional Budget Office for the Subcommittee on Priorities and Economy in Government of the Joint Economic Committee. Washington: October 26, 1976, 13 pp. plus tables.

3. Colonel James N. Hockney, United States Air Force, served as principal advisor on U.S. airlift during preparation of this section. For general background see U.S. Congress. House. *Hearings on H.R. 2637 and the Posture of the U.S. Military Airlift,* Before the Committee on Armed Services. 95th Congress, 1st Session. Washington: U.S. Govt. Print. Off., 1977, 187 pp.

4. U.S. strategic airlift at an early stage was coupled with prepositioned stocks of "heavy equipment and bulk supplies which could be quickly 'married up' with lightly equipped land force units airlifted into [selected areas]." McNamara, Robert S., *Statement on the FY 1969 Defense Budget,* p. 140.

5. The last C-133 phased out of the active Air Force in 1971. A few C-124s remained with reserve components until 1974. The U.S. Civil Reserve Air Fleet retired its last piston-powered transports in 1968, except for three with Reeve Aleutian Airline in Alaska, according to telephonic contact with MAC officials on October 14, 1977.

6. Military Airlift Command superseded the Military Air Transport Service on New Year's Day, 1966.

7. "DOD's consolidation of [tactical and strategic] airlift forces is now virtually complete. MAC has assumed effective control of C-130 assets in the United States and will coordinate C-130 movements overseas." To increase efficiency, "the President has decided to designate MAC a 'specified' command." Rumsfeld, Donald H., *Annual Defense Department Report on the FY 1978 Budget,* p. 236.

8. *Ibid.,* pp. 230, 231, 232, 233, 234, 236.

9. U.S. Congress. House. "The Posture of Military Airlift." A report by the Research and Development Subcommittee of the Committee on Armed Services. 94th Congress, 2d Session. Washington: U.S. Govt. Print. Off., April 9, 1976, p. 28.

10. "Mobility Forces," Congressional Budget Office, p. 3.

11. C-5 aircraft have always been equipped with refueling receptacles, but crews were not qualified during the emergency airlift to Israel in 1973. Consequently, they not only were compelled to take on fuel at politically sensitive Lajes Field in the Azores enroute, but consumed 1.3 pounds of POL at Lod Airport in Israel for every pound of equipment delivered. *Ibid.,* p. 15.

Present U.S. aircraft could carry 38 percent more outsize cargo if refueled in flight, according to a recent MAC study.

12. Brown, George S., *United States Military Posture for FY 1978,* p. 94.

13. "Mobility Forces," Congressional Budget Office, p. 7, amended by Air Force comments on a draft of this study, March 7, 1977.

14. Brown, George S., *United States Military Posture for FY 1978,* p. 95.

15. CRAF callups, by model and series, can be in three stages. The first two afford extensive voluntary civil augmentation airlift in times of limited crisis. Commander, MAC is authorized to activate Stage I. Stage II requires Defense Secretary approval. Stage III provisions, connected with grave national emergencies declared by Congress, the President, or (under specified conditions) the Office of Preparedness, permit requisitioning of the entire CRAF. To date, none of those plans have been implemented. Commitments during the Vietnam conflict comprised voluntary expansion of peacetime contracts. U.S. Congress. House. "The Posture of Military Airlift," pp. 31–32.

16. Air Force comments on a draft of this study, March 4, 1977. To put 30-day lift capacities in perspective, a single armored division with accompanying supplies (computed at 422 pounds per man day) weighs 55,900 tons. A mechanized division weighs 49,710. Infantry divisions, which make up most of our National Guard, weigh 29,370 each. Figures were furnished by Army DCSLOG planners on February 4, 1977.

17. U.S. Congress. House. "The Posture of Military Airlift," p. 18.

18. Rainville, R. C., *Strategic Mobility and the Nixon Doctrine*, pp. 51–52, 73. The study cited is out of date, but C-5 holdings have stayed constant at 70 and similar delivery delays could be expected today.

19. Large, irregular items such as vehicles often fill the cigar-shaped C-141 cargo compartment long before allowable cargo load (ACL) limits are reached in terms of pounds. That phenomenon, called "cubing out," has produced a prototype program for a "stretch" version of the C-141, which (if procured) would increase lift capacity about 30 percent.

20. C-141s would have proved useless during the 1973 airlift to Israel if Portugal had refused landing rights at Lajes field. The same tonnage could have been delivered with 57 fewer sorties while saving 5 million gallons of gas if in-flight refueling had been feasible. U.S. Congress. House. "The Posture of Military Airlift," p. 15.

21. A sortie is one round trip by one aircraft.

22. Statistics were received telephonically from staff officers of the 82d Airborne Division in April 1975.

23. MAC Monthly Reserve Air Fleet Summary.

24. Rainville, R. C. *Strategic Mobility and the Nixon Doctrine*, p. 49.

25. Brown, George S., *United States Military Posture for FY 1978*, p. 96.

26. Rumsfeld, Donald H., *Annual Defense Department Report for FY 1978*, p. 230.

27. Schott, Terry L. "Soviet Air Transportation: Projection of Power," *U.S. Army Aviation Digest*, July 1976, p. 14.

28. Four Soviet flight corridors to Ethiopia take the following routes: 1) southwest from Tashkent across Afghanistan and Iran to the Arabian Sea, thence over the Strait of Hormuz and Aden to Addis Ababa; 2) Georgiyevak to Oman and Addis Ababa; 3) Georgiyevak to Damascus and the Sinai, then south along the Red Sea; and 4) Georgiyevak to Nicosia, Cyprus, Baghdad, Basra, Riyadh, and South Yeman. Two routes overfly Turkey, two others take a good look at oil fields in Iran. Cooley, John, "Spying on Iran, Saudi Oil Fields?," *Christian Science Monitor*, January 11, 1978, p. 1; "Soviet Arms for Ethiopia Jam Sealanes," *Washington Post*, January 20, 1978, p. A30.

29. Brown, George S., *United States Military Posture for FY 1978*, p. 94.

30. DIA comments on a draft of this study, September 9, 1977.

31. U.S. Congress. House. "The Posture of Military Airlift," p. 7.

32. Turbiville, Graham H., "Soviet Airborne Forces: Increasingly Powerful Factor in the Equation," *Army Magazine*, April 20, 1976, p. 22; Schott, Terry L., "Soviet Air Transportation," pp. 14–16. Supplemented by DIA comments on a draft of this study, September 9, 1977.

33. DIA comments on a draft of this study, March 3, 1977.

34. Erickson, John, "Soviet-Warsaw Pact Force Levels," p. 51; Turbiville, Graham H., "Soviet Airborne Forces," pp. 22, 27.

35. Turbiville, Graham H., "Soviet Airborne Forces," p. 27.

36. Erickson, John, "Soviet-Warsaw Pact Force Levels," p. 51; Bramlett, David A.,

"Soviet Airmobility: An Overview," *Military Review*, January 1977, pp. 16–18, 24–25.

37. Preoccupation with rapid-response sealift is summarized in McNamara, Robert S., *Statement on the FY 1969 Defense Budget*, pp. 140–144.

38. See, for example, Collins, Gerald W., "Building Bridges. . . . Not Barriers," and Moore, Sam H., "Sealift as an Element of Strategic Mobility." Both contained in *Proceedings of the 1977 World Wide Strategic Mobility Conference*. Sponsored by the Organization of the Joint Chiefs of Staff, Logistics Directorate. Washington: National Defense University, 1977.

39. The U.S. National Defense Reserve Fleet (NDRF) is a shadow of its former self. Recent status was reviewed in "Age, Neglect This Fleet's Only Enemies," *Washington Star*, October 1, 1977, p. F-3.

40. "DOD-controlled sealift is probably insufficient to support even a minor contingency in a timely fashion, so we are heavily dependent on the U.S. Merchant Marine and, in the case of a NATO conflict, on the commercial fleets of our NATO allies as well," according to Deputy Secretary of Defense Charles W. Duncan, Jr. However, "present arrangements by the NATO Planning Board for Ocean Shipping . . . . [do] not provide for augmentation of the U.S. ships by European merchant ships unless and until hostilities have started." That may be too late, says Admiral Isaac C. Kidd, Jr., Supreme Allied Commander Atlantic. The availability of allies for non-NATO contingencies is also less than certain. Quotes contained in Duncan's Keynote Address and Kidd's presentation on NATO Strategic Mobility, *Proceedings of the 1977 World Wide Strategic Mobility Conference*.

41. W. J. Amoss, Jr., President of the Lykes Brothers Steamship Co., Inc., sums up the situation in these words: "For many years, the Defense Department and the Maritime industry have had a tentative relationship. . . . We have failed to exploit the rich potential for planning and development. This, despite some conspicuously kind words that are cast in the direction of the Merchant Marine by the Navy's top brass." Many associates share his sentiments. Good intentions have not translated ideals into action. "The Horrible Mistake," *Ibid.*, p. II-E-4.

42. *Understanding Soviet Naval Developments*. Washington: Office of the Chief of Naval Operations, April 1975, pp. 51–53.

43. Ackley, Richard T., "The Soviet Merchant Fleet," *U.S. Naval Institute Proceedings*, February 1976, pp. 27–37.

44. The combined force of Soviet and East European merchant ships, which carried several million tons of cargo from Black Sea ports to Haiphong, was a prominent logistic link for communist insurgents in Southeast Asia. Joint Soviet-satellite exercises have been common since 1958.

45. Something like 10 Soviet merchant ships in various capacities supported Okean-75. The magnitude of that exercise was immense. See summary in Watson, Bruce W. and Walton, Margurite A., "Okean-75," *Naval Institute Proceedings*, July 1976, reprinted in *Congressional Record*, August 24, 1976, pp. S14339–S14341.

46. Early expansionist aims and efforts of the Soviet Merchant Marine are expounded in *Soviet Sea Power, Special Report Series: No. 10*, Washington: The Center for Strategic and International Studies, Georgetown University, June 1969, pp. 73–91.

47. Captains of selected merchant ships, for example, possess packets to be opened when ordered in emergency. Those "Last Testament" documents should significantly improve signal communications, reduce routing problems, and otherwise help preserve carriers and cargoes. All merchant ships at sea provide defense controllers with a "noon position", so that continuous plots may be maintained and assembly accelerated on call. The sum total of such steps, however, is still few. Amoss, W. J., *Proceedings of the 1977 World Wide Strategic Mobility Conference*, p. II-E-3.

48. *Ibid.*, p. II-E-2. In addition to Amoss, who is President of the Lykes Brothers Steamship Co., Inc., opinions were expressed by presidents of U.S. Lines, American President Lines, American Export Lines, Farrell Lines, Delta Lines, and Moore McCormack Lines.

49. *Ibid.*, p. II-E-3/4.

50. Break-bulk ships, as opposed to those constructed to carry containers, transport undifferentiated dry cargo of various sizes and shapes. They suit military needs very well. "Tramps" are owned by independent operators, who haul cargoes of opportunity without regard for schedules or routes.

51. Containers are rectangular steel boxes, eight feet square in cross-section. Standard lengths are 20, 24, 35, and 40 feet. Each can be carried on a trailer, railroad flat car, or in a barge. They stack vertically in container cells and on top of strong hatch covers, side-by-side, so that loading is simple and no space is wasted.

52. Approximately 400 dry cargo ships were needed to sustain operations in Vietnam, because unloading and clearance facilities were inadequate. Consequently, scores of merchantmen constantly anchored offshore or queued in Thai harbors waiting their turn, extending turn-around times. New container ships transferred cargo to old self-sustainers or LSTs at Cam Ranh Bay. Many of those useful craft, that saw yeoman service, have since been retired. Chase, John D., *U.S. Merchant Marine—For Commerce and Defense*, pp. 133–134; Brown, George S., *United States Military Posture for FY 1978*, p. 98.

53. The Merchant Marine Act of 1936, as amended in 1970, prescribes a fleet "capable of serving as a naval and military auxiliary in time of war or national emergency declared by Presidential proclamation." In such case, "it shall be lawful for the Secretary of Commerce to requisition or purchase any vessel or other watercraft owned by citizens of the United States, or under construction in the United States, or for any period during such emergency to requisition or charter the use of any such property." Title 46, Sections 1101 and 1242, United States Code.

54. Kendall, Lane C., "Capable of Serving as a Naval and Military Auxiliary. . . ." *U.S. Naval Institute Proceedings,* May 1971, pp. 213–214, 214–215.

55. "The National Defense Reserve Fleet—Can it Respond to Future Contingencies?" Report to the Congress by the Comptroller General of the United States, Washington: General Accounting Office, October 6, 1976, p. 2.

56. Mariner class ships are newer, larger, and faster than Victory ships, but configurations are similar. Twenty-six were available for exchange during the two-year period (January 2, 1975 to January 2, 1977) permitted by Public Law 93–605. Not one was traded pursuant to its provisions. U.S. Congress. House. *Vessels Traded into National Defense Reserve Fleet.* Report No. 95–727. 95th Congress, 1st Session. Washington: U.S. Govt. Print. Off., October 20, 1977, pp. 2–3.

57. Cargo ship speed is an important factor for fast turn-around times. Steaming at a steady 15 knots, a Victory ship would take four days plus four hours longer than a 20-knot C-4 Challenger to travel 6,000 miles.

58. "The National Defense Reserve Fleet—Can it Respond to Future Contingencies?;" pp. 3–4; telephonic conversation with MSC planners on February 9, 1977.

59. The "National Defense Reserve Fleet—Can it Respond to Future Contingencies?," pp. 4–13, 32.

60. The present list of 30 ships will change in size, composition, and capability if MSC receives approval to swap a few Victory ships for more modern models.

61. Discussions with members of the military transportation community in January and February 1978.

62. Chase, John D., "U.S. Merchant Marine—For Commerce and Defense," pp. 140–143.

63. *Ibid.*, p. 140; Kendall, Lane C., "Capable of Serving as a Naval and Military Auxiliary. . . ." pp. 216, 219.

64. For general surveys of Soviet strategic sealift, see Prina, Edgar L., "Soviet Merchant Marine Takes a Great Leap Forward," *Sea Power,* December 1977, pp. 9–12 and Ackley, Richard T., "The Soviet Merchant Marine," *U.S. Naval Institute Proceedings,* February 1976, pp. 27–37.

65. "Self-sustaining" in merchant marine terms connotes ships that can load and

unload themselves, using the ship's booms, cranes, and other cargo-handling apparatus.

66. Briefing by Larry Luckworth, U.S. Naval Intelligence Support Center, Washington, May 1976, pp. 1–2 of text; *Understanding Soviet Naval Developments*, pp. 51–53; Brown, George S., *United States Military Posture for FY 1978*, p. 97. Sources refer to ship characteristics, not Soviet use.

67. Chase, John D. "U.S. Merchant Marine—for Commerce and Defense," pp. 134–135, 141; Rumsfeld, Donald H., *Annual Defense Department Report for FY 1978*, p. 237; *Izvestia*, December 27, 1976.

68. Marine Corps comments on a draft of this study, August 31, 1977.

69. Russian broad gauge tracks are five feet wide. Standard gauge tracks in satellite states are 4 feet 8½ inches.

III

NATO AND THE WARSAW PACT

PART I

Fundamental Focus

Books I and II survey U.S. and Soviet armed services as separate entities. Complete assessment of comparative strengths, however, must also consider alliance systems. This case study covers NATO and the Warsaw Pact, the world's two strongest coalitions.

U.S. and Soviet conflicting security interests converge in Western Europe. Both superpowers prize that region for political, economic, military, technological, and cultural reasons. Its significance in our case is vital[1] for if the Soviets add that prodigious source of strength to their present holdings, the power balance might shift so far in their favor that this country could not compete.

Attention focuses on the crucial center sector,[2] where both sides concentrate great combat power in constant and contiguous confrontation. That is the point of decision. If defense fails there, NATO can forget the flanks.

Alliance Arrangements

America's deterrent and defense commitments in Europe were formally confirmed in 1949, when 12 countries created the Atlantic Alliance in response to Soviet pressure.[3] (See Annex E for full text.) Stalin had already incarcerated nine countries behind the Iron Curtain,[4] and showed no inclination to stop. Collective security seemed the only answer for West European states, which had been badly weakened by World War II.[5]

The Warsaw Pact, which appeared six years later, coordinates security efforts of satellite states that already were tied tightly to the Soviet Union and each other by a series of bilateral treaties.[6] The text closely parallels NATO's compact on paper (Annex F), but similarities are superficial in practice.[7]

Superpowers in each case overshadow colleagues, with one decisive difference. U.S. leadership is approved by peers. Soviet control over subordinates is compulsory.

Comparative Security Commitments

Security teeth in the Atlantic Treaty are contained in Article 5, which asserts that "an armed attack against one or more [members] . . . . shall be considered an attack against them all," obligating each signatory to take "such action as it deems necessary, including the use of armed force."

Contrary to popular misconception, however, nothing in NATO accords requires an automatic declaration of war or any other reflex action by affiliated countries, except consultation. Our State Department submits that the shape, extent, and timing of U.S. responses "would in the final analysis depend on the nature of the attack, the defensive capacity of the state or states attacked, and other relevant circumstances."[8]

Security commitments in the Warsaw Treaty look much the same on the surface. Article 4 stipulates that each signatory "shall immediately, either individually or in agreement with other Parties . . . . come to the assistance of the state or states attacked with all such means as it deems necessary, including armed force."

The coalition is entirely defensive, according to highly-placed and authoritative Soviet spokesmen. The definition of "defense", however, is somewhat different in the communist context than in standard U.S. dictionaries. As the Soviets see it, defense of "revolutionary attainments and the cause of peace" permits initiatives not allowable in NATO's camp, including preemptive action.[9]

Contracting parties may indeed "consult with one another," as prescribed in Article 3, but Satellite statesmen have little say concerning the character of collective response to contingencies.

Security arrangements are skewed when it comes to internal conflict. Collective defense obligations, for example, were inoperative from our standpoint when Russian troops overran Hungary in 1956 and quashed rebellious Czechs in 1968. "Assistance" rendered in each case was cited as "defending the attainments of socialism."[10]

Comparative Command Structures

Warsaw Pact capabilities are essentially continental, except for the Soviet sponsor.[11] NATO's operational area includes the North Atlantic. Respective requirements, plus political peculiarities, shape respective command structures.

NATO Structure

This short section traces NATO's chain of command from top civilians to combatants, with special attention to control over forces that face the Warsaw Pact along the Iron Curtain (Figure 39).

North Atlantic Council

The North Atlantic Council, NATO's senior authority, "provides a unique forum for consultation and promulgates policy decisions. Each year, the Foreign Minister of a member state is elected President, selection being made in alphabetical order of countries. A Secretary General chairs all working sessions. Ambassadors from the 15 sovereign countries, which are coequal, represent their foreign ministers at the Council in Permanent Session.[12]

Collective security policy is the prime concern of the Defense Planning Committee, an integral element of the Council. It too is chaired by the Secretary General, along with the Nuclear Defense Affairs Committee and its affiliate, the Nuclear Planning Group.[13]

The North Atlantic Council meets twice a year at ministerial level. Foreign Ministers represent their respective countries, but defense and finance secretaries often attend. Prime Ministers and the U.S. President were present in 1957, 1974–75, and 1977.[14]

Decisions, even in times of intense crisis, "are not taken by majority vote, but by common consent," a complicated process that involves considerable compromise and necessarily "demands time and patience." Collocating the North Atlantic Council with its Military Committee in Brussels has helped improve the machinery.[15]

Military Committee

Chiefs of Staff from member countries (the JCS Chairman in our case) make up NATO's Military Committee, which advises the North Atlantic Council/Defense Planning Committee on security matters, and promulgates policy decisions predicated on their approval. Its Presidency rotates among nations annually in order of the English alphabet. A Chairman, elected by the Chiefs of Staff for a two-year period, presides over all sessions. That term may be extended.[16]

Since the Chiefs normally meet just twice a year (more often if necessary), each nation appoints a full-time Military Representative to the Committee in Permanent Session. An International Military Staff supports. Its three-star Director may be drawn from any member State, as long as his nationality is different than that of the Chairman. The staff "prepares plans, initiates studies and recommends policy on matters of a military nature referred . . . . by various national or NATO authorities." It also acts as executive agent to ensure that policy decisions are implemented as directed by subordinate commands.[17]

Figure 39

NATO COMMAND STRUCTURE

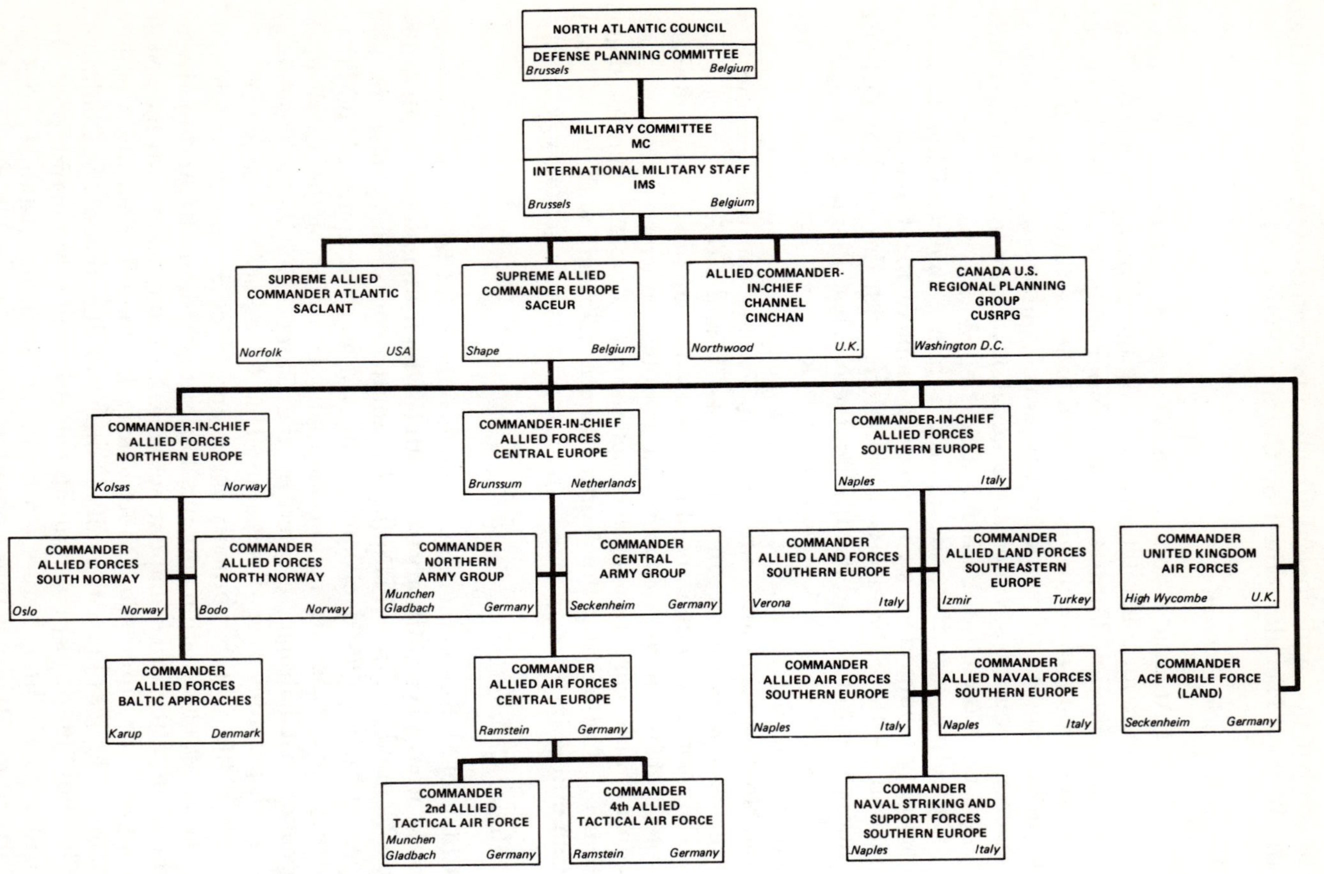
NORTH ATLANTIC COUNCIL
DEFENSE PLANNING COMMITTEE
Brussels Belgium
MILITARY COMMITTEE MC
INTERNATIONAL MILITARY STAFF IMS
Brussels Belgium
SUPREME ALLIED COMMANDER ATLANTIC SACLANT
Norfolk USA
SUPREME ALLIED COMMANDER EUROPE SACEUR
Shape Belgium
ALLIED COMMANDER-IN-CHIEF CHANNEL CINCHAN
Northwood U.K.
CANADA U.S. REGIONAL PLANNING GROUP CUSRPG
Washington D.C.
COMMANDER-IN-CHIEF ALLIED FORCES NORTHERN EUROPE
Kolsas Norway
COMMANDER ALLIED FORCES SOUTH NORWAY
Oslo Norway
COMMANDER ALLIED FORCES NORTH NORWAY
Bodo Norway
COMMANDER ALLIED FORCES BALTIC APPROACHES
Karup Denmark
COMMANDER-IN-CHIEF ALLIED FORCES CENTRAL EUROPE
Brunssum Netherlands
COMMANDER NORTHERN ARMY GROUP
Munchen Gladbach Germany
COMMANDER CENTRAL ARMY GROUP
Seckenheim Germany
COMMANDER ALLIED AIR FORCES CENTRAL EUROPE
Ramstein Germany
COMMANDER 2nd ALLIED TACTICAL AIR FORCE
Munchen Gladbach Germany
COMMANDER 4th ALLIED TACTICAL AIR FORCE
Ramstein Germany
COMMANDER-IN-CHIEF ALLIED FORCES SOUTHERN EUROPE
Naples Italy
COMMANDER ALLIED LAND FORCES SOUTHERN EUROPE
Verona Italy
COMMANDER ALLIED LAND FORCES SOUTHEASTERN EUROPE
Izmir Turkey
COMMANDER ALLIED AIR FORCES SOUTHERN EUROPE
Naples Italy
COMMANDER ALLIED NAVAL FORCES SOUTHERN EUROPE
Naples Italy
COMMANDER NAVAL STRIKING AND SUPPORT FORCES SOUTHERN EUROPE
Naples Italy
COMMANDER UNITED KINGDOM AIR FORCES
High Wycombe U.K.
COMMANDER ACE MOBILE FORCE (LAND)
Seckenheim Germany

Combatant Commands

The Supreme Allied Commander Europe (SACEUR), Supreme Allied Commander Atlantic (SACLANT), and Allied Commander-in-Chief Channel (CINCHAN) develop and coordinate military plans for their interrelated regions.

Allied Command Atlantic SACLANT, under supervision of the Military Committee, develops defense plans for Atlantic areas from the North Pole to the Tropic of Cancer, including all contiguous coastal waters except the English Channel (Map 14).[18] Should war occur, Allied Command Atlantic would strive to keep essential SLOCs open, "conduct conventional and nuclear operations against enemy naval bases and airfields," and assist SACEUR as required.[19]

A small Standing Naval Force of destroyer class ships drawn from assorted member countries has been under SACLANT's peacetime orders since 1967. It carries out training programs and port calls while flying the NATO flag. Assigned ships rotate, so many crews can gain experience with multinational teams in command/control procedures, communications, surveillance, tactics, and integrated operations. The entire contingent can deploy rapidly to trouble spots in times of tension.[20]

Channel Command Channel Command covers the English Channel choke point and North Sea approaches from Lands End to a line that connects Scotland with central Denmark. Its primary purpose is to control that sluiceway in war with air and sea elements. NATO's Standing Naval Force Channel, a flotilla of mine countermeasures ships, serves CINCHAN in peacetime.[21]

Allied Command Europe Allied Command Europe, commonly called ACE, stretches from the North Cape of Norway to North Africa, and from the Pillars of Hercules to Turkey's frontier with Persia.[22] Peacetime activities prepare assigned and earmarked elements to function effectively as a unified force in war. SACEUR, like SACLANT, "has right to direct access to the Chiefs-of-Staff of any [NATO] powers and, in certain circumstances, to Defense Ministers and Heads of Government."[23]

Three subordinate commands share SACEUR's great load. Allied Forces Northern Europe stands guard in Norway and covers the Kattegat. Allied Forces Southern Europe secures NATO's Mediterranean flank. Allied Forces Central Europe, whose components include Northern Army Group (NORTHAG), Central Army Group (CENTAG), and Allied Air Forces Central Europe (AAFCE), is the basic bulwark between the Baltic and the Alps. (See Figure 39 for further breakout.)[24]

Map 14
NATO AREAS OF RESPONSIBILITY

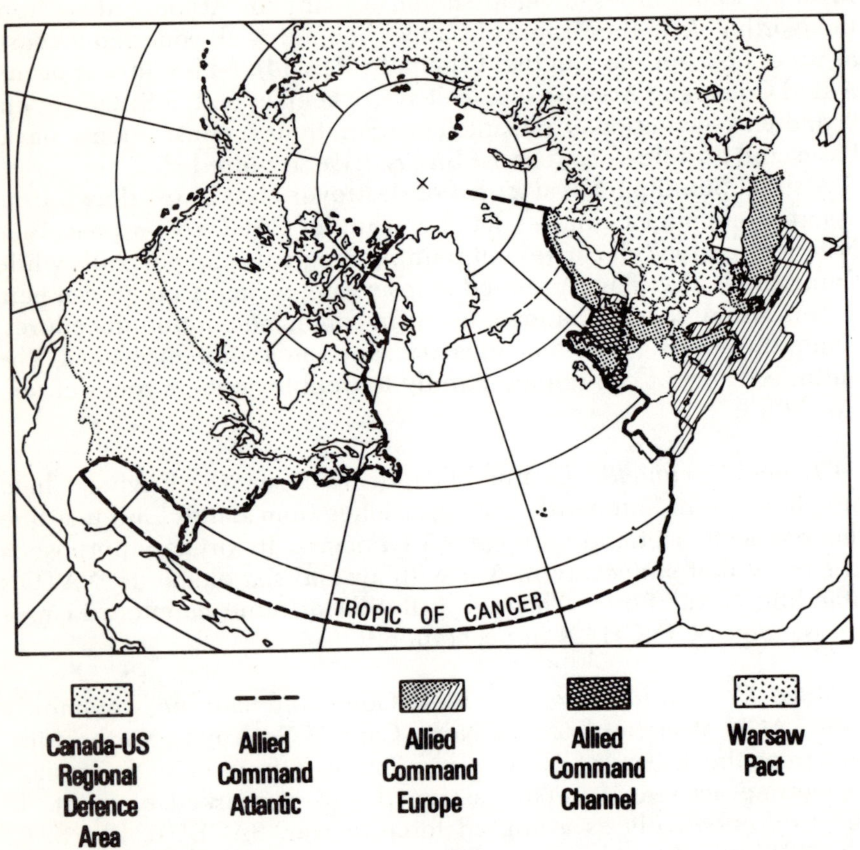

The ACE Mobile Force, first constituted in 1960, makes use of selected land and air units earmarked for immediate commitment to any threatened area, especially on NATO's north and south flanks. The package couples a three-battalion light brigade (one of which is U.S.) with a composite air wing that includes a fighter-bomber squadron and tactical transports. The intent is to deter limited aggression and demonstrate solidarity in times of intense tension, when perhaps only one or two NATO countries are directly endangered.[25]

Warsaw Pact Structure

Warsaw Pact institutional structure seems to reflect strong Soviet politico-military influence all the way down the chain of command (Figure 40), although official sources refer infrequently to relationships or responsibilities.

Political Consultative Committee

Signatories to the Treaty, in accord with Article 6, contracted to set up a Political Consultative Committee, which acts as a Soviet-controlled counterpart of NATO's North Atlantic Council. Each associate contributes "a member of its Government or . . . . another specifically appointed representative." In full formal order, it reportedly consists of First Secretaries (topped by Secretary General Brezhnev) of respective communist parties, plus Chiefs of State, Foreign Ministers, and Defense Ministers from each participating country. The Joint Secretariat, with a Soviet official in charge, remains in Moscow. So does a Standing Commission, whose function is to formulate foreign policy recommendations for the Pact. Performance, however, has been sporadic.[26]

Council of Defense Ministers

The Council of Defense Ministers was conceived in 1969, as a result of efforts to reduce satellite resentment after repressions for the preceding two decades. It appears to be a rather inactive agent, meeting rarely at irregular intervals to review (and presumably approve) recommendations by the military CINC.[27]

Joint High Command Member States, according to Article 5 of the Warsaw Treaty, consented "to establish a Joint Command of the armed forces that by agreement . . . . shall be assigned." A Marshal of the Soviet Union has always been Commander-in-Chief, just as NATO's SACEUR and SACLANT have always been American generals and admirals.[28] Choice, however, is by active consensus in the Atlantic Alliance. Passive acquiescence shapes selection processes in the Warsaw Pact. "Ministers of Defense or other military leaders of the signatory states . . . . serve as Deputy Commanders-in-Chief . . . . and shall command the armed forces assigned by their respective" countries. The entire entourage is stationed in Moscow.[29]

A Military Council within the Joint High Command is the major innovation resulting from reforms. It seems analogous to NATO's Military Committee when seen on a chart, but Soviet control is supercentralized. The CINC, for example, is Chairman. His Deputy, the Chief of Staff, probably the Inspector General, and a senior political officer,

Figure 40
WARSAW PACT COMMAND STRUCTURE

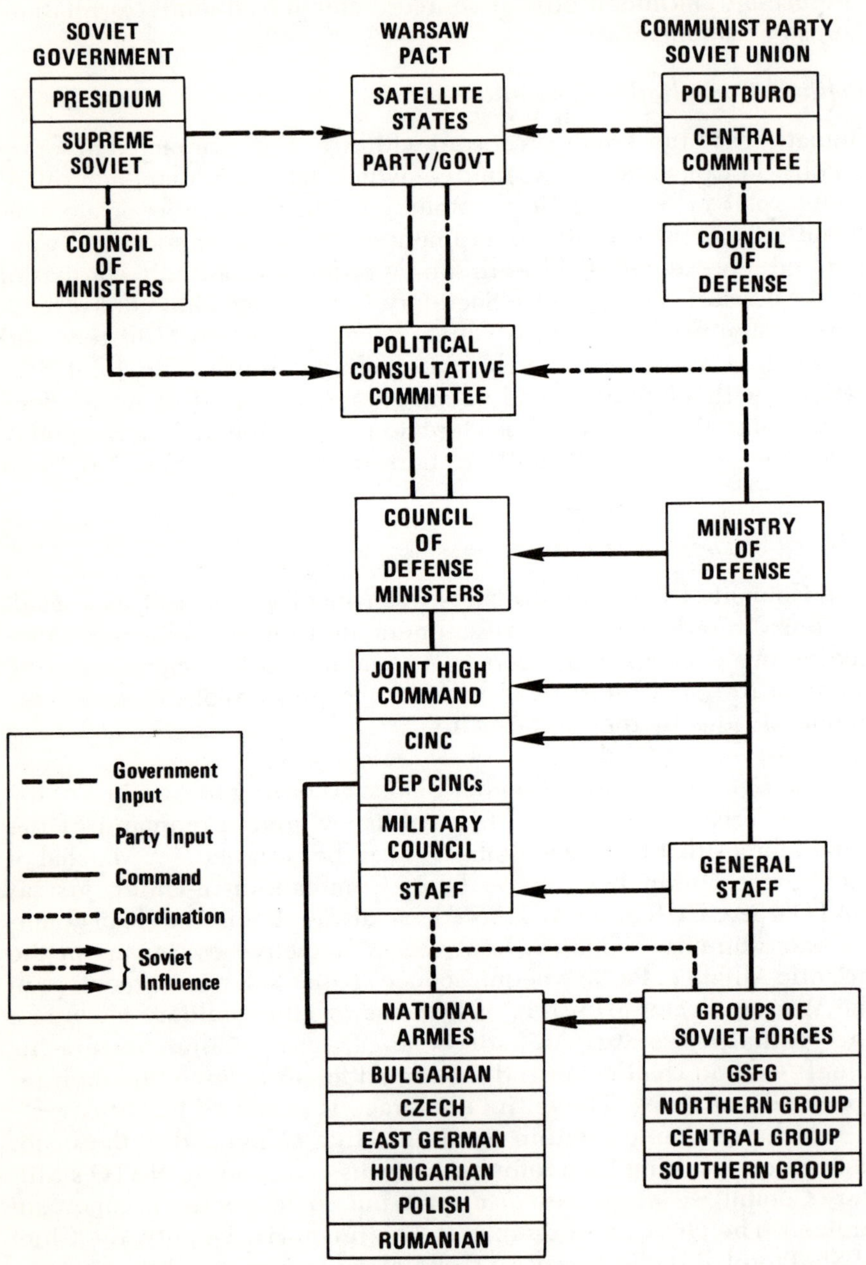

all Soviet, sit at the table. As a sop, the Council also includes a lieutenant general or vice admiral from each satellite state, who collectively participate in discussions, if not the decision process. Access of that sort is a considerable concession.[30]

The Staff of the Joint Armed Forces of the Warsaw Treaty States, as officially titled, operates under the aegis of a Soviet Chief and First Deputy. East European representatives at the two-star level are relegated to less prestigious posts. Little is publicly known about the Joint Staff, but the Deputy CINC, writing in Red Star (May 14, 1972), revealed that important tasks include planning, troop dispositions, training, and large-scale exercises. Standardization of weapons, equipment, and procedures is another central concern. The Joint Staff likely also controls sizable Soviet Military Liaison Missions, which are assigned to each satellite Defense Ministry.[31]

Structural Net Assessment

The two coalitions share some significant structural shortcomings.

Political infidelity, poor motivation, or both are commonly cited as Warsaw Pact weaknesses,[32] but in fact afflict NATO as well. Increasing strength of Eurocommunism, for example, causes insecurity and instability in The North Atlantic Alliance. Britain, which once was a NATO bulwark, is losing abilities. France has not been a full NATO partner militarily for more than a decade, during which time the Alliance has suffered all sorts of ills, many associated with lack of space for dispersion. Relations reportedly are improving, but the two French divisions in Germany still have no operational sectors, and no agreed strategy integrates their efforts in emergency.[33]

Neither side could function effectively in combat without first shifting from peacetime to wartime command footing.

The Warsaw Pact almost certainly would be subordinate to the Soviet General Staff, or some higher agency, since its known command/control capabilities are essentially administrative.[34] Most of NATO's armed forces are normally under national control. Converting to a simple, straightforward structure would be a complex process, especially under pressures caused by fluid conflict. Indeed, associated C^3 problems could impinge on NATO's survival prospects at least as much as the physical balance of forces.[35]

Perhaps most important of all, unity of command coupled with strategic initiative affords strength to the communist side that NATO's coalition of 15 independent nations would find difficult to duplicate under duress.

Soviet forces furnish a far greater share of Warsaw Pact combat power than U.S. counterparts contribute to NATO.[36] Close integration is enhanced, because strategy, tactics, and command decisions derive directly from the Kremlin. Advantages are apparent, compared with the Atlantic Alliance, which relies on committee decisions at top leadership levels (not in combat units) during crises.

Arms and equipment, produced in satellite states as well as the Soviet Union, are sufficiently standard to reduce duplicate R&D programs, which cuts costs. Common items simplify logistic support and foster flexibility. NATO, in contrast, is afflicted with incompatible accoutrements and supplies. Neither ammunition nor repair parts are readily interchangeable between combat forces of different countries that share common causes and boundaries.[37] Conflicting politico-military and economic interests preclude early resolution of resultant problems.[38]

This assessment in no way suggests that the Warsaw Pact is perfect, despite central control. It simply contends that NATO must maintain a strong posture if it plans to compete successfully with power that is mostly Soviet.[39]

Footnotes

1. The only vital national interest, by definition, is survival. States cease to exist if they fail to safeguard that essential. Serious threats to survival therefore compel stringent countermeasures.

2. NATO's center sector is herein construed to include the continental countries of Denmark, the Federal Republic of Germany, France, the Low Countries, and Luxembourg.

3. Belgium, Canada, Denmark, France, Iceland, Italy, Luxembourg, the Netherlands, Norway, Portugal, the United Kingdom, and the United States were charter members who signed the Atlantic Treaty on April 4, 1949. Greece and Turkey acceded concurrently on February 18, 1952. The Federal Republic of Germany was admitted in 1955.

4. The Soviet Union annexed Estonia, Latvia, Lithuania, and a piece of Finland in 1940. Parts of Czechoslovakia, eastern Germany, Poland, and Romania followed in 1945. Albania, Bulgaria, Czechoslovakia, East Germany, Hungary, Poland, and Romania became Soviet satellites between 1946 and 1948.

5. For background summary, see *NATO Facts and Figures*. Brussels: NATO Information Service, January 1976, pp. 11–24, 247–250.

6. The Soviet Union, Albania, Bulgaria, Czechoslovakia, East Germany, Hungary, Poland, and Romania signed the Warsaw Treaty on May 21, 1955. Albania left the alliance in September 1968.

7. For background summary, see Mackintosh, Malcolm, "The Evolution of the Warsaw Pact." Adelphi Papers No. 58. London: Institute for Strategic Studies, June 1969, 25 pp.

8. U.S. Congress. Senate. Subcommittee on United States Security Agreements and

Commitments Abroad of the Committee on Foreign Relations. *United States Security Agreements and Commitments Abroad: Greece and Turkey. Hearings. Part* 7. 91st Congress, 2d Session. Washington: U.S. Govt. Print. Off., 1970, pp. 1772–1773. See also *NATO Facts and Figures,* pp. 22–23.

9. Yakubovsky, Ivan I., "Bastion of Peace and National Security," *Journal of Military History,* No. 3, March 1971, pp. 20–31. Quoted in Clemens, Walter C., Jr., "NATO and the Warsaw Pact: Comparisons and Contrasts," *Parameters,* Fall 1974, p. 16.

10. *Ibid.,* pp. 16–17.

11. Every Soviet satellite except land-locked Hungary and Czechoslovakia has some sort of navy. Some ships occasionally operate in the Mediterranean and Norwegian Seas, but most are confined to the Baltic and Black Seas.

12. *NATO Facts and Figures,* pp. 204, 205, 209.

13. *Ibid.,* pp. 58, 109, 204, 209. The Defense Planning Committee includes representatives from every nation that participates in NATO's integrated military structure. France currently is excluded. The Nuclear Defense Affairs Committee (NDAC) embraces all but France, Iceland, and Luxembourg. Its subsidiary, the Nuclear Planning group, comprises seven or eight member nations from the NDAC.

14. *Ibid.,* p. 207.

15. *Ibid.,* pp. 96, 111.

16. *Ibid.,* pp. 204, 218–219, 221. France has furnished a mission to the Military Committee, instead of its Chief of Staff, since withdrawing from integrated defense arrangements of the Alliance in 1966. Iceland sends a civilian, because it has no armed services.

17. *Ibid.,* pp. 218, 221.

18. U.S. CINCLANT also is SACLANT. His area of responsibility in the former capacity exceeds SACLANT's jurisdiction, as shown on Map 1.

19. *NATO Facts and Figures,* pp. 223–225.

20. *Ibid.,* p. 109.

21. *Ibid.,* pp. 225–227.

22. U.S. CINCEUR also is SACEUR. His area of responsibility in the former capacity exceeds SACEUR's jurisdiction, as shown on Map 1.

23. *NATO Facts and Figures,* pp. 221–222.

24. *Ibid.*

25. *Ibid.,* pp. 50, 108, 109, 222. Supplemented by JCS (J-5) on February 3, 1978.

26. Erickson, John, *Soviet-Warsaw Pact Force Levels,* p. 65; Remington, Robin Alison, *The Warsaw Pact: Case Studies in Communist Conflict Resolution."* Cambridge, Mass.: The MIT Press, 1971, pp. 17–18; Mackintosh, Malcolm, "The Evolution of the Warsaw Pact," p. 2–3.

27. "The meeting of the Political Consultative Committee in Budapest on March 26, 1969, which authorized the reorganization of the Pact's structure, lasted only 2 hours—presumably all the hard preparatory work had already been done in Moscow." Mackintosh, Malcolm, "The Warsaw Pact Today," *Survival,* May/June 1974, p. 123.

28. Marshal of the Soviet Union Viktor G. Kulikov, most recently Chief of the Soviet General Staff, was promoted to that rank on January 8, 1977 and appointed Warsaw Pact CINC. He filled a post vacant since November 1976, when his predecessor Marshal Ivan I. Yakubovsky died.

29. Addendum to the Warsaw Treaty.

30. Mackintosh, Malcolm, "The Warsaw Pact Today," p. 123.

31. *Ibid.,* pp. 123–124.

32. Not all students of the subject agree that satellite states are unreliable Soviet allies. For detailed discussion, which concludes "that the Warsaw Pact would act in concert against NATO, with the possible exception of Hungary and parts of Czechoslovakia," see Papworth, Peter M., "The Integrity of the Warsaw Pact," *Air University Review,* March-April 1977, pp. 16–23; and Part II, May-June 1977, pp. 47–59.

33. *The Military Balance, 1977–1978*. London: International Institute for Strategic Studies, 1977, p. 103; *The Strategic Survey, 1976*. London: International Institute for Strategic Studies, 1977, pp. 61–71.

34. When Soviet troops repulsed the Czech rebellion in 1968 with satellite assistance, Marshal Yakubovsky, then the Pact CINC, passed control to a forward echelon of the Soviet High Command under the Chief of Soviet Ground Forces. Mackintosh, Malcolm, "The Warsaw Pact Today", p. 122. See also Erickson, John, *Soviet-Warsaw Pact Force Levels,* p. 67.

35. The DOD Director of Net Assessment expressed special concern for NATO's command/control and communications problems in comments on an early draft of this study, September 14, 1977. No spectacular change for the better has yet been observed.

36. The United States consistently contributes about 10 percent of NATO's ground forces, 20 percent of its naval forces, and a quarter of its tactical air forces. An additional 50,000 American specialists (such as subordinate elements of Defense Communications Agency), are stationed in Europe, but are not controlled by U.S. European Command (EUCOM).

37. U.S. Congress. Senate. *NATO and the New Soviet Threat*. Report of Senator Sam Nunn and Senator Dewey Bartlett to the Committee on Armed Services. 95th Congress, 1st Session. Washington: U.S. Govt. Print. Off., 1977, p. 10.

38. U.S. Congress. House. *NATO Standardization: Political, Economic, and Military Issues for Congress.* Report to the Committee on International Relations by the Congressional Research Service. Washington, March 29, 1977. 58 pp.; Mayer, Andrew, *NATO Standardization and Defense Procurement Statutes,* Washington, Congressional Research Service, January 26, 1978, 15 pp.

A view which suggests that standardization has several drawbacks is described in Daniels, John K., "NATO Standardization—The Other Side of the Coin," *National Defense,* January-February 1977, pp. 301–304. See also comments by Senator Dewey F. Bartlett and General James H. Polk (USA, Ret.), *NATO Arms Standardization: Two Views*. Washington: American Enterprise Institute for Public Policy Research, 1977, 24 pp. (Polk is opposed.)

39. "Optimistic assessments" tend to view the Warsaw Pact's "hierarchical rigidity . . . . as inhibiting individual and lower-level initiatives, incapable of rectifying errors in data or judgment, and because of internal secrecy and distrust, more cumbersome than NATO." Soviet-Pact relationships are considered insecure. *Assessing the NATO/Warsaw Pact Military Balance*. Washington: Congressional Budget Office, December 1977, pp. 27–28, 29–30.

PART II

NATO's Center Sector

SACEUR's center sector is the most populous and productive part of Europe. It also is the only place where the Warsaw Pact, with collective strength, could bring primary power to bear.

Perceived Threats

Soviet power alone would pose serious potential threats to NATO's center sector, even if most satellite forces were pinned down for local security and air defense purposes, which is no longer a likely case.

All six East German divisions apparently play parts in Soviet plans. Czechoslovakia and Poland also contribute offensive capabilities. The political reliability of non-Soviet forces seems less shaky than popularly presumed, according to on-the-scene authorities, who point out that military elites in Eastern Europe have been pretty well purged of capricious elements.[1]

Warsaw Pact Capabilities

The Soviets, in concert with selected allies, could exercise all or part of the following combat capabilities,[2] if they chose to run serious risks:

—Inflict catastrophic damage on the Continental United States with strategic nuclear weapons as a prelude to war in Europe.

—Invade Western Europe with little warning, using air and ground forces now in East Germany and Czechoslovakia.

—Support conventional operations with tactical nuclear weapons targeted against NATO forces, airfields, ports, command/control centers, and supply installations.

—Challenge NATO for air superiority over Western Europe.
—Reinforce initial efforts rapidly with ready reserves in European Russia and Poland.
—Seriously inhibit reinforcement and resupply from the United States by interdicting trans-Atlantic air and sea lanes.
—Mobilize additional combat power.

Soviet Intentions

Capabilities just enumerated are tempered by Soviet intentions, which separate *possibilities* from *probable courses of action.*[3]

History indicates that the Kremlin's hierarchy is essentially conservative, despite its revolutionary tradition. National character, communist doctrine, and unshakable convictions that time is generally on their side tend to repress impulses and reduce unwarranted risks. Political, economic, social, psychological, and technological competition have superseded naked force as policy tools since the Cuban missile crisis, although military power looms increasingly large as a possible option.

Bearing that backdrop in mind, premeditated Soviet attacks across the Iron Curtain, even for limited objectives, seem likely to occur only if Moscow entertains serious doubts concerning NATO's defense abilities and/or resolve. Even then, issues would have to be immediate and immense, unless Kremlin leaders believed *actual risks* were low in relation to *anticipated gains*.

Whether those conditions will soon be satisfied is subject to conjecture in the U.S. intelligence community and among net assessment specialists. One scholar, whose views are widely shared, suggests that if "Soviet leaders want to assimilate Western Europe's resources and bend its political processes to their will . . . . they might think of better ways than a direct military assault." The preferred alternative could well be "a combination of enticements and pressures" aimed at "a growing sense of [NATO's] impotence in the face of preponderant Soviet military power."[4]

Soviet Strategy

Long-term allegiance of common people in Soviet satellite states is something less than assured. Supply lines through those countries could become insecure. Protracted combat would allow time for Pact forces to defect on the battlefield and civilian rebels to cut routes in the rear.[5]

Three objectives thus seem essential if the Soviets sought to overrun SACEUR's center sector: early destruction of NATO's defense; early occupation of NATO territory; and early isolation of Western Europe from its U.S. ally.[6] Concepts accordingly stress shock, surprise, and exploitation.[7] Conventional and nuclear capabilities would likely be used in combinations best suited to occasions, without strong scruples concerning collateral casualties and damage.[8]

NATO's Counter Strategy

NATO's common sense of purpose and associated policies form the framework within which strategic concepts must be shaped to counter Warsaw Pact threats.[9]

NATO's Common Interests

Most U.S. interests in Europe coincide with those of our NATO allies, but emphases differ. Europe's survival and independence, for example, would be *directly* endangered by Soviet aggression. America's would not. Some choices that are seemingly open to us are not open to the rest of NATO. That condition has complicated the formulation of an agreed NATO strategy since the mid-1960s, when burgeoning Soviet nuclear strike forces caused West Europeans to question whether the United States would risk general nuclear war to satisfy interests that are not immediately vital. If Moscow ever seriously entertained serious doubts concerning U.S. conventional commitments, NATO's credibility could be shattered.

NATO's Deterrent/Defense Objectives

To satisfy its security interests despite potential threats, NATO seeks to deter all forms of Warsaw Pact aggression, from encroachment to general war, and to defend NATO territory without serious loss or damage should dissuasion fail (Figure 41).

Strategists in Western Europe understandably stress deterrence even more than their U.S. counterparts. Extensive hostilities on NATO soil would be "limited" from the U.S. standpoint, but could be lethal to our partners. Should war occur, *our* overriding objective would be to obviate damage to the United States. *Theirs* would be to safeguard Free Europe.

Those schisms in defense priorities shape opposing schools of thought, whose views differ regarding what stance would best ensure deterrence, and where the war should be fought if battle were unavoidable.

NATO's Supporting Policies

Fundamental policies that shape NATO's military planning are summarized in Figure 41.

FIGURE 41 THE FRAMEWORK FOR NATO'S STRATEGY

OBJECTIVES	
Deterrent Objectives	*Defense Objectives*[1]
Prevent General Nuclear War Prevent Local Nuclear War Prevent Conventional War Prevent Encroachment	Stabilize the Situation Expeditiously Repel Invaders Limit Damage to NATO
POLICIES	
Deterrence/Defense	*Burden-Sharing*
Limited War Second Strike Containment (not Rollback) Flexible Response Forward Defense High Nuclear Threshold Minimum Civilian Casualties Minimum Collateral Damage Central Control Non-provocative Posture Comprehensive Capabilities Lowest Credible Force Levels Heavy Reliance on: CONUS Reserves Mobilization	Fundamental Philosophy: An attack against one member is an attack against all, whether it occurs on the flanks or in the center sector. U.S. Provides: Primary Nuclear Capability Most Sea Power Substantial Air Power Substantial Land Power Europe Provides: Most Land Power Limited Nuclear Capability Limited Sea Power Substantial Air Power Installations and Facilities[2]

[1]Each defense objective applies equally to general nuclear war and encroachment.
[2]United States pays construction costs in many cases.

Obvious contradictions between policies and objectives, between various policies, between official policies and member state proclivities, and between NATO policies and Soviet military doctrine all cause compromises and increasing controversy.

NATO's Strategic Concepts

Policies constitute separate guidelines. Strategy is the concept of operations that ties them together.

The Switch to Flexible Response

NATO's deterrent and defense posture originally was predicated on threats of massive retaliation against the U.S.S.R. in the event the

Warsaw Pact provoked a war in Western Europe. That simple, relatively low-cost strategy sufficed as long as U.S. nuclear capabilities were markedly superior to Moscow's. As the Soviets strengthened their position, massive retaliation gradually lost credibility as a deterrent. Worse yet, if deterrence foundered, massive retaliation guaranteed a general nuclear war which NATO could not "win" in any sense of achieving a favorable outcome.

A sweeping strategic reappraisal therefore culminated in the mid-1960s. Predominantly conventional defenses soon were deemed too expensive. Predominantly tactical nuclear defenses were deemed too unpredictable. Neither of those tacks could cope with a wide range of contingencies. After prolonged debate, a consensus eventually prevailed in NATO councils that the low-option, low-credibility, high-risk strategy of Massive Retaliation was imprudent. In December 1967, the Alliance therefore embraced a complex, costly strategy called Flexible Response, which could contribute credibly to deterrence and would afford multiple war-fighting options if a conflict erupted.[10] (See Figure 42 for a comparison of NATO's past and present strategies.)

Current Strategic Summary

America's strategic retaliatory forces, with their Assured Destruction capability, provide the primary deterrent to general nuclear war between NATO and the Soviet Union (but do *not* similarly discourage Soviet use of tactical nuclear weapons, whose utility will shortly be shown).

NATO's strategy for limited war within its center sector contemplates a strong forward defense, to repel invaders immediately or contain them as near the Iron Curtain as possible. That concept demands sufficient versatility to cope with aggression at the most appropriate level on the conflict scale, and to escalate under full control, if necessary. Nuclear weapons are held in reserve, ready for use whenever and wherever decision-makers decree.

In essence, NATO strives to deny the Soviets any hope of success unless they attack with such weight that compelling U.S. interests would be compromised, and the risk of rapid escalation would be excessive.

Comparative Force Posture Trends

NATO needs credible strength to support its deterrent strategy, which forfeits freedom of action to prospective foes whose posture also features tight central control. As it stands, however, the Alliance not only is outclassed quantitatively in almost every conventional category on

FIGURE 42 PAST AND PRESENT NATO STRATEGIES COMPARED

	Massive Retaliation	*Flexible Response*
Type War		
Global; General[1]	X	X
Regional; Limited		X
Main Theater of Operations		
U.S. - U.S.S.R.	X	
Western Europe		X
Main Objectives		
Deterrence	X	X
Defense		X
Options if Deterrence Fails		
Sustained Defense		X
Available Forces Only		X
Reinforcement		X
Conventional Only		X
Tactical Nuclear Assistance		X
"Tripwire" Defense[2]	X	
Strategic Bombardment	X	X
Special Requirements		
U.S. Nuclear Superiority	X	
U.S. Nuclear Sufficiency		X
Local Air Supremacy		X
Sea Control		X
Strategic Mobility		X
Mobilization		X
Force Requirements		
Specialized	X	
Comprehensive		X

[1]General war is the last resort option of flexible response.

[2]"Tripwire" forces are largely symbolic. Defensive *capabilities* may be considerable, but the *intent* is to trigger a massive response if the contingent is attacked.

prospective battlefields and in backup, but its qualitative edge is fast fading. (See Figure 43 at the end of this sub-section.)

Quantitative Comparisons

NATO's conventional complement is smaller today than during the time of Massive Retaliation, when it simply served as a "tripwire". German contingents along the Iron Curtain are the only exception. France remains a member, but its divisions and tactical aircraft, not now under NATO control, would be difficult to reinsert into the current command structure if push came quickly to shove.[11]

Soviet forces alone substantially outnumber NATO in most instances. Twenty-five Category I divisions in East Germany and Czechoslovakia compare favorably with 22 NATO divisions in West Germany. Soviet tanks, aircraft, and artillery in those two countries exceed NATO's total. Assault forces from satellite states almost double our rival's numerical strength.[12]

Soviet reinforcements could reach the current line of contact more rapidly and in much greater quantities than forces from the United States, which contains nearly all of NATO's uncommitted combat strength.[13] Personnel airlifted from European Russia could quickly relieve five Category I divisions deployed in Czechoslovakia since the abortive uprising in 1968, along with two in Poland and four more in Hungary. No equipment, however, is prepositioned for their use. Forward-deployed forces could be further strengthened on short notice from eight armies composed of 29 divisions (three are airborne) and 6,800 main battle tanks that now are maintained in the Baltic, Belorussian, and Carpathian Military Districts.[14]

Friendly forces consequently are poorly prepared to absorb attrition, which could be awesome during early stages of an all-out war.

Qualitative Comparisons

NATO's firepower and mobility have improved immensely since the days of Massive Retaliation. Precision-guided munitions, anti-tank guided missiles, helicopters, and the world's finest fighter aircraft afford advantages not available to conventional forces in the past.

Soviet progress, however, has been more rapid. Ground combat firepower, mobility, and staying power have been beefed up.[15] T-72 tanks are arriving in considerable numbers. BMP armored fighting vehicles, with a 76mm gun and Sagger anti-tank missiles, are superior to NATO's armored personnel carriers, which have no firing port in the troop compartment and are armed with a single machine gun. (German APCs are the sole exception).[16] Mobile AT missiles merge with armored formations. A shift is under way from towed to self-propelled artillery, which eventually will enable many battalions to support fast-moving tanks. Soviet guns in general not only outnumber, but out-range NATO's, and have higher rates of fire.[17] Engineer bridging capabilities, unequalled in the world, suggest that Western Europe's wide streams could be crossed quickly.[18] How well Soviet logistic systems could sustain deep armored thrusts, which consume huge quantities of ammunition and POL, is uncertain.[19]

Mobile air defense systems, being emended and extended in light of Middle East experience, free many fighter-interceptors for other missions. Some Front Aviation regiments have 25 percent more aircraft than they did in 1970. Concrete shelters and increased dispersal assure their security better than in previous years. New types of tactical aircraft afford a four-fold improvement in payload and range that would allow them to strike critical targets deep in NATO territory without first redeploying from peacetime bases well behind present frontiers. Armed helicopters are helping to bolster close air support abilities, which got short shrift in the 1960s.[20]

NATO never has matched Moscow's medium- and intermediate-range ballistic missiles (MRBMs, IRBMs), which are being supplemented or supplanted by a mobile model (SS-20) with MIRVs.[21] Increased stocks of tactical nuclear weapons, such as Scaleboards, Frogs, and Scuds, cover targets as close as 10 and as far as 500 miles from firing points. Chemical warfare capacities of all kinds are considerable. NATO has little defense against such threats.[22]

The Crux

No change by itself is crucial, but emerging Soviet capabilities, with great stress on offensive shock power, create a new strategic environment when considered in combination. NATO obviously has made some significant progress during the period surveyed by this study. However, it failed to keep pace, because members (including the United States) compromised on requirements.[23] Consequently, the overall balance has not been so lopsided since the early 1950s, before NATO's bulwark was complete.

Deterrent/Defense Dynamics

Neither NATO nor the Warsaw Pact can stamp strategies "APPROVED" and stash them on the shelf. Dynamic interactions between capabilities and/or intentions on both sides constantly alter equations. The following survey summarizes special issues. Some are just taking shape. Others are long-standing.

The Issue of Surprise

Soviet armed forces facing NATO are fast adopting a credible offensive posture that was absent a few years ago.[24] Several new options now seem open.[25] Assessing plausible courses of action, then assigning priorities, consequently is an increasingly subjective, scenario-dependent process shot full of assumptions, because U.S and NATO analysts at best must work with a factual fabric full of holes.

Traditional Warning Time

NATO's deterrent and defense plans at the start of this decade were predicated on substantial strategic warning. Most analyses predicted that the Warsaw Pact would need to mobilize before launching a large attack. Any reciprocal buildup by the Atlantic Alliance would lag by several days, due to detection and collective decision difficulties.[26] Pact strength, according to that scenario, would reach a plateau 30 days after mobilization began (M+30), but force ratios in their favor would peak about M+14.[27]

Concern For Sudden Attack

Contingencies of that sort are still important,[28] but the likelihood of attacks with little notice now looms large in the minds of many NATO planners. Soviet and satellite forces, they suspect, could simulate maneuvers, then suddenly scoot for the Channel coast,[29] just as Soviet troops struck the Czechs by surprise in 1968.[30]

One report and contemporary commentary in particular turned a public spotlight on the subject in the recent past. It concluded that the Warsaw Pact could quickly overwhelm NATO with 29 first-class divisions. Lead elements would crack the crust three hours after leaving casernes. "A second wave would cross [the frontier] seven hours later and a third six hours after that . . . . without 'political warning' on which so much NATO planning depends." Within 48 hours, lightly-opposed Pact spearheads would be west of the Rhine, and still rolling.[31]

Restudy

Such contentions, however unconfirmed, served a useful purpose, by stimulating fresh study of surprise attack scenarios. Officials on both sides of the Atlantic, including those in the U.S. intelligence community, took part.[32] Pact readiness and travel times were subject to special scrutiny.

Tightly-controlled Pact forces, they found, are on constant tap. Few enlisted men are accompanied by families, and none have much free time.

Still, readiness among satellite units scores low marks in relation to NATO counterparts. That fact assumes significance if, as EUCOM planners see it, all six East German, several Czech, and perhaps 10 Polish divisions would participate in a full-scale assault by the Warsaw Pact.[33] Category I divisions, their best quality, in no case seem to exceed 75 percent of authorized personnel strength.[34] U.S. divisions manned at that level are rated C-4, or "not ready".[35]

Some Soviet forces too are a long way from being "loaded and locked."[36] "A large number" of tanks in "short-term storage . . . . can be made ready for combat without [much] delay."[37] Trained crews, however, are another matter, considering the high annual turnover of two-year conscripts and the understrength status of some units. Commissioned pilots fly a third fewer hours than those in USAFE (15 hours a month, on the average, versus 20–25).[38]

Current Pact dispositions (Map 15), route capacities, and transport capabilities are fairly well confirmed. Speculation concerning the speed of mobilization most certainly is not. Neither are marshalling times and movement control measures. Skeptics, for example, recall scandalous conduct during the Czech rebellion. "Soviet tanks and armored personnel carriers blithely poured into narrow bottlenecks,

Map 15
SOVIET FORWARD DEPLOYMENTS

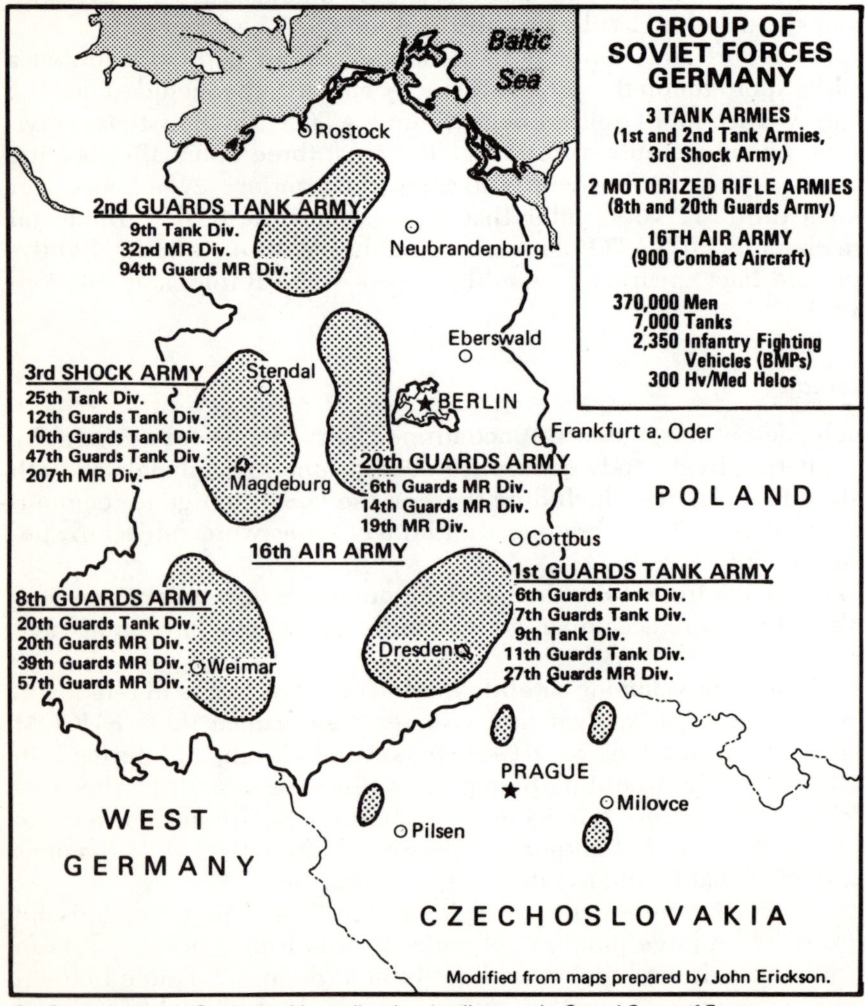

Five Soviet divisions in Czechoslovakia are directly subordinate to the Central Group of Forces. One division, near Zvolen, is off the map in eastern Czechoslovakia

causing rush-hour-style traffic jams that would have provided tempting targets in a real war."[39]

In short, cumulative management difficulties of the kind just discussed cause officials to look askance at radical assumptions. "The scenario in which the balance looks least favorable to the West is," as one authority put it, "a complete surprise attack, with no political warning. But that is probably the least likely scenario, also."[40]

Current SHAPE Assessments

A "bolt from the blue", in which Soviet theater ballistic missiles blast key installations in Western Europe without warning, is possible but not probable, according to SHAPE and EUCOM staffs. SACEUR cites 48 hours as a rock-bottom, high-risk option for the Warsaw Pact. That is the minimum time it would take to convert Category II divisions to Category I. Perhaps 85 percent of all fighter/attack aircraft could support, if they "stood down" for maintenance during that period. Most naval participants, however, would need more notice. A preparatory period of 8–14 days apparently would optimize Pact opportunities for success. Advantages diminish thereafter, because of NATO's counter buildup.[41]

Watching the Warsaw Pact

Since current wisdom indicates that the Soviets likely would not "launch an attack without taking certain fundamental preparatory measures," EUCOM continually monitors a "watch list" that contains 505 discrete indicators (more than 700, counting subsets).[42] Component commands compile reports daily, and submit to the Deputy CINC.[43]

Weights assigned each item vary with courses of action open to the Warsaw Pact. Submarines and surface ships leaving port for security purposes would provide a clear tipoff in some cases, but not occur in others. Several conceivable plans could be executed successfully without evacuating Soviet cities. And so on.[44]

The Irreducible Requirement

"Too simplified a view of surprise dominates most discussion," says DOD's Director of Net Assessment. "The speed of transition from a normal peacetime posture" is important, but deception (which can be self-induced) could sometimes conceal the true purpose of open preparations over extended periods of time.[45]

"It is human nature to seek some unique and unequivocal signal of [impending] attack," but in fact "we have to accept the fate of uncertainty, and learn to live with it." Awareness, if it comes at all, may be so ambiguous that leaders spurn precautions until too late. Fever pitch, induced among defenders during crises, can be cooled by false alarms and endless tension.[46]

NATO consequently can neither count on clear notice nor stay on constant alert. The safest course is to plan on war without strategic warning, and produce the proper support.

Pact Avenues of Approach

Three strategically significant thoroughfares cut across the Iron Curtain from satellite states to SACEUR's center sector (Map 16).

The northernmost avenue, which is tailor-made for tanks, traverses flat to rolling terrain over first-rate roads that reach past the Ruhr and Rhine.[47] A lattice of small streams would only slightly slow the advance of trained troops with engineer bridging equipment.[48] (See section on urban sprawl for constraints.)

Topography is tighter in the center and south, where two less propitious approaches breach a mountain barrier along the Czech and East German borders. The first, called the Fulda Gap, bisects the boundary between U.S. and West German corps, before funneling into Frankfurt (Map 17). The Hof Corridor, a broader belt, heads almost south toward Bavaria. The road net is good, but woods and rough ground restrict rapid cross-country movement.

NATO's Present Dispositions

NATO's much-criticized dispositions athwart those three avenues result from historical accidents rather than strategic design. In large part, they parallel British, French, and American occupation zones at the end of World War II.

Northern Army Group (NORTHAG) contains four corps: Dutch, West German, British, and Belgian, disposed from north to south in that sequence. Together, they include 11 divisions, but none are deployed on line along the front, which measures about 400 km (250 mi) at the East German border.[49]

Central Army Group (CENTAG) is assigned frontage from its common boundary with NORTHAG to the Alps (600 km/375 mi). Two West German corps cover the flanks, with U.S. V and VII Corps in the center. Thirteen and 2/3 divisions include a Canadian brigade group and French forces in CENTAG's southwest corner.[50]

The *Bundeswehr*, being split, shares responsibility for the crucial North German Plain with badly weakened Britain[51] and a mixed bag from the Low Countries. The United States, with its great strength, stands guard over the least dangerous avenues, and the most easily defended terrain. Positioning forces well to the rear protects them from sudden attack, but poorly supports the stated forward strategy. Five out of six Dutch brigades, for example, are stationed in Holland.

Map 16

PRIMARY AVENUES OF APPROACH FOR WARSAW PACT

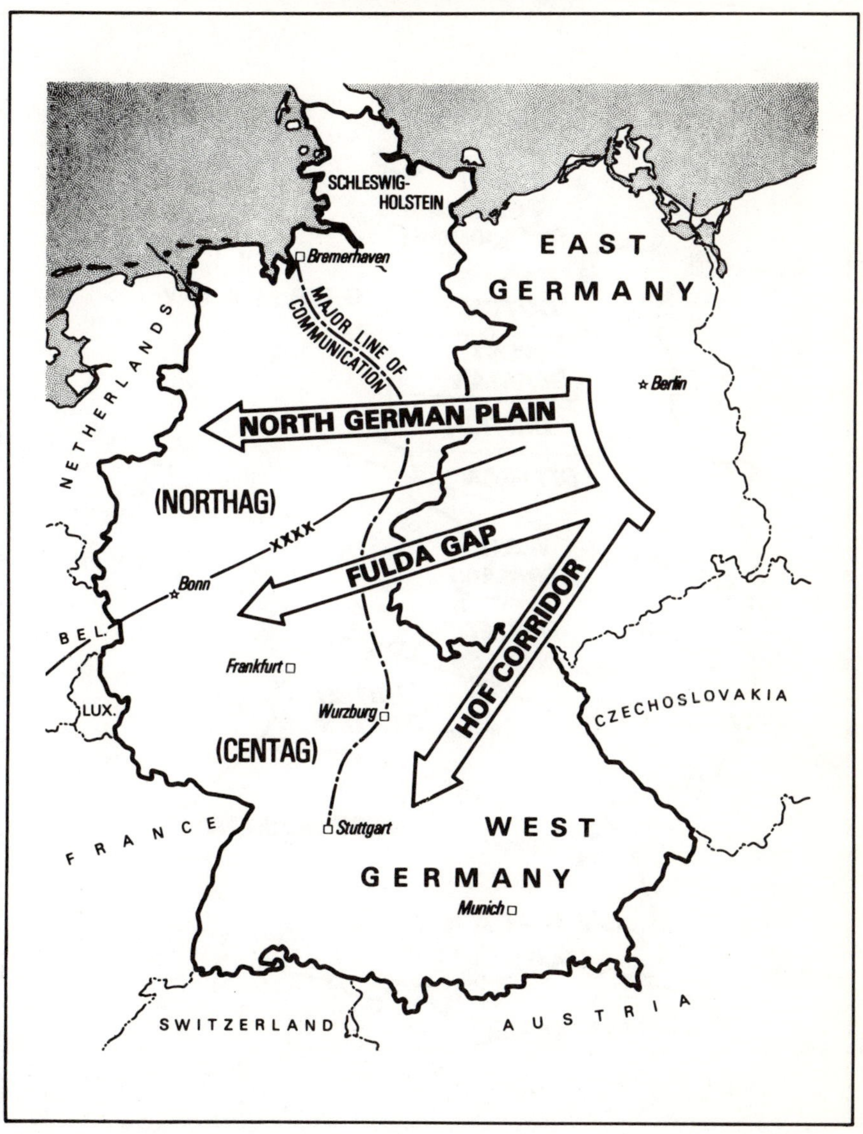

SOURCE: Adapted from Richard Lawrence and Jeffrey Record, *U.S. Force Structure in NATO* (Washington, D.C.: The Brookings Institution, 1974), p. 31.

Map 17

MILITARY SECTORS IN NATO's CENTRAL REGION

SOURCE: Adapted from Richard Lawrence and Jeffrey Record, *U.S. Force Structure in NATO* (Washington, D.C.: The Brookings Institution, 1974),.p. 31 and also from U.S. Army materials.

Both "forward" French divisions, the Canadian brigade, and substantial other forces behind the Rhine would be unable to reinforce quickly if the bridges were blown.[52]

Amending such maldeployments would make military sense, but the cost of moving is immense, and diplomatic difficulties are discouraging. A U.S. brigade will shift from southern Germany to NORTHAG by the end of 1978, but no major American or allied improvements are impending.[53]

Conventional Defense

NATO needs to decide in peacetime the proper deployment for war. Forces concentrated for conventional combat could expect unprecedented casualties if the enemy initiated nuclear conflict. Forces dispersed to escape the effects of nuclear weapons would be poorly prepared for classic defense. Compromise solutions are ill-suited for either environment.[54]

AFCENT now is disposed for conventional combat, presuming the Soviets would withhold nuclear weapons during the opening stage. Any surprise attack would be met, and repulsed if possible, by forces presently in place. If those elements were unable to stem the tide alone, they would strive to buy time for NATO to reinforce, make calculated decisions concerning escalation, or negotiate a solution.

The prescription for forward defense originally was a *political expedient* to ensure wholehearted participation by West Germany, which has persistently rejected any proposition that arbitrarily cedes German ground.[55] The objective, therefore, has always been to block major attacks and restore the status quo quickly.

That task is imposing. The present line of contact would be difficult to defend, particularly along the flat northern plain, but forward defense has been a *military necessity* since 1967, when President de Gaulle evicted NATO from France.[56] The first sharp Soviet surge could sever present supply lines, which radiate from Bremerhaven, Rotterdam, and Antwerp, then run closely behind and parallel to the prospective front. Airfields also could be overrun.

NATO can no longer defend in depth. Its forces formerly could fence with the foe all the way to the Pyrenees if necessary, along established lines of supply and communication. At West Germany's waist, the theater now is barely 130 miles wide, about the same distance that separates Washington from Philadelphia. Maneuver room for armies is at a premium. NATO forces and facilities are fearfully congested (Map 18). Every lucrative military target, including command and control centers, airbases, ports, and supply depots, is within reach of Soviet IRBMs and MRBMs. An enemy breakthrough would compel NATO to retreat across Belgium toward Dunkerque or south

Map 18
MAJOR U.S. MILITARY INSTALLATIONS IN WEST GERMANY

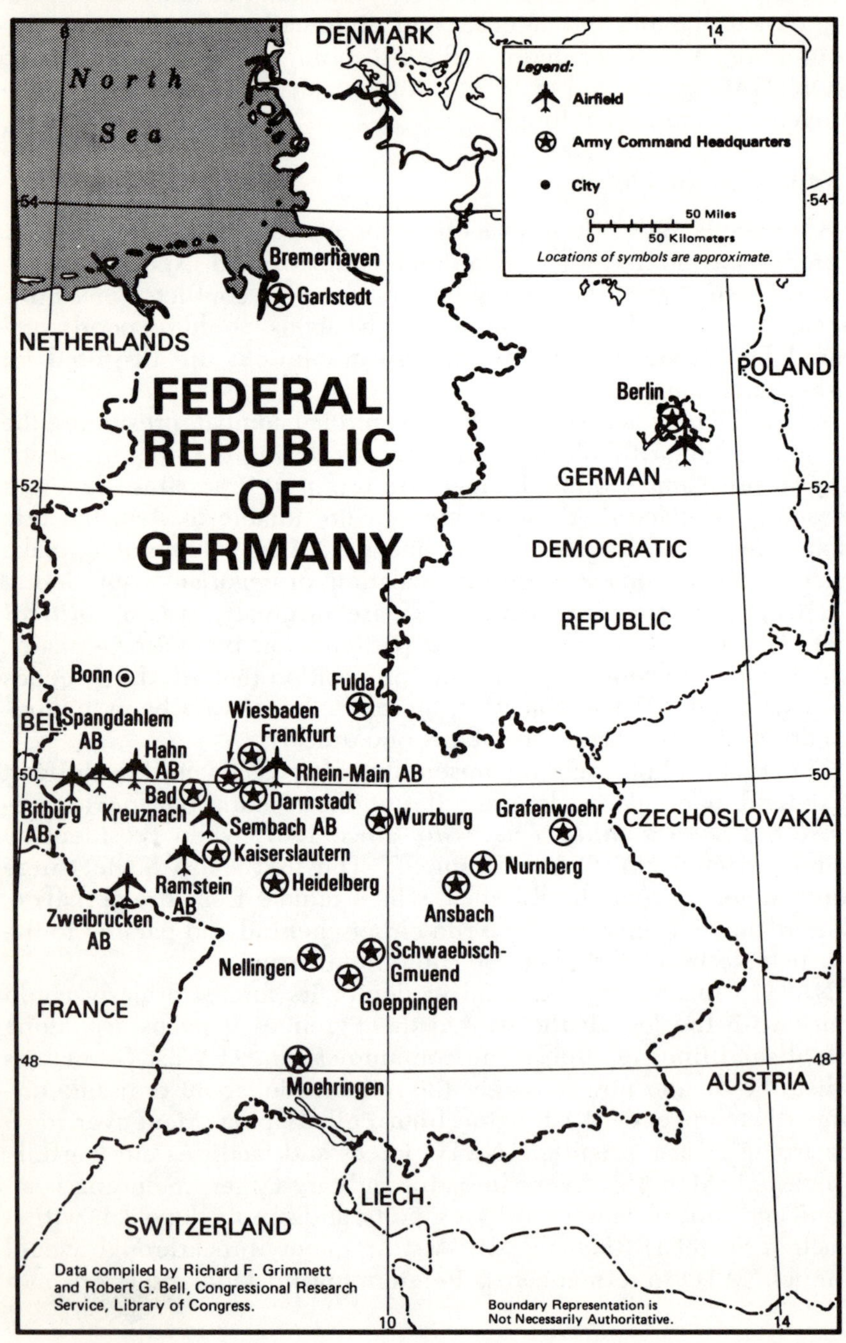

North Sea
DENMARK
Legend:
Airfield
Army Command Headquarters
City
0 50 Miles
0 50 Kilometers
Locations of symbols are approximate.
Bremerhaven
Garlstedt
NETHERLANDS
POLAND
FEDERAL REPUBLIC OF GERMANY
Berlin
GERMAN
DEMOCRATIC
REPUBLIC
Bonn
Fulda
BEL.
Spangdahlem AB
Wiesbaden
Frankfurt
Hahn AB
Rhein-Main AB
Bad Kreuznach
Darmstadt
Bitburg AB
Sembach AB
Wurzburg
Grafenwoehr
CZECHOSLOVAKIA
Kaiserslautern
Nurnberg
Ramstein AB
Heidelberg
Ansbach
Zweibrucken AB
Schwaebisch-Gmuend
Nellingen
Goeppingen
FRANCE
Moehringen
AUSTRIA
LIECH.
SWITZERLAND
Data compiled by Richard F. Grimmett and Robert G. Bell, Congressional Research Service, Library of Congress.
Boundary Representation is Not Necessarily Authoritative.

toward the Alpine wall. Even if France invited NATO back in emergency, many handicaps would remain, since facilities there have deteriorated or been dismantled.[57]

NATO's freedom of choice obviously would be constricted under present circumstances, and decision times compressed. How long the Atlantic Alliance could hold along the Iron Curtain would depend on a host of variables, including—but not restricted to—the nature of the conflict (nuclear or non-nuclear); the scale of Soviet attack (comprehensive or limited objectives); the amount of warning (hours, days, or weeks); the capabilities of opposing forces; NATO's will; and the weather. If strong enemy elements cracked through the crust, our main line of resistance could be enveloped, unless friendly forces quickly regrouped behind the unfordable Rhine, the first major defensible terrain feature to the rear.

Tactical Nuclear Defense

If conventional defenses prove unsatisfactory, NATO plans to use tactical nuclear weapons, after consultation among its members.[58] The time, place, and circumstances under which the Alliance would "go nuclear" have deliberately been left vague to complicate Warsaw Pact planning.

Rationale For a High Nuclear Threshold

Early resort to nuclear weapons theoretically could improve NATO's ability to sustain a strong forward defense, but a high threshold (crossed only after pressures became unbearable) would be salutary for several reasons.

Severe civilian casualties and collateral damage appear unavoidable if tactical nuclear weapons were exploded in large numbers.[59] Limited target acquisition capabilities make it technically impossible to deliver ordnance infallibly onto military forces on the move. Moreover, in a war for survival, the temptation to engage "suspected" targets would be high. Numerous deaths from accidental fallout probably would follow, even if both sides agreed to abstain from surface and subsurface detonations. Neutron weapons available to NATO, but not the Warsaw Pact, would alleviate such problems very little.[60]

Controls would be tenuous. Nuclear weapons could be administered very selectively—for defensive purposes only; on NATO territory only; against military targets only; using air bursts only or atomic land mines only; and low yields only—but none of those restrictions would be as readily distinguishable by the enemy as the "firebreak" between nuclear and conventional combat.

Since the first side to disregard restraints might accrue a decisive advantage, the pressures to escalate would be enormous. Surprise Soviet missile strikes on key installations at the onset of a war could cripple NATO. The absence of an ABM shield therefore constitutes a potentially fatal flaw for our side, but not for the Soviet Union.[61]

Theater Nuclear Force Requirements

Force requirements for tactical nuclear warfare might *exceed* those for conventional combat. NATO's forward defense forces have to be strong enough to make the enemy mass. Otherwise, Soviet assault troops would present few profitable targets. However, friendly formations would also suffer from nuclear attack. Eventual ascendance thus might be attained by the side with the greatest reserves of materiel and trained manpower.[62]

NATO unfortunately has few readily accessible reserves. All major ground combat forces are committed. On-the-spot fighter squadrons are insufficient to perform assigned tasks. If conflict occurred, early augmentation of elements now in place would be imperative.

Special Problems

Several special problems condition deterrent and defense demands in SACEUR's center sector. This section silhouettes four.

Reinforcements and Resupply

To function effectively, NATO must be able to move immense amounts of men and materiel from the United States to Europe on a continuing basis.

The throughput capacity of ports and airfields at both ends is adequate, *provided most installations in Western Europe escape early destruction.* Peacetime aerial ports would be supplemented in emergency by other military airfields suitable for transport aircraft and, if necessary, by civilian facilities (subject to political approval and the tactical situation). Benelux seaports that presently serve NATO would continue to do so in war. Either Rotterdam or Antwerp alone has sufficient capability to handle U.S. needs,[63] but the threat of ballistic missile attacks and naval mine blockades casts a cloud over every base.

SACLANT must be able to contain Soviet attacks on SLOCs to the Middle East and across the Atlantic if the Alliance is to survive. Failure to keep essential avenues open indefinitely in the face of concerted campaigns could cause NATO's defense to collapse from logistic starvation, even if the land war went favorably.

Arms Control

American efforts since 1965 to improve stability in NATO's center sector by Mutual and Balanced Force Reductions (MBFR) have been frustrated by politico-military and geographic circumstances.[64] The fifth year of fruitless talks ended on December 15, 1977, then reconvened the following month.[65]

One proposal would delete identical percentages on each side, but that apparently fair approach would favor the Warsaw Pact, which has many more tanks, troops, and tactical aircraft than NATO. The larger the reduction, the greater the risk. Soviet columns could concentrate to attack at any desired point, while fewer forward defenders would be deployed along a linear front whose great length remained unchanged.[66] Defensive posture would be improved if reductions produced numerical parity, but the Soviets so far spurn any such relationship.

Beyond that, American armed services would have to withdraw 6,000 km (3,200 nm) across the Atlantic, while Soviet counterparts could be repositioned in Western Russia, one-tenth as far away.[67] They could return to attack positions over land routes more readily than air and water transport could move U.S. reinforcements, even if our heavy equipment, such as tanks, stayed in place.[68]

More than 100,000 Russian troops in East Germany, for example, have rotated rapidly with Aeroflot support. Soviet road and rail routes would be subject to interdiction in wartime, but reinforcements could shuttle across satellite states with impunity before any conflict erupted, probably (but not necessarily) forfeiting surprise.[69]

Should NATO receive a nuclear attack by ballistic missiles (or aircraft) at an early stage, chances are slight that essential port and airfield facilities would remain in condition to receive U.S. units from CONUS.

Urban Sprawl

"The whole subject of combat in built-up areas is one in which the U.S. Army is not well versed."[70] Neither are NATO's other armies, nor presumably the Warsaw Pact. Doctrine centers on tactical techniques, such as house-to-house fighting,[71] but "the larger problem of conducting operations in continuous and contiguous built-up areas" involves untested principles.[72]

That circumstance assumes immense significance, since urban fighting would surely ensue if NATO's forward defense failed or allied forces fell back deliberately for any reason.

Environmental Developments Typical villages in Central Europe (population 1,000 or less) comprise stone, brick, or concrete buildings in a cluster, with lightly-constructed structures on the outskirts. Each is a potential strongpoint. The trend is toward continuous strips between villages, towns, and small cities (population up to 100,000) that facilitate linear fortification.[73]

Conterminous cities, such as Frankfurt, Mainz, and Hanau, are melding into megalopoli. Ruhr and Rhine-Main River complexes "will form a single gigantic urban barrier 300 kilometers [190 miles] long, stretching down the Rhine from Bonn to the Hook of Holland" in the 1980s. Modern versions of von Schlieffen's grand envelopment plan would be close to worthless, without a gap in that solid wall.[74]

Concentric rings commonly circumscribe picturesque cores, where medieval architects combined stout construction with crooked streets to form "canyons". Residential and commercial areas, with rectangular traffic patterns, typically surround inner cities. Buildings, set close to curbs, sometimes encircle courtyards. Low-density suburbs spread irregular shapes in diverse directions. Boulevards and parks abound.[75]

Cumulative effects, already considerable, will increasingly constrain large-scale military operations, even in ostensibly open areas, such as the North German Plain.

U.S. Defensive Doctrine Villages in close proximity, perhaps a mile or two apart, can be converted quickly into mutually-supporting defensive positions by well-trained troops. Thick walls provide protection. The same is true of towns and cities. Enemy armor may occasionally bypass, but must reduce resistance that blocks supply lines or otherwise upsets plans. Consequent sideshows, which are costly in terms of time and casualties, slow the foe's forward momentum and blunt his basic attack.[76]

Defending any city, even a small one, *"may be tantamount to a decision to destroy it."* Political considerations weigh heavily, "particularly if the city has a cultural or historical significance," since even successful operations may leave little more than rubble.[77]

Strategic Dilemmas Defensive advantages could be decisively diluted if the Soviets deliberately adopted "city hugging" tactics to reduce the danger of counter strikes. So doing would retard their rate of advance, but armor and mobile infantry might still move rapidly through suburbs, secured physically and psychologically by NATO's likely reluctance to raze its own cities in response.[78]

Deterrent and defense concepts for SACEUR's crucial center sector consequently require serious reconsideration.[79]

Beleaguered Berlin

Berlin, a potential powder keg 100 miles behind enemy lines, is strategically significant to both sides. As a transportation and communications center, it controls nearly every high-speed east-west avenue that leads from Warsaw Pact states into NATO's positions. It is the unofficial capital of both Germanies, with political, economic, and cultural connotations. Most of all, Berlin has been a psychological symbol since the late 1940s. The last serious confrontation over that city took place in 1961, before President Kennedy's "Ich bin ein Berliner!" speech and Soviet comeuppance in Cuba the following year, but similar crises could still occur.[80]

It once was popular in U.S. circles to call Berlin a "testing place of Western courage and will," but that beleaguered city is almost completely cut off from conventional support.

Four roads, four rail lines, and one barge canal technically tie Berlin to West Germany (Map 19). Only two, however, the railway and Autobahn to Helmstedt, have ever been open to NATO's military traffic. All can be sealed at Soviet pleasure. So can three supplemental air corridors, each about 20 miles wide, which are subject to interdiction by Warsaw Pact interceptors and surface-to-air missiles (SAMs).[81]

Berlin would be tactically indefensible if communist troops chose to swallow the resident garrison.[82] Fast relief would be beneficial, but NATO is poorly prepared for rescue operations. Its strategy is essentially defensive, and its forces are not structured for deep penetration purposes.[83]

NATO's Newest Initiatives

NATO's newest initiatives, designed essentially to strengthen deterrent and defense capabilities in the center sector,[84] concentrate on a packet prepared by our Secretary of Defense and presented to the Atlantic Council by President Carter in May 1977.[85] Three key tasks take priority: readiness; rapid reinforcement; and rapport.[86]

Short-Term Initiatives

Defense ministers, following guidelines laid down by respective Governments, soon directed NATO's military authorities to develop "early alliance improvements." Allied capitals reportedly received proposals "with spirit and enthusiasm." Results are anticipated "in these high priority areas by the end of 1978."[87]

Readiness and Reinforcement

Short-term steps to cultivate readiness and rapid reinforcement accentuate accelerated reaction in emergency by the United States, Canada, and the United Kingdom, together with improved procedures for receiving and transshipping those forces once they reach the continent. Expanded exercises that simulate combat conditions will test results. Most nations also have been asked to increase active duty military manning levels, promote reserve component training, and modernize their mobilization machinery.[88] NATO's tactical air power is also receiving strong stress.[89]

Map 19
BERLIN AND VICINITY

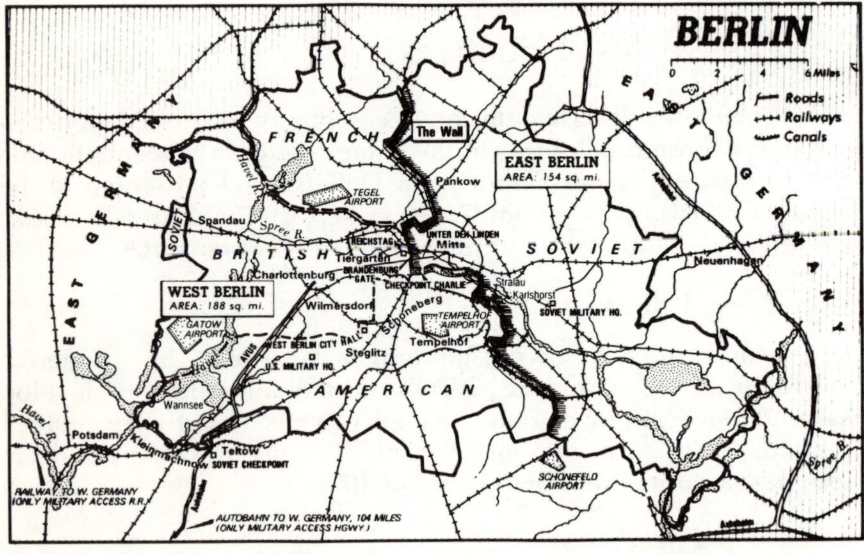

Antitank Guided Missiles

Soviet superiority in tanks causes serious concern in SHAPE. Soviet mobile air defense missiles substantially offset counter capabilities supplied by allied tactical aircraft. NATO's "thin-skinned" AT systems on the ground could suffer severe attrition from Soviet artillery.[90]

Anti-armor initiatives therefore stress additional ATGM deployments, especially of TOWs, many mounted on helicopters.[91] Modern range-finders with infrared and laser components are part of the package. Since some NATO countries now are "haves" in this category, while others are nearly "have nots", decision-makers hope to reduce disparities during the dispensement process. EUCOM staff officers, however, sadly note no plans to furnish antitank guns, which can function effectively (say, in cities) where most missiles cannot.[92]

War Reserve Ammunition

NATO defense chiefs on December 6, 1977, approved proposals to increase stocks of air-to-air, air-to-ground, and assorted antitank missiles, along with artillery and mortar ammunition, after specialists from 14 countries hammered out "enhanced consumption rates" at SHAPE's Technical Center.[93]

Plans, however, take time to implement. Added allowances, for example, recently were authorized U.S. Army Europe (USAREUR), but acquisition is contingent on funds, storage capacity, and suitable covered construction, all of which are currently insufficient.[94] Meanwhile, "the separation of many USAREUR combat formations from immediate access to their ammunition; the concentration of ammunition storage sites in a manner .... [that tempts] a preemptive Soviet air attack; and the disposition of much of USAREUR's ammunition west of the Rhine (including England) all combine to raise serious questions about USAREUR's true readiness for combat."[95]

Long-Term Initiatives

NATO's Defense Planning Committee has identified "10 long-term priority program areas." Instructions to each affiliated task force "stress the need to project at least 10 years in the future."[96]

Readiness Task Force

Long-range readiness amplifies short-term steps just discussed. The aim is to improve "responsiveness of standing forces, selected reserve units and civil support in crisis, time of tension or during hostilities." NATO's alert apparatus, armor/AT capabilities, competence in coping with Soviet CBR attacks, and creative combinations of new weapons systems are singled out for special attention.[97]

Reinforcement Task Force

Strategic army reserves in CONUS depend on quick reaction airlift coupled with prepositioned stocks, which were in sad shape at the end of 1976. Shortfalls were pronounced and maintenance poor.[98] Recovery, according to EUCOM, is now close to complete but DOD, after a recent review of the U.S. Five Year Defense Program (FYDP), recommends "adding several sets of [division] equipment to the present two and one-third." Authorities "will also seek further enhancement of badly needed strategic airlift."[99]

Reserve Mobilization Task Force

Reserve mobilization is a "companion piece" to reinforcement. Since NATO's European reserves currently are restricted to fillers for regular forces, some of our allies might "contribute greatly to improvements in the military balance", if they organized, trained, and equipped sizable backup structures (other than paramilitary and territorial forces) to support standing establishments.[100]

Naval Task Force

The task force to strengthen NATO's naval posture will strive to correct "serious deficiencies in combat capabilities" by fostering "a joint, collective fighting force," which presently exists in principle, but not entirely in practice.

The potential is promising. NATO's non-U.S. navies not only are considerable, but complement our fleets very nicely (Figure 44). Their aircraft carriers and most shore-based air power are well suited for ASW. Other surface ships, coastal combatants, and submarines, conducting coordinated, close-in defensive operations, could constrain or close Soviet naval options in waters their skippers know well.[101]

Air Defense Task Force

NATO's Improved Hawk belt, combined with Nike Hercules and NADGE (NATO's Air Defense Ground Environment),[102] is perhaps the most closely knit component in SACEUR's center sector. Scandalous shortages in 1976[103] are being corrected, although funding deficiencies are causing schedules to slip. All Hawk batteries now have their basic load. Standby stocks will be boosted. Each battalion has 1,160 extra men to help with maintenance.[104]

Soviet Front Aviation, however, is fast undercutting confidence in NATO's current setup. The air defense task force, in close collaboration with its naval counterpart, consequently "will cover all aspects .... Its goal is to achieve the kind of integrated complex of weapons, organization and air command and control systems that is needed to deal effectively with the increasing Warsaw Pact threat.[105] Air base dispersion to reduce vulnerability plays an important part.[106] So do F-15 squadrons, which far outstrip AAFCE's other interceptors.

C³ Task Force

The command/control and communications task force seeks greater commonality in doctrine, procedures, organizational structure, per-

FIGURE 44 NATO NAVIES
(Excluding United States)

	Aircraft Carriers	Attack Sub-marines	Cruisers and Destroyers	Frigates and Corvettes	Patrol Ships	Mine Warfare Ships
Belgium	0	0	0	2	0	29
Britain	3	27	13	57	11	38
Canada	0	3	4	19	6	0
Denmark	0	6	0	10	37	14
France	2	21	22	22	32	38
W. Germany	0	24	17	5	40	57
Greece	0	6	15	0	24	16
Italy	0	8	7	20	6	44
Netherlands	0	6	11	12	5	37
Norway	0	15	0	7	52	15
Portugal	0	3	0	17	17	18
Turkey	0	14	12	2	65	34
Total	5	133	101	173	295	340

Source: Modified from *Arms, Men, and Military Budgets: Issues for Fiscal Year 1979*, p. 69.

sonnel, equipment, and facilities. "This is a difficult goal in a complex field, to which a great deal of effort must be devoted if the Allies are to be able to fight optimally together as a coalition."[107]

Visible signs include the physical affiliation of national headquarters with NATO wartime functions and collocation to simplify contact between air/ground commanders and staffs. DOD consequently supports plans to put CENTAG, 4th ATAF, the ACE Mobile Force, and USAREUR at least figuratively under the same roof. Such concentration, of course, also creates compact targets. Extensive efforts are thus underway to "harden" headquarters and interconnecting communications. Each complex, when complete, could take conventional hits, but none could withstand nuclear shocks, and CBR contamination could cause trouble. Redundant relay centers, switches, and routes should strengthen survival prospects.[108]

Electronic Warfare Task Force

Fast-growing Soviet EW capabilities and countermeasures span the full active and passive spectrum.[109] NATO, in comparison, so far has scarcely scratched. That asymmetry, if uncorrected, could critically curtail allied concepts of deterrence and defense.[110]

Electronic warfare consequently is one of NATO's two top-priority projects (C^3 is the other). An expansive scope includes intelligence, equipment components and systems, manpower, management, and money.[111]

Rationalization Task Force

Parties responsible for each long-term research, development, and arms production program "will work on specific standardization and interoperability measures in their respective areas." A special "rationalization" task force[112] will try to tie those segments together into a "harmonious" whole.[113] Standardization, interoperability, interchangeability, and compatibility of systems and supplies are special parts of the package.[114]

Consumer Logistics Task Force

NATO's logistic apparatus, predicated on separate supply and maintenance arrangements for each member state, leaves a lot to be desired. Stock levels for selected items vary from 90 days or more in some countries to a week or less in others. Cross-servicing capacities for a hodge-podge of arms and equipment are quite limited. Shortages between authorized and actual inventories are common.[115] The north-south line of communication, which is perpendicular to east-west Pact invasion routes instead of parallel, may pose the most pressing problem of all: "defense of [that] LOC is in essence the defense of Central Europe and involves [NATO's] entire defense strategy."[116] (See Maps 16–17.)

A consumer logistics task force is therefore commissioned to "prepare an improved NATO logistics structure, steps for better common logistics support," and improved civil participation in military plans and operations.[117]

NATO's Nuclear Planning Group

Last, but not least, NATO's Nuclear Planning Group "will develop a draft long-term program to insure that [Allied] theater nuclear forces continue to perform their key role in deterrence." Strategy, tactics, doctrine, and new systems, such as ground-launched cruise missiles (GLCMs), are presently under study.[118]

The Bottom Line

NATO's newest initiatives could turn present trends around, if pursued to successful conclusions. At this stage, however, most are more shadow than substance. Predictions concerning their contributions to the NATO/Warsaw Pact military balance may thus be a bit premature.

FIGURE 43 NATO's CENTER SECTOR:
Statistical Summary

	1970			1977		
	United States	*Soviet Union*	*U.S. Standing*	*United States*	*Soviet Union*	*U.S. Standing*
Personnel[1]	240,000	680,000	−440,000	275,000	730,000	−455,000
Divisions[2]						
Committed[3]						
Armor	2	14	− 12	2	14	− 12
Other	3	13	− 10	3	13	− 10
Total	5	27	− 22	5	27	− 22
Ready Reinforcements[4]						
Armor	2	10	− 8	2	10	− 8
Other	9	6	+ 3	9	6	+ 3
Total	11	16	− 5	11	16	− 5
Sub-total	16	43	− 27	16	43	− 27
First-Line Reserves[5]						
Armor	2	4	− 2	2	4	− 2
Other	10	11	− 1	10	12	− 2
Total	12	15	− 3	12	16	− 4
Total Divisions	28	58	− 30	28	59	− 31

FIGURE 43 (cont'd)

	1970			1977		
	United States	*Soviet Union*	*U.S. Standing*	*United States*	*Soviet Union*	*U.S. Standing*
Medium Tanks[6]	2065	16,000	−13,035	4300	18,000	−13,700
Tactical Aircraft[7]						
Bombers	0	50	− 50	0	0	—
Ground Attack	180	500	− 320	300	400	− 100
Interceptors	0	350	− 350	0	650	− 650
Total	180	900	− 720	300	1050	− 750
MRBM/IRBM	0	650	− 650	0	550	− 550
	1970[8]			*1977*[8]		
	NATO	*Warsaw Pact*	*NATO Standing*	*NATO*	*Warsaw Pact*	*NATO Standing*
Personnel[1]	1,523,300	1,190,000	+333,300	1,409,000	1,600,000	−191,000
Divisions[2]						
Committed[3]						
Armor	8	24	− 16	8	24	− 16
Other	22	28	− 6	28	26	+ 2
Total	30	52	− 22	36	50	− 14
Ready Reinforcements[4]						
Armor	2	14	− 12	2	10	− 8
Other	10	7	+ 3	10	6	+ 4
Total	12	21	− 9	12	16	− 4
Sub-total	42	73	− 31	48	66	− 18

First-line Reserves[5]						
Armor	2	2	par	2	6	– 4
Other	11	13	– 2	11	18	– 7
Total	13	15	– 2	13	24	– 11
Total Divisions	55	88	– 33	61	90	– 29
Medium Tanks[6]	6535	14,500	–7965	7400	22,000	–14,600
Tactical Aircraft[7]						
Bombers	15	100	– 85	185	100	+ 85
Ground Attack	1640	800	+ 840	1500	800	+ 700
Interceptors	470	1600	–1130	400	1700	– 1300
Total	2125	2500	– 375	2085	2600	– 515
MRBM/IRBM	0	650	– 650	0	550	– 550

[1]Personnel strengths are active forces only for U.S./NATO, but include Soviet Category III divisions.

[2]U.S., West German, and Soviet divisions have increased in size since 1970. Three German divisions, for example, had only two brigades each at that time. All 12 now have three brigades. The British Army has the same total number of brigades as in 1970, but has added a division headquarters.

These charts do not reflect NATO's increased strength in separate brigades and regiments, which are included in some computations as "division equivalents." The IISS *Military Balance, 1977–1978*, for example, shows 27 NATO divisions (excluding France), including 10 armored divisions, by counting division equivalents (3 brigades = 1 division).

[3]U.S./NATO committed divisions include all active divisions in NATO's center sector. SOVIET/Warsaw Pact counterparts are limited to divisions in East Germany, Czechoslovakia, and Poland. All are Category I.

[4]U.S./NATO ready reinforcements include all other active U.S. Army divisions, less one in Korea; two U.S. Marine Corps Amphibious Force (MAF) division/wing teams; six French divisions; and one British division in the U.K. Soviet lists are restricted to Category I and II divisions in the Baltic, Belorussian, and Carpathian Military Districts. There are no satellite state divisions in this class.

[5]U.S./NATO first-line reserves include one active U.S. Army division; two U.S. Marine MAFs; all eight U.S. National Guard divisions; and one Dutch reserve division. Warsaw Pact forces are Category III divisions, including those in the Baltic, Belorussian, and Carpathian Military Districts of European Russia. Every U.S. division, active and reserve component, is shown. The Soviet Union has 112 others, some Categories I and II. Many of those would be available for service in Central Europe if a crisis arose.

[6]U.S./NATO medium tank statistics include U.S. prepositioned stocks in unit sets (POMCUS), war reserve stocks (PWRMS), plus 130 in divisions that serve as maintenance float. The number of Warsaw Pact reserve stock tanks is not ascertainable.

[7]Aircraft statistics exclude U.S. dual-based forces in CONUS.

[8]NATO and Warsaw Pact comparisons include the United States and Soviet Union. French Army and Air Force totals are included in all categories, even though those forces are not under NATO control and only two divisions are deployed in Germany.

FIGURE 43 (Con't) NATO'S CENTER SECTOR

	1970	1977
NATO DIVISIONS		
Committed Divisions		
In West Germany		
Belgium	2	2
Britain	2	3
France	2	2
U.S.	4	5
West Germany	12	12
Total	22	24
Elsewhere		
Belgium	0	1
Denmark	1	1
France[1]	5	8
Netherlands	2	2
Total	8	12
Grand Total	30	36
Ready Reinforcements		
Britain	1	1
U.S.	11	11
Total	12	12
First-Line Reserves		
Netherlands	1	1
U.S.	12	12
Total	13	13
Grand Total	55	61

[1]French forces, not under NATO control, include three divisions from Territorial Defense Forces and two from Strategic Reserve.

FIGURE 43 (Con't) NATO'S CENTER SECTOR

	1970	1977			
WARSAW PACT DIVISIONS	*Total*	*Total*	*Category* I	II	III
In Czechoslovakia					
Czech[1]					
Tank	5	5	3	0	2
Motor Rifle	5	5	4	0	1
Total	10	10	7	0	3
Soviet					
Tank	3	3	3	0	0
Motor Rifle	2	2	2	0	0
Total	5	5	5	0	0
Grand Total	15	15	12	0	3
In East Germany					
East German					
Tank	2	2	2	0	0
Motor Rifle	4	4	4	0	0
Total	6	6	6	0	0
Soviet					
Tank	10	10	10	0	0
Motor Rifle	10	10	10	0	0
Total	20	20	20	0	0
Grand Total	26	26	26	0	0
In Poland					
Polish[2]					
Tank	5	5	5	0	0
Motor Rifle	8	8	3	1	4
Other	2	2	2	0	0
Total	15	15	10	1	4
Soviet					
Tank	2	2	2	0	0
Motor Rifle	0	0	0	0	0
Total	2	2	2	0	0
Grand Total	17	17	12	1	4

[1]Czech divisions shown as Cat III were considered Cat II in 1970.

[2]Five Polish motor rifle divisions were considered Cat I in 1970. The other three were considered Cat II.

FIGURE 43 (Con't) NATO'S CENTER SECTOR

WARSAW PACT DIVISIONS	1970 Total	1977 Total	Category I	Category II	Category III
Total Committed					
Non-Soviet					
Tank	12	12	10	0	2
Motor Rifle	17	17	11	1	5
Other	2	2	2	0	0
Total	31	31	23	1	7
Soviet					
Tank	15	15	15	0	0
Motor Rifle	12	12	12	0	0
Total	27	27	27	0	0
Grand Total	58	58	50	1	7

Footnotes

1. Roundtable discussion with staff officers at Supreme Headquarters Allied Powers Europe (SHAPE), November 17, 1977. See also Erickson, John, *Soviet-Warsaw Pact Force Levels*, pp. 67, 79. Reinforced by DIA comments on this study in February 1978.

2. Capabilities constitute the ability of countries or coalitions to execute specific courses of action at specific times and places. Fundamental components can be quantified and compared—so many tanks, ships, and planes with particular characteristics. Time, space, climate, terrain, organizational structures, and so on can also be calculated with reasonable reliability. Capabilities rarely are subject to rapid change. Technological breakthroughs, typified by the advent of atomic weapons, sometimes cause exceptions.

3. Intentions deal with the determination of countries or coalitions to use their capabilities in specific ways at specific times and places. Interests, objectives, policies, principles, and commitments all play important parts. National will is the integrating factor. Intentions are tricky to deal with, since they are subjective and changeable states of mind, but estimates of capabilities and intentions in combination are essential for decision-makers who hope to design sound strategies.

4. Wolfe, Thomas W., "Soviet Military Capabilities and Intentions in Europe." A chapter in *Soviet Strategy in Europe.* Ed. by Richard Pipes. Menlo Park, Calif.: Stanford Research Institute, 1977, pp. 160–161.

5. The Soviet Union fought a protracted war in 1941–1945. Internal security was never a serious problem, even in the Ukraine, after that defensive contest turned into a

struggle for survival by *all* factions in the face of Nazi Germany. Circumstances thus were quite different than might pertain in subjugated states today if the Warsaw Pact waged an offensive war against NATO.

6. Soviet theater doctrine is discussed in Book II under ground forces, tactical air combat forces, and general purpose navies.

7. Rumsfeld, Donald H., *Annual Defense Department Report for FY 1977*, pp. 101–102; Betit, Eugene D., "Soviet Tactical Doctrine and Capabilities and NATO's Strategic Defense," *Strategic Review*, Fall 1976, pp. 95–107; Erickson, John, "Trends in the Soviet Combined Arms Concept," *Strategic Review*, Winter 1977, pp. 38–53.

8. "We believe that in a conflict with NATO the Soviets foresee three general levels of conflict: a war conducted with nonnuclear weapons only, war in which the use of nuclear weapons is confined to the theater of operations, and strategic nuclear warfare. Doubtless any decision to initiate strategic nuclear warfare would be made only by the top political leadership; however, escalation from the nonnuclear to the theater nuclear level probably would be dictated more by military . . . . than by political factors," predicated on assessments of relative advantage. DIA comments on a draft of this study, September 9, 1977.

For comprehensive coverage, see Davis, Jacquelyn K. and Pfaltzgraff, Robert L., Jr., *Soviet Theater Strategy: Implications for NATO, USSI Report 78-1*. Washington: United States Strategic Institute, 1978. 54 pp.

9. Sections on NATO strategy depend primarily on Collins, John M., *Grand Strategy: Principles and Practices*. pp. 129–140.

10. Pfaltzgraff, Robert L., Jr., *The Atlantic Community: A Complex Imbalance*. New York: Van Nostrand Reinhold, Co., 1969, pp. 37–69.

11. *The Military Balance, 1970–1971*. London: International Institute for Strategic Studies, 1970, pp. 22–30, and *The Military Balance, 1977–1978*, pp. 16–28.

12. DIA comments on a draft of this study, September 9, 1977; roundtable discussions with staff officers at SHAPE and EUCOM on November 17–18, 1977.

13. Most European reserves are simply scheduled to bring existing formations up to strength. *The Military Balance, 1977–1978*, pp. 104–106.

14. Erickson, John, *Soviet-Warsaw Pact Force Levels*, pp. 69–71. Updated by DIA comments on this draft in February 1978.

15. Erickson, John, *The Ground Forces in Soviet Military Policy*, pp. 1–42.

16. Magnesium armor on BMPs proved disadvantageous during the Yom Kippur conflict between Arab States and Israel. Gas tanks on the rear door are also undesirable.

17. Miller, Edward A. and Cooksey, Howard H., "Evaluation of Soviets' Overall Threat: Analysis of Potential Factors," *Army Research and Development News Magazine*, March-April 1977, p. 22.

18. Egyptian troops using Soviet engineer bridging in October 1973 crossed the Suez Canal in great strength and in far faster time than Israeli intelligence previously indicated was possible.

19. Coverage was compiled from Erickson, John, *Soviet-Warsaw Pact Force Levels*, pp. 74–75; Schemmer, Benjamin F., "Soviet Build-up on Central Front Poses New Threat to NATO." *Armed Forces Journal*, December 1976, pp. 30–33; U.S. Congress. Senate. *NATO and the New Soviet Threat*, pp. 4–5; *The Military Balance, 1976*–1977, pp. 101–102.

20. Berman, Robert P., *Soviet Air Power in Transition*, pp. 54–55, 68–73; Erickson, John, *Soviet-Warsaw Pact Force Levels*, pp. 74, 75–76; Schemmer, Benjamin F., "Soviet Build-up on Central Front Poses New Threat to NATO," pp. 31–32; U.S. Congress. Senate. *NATO and the New Soviet Threat*, pp. 5–6.

21. SS-4 and SS-5 MRBMs/IRBMs, installed around 1960, have ranges of roughly 1,200 and 2,300 miles respectively. Each, armed with a single one-megaton warhead, is sufficiently accurate to hit within a mile or less of its target half the time. SS-20s, which carry three MIRVs each, reportedly have CEPs that approximate 440 yards over 2,500

miles. Beecher, William, "Portable Red Missiles Housed in 'Garages,' " *Washington Star*, January 9, 1977, p. 9; *The Military Balance, 1976–1977*, p. 73.

22. Miller, Edward A. and Cooksey, Howard H., "Evaluation of Soviets' Overall Threat," p. 22; U.S. Congress. House. *NATO and U.S. Security*. Report of the Committee Delegation to NATO Submitted to the Committee on Armed Services. (H.A.S.C. No. 95–18). 95th Congress, 1st Session. Washington: U.S. Govt. Print. Off., 1977, p. 16; U.S. Congress. Senate. *NATO Posture and Initiatives. Hearings Before the Subcommittee on Manpower and Personnel of the Committee on Armed Services, August 3, 1977*. 95th Congress, 1st Session. Washington: U.S. Govt. Print. Off., 1977, p. 54; *Growing Dimensions of Security*. Washington: The Atlantic Council of the United States, November 1977, pp. 32–34.

23. U.S. Congress. House. *NATO and U.S. Security*, p. 3; U.S. Congress. Senate. *NATO Posture and Initiatives*, pp. 18–19.

24. Aspin, Les, "A Surprise Attack on NATO—Refocusing the Debate." *NATO Review*, April 1977, pp. 7–8.

25. Stefan T. Possony advances five Soviet courses of offensive action in "NATO and the Dawn of New Technology, Part II," *Defense and Foreign Affairs*, November 1976, pp. 18–25.

26. DOD planners, for force-sizing purposes, originally sought to determine what threat NATO would face if the Warsaw Pact took 30 days to mobilize before attempting a breakthrough. Time transformed that study into the so-called "23/30 scenario," which predicted the Pact would in fact attack about M+30. NATO mobilization would lag a full week, allowing no more than 23 days to fill before the onslaught started. Other contingencies, of course were considered, but 23/30 was stressed. Aspin, Les, "A Surprise Attack on NATO," p. 7; "Assessing the NATO/Warsaw Pact Military Balance," *CBO*, pp. 21–22.

27. For a typical unclassified estimate predicated on the 23/30 scenario, see Fowler, Delbert M., "How Many Divisions? A NATO-Warsaw Pact Assessment," *Military Review*, November 1972, pp. 76–88.

28. Mounting a major attack with even a week's preparation seems a low-priority prospect to some serious students of Warsaw Pact capabilities. Robert Lucas Fischer, for one, feels that "immediate results would be most difficult to predict, making [short-notice] attack unattractive as a deliberate choice." He finds the 23/30 scenario more credible. *Defending the Central Front: The Balance of Forces*. Adelphi Papers No. 127. London: International Institute for Strategic Studies, 1976, pp. 15–25.

29. Flights of up to 40 Pact bombers, for example, repeatedly burst across the Baltic toward southern Denmark during winter exercises early in 1977, then broke off just before crossing the border. Alert times would have been close to zero if they had continued on course toward targets. Miller, Edward A. and Cooksey, Howard H., "Evaluation of Soviets' Overall Threat," p. 1.

30. Wolfe, Thomas W., *Soviet Power in Europe, 1945–1970*, pp. 473–477.

31. The basic report, "prepared by a senior officer of NATO's armed forces," was summarized in "Surprise Attack Could Make Nuclear Weapons Useless," *The Times* (London), March 15, 1976, p. 1. A commentary by Lord Chalfont, Britain's former Secretary of State for Foreign and Commonwealth Affairs (1964–1970), appeared in the same issue as "The West Must Act to Defend Itself While it Still Has the Chance," p. 12. NATO spokesmen subsequently called the cited study "a vast oversimplification of a very complex issue" with "no official status whatsoever." *Atlantic News*, Brussels, March 17, 1976, p. 2.

32. U.S. Congress. Senate. *NATO Posture and Initiatives*, p. 29.

33. Roundtable discussion with EUCOM staff officers on November 18, 1977.

34. *The Military Balance, 1977–1978*, p. 13; Aspin, Les, "A Surprise Attack on NATO," p. 10.

35. Any U.S. Army active or reserve component division is automatically classified C-4 if less than 75 percent of authorized wartime personnel are assigned; or if less than

68 percent of assigned personnel are fully qualified in their Military Occupational Specialty (MOS); or if more than 10 percent of reportable line equipment is less than 70 percent filled; or if less than 70 percent of all arms and equipment passes readiness inspection; or if the division would take more than seven weeks to become fully trained. Army Regulation 220-1, Unit Readiness Reporting, p. A-1/2.

36. Soviet concern for readiness recently resulted in a special conference at the Ministry of Defense for top military commanders summoned from "Central Europe, the Far East and Russia's frontiers." Middleton, Drew, "Moscow Said to Call Generals to Talks," *New York Times*, November 25, 1977, p. 8.

37. Lieutenant General Samuel V. Wilson, former Director of DIA, quoted in U.S. Congress. Joint Economic Committee. "Allocation of Resources in the Soviet Union and China—1977," p. 77.

38. Roundtable discussion with SHAPE staff officers on November 17, 1977; DIA comments on this study, February 1978.

39. Aspin, Les, "A Surprise Attack on NATO," pp. 9–10; "Assessing the NATO/Warsaw Pact Military Balance," *CBO*, pp. 20–21, 31.

40. Comments on a draft of this study by Andrew Marshall, DOD Director of Net Assessment, September 14, 1977.

41. Conversation with the Deputy CINCEUR on November 18, 1977; roundtable discussion with SHAPE and EUCOM staffs on November 17–18, 1977; Middleton, Drew, "Haig Lifts Estimate of NATO Alert Time," *New York Times*, September 15, 1977, p. 10; Schemmer, Benjamin F., "Haig Now Says NATO Can Expect 8–14 days Warning, Not 48 Hours," *Armed Forces Journal*, October 1977, pp. 16–17.

42. The quote is SACEUR's, contained in Schemmer, Benjamin F., "Haig Now Says NATO Can Expect 8–14 Days Warning," p. 17. Indicator data was derived from personal conversation with Deputy CINCEUR on November 18, 1977 and roundtable discussion with EUCOM staff same date. See also Aspin, Les, "A Surprise Attack on NATO," p. 10, and Currie, William, "Haig's Views on What May Cause a War," *Chicago Tribune*, September 26, 1977, p. 27.

Selected indicators are discussed in *Field Manual (FM) 30-102, Opposing Forces Europe*. Washington: Department of the Army, November 8, 1977, pp. 2–26 to 2–32.

43. SACEUR, who is also U.S. CINCEUR, concentrates on *Allied* matters. Since SHAPE, at Casteau, Belgium (near Brussels), is far distant from EUCOM at Stuttgart, he delegates daily command of *American* forces to Deputy CINCEUR, a four-star general.

44. Schemmer, Benjamin F., "Haig Now Says NATO Can Expect 8–14 Days Warning," p. 17; Aspin, Les, "A Surprise Attack on NATO," p. 10; and Currie, William, "Haig's Views on What May Cause a War," p. 27.

45. Comments on a draft of this study by Andrew Marshall, DOD Director of Net Assessment, September 14, 1977.

46. Critchley, Julian, British Member of Parliament and Chairman of the Defense and Armaments Committee of the Western European Union Assembly, "Warnings and Response," *NATO Review*, April 1977, pp. 14–18, 27.

47. An offshoot of the North German Plain dead-ends at Hamburg, a shallow but lucrative goal.

48. Feld-marschall Graf von Schlieffen, Chief of the German General Staff from 1891 to 1906, saw the North German Plain and Belgium, plus the French provinces of Picardy, eastern Normandy, and Ile-de-France, as a single corridor, sufficient for 34 of the Kaiser's divisions to outflank Allied opponents "if the last man on the right brushed the [English] Channel with his sleeve."

49. *U.S. Air and Ground Conventional Forces for NATO: Overview*. Washington: Congressional Budget Office, January 1978, pp. 9–11; Lawrence, Richard D. and Record, Jeffrey, *U.S. Force Structure in NATO: An Alternative*. Washington: The Brookings Institution, 1974, pp. 27–28.

50. *Ibid.*

51. See, for example, Edmonds, Martin H. A., "British Defense Capabilities and

Commitments," *Air University Review*, July-August 1977, pp. 70–80.

52. U.S., Congress, Senate, *NATO and the New Soviet Threat*, p. 12.

53. Some difficulties are discussed in Brown, Harold, *Department of Defense Annual Report for FY 1979*, pp. 237–238.

54. Amme, Carl H., Jr., *NATO Without France*. Stanford, Calif.: The Hoover Institution on War, Revolution and Peace, 1967, pp. 117–121.

55. Amme, Carl H., Jr., "National Strategies Within the Alliance: West Germany," *NATO's Fifteen Nations*, August-September 1972, p. 82.

56. For implications of de Gaulle's decision to evict NATO's forces from France, see Moon, Gordon A., II, "Uncertain Future," *Army Magazine*, March 1967, pp. 38–42 and "Invasion in Reverse," *Army Magazine*, February 1967, pp. 24–30.

57. France has not undertaken any agreement to rejoin NATO militarily. The use of French forces and territory in time of crisis would be subject to political decision. NATO planners therefore treat that possibility as one of many contingencies.

58. Literature on theater nuclear weapons and warfare is almost endless. For basic background, see Schlesinger, James R., *The Theater Nuclear Force Posture in Europe: A Report to the United States Congress in Compliance With Public Law 93-365*. Washington: Department of Defense, 1975, 30 pp.; *Planning U.S. General Purpose Forces: The Theater Nuclear Forces*. Washington: Congressional Budget Office, January 1977, 45 pp.; Gessert, Robert A. and Seim, Harvey B., *Improving NATO's Theater Nuclear Posture: A Reassessment and a Proposal*. Washington, Georgetown University: Center for Strategic and International Studies, April 1977, 33 pp.; Gray, Colin, "Theater Nuclear Weapons: Doctrines and Postures," *World Politics*, January 1976, pp. 300–314; Record, Jeffrey, "Theater Nuclear Weapons: Begging the Soviets to Pre-empt," *Survival*, September/October 1977, pp. 208–211; Galen, Justin, "Tactical Nuclear Balance, Part I: Recent Force Trends and Improvements," *Armed Forces Journal*, December 1977, pp. 29–34 and "Theater Nuclear Balance, Part II: The NATO/Warsaw Pact Imbalance," *Armed Forces Journal*, January 1978, p. 20–29.

59. Possibilities that Soviet theater nuclear strikes could "be simultaneously massive and designed to be discriminant . . . . without sacrificing basic military effectiveness" are being explored by U.S. analysts. The issue "is whether or not a nuclear war can be fought in Europe without destroying . . . . the very prize [the Soviets] seek to capture." Conclusions are still "highly speculative", but stimulate further thought. Douglass, Joseph D., Jr., *A Soviet Selective Targeting Strategy Toward Europe*. Washington: System Planning Corporation, Revised August 1977, 47 pp. To put that paper in perspective, see his *The Soviet Theater Nuclear Offensive, Studies in Communist Affairs, Vol. I*, published under auspices of the U.S. Air Force, 1976. 127 pp.

60. Procurement funds for enhanced radiation W70-3 warheads to fit Lance missiles were first contained in *H.R. 7553, the FY 1978 Public Works for Water and Power Development and Energy Research and Development Bill* submitted by the U.S. Energy Research and Development Administration (ERDA). Similar projectiles reportedly are planned for 8-inch and 155mm howitzers, according to the *Washington Post* June 24, 1977, p. 41. The purported purpose is to destroy point targets, particularly tanks, while confining collateral casualties and damage. For basic issues, see Bell, Robert G., *Pro/Con Analysis of the Neutron Bomb*. Washington: Congressional Research Service, June 27, 1977, 7 pp.; " 'Neutron Bomb' Poses Dilemma for Congress," *Congressional Quarterly*, July 9, 1977, pp. 1403–1407; Miettinen, Jorma K., "Enhanced Radiation Warfare," *Bulletin of the Atomic Scientists*, September 1977, pp. 32–37.

61. If the Soviets struck first with MRBMs and IRBMs, "it is doubtful that NATO could successfully accomplish any Western European defense plan. In the next five to ten years this force will probably change from a fixed-site . . . . to a road-mobile force, delivering MIRVed warheads [the SS-20 is the vanguard]. Although the system(s) will probably be relatively soft, their mobility will drastically degrade NATO's ability to target the launchers." DIA comments on a draft of this study, September 9, 1977.

62. Enthoven, Alain C. and Smith, K. Wayne, *How Much is Enough?* New York: Harper and Row, 1971, p. 125.

63. U.S., Congress, Senate, *Hearings Before the Senate Armed Services Committee on FY 1973 Authorization for Military Procurement.* Part 2 of 6 Parts. 92d Congress, 1st Session. Washington: U.S. Govt. Print. Off., 1972, pp. 642, 1195; and U.S., Congress, House, *Hearings Before the Special Subcommittee on North Atlantic Treaty Organization Commitments of the Armed Services Committee.* 92d Congress, 1st Session. Washington: U.S. Govt. Print. Off., 1972, p. 13344.

64. U.S. MBFR endeavors date from November, 1965, when an arms control committee composed of distinguished private experts expressed its belief that "the United States should encourage an examination of the problem of parallel troop reductions in . . . . Germany by the United States and Soviet Union." The group recommended equitable adjustments on both sides, "which would preserve the balance at less cost and strain for each." "Report of the Committee on Arms Control and Disarmament of the National Citizens' Commission on International Cooperation," November 28, 1965. *Documents on Disarmament,* 1965, United States Arms Control and Disarmament Agency. Washington: U.S. Govt. Print. Off., 1966, p. 570.

For discussion of subsequent issues, see Schandler, Herbert Y., "Mutual and Balanced Force Reductions (MBFR)." Contained in *Major U.S. Foreign and Defense Policy Issues,* A Compilation of Papers Prepared for the Commission on the Operation of the Senate by the Congressional Research Service, Library of Congress. Washington: U.S. Govt. Print. Off., 1977, pp. 127–131.

65. Bourne, Eric, "East, West Renew Troop Cut Talks," *Christian Science Monitor,* January 31, 1978, p. 4.

66. Sandström, Anders, "M(B)FR: A Non-Starter or a Slow Starter?", *Cooperation and Conflict,* 1976, pp. 79, 80.

67. *Ibid.;* Ruehl, Lothar, "The Negotiations on Force Reductions in Central Europe," *NATO Review,* October 1976, pp. 19–20.

68. James R. Schlesinger during his nomination hearings in 1973 indicated that "with our airlift capabilities, we are able to redeploy [ground] combat troops very quickly, in fact more quickly in a number of respects than the Soviets can in a location closer at hand . . . . The difficulties of redeployment may be less for us than they are for our possible opponents." U.S. Congress, Senate, Committee on Armed Services. Nomination of James R. Schlesinger to be Secretary of Defense. *Hearings.* 93d Congress, 1st Session. June 18, 1973. Washington: U.S. Govt. Print. Off., 1973, p. 96.

Since then, the Soviets have improved their airlift capabilities considerably, even though 130 AN-12 tactical transports have left the active military inventory.

69. One proposal, which would add warning time instead of reducing troops, perhaps could break the MBFR barrier. Three prerequisites are prescribed: international observers at installations on each side to inhibit offensive preparations; strict limitations on the size and scope of maneuvers; and restrictions on the number of troops that can rotate to and from Central Europe in any particular period. "Should the Pact take any of those forbidden steps, it would be like ringing a firebell in all the NATO capitals. . . ." Aspin, Les, "A Surprise Attack on NATO," pp. 11–13.

70. *FM 100-5, Operations,* pp. 14–19.

71. Donnelly, C. N., "Soviet Techniques for Combat in Built up Areas," *International Defense Review,* April 1977, pp. 238–242; Scharfen, John C. and Deane, Michael J., "To Fight the Russians in Cities, Know Their Tactics," *Marine Corps Gazette,* January 1977, pp. 38–42.

72. *FM 100-5, Operations,* pp. 14–19.

73. *Ibid.,* pp. 14–18/14–20.

74. *Ibid.,* pp. 14–15/14–17, 14–23; Bracken, Paul, "Urban Sprawl and NATO Defense," *Survival,* November/December 1976, p. 256.

75. Bracken, Paul, "Urban Sprawl and NATO Defense," pp. 254–255.

76. "A typical defensive position for a NATO armored brigade on the East German border contains about 85 villages." Combined with forests, they "comprise nearly 60 percent of the available terrain . . . . Warsaw Pact forces attacking tanks would be unable to bypass one village without almost immediately running into another." Bracken, Paul, "Urban Sprawl and NATO Defense," p. 255; *FM 100-5, Operations,* pp. 14–19/14–21.

77. *FM 100-5, Operations,* pp. 14–22. For details, see *FM 9–10, Military Operations in Built-Up Areas.*

78. Bracken, Paul, "Urban Sprawl and NATO Defense," pp. 257–259.

79. *Ibid.,* pp. 259–260 summarizes several corrective courses of action. Strengths seem outweighed by weakness in each instance.

80. Shick, James M., *The Berlin Crisis, 1958–1962.* Philadelphia: University of Pennsylvania Press, 1971. 236 pp.

81. Soviet and satellite forces have blocked entryways to Berlin only once since World War II, not counting intermittant interruptions. The Berlin Airlift lasted from June 1948 to May 1949, before that barrier was lifted. President Kennedy reinforced the U.S. Berlin contingent in 1961 and called up substantial reserves, but in response to anxieties over the Wall, rather than access routes.

82. General Maxwell D. Taylor, when still Army Chief of Staff, admitted that "Berlin has always been untenable. . . . A surprise attack, or [even] an attack with warning, could never be effectively resisted locally by military means. We have known that; we have accepted the fact that such is inevitable." Nothing essential has changed. U.S., Congress, Senate, *Hearings on Major Defense Matters Before the Preparedness Investigating Subcommittee of the Committee on Armed Services,* March 11–13, 1959. Part I. Washington: U.S. Govt. Print. Off., 1959, pp. 6, 15.

83. Western powers registered protests when Soviet troops squashed East Berlin's rebellion in 1953, but NATO never seriously considered committing corps-sized relief columns, which would have been necessary. No subsequent changes in NATO's capabilities would support a more rigorous response.

84. Deficiencies are discussed in some detail by Senators Sam Nunn and Dewey F. Bartlett in *NATO and the New Soviet Threat,* pp. 13–30.

85. President Carter pledged greater support for NATO in his speech to the Atlantic Council in May, 1977, and reinforced his remarks in Brussels at the beginning of 1978. The U.S. FY 1979 defense budget proposal is demonstrative proof that he meant what he said. As Secretary Brown put it, that request "first places particular priority and emphasis on weapons systems in support of the NATO alliance." Curtis, Wilkie, "Allies Welcome Pledge to Strengthen NATO," *Boston Globe,* May 11, 1977, p. 1; Walsh, Edward, "Carter Will Increase U.S. forces in Europe," *Washington Post,* January 7, 1978, p. 1; Weinraub, Bernard, "Higher Outlay Emphasizes Buildup in Aid to NATO," *New York Times,* January 24, 1978, p. 15.

86. Defense Secretary Harold Brown describes NATO's newest initiatives in U.S., Congress, Senate, *NATO Posture and Initiatives,* pp. 3–7; see also Currie, William, "Gen. Haig Takes Command," *Chicago Tribune,* November 1977, p. 9.

87. U.S., Congress, Senate, *NATO Posture and Initiatives,* pp. 4–5.

88. *Ibid.,* p. 5.

89. For initiatives related to tactical air power, see Robinson, Clarence A., Jr. and Brown, David A., "NATO: The New Challenge," a special issue of *Aviation Week and Space Technology,* 1977. 49 pp.

90. Roundtable discussions with SHAPE and EUCOM staff officers on November 17–19, 1977.

91. Brown, David A., "Cobra Bolsters U.S. Stance in Europe," *Aviation Week and Space Technology,* November 14, 1977, pp. 40–42; and Brown, David A., "Helicopters Play New Role in Europe," *Aviation Week and Space Technology,* November 28, 1977, pp. 62–63, 65, 69.

92. U.S., Congress, Senate, *NATO Posture and Initiatives*, p. 5; roundtable discussion with EUCOM staff officers on November 18, 1977.

93. U.S., Congress, Senate, *NATO Posture and Initiatives*, pp. 5, 44; Getler, Michael, "NATO Agrees on Weapons Stockpile," *Washington Post*, December 7, 1977, p. 28.

94. U.S., Congress, Senate, *NATO Posture and Initiatives*, pp. 44, 55–56.

95. U.S., Congress, Senate, *NATO and the New Soviet Threat*, pp. 13–14.

96. U.S., Congress, Senate, *NATO Posture and Initiatives*, pp. 5–8.

97. *Ibid.*, p. 6.

98. U.S., Congress, Senate, *NATO and the New Soviet Threat*, p. 14; U.S., Congress, House, *NATO and U.S. Security*, p. 17.

99. Roundtable discussion with EUCOM staff officers on November 18, 1977; Brown, Harold, *Department of Defense Annual Report for FY 1979*, p. 140; U.S., Congress, Senate, *NATO Posture and Initiatives*, pp. 6, 64, 75–78.

100. U.S., Congress, Senate, *NATO Posture and Initiatives*, p. 6.

101. Hoeber, Francis P., Kassing, David B., and Schneider, William, Jr., *Arms, Men, and Military Budgets: Issues for Fiscal Year 1979*. New York: Crane, Russak & Co., Inc., 1977, pp. 68–70. See also Garde, Hans, "The Influence of Navies on the European Central Front," and Palmer, Joseph M., "The Channel Command, Sea Highway to Europe," both in *U.S. Naval Institute Proceedings*, May 1976, pp. 160–175; 176–189.

102. NATO's NADGE screen scans the skies from northern Norway to Italy's heel, then tracks through Thrace to eastern Turkey. Its fully-integrated, semi-automatic sites take care of missile and aircraft warning. They also direct air defense in response to proven and possible threats. For general discussion, see Bosch, J. L., "As NADGE Nears Completion, Follow-on Organization Prepares to Take Over," *NATO Review*, No. 1, 1973, pp. 12–14.

103. U.S., Congress, Senate, *NATO and the New Soviet Threat*, p. 15.

104. U.S., Congress, Senate, *NATO Posture and Initiatives*, pp. 7, 50, 61, 63.

105. *Ibid.*, pp. 7, 51, 63, 72; U.S., Congress, House, *NATO and U.S. Security*, p. 7; Robinson, Clarence A., Jr. and Brown, David A., *NATO: The New Challenge*. See especially pp. 8, 22, 30–35.

106. "More NATO Sites Sought," *Air Force Times*, November 14, 1977, p. 2; "DOD Should Study U.S. Air Force's NATO Airbasing Requirement, GAO Says," *Aerospace Daily*, November 2, 1977, p. 13; U.S., Congress, Senate, *NATO Posture and Initiatives*, p. 61.

107. U.S., Congress, Senate, *NATO Posture and Initiatives*, p. 7.

108. *Ibid.*, pp. 59, 61, 64; roundtable discussion with EUCOM staff officers, November 18, 1977.

109. For EW trends and implications, see Currie, Malcolm R., "Economic Warfare," Supplement to the *Air Force Policy Letter for Commanders*, No. 2–1977, February 1977, pp. 2–13; "The Importance of Electronic Warfare to the National Defense Posture," *Commanders Digest*, December 9, 1976, 8 pp.; "The Electronic Air Force," a special section in *Air Force Magazine*, July 1977, pp. 29–79.

110. Roundtable discussion with EUCOM staff officers on November 18, 1977; U.S., Congress, Senate, *NATO Posture and Initiatives*, p. 7.

111. *Ibid.*

112. Special Assistants to the Chief of Staff (SPACOS) produced a SHAPE paper on May 11, 1976 entitled "The Definitional Jungle." As updated informally for the author in November 1977, it described "rationalization" as the "all encompassing umbrella for . . . . making the Alliance, militarily, work more off the same score of music, materially, tactically, doctrinally, etc:

"Rationalization—Overall concept of realigning Alliance defense efforts to insure more efficient use of resources. This encompasses standardization, interoperability, and more.

"Standardization—The process by which member nations achieve the closest practicable cooperation among forces, the most efficient use of research, development, and production resources and agree to adopt common or compatible procedures, supplies, weapons, and doctrine. Can lead to two levels of achievement:

—"Commonality of equipment, i.e. precisely the same equipments among forces.

—"Interchangeability—Use of component parts of one country (e.g. ammunition) in the equipment of another.

"Interoperability—The ability of systems, units, or forces to provide services to and accept services from other systems, units or forces and to use the services so exchanged to enable them to operate effectively together, e.g. the capability of different equipment to work with each other.

"Compatibility—The assurance that equipments will at least not interfere with each other's operations."

113. "The optimum utilization of the military and industrial resources of the alliance has not occurred—with significant adverse effects on the military capability of NATO . . . . Most efforts have been frustrated by considerations of national pride and domestic economic welfare." U.S., Congress, House, *Report of the Committee Delegation to NATO concerning NATO and U.S. Security*, p. 5. Associated problems are addressed in *Standardization in NATO: Improving the Effectiveness and Economy of Mutual Defense Efforts*. Washington: Comptroller General (GAO), January 18, 1978, 50 pp.; Robinson, Clarence A., Jr. and Brown, David A., *NATO: The New Challenge*, pp. 42–49.

114. U.S., Congress, Senate, *NATO Posture and Initiatives*, pp. 7, 9–12.

115. U.S., Congress, Senate, *NATO and the New Soviet Threat*, pp. 13–16, 18, 20; roundtable discussion with EUCOM staff officers, November 18, 1977.

116. Quotation by Defense Secretary Brown is from U.S., Congress, Senate, *NATO Posture and Initiatives*, p. 65. Repeated proposals to relocate NATO's peacetime LOC from Bremerhaven to the U.S. sector have foundered on political and financial obstacles. American forces plan to use ports in France or the Benelux countries if war occurs, but no funds, personnel, or facilities have ever been furnished for that purpose. Lawrence, Richard D., and Record, Jeffrey, *U.S. Force Structure in NATO*, pp. 87–88.

117. U.S., Congress, Senate, *NATO Posture and Initiatives*, p. 7.

118. *Ibid.* For background concerning GLCMs, see Oka, Takashi, "NATO: The Cruise Missile Dilemma," *Christian Science Monitor*, December 21, 1977, p. 12; Burns, Michael K., "SALT Won't Bar Cruise Missile from NATO, U.S. Assures Allies," *Baltimore Sun*, December 8, 1977, p. 4; "Cruise For Europe," *The Economist* (London), September 24, 1977, p. 14; and Franke, Friedrich, "A Wonder Weapon for the West?—NATO Can Be More Effective With the New Cruise Missile," *Cologne Rheinischer Merkur*, June 24, 1977, p. 28 (reprinted in English as "Cruise Missile's Effect on European Defense Examined," Joint Publications Research Service, CIA, July 1977, pp. 1–5); Svetlich, William G., *Cruise Missile Issues and Management* Washington: Headquarters Air Force Systems Command, July 22, 1977, 12 pp., plus charts.

PART III

NATO's Flanks

Wartime naval activities on NATO's north and south flanks would bear indirectly on land battles in the center, but outcomes could have far-reaching influence.

NATO's Northern Flank

NATO's far northern flank controls exits from and access to the ice-free Kola coast (Map 20), which houses immense Soviet submarine packs, plus more than half of all Soviet surface combatants.[1] If adjacent Norway fell into hostile hands, forward-based fighters and bombers, including missile-armed naval Backfires, could extend Gorshkov's sea-denial capabilities far over open ocean, to the detriment of NATO navies and merchant shipping. Timely arrival of NATO's much-needed reinforcements and supplies would, at the very least, be in question. The strategic significance to *both* sides is consequently critical.

Nevertheless, Norway permits no NATO forces on its soil, except in national emergency. The Alliance therefore secures that sensitive area with a single Norwegian brigade, whose in-place opposition comprises one Soviet motorized rifle division and a naval infantry regiment, the latter being buttressed with air cushion vehicles and amphibious craft for assault purposes. They are backed by seven more divisions (one airborne) located elsewhere in the Leningrad Military District. Soviet tactical air strength in the area is substantial.

Map 20
NATO's North Flank

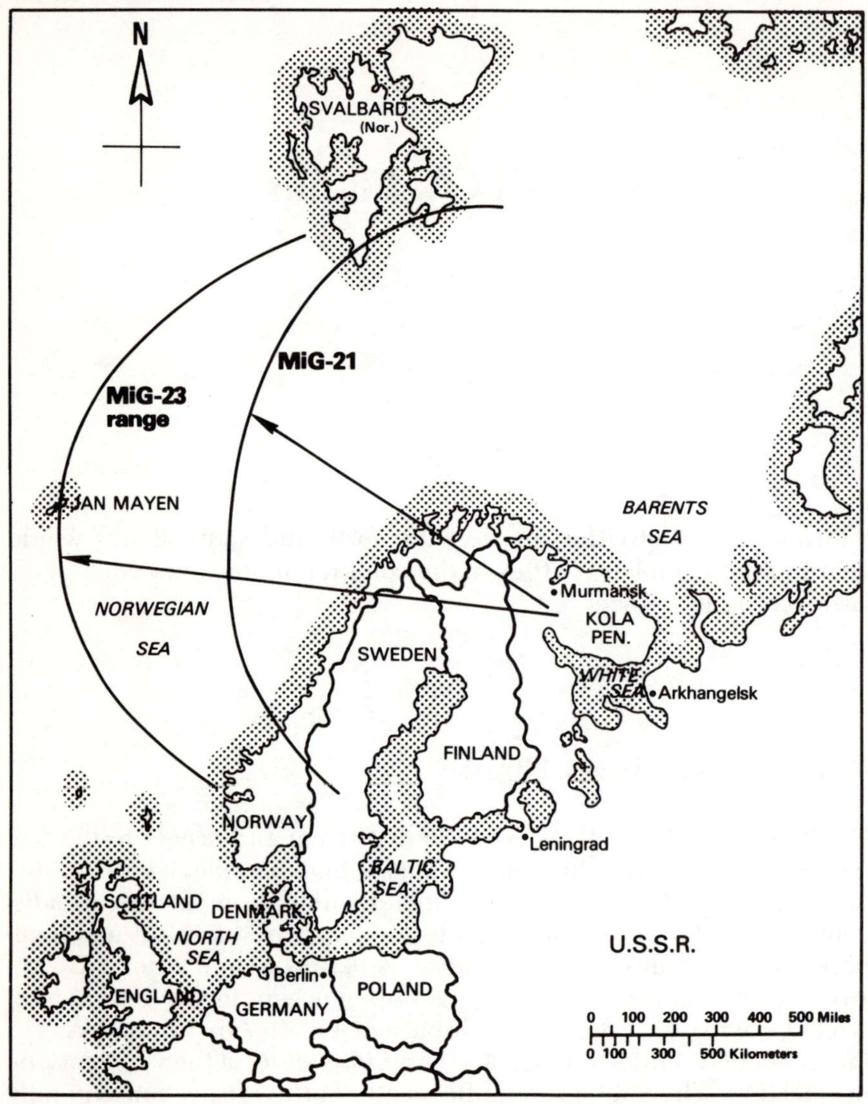

Fears of surprise attack on that flank, followed by a *fait accompli*, thus cause serious concern among Alliance officials. NATO's risk-gain ratios in such case would severely constrain realistic response, regardless of treaty commitments that consider an attack on one an attack on all.[2]

NATO's Southern Flank

A great Alpine abatis separates NATO's center and southern sectors into two distinct theaters that largely lack mutual support and are only marginally related.[3] (See Map 21.)

North of that barrier, NATO comprises a contiguous coalition for security purposes. Threats against one state are threats against all. Deterrent and defensive schemes stress land power. Other forces are complementary.

Collective security measures of Mediterranean states are somewhat less cohesive. Members are not only cut off from NATO's nucleus, they are isolated from each other. Common threats are uncommon. Common fronts are infeasible. Three sub-theaters thus exist: Italy; Greece, plus Turkish Thrace; and Asia Minor. Deterrence and defense depend strongly on sea power, screened from the air.

The Balance Ashore

The United States furnishes few ground combat or tactical air forces for use on NATO's south flank, but even so, the Warsaw Pact is badly outnumbered in most categories, as Figure 45 shows. Tanks comprise the salient exception. Interceptor aircraft on both sides influence air supremacy indirectly, but are expressly designed for defense.

NATO's land-based forces, being geographically separate, can not concentrate, but neither can prospective foes. Enemy breakthroughs in any locale would be isolated. Mass assaults from the Balkans, for example, might menace Greece and Turkey (the most exposed countries), but other states would stay secure from Italy through Iberia.

The Balance Afloat

NATO not only outnumbers its rivals at sea, but enjoys other advantages. Soviet staying power and surge capabilities, for example, depend almost completely on freedom of passage through the Turkish Straits, which likely would be closed in time of war.

Logistic lines from the Black Sea are short but, being controlled by NATO at present, are constrained. Moscow maintains no formal base rights in the Mediterranean, merely a presence. Underway replenishment procedures are still limited. Many anchorages, which simplify peacetime resupply and overlook every choke point from Suez to Gibraltar, probably would prove untenable in war.

Overall Soviet opportunities to compete with Sixth Fleet in the eastern Mediterranean are nevertheless impressive, especially if conflict were short.[4]

Map 21
Mediterranean Basin

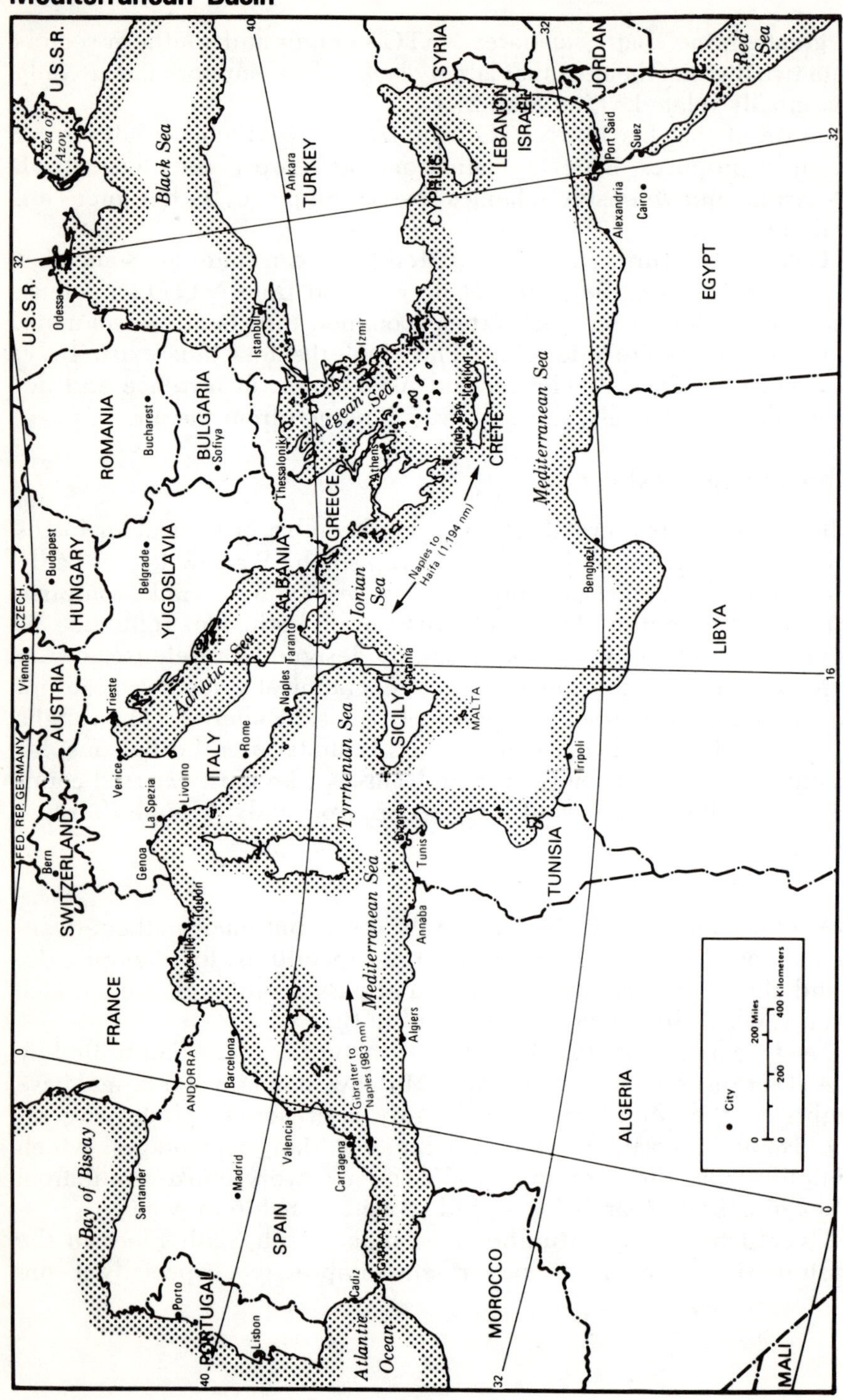

FIGURE 45 NATO's SOUTH FLANK
Statistical Summary
(Committed Forces Only)

FORCES ASHORE

	NATO	*Warsaw Pact*	*Soviet Union*
Combat Troops, Direct Support	840,000	540,000	200,000
Divisions			
Armored	2	4	2
Other	32	24	2
Total	34	28	4
Tanks	4,000	7,500	2,750
Tactical Bombers	0	60	60
Ground Attack Aircraft	625	200	125
Interceptors	200	500	425

FORCES AFLOAT

	Mediterranean Members of NATO	*U.S. Sixth Fleet*	*Soviet Union*
Surface Combatants			
Attack Carriers	2	2	0
ASW Carriers	0	0	0–1
Helicopter Carriers	0	1	0–1
Cruisers	2	3	1–3
Destroyers/Frigates/ Corvettes	56	12	7–9
Total	60	18	8–14
Attack Submarines	40	14	9–11
Grand Total	100	32	17–25
Naval Aircraft	111	200	15
Fighter Squadrons	0	4	0
Attack Squadrons	2	6	1

NOTE: NATO ground forces include U.S. and British units. Air strengths exclude U.S. dual-based squadrons. Normal naval deployments in the Mediterranean are shown. NATO includes Greece, Turkey, and Italy, plus 2 French attack carriers, 1 cruiser, 13 of the 56 escorts, and 111 naval aircraft (80 afloat). Soviet naval figures exclude a substantial fleet of ships home-ported in the Black Sea. The number in the Mediterranean is 20–23 on the average, depending on what mix is present at any given time.

Maneuver room is minimal in the Mediterranean, but Soviet submarines still are difficult to detect in those shallow waters, where thermal layers and many merchantmen confuse ASW devices by distorting sounds. Anti-ship cruise missiles also inject serious uncertainties into strategic equations. Peacetime contacts with Sixth Fleet are so close that U.S. reactions to sneak attacks might be measured in seconds.

The western Mediterranean is a much different matter. Soviet abilities to conduct combat operations in that area against numerically superior NATO are strictly limited, for short wars as well as long ones.[5]

Connections with Center Sector

Soviet breakthroughs along NATO's south flank would cause psychological shock waves to buffet the Atlantic Alliance, but the center sector could still stand.

Greek and Turkish armed forces defend a discrete region, nothing more. Reducing freedom of action for Soviet reserves in south Russia is their only direct connection with plans and operations in Western Europe. Airfields, NADGE installations,[6] and most communications sites are only significant locally. Aegean ports improve Sixth Fleet's posture in the eastern Mediterranean, but are not crucial beyond that basin.

If war ensued with the Warsaw Pact, far distant France would be free from fear of waterborne invasion if NATO held the Sicilian narrows. Italy would still be intact, subject to incursions only by airborne/amphibious assaults across the Adriatic (specialized Soviet sealift being in short supply), or along difficult axes in northern Yugoslavia. Assuming the Italian outlier fell, aggressors still would have to breach the Alpine obstacle before they could overrun NATO's heartland.

All told, therefore, the Mediterranean seems an unlikely avenue for compromising NATO's center sector by direct military action.[7] The southeast flank, however, takes on different connotations when connected with U.S. security policies, plans, programs, and prospects in the Middle East. Turkey in particular directly influences U.S. abilities to abridge Soviet adventurism in that area. The loss of Middle East oil would have an immediate and inimical impact on all of NATO.[8]

Footnotes

1. For Soviet strength along the Kola coast and implications for NATO ships, see Steinhaus, R., "The Northern Flank," a paper delivered at a symposium sponsored by the American Enterprise Institute in Washington, D.C., October 6, 1977, 40 pp.; Moulton, J. L., "Northern Flank," *Navy International,* May 1977, pp. 4–9; Erickson, John, "The Northern Theater: Soviet Capabilities and Concepts," *Strategic Review,* Summer 1976, pp. 67–82; Sharp, John, "The Northern Flank," *Journal of the Royal United Services Institute (RUSI),* December 1976, pp. 10–16.

2. For divergent views concerning the utility of U.S. Marines on NATO's northern flank, see Miles, Perry W. and Taber, Richard D., Sr., "USMC and NATO: Two Perspectives," *Marine Corps Gazette,* December 1977, pp. 31–37.

3. NATO's south flank includes Italy, Greece (which has withdrawn forces from the Alliance, at least for the moment), and Turkey. Opponents are primarily Bulgaria, Romania, Hungary, and forces from southwestern U.S.S.R.

4. Moscow massed 95 ships south of Turkey during the Arab-Israeli outburst of 1973 (Sixth Fleet totalled 60, including three attack carriers), plus 30 in the Indian Ocean, a spectacular feat for a force devoted to coastal defense in the recent past.

5. For further background, see U.S. Congress. Senate. *U.S. Naval Forces in Europe.* Report of Senator Gary Hart to the Committee on Armed Services, 95th Congress, 1st Session. Washington: U.S. Govt. Print. Off., 1977, 9 pp.

6. A full discussion of U.S. bases is contained in U.S. Congress. House. *United States Military Installations and Objectives in the Mediterranean.* Report prepared for the Subcommittee on Europe and the Middle East of the Committee on International Relations by the Congressional Research Service. Washington, March 27, 1977, 95 pp.

7. For further background, see Rivero, Horacio, "Why a U.S. Fleet in the Mediterranean?" *United States Naval Institute Proceedings,* May 1977, pp. 66–89; and Milton, T.R., "NATO's Troubled Southern Flank," *Strategic Review,* Fall 1975, pp. 27–31.

8. U.S. Congress. Senate. *Oil Fields as Military Objectives,* pp. 5, 7, 27–28.

IV

ISSUES AND OPTIONS

PART I

Issues

Comparing Postures

A mirror image between U.S. and Soviet armed services is neither necessary nor desirable. Some asymmetries are safe. Others cause insecurity.

Statistics and capabilities are far from synonymous. Twelve MIGs on a tally sheet are not very meaningful. Neither are squadrons, unless considered in context with crews, training, tactics, doctrine, deployment patterns, subordination, and ground support. Battalion teams, not isolated landing craft and marines, take contested beaches.

Quantitative asymmetries are important when similar systems on each side (such as divisions) compete with each other in combat. Quality counts, but a prudent statistical balance must be maintained, because there are points beyond which mass matters more than excellence.[1] Land, sea, and air forces alike lack flexibility if numbers are too few compared with competitors and commitments.

Correlation between similar forces on each side is militarily and, more often than not, politically immaterial when offensive systems face dissimilar opposition. If the Soviets, for example, chose to deploy Backfire bombers en masse, there would be no call for SAC to match their action with more aircraft. Stronger defense would make more sense.

Strengths of one sort sometimes compensate for weakness elsewhere in the same category. Antitank guns could stop Soviet armor more surely than TOWs on occasion. SAMs complement interceptor aircraft. And so on. Analysts must consider combinations, instead of single systems, to ascertain whether cumulative capabilities (not just numbers) are short or sufficient.

Asymmetrical capabilities would sometimes still exist, even if forces on the two sides were identical in size, structure, and potential power. Soviet preemptive employment of ICBMs or anti-ship cruise missiles, to cite a pair of examples, would pose counterforce perils far out of proportion to U.S. response restrained by second-strike concepts and our unaggressive stance.

In short, what we *have* makes less difference than what we can *do* on demand, despite all opposition.[2]

Appraising Problems

Concluding which trends in the U.S./Soviet military balance are "good" and which are "bad" is beyond the scope of this study. Several subjects, however, seem to merit special consideration, so that readers can conclude for themselves whether U.S. interests, aims, and assets are compatible.[3]

Strategic Nuclear Issues

Contemporary issues which directly influence U.S. survival and security prospects can be derived from Figure 46:[4]

- — Does credible nuclear deterrence depend on a flexible U.S. stance?
- — If so, can we attain sufficient flexibility by pursuing policies that:
  - — Stress countervalue capabilities, but slight counterforce?
  - — Stress retaliatory capabilities, but slight defense?
  - — Seek peacetime parity in undefended, fixed-site, second-strike ICBMs, which could suffer heavy initial casualties if war occurred?[5]
- — To what extent do U.S. interests depend on Soviet cooperation in SALT? Is that extent satisfactory?
- — If SALT should fail, must U.S. forces match Moscow's nuclear buildup to satisfy stability?
- — Would city defense add to or subtract from U.S. nuclear deterrent capabilities?

Conventional Issues

Possible contradictions between available U.S. assets and announced U.S. aims are apparent in Figure 47. The following questions concern present and projected abilities of America's armed forces to fulfill fundamental functions in support of the interests shown:

- — Does credible conventional deterrence depend on a flexible U.S. stance?

FIGURE 46 U.S. STRATEGIC NUCLEAR PURPOSE AND POLICIES
A Selected Synopsis

NATIONAL SECURITY INTERESTS	
Survival	Peace
Security	Power
Stability	Prosperity
Credibility	Freedom of Action

STRATEGIC NUCLEAR OBJECTIVES

Consistent, Past and Present

Deter Nuclear War
Punish Foe if Deterrence Fails

Past	*Present*
Disarm the Enemy	Contain Conflict Quickly
Limit Damage and Casualties	Negotiate Quick Settlement
Win the War	

STRATEGIC NUCLEAR POLICIES

Consistent, Past and Present

Second-Strike
Quality Over Quantity

Past	*Present*
Massive Retaliation	Flexible Response
Strong Counterforce	Strong Countervalue
Balanced Defense	Abandon Defense
Superiority/Sufficiency	Essential Equivalence
Arms Control Convenient	Arms Control Critical

NOTE: Not all past objectives and policies occurred concurrently.

— If so, can we attain sufficient flexibility by pursuing policies that:
  — Make it difficult to maintain the current peacetime force at stated personnel standards?
  — Make rapid mobilization impossible in emergency?
  — Impede force modernization, by devoting more than half of every defense dollar to pay and allowances?
  — Increase reliance on allies to safeguard U.S. interests, while curtailing military assistance?
  — Leave little in reserve to cope with contingencies, without undercutting deterrent/defense capabilities in Europe?

Figure 47 U.S. PURPOSE AND POLICIES FOR CONVENTIONAL FORCES
A Selected Synopsis

NATIONAL SECURITY INTERESTS	
Survival	Peace
Security	Power
Stability	Prosperity
Credibility	Freedom of Action

GENERAL PURPOSE OBJECTIVES

Consistent, Past and Present

Freedom of the Seas
General Naval Supremacy
General Air Supremacy
Satisfy Overseas Commitments

Past	*Present*
Universal Containment	Selective Containment
Slight Stress on Deterrence	Strong Stress on Deterrence
2½-War Capability	1-Plus War Capability
Defeat Insurgencies	Reinforce/Resupply Overseas

GENERAL PURPOSE POLICIES

Consistent, Past and Present

Quality Over Quantity	Cyclical Cutbacks
Firepower Over Manpower	Sustained Combat

Past	*Present*
Stress Nuclear Strength	Flexible Response
Stress Forward Deployment	Stress CONUS Reserves
Draft	All-Volunteer Force
Stress U.S. Active Strength	Stress Total Force
Military Aid Expansive	Military Aid Selective
Balanced Mobility Force	Stress Airlift, Slight Sealift

NOTE: Not all past objectives and policies occurred concurrently.

— Furnish airlift to commit forces quickly, but forego sustaining sealift?

— If regional war should occur with the Soviet Union, would U.S. security interests and commitments overseas be well served by force levels that:

— Compel our Army to adopt a complex defensive doctrine that strains credibility?

— Constrain our Navy's ASW and escort capabilities despite increased Soviet submarine threats?

— Finally, did U.S. decision-makers positively or negatively affect America's interests in peace and stability when they dropped the aim of defeating insurgencies?

Footnotes

1. Qualitative considerations include, but are not confined to, technological characteristics, education, training, morale, motivation, discipline, and leadership. Superiority in all or most instances can enable numerically inferior forces to compete successfully, categorically or within limits, according to circumstance. Conversely, great quantitative superiority can prove insufficient if serious shortcomings are evident in even one of those entries.

2. "Do" in this context connotes the complete range of politico-military powers across a spectrum of possibilities that starts with shaping peacetime perceptions and culminates with spasmic nuclear combat.

3. The Soviet Union is plagued with its own set of problems. This section concentrates on potential *U.S.* problems which, if confirmed, would call for *U.S.* solutions, taking Soviet circumstances into account.

4. Issues summarized in this section were identified and discussed indirectly earlier in this document. Spartan treatment here is done deliberately to spotlight central concerns.

5. Quantitative requirements for U.S. fixed-site ICBMs, for example, were directly dependent on numbers of rival launchers as long as each Soviet missile mounted a single warhead. The balance between U.S. silos and Soviet countersilo MIRVs is becoming much more important.

PART II

Options

The primary mission of U.S. defense decision-makers is to match realistic ends with measured means, minimizing risks in the process. Congress, which assesses issues and corrective courses of action in concert with the Executive Branch, might find the following methods useful.

Ascertaining Real Requirements

National security interests, objectives, and commitments, combined with military missions, constitute requirements. Some shortfalls would assume less significance if they could be safely reduced or rescinded.

Review U.S. Interests

A fundamental review of U.S. foreign policy to identify which interests are essential, which are of secondary importance, and which are irrelevant, ranks first in order of importance. Cogent questions include:

— Are U.S. national security interests inseparable from our connections with other states? Why? Which ones?

— Does U.S. economic prosperity demand input from other countries? Which countries? What items? How much? What consequences would be caused by loss?

— Does the United States have a moral obligation to help safeguard countries overseas? If so, which ones?

Review U.S. Objectives

Amending America's national security objectives could basically affect the way available forces influence the U.S./Soviet balance, whether interests change or not.

There is very little latitude for improving relationships between U.S. ends and means by altering strategic nuclear objectives. Deterring general war, generally acclaimed as the most important of all aims, is not negotiable. Neither is protection for this country if deterrence fails, although lip service or less is presently paid to CONUS defense. Consequently, the only significant opportunities for adjustment concern safeguards for other states whose security is closely tied to our own.

Answers to questions of the following kind would help sort out the issues:

— Should the United States still seek to contain Soviet expansion? To contain the spread of Soviet influence through the use of proxies? If so, where? Under what circumstances?

— Is maintaining a global balance of power an imperative U.S. objective? Regional balances? Why? Where?

— Should the United States strive to deter regional wars? What kinds (conventional, tactical nuclear, revolutionary)? Why? Where?

— Should this country be able to cope with one major and one minor contingency concurrently if regional conflicts occur? What kinds? Why? Where?

— Wherever answers seem to be "no," what substitute objectives would satisfy U.S. interests?

Review U.S. Commitments

Downgrading or discontinuing certain commitments in consonance with altered interests and objectives could help correct military imbalances between the United States and the Soviet Union if forces freed from inconsequential areas were shifted to sites of crucial concern. (See Figure 16 and Annex F.) Associated questions include:

— Which commitments contribute least to U.S. security?

— Would inimical implications arise if they were scrapped?

— What forces would be freed? In what numbers?

— What use would they be elsewhere?

Review U.S. Military Roles and Missions

Title 10, United States Code and related DOD Instructions assign roles/missions to U.S. armed forces (see Annex E for details). Mismatched ends and means ensue when strength is insufficient to fulfill assigned functions. "It is the intent of Congress," for example, to provide combat power capable of "overcoming [*not just deterring*] any nations responsible for aggressive acts" that imperil U.S. peace and security, but U.S. war-winning capabilities and intentions with respect to the Soviet Union have been absent for many years.

Removing unrealistic requirements and/or revising resources would bring U.S. assets and aims into better balance. Several questions thus seem in order:

— Should strategic nuclear roles/missions be segregated from those for conventional forces? In either instance,

— Is war-winning an essential requirement? If not, what should be substituted? Deterrent capabilities only? Conflict control capabilities? How would changes affect U.S. security?

— Should U.S. armed forces be charged with conducting *prompt* combat operations? If so, how promptly? On what scale? Where? Globally or in selected regions? Relate to active force requirements, the readiness of reserve components, and Soviet threats.

— Should U.S. armed forces be charged with conducting *sustained* combat operations? Under what conditions? Relate to total force size and tooth-to-tail ratios.

— Should this country seek to gain and maintain *general* air and naval supremacy? What are the alternatives? How would adjustments affect the U.S./Soviet balance?

Adjusting Policy Guidelines

Prevailing U.S. policies cause many asymmetries between U.S. and Soviet armed forces. Some mismate ends with means. Each should be analyzed to ascertain its continued advisability.

Review Strategic Nuclear Policies

— What policy would best deter a Soviet first strike? Deterrence based mainly on city targeting or selective capabilities to cope with assorted options?

— What blend of offensive and defensive forces would best preserve deterrence? Would that same blend significantly protect the American people and production base if preventive measures should fail? If not, what compromise, if any, is advisable?

— How well do U.S. SALT II objectives and negotiating policies serve this country's interests? What advantages and disadvantages are evident? What alternatives?

Review General Purpose Policies

— Under what circumstances could the United States unilaterally reduce its arms without endangering security? Relate to U.S. objectives and Soviet capabilities.

— Does a high nuclear threshold in NATO Europe best serve U.S. purposes?. Would changes in policy strengthen or undercut deterrence? In what ways? Would increased risks be serious or inconsequential? Why?
— Are forward defense policies obsolete? If not, what is the optimum balance between U.S. forces in overseas areas and those in strategic reserve?
— Is military assistance an effective policy? How does it improve U.S. security? To what extent? In what areas?
— Should the United States institute stringent controls over the sale of conventional arms? Would the Soviets or others sell where we decline? If so, how would it affect our security?
— Is continued dependence on foreign-flag shipping a sound U.S. policy? Relate to U.S. objectives and commitments. What cost-effective alternatives would improve this country's security?

Adjusting Available Means

Ends, identified as interests, objectives, commitments, and military missions, must equate with money, manpower, and materiel, which amount to means.

Review Manpower Matters

— Should present pay and allowances policies be perpetuated? If not, what options are feasible? Reduced pay scales for regular forces? Constant scales that disregard cost-of-living increases? Lower scales for conscripts if we return to the draft?
— Does the All-Volunteer Force permit an acceptable balance between U.S. and Soviet forces, given other commitments? If not, would conscription be preferable? If not, what other possibilities are open?
— Are U.S. total force concepts sound? If so, should the balance between active and reserve components stay constant or change? Between U.S. forces and allies? In what ways? What substitute policies should be considered? Relate to specific regions, such as Europe and Korea.

Review U.S. Force Structure

Significant improvements in the U.S./Soviet military balance could ensue if ways were found to reduce excessive redundancy and extraneous capabilities, whatever the cause. Answers to questions of the following kind would assist:

— Is a nuclear triad essential to U.S. survival and security. If not, how many systems are essential? Two? Four? More? Why?

— If the structure selected contains one or more components of the present triad, what modernization measures (if any) would be mandatory to maintain a credible posture?
— If any change to the present structure seems required, what combination of systems would be most suitable? Would costs be commensurate with projected threats?
— What force level for each system would serve best? Full justification should pay particular attention to pre- and post-launch survival prospects, plus targeting problems.
— Should air defense aircraft be replaced entirely by surface-to-air missiles? If not, what mix would be most advantageous? To what extent should tactical fighters supplant specialized interceptors for continental air defense?
— Should U.S. tactical nuclear capabilities include IRBMs/MRBMs? Compare strengths and weaknesses with those of tactical aircraft.
— Could much larger inventories of less sophisticated weapons increase U.S. capabilities at reduced costs? What would be the optimum distribution of high-cost, high-performance items to relatively low-cost, low-performance items in specific systems (the so-called hi-lo mix)?
— To what extent could lightly-armored, low-cost fighting vehicles supplant U.S. tanks in NATO Europe? What missions would suffer? How would overall security be influenced in consequence?
— Does continued emphasis on large surface combatants contribute significantly to the U.S./Soviet naval balance? Would capabilities increase if many small, fast ships took their place? Relate to survivability in conventional and nuclear attack environments.
— Would fast, comparatively cheap, easy-to-service gas turbine engines serve future U.S. cruisers and destroyers better than nuclear power? What credits would accrue? What debits could be expected?
— How seriously does the shortage of amphibious lift affect the ability of U.S. Marines to conduct division-sized amphibious assaults? What difference does it make? Relate to American support for NATO's flanks and Middle East contingencies.
— What risks do we run by slighting naval mine warfare capabilities?
— What risks do we run by slighting chemical warfare capabilities? Special concern for chemical defense.
— What advantages would accrue from increased cooperation with NATO on R&D, procurement, and standardization? What disadvantages?

Review U.S. Budget Procedures

Inflation, recession, balance of payments problems, and dollar devaluations inhibit efforts to create U.S. military capabilities that can compete successfully with the Soviet Union. So do defense budget procedures. Two in particular bear review:

— The Congress generally judges individual programs *in isolation.* To what extent would ends and means merge more successfully if Congress consistently examined manpower and materiel *interrelationships* within and between the several Services? What procedural adjustments would be required?

— Total life cycle costs of competitive systems still are not clear. How could DOD and the Congress better assess long-term expenditures in relation to expected capabilities for proposed weapons and equipment?

WRAP-UP

The Present Balance in Perspective

The Soviet Union, alone among all countries in the world today, has sufficient strength to challenge America militarily in many areas of mutual interest overseas and bring decisive power to bear on our homeland. Other countries, large and small, pose additional threats that our leaders may wish to deter or deal with successfully, but the balance between U.S. and Soviet armed forces is critical.

Few trends over the past 15 years are positive from this country's standpoint.[1]

Quantitative changes since the Cuban missile crisis favor the Soviet Union, with scattered exceptions. U.S. *qualitative* superiority, less pronounced than in the past, is slowly slipping away. As it stands:

— High manpower costs inhibit force modernization much more in the United States than in the Soviet Union.

— U.S. technological supremacy shows signs of perishability that results more from policies than potential.

— Soviet nuclear strength increasingly endangers our static force of ICBMs and undefended cities.

— Only a handful of U.S. divisions are free to contend with contingencies without undercutting U.S. capabilities in Europe.

— The U.S. Navy is poorly prepared to cope with Soviet antiship cruise missiles, which severely constrain its mission capabilities.

— The U.S. Merchant Marine could support small-scale contingencies, but even modest attrition from Soviet attacks would sap it quickly.

— Emerging Soviet offensive strength is creating a new range of threats against NATO, whose forces cannot stand large losses.

Mutual Assured Destruction seems less mutual than it was in the last decade. America's land, sea, and air forces alike would be hard pressed to support NATO plans at existing levels and deal concurrently with large-scale diversions, including those caused or sustained by the Kremlin in spots that contain U.S. life lines.

In short, current trends curtail U.S. freedom of action. The upshot abridges abilities of U.S. armed services to deter attacks on the United States, defend this country effectively if deterrence should fail, and safeguard associates whose security is closely linked with our own.

The Problem of U.S. Priorities

Congress and the Executive Branch, which focus on forces and funds, clash annually over expensive programs, each considered essentially in isolation, and each with a life of its own. Economic considerations and technological excellence, rather than pressing requirements, often are the tests. American armed services consequently suffer from structural deficiencies and conceptual shortcomings, including force posture standards that frequently depend on Soviet deployments instead of U.S. demands.

Not all asymmetries in the U.S./Soviet military balance need to be corrected. Some are meaningful only in special context, or are immaterial. Several current samples serve to make that point:

— Soviet military budgets are much bigger than those of the United States, but that imbalance by itself proves little in terms of comparative strength.

— Better bombers, combined with more and bigger ballistic missiles, MIRVs, and MARV, would improve U.S. countersilo capabilities very little, because of our second-strike strategy.

— Matching Moscow's SLBM buildup would serve little purpose, since essential U.S. missions depend on survivable systems, not more submarines, missiles, or warheads.

— Soviet Backfire bombers have a direct bearing on U.S. air defense needs, but are unrelated to requirements for American counterparts or cruise missiles.

— Soviet manpower statistics, which overshadow our own immensely, have only modest meaning militarily, *except* for ground combat forces that compete man to man.

— Civil defense evacuation capabilities, even if extensive, would secure U.S. citizens less successfully than those in Soviet cities.

— NATO will always have more to lose from tactical nuclear combat than the Warsaw Pact, no matter how much we improve its weapons.

Some U.S. shortcomings would lose significance if our leaders scaled down overseas interests, accepting uncertain costs related to reduced world power status, the possible loss of Free World leadership, and long-range security. Others could be corrected, entirely or in part, by policy changes, over which we have complete control. A third course of action could contribute by scrapping inappropriate capabilities.

Step One in the process of obtaining a better balance between American and Soviet military strength is to ascertain our true requirements, based on imperative U.S. interests, objectives, and commitments. Step Two is to reshape U.S. force posture.

More money may be essential, but bolstering budgets would produce few benefits unless U.S. leaders stand back, survey the strategic forest instead of the tactical trees, challenge assumptions, subordinate special interests, stress proven principles, and press for practical change. Most options may seem politically or economically *unattractive*, but straight line projections in many cases could prove *unacceptable* from national security standpoints.

Sound conclusions would allow Congress and the Executive Branch in concert to chart a course that assures America's ability to deter and, if need be, defend successfully against any sort of Soviet armed aggression into the twenty-first century.

Footnote

1. President Carter expressed serious concern over trends in the U.S./Soviet military balance when he delivered a major address on defense and foreign policy at Wake Forest University on March 17, 1978. See excerpts from Carter's Speech on "Defense Policy and Soviet Ties," *New York Times*, March 18, 1978, p. 9; Beecher, William, "Carter Warns of 'Massive' Soviet Buildup," *Boston Globe*, March 18, 1978, p. 1.

Annex A
GLOSSARY

ABM: *See* Ballistic Missile Defense.

ACTIVE DEFENSE: The employment of weapons systems to deter, deflect, or otherwise defeat enemy offensive forces. The term commonly connotes defensive forces, such as interceptor aircraft and antiballistic missiles, but friendly offensive forces customarily contribute. *See also* Passive defense.

ADMINISTRATIVE SUPPORT: Personnel and logistical management. *See also* Logistics.

AEROSPACE DEFENSE: An inclusive term encompassing all measures to intercept and destroy hostile aircraft, missiles, and space vehicles, or otherwise neutralize them. *See also* Air defense and Ballistic missile defense.

AGGRESSION: The first use of armed force to satisfy political, economic, or social aims. *See* Armed Aggression.

AIRBORNE FORCES, OPERATIONS: Ground combat and airlift forces designed primarily to conduct parachute and/or other type air assaults that open up new areas of operation; the employment of such forces in combat. *See also* Airmobile forces, operations.

AIRBORNE WARNING AND CONTROL SYSTEM: An aircraft-mounted radar system designed to detect and track attacking enemy bombers and cruise missiles, then direct defensive actions. Fast reaction computers and reliable communications are featured.

AIR DEFENSE: All measures to intercept and destroy hostile aircraft and cruise missiles, or otherwise neutralize them. Equipment includes interceptor aircraft, surface-to-air missiles, surveillance devices, and ancillary installations.

AIR-LAUNCHED BALLISTIC MISSILE: Any ballistic missile transported by and launched from land- or sea-based aircraft and/or lighter-than-air conveyances, such as blimps, balloons, and dirigibles.

AIRMOBILE FORCES, OPERATIONS: Ground combat units using assigned and/or attached fixed- and rotary-wing aircraft under their control to maneuver rapidly within given areas of operation; the employment of such forces in combat. *See also* Airborne forces, operations.

AIR SUPERIORITY: Dominance in the air to a degree that permits friendly land, sea, and air forces to operate at specific times and places without prohibitive interference by enemy air forces.

ALBM: *See* Air-launched ballistic missile.

ALCM: *See* Cruise missile.

ALERT SYSTEM: Personnel and communications devices of all sorts (such as radios, telephones, and sirens) needed to transmit warnings from surveillance elements to defense forces and/or the general populace.

AMPHIBIOUS OPERATIONS: An assault on a hostile shore launched from the sea by naval and ground forces trained, organized and equipped for that purpose. *See also* Amphibious ships.

AMPHIBIOUS SHIPS: Navy vessels specifically designed to transport, land, and support forces in amphibious assault operations, loading and unloading without external assistance. *See also* Amphibious operations.

ANTIBALLISTIC MISSILE: Any missile capable of destroying hostile ballistic missiles or their payloads in flight at short, medium, or long-range inside or outside the atmosphere. It may be armed with any sort of weapon (laser, maser, nuclear, or conventional), and may be single-, dual-, or multipurpose (such as anti-missile and anti-aircraft).

ANTISUBMARINE WARFARE: All measures to reduce or nullify the effectiveness of hostile submarines; in relation to this study, specifically concerns operations to detect, locate, track, and destroy submarines used for strategic nuclear and conventional purposes.

APPLIED RESEARCH: The use of basic scientific knowledge to solve technological problems. *See also* Basic research.

AREA DEFENSE: All measures to protect key targets of any kind (cities, for example) by engaging enemy forces at a considerable distance. *See also* Point target.

AREA TARGET: A target whose dimensions encompass two or more geographic coordinates on operational maps. Cities are representative.

ARMED AGGRESSION: The first use of armed force to satisfy political, economic, or social aims.

ARMS CONTROL: Explicit or implicit international agreements that govern the numbers, types, characteristics, deployment, and use of armed forces and armaments. *See also* Arms limitation; Disarmament.

ARMS LIMITATION: An agreement to restrict quantitative holdings of or qualitative improvements in specific armaments or weapons systems. *See also* Arms control; Disarmament.

ASSUMPTION: A supposition concerning the current situation or future events, presumed to be true in the absence of positive proof to the contrary. Used for planning and decision-making purposes.

ASSURED DESTRUCTION: A highly reliable ability to inflict unacceptable damage on any aggressor or combination of aggressors at any time during the course of a nuclear exchange, even after absorbing a surprise first strike.

ASW: *See* Antisubmarine warfare.

ATTACK AIRCRAFT: Tactical aircraft used primarily for interdiction and close air support purposes. *See also* Fighter aircraft.

ATTACK CARRIER: An aircraft carrier designed to accommodate high-performance fighter/attack aircraft whose primary purpose is to project offensive striking power against targets ashore and afloat.

ATTACK SUBMARINE: A submarine designed primarily to destroy enemy merchant shipping and naval vessels, including other submarines.

AWACS. *See* Airborne warning and control system.

BALANCE: *See* Military balance; Strategic balance.

BALLISTIC MISSILE: A pilotless projectile propelled into space by one or more rocket boosters. Thrust is terminated at some early stage, after which reentry vehicles follow trajectories that are governed mainly by gravity and aerodynamic drag. Mid-course corrections and terminal guidance permit only minor modifications to the flight path. *See also* Reentry vehicle.

BALLISTIC MISSILE DEFENSE: All measures to intercept and destroy hostile ballistic missiles, or otherwise neutralize them. Equipment includes weapons; target acquisition, tracking and guidance radars; and ancillary installations. *See also* Air defense.

BALLISTIC MISSILE EARLY WARNING SYSTEM: An electronic surveillance screen designed to detect attacks by ballistic missiles and notify authorities. The three U.S. BMEWS stations, tied to NORAD's Operations Center, also have tracking capabilities.

BASIC RESEARCH: All efforts to increase knowledge of natural environments and scientific phenomena. *See also* Applied research.

BATTLE MANAGEMENT: Command/control personnel, equipment, and procedures needed to evaluate and direct military operations as situations develop so that appropriate adjustments in force deployments and tactics proceed efficiently.

BIOLOGICAL WARFARE: The use of living microorganisms (such as bacteria and viruses), toxic agents derived from dead microorganisms, and plant growth regulators to produce lethal or nonlethal casualties among humans, animals, and/or plants; defenses against such actions. *See also* Chemical warfare.

BLAST SHELTER: Any structure, natural or manmade, that provides substantial protection against overpressures caused by nuclear explosions. Effectiveness is determined by the yield of the weapon, proximity to ground zero, and durability of the structure. Subterranean sites, such as subway stations, caves, and mine shafts, are most effective. Protection against fallout is a bonus effect. *See also* Fallout shelter.

BMD: *See* Ballistic missile defense.

BMEWS: *See* Ballistic Missile Early Warning System.

BOMB: An explosive weapon without propulsion which is dropped from any sort of aircraft. Gravity and speeds at release time exert primary forces on conventional types, but "smart" bombs can be steered by electronic or other means.

BW: *See* Biological Warfare

CALCULATED RISK: The deliberate acceptance of gaps between ends and means in accord with estimates that enemies are unlikely to initiate actions that will interfere unacceptably with friendly aims. *See also* Intention; Risk.

CAPABILITY: The ability of a country or coalition of countries to execute specific courses of action. Capabilities are conditioned by many variables, including the balance of military forces, time, space, terrain, and weather. *See also* Intention.

CD: *See* Civil Defense.

CEP: *See* Circular Error Probable.

CHEMICAL WARFARE: The use of asphyxiating, poisonous, and corrosive gases, flames, aerosols, liquid sprays, and smoke of various sorts to produce lethal or nonlethal casualties among humans and animals and/or damage to plants and material; defense against such actions. *See also* Biological warfare.

CIRCULAR ERROR PROBABLE: The radius of a circle within which half of all missiles/projectiles delivered by any given weapons system are expected to land. Used to indicate and compare accuracies.

CIVIL DEFENSE: Passive measures designed to minimize the effects of enemy action on all aspects of civil life, particularly to protect the population and production base. Includes emergency steps to repair or restore vital utilities and facilities.

CIVIL RESERVE AIR FLEET: U.S. commercial aircraft and crews allocated in emergency for exclusive military use in international and domestic service.

CLOSE AIR SUPPORT: Air strikes against targets near enough to ground combat units that detailed coordination between participating air and ground elements is required.

COLD LAUNCH: A "pop up" technique that ejects ballistic missiles from silos or submarines using power plants that are separate from the delivery vehicles. Primary ignition is delayed until projectiles are safely clear of the launcher.

COLD WAR: A state of international tension at the lower end of the conflict spectrum, wherein political, economic, technological, sociological, psychological, paramilitary, and military measures short of sustained armed combat are orchestrated to attain national objectives.

COLLATERAL CASUALTIES AND DAMAGE: Physical harm done to persons and property collocated with or adjacent to targets. Collateral effects may be welcome or unwanted, depending on circumstances.

COMBAT POWER: A compilation of capabilities related to a specific military balance between countries or coalitions. Ingredients include numbers and types of forces; technological attributes of weapons and equipment; discipline; morale; pride; confidence; hardiness; élan; loyalty; training; combat experience; command/control arrangements; staying power, and leadership. Combat power is illusory unless accompanied by the national will to use it as required. *See also* Military balance; National will.

COMMAND AND CONTROL: An arrangement of facilities, equipment, personnel, and procedures used to acquire, process, and disseminate data needed by decision-makers to plan, direct, and control operations.

COMMITMENT: An obligation or pledge to carry out or support a given national policy. *See also* National security policies.

CONFLICT SPECTRUM: A continuum of hostilities that ranges from sub-crisis maneuvering in cold-war situations to the most violent form of general war.

CONTAINMENT: Measures to discourage or prevent the expansion of enemy territorial holdings and/or influence. Specifically, a U.S. policy directed against communist expansion.

CONTINGENCY PLANS AND OPERATIONS: Preparation for major events that can reasonably be anticipated and that probably would have a detrimental effect on national security; actions in case such events occur.

CONTROLLED COUNTERFORCE WAR: War in which one or both sides concentrate on reducing enemy strategic retaliatory forces in a bargaining situation, and take special precautions to minimize collateral casualties and damage. *See also* Controlled war.

CONTROLLED WAR: A war waged in response to the continuous receipt and evaluation of information concerning changes in the situation, combined with the competence to adjust accordingly. *See also* Controlled counterforce war.

CONVENTIONAL (FORCES, WAR, WEAPONS): Military organizations, hostilities, and hardware that exclude nuclear, chemical, and biological capabilities.

COST EFFECTIVENESS: A condition that matches ends with means in ways that create maximum capabilities at minimum expense.

COUNTER CITY: *See* Countervalue.

COUNTERFORCE: The employment of strategic air and missile forces to destroy, or render impotent, military capabilities of an enemy force. Bombers and their bases, ballistic missile submarines, ICBM silos, ABM and air defense installations, command and control centers, and nuclear stockpiles are typical counterforce targets. *See also* Countervalue.

COUNTERVALUE: A strategic concept which calls for the destruction or neutralization of selected enemy population centers, industries, resources, and/or institutions which constitute the social fabric of a society. *See also* Counterforce.

CRAF: *See* Civil Reserve Air Fleet.

CREDIBILITY: Clear evidence that capabilities and intentions are sufficient to support purported policies.

CRISIS RELOCATION: A civil defense measure that involves evacuating people from cities to comparative safehavens in the surrounding countryside as one means of constraining casualties in nuclear conflict. Displacement can be a preemptive move or take place upon receipt of strategic warning. *See also* Dispersal; Evacuation.

CRUISE MISSILE: A pilotless aircraft, propelled by an airbreathing engine, that operates entirely within the earth's atmosphere. Thrust continues throughout its flight. Air provides most of the lift. Inflight guidance and control can be accomplished remotely or by onboard equipment. Conventional and nuclear warheads are available.

CRUISER: A large, long-endurance surface warship armed for independent offensive operations against surface ships and land targets. Also acts as an escort to protect aircraft carriers, merchantmen, and other ships against surface or air attack. May have an antisubmarine capability. Own aircraft-handling capability restricted to one or two float planes, helicopters, or other short take-off and landing types.

CW: *See* Chemical Warfare

DAMAGE LIMITATION: Active and/or passive efforts to restrict the level and/or geographic extent of devastation during war. Includes counterforce actions of all kinds, as well as civil defense measures. *See also* Counterforce; Civil defense.

DEFENSE: Measures taken by a country or coalition of countries to resist political, military, economic, social, psychological, and/or technological attacks. Defensive capabilities reinforce deterrence, and vice versa. *See also* Deterrence.

DEFENSE-IN-DEPTH: Protective measures in successive positions along axes of enemy advance, as opposed to a single line of resistance. Designed to absorb and progressively weaken enemy penetrations.

DEPLOYMENT: The allocation of manpower and/or materiel to operational units; positioning those units in desired areas.

DEPRESSED TRAJECTORY: The flight path of a ballistic missile fired at an angle to the ground significantly lower than standard launches. Such shots have short flight times and are invisible to line-of-sight radars longer than attacks along conventional arcs.

DESTROYER: A medium-sized warship configured to escort and protect other ships against air, submarine, and surface attacks. May also be used for independent offensive operations against enemy ships or land targets. Some embark one or two helicopters.

DETENTE: Lessening of tensions in international relations. May be achieved formally or informally.

DETERRENCE: Steps taken to prevent opponents from initiating armed actions and to inhibit escalation if combat occurs. Threats of force predominate. *See also* Defense; Escalation.

DEVELOPMENT: A three-phase process. Phase I, Concepts; identifies options, sets priorities, and defines the project. Exploration and experimentation take place. Phase II, Validation; produces "brass board" models used to establish program characteristics, including technical problems, costs, and schedules. Phase III, Engineering; terminates with "hardware" models (prototypes) ready for test and evaluation. *See also* Applied research; Basic research; Deployment; Test and Evaluation.

DEW LINE: *See* Distant Early Warning Line.

DISARMAMENT: The reduction of armed forces and/or armaments as a result of unilateral initiatives or international agreement. *See also* Arms control; Arms limitation.

DISPERSAL: A civil defense measure that physically separates industrial plants and other elements of the national production base, either within cities or in outlying areas, to reduce destruction during a nuclear war.

The term also applies to Soviet crisis relocation plans which prescribe the dispersion of city caretaker crews to safehavens in surrounding areas during off-duty hours.

DISTANT EARLY WARNING LINE: The northernmost stations in NORAD's air defense surveillance system. The line, which stretches across the arctic from Alaska to the Atlantic, currently comprises 31 isolated radar stations.

DIVISION EQUIVALENT: Separate brigades, regiments, and comparable combat forces whose aggregate capabilities approximate those of a division, except for staying power.

ECCM: *See* Electronic counter-countermeasures.

ECM: *See* Electronic countermeasures.

ELECTRONIC COUNTERMEASURES: A form of electronic warfare that prevents or degrades effective enemy uses of the electromagnetic spectrum. Jamming is a typical tactic. *See also* Electronic counter-countermeasures.

ELECTRONIC COUNTER-COUNTERMEASURES: A form of electronic warfare taken to insure effective use of the electromagnetic spectrum despite enemy ECM efforts. *See also* Electronic countermeasures.

ENDS: National security interests, objectives, and commitments, along with military roles and missions, which establish aims to be accomplished. *See also* Means.

ESCALATION: An increase, deliberate or unpremeditated, in the scope and/or intensity of a conflict.

ESCORT: Cruisers, destroyers, frigates, and other surface warships expressly configured to defend other ships against enemy attack. May be multipurpose (e.g. anti-air, anti-submarine) or unipurpose. May also be assigned independent offensive missions. *See also* Cruiser; Destroyer; Frigate.

ESSENTIAL EQUIVALENCE: A force structure standard that demands capabilities approximately equal in overall effectiveness to those of particular opponents, but does not insist on numerical equality in all cases. *See also* Parity.

EVACUATION: A civil defense measure that seeks to reduce casualties in a nuclear war by dispatching city populations to safehavens in the surrounding countryside. *See also* Crisis relocation; Dispersal.

FALLOUT: The precipitation of radioactive particles from clouds of debris produced by nuclear blasts. Dangers from surface bursts are most severe, because huge amounts of material are sucked up mushroom stems. Winds aloft may then waft a deadly mist over immense areas.

FALLOUT SHELTER: Any structure, natural or manmade, that provides substantial protection against radioactive particles precipitated from clouds of debris caused by nuclear blasts. *See also* Blast shelter.

FIGHTER AIRCRAFT: Tactical aircraft used primarily to gain and maintain air superiority. *See also* Attack aircraft.

FIRST-STRIKE: The first offensive move of a war. As applied to general nuclear war, it implies the ability to eliminate effective retaliation by the opposition. *See also* Second-strike.

FIRST USE: The initial employment of specific military measures, such as nuclear weapons, during the conduct of a war. A belligerent could execute a second strike in response to aggression, yet be the first to employ nuclear weapons. *See also* First-strike.

FLEXIBILITY: Capabilities that afford countries and weapons systems a range of options, and facilitate smooth adjustment when situations change. *See also* Flexible response.

FLEXIBLE RESPONSE: A strategy predicated on meeting aggression at an appropriate level or place with the capability of escalating the level of conflict if required or desired. *See also* Flexibility.

FOBS: *See* Fractional Orbit Bombardment System.

FORWARD BASE: A military installation maintained on foreign soil or on a distant possession that is conveniently located with regard to actual or potential areas of operations.

FORWARD DEFENSE: A strategic concept which calls for containing or repulsing military aggression as close to the original line of contact as possible to protect important areas.

FRACTIONAL ORBIT BOMBARDMENT SYSTEM: A method of launching ballistic missiles into low orbit (about 100 miles). Retrorockets fired after less than one revolution permit a rapid descent to targets, reducing defensive radar reaction times. FOBS attacks from the Soviet Union could approach the United States from the south, thus circumventing most of our current surveillance and tracking devices.

FREE ROCKET: A missile with completely self-contained propellant package that is neither guided nor controlled in flight.

FRIGATE: A medium to small surface warship configured to escort and protect other ships against surface, air, or submarine attack. May embark one or two helicopters. *See also* Escort.

FROG: *See* Free rocket.

GAP FILLER RADAR: Small, unattended air defense surveillance radars once used by the United States to supplement long-range radars whose line-of-sight coverage was interrupted by terrain masks or other phenomena.

GENERAL PURPOSE FORCES: All combat forces not designed primarily to accomplish strategic offensive/defensive or strategic mobility missions.

GENERAL WAR: Armed conflict between major powers in which the national survival of one or more belligerent is in jeopardy. Commonly reserved for a showdown between the United States and U.S.S.R., featuring nuclear weapons.

GUIDED MISSILE: Any unmanned missile whose trajectory or flight path can be corrected by internal or external mechanisms. *See also* Guided munitions.

GUIDED MUNITIONS: Any bomb or missile warhead that can be steered to its target by internal or external mechanisms. *See also* Guided missile; Maneuverable reentry vehicle.

HARD-SITE ICBM: Any ICBM in a silo that provides substantial protection against nuclear attack. *See also* Hard target; Intercontinental ballistic missile.

HARD TARGET: A point or area protected to some significant degree against the blast, heat, and radiation effects of nuclear explosions of particular yields. *See also* Soft target.

HEAVY BOMBER: A multi-engine aircraft with intercontinental range, designed specifically to engage targets whose destruction would reduce an enemy's capacity and/or will to wage war. *See also* Medium bomber.

HEAVY ICBM: U.S. Titan II; Soviet SS-7, SS-8, SS-9, SS-18, SS-19 for purposes of this study. *See also* Light ICBM.

HEAVY TANK: Tanks weighing more than 60 tons are generally designated as "heavies," although the United States no longer uses heavy, medium, and light as classifications. *See also* Light tank; Medium tank.

HIGH-RISK AREA: Major military installations; metropolises; lesser cities of great industrial, commercial, or transportation value; lesser cities situated next to major military targets.

HIGH THRESHOLD: An intangible line between levels and types of conflict across which one or more antagonists plan to escalate with great reluctance after other courses of action fail, or which they could be compelled to cross only if subjected to immense pressures. *See also* Low threshold and Threshold.

HI-LO MIX: Mingling high-cost, high performance items with relatively low-cost, low performance items in any given weapons category to achieve the best balance between quantity and quality in ways that maximize capabilities and minimize expense.

ICBM: *See* Intercontinental ballistic missile.

INERTIAL GUIDANCE: A system that measures acceleration and relates it to distances traveled in certain directions. Designed to steer ballistic missiles over pre-determined courses, using data generated solely by devices in the missiles.

INTENTION: The determination of a country or coalition to use capabilities in specific ways at specific times and places. Intentions are conditioned by many variables, including interests, objectives, policies, principles, commitments, and national will. *See also* Capability; National will.

INTERCEPTOR: An air defense aircraft designed to identify and/or destroy hostile airbreathing weapons systems such as bombers and cruise missiles.

INTERCONTINENTAL BALLISTIC MISSILE: A ballistic missile with a range of 3,000 to 8,000 nautical miles. *See also* Ballistic missile.

INTERDICTION: Operations to prevent or impede enemy use of an area or route.

INTERESTS: *See* National security interests.

INTERMEDIATE-RANGE BALLISTIC MISSILE: A ballistic missile with a range of 1,500 to 3,000 nautical miles. *See also* Ballistic missile.

IRBM: *See* Intermediate-range ballistic missile.

KILOTON: The yield of a nuclear weapon equivalent to 1,000 tons of TNT (trinitrotoluene). *See also* Megaton.

KT: *See* Kiloton.

LASER (Light Amplification by Stimulated Emission of Radiation): Light beams which can be focused to provide force that has potential applications for military weapons. *See also* Maser.

LAUNCH-ON-WARNING: Retaliation triggered in time to prevent any pre-launch attrition to friendly strike forces by enemy nuclear attacks already in progress.

LIGHT ICBM: U.S. Minutemen; Soviet SS-11, SS-13, SS-16, SS-17 for purposes of this study. *See also* Heavy ICBM.

LIGHT TANK: Tanks weighing less than 40 tons are generally designated as "light," although the United States no longer uses heavy, medium, and light classifications. *See also* Heavy tank; Medium tank.

LIMITED WAR: Armed encounters, exclusive of incidents, in which one or more major powers or their proxies voluntarily exercise various types and degrees of restraint to prevent unmanageable escalation. Objectives, forces, weapons, targets, and geographic areas all can be limited.

LINES OF COMMUNICATION: Land, sea, and aerospace routes essential to the conduct of international security affairs, particularly the deployment of armed forces and associated logistic support.

LOGISTICS: Plans and operations associated with the design, development, acquisition, storage, movement, distribution, maintenance, evacuation, and hospitalization of personnel; the acquisition or construction, maintenance, operation, and disposition of facilities; and the acquisition or furnishing of services.

LOITER TIME: The length of time an aircraft can remain aloft in any given location, pending receipt of further orders. Depends primarily on fuel capacity, consumption rates, refueling capabilities, and pilot fatigue. Loiter capabilities for missiles are a future possibility.

LOOK-DOWN, SHOOT-DOWN CAPABILITY: Airborne radars that discriminate aerial targets from ground clutter below, combined with air-to-air weapons systems that can destroy supersonic targets. The system alleviates low-level air defense problems associated with ground surveillance and tracking radars.

LOW THRESHOLD: An intangible line between levels and types of conflict across which one or more antagonists plan to escalate with scant regret, or which they would be compelled to cross quickly if subjected to pressures. *See also* High threshold and Threshold.

MAD: *See* Magnetic anomaly detection.

MAGNETIC ANOMALY DETECTION: ASW equipment designed to pinpoint the location of hostile submarines by detecting disturbances in normal magnetic fields of force.

MANEUVERABLE REENTRY VEHICLE: A missile warhead or confusion device that can be steered to its target by internal or external mechanisms. *See also* Penetration aid; Warhead.

MANUAL CONTROL CENTER: A U.S. air defense facility designed to receive early warning of unidentified and/or hostile aircraft, then direct intercept operations. Capabilities are severely constrained, since all functions depend on actions by on-site personnel. *See also* Semi-Automatic Ground Environment; Regional Operations Control Center.

MARV: *See* Maneuverable reentry vehicle.

MASER (Microwave Amplification by Stimulated Emission of Radiation): Beams of very short electromagnetic waves which can be focused to provide energy that has potential applications for city defense weapons. *See also* Laser.

MASSIVE RETALIATION: The act of countering aggression of any type with tremendous destructive power; particularly a crushing nuclear response to any provocation deemed serious enough to warrant military action.

MCC: *See* Manual Control Center.

MEANS: Money, manpower, materiel, and other resources converted into capabilities that contribute to the accomplishment of national security aims. *See also* Capability; Ends.

MEDIUM BOMBER: A multi-engined aircraft that lacks intercontinental range without in-flight refueling, but is suitable for strategic bombing on one-way intercontinental missions, even lacking tanker support.

MEDIUM-RANGE BALLISTIC MISSILE: A ballistic missile with a range of 600 to 1,500 nautical miles. *See also* Ballistic missile.

MEDIUM TANK: Tanks weighing between 40 and 60 tons generally are designated as "mediums," although the United States no longer uses heavy, medium, and light classifications. *See also* Heavy tank; Light tank.

MEGATON: The yield of a nuclear weapon equivalent to 1,000,000 tons of TNT (trinitrotoluene); 1,000 kilotons, *See also* Kiloton.

MERCHANT MARINE: All non-military vessels of a nation, publicly- and privately-owned, together with crews, which engage in domestic and/or international trade and commerce.

MID-COURSE CORRECTION: Adjustment of a ballistic missile flight path between boost and reentry phases.

MILITARY BALANCE: The comparative combat power of two competing countries or coalitions. *See also* Combat power; Strategic balance.

MILITARY POWER: *See* Combat power.

MILITARY STRATEGY: The art and science of employing military power under all circumstances to attain national security objectives by applying force or the threat of force. *See also* Tactics.

MIRV: *See* Multiple independently targetable reentry vehicle.

MISSION: A function or task assigned to specific armed forces.

MOBILE MISSILE: Any ballistic or cruise missile mounted on and/or fired from a movable platform, such as a truck, train, ground effects machine, ship, or aircraft.

MOBILIZATION: The act of preparing for war or other emergencies by assembling and organizing raw materials; focusing industrial efforts on national security objectives; marshalling and readying Reserve and National Guard units and individuals for active military service; and/or activating and readying new military organizations filled with personnel inducted from civilian life.

MRBM: *See* Medium-range ballistic missile.

MRV: *See* Multiple reentry vehicle.

MT: *See* Megaton.

MULTIPLE INDEPENDENTLY TARGETABLE REENTRY VEHICLE: A missile payload comprising two or more warheads that can engage separate targets. *See also* Multiple reentry vehicle; Reentry vehicle.

MULTIPLE REENTRY VEHICLE: A missile payload comprising two or more warheads that engage the same target. *See also* Multiple independently targetable reentry vehicle; Reentry vehicle.

MUTUAL ASSURED DESTRUCTION: Reciprocal capabilities of two or more rivals to inflict unacceptable damage on each other at any time during the course of a nuclear war, even after absorbing a surprise first strike. *See also* Assured Destruction.

NATIONAL COMMAND AUTHORITIES: The top national security decision-makers of a country. In the United States, they are limited to the President, the Secretary of Defense, and their duly deputized alternates or successors.

NATIONAL INTERESTS: A highly generalized concept of elements that constitute a state's compelling needs, including self-preservation, independence, national integrity, military security, and economic well-being.

NATIONAL MILITARY COMMAND SYSTEM: The priority component of the World-wide Military Command and Control System, designed to support the National Command Authorities and the Joint Chiefs of Staff. NORAD and its affiliates are key centers. *See also* World-wide Military Command and Control System.

NATIONAL OBJECTIVES: The fundamental aims, goals, or purposes of a nation toward which policies are directed and energies are applied. These may be short-, mid-, or long-range in nature.

NATIONAL POLICIES: Broad courses of action or statements of guidance adopted by a government in pursuit of national objectives.

NATIONAL POWER: The sum total of any nation's capabilities or potential derived from available political, economic, military, geographic, social, scientific, and technological resources. Leadership and national will are the unifying factors.

NATIONAL SECURITY: The protection of a nation from all types of external aggression, espionage, hostile reconnaissance, sabotage, subversion, annoyance, and other inimical influences. *See also* National security interests, National security objectives, and National security policies.

NATIONAL SECURITY INTERESTS: Those national interests primarily concerned with preserving a state from harm. *See also* National interests and National security.

NATIONAL SECURITY OBJECTIVES: Those national objectives primarily concerned with shielding national interests from threats, both foreign and domestic. *See also* National objectives and National security.

NATIONAL SECURITY POLICIES: Those national policies which provide guidance primarily for attaining national security objectives. *See also* National policies and National security.

NATIONAL WILL: The temper and morale of the people, as they influence a nation's ability to satisfy national security interests and/or attain national security objectives.

NAVAL SUPERIORITY: Dominance on the high seas to a degree that permits friendly land, aerospace, and naval forces to operate at specific times and places on, over, or adjacent to the high seas without prohibitive interference by enemy naval elements. *See also* Sea control.

NCA: *See* National Command Authorities.
NMCS: *See* National Military Command System.
NORAD: *See* North American Air Defense Command.

NORTH AMERICAN AIR DEFENSE COMMAND: A combined U.S. and Canadian headquarters responsible for global aerospace surveillance and the defense of North America against air and ballistic missile attack. Capabilities in the latter regard currently are confined to early warning.

NUCLEAR DELIVERY SYSTEM: A nuclear weapon, together with its means of propulsion and associated installations. Includes carriers such as aircraft, ships, and motor vehicles. *See also* Nuclear weapon.

NUCLEAR WEAPON: A bomb, missile warhead, or other deliverable ordnance item (as opposed to an experimental device) that explodes as a result of energy released by atomic nuclei through fission, fusion, or both. *See also* Nuclear delivery system.

NUCLEAR YIELD: The explosive power of a nuclear bomb or warhead expressed in kilotons or megatons.

OBJECTIVE: *See* National security objectives.

OPERATIONS AND MAINTENANCE: All activities of armed forces, in peace and in war, to carry out strategic, tactical, training, logistic, and administrative missions.

OTH RADAR: *See* Over-the-horizon radar.
OTH-B RADAR: *See* Over-the-horizon backscatter radar.

OVER-THE-HORIZON BACKSCATTER RADAR: An OTH radar that transmits signals that extend beyond line-of-sight along the ground. Effective range is about 1,800 miles. If signals detect an airborne target, return waves reflect back along the same path to a receiver near the transmitter. *See also* Over-the-horizon radar.

OVER-THE-HORIZON RADAR: A surveillance radar whose signals hug the earth's surface for distances well beyond line-of-sight, bounce off the ionosphere and return to earth several times in sawtoothed waves, finally activating a receiver on the far side of the globe. Data gathered is very general, and must be confirmed/refined by other sources. *See also* Over-the-Horizon Backscatter Radar.

OVERKILL: Destructive capabilities in excess of those which logically should be adequate to destroy specified targets and/or attain specific security objectives.

PAR: *See* Perimeter Acquisition Radar.

PARITY: A force structure standard which demands that capabilities of specific forces and weapons systems be approximately equal in effectiveness to enemy counterparts. *See also* Essential equivalence.

PASSIVE DEFENSE: All measures, other than the application of armed force, taken to deter or minimize the effects of enemy actions. These include the use of cover, concealment, dispersion, protective construction, mobility, and subterfuge. *See also* Active defense.

PAYLOAD: The weapon and/or cargo capacity of any aircraft or missile system, expressed variously in pounds; numbers of bombs, air-to-air and air-to-surface missiles, CW canisters, guns, sensors, ECM packets, etc; and in terms of missile warhead yields (kilotons, megatons).

PENAID: *See* Penetration aid.

PENETRATION AID: Any confusion device (such as decoys, chaff, and electronic countermeasures) or defense suppression weapon (such as standoff missiles) used by strategic offensive forces to assist in striking targets.

PERIMETER ACQUISITION RADAR: That segment of the U.S. Sentinel and Safeguard ABM systems which was designed to track ballistic missiles beginning at a maximum range of about 1,000 miles and predict probable impact points.

POINT DEFENSE: All measures to protect key targets of any kind (cities for example) by engaging enemy forces during terminal stages of the attack. *See also* Area defense.

POINT TARGET: A target whose dimensions are small enough to be identified by a single coordinate on operational maps. Missile silos are representative.

POLICY: *See* National security policies.

POST-LAUNCH SURVIVABILITY: The ability of any given delivery system to breach enemy defenses and attack designated targets. *See also* Pre-launch survivability.

POSTURE: The combined strategic intentions, capabilities, and vulnerabilities of a country or coalition of countries, including the strength, disposition, and readiness of its armed forces.

PRECISION-GUIDED MUNITIONS: *See* Guided Munitions.

PREEMPTIVE WAR: Conflict initiated on the basis of incontrovertible evidence that an enemy attack is imminent. *See also* Preventive war.

PRE-LAUNCH SURVIVABILITY: The ability of any given delivery system to weather a surprise first-strike successfully and retaliate. *See also* Post-launch survivability.

PREVENTIVE WAR: Conflict initiated in the belief that armed combat, while not imminent, is inevitable, and that to delay would involve greater risk. *See also* Preemptive war.

PRODUCTION BASE: Indigenous assets that provide food, clothing, housing, and other items needed to sustain a national population in peacetime and reconstitute after being ravaged by war, including raw materials as well as commerce, industry, transportation, and power facilities.

PROXY WAR: A form of limited war in which great powers avoid a direct military confrontation by furthering their national security interests and objectives through conflict in which associates, not principals, participate. *See also* Limited war.

RADAR CROSS-SECTION: The picture produced by recording radar waves reflected from a given target surface. The size of the image is not determined entirely by the size of objects. Structural shape, the refractory characteristics of materials, and locations with regard to receivers all are important.

RAPID RELOAD CAPABILITY: The ability of a delivery system to conduct multiple strikes. Land-mobile missiles and hard-site ICBMs have the potential. Submarines conceivably could be replenished at sea, but a significantly greater time lag would occur.

READINESS: The ability of specific armed forces to respond in times allotted and thereafter perform assigned missions effectively.

REENTRY VEHICLE: That part of a ballistic missile designed to reenter the earth's atmosphere during terminal stages of its trajectory.

REGIONAL OPERATIONS CONTROL CENTER: A U.S. air defense facility designed to direct peacetime airspace sovereignty operations after replacing SAGE. Military radars, assisted by sets belonging to the Federal Aviation Administration, will furnish input. *See also* Manual Control Center; Semi-Automatic Ground Environment.

REINFORCEMENT: Augmenting military capabilities in any given area by introducing locally-available and/or strategic reserves. *See also* Strategic reserve.

RELOCATION: *See* Crisis relocation.

RESEARCH: *See* Applied research; Basic research.

RESERVE COMPONENT: Armed forces not in active service. U.S. Reserve Components include the Army National Guard and Army Reserve; the Naval Reserve; the Marine Corps Reserve; the Air National Guard, and Air Force Reserve.

RESERVES: *See* Reserve component; Strategic reserve.

RISK: The danger of disadvantage, defeat, or destruction that results from a gap between ends and means. *See also* Calculated risk.

ROCC: *See* Regional Operations Control Center.

ROLE: *See* Mission.

RV: *See* Reentry vehicle.

SAGE: *See* Semi-Automatic Ground Environment.

SALT: *See* Strategic Arms Limitation Talks.

SEA CONTROL: The employment of naval forces, supplemented by land and aerospace forces as appropriate, to destroy enemy naval forces, suppress enemy oceangoing commerce, protect vital shipping lanes, and establish local superiority in areas of naval operations. *See also* Naval superiority.

SECOND-STRIKE: A strategic concept which excludes preemptive and preventive actions before the onset of a war. After an aggressor initiates hostilities, the defender retaliates. In general nuclear war, this implies the ability to survive a surprise first strike and respond effectively. *See also* First-strike.

SEMI-AUTOMATIC GROUND ENVIRONMENT: A network of U.S. air defense facilities designed to receive early warning of unidentified and/or hostile aircraft, then direct intercept operations. Our standard capability since the early 1960s. *See also* Manual Control Center; Regional Operations Control Center.

SHELTER: *See* Blast shelter; Fallout shelter.

SILO: Underground facilities for a hard-site ballistic missile and/or crew, designed to provide pre-launch protection against atomic effects. High-yield, precision weapons are needed to destroy the most durable construction.

SINGLE-INTEGRATED OPERATIONAL PLAN: The U.S. contingency plan for strategic retaliatory strikes in event of a nuclear war. Targets, timing, tactics, and force requirements are considered for a variety of responses. Prepared by the Joint Strategic Target Planning Staff, which is collocated with SAC Headquarters at Offutt AFB outside Omaha, Nebraska.

SIOP: *See* Single Integrated Operational Plan.

SLANT RANGE: The line-of-sight distance between two points not at the same elevation.

SLBM: *See* Submarine/sea-launched ballistic missile.

SLCM: *See* Submarine/sea-launched cruise missile.

SOFT TARGET: A target not protected against the blast, heat, and radiation produced by nuclear explosions. There are many degrees of softness. Some missiles and aircraft, for example, are built in ways that ward off certain effects, but they are "soft" in comparison with shelters and silos. *See also* Hard target.

SPECIFIED COMMAND: A top-echelon U.S. combatant organization with regional or functional responsibilities, which normally is composed of forces from one military service. It has a broad, continuing mission and is established by the President, through the Secretary of Defense, with the advice and assistance of the Joint Chiefs of Staff. *See also* Unified command.

STABILITY: *See* Strategic stability.

STANDOFF MISSILE: An air-to-surface missile carried by military aircraft for air defense suppression purposes or to strike primary targets. Permits aircraft to attack multiple targets without physically penetrating to any of them, thus reducing fuel requirements and dangers to crews.

STRATEGIC AIR WAR: Aerospace operations directed against the enemy's war-making capacity. Typical targets include industry, stockpiles of raw materials and finished products, power systems, transportation and communication centers, strategic weapons systems, and cities.

STRATEGIC AIRLIFT: Transport aircraft, both military and civilian, used to move armed forces, equipment, and supplies expeditiously over long distances, especially intercontinentally. *See also* Tactical airlift.

STRATEGIC ARMS LIMITATION TALKS: Negotiations between the United States and the Soviet Union to curtail the expansion of, and if possible reduce, strategic offensive and defensive weapons systems of both countries in an equitable fashion. *See also* Arms control; Arms limitation.

STRATEGIC BALANCE: The comparative national power of two competing countries or coalitions. *See also* Military balance; National power.

STRATEGIC DEFENSE: The strategy and forces designed primarily to protect a nation, its outposts and/or allies from the hazards of general war. It features defense against missiles, both land- and sea-launched, and long-range bombers. *See also* Strategic offense.

STRATEGIC MOBILITY: The ability to shift personnel, equipment, and supplies effectively and expeditiously between theaters of operation. *See also* Strategic airlift; Strategic sealift; Tactical mobility.

STRATEGIC OFFENSE: The strategy and forces designed primarily to destroy the enemy's war-making capacity during general war or to so degrade it that the opposition collapses. *See also* Strategic defense; Strategic retaliatory (concepts and forces).

STRATEGIC RESERVE: Uncommitted forces of a country or coalition of countries which are intended to support national security interests and objectives, as required.

STRATEGIC RETALIATORY (CONCEPTS AND FORCES): Second-strike strategies and forces designed primarily to destroy the enemy's war-making capacity during general war or to so degrade it that the opposition collapses. *See also* Strategic defense; Strategic offense.

STRATEGIC SEALIFT: Naval and merchant ships, together with crews, used to move armed forces, equipment, and supplies over long distances, especially intercontinentally.

STRATEGIC STABILITY: A state of equilibrium which encourages prudence by opponents facing the possibility of general war. Tendencies toward an arms race are restrained, since neither side has undue advantage.

STRATEGIC WARNING: Notification that enemy offensive operations of any kind may be imminent. The alert may be received minutes, hours, days, or longer before hostilities commence. *See also* Tactical warning.

SUBMARINE/SEA-LAUNCHED BALLISTIC MISSILE: Any ballistic missile transported by and launched from a ship. May be short-, medium-, intermediate-, or long-range. *See also* Ballistic missile.

SUBMARINE/SEA-LAUNCHED CRUISE MISSILE: Any air-breathing missile transported by and launched from a ship. May be short-, medium-, intermediate-, or long-range. *See also* Cruise missile.

SUFFICIENCY: A force structure standard that demands capabilities adequate to attain desired ends without undue waste. Superiority thus is essential in some circumstances; parity/essential equivalence suffices under less demanding conditions; and inferiority, qualitative as well as quantitative, is sometimes acceptable. *See also* Superiority; Essential equivalence; and Parity.

SUPERIORITY: A force structure standard that demands capabilities markedly greater than those of opponents.

SURVIVABILITY: The ability of armed forces and civilian communities to withstand attack and still function effectively. It is derived mainly from active and passive defenses. *See also* Pre-launch survivability; Post-launch survivability.

TACTICAL AIRCRAFT: Land- and carrier-based aircraft designed primarily as general purpose forces. Selected U.S. elements are routinely assigned strategic nuclear missions. *See also* General purpose forces.

TACTICAL AIRLIFT: Transport aircraft (military only in the United States) used to move armed forces, equipment, and supplies expeditiously within theaters of operation. *See also* Strategic airlift.

TACTICAL MOBILITY: The ability to shift personnel, equipment, and supplies effectively and expeditiously within a theater of operations, using air, ground, or water-borne transport. *See also* Strategic mobility.

TACTICAL NUCLEAR FORCES, WEAPONS, OPERATIONS: Nuclear combat power expressly designed for deterrent, offensive, and defensive purposes that contribute to the accomplishment of localized military missions; the threatened or actual application of such power. May be employed in general as well as limited wars. *See also* General war; Limited war.

TACTICAL WARNING: Notification that enemy offensive operations of any kind are in progress. The alert may be received at any time from the moment the attack is launched until its effect is felt. *See also* Strategic warning.

TACTICS: The detailed methods used to carry out strategic designs. Military tactics involve the employment of units in combat, including the arrangement and maneuvering of units in relation to each other and/or to the enemy. *See also* Military strategy.

TERCOM: *See* Terrain Contour Matching.

TERMINAL GUIDANCE: In-flight corrections to the trajectory of a ballistic or cruise missile during its final approach to the target, for the purpose of improving accuracy. *See also* Mid-course correction.

TERRAIN CONTOUR MATCHING: A system that correlates contour map data with terrain being overflown by ballistic or cruise missiles. The results provide position fixes at intervals. These can be used to correct inertial guidance errors, and thereby improve accuracy. *See also* Inertial guidance; Mid-course corrections.

TEST AND EVALUATION: The final stage of research and development before procuring and deploying new weapons and equipment. Contractors and military services both analyze and evaluate the performance of basic components and all support items needed to operate and maintain the system. *See also* Applied research; Basic research; Deployment; Development.

TEXAS TOWERS: Air defense surveillance sites on the continental shelf, formerly used to extend coverage off the U.S. East Coast.

THEATER AIR DEFENSE FORCES: Interceptor aircraft and surface-to-air missiles designed primarily to support tactical forces. Some can be adapted for strategic defense.

THEATER OF OPERATIONS: A geographical area outside the United States for which the commander of a U.S. unified or specified command has been assigned military responsibility. *See also* Specified command; Unified command.

THREAT: The capabilities, intentions, and actions of actual or potential enemies to prevent or interfere with the successful fulfillment of national security interests and/or objectives.

THRESHOLD: An intangible and adjustable line between levels and types of conflict, such as the separation between nuclear and nonnuclear warfare. The greater the reluctance to use nuclear weapons, the higher the threshold. *See also* High threshold; Low threshold.

THROW WEIGHT: The payload capacity of a ballistic missile expressed in aggregate poundage for reentry vehicles of all types (warheads, decoys). *See also* Payload.

TIME-SENSITIVE TARGET: Any counterforce target which is vulnerable only if it can be struck before it is launched (as with bombers and missiles) or redeploys (as with ground combat troops and ships).

TOOTH-TO-TAIL RATIO: The proportion of combat forces to administrative/logistic support in a nation's armed forces and in specific military organizations, such as divisions, air wings, and fleets.

TRIAD: Any group of three military elements with separate characteristics but common basic missions. Specifically, the tripartite U.S. strategic retaliatory force, which comprises manned bombers, intercontinental ballistic missiles, and ballistic-missile submarines.

TRIPWIRE: A largely symbolic force positioned on an ally's soil to advertise the owner's commitment to a particular country or coalition of countries. Attacks against the token contingent would trigger a massive response.

TUBE ARTILLERY: Howitzers and guns, as opposed to rockets and guided missiles. May be towed or self-propelled.

UNIFIED COMMAND: A top-echelon U.S. combatant organization with regional or functional responsibilities, which normally is composed of forces from two or more military services. It has a broad, continuing mission and is established by the President, through the Secretary of Defense, with the advice and assistance of the Joint Chiefs of Staff. When authorized by the JCS, commanders of unified commands established by the President may form one or more subordinate unified commands within their jurisdictions. *See also* Specified command.

VULNERABILITY: The susceptibility of any country, military force, or weapons system to any action by any means through which its effectiveness may be diminished.

WARHEAD: That part of a ballistic or cruise missile which contains explosives.

WEAPON: *See* Nuclear weapon.

WEAPONS SYSTEM: Any instrument designed for offensive and/or defensive combat, together with support components required for effective operations (such as an ABM system, comprising two types of radar and two types of missile).

WILL: *See* National Will.

WORLD-WIDE MILITARY COMMAND AND CONTROL SYSTEM: Provides the means for operational direction and administrative support of U.S. armed forces deployed globally. Components include the Advanced Airborne Command Post (AABNCP), satellite communications, the National Emergency Airborne Command Post (NEACP), the Post-Attack Command and Control System (PAACS), communications systems for ballistic missile submarines, the WWMCCS Information System, and Commander-in-Chief (CINC) programs. *See also* National Military Command System.

WWMCCS: *See* World-Wide Military Command and Control System.

YIELD: *See* Nuclear yield.

Annex B

Abbreviations

A-	Attack Aircraft
AA(A)	Antiaircraft (Artillery)
AAFCE	Allied Air Forces Central Europe
ABM	Antiballistic Missile
ABRES	Advanced Ballistic Reentry System
ACDA	Arms Control and Disarmament Agency
ACE	Allied Command Europe
ACL	Allowable Cargo Load
ADCOM	Aerospace Defense Command
AE	Ammunition Ship
AF	Stores Ship
AFB	Air Force Base
AFLANT	Air Force Atlantic Command
AFM-	Air Force Manual
AFRED	Air Force Readiness Command
AFS	Combat Stores Ship
AFSO	Air Force Southern Command
AFV	Armored Fighting Vehicle
AGI	Auxilliary, Intelligence Collector
AGM	Air-to-Ground Missile
AH-	Attack Helicopter
AIM	Air Intercept Missile
AIMVAL	Air Intercept Missile Evaluation
AIR	Air Intercept Rocket
AK	Cargo Ship
ALBM	Air-Launched Ballistic Missile
ALCM	Air-Launched Cruise Missile

Ammo	Ammunition
AN-	Antonov Aircraft
ANG	Air National Guard
ANZUS	Australia-New Zealand-United States
AO	Fleet Oiler
AOE	Fast Combat Support Ship
AOR	Replenishment Oiler
APC	Armored Personnel Carrier
AR	Repair Ship
ARADCOM	Army Air Defense Command
ARNG	Army National Guard
ARPA	Advanced Research Projects Agency
Arty	Artillery
AS	Submarine Tender
ASM	Air-to-Surface Missile
ASROC	Antisubmarine Rocket
ASW	Antisubmarine Warfare
AT	Antitank
ATAF	Allied Tactical Air Force
ATGM	Antitank Guided Missile
Aux	Auxilliary
AV-	Attack Aircraft, Vertical or Short Take-off and Landing
AWACS	Airborne Warning and Control System
B-	Bomber
Be-	Beriev Aircraft
BMEWS	Ballistic Missile Early Warning System
BMP	Infantry Combat Vehicle (Soviet)
Bn	Battalion
C-	Cargo Aircraft; Readiness Condition
C^3	Command/Control and Communications
CAS	Close Air Support
Cat	Category
Cav	Cavalry
CBR	Chemical, Biological, Radiological
CD	Civil Defense
CENTAG	Central Army Group
CEP	Circular Error Probable
CFV	Cavalry Fighting Vehicle
CG	Guided Missile Cruiser
CGN	Guided Missile Cruiser, Nuclear-Powered
CGS	Command and General Support
CH-	Cargo Helicopter
Chem	Chemical

CHG	Antisubmarine Warfare Helicopter Carrier
CIA	Central Intelligence Agency
CINC	Commander-in-Chief
CINCEUR	Commander-in-Chief, European Command
CINCHAN	Commander-in-Chief, Channel Command
CINCPAC	Commander-in-Chief, Pacific Command
CL	Light Cruiser
Cmd	Command
Co	Company
CoComCo	Consultative Group Coordinating Committee
Compt	Comptroller
CONAD	Continental Air Defense Command
CONUS	Continental United States
CPB	Charged Particle Beam
CPSU	Communist Party of the Soviet Union
CRAF	Civil Reserve Air Fleet
CUSRPG	Canadian-U.S. Regional Planning Group
CV	Aircraft Carrier
CVA	Attack Aircraft Carrier
CVAN	Attack Aircraft Carrier, Nuclear-Powered
CVN	Aircraft Carrier, Nuclear-Powered
CVS	Antisubmarine Warfare Aircraft Carrier
CVSG	Antisubmarine Warfare Guided Missile Aircraft Carrier
DCA	Defense Communications Agency
DCPA	Defense Civil Preparedness Agency
DCSLOG	Deputy Chief of Staff, Logistics
DCSOPS	Deputy Chief of Staff, Operations
DD	Destroyer
DDG	Guided Missile Destroyer
DDR&E	Director, Defense Research and Engineering
Def	Defense, Defensive
DEW	Distant Early Warning (Line)
DIA	Defense Intelligence Agency
Div	Division
DMC	Defense Manpower Commission
DMZ	Demilitarized Zone
DOD	Department of Defense
DOSAAF	All-Union Voluntary Society for Assistance to the Army, Air Force, and Navy
DPR	Democratic Peoples Republic
Dwt	Deadweight Ton

ECCM	Electronic Counter Countermeasures
ECM	Electronic Countermeasures
ELF	Extremely Low Frequency
Engr	Engineer
ERDA	Energy Research and Development Administration
EUCOM	European Command
EUSC	Effective U.S. Controlled Fleet
F-	Fighter Aircraft
FA	Field Artillery
FBIS	Foreign Broadcast Information Service
FF	Frigate
FFG	Guided Missile Frigate
FFL	Small Frigate
FM-	Field Manual
FOBS	Fractional Orbit Bombardment System
FROG	Free Rocket Over Ground
FY	Fiscal Year
FYDP	Five-Year Defense Program
GAO	Government Accounting Office
GKO	State Committee for Defense
GLCM	Ground-Launched Cruise Missile
GNP	Gross National Product
GSFG	Group of Soviet Forces Germany
H. Con. Res.	House Concurrent Resolution
HE	High Explosive
Helo	Helicopter
HHC	Headquarters and Headquarters Company
Hi-Lo	High-Low
H.J. Res.	House Joint Resolution
How	Howitzer
Hq	Headquarters
ICBM	Intercontinental Ballistic Missile
IFV	Infantry Fighting Vehicle
IL-	Ilyushin Aircraft
IMS	International Military Staff (NATO)
Inf	Infantry
IR	Infrared
IRBM	Intermediate-Range Ballistic Missile
IRR	Individual Ready Reserve

J-2	Joint Staff, Intelligence
J-5	Joint Staff, Plans and Policy
JCS	Joint Chiefs of Staff
JTF	Joint Task Force
K	Warhead Lethality Factor
KA-	Kamov Aircraft
KC-	Tanker Aircraft
KGB	Committee for State Security
KISS	Keep it Simple, Stupid
Km	Kilometer
KT	Kiloton
LAMPS	Light Airborne Multipurpose System
LANTCOM	Atlantic Command
LASH	Lighter Across the Shore
LAW	Light Antitank Weapon
LCC	Amphibious Command Ship
LCM	Landing Craft Mechanized
Lchr	Launcher
LCPL	Landing Craft, Personnel
LCU	Landing Craft, Utility
LCVP	Landing Craft, Vehicle, Personnel
LHA	Amphibious Assault Ship
LKA	Amphibious Cargo Ship
LOC	Line of Communication
LPA	Amphibious Transport
LPD	Amphibious Transport, Dock
LPH	Landing Platform, Helicopter
LPSS	Amphibious Transport, Submarine
LSD	Landing Ship, Dock
LSM	Landing Ship, Mechanized
LST	Landing Ship, Tank
LVTP	Landing Vehicle, Tracked, Personnel
M-	Model
MAC	Military Airlift Command
MAD	Mutual Assured Destruction; Magnetic Anomaly Detection
MAF	Marine Amphibious Force
Maint	Maintenance
MAP	Military Assistance Program
MARAD	Maritime Administration
MARV	Maneuverable Reentry Vehicle
MATS	Military Air Transport Service

Max	Maximum
MBFR	Mutual and Balanced Force Reductions
MC	Military Committee
MCC	Military Control Center
Med	Medium
MI-	Mil Aircraft
MIG-	Mikoyan Aircraft
MIRV	Multiple Independently Targetable Reentry Vehicle
MIT	Massachusetts Institute of Technology
MK-	Mark
MM	Minuteman
Mod	Model
MOS	Military Occupational Specialty
MR	Motor Rifle
MRA	Manpower and Reserve Affairs
MRA&L	Manpower, Reserve Affairs, and Logistics
MRBM	Medium-Range Ballistic Missile
MRV	Multiple Reentry Vehicle
MSC	Military Sealift Command
MSF	Fleet Minesweeper
MSR	Minesweeper, Patrol; Main Supply Route
MT	Megaton
Mtzd	Motorized
MX	Missile, Experimental
MVD	Ministry of Internal Affairs
MYA	Myasishchev Aircraft
NADGE	NATO's Air Defense Ground Environment
NATO	North Atlantic Treaty Organization
NCA	National Command Authorities
NDAC	Nuclear Defense Affairs Committee (NATO)
NDRF	National Defense Reserve Fleet
NKVD	People's Commissariat of the Interior
NORAD	North American Air Defense Command
NORTHAG	Northern Army Group
Nr	Number
NSA	National Security Agency
NSC	National Security Council
OASD	Office, Assistant Secretary of Defense
OCS	Officer Candidate School
Off	Offense; Offensive
OJCS	Office, Joint Chiefs of Staff

OSD	Office, Secretary of Defense
OTH	Over-the-Horizon
P-	Pursuit Aircraft
PACOM	Pacific Command
Para	Paratroops
Pax	Passengers
Penaid	Penetration Aid
PGG	Patrol Combatant
PGM	Precision-Guided Munitions; Patrol Combatant, Missile
P.L.	Public Law
POL	Petrol, Oil, and Lubricants
Politburo	Political Bureau
POMCUS	Prepositioned Overseas Material Configured to Unit Sets
PONAST	Post Nuclear Attack Study
PRM	Presidential Review Memorandum
PT	Patrol Boat
PTG	Guided Missile Patrol Boat
Pub.	Publication
PVO	Air Defense Forces (Soviet)
RA	Reserve Affairs; Regular Army
Radar	Radio Detection and Ranging
R&D	Research and Development
RDT&E	Research, Development, Test, and Engineering
Recon	Reconnaissance
REDCOM	Readiness Command
REDCON	Readiness Condition
Regt	Regiment
RF-	Reconnaissance (Fighter) Aircraft
RL	Rocket Launcher
ROCC	Regional Operations Control Center
ROTC	Reserve Officers Training Corps
RPG	Rocket-Propelled Grenade
S-	Antisubmarine Warfare Aircraft
SA-	Surface-to-Air
SAC	Strategic Air Command
SACEUR	Supreme Allied Commander Europe
SACLANT	Supreme Allied Commander Atlantic
SAGE	Semi-Automatic Ground Environment
SALT	Strategic Arms Limitation Talks

SAM	Surface-to-Air Missile
SAT	Scholastic Aptitude Test
SeaBee	Construction Battalion; Sea Barge
SEATO	Southeast Asia Treaty Organization
SH-	Antisubmarine Warfare Helicopter
SHAPE	Supreme Headquarters, Allied Powers Europe
SIOP	Single Integrated Operational Plan
S.J. Res.	Senate Joint Resolution
SLBM	Sea/Submarine-Launched Ballistic Missile
SLCM	Sea/Submarine-Launched Cruise Missile
SLOC	Sea Line of Communication
Sonar	Sound Navigation and Ranging
SOUTHCOM	Southern Command
SPACOS	Special Assistants to the Chief of Staff
Sqdn	Squadron
SRAM	Short-Range Attack Missile
SRF	Strategic Rocket Forces
SS	Submarine; *Schutzstaffel*
SSB	Ballistic Missile Submarine
SSBN	Ballistic Missile Submarine, Nuclear-Powered
SSG	Guided Missile Submarine
SSM	Surface-to-Surface Missile
SSN	Submarine, Nuclear-Powered
SS-N-	Surface-to-Surface Missile, Navy
Strat	Strategic
SU-	Sukhoi Aircraft
SUBROC	Submarine Rocket
Svc	Service
T-	Tank
TAC	Tactical Air Command
TERCOM	Terrain Contour Matching
Tk	Tank
T/O	Take-off
TOW	Tube-Launched, Optically-Tracked, Wire-Guided
TRADOC	Training and Doctrine Command
Trans	Transport; Transportation
UE	Unit Equipment
UH-	Utility Helicopter
UK	United Kingdom
USAF	United States Air Force

USAFE	United States Air Forces Europe
USAREUR	United States Army Europe
USMC	United States Marine Corps
USMCR	United States Marine Corps Reserve
USNAVEUR	United States Navy Europe
VLF	Very Low Frequency
VSTOL	Vertical/Short Take-off and Landing
VTOL	Vertical Take-off and Landing
VVS	Soviet Air Force
WWMCCS	Worldwide Military Command and Control System
X-	Experimental
YAK	Yakolev Aircraft

Annex C

Nicknames for Selected Weapons Systems

UNITED STATES

	Designation	*Nickname*
MISSILES		
Strategic		
ICBM	LGM-30F/G	Minuteman II/III
	LGM-25C	Titan II
SLBM	UGM-27C	Polaris A-3
	UGM-73A	Poseidon C-3
	UGM-93A	Trident C-4
ALCM	AGM-86	(None)
SLCM	(None)	Tomahawk
Tactical Surface-to-Surface	MGM-20A	Sergeant
	MGM-31A	Pershing
	MGM-52C	Lance
	RGM-84	Harpoon
Air-to-Surface	AGM-12	Bullpup
	AGM-45	Shrike
	AGM-65	Maverick
	AGM-69A	SRAM
	AGM-78	Standard
	AGM-84	Harpoon
Surface-to-Air	CIM-10B	BOMARC
	MIM-14B	Nike-Hercules

MISSILES	*Designation*	*Nickname*
Surface-to-air	MIM-23A	Hawk
	XMIM-104	SAM-D
Shipborne	AIM-54L	Phoenix
	RIM-2F	Terrier
	RIM-8G	Talos
	RIM-24B	Tartar
Air-to-Air	AIR-2	Genie
	AIM-4	Falcon
	AIM-7	Sparrow
	AIM-9	Sidewinder
AIRCRAFT		
Bombers	B-52	Stratofortress
	FB-111	(None)
Fighter	F-4	Phantom
	F-5	Tiger
	F-8	Crusader
	F-14	Tomcat
	F-15	Eagle
	F-16	(None)
	F-100	Super Sabre
	F-101	Voodoo
	F-102	Delta Dagger
	F-105	Thunderchief
	F-106	Delta Dart
	F-111	(None)
Attack	A-4	Skyhawk
	A-6	Intruder
	A-7	Corsair
	A-10	Thunderbolt II
	AV-8	Harrier
	P-3	Orion
	S-2	Tracker
	S-3	Viking
Helicopters	AH-1	Cobra
	CH-34	Choctaw
	CH-37	Mojave
	CH-46	Sea Knight
	CH-47	Chinook
	CH-53	Sea Stallion
	CH-54	Flying Crane
	SH-3	Sea King
	UH-1	Iroquois

UNITED STATES

	Designation	*Nickname*
AIRCRAFT		
Airlift	C-5	Galaxy
	C-7	Caribou
	C-97	Stratofreighter
	C-119	Flying Boxcar
	C-123	Provider
	C-124	Globemaster
	C-130	Hercules
	C-133	Cargomaster
	C-141	Starlifter
	KC-135	Stratotanker
ARTILLERY	M-101	105mm Howitzer
	M-102	105mm Howitzer
	M-107	175mm Gun
	M-109	155mm Howitzer
	M-110	8-inch Howitzer
	M-114	155mm Howitzer
ANTI-TANK	M-47	Dragon
	BGM-71A	TOW
ARMOR		
Tanks	M-48	(None)
	M-60	(None)
	M-551	Sheridan
APC	M-113	(None)
	LVTP-7	(None)

SOVIET UNION

MISSILES		
Strategic		
ICBM	SS-7	Saddler
	SS-8	Sasin
	SS-9	Scarp
	SS-11	Sego
	SS-13	Savage
	SS-17	(None)
	SS-18	(None)
	SS-19	(None)
SLBM	SS-N-4	Sark
	SS-N-5	Serb
	SS-N-6	Sawfly
	SS-N-8	Sasin
	SS-NX-17	(None)
	SS-NX-18	(None)
IRBM	SS-5	Skean
	SS-20	(None)

SOVIET UNION

	Desination	*Nickname*
MRBM	SS-4	Sandal
ABM	ABM-1	Galosh
Tactical Surface-to-Surface	SS-1B	SCUD A
	SS-1C	SCUD B
	SS-12	Scaleboard
Shipborne	SS-N-1	Scrubber
	SS-N-2	Styx
	SS-N-3	Shaddock
	SS-N-9	(None)
	SS-N-10	(None)
	SS-N-11	(None)
	SS-N-13	(None)
	SS-N-14	(None)
Air-to-Surface	AS-2	Kipper
	AS-3	Kangaroo
	AS-4	Kitchen
	AS-5	Kelt
	AS-6	Kingfish
	AS-7	Kerry
Surface-to-Air	SA-1	Guild
	SA-2	Guideline
	SA-3	Goa
	SA-4	Ganef
	SA-5	Gammon
	SA-6	Gainful
	SA-7	Grail
	SA-8	Gecko
	SA-9	Gaskin
Shipborne	SA-N-1	Goa
	SA-N-3	(None)
	SA-N-4	(None)
Air-to-Air	AA-1	Alkali
	AA-2	Atoll
	AA-3	Anab
	AA-5	Ash
	AA-6	Acrid
	AA-7	Apex
	AA-8	Aphid

SOVIET UNION

	Designation	*Nickname*
AIRCRAFT		
Bombers	IL-28	Beagle
	M-4	Bison
	TU-16	Badger
	TU-22	Blinder
	TU-26	Backfire
	TU-95	Bear
Fighter/Attack	MIG-17	Fresco
	MIG-19	Farmer
	MIG-21	Fishbed
	MIG-23	Flogger
	MIG-25	Foxbat
	SU-7	Fitter-A
	SU-9	Fishpot
	SU-17	Fitter-C
	SU-19	Fencer
Recon/ Intercept	SU-15	Flagon
	TU-28	Fiddler
	TU-126	Moss
	YAK-25	Flashlight
	YAK-28	Firebar
Naval Patrol	BE-6	Madge
	BE-12	Mail
	IL-38	May
	YAK-36	Forger (VTOL)
Helicopters	KA-25	Hormone
	MI-4	Hound
	MI-6	Hook
	MI-8	Hip
	MI-10	Harke
	MI-12	Homer
	MI-24	Hind
Airlift	AN-12	Cub
	AN-22	Cock
	IL-76	Candid
ARTILLERY	M-43	152mm
	M-46	130mm

SOVIET UNION

	Designation	*Nickname*
ARTILLERY	M-55	203.2mm
	M-1938	122mm
	M-1955	100mm
	M-1975	152mm (SP)
	S-23	180mm
ANTI-TANK	AT-1	Snapper
	AT-2	Swatter
	AT-3	Sagger
ARMOR		
Tanks	T-55	(None)
	T-62	(None)
	T-72	(None)
APC/AFV	BTR-50P	(None)
	BTR-60P	(None)
	BTR-152	(None)
	BMP-76PB	(None)

ANNEX D

Roles and Missions U.S. Armed Forces

Congress, in accord with Title 10, United States Code, confirms fundamental functions for each U.S. military Service. The Department of Defense, with Presidential approval, prescribes primary and collateral functions in greater detail. Forces should be sufficient to fulfill each function effectively.

Army

Title 10 Functions (Chapter 307, Section 3062):

(a) It is the intent of Congress to provide an Army that is capable, in conjunction with the other armed forces, of—

(1) preserving the peace and security, and providing for the defense, of the United States, the Territories, Commonwealths, and possessions, and any areas occupied by the United States;

(2) supporting the national policies;

(3) implementing the national objectives; and

(4) overcoming any nations responsible for aggressive acts that imperil the peace and security of the United States.

(b) In general, the Army, within the Department of the Army, includes land combat and service forces and such aviation and water transport as may be organic therein. It shall be organized, trained, and equipped primarily for prompt and sustained combat incident to operations on land. It is responsible for the preparation of land forces necessary for the effective prosecution of war except as otherwise assigned and, in accordance with integrated joint mobilization plans, for the expansion of the peacetime components of the Army to meet the needs of war.

(c) The Army consists of—

(1) the Regular Army, the Army National Guard of the United States, the Army National Guard while in the service of the United States, and the Army Reserve; and

(2) all persons appointed or enlisted in, or conscripted into, the Army without component.

(d) The organized peace establishment of the Army consists of all—

(1) military organizations of the Army with their installations and supporting and auxiliary elements, including combat, training, administrative, and logistic elements; and

(2) members of the Army, including those not assigned to units, necessary to form the basis for a complete and immediate mobilization for the national defense in the event of a national emergency. Aug. 10, 1956, c. 1041, 70A Stat. 166.

DOD Directive 5100.1:

A. *Functions of the Department of the Army* The Department of the Army is responsible for the preparation of land forces necessary for the effective prosecution of war except as otherwise assigned and, in accordance with integrated mobilization plans, for the expansion of the peacetime components of the Army to meet the needs of war.

The Army, within the Department of the Army, includes land combat and service forces and such aviation and water transport as may be organic therein.

1. Primary Functions of the Army. a. To organize, train, and equip Army forces for the conduct of prompt and sustained combat operations on land—specifically, forces to defeat enemy land forces and to seize, occupy, and defend land area.

b. To organize, train and equip Army air defense units, including the provision of Army forces as required for the defense of the United States against air attack, in accordance with doctrines established by the Joint Chiefs of Staff.

c. To organize and equip, in coordination with the other Services, and to provide Army forces for joint amphibious and airborne operations, and to provide for the training of such forces, in accordance with doctrines established by the Joint Chiefs of Staff.

(1) To develop, in coordination with the other Services, doctrines, tactics, techniques, and equipment of interest to the Army for amphibious operations and not provided for in Section V, paragraph B 1 b (3) and paragraph B 1 d.

(2) To develop, in coordination with the other Services, the doctrines, procedures, and equipment employed by Army and Marine Forces in airborne operations. The Army shall have primary interest in the development of those airborne doctrines, procedures, and equipment which are of common interest to the Army and the Marine Corps.

d. To provide an organization capable of furnishing adequate, timely, and reliable intelligence for the Army.

e. To provide forces for the occupations of territories abroad, to include initial establishment of military government pending transfer of this responsibility to other authority.

f. To formulate doctrines and procedures for the organizing, equipping, training, and employment of forces operating on land, except that the formulation of doctrines and procedures for the organization, equipping, training, and employment of Marine Corps units for amphibious operations shall be a function of the Department of the Navy, coordinating as required by Section V, paragraph B 1 b (3).

g. To conduct the following activities:

(1) The administration and operation of the Panama Canal.

(2) The authorized civil works program, including projects for improvement of navigation, flood control, beach erosion control, and other water resource developments in the United States, its territories, and its possessions.

(3) Certain other civil activities prescribed by law.

2. *Collateral Functions of the Army—To train forces:* a. To interdict enemy sea and air power and communications through operations on or from land.

Navy and Marine Corps

Title 10 Functions (Chapter 503, Sections 5012, 5013):

Navy

(a) The Navy, within the Department of the Navy, includes, in general, naval combat and service forces and such aviation as may be organic therein. The Navy shall be organized, trained, and equipped primarily for prompt and sustained combat incident to operations at sea. It is responsible for the preparation of naval forces necessary for the effective prosecution of war except as otherwise assigned and is generally responsible for naval reconnaissance, antisubmarine warfare, and protection of shipping.

(b) All naval aviation shall be integrated with the naval service as part thereof within the Department of the Navy. Naval aviation consists of combat and service and training forces, and includes land-based naval aviation, air transport essential for naval operations, all air weapons and air techniques involved in the operations and activities of the Navy, and the entire remainder of the aeronautical organization of the Navy, together with the personnel necessary therefor.

(c) The Navy shall develop aircraft, weapons, tactics, technique, organization, and equipment of naval combat and service elements. Matters of joint concern as to these functions shall be coordinated between the Army, the Air Force, and the Navy.

(d) The Navy is responsible, in accordance with integrated joint mobilization plans, for the expansion of the peacetime components of the Navy to meet the needs of war. Aug. 10, 1956, c. 1041, 70A Stat. 277.

Marine Corps

(a) The Marine Corps, within the Department of the Navy, shall be so organized as to include not less than three combat divisions and three air wings, and such other land combat, aviation, and other services as may be organic therein. The Marine Corps shall be organized, trained, and equipped to provide fleet marine forces of combined arms, together with supporting air components, for service with the fleet in the seizure or defense of advanced naval bases and for the conduct of such land operations as may be essential to the prosecution of a naval campaign. In addition, the Marine Corps shall provide detachments and organizations for service on armed vessels of the Navy, shall provide security detachments for the protection of naval property at naval stations and bases, and shall perform such other duties as the President may direct. However, these additional duties may not detract from or interfere with the operations for which the Marine Corps is primarily organized.

(b) The Marine Corps shall develop, in coordination with the Army and the Air Force, those phases of amphibious operations that pertain to the tactics, technique, and equipment used by landing forces.

(c) The Marine Corps is responsible, in accordance with integrated joint mobilization plans, for the expansion of peacetime components of the Marine Corps to meet the needs of war. Aug. 10, 1956, c. 1041, 70A Stat. 278.

DOD Directive 5100.1:

B. Functions of the Department of the Navy The Department of the Navy is responsible for the preparation of Navy and Marine Corps forces necessary for the effective prosecution of war except as otherwise assigned and, in accordance with integrated mobilization plans, for the expansion of the peacetime components of the Navy and Marine Corps to meet the needs of war.

Within the Department of the Navy, the Navy includes naval combat and service forces and such aviation as may be organic therein, and the Marine Corps includes not less than three combat divisions and three air wings and such other land combat, aviation, and other services as may be organic therein.

1. Primary Functions of the Navy and the Marine Corps a. To organize, train, and equip Navy and Marine Corps forces for the conduct of prompt and sustained combat operations at sea, including operations of sea-based aircraft and land-based naval air components—specifically, forces to seek out and destroy enemy naval forces and to suppress enemy sea commerce, to gain and maintain general naval supremacy, to control vital sea areas and to protect vital sea lines of communication, to establish and maintain local superiority (including air) in an area of naval operations, to seize and defend advanced naval bases, and to conduct such land and air operations as may be essential to the prosecution of a naval campaign.

b. To maintain the Marine Corps, having the following specific functions:

(1) To provide Fleet Marine Forces of combined arms, together with supporting air components, for service with the Fleet in the seizure or defense of advanced naval bases and for the conduct of such land operations as may be essential to the prosecution of a naval campaign. These functions do not contemplate the creation of a second land Army.

(2) To provide detachments and organizations for service on armed vessels of the Navy, and security detachments for the protection of naval property at naval stations and bases.

(3) To develop, in coordination with the other Services, the doctrines, tactics, techniques, and equipment employed by landing forces in amphibious operations. The Marine Corps shall have primary interest in the development of those landing force doctrines, tactics, techniques,and equipment which are of common interest to the Army and the Marine Corps.

(4) To train and equip, as required, Marine Forces for airborne operations, in coordination with the other Services and in accordance with doctrines established by the Joint Chiefs of Staff.

(5) To develop, in coordination with the other Services, doctrines, procedures, and equipment of interest to the Marine Corps for airborne operations and not provided for in Section V, paragraph A 1 c (2).

c. To organize and equip, in coordination with the other Services, and to provide naval forces, including naval close air-support forces, for the conduct of joint amphibious operations, and to be responsible for the amphibious training of all forces assigned to joint amphibious operations in accordance with doctrines established by the Joint Chiefs of Staff.

d. To develop, in coordination with the other Services, the doctrines, procedures, and equipment of naval forces for amphibious operations, and the doctrines and procedures for joint amphibious operations.

e. To furnish adequate, timely, and reliable intelligence for the Navy and Marine Corps.

f. To organize, train, and equip naval forces for naval reconnaissance, antisubmarine warfare, and protection of shipping, and mine laying, including the air aspects thereof, and controlled mine field operations.

g. To provide air support essential for naval operations.

h. To provide sea-based air defense and the sea-based means for coordinating control for defense against air attack, coordinating with the other Services in matters of joint concern.

i. To provide naval (including naval air) forces as required for the defense of the United States against air attack, in accordance with doctrines established by the Joint Chiefs of Staff.

j. To furnish aerial photography as necessary for Navy and Marine Corps operations.

2. *Collateral Functions of the Navy and the Marine Corps—To train forces:* a. To interdict enemy land and air power and communications through operations at sea.

b. To conduct close air and naval support for land operations.

c. To furnish aerial photography for cartographic purposes.

d. To be prepared to participate in the overall air effort as directed.

e. To establish military government, as directed, pending transfer of this responsibility to other authority.

Air Force

Title 10 Functions (Chapter 817, Section 8062):

(a) It is the intent of Congress to provide an Air Force that is capable, in conjunction with the other armed forces, of—

(1) preserving the peace and security, and providing for the defense, of the United States, the Territories, Commonwealths, and possessions, and any areas occupied by the United States;

(2) supporting the national policies;

(3) implementing the national objectives; and

(4) overcoming any nations responsible for aggressive acts that imperil the peace and security of the United States.

(b) There is a United States Air Force within the Department of the Air Force.

(c) In general, the Air Force includes aviation forces both combat and service not otherwise assigned. It shall be organized, trained, and equipped primarily for prompt and sustained offensive and defensive air operations. It is responsible for the preparation of the air forces necessary for the effective prosecution of war except as otherwise assigned and, in accordance with integrated joint mobilization plans, for the expansion of the peacetime components of the Air Force to meet the needs of war.

(d) The Air Force consists of—

(1) the Regular Air Force, the Air National Guard of the United States, the Air National Guard while in the service of the United States, and the Air Force Reserve;

(2) all persons appointed or enlisted in, or conscripted into, the Air Force without component; and

(3) all Air Force units and other Air Force organizations, with their installations and supporting and auxiliary combat, training, administrative, and logistic elements; and all members of the Air Force, including those not assigned to units; necessary to form the basis for a complete and immediate mobilization for the national defense in the event of a national emergency.

(e) Subject to subsection (f) of this section and chapter 831 of this title, the authorized strength of the Air Force is 70 Regular Air Force groups and such separate Regular Air Force squadrons, reserve groups, and supporting and auxiliary regular and reserve units as required.

(f) There are authorized for the Air Force 24,000 serviceable aircraft or 225,000 airframe tons of serviceable aircraft, whichever the Secretary of the Air Force considers appropriate to carry out this section. This subsection does not apply to guided missiles. Aug. 10, 1956, c. 1041, 70A Stat. 493.

DOD Directive 5100.1:

C. Functions of the Department of the Air Force The Department of the Air Force is responsible for the preparation of the air forces necessary for the effective prosecution of war except as otherwise assigned and, in accordance with integrated mobilization plans, for the expansion of the peacetime components of the Air Force to meet the needs of war.

The Air Force, within the Department of the Air Force, includes aviation forces, both combat and service, not otherwise assigned.

1. Primary Functions of the Air Force a. To organize, train, and equip Air Force forces for the conduct of prompt and sustained combat operations in the air—specifically, forces to defend the United States against air attack in accordance with doctrines established by the Joint Chiefs of Staff, to gain and maintain general air supremacy, to defeat enemy air forces, to control vital air areas, and to establish local air superiority except as otherwise assigned herein.

b. To develop doctrines and procedures, in coordination with the other Services, for the unified defense of the United States against air attack.

c. To organize, train, and equip Air Force forces for strategic air warfare.

d. To organize and equip Air Force forces for joint amphibious and airborne operations, in coordination with the other Services, and to provide for their training in accordance with doctrines established by the Joint Chiefs of Staff.

e. To furnish close combat and logistical air support to the Army, to include air lift, support, and resupply of airborne operations, aerial photography, tactical reconnaissance, and interdiction of enemy land power and communications.

f. To provide air transport for the armed forces, except as otherwise assigned.

g. To develop, in coordination with the other Services, doctrines, procedures, and equipment for air defense from land areas, including the continental United States.

h. To formulate doctrines and procedures for the organizing, equipping, training, and employment of Air Force forces.

i. To provide an organization capable of furnishing adequate, timely, and reliable intelligence for the Air Force.

j. To furnish aerial photography for cartographic purposes.

k. To develop, in coordination with the other Services, tactics, techniques, and equipment of interest to the Air Force for amphibious operations and not provided for in Section V, paragraph B 1 b (3) and paragraph B 1 d.

l. To develop, in coordination with the other Services, doctrines, procedures, and equipment employed by Air Force forces in airborne operations.

2. Collateral Functions of the Air Force—To train forces: a. To interdict enemy sea power through air operations.

b. To conduct antisubmarine warfare and to protect shipping.

c. To conduct aerial mine-laying operations.

Annex E

SALT ABM Treaty and Interim Agreement on the Limitation of Offensive Weapons Systems

Treaty between the United States of America and the Union of Soviet Socialist Republics on the Limitation of Anti-Ballistic Missile Systems, With Associated Protocol[1]

Signed May 26, 1972; ratification advised by the Senate August 3, 1972; ratified by the President and entered into force October 3, 1972.

The United States of America and the Union of Soviet Socialist Republics, hereinafter referred to as the Parties,

Proceeding from the premise that nuclear war would have devastating consequences for all mankind,

Considering that effective measures to limit anti-ballistic missile systems would be a substantial factor in curbing the race in strategic offensive arms and would lead to a decrease in the risk of outbreak of war involving nuclear weapons,

Proceeding from the premise that the limitation of anti-ballistic missile systems, as well as certain agreed measures with respect to the limitation of strategic offensive arms, would contribute to the creation of more favorable conditions for further negotiations on limiting strategic arms,

Mindful of their obligations under Article VI of the Treaty on the Non-Proliferation of Nuclear Weapons,

Declaring their intention to achieve at the earliest possible date the cessation of the nuclear arms race and to take effective measures toward reductions in strategic arms, nuclear disarmament, and general and complete disarmament,

1. 23 UST 3435; TIAS 7503.

Desiring to contribute to the relaxation of international tension and the strengthening of trust between States,

Have agreed as follows:

Article I

1. Each Party undertakes to limit anti-ballistic missile (ABM) systems and to adopt other measures in accordance with the provisions of this Treaty.

2. Each Party undertakes not to deploy ABM systems for a defense of the territory of its country and not to provide a base for such a defense, and not to deploy ABM systems for defense of an individual region except as provided for in Article III of this Treaty.

Article II

1. For the purposes of this Treaty an ABM system is a system to counter strategic ballistic missiles or their elements in flight trajectory, currently consisting of:

(a) ABM interceptor missiles, which are interceptor missiles constructed and deployed for an ABM role, or of a type tested in an ABM mode;

(b) ABM launchers, which are launchers constructed and deployed for launching ABM interceptor missiles; and

(c) ABM radars, which are radars constructed and deployed for an ABM role, or of a type tested in an ABM mode.

2. The ABM system components listed in paragraph 1 of this Article include those which are:

(a) operational;
(b) under construction;
(c) undergoing testing;
(d) undergoing overhaul, repair or conversion; or
(e) mothballed.

Article III

Each party undertakes not to deploy ABM systems or their components except that:

(a) within one ABM system deployment area having a radius of one hundred and fifty kilometers and centered on the Party's national capital, a Party may deploy; (1) no more than one hundred ABM launchers and no more than one hundred ABM interceptor missiles at launch sites, and (2) ABM radars within no more than six ABM radar complexes, the area of each complex being circular and have a diameter of no more than three kilometers; and

(b) within one ABM system deployment area having a radius of one hundred and fifty kilometers and containing ICBM silo launchers, a

Party may deploy: (1) no more than one hundred ABM launchers and no more than one hundred ABM interceptor missiles at launch sites, (2) two large phased-array ABM radars comparable in potential to corresponding ABM radars operational or under construction on the date of signature of the Treaty in an ABM system deployment area containing ICBM silo launchers, and (3) no more than eighteen ABM radars each having a potential less than the potential of the smaller of the above-mentioned two large phased-array ABM radars.

Article IV

The limitations provided for in Article III shall not apply to ABM systems or their components used for development or testing, and located within current or additionally agreed test ranges. Each Party may have no more than a total of fifteen ABM launchers at test ranges.

Article V

1. Each Party undertakes not to develop, test, or deploy ABM systems or components which are sea-based, air-based, space-based, or mobile land-based.

2. Each Party undertakes not to develop, test, or deploy ABM launchers for launching more than one ABM interceptor missile at a time from each launcher, nor to modify deployed launchers to provide them with such a capability, nor to develop, test, or deploy automatic or semi-automatic or other similar systems for rapid reload or ABM launchers.

Article VI

To enhance assurance of the effectiveness of the limitations on ABM systems and their components provided by this Treaty, each Party undertakes:

(a) not to give missiles, launchers, or radars, other than ABM interceptor missiles, ABM launchers, or ABM radars, capabilities to counter strategic ballistic missiles or their elements in flight trajectory, and not to test them in an ABM mode; and

(b) not to deploy in the future radars for early warning of strategic ballistic missile attack except at locations along the periphery of its national territory and oriented outward.

Article VII

Subject to the provisions of this Treaty, modernization and replacement of ABM systems or their components may be carried out.

Article VIII

ABM systems or their components in excess of the numbers or outside the areas specified in this Treaty, as well as ABM systems or their components prohibited by this Treaty, shall be destroyed or dismantled under agreed procedures within the shortest possible agreed period of time.

Article IX

To assure the viability and effectiveness of this Treaty, each Party undertakes not to transfer to other States, and not to deploy outside its national territory, ABM systems or their components limited by this Treaty.

Article X

Each Party undertakes not to assume any international obligations which would conflict with this Treaty.

Article XI

The Parties undertake to continue active negotiations for limitations on strategic offensive arms.

Article XII

1. For the purpose of providing assurance of compliance with the provisions of this Treaty, each Party shall use national technical means of verification at its disposal in a manner consistent with generally recognized principles of international law.

2. Each Party undertakes not to interfere with the national technical means of verification of the other Party operating in accordance with paragraph 1 of this Article.

3. Each Party undertakes not to use deliberate concealment measures which impede verification by national technical means of compliance with the provisions of this Treaty. This obligation shall not require changes in current construction, assembly, conversion, or overhaul practices.

Article XIII

1. To promote the objectives and implementation of the provisions of this Treaty, the Parties shall establish promptly a Standing Consultative Commission, within the framework of which they will:

(a) consider questions concerning compliance with the obligations assumed and related situations which may be considered ambiguous;

(b) provide on a voluntary basis such information as either Party considers necessary to assure confidence in compliance with the obligations assumed;

(c) consider questions involving unintended interference with national technical means of verification;

(d) consider possible changes in the strategic situation which have a bearing on the provisions of this Treaty;

(e) agree upon procedures and dates for destruction or dismantling of ABM systems or their components in cases provided for by the provisions of this Treaty;

(f) consider, as appropriate, possible proposals for further increasing the viability of this Treaty, including proposals for amendments in accordance with the provisions of this Treaty;

(g) consider, as appropriate, proposals for further measures aimed at limiting strategic arms.

2. The Parties through consultation shall establish, and may amend as appropriate, Regulations for the Standing Consultative Commission governing procedures, composition and other relevant matters.

Article XIV

1. Each Party may propose amendments to this Treaty. Agreed amendments shall enter into force in accordance with the procedures governing the entry into force of this Treaty.

2. Five years after entry into force of this Treaty, and at five year intervals thereafter, the Parties shall together conduct a review of this Treaty.

Article XV

1. This Treaty shall be of unlimited duration.

2. Each Party shall, in exercising its national sovereignty, have the right to withdraw from this Treaty if it decides that extraordinary events related to the subject matter of this Treaty have jeopardized its supreme interests. It shall give notice of its decision to the other Party six months prior to withdrawal from the Treaty. Such notice shall include a statement of the extraordinary events the notifying Party regards as having jeopardized its supreme interests.

Article XVI

1. This Treaty shall be subject to ratification in accordance with the constitutional procedures of each Party. The Treaty shall enter into force on the day of the exchange of instruments of ratification.

2. This Treaty shall be registered pursuant to Article 102 of the Charter of the United Nations.

Done at Moscow on May 26, 1972, in two copies, each in the English and Russian languages, both texts being equally authentic.

For the United States of America:

RICHARD NIXON,
President of the United States of America.

For the Union of Soviet Socialist Republics:

L. I. BREZHNEV,
General Secretary of the Central Committee of the CPSU.

Protocol to the Treaty Between the United States of America and the Union of Soviet Socialist Republics on the Limitation of Anti-Ballistic Missile Systems[1]

Signed at Moscow July 3, 1974; ratification advised by the Senate November 10, 1975; entered into force May 24, 1976

The United States of America and the Union of Soviet Socialist Republics, hereinafter referred to as the Parties,

Proceeding from the Basic Principles of Relations between the United States of America and the Union of Soviet Socialist Republics signed on May 29, 1972,

Desiring to further the objectives of the Treaty between the United States of America and the Union of Soviet Socialist Republics on the Limitation of Anti-Ballistic Missile Systems signed on May 26, 1972, hereinafter referred to as the Treaty,

Reaffirming their conviction that the adoption of further measures for the limitation of strategic arms would contribute to strengthening international peace and security,

Proceeding from the premise that further limitation of anti-ballistic missile systems will create more favorable conditions for the completion of work on a permanent agreement on more complete measures for the limitation of strategic offensive arms,

Have agreed as follows:

Article I

1. Each Party shall be limited at any one time to a single area out of the two provided in Article III of the Treaty for deployment of anti-ballistic missile (ABM) systems or their components and accordingly shall not exercise its rights to deploy an ABM system or its components in the second of the two ABM system deployment areas permitted by Article III of the Treaty, except as an exchange of one permitted area for the other in accordance with Article II of this Protocol.

2. Accordingly, except as permitted by Article II of this Protocol: the United States of America shall not deploy an ABM system or its

1. TIAS 8276.

components in the area centered on its capital, as permitted by Article III(a) of the Treaty, and the Soviet Union shall not deploy an ABM system or its components in the deployment area of intercontinental ballistic missile (ICBM) silo launchers permitted by Article III(b) of the Treaty.

Article II

1. Each Party shall have the right to dismantle or destroy its ABM system and the components thereof in the area where they are presently deployed and to deploy an ABM system or its components in the alternative area permitted by Article III of the Treaty, provided that prior to initiation of construction, notification is given in accord with the procedure agreed to by the Standing Consultative Commission, during the year beginning October 3, 1977, and ending October 2, 1978, or during any year which commences at five year intervals thereafter, those being the years for periodic review of the Treaty, as provided in Article XIV of the Treaty. This right may be exercised only once.

2. Accordingly, in the event of such notice, the United States would have the right to dismantle or destroy the ABM system and its components in the deployment area of ICBM silo launchers and to deploy an ABM system or its components in an area centered on its capital, as permitted by Article III(a) of the Treaty, and the Soviet Union would have the right to dismantle or destroy the ABM system and its components in the area centered on its capital and to deploy an ABM system or its components in an area containing ICBM silo launchers, as permitted by Article III(b) of the Treaty.

3. Dismantling or destruction and deployment of ABM systems or their components and the notification thereof shall be carried out in accordance with Article VIII of the ABM Treaty and procedures agreed to in the Standing Consultative Commission.

Article III

The rights and obligations established by the Treaty remain in force and shall be complied with by the Parties except to the extent modified by this Protocol. In particular, the deployment of an ABM system or its components within the area selected shall remain limited by the levels and other requirements established by the Treaty.

Article IV

This Protocol shall be subject to ratification in accordance with the constitutional procedures of each Party. It shall enter into force on the day of the exchange of instruments of ratification and shall thereafter be considered an integral part of the Treaty.

Done at Moscow on July 3, 1974, in duplicate, in the English and Russian languages, both texts being equally authentic.

For the United States of America:

RICHARD NIXON,
President of the United States of America.

For the Union of Soviet Socialist Republics:

L. I. BREZHNEV,
General Secretary of the Central Committee of the CPSU.

SALT I
Interim Agreement of 1972

Interim Agreement Between the United States of America and the Union of Soviet Socialist Republics on Certain Measures With Respect to the Limitation of Strategic Offensive Arms, With Associated Protocol[1]

Signed at Moscow on May 26, 1972; Related joint resolution approved September 30, 1972 [Public Law 92-448]; Approved by the President of the United States of America October 3, 1972; Entered into force October 3, 1972.

The United States of America and the Union of Soviet Socialist Republics, hereinafter referred to as the Parties,

Convinced that the Treaty on the Limitation of Anti-Ballistic Missile Systems and this Interim Agreement on Certain Measures with Respect to the Limitation of Strategic Offensive Arms will contribute to the creation of more favorable conditions for active negotiations on limiting strategic arms as well as to the relaxation of international tension and the strengthening of trust between States,

Taking into account the relationship between strategic offensive and defensive arms,

Mindful of their obligations under Article VI of the Treaty on the Non-Proliferation of Nuclear Weapons,

Have agreed as follows:

1. 23 UST 3462: TIAS 7504. The Interim Agreement expired on October 3, 1977. However, both the United States and the Soviet Union issued parallel statements announcing that they would continue to observe the limitations on strategic buildups which were contained in the agreement.

Article I

The Parties undertake not to start construction of additional fixed land-based intercontinental ballistic missile (ICBM) launchers after July 1, 1972.

Article II

The Parties undertake not to convert land-based launchers for light ICBMs, or for ICBMs of older types deployed prior to 1964, into land-based launchers for heavy ICBMs of types deployed after that time.

Article III

The Parties undertake to limit submarine-launched ballistic missile (SLBM) launchers and modern ballistic missile submarines to the numbers operational and under construction on the date of signature of this Interim Agreement, and in addition to launchers and submarines constructed under procedures established by the Parties as replacements for an equal number of ICBM launchers of older types deployed prior to 1964 or for launchers on older submarines.

Article IV

Subject to the provisions of this Interim Agreement, modernization and replacement of strategic offensive ballistic missiles and launchers covered by this Interim Agreement may be undertaken.

Article V

1. For the purpose of providing assurance of compliance with the provisions of this Interim Agreement, each Party shall use national technical means of verification at its disposal in a manner consistent with generally recognized principles of international law.

2. Each Party undertakes not to interfere with the national technical means of verification of the other Party operating in accordance with paragraph 1 of this Article.

3. Each Party undertakes not to use deliberate concealment measures which impede verification by national technical means of compliance with the provisions of this Interim Agreement. This obligation shall not require changes in current construction, assembly, conversion, or overhaul practices.

Article VI

To promote the objectives and implementation of the provisions of this Interim Agreement, the Parties shall use the Standing Consultative Commission established under Article XIII of the Treaty on the Limitation of Anti-Ballistic Missile Systems in accordance with the provisions of that Article.

Article VII

The Parties undertake to continue active negotiations for limitations on strategic offensive arms. The obligations provided for in this Interim Agreement shall not prejudice the scope or terms of the limitations on strategic offensive arms which may be worked out in the course of further negotiations.

Article VIII

1. This Interim Agreement shall enter into force upon exchange of written notices of acceptance by each Party, which exchange shall take place simultaneously with the exchange of instruments of ratification of the Treaty on the Limitation of Anti-Ballistic Missile Systems.

2. This Interim Agreement shall remain in force for a period of five years unless replaced earlier by an agreement on more complete measures limiting strategic offensive arms. It is the objective of the Parties to conduct active follow-on negotiations with the aim of concluding such an agreement as soon as possible.

3. Each Party shall, in exercising its national sovereignty, have the right to withdraw from this Interim Agreement if it decides that extraordinary events related to the subject matter of this Interim Agreement have jeopardized its supreme interests. It shall give notice of its decision to the other Party six months prior to withdrawal from this Interim Agreement. Such notice shall include a statement of the extraordinary events the notifying Party regards as having jeopardized its supreme interests.

Done at Moscow on May 26, 1972, in two copies, each in the English and Russian languages, both texts being equally authentic.

For the United States of America:

RICHARD NIXON,
President of the United States of America.

For the Union of Soviet Socialist Republics:

L. I. BREZHNEV,
General Secretary of the Central Committee of the CPSU.

Protocol to the Interim Agreement Between the United States of America and the Union of Soviet Socialist Republics on Certain Measures with respect to the Limitation of Strategic Offensive Arms

Signed at Moscow May 26, 1972

The United States of America and the Union of Soviet Socialist Republics, hereinafter referred to as the Parties,

Having agreed on certain limitations relating to submarine-launched ballistic missile launchers and modern ballistic missile submarines, and to replacement procedures, in the Interim Agreement,

Have agreed as follows:

The Parties understand that, under Article III of the Interim Agreement, for the period during which that Agreement remains in force:

The U.S. may have no more than 710 ballistic missile launchers on submarines (SLBMs) and no more than 44 modern ballistic missile submarines. The Soviet Union may have no more than 950 ballistic missile launchers on submarines and no more than 62 modern ballistic missile submarines.

Additional ballistic missile launchers on submarines up to the above-mentioned levels, in the U.S.—over 656 ballistic missile launchers on nuclear-powered submarines, and in the U.S.S.R.—over 740 ballistic missile launchers on nuclear-powered submarines, operational and under construction, may become operational as replacements for equal numbers of ballistic missile launchers of older types deployed prior to 1964 or of ballistic missile launchers on older submarines.

The deployment of modern SLBMs on any submarine, regardless of type, will be counted against the total level of SLBMs permitted for the U.S. and the U.S.S.R.

This Protocol shall be considered an integral part of the Interim Agreement.

Donc at Moscow this 26th day of May, 1972.

For the United States of America:

RICHARD NIXON,
President of the United States of America.

For the Union of Soviet Socialist Republics:

L. I. BREZHNEV,
General Secretary of the Central Committee of the CPSU.

Agreed Interpretations and Unilateral Statements

1. Agreed Interpretations

(a) *Initialed Statements.*—The texts of the statements set out below were agreed upon and initialed by the Heads of the Delegations on May 26, 1972.

[A]

The Parties understand that, in addition to the ABM radars which may be deployed in accordance with subparagraph (a) of Article III of the Treaty, those non-phased-array ABM radars operational on the date of signature of the Treaty within the ABM system deployment area for defense of the national capital may be retained.

[B]

The Parties understand that the potential (the product of mean emitted power in watts and antenna area in square meters) of the smaller of the two large phased-array ABM radars referred to in subparagraph (b) of Article III of the Treaty is considered for purposes of the Treaty to be three million.

[C]

The Parties understand that the center of the ABM system deployment area centered on the national capital and the center of the ABM system deployment area containing ICBM silo launchers for each Party shall be separated by no less than thirteen hundred kilometers.

[D]

The Parties agree not to deploy phased-array radars having a potential (the product of mean emitted power in watts and antenna area in square meters) exceeding three million, except as provided for in Articles III, IV and VI of the Treaty, or except for the purposes of tracking objects in outer space or for use as national technical means of verification.

[E]

In order to insure fulfillment of the obligation not to deploy ABM systems and their components except as provided in Article III of the Treaty, the Parties agree that in the event ABM systems based on other physical principles and including components capable of substituting for ABM interceptor missiles, ABM launchers, or ABM radars are created in the future, specific limitations on such systems and their components would be subject to discussion in accordance with Article XIII and agreement in accordance with Article XIV of the Treaty.

[F]

The Parties understand that Article V of the Treaty includes obligations not to develop, test or deploy ABM interceptor missiles for the delivery by each ABM interceptor missile of more than one independently guided warhead.

[G]

The Parties understand that Article IX of the Treaty includes the obligation of the U.S. and the USSR not to provide to other States technical descriptions or blueprints specially worked out for the construction of ABM systems and their components limited by the Treaty.

Interim Agreement

[H]

The Parties understand that land-based ICBM launchers referred to in the Interim Agreement are understood to be launchers for strategic ballistic missiles capable of ranges in excess of the shortest distance between the northeastern border of the continental U.S. and the northwestern border of the continental USSR.

[I]

The Parties understand that fixed land-based ICBM launchers under active construction as of the date of signature of the Interim Agreement may be completed.

[J]

The Parties understand that in the process of modernization and replacement the dimensions of land-based ICBM silo launchers will not be significantly increased.

[K]

The Parties understand that dismantling or destruction of ICBM launchers of older types deployed prior to 1964 and ballistic missile launchers on older submarines being replaced by new SLBM launchers on modern submarines will be initiated at the time of the beginning of sea trials of a replacement submarine, and will be completed in the shortest possible agreed period of time. Such dismantling or destruction, and timely notification thereof, will be accomplished under procedures to be agreed in the Standing Consultative Commission.

[L]

The Parties understand that during the period of the Interim Agreement there shall be no significant increase in the number of ICBM or

SLBM test and training launchers, or in the number of such launchers for modern land-based heavy ICBMs. The Parties further understand that construction or conversion of ICBM launchers at test ranges shall be undertaken only for purposes of testing and training.

(b) *Common Understandings.*—Common understanding of the Parties on the following matters was reached during the negotiations:

A. Increase in ICBM Silo Dimensions

Ambassador Smith made the following statement on May 26, 1972:

"The Parties agree that the term 'significantly increased' means that an increase will not be greater than 10–15 percent of the present dimensions of land-based ICBM silo launchers."

Minister Semenov replied that this statement corresponded to the Soviet understanding.

B. Location of ICBM Defenses

The U.S. Delegation made the following statement on May 26, 1972:

"Article III of the ABM Treaty provides for each side one ABM system deployment area centered on its national capital and one ABM system deployment area containing ICBM silo launchers. The two sides have registered agreement on the following statement: 'The Parties understand that the center of the ABM system deployment area centered on the national capital and the center of the ABM system deployment area containing ICBM silo launchers for each Party shall be separated by no less than thirteen hundred kilometers.' In this connection, the U.S. side notes that its ABM system deployment area for defense of ICBM silo launchers, located west of the Mississippi River, will be centered in the Grand Forks ICBM silo launcher deployment area." (See Initialed Statement [C].)

C. ABM Test Ranges

The U.S. Delegation made the following statement on April 26, 1972:

"Article IV of the ABM Treaty provides that 'the limitations provided for in Article III shall not apply to ABM systems or their components used for development or testing, and located within current or additionally agreed test ranges.' We believe it would be useful to assure that there is no misunderstanding as to current ABM test ranges. It is our understanding that ABM test ranges encompass the area within which ABM components are located for test purposes. The current U.S. ABM test ranges are at White Sands, New Mexico, and at Kwajalein Atoll, and the current Soviet ABM test range is near Sary Shagan in Kazakhstan. We consider that non-phased array radars of types used for range safety or instrumentation purposes may be located outside of ABM test ranges. We interpret the reference in Article IV to 'additionally agreed test ranges' to mean that ABM components will not be located at any other test ranges without prior agreement between our Governments that there will be such additional ABM test ranges."

On May 5, 1972, the Soviet Delegation stated that there was a common understanding on what ABM test ranges were, that the use of the types of non-ABM radars for range safety or instrumentation was not limited under the Treaty, that the reference in Article IV to "additionally agreed" test ranges was sufficiently clear, and that national means permitted identifying current test ranges.

D. Mobile ABM Systems

On January 28, 1972, the U.S. Delegation made the following statement:

"Article V(I) of the Joint Draft Text of the ABM Treaty includes an undertaking not to develop, test, or deploy mobile land-based ABM systems and their components. On May 5, 1971, the U.S. side indicated that, in its view, a prohibition on deployment of mobile ABM systems and components would rule out the deployment of ABM launchers and radars which were not permanent fixed types. At that time, we asked for the Soviet view of this interpretation. Does the Soviet side agree with the U.S. side's interpretation put forward on May 5, 1971?"

On April 13, 1972, the Soviet Delegation said there is a general common understanding on this matter.

E. Standing Consultative Commission

Ambassador Smith made the following statement on May 22, 1972:

"The United States proposes that the sides agree that, with regard to initial implementation of the ABM Treaty's Article XIII on the Standing Consultative Commission (SCC) and of the consultation Articles to the Interim Agreement on offensive arms and the Accidents Agreement,[1] agreement establishing the SCC will be worked out early in the follow-on SALT negotiations; until that is completed, the following arrangements will prevail: when SALT is in session, any consultation desired by either side under these Articles can be carried out by the two SALT Delegations: when SALT is not in session, *ad hoc* arrangements for any desired consultations under these Articles may be made through diplomatic channels."

1. See Article 7 of Agreement to Reduce the Risk of Outbreak of Nuclear War Between the United States of America and the Union of Soviet Socialist Republics, signed Sept. 30, 1971, p. 45.

Minister Semenov replied that, on an *ad referendum basis,* he could agree that the U.S. statement corresponded to the Soviet understanding.

F. Standstill

On May 6, 1972, Minister Semenov made the following statement:

"In an effort to accommodate the wishes of the U.S. side, the Soviet Delegation is prepared to proceed on the basis that the two sides will in fact observe the obligations of both the Interim Agreement and the ABM Treaty beginning from the date of signature of these two documents."

In reply, the U.S. Delegation made the following statement on May 20, 1972:

"The U.S. agrees in principle with the Soviet statement made on May 6 concerning observance of obligations beginning from date of signature but we would like to make clear our understanding that this means that, pending ratification and acceptance, neither side would take any action prohibited by the agreements after they had entered into force. This understanding would continue to apply in the absence of notification by either signatory of its intention not to proceed with ratification or approval."

The Soviet Delegation indicated agreement with the U.S. statement.

2. Unilateral Statements

(a) The following noteworthy unilateral statements were made during the negotiations by the United States Delegation:

A. Withdrawal from the ABM Treaty

On May 9, 1972, Ambassador Smith made the following statement:

"The U.S. Delegation has stressed the importance the U.S. Government attaches to achieving agreement on more complete limitations on strategic offensive arms, following agreement on an ABM Treaty and on an Interim Agreement on certain measures with respect to the limitation of strategic offensive arms. The U.S. Delegation believes that an objective of the follow-on negotiations should be to constrain and reduce on a long-term basis threats to the survivability of our respective strategic retaliatory forces. The USSR Delegation has also indicated that the objectives of SALT would remain unfulfilled without the achievement of an agreement providing for more complete limitations on strategic offensive arms. Both sides recognize that the initial agreements would be steps toward the achievement of more complete limitations on strategic arms. If an agreement providing for more complete strategic offensive arms limitations were not achieved within five years, U.S. supreme interests could be jeopardized. Should that occur, it would constitute a basis for withdrawal from the ABM Treaty. The U.S. does not wish to see such a situation occur, nor do we believe that the USSR does. It is because we wish to prevent such a situation that we emphasize the importance the U.S. Government attaches to achievement of more complete limitations on strategic offensive arms. The U.S. Executive will inform the Congress, in connection with Congressional consideration of the ABM Treaty and the Interim Agreement, of this statement of the U.S. position."

B. Land-Mobile ICBM Launchers

The U.S. Delegation made the following statement on May 20, 1972:

"In connection with the important subject of land-mobile ICBM launchers, in the interest of concluding the Interim Agreement the U.S. Delegation now withdraws its proposal that Article I or an agreed statement explicitly prohibit the deployment of mobile land-based ICBM launchers. I have been instructed to inform you that, while agreeing to defer the question of limitation of operational land-mobile ICBM launchers to the subsequent negotiations on more complete limitations on strategic offensive arms, the U.S. would consider the deployment of operational land-mobile ICBM launchers during the period of the Interim Agreement as inconsistent with the objectives of that Agreement."

C. Covered Facilities

The U.S. Delegation made the following statement on May 20, 1972:

"I wish to emphasize the importance that the United States attaches to the provisions of Article V, including in particular their application to fitting out or berthing submarines."

D. "Heavy" ICBMs

The U.S. Delegation made the following statement on May 26, 1972:

"The U.S. Delegation regrets that the Soviet Delegation has not been willing to agree on a common definition of a heavy missile. Under these circumstances, the U.S. Delegation believes it necessary to state the following: The United States would consider any ICBM having a volume significantly greater than that of the largest light ICBM now operational on either side to be a heavy ICBM. The U.S. proceeds on the premise that the Soviet side will give due account to this consideration."

E. Tested in ABM Mode

On April 7, 1972, the U.S. Delegation made the following statement:

"Article II of the Joint Text Draft uses the term 'tested in an ABM mode,' in defining ABM components, and Article VI includes certain obligations concerning such testing. We believe that the sides should have a common understanding of this phrase. First, we would note that the testing provisions of the ABM Treaty are intended to apply to testing which occurs after the date of signature of the Treaty, and not to any testing which may have occurred in the past. Next, we would amplify the remarks we have made on this subject during the previous Helsinki phase by setting forth the objectives which govern the U.S. view on the subject, namely, while prohibiting testing of non-ABM components for ABM purposes: not to prevent testing of ABM components, and not to prevent testing of non-ABM components for non-ABM purposes. To clarify our interpretation of 'tested in an ABM mode,' we note that we would consider a launcher, missile or radar to be 'tested in an ABM mode' if, for example, any of the following events occur: (1) a launcher is used to launch an ABM interceptor missile, (2) an interceptor missile is flight tested against a target vehicle which has a flight trajectory with characteristics of a strategic ballistic missile flight trajectory, or is flight tested in conjunction with the test of an ABM interceptor missile or an ABM radar at the same test range, or is flight tested to an altitude inconsistent with interception of targets against which air defenses are deployed, (3) a radar makes measurements on a cooperative target vehicle of the kind referred to in item (2) above during the reentry portion of its trajectory or makes measurements in conjunction with the test of an ABM interceptor missile or an ABM radar at the same test range. Radars used for purposes such as range safety or instrumentation would be exempt from application of these criteria."

F. No-Transfer Article of ABM Treaty

On April 18, 1972, the U.S. Delegation made the following statement:

"In regard to this Article [IX], I have a brief and I believe self-explanatory statement to make. The U.S. side wishes to make clear that the provisions of this Article do not set a precedent for whatever provision may be considered for a Treaty on Limiting Strategic Offensive Arms. The question of transfer of strategic offensive arms is a far more complex issue, which may require a different solution."

G. No Increase in Defense of Early Warning Radars

On July 28, 1970, the U.S. Delegation made the following statement:

"Since Hen House radars [Soviet ballistic missile early warning radars] can detect and track ballistic missile warheads at great distances, they have a significant ABM potential. Accordingly, the U.S. would regard any increase in the defenses of such radars by surface-to-air missiles as inconsistent with an agreement."

* * * * * * *

The following noteworthy unilateral statement was made by the Delegation of the U.S.S.R. and is shown here with the U.S. reply:

On May 17, 1972, Minister Semenov made the following unilateral "Statement of the Soviet Side":

"Taking into account that modern ballistic missile submarines are presently in the possession of not only the U.S., but also of its NATO allies, the Soviet Union agrees that for the period of effectiveness of the Interim 'Freeze' Agreement the U.S. and its NATO allies have up to 50 such submarines with a total of up to 800 ballistic missile launchers thereon (including 41 U.S. submarines with 656 ballistic missile launchers). However, if during the period of effectiveness of the Agreement U.S. allies in NATO should increase the number of their modern submarines to exceed the numbers of submarines they would have operational or under construction on the date of signature of the Agreement, the Soviet Union will have the right to a corresponding increase in the number of its submarines. In the opinion of the Soviet side, the solution of the question of modern ballistic missile submarines provided for in the Interim Agreement only partially compensates for the strategic imbalance in the deployment of the nuclear-powered missile submarines of the USSR and the U.S. Therefore, the Soviet side believes that this whole question, and above all the question of liquidating the American missile submarine bases outside the U.S., will be appropriately resolved in the course of follow-on negotiations."

On May 24, Ambassador Smith made the following reply to Minister Semenov:

"The United States side has studied the 'statement made by the Soviet side' of May 17 concerning compensation for submarine basing and SLBM submarines belonging to third countries. The United States does not accept the validity of the considerations in that statement."

On May 26 Minister Semenov repeated the unilateral statement made on May 17. Ambassador Smith also repeated the U.S. rejection on May 26.

Annex F

North Atlantic Treaty

Washington D.C., April 4, 1949

The Parties to this Treaty reaffirm their faith in the purposes and principles of the Charter of the United Nations and their desire to live in peace with all peoples and all governments.

They are determined to safeguard the freedom, common heritage and civilization of their peoples, founded on the principles of democracy, individual liberty and the rule of law.

They seek to promote stability and well-being in the North Atlantic area.

They are resolved to unite their efforts for collective defense and for the preservation of peace and security.

They therefore agree to this North Atlantic Treaty:

Article 1

The Parties undertake, as set forth in the Charter of the United Nations, to settle any international dispute in which they may be involved by peaceful means in such a manner that international peace and security and justice are not endangered, and to refrain in their international relations from the threat or use of force in any manner inconsistent with the purposes of the United Nations.

Article 2

The Parties will contribute toward the further development of peaceful and friendly international relations by strengthening their free institutions, by bringing about a better understanding of the principles upon which these institutions are founded, and by promoting conditions of stability and well-being. They will seek to eliminate conflict in their international economic policies and will encourage economic collaboration between any or all of them.

Article 3

In order more effectively to achieve the objectives of this Treaty, the Parties, separately and jointly, by means of continuous and effective self-help and mutual aid, will maintain and develop their individual and collective capacity to resist armed attack.

Article 4

The Parties will consult together whenever, in the opinion of any of them, the territorial integrity, political independence or security of any of the Parties is threatened.

Article 5

The Parties agree that an armed attack against one or more of them in Europe or North America shall be considered an attack against them all and consequently they agree that, if such an armed attack occurs, each of them, in exercise of the right of individual or collective self-defense recognized by Article 51 of the Charter of the United Nations, will assist the Party or Parties so attacked by taking forthwith, individually and in concert with the other Parties, such action as it deems necessary, including the use of armed force, to restore and maintain the security of the North Atlantic area.

Any such armed attack and all measures taken as a result thereof shall immediately be reported to the Security Council. Such measures shall be terminated when the Security Council has taken the measures necessary to restore and maintain international peace and security.

Article 6[1]

For the purpose of Article V an armed attack on one or more of the Parties is deemed to include an armed attack on the territory of any of the Parties in Europe or North America, on the Algerian Departments of France,[2] on the occupation forces of any Party in Europe, on the

1. The definition of the territories to which Article V applies has been revised by Article II of the Protocol to the North Atlantic Treaty on the accession of Greece and Turkey.

2. On January 16, 1963, the North Atlantic Council has heard a declaration by the French Representative who recalled that by the vote on self-determination on July 1, 1962, the Algerian people had pronounced itself in favour of the independence of Algeria in co-operation with France. In consequence, the President of the French Re-

islands under the jurisdiction of any Party in the North Atlantic area north of the Tropic of Cancer or on the vessels or aircraft in this area of any of the Parties.

Article 7

This Treaty does not affect, and shall not be interpreted as affecting, in any way the rights and obligations under the Charter of the Parties which are members of the United Nations, or the primary responsibility of the Security Council for the maintenance of international peace and security.

Article 8

Each Party declares that none of the international engagements now in force between it and any other of the Parties or any third State is in conflict with the provisions of this Treaty, and undertakes not to enter into any international engagement in conflict with this Treaty.

Article 9

The Parties hereby establish a Council, on which each of them shall be represented, to consider matters concerning the implementation of this Treaty. The Council shall be so organized as to be able to meet promptly at any time. The Council shall set up such subsidiary bodies as may be necessary; in particular it shall establish immediately a defense committee which shall recommend measures for the implementation of Articles III and V.

Article 10

The Parties may, by unanimous agreement, invite any other European State in a position to further the principles of this Treaty and to contribute to the security of the North Atlantic area to accede to this Treaty. Any State so invited may become a Party to the Treaty by depositing its instrument of accession with the Government of the United States of America. The Government of the United States of America will inform each of the Parties of the deposit of each such instrument of accession.

public had on July 3, 1962, formally recognized the independence of Algeria. The result was that the 'Algerian departments of France' no longer existed as such, and that at the same time the fact that they were mentioned in the North Atlantic Treaty had no longer any bearing.

Following this statement the Council noted that insofar as the former Algerian Departments of France were concerned, the relevant clauses of this Treaty had become inapplicable as from July 3, 1962.

Article 11

This Treaty shall be ratified and its provisions carried out by the Parties in accordance with their respective constitutional processes. The instruments of ratification shall be deposited as soon as possible with the Government of the United States of America, which will notify all the other signatories of each deposit. The Treaty shall enter into force between the States which have ratified it as soon as the ratifications of the majority of the signatories, including the ratifications of Belgium, Canada, France, Luxembourg, the Netherlands, the United Kingdom and the United States, have been deposited and shall come into effect with respect to other States on the date of the deposit of their ratifications.

Article 12

After the Treaty has been in force for ten years, or at any time thereafter, the Parties shall, if any of them so requests, consult together for the purpose of reviewing the Treaty, having regard for the factors then affecting peace and security in the North Atlantic area, including the development of universal as well as regional arrangements under the Charter of the United Nations for the maintenance of international peace and security.

Article 13

After the Treaty has been in force for twenty years, any Party may cease to be a Party one year after its notice of denunciation has been given to the Government of the United States of America, which will inform the Government of the other Parties of the deposit of each notice of denunciation.

Article 14

This treaty, of which the English and French texts are equally authentic, shall be deposited in the archives of the Government of the United States of America. Duly certified copies will be transmitted by that Government to the Governments of other signatories.

Protocol to the North Atlantic Treaty on the accession of Greece and Turkey

London, October 22, 1951

The Parties to the North Atlantic Treaty, signed at Washington on April 4, 1949,

Being satisfied that the security of the North Atlantic area will be enhanced by the accession of the Kingdom of Greece and the Republic of Turkey to that Treaty,

Agree as follows:

Article 1

Upon the entry into force of this Protocol, the Government of the United States of America shall, on behalf of all the Parties, communicate to the Government of the Kingdom of Greece and the Government of the Republic of Turkey an invitation to accede to the North Atlantic Treaty, as it may be modified by Article II of the present Protocol. Thereafter the Kingdom of Greece and the Republic of Turkey shall each become a Party on the date when it deposits its instruments of accession with the Government of the United States of America in accordance with Article X of the Treaty.

Article 2

If the Republic of Turkey becomes a Party to the North Atlantic Treaty, Article VI of the Treaty shall, as from the date of the deposit by the Government of the Republic of Turkey of its instruments of accession with the Government of the United States of America, be modified to read as follows:

'For the purpose of Article 5, an armed attack on one or more of the Parties is deemed to include an armed attack:

i. on the territory of any of the Parties in Europe or North America, on the Algerian Departments of France, on the territory of Turkey or on the islands under the jurisdiction of any of the Parties in the North Atlantic area north of the Tropic of Cancer;

ii. on the forces, vessels, or aircraft of any of the Parties, when in or over these territories or any other area in Europe in which occupation forces of any of the Parties were stationed on the date when the Treaty entered into force or the Mediterranean Sea or the North Atlantic area north of the Tropic of Cancer.'

Article 3

The present Protocol shall enter into force when each of the Parties to the North Atlantic Treaty has notified the Government of the United States of America of its acceptance thereof. The Government of the United States of America shall inform all the Parties to the North Atlantic Treaty of the date of the receipt of each such notification and of the date of the entry into force of the present Protocol.

Article 4

The present Protocol, of which the English and French texts are equally authentic, shall be deposited in the Archives of the Government of the United States of America. Duly certified copies thereof shall be transmitted by that Government to the Governments of all the Parties to the North Atlantic Treaty.

Protocol to the North Atlantic Treaty on the accession of the Federal Republic of Germany

Paris, October 23, 1954

The Parties to the North Atlantic Treaty signed at Washington on April 4, 1949,

Being satisfied that the security of the North Atlantic area will be enhanced by the accession of the Federal Republic of Germany to that Treaty, and

Having noted that the Federal Republic of Germany has, by a declaration dated October 3, 1954, accepted the obligations set forth in Article 2 of the Charter of the United Nations and has undertaken upon its accession to the North Atlantic Treaty to refrain from any action inconsistent with the strictly defensive character of that Treaty, and

Having further noted that all member governments have associated themselves with the declaration also made on October 3, 1954, by the Governments of the United States of America, the United Kingdom of Great Britain and Northern Ireland and the French Republic in connection with the aforesaid declaration of the Federal Republic of Germany,

Agree as follows:

Article 1

Upon the entry into force of the present Protocol, the Government of the United States of America shall on behalf of all the Parties communicate to the Government of the Federal Republic of Germany an invitation to accede to the North Atlantic Treaty. Thereafter the Federal Republic of Germany shall become a Party to that Treaty on the date when it deposits its instruments of accession with the Government of the United States of America in accordance with Article 10 of the Treaty.

Article 2

The present Protocol shall enter into force, when (a) each of the Parties to the North Atlantic Treaty has notified to the Government of the United States of America its acceptance thereof, (b) all instruments of ratification of the Protocol modifying and completing the Brussels Treaty have been deposited with the Belgian Government, and (c) all instruments of ratification or approval of the Convention on the Presence of Foreign Forces in the Federal Republic of Germany have been deposited with the Government of the Federal Republic of Germany. The Government of the United States of America shall inform the other Parties to the North Atlantic Treaty of the date of the receipt of each notification of acceptance of the present Protocol and of the date of the entry into force of the present Protocol.

Article 3

The present Protocol, of which the English and French texts are equally authentic, shall be deposited in the Archives of the Government of the United States of America. Duly certified copies thereof shall be transmitted by that Government to the Governments of the other Parties to the North Atlantic Treaty.

Annex G

Warsaw Treaty

New Times 21 (May 21, 1955), Moscow

Treaty

of Friendship, Cooperation and Mutual Assistance Between the People's Republic of Albania, the People's Republic of Bulgaria, the Hungarian People's Republic, the German Democratic Republic, the Polish People's Republic, the Rumanian People's Republic, the Union of Soviet Socialist Republics and the Czechoslovak Republic

The Contracting Parties reaffirming their desire for the establishment of a system of European collective security based on the participation of all European states irrespective of their social and political systems, which would make it possible to unite their efforts in safeguarding the peace of Europe; mindful, at the same time, of the situation created in Europe by the ratification of the Paris agreements, which envisage the formation of a new military alignment in the shape of "Western European Union," with the participation of a remilitarized Western Germany and the integration of the latter in the North-Atlantic bloc, which increases the danger of another war and constitutes a threat to the national security of the peaceable states; being persuaded that in these circumstances the peaceable European states must take the necessary measures to safeguard their security and in the interests of preserving peace in Europe; guided by the objects and principles of the Charter of the United Nations Organization; being desirous of further promoting and developing friendship, cooperation and mutual assistance in accordance with the principles of respect for the independence and sovereignty of states and of noninterference in their internal affairs, have decided to conclude the present Treaty of Friendship, Cooperation and Mutual Assistance and have for that purpose appointed as their plenipotentiaries: the Presidium of the People's Assembly of the People's Republic of Albania: Mehmet Shehu, Chairman of the Council of Ministers of the People's Republic of Albania; the Presidium of the People's Assembly of the People's Republic of Bulgaria: Vulko Chervenkov, Chairman of the Council of Ministers of the People's Republic of Bulgaria; the Presidium of the Hungarian People's Republic: Andras Hegedüs, Chairman of the Council of Ministers of the Hungarian People's Republic; the President of the German Democratic Republic: Otto Grotewohl, Prime Minister of the German Democratic Republic; the State Council of the Polish People's Republic: Józef Cyrankiewicz, Chairman of the Council of Ministers of the Polish People's Republic; the Presidium of the Grand National Assembly of the Rumanian People's Republic: Gheorghe Gheorghiu-Dej, Chairman of the Council of Ministers of the Rumanian People's Republic; the Presidium of the Supreme Soviet of the Union of Soviet Socialist Republics: Nikolai Alexandrovich Bulganin, Chairman of the Council of Ministers of the U.S.S.R.; the President of the Czechoslovak Republic: Viliam Široký, Prime Minister of the Czechoslovak Republic, who, having presented their full powers, found in good and due form, have agreed as follows:

Article I

The Contracting Parties undertake, in accordance with the Charter of the United Nations Organization, to refrain in their international relations from the threat or use of force, and to settle their international disputes peacefully and in such manner as will not jeopardize international peace and security.

Article 2

The Contracting Parties declare their readiness to participate in a spirit of sincere cooperation in all international actions designed to safeguard international peace and security, and will fully devote their energies to the attainment of this end.

The Contracting Parties will furthermore strive for the adoption, in agreement with other states which may desire to cooperate in this, of effective measures for universal reduction of armaments and prohibition of atomic, hydrogen and other weapons of mass destruction.

Article 3

The Contracting Parties shall consult with one another on all important international issues affecting their common interests, guided by the desire to strengthen international peace and security.

They shall immediately consult with one another whenever, in the opinion of any one of them, a threat of armed attack on one or more of the Parties to the Treaty has arisen, in order to ensure joint defense and the maintenance of peace and security.

Article 4

In the event of armed attack in Europe on one or more of the Parties to the Treaty by any state or group of states, each of the Parties to the Treaty, in the exercise of its right to individual or collective self-defense in accordance with Article 51 of the Charter of the United Nations Organization, shall immediately, either individually or in agreement with other Parties to the Treaty, come to the assistance of the state or states attacked with all such means as it deems necessary, including armed force. The Parties to the Treaty shall immediately consult concerning the necessary measures to be taken by them jointly in order to restore and maintain international peace and security.

Measures taken on the basis of this Article shall be reported to the Security Council in conformity with the provisions of the Charter of the United Nations Organization. These measures shall be discontinued immediately the Security Council adopts the necessary measures to restore and maintain international peace and security.

Article 5

The Contracting Parties have agreed to establish a Joint Command of the armed forces that by agreement among the Parties shall be assigned to the Command, which shall function on the basis of jointly established principles. They shall likewise adopt other agreed measures necessary to strengthen their defensive power, in order to protect the peaceful labours of their peoples, guarantee the inviolability of their frontiers and territories, and provide defense against possible aggression.

Article 6

For the purpose of the consultations among the Parties envisaged in the present Treaty, and also for the purpose of examining questions which may arise in the operation of the Treaty, a Political Consultative Committee shall be set up, in which each of the Parties to the Treaty shall be represented by a member of its Government or by another specifically appointed representative.

The Committee may set up such auxiliary bodies as may prove necessary.

Article 7

The Contracting Parties undertake not to participate in any coalitions or alliances and not to conclude any agreements whose objects conflict with the objects of the present Treaty.

The Contracting Parties declare that their commitments under existing international treaties do not conflict with the provisions of the present Treaty.

Article 8

The Contracting Parties declare that they will act in a spirit of friendship and cooperation with a view to further developing and fostering economic and cultural intercourse with one another, each adhering to the principle of respect for the independence and sovereignty of the others and non-interference in their internal affairs.

Article 9

The present Treaty is open to the accession of other states irrespective of their social and political systems, which express their readiness by participation in the present Treaty to assist in uniting the efforts of the peaceable states in safeguarding the peace and security of the peoples. Such accession shall enter into force with the agreement of the Parties to the Treaty after the declaration of accession has been deposited with the Government of the Polish People's Republic.

Article 10

The present Treaty is subject to ratification, and the instruments of ratification shall be deposited with the Government of the Polish People's Republic.

The Treaty shall enter into force on the day the last instrument of ratification has been deposited. The Government of the Polish People's Republic shall notify the other Parties to the Treaty as each instrument of ratification is deposited.

Article 11

The present Treaty shall remain in force for twenty years. For such Contracting Parties as do not at least one year before the expiration of this period present to the Government of the Polish People's Republic a statement of denunciation of the Treaty, it shall remain in force for the next ten years.

Should a system of collective security be established in Europe, and a General European Treaty of Collective Security concluded for this purpose, for which the Contracting Parties will unswervingly strive, the present Treaty shall cease to be operative from the day the General European Treaty enters into force.

Done in Warsaw on May 14, 1955, in one copy each in the Russian, Polish, Czech and German languages, all texts being equally authentic. Certified copies of the present Treaty shall be sent by the Government of the Polish People's Republic to all the Parties to the Treaty.

In witness whereof the plenipotentiaries have signed the present Treaty and affixed their seals.

For the Presidium of the People's Assembly of the People's Republic of Albania

MEHMET SHEHU

For the Presidium of the People's Assembly of the People's Republic of Bulgaria

VULKO CHERVENKOV

For the Presidium of the Hungarian People's Republic

ANDRAS HEGEDÜS

For the President of the German Democratic Republic

OTTO GROTEWOHL

For the State Council of the Polish People's Republic

JOZEF CYRANKIEWICZ

For the Presidium of the Grand National Assembly of the Rumanian People's Republic

GHEORGHE GHEORGHIU-DEJ

For the Presidium of the Supreme Soviet of the Union of Soviet Socialist Republics

NIKOLAI ALEXANDROVICH BULGANIN

For the President of the Czechoslovak Republic

VILIAM ŠIROKÝ

Establishment of a Joint Command

of the Armed Forces of the Signatories to the Treaty of Friendship, Cooperation and Mutual Assistance

In pursuance of the Treaty of Friendship, Cooperation and Mutual Assistance between the People's Republic of Albania, the People's Republic of Bulgaria, the Hungarian People's Republic, the German Democratic Republic, the Polish People's Republic, the Rumanian People's Republic, the Union of Soviet Socialist Republics and the Czechoslovak Republic, the signatory states have decided to establish a Joint Command of their armed forces.

The decision provides that general questions relating to the strengthening of the defensive power and the organization of the Joint Armed Forces of the signatory states shall be subject to examination by the Political Consultative Committee, which shall adopt the necessary decisions.

Marshall of the Soviet Union I. S. Konev has been appointed Commander-in-Chief of the Joint Armed Forces to be assigned by the signatory states.

The Ministers of Defense or other military leaders of the signatory states are to serve as Deputy Commanders-in-Chief of the Joint Armed Forces, and shall command the armed forces assigned by their respective states to the Joint Armed Forces.

The question of the participation of the German Democratic Republic in measures concerning the armed forces of the Joint Command will be examined at a later date.

A Staff of the Joint Armed Forces of the signatory states will be set up under the Commander-in-Chief of the Joint Armed Forces, and will include permanent representatives of the General Staffs of the signatory states.

The Staff will have its headquarters in Moscow.

The disposition of the Joint Armed Forces in the territories of the signatory states will be effected, by agreement among the states, in accordance with the requirements of their mutual defense.

INDEX

Index

B

C

D

E

F

J

K

L

M

N

O

P

Q

R

S

T

U

V

W